Celestial Navigation

A Complete Home Study Course

Second Edition

by

David Burch

STARPATH®

www.starpathpublications.com

ISBN 978-0-914025-46-7

Published by

Starpath Publications

3050 NW 63rd Street, Seattle, WA 98107

Manufactured in the United States of America

www.starpathpublications.com

10 9 8 7

Cover, book design, and figures by Tobias Burch.

Cover moon photograph courtesy of Stuart Lowe.

·SPHERA· ·MVNDI·
Hey, My Friend, Is it not best to learn the traditional methods of celestial navigation before starting with that calculator?
???

Table of Contents

Chapter 8. Planet Sights

Chapter 9. Moon Sights

Chapter 10. Principles

Chapter 11. In Depth

Appendix

Preface

Our goal is to teach readers how to do celestial navigation and do it well. This book evolved from interactions with many thousands of students over the past 20 years, both in the classroom and in online training. The structure of the book reflects that which we have learned. One influence of that experience was to break up the early study between tables and number crunching with hands on plotting exercises. Another is to teach how to do it as quickly as possible up front, and only after that, or during that, do we fill in details of the practice and theory. The goal is to get readers carrying out the full process from beginning to end, so they can then be practicing the process and catching mistakes early, as we slowly add the background. In short, the background goes to the back.

Practical, self-reliant celestial navigation is easy to do. It is done basically the same today as it was 100 years ago, and as it will likely be done 100 years from now. We risk losing sight of that if we choose to understand all the math and science background before getting started on the actual navigation, which itself requires no math beyond arithmetic. We have a proven compromise at hand. There are "In-Depth" references to the back of the book at each stage of the learning for those who are more comfortable having the background at hand. Many readers, however, will follow the background more readily once they know how it works in practice.

We have also learned that a well-designed work form is key to versatile cel nav practice. Our unique forms guide you through the process, step by step. They make all sights essentially the same, and provide an easy reminder of the next step at each stage.

Preface to the Second Edition

We are pleased to say that after 10 more years of using this text we do not find reason to change the basic approach and methods of the teaching. We still use most of the same examples, which are now quite old, but that is the beauty of celestial navigation. It has not changed; so we do not benefit in any way from making all new examples, which would bring with them more chance of error in a book of many numbers.

We have, however, notably improved and expanded the book. Each section has been updated and reformatted for a clearer presentation, often in response to student questions over the years. New graphics have been added and older ones all updated. There is new content in the text, especially in the "In-Depth" chapter including more detailed discussion of the sailings and more background on the principles. And new sections on general ocean navigation tactics and new sections on optimizing the fixes. We have also updated the electronic navigation section, and we no longer explain systems we will never see again!

Starpath instructors remain at hand to answer questions about the subject and we maintain an online support page for this book at www.starpath.com/celnavbook.

Acknowledgements

This book has benefited from the input from many students over the years and we remain grateful to have this ongoing practical feedback. For the Second Edition we received much appreciated help from Lanny Petitjean who reviewed the full text with valuable suggestions throughout. And we are pleased to thank Captain Louise Orion of Blue Planet Cruising for sharing her expertise in both celestial navigation and editing by providing many useful suggestions to Chapter 10.

INTRODUCTION

About this Book

These study materials (text, examples, and practice exercises, along with the table selections and work forms in the Appendix) are used for classroom, home study, and online courses throughout the US. With home study, readers do not have the benefit of classroom discussion, but they do have the benefit of using materials that more than 30,000 celestial navigation students have used before them. Hopefully most of the questions that might come up are already answered.

The materials you have in this book are the basis for all three learning formats. For those who might like a classroom course, the Calendar section of starpath.com lists courses around the country that use this textbook and related materials. Online courses are also available that provide direct contact with instructors and individually graded practice quizzes. Various levels of certification are also available.

Without either of those options, however, we feel confident you can learn practical and versatile celestial navigation from these materials alone, studying at home on your own. Thousands have done so, and gone on to cross oceans or circumnavigate the globe.

Hands-on instruction with sextant sights might seem like the main factor missed in home-study learning, but here too, our experience with so many past students helps again. We have a thorough section on sextant handling and how to read the dials, along with crucial steps to taking good sights. Follow these procedures and you will learn quickly how to use the sextant.

In fact, the challenge of using a sextant is not as high as one might guess from scuttlebutt on the topic. The ingenuity of sextant design is not its ability to measure accurate angles—this could be done on land two centuries before sextants were invented—but rather it was its unique double reflection design that lets you measure accurate angles when you are bouncing around in a seaway. Standing still on a beach or the edge of a lake, you will learn the process quickly, and the ingenuity of the instrument design will let you carry these new-found skills on to the rolling platform of a boat at sea.

Also, you will learn shortly that a real beauty of celestial navigation is its transparency. If you make a mistake, it will be obvious, and if you keep careful records of all the data that went into the sight process and analysis, you will be able to find that mistake. If you have a friend or teacher who is familiar with celestial navigation, they can also look at the data and help you learn what went wrong. Part of the learning process is exactly that. Learning the pitfalls of possible mistakes and how to avoid them. This course offers so many practice examples that you will have this under control before you set off. It is obviously much better to make all the mistakes on land, and save your time at sea for other matters.

The various subjects covered in our materials, and the relative emphasis given them in the course, is based on the latest information on these subjects—some of which is changing, though most is not—and our actual experience at sea (mostly under sail) covering more than 70,000 miles, of which about 25% were navigated by celestial alone (See *Hawaii by Sextant*, Starpath Publications, 2014). We concentrate on practical matters, presented and explained in a manner that we have learned (from classroom experience) suits most students best.

The various procedures of celestial navigation are presented in a step-by-step manner, with numerous examples and many practice problems. This is a practical approach, but not a cookbook approach. We delegate the astronomical and mathematical backbones of celestial navigation to Chapter 10 because these details can in fact distract from learning how to do it. We can promise, however, that by the end of the course, you will know how to do it, and do it well, and also know how it works.

You will notice that some of the practice examples and sample data pages date from the late 70's, when we first started teaching celestial navigation. Don't be alarmed by these dates. The *Nautical Almanac* pages that we teach from that originated in 1978 are identical to those printed today, and likely will be the same 30 years from now. One might be tempted to change all the examples to the present date to make them look up to date, but in reality there is no difference in the learning whatsoever, and by not doing this we avoid the chance of introducing typographic errors. There are a lot of numbers in a course on cel nav, so this is an important step toward maintaining the integrity of the materials.

Are You Nervous About Learning Celestial Navigation?

You will soon see that celestial navigation is an impressive and very rewarding thing to learn about; it is also an unusual subject in that it is technical stuff that many non-technical people want to learn. For people who do not routinely deal with numbers, graphs, or other technical matters, the onset of this course might well be more of a challenge than it is for those who are already comfortable with numerical work. If you do not work with numbers on a daily basis, your worries might be reinforced after skimming through this book, filled with numbers, tables, forms, and strange looking plots. Please let me assure you, however, that the chart and paperwork of celestial navigation looks more complicated than it is.

There is sophisticated science and mathematics buried in the subject, but it is well buried. The actual practice has evolved into a systematic process requiring no math beyond arithmetic and no science beyond reading the dials of a sextant and watch. The key to success is an organized approach to the paperwork and prudent tips on sextant use. This course is designed with that in mind. The course approaches the subject step by step, with planned changes in subject matter that lets earlier parts settle in, followed by a review of the past before proceeding on to something new. By the end of the course, the parts of this book that might have looked overwhelming at first will then be familiar. Step by step, you will have learned it all. In the end, as you flip through the book again, you will rightfully be proud of the accomplishment.

Thousands of people have used these notes to learn celestial. People in their early teens to people in their early 80's. People from every profession and every walk of life. Sailors who have spent years on the water, as well as those who have never been on a boat. The vast majority were totally unfamiliar with celestial to begin with, but we are equally proud of our success with those who have "tried every course available" and did not succeed until now. Our reputation is based on our record. Anyone who wants to learn celestial can do it with this course. That is our job.

How to do the Home Study Course

We suggest that you divide your study into sections that follow the Table of Contents. This is very similar to the way we present the materials in a classroom or online course. It divides up the course into sections, with logical breakpoints in between. It structures the reading and practice exercises. Answers are provided along with solutions in most cases in the back of the book. If you cannot get the right answer on a practice exercise, rework one of the illustrative examples to double-check your procedure. If you have trouble finding an error, it is often easier to start from scratch with a clean slate, rather than going back over the numbers of a completed solution.

As you work through the practice, keep a bound notebook of your work, with each problem labeled carefully—as opposed to just using loose sheets of paper that may get lost. If a question or concern arises, jot it down and date it so you don't forget it. This is especially valuable practice for general questions or curiosities that have not stopped your progress. Most of these questions will likely be answered as you progress through the book. They will also be useful if you choose to work with an instructor later on or post questions in an online forum.

Frequently Asked Questions

How Long Does the Course Take?

The Starpath classroom course was eight 3-hour classes, with the assumption that students spent at least an equivalent amount of time outside of the classroom. We have estimated that our online version of the course would take about 70 hr, but some students spend more time than that. The time spent depends on the number of practice exercises needed to master a topic as well as how much of the special In-Depth material from Chapter 11 you choose to cover. Most classroom courses include some, but not all of that material.

Do I Need a Sextant to do the Course?

The answer to that is No, but you will eventually need one to do real sights. You can actually work though the course without one and get the sextant later—in fact, it is even best to read through Chapter 2 on sextants before making your choice. But once that chapter is presented, the practice exercises simply start out saying "the sextant reads such-and-such at time such-and such" and you can work out your position lines from that.

When you start doing sights, be sure to keep careful records of your work. Take a notebook and record *everything* about the sight session. Use a GPS to know your exact location, and use it as well to check your watch time. Note the times of all sights, the height of eye above water level, the height of the tide at the time, the index correction, plus how and how often you checked it. If you use more than one sextant, which sextant goes with which sight, etc. Do not throw out sights—make a note on it, but keep it. If you do all this, you will eventually be able to figure out what is wrong if you do not get a good fix or good LOPs. That is the beauty of celestial navigation.

What Sight Reduction Tables Are Used?

This question may or may not make sense to you at this point, depending on where you are starting, but it is a question that comes up frequently. The answer is we teach the use of them all in this book, and our work forms can be used with any of the tables. The Table Selections we provide are from Pub. 249 and our solutions use those tables, but any version could be used to work the problems. Toward the end of the course we encourage students to consider the

NAO Tables included in each edition of the almanac. And we have examples from Pub. 229. Those preparing for a USCG exam will have to eventually use Pub. 229. (Again, if this question and answer does not make sense, do not worry about it. It will all be clear very shortly.)

More Support?

For extra help see www.starpath.com/celnavbook. There are multiple resources there related to this book and the general study of celestial navigation, including several organizations and discussion groups that specialize in cel nav. There are also links to schools around the country that use this text for their courses. Sextants and related tools and materials are also available.

Tools of the Trade

The following is a list of the equipment and materials needed to do celestial navigation at sea. This is not a list of what you need for the course. Everything needed for the course is provided in this book except for standard plotting tools. We include this list early in the notes, only because it is consistently an early question we get in class. And it is certainly reasonable to wonder "What am I going to need after I learn this stuff and what will it cost?"

Celestial Equipment Needed Underway

Approximate 2019 prices are shown; options and alternatives are discussed later.

Metal Sextant	$800
Plastic backup sextant	$49
Two Watches	$80
Nautical Almanac	$30
Universal Plotting Sheets	$11
Work Forms	$13
Sight Reduction Tables	$60
2102-D Star Finder	$50
Plotting tools	$75
Notebook	$10
Large waterproof cases	$15

The total cost is about $400 plus a sextant, but a radio of some kind is required to confirm the watch times. Generally, the minimum radio equipment one should consider for an ocean crossing is a SW receiver capable of receiving the high seas weather. Dependable portable models cost about $300. These will provide very good time signal reception, but it is not clear that this should be counted in as a celestial expense. You can, in fact, get accurate time from your GPS while it is working, but the radio is still the safest source. (Connected to a network, your cellphone also gives accurate time.)

If you happen to have a SSB transceiver or satellite phone on board for high-seas communication, then it will provide excellent weather and time signal coverage as well. It is a toss up these days as to which is best, if only one is to be had. Satellite phones are more convenient, but cost more to operate.

Celestial Terminology

Learning celestial navigation can be thought of in terms of several goals:

- Learning how to use a sextant to take sights (usually mastered in a few hours with good instructions).
- Learning how to use a dozen or so new tables (similar to learning to use a phone book or tide table for the first time).
- Learning a bookkeeping procedure for what to do with the numbers we get from the tables (we use a work form to guide us through this step; the only math required is adding and subtracting).
- Learning a new plotting procedure for putting the numerical results onto a chart (takes only an hour or so to master using our instructions).
- Learning a couple dozen or so new terms, which is the subject of this section.

Many of the terms to be used are already familiar, but we need to add precision to the meanings. Some celestial terms have recognizable origins (i.e., *zenith* is indeed the point overhead, as *sextant angle* is indeed the angle we measure with a sextant), but many terms have obscure names (sextant angle is usually called sextant height or sextant altitude; zenith distance is actually an angle, not a distance; ZD stands for zone description, not zenith distance, and so on). There is a temptation to rename some terms to simplify the learning (which some books give in to), but in the long run this is a serious disservice. It is best to stick with traditional terminology so everyone can speak the same language and read the same books.

Keeping these terms straight does not come instantly, but slowly it falls into place. To help with this, there is a thorough glossary at the back of the book, and we list new terms at the end of each Chapter.

How this Book is Structured

The body of the text presents a sequence of topic discussions with a few worked out numerical examples showing how the tables and forms are used to complete the task at hand, followed by practice exercises for the reader. Answers and selected solutions are in the back of the book, which also includes blank work forms and plotting sheets that can be photocopied as needed. High resolution pdfs of the forms and plotting sheets are available for free download at www.starpath.com/celnavbook. The philosophy of the presentation is outlined in the Preface.

Glossary

At the end of each chapter we include a list of the new terms defined or introduced in that chapter. The defined terms might appear later in the text without further definition. Please double-check these terms in the Glossary to complete that Chapter.

The Glossary is meant to be more than just a list of definitions. There are details there that do not appear elsewhere in the book. Also, frequent questions about more technical meanings of some terms are answered only in the Glossary to keep this information from distracting from the course. In this sense, the Glossary is a mini encyclopedia.

As the course progresses and more terms are introduced, refer to the Glossary frequently to remind yourself of the meanings and interrelationships of the various terms.

Abbreviations

Cel nav is filled with abbreviations. We stick with the standard abbreviations for standard terms regardless of our own interpretation of the logic. Then when referring to standard references you will be at home. This terminology is part of the learning process, i.e., ZD is zone description, not zenith distance, which is a lower-case z. Likewise, Z is a relative bearing (azimuth angle) whereas Zn is a true bearing (azimuth), and so on.Í

To help with this we have a list of abbreviations at the end of the Glossary, which could be a useful resource. We have also added a few editorial ones that are not standard to simplify the presentation, such as NA for *Nautical Almanac*, and T-2 to refer to the second table in our Table Selections.

Tables Selections

This section provides all the table data needed to work the standard exercises in the book. These are historic values in some cases, but this does not affect the learning as the procedures and table layouts have not changed. For your own navigation at home or underway you will need access to full sets of the sight reduction tables and a current *Nautical Almanac*, both are available online as free downloads (www.starpath.com/celnavbook).

Links to In-Depth Topics

Throughout the book you will periodically see at the bottom of the page a cross reference link to a section of Chapter 11 on In-Depth topics. These are presented in the book whenever there is related extra material available. The In-Depth or special topics are removed to that section so they do not distract from the main progress of the course.

Sometimes these include new material that might be of interest to you but is not crucial to the content of the course, and sometimes they are just extra practice on a detail now being covered. These extra topics are not all specifically celestial navigation, but they are all related to doing or learning ocean navigation. Two samples are shown below.

...In Depth

11.1 *Bowditch* and other Resources

Our text is self-contained, providing all the information required for safe efficient navigation, but the quest for more details may come up, so we list standard and unique resources in this section...

...In Depth

11.2 Taking Your Departure

There are navigation procedures from the early days of sailing ships that have wandered out of the textbooks, but some remain valuable in modern times. In this section we help one wander back in...

Chapter 1

Background & Overview

1.1 Overview of Ocean Navigation

Navigation means two things: knowing where you are and choosing a safe, efficient route to where you want to go. The first aspect of navigation, finding and keeping track of position (out of sight of land), is the goal of this course on ocean navigation. The second aspect, choosing a route, is covered in *Modern Marine Weather* (Starpath Publications, 2013), since route planning for ocean-going yachts is more a matter of wind and current than it is of pure geographical navigation. These are equally important aspects of ocean navigation, but they are different subjects.

On inland and coastal waters we usually navigate using charted landmarks. This type of navigation is called piloting. If I sail up the Sound or down the coast going from one headland to the next, I am piloting. If I find my way home by going to Sears and turning left, I am piloting. Piloting is the technical name for the usual way we get from place to place. On inland and coastal waters, piloting techniques include natural ranges, depth sounding, bearing fixes, and the various methods of finding distance off by angle measurements. These techniques and the philosophy of navigation near land are covered in our book *Inland and Coastal Navigation* (Starpath Publications, 2014).

To keep track of our intermediate position as we sail from one landmark to the next we use dead reckoning—an unusual term used by mariners since the late 1500s. To navigate by dead reckoning (DR), we deduce our new position, as we move away from a known position, using the shipboard instruments—primarily the compass, which tells us which way we went, and the ship's log (odometer), which tells us how far we went. We also need a logbook to record how far we went on each heading and when we made course changes. We can then plot our course on a chart or plotting sheet, 10 miles this way, then 5 miles that way, and so on, and this way keep track of our position. An accurate logbook and careful dead reckoning are always the keys to good navigation, regardless of what other navigation aids we may have on board.

But no vessel can travel far by dead reckoning alone. Small errors in the compass or log accumulate with time, and even with precise instruments we can't hold a precise course in all wind and sea conditions. Besides this, we have no way of knowing the effects of ocean currents while we navigate by dead reckoning alone. Dead reckoning tells us our track through the water, but it does not tell us anything about the motion of the water itself. It is like knowing exactly where you are in a large bathtub, but not knowing where the bathtub is. Typical ocean currents (averaged worldwide) might drift us off course by 10 to 20 miles a day; in extreme cases (such as the Gulf Stream) the current drift could be as large as 50 to 100 miles a day. Other sources of DR error are even more likely, such as changing course and forgetting to log it, or not really steering the average course we thought we were, because of brief but consistent course alterations at each wave in a seaway. These and other influences on DR accuracy are discussed later in this course.

To keep track of our position over a long voyage we must periodically check and correct our dead reckoning. In the ocean we do this with celestial navigation—the subject of this book. In sight of land we might do this by taking bearings to various landmarks. Two crossed bearing lines tell us where we are—gives us a position fix. We can then compare our true position, our fix, with where we thought we were on the basis of our dead reckoning. This usually tells us something about the accuracy of our dead reckoning—especially if we are right where we thought we were.

If we are not where we thought we were, we have more work to do to figure out why. In this case we must keep a record of our dead reckoning errors long enough to spot a trend, or a distinct lack of trend. And maybe then we can figure out if our errors are due to currents, instrument error, or helmsmanship. Oftentimes apparent errors in DR are just errors in the logbook entries—after neglecting to promptly record a course change, we err in reconstructing what we did do, or when we did it. The best way to keep track of DR errors in the ocean is to record how far off the fix was from the DR position and in what direction. Also record how many miles you have logged since the last fix and how long in time you have sailed since the last fix. For example, fix position 4.9 miles from DR in direction 225 T; error occurred during a 38-mile run that lasted 6 hours and 20 minutes. Although the magnitudes of the numbers will be different, the same information is crucial to good inland navigation as well. Later in the course we discuss how to analyze this type of important information.

In any event, once we have a true position fix from whatever means, we restart our DR from the new position and abandon our previous DR track on the chart. Any long voyage proceeds as a series of position fixes, with navigation by DR in between the fixes. And throughout this process, the on-going goal of the navigator is to improve the accuracy of the dead reckoning. The reason for this is simple: we may get caught without any means of doing a position fix (sky or horizon obscured at sea, or socked in by the fog inland), in which case we must rely entirely on dead reckoning. If this happens we want to be sure our dead reckoning is right. No surprises. At this point, it is too late to learn. In a very real sense, the main goal of celestial navigation is to test the DR. The most successful approach to ocean navigation is to outright assume that you are going to DR across the ocean and then use each successive celestial fix to fine tune your ability to predict your position by log and compass—and any knowledge of the sea and your boat's performance that you glean from this endeavor. The best celestial navigator in the world will be nervous if he doesn't know his DR accuracy, and the last three days of the voyage are covered with clouds so no sun nor stars can be seen, especially in a circumstance where GPS might not be available.

As a side note, if you count on the electronics to get you in, you are putting your reputation—not to mention, possibly, your safety—into the hands of a circuit board in salty air. Whenever you miss the mark, regardless of the reason, even when it was not a threat to safety or even much of an inconvenience, you inevitably lose a bit of intangible rapport with your crew. They will buy the explanations for errors the first few times, but eventually they will start making their own evaluations of which way to go, and this can lead to conflict, especially if decisions must be made under stress, in a storm for example. In short, the value of pursuing accurate DR as a general goal can have farther reaching implications than one might guess.

The interplay between DR and position fixing is the same on inland waters as it is at sea. The only difference at sea, out of sight of land, is the way we get our position fixes. We can't use bearings; there are no landmarks at sea. The answer is either celestial navigation or some form of electronic navigation like GPS. (Radar and radio direction finding are just sophisticated ways of taking bearings. These methods can only be used on inland and coastal waters, though they do often work for some distance out of visible sight of land.)

Celestial navigation is in many ways the most reliable. You do it all yourself with simple instruments and tables. There are no electronic components to fail, and it takes no electric power. You do not depend on any land-based source of information, assuming you know what time it is (we cover prudent timekeeping procedures in this course, as well as finding time from the moon if need be). You use the positions of the sun and stars, which, by anyone's evaluation, must be the most reliable guides imaginable. If you can't count on the stars, you can't count on anything.

The personal accomplishment of doing it is also very satisfying. With a set of equipment that you can fit in a shoe box, if you trim it to the basics, you can find your position on earth, on your own, to within a mile or so—which is quite an accomplishment, considering that the earth's surface spans some 200 million square miles.

These days the competitor for ocean position fixing is GPS. As a rule, it is dependable and inexpensive, but it remains a black box. If it says the fix is good, we have to believe it. If it says it is not good, we have to wait till it says it is good, and again, believe it. If we rely on GPS alone to cross an ocean, we will not know if it is right until the last day.

Celestial navigation, on the other hand, is inexpensive and transparent. It is easy to tell if we make a mistake. A bad fix is just as obvious as a good one. If we do spot a mistake, we know and understand all possible sources of the error. With very little training, there are no mysteries in celestial navigation. The basic equipment we need for celestial navigation is a sextant, a chronometer, an almanac, and a set of sight reduction tables. We also need the standard equipment of all navigation: paper, pencil, and plotting tools.

The sextant is a handheld instrument used to measure the angular height of the sun or stars above the horizon. We can also use the moon or the visible planets: Venus, Jupiter, Mars, and Saturn. Sextants are basically rugged instruments with few moving parts, but they are precision instruments, so they must be treated carefully. If you dropped a sextant, you would probably break or bend some part of it, but it is likely to still be usable. This is not something you want to test. It's good practice to carry an inexpensive plastic backup sextant. Sextants are discussed in Chapter 2. The minimum cost of a quality instrument is about $660 or so in 2015.

We also need a chronometer. A chronometer is just a watch that gains or loses time at a constant rate. In the old days, this was a major expense, greater-than or equal to the sextant cost. These days, this means just about any quartz watch. If we take two of them (one as backup), it still costs only $80 or so for good waterproof models, with 24-hour scales, stopwatches, alarms, good lighting, etc.

And finally, we need two books: the *Nautical Almanac* that costs about $30, and a set of Sight Reduction Tables that cost anywhere from nothing to about $60, depending on the set we choose—nothing is an option, because there

...In Depth

11.3 Electronic Navigation at Sea

This is a course on cel nav, not electronics, but it still helps to keep all navigation options in perspective, so we add these notes on GPS and other electronic aids...

is a set of these in the *Nautical Almanac* as of 1989. And that's it—less than $1,000 for a full set of adequate equipment that will take your boat anywhere in the world, independent of what goes on elsewhere in the world. At the other extreme, you could cut the cord and sail off with as little as $100 invested in celestial navigation gear and still do it safely, but it would take more work. If you are to rely on celestial, there is no substitute for a good sextant.

The previous discussion is not meant to imply that electronics are not worthwhile. I would be the first to want them all on board for an ocean passage, as would any insurance company... or Admiralty Court if a question of liability ever arose. The main point is, despite the convenience of electronic navigation, celestial equipment and your knowledge of how to use it are the things you can count on. In actual practice, you might well end up using GPS most of the time, but it still must be checked periodically with celestial. When it comes to confidence in a position, there is not much that can beat three star lines crossing at the same point on your plotting sheet. Furthermore, one must realistically admit that GPS on a small boat at sea will someday fail, and this can just as well happen when it matters as when it doesn't. It is outright certain that it will one day fail. Ask anyone who has sailed a yacht for a long distance in the ocean. If theirs has not failed, they know someone whose has. The practical approach is to learn celestial, practice it till you are confident with it, and then use GPS whenever you can.

Celestial navigation is aesthetically satisfying, and it is part of the tradition of the sea that makes sailing so attractive. But it does take some time to do right, which can be at a premium to the skipper underway. As far as manning the boat is concerned, a GPS is worth about a quarter of a crew member on a long ocean passage. Prudent ocean navigation by *celestial alone* will take someone about one quarter of their on-watch time to do the job.

1.2 Overview of Celestial Navigation

Celestial navigation can mean many things, but mostly it means using a sextant to measure the angular heights of a few stars, and a watch to record the corresponding times, and then comparing this information with the known locations of these stars at the time you looked at them. You end up with your latitude and longitude. The entire process takes about an hour or so, and is described in detail in the next section. Star and planet sights are done during morning or evening twilight, while both stars and horizon are visible. Sun and moon sights can be taken throughout the day, but we cannot very often take sights at night, because the horizon is not visible. Artificial horizons and bubble sextants, although useful on land, essentially do not work from a moving vessel underway.

"Taking a star sight" (sometimes called "shooting a star") is the name of the process of using a sextant to measure the angular height of a star above the horizon, and then noting the precise time you did it. Chapter 2 covers this step. The term "sight reduction" is the name of the bookwork and paperwork of celestial navigation. The special tables you need to find your position are a *Nautical Almanac*, to tell you where the stars were when you did the sights, and sight reduction tables, to do the computations. The paperwork is followed by a few minutes of special chart work, and you're done.

Once the procedures are learned, celestial navigation is easy to do, and easy to comprehend—that is, if you make a mistake, it is usually easy to spot it and correct it. Providing you know the right time, it is rare to be fooled by it. Each star sight you take yields one line on your chart. If the lines from three different stars all cross at the same point, then that intersection is where you must be. There is no mistake (other than an unknown watch error) that will get you three lines that cross somewhere you aren't. Even if your watch is wrong, the latitude of the intersection will be your correct latitude; but the longitude will be off in proportion to the watch error.

If you do make a mistake and can't correct it, it's probably not too serious. At the next opportunity, take another set of sights. In other words, if your celestial fails once, you can recover. When an electronic navigation aid fails, it usually fails for good, or at least for as long as you remain in that part of the ocean.

Celestial navigation is accurate—even more accurate than we usually need or care to take advantage of. Celestial accuracy can be pushed down to about ±0.5 miles or so, but realistically, we won't often want to spend the extra time and energy to get to this limit. We can achieve 1 or 2 miles accuracy with much less work. The main influence on celestial accuracy in actual practice is how we average a series of sights and how we correct each of them for the motion of the boat during the time we are taking the sights. As far as the actual sextant use and sight taking are concerned, in typical conditions, someone who has taken 1,000 sights will not do much better than someone who has taken only 50 sights, providing each analyzes the sights properly. The more experienced person might do better in unfavorable conditions such as rough seas, cloudy skies, or faint stars, but most sights are not in these conditions. The point is that the sight-taking itself is usually not the main influence on the final accuracy of a typical fix.

Celestial sights take about 30 minutes to complete, and if you are moving at 7 knots during this period, you moved 3.5 miles during the time you were figuring out where you were. Obviously, this must be accounted for if we are to claim an accuracy of less than 1 mile or so.

As a rule, we can expect a routine accuracy of some 2 or 3 miles providing we use good procedures, but nothing fancy, and maybe as bad as twice that in the worst conditions with a limited number of sights. If celestial sights end up leaving us uncertain of our position by as much as 10 or 15 miles, then we are making a mistake somewhere, and we should track it down and double-check our general procedures.

Do not be discouraged by the occasional stories you might hear about how difficult celestial is from a small boat, bouncing around in the waves. First of all, rough conditions are much less common than good conditions along typical cruising routes in typical cruising seasons. Furthermore, most reported difficulties can be traced to a lack of preparation in the proper procedures. When we run across a point or procedure that is important to do properly, we will stress it, and try to explain the reasons for doing it in the suggested way. In some cases, it is indeed difficult if not done properly.

In this course we will stress the importance of doing moon, planet, and star sights, not just sun sights. You will likely hear, however, of sailors reporting that they sailed around the world, or all their lives, and never took any sights but sun sights. This may be the case, but such statements can be evaluated only by looking into the details of such voyages.

To add to such stories, we have taught celestial to top-of-the-line professional skippers of commercial ships and luxury power yachts who had been around the world numerous times without taking *any* sights or even knowing how to. For that matter, the vast majority of all vessels that ply the oceans daily never take celestial sights. Most are power-driven with GPS backing up GPS or other electronics; and in a power-driven vessel, you don't have to worry about navigation if the power fails. If the power fails, you aren't going anywhere. But when a sailor makes such statements, we need to know more about the boat, the skipper, and the level of success that is being claimed. What other equipment did they have? To what extent did they use celestial at all? Did they indeed make the landfalls they sought in each case? What was their range under power (that allowed for correcting navigation errors)? And were they otherwise prudent skippers to begin with?

It is certainly not prudent to rely on celestial navigation alone and then use only the sun. Sparing the details for now, the simple truth is that if you navigate by the sun alone, you gradually lose information about your longitude, no matter how careful you are and no matter how sophisticated your methods are. If the only thing you see in your sextant for two or three weeks is the sun, you won't know your longitude for certain until you see a landmark. The usual reason for doing only sun sights is not knowing how to do star sights. Nearly any navigator who knows how to do star sights will do star sights, because they know that this is the one way to be certain of your position. Sun sights alone will never give you this confidence, because, in mathematical fact, the certainty is not there to be given. A sun–moon fix will do it, but not the sun alone. We stress the limits of navigation by sun alone, because there are many books that claim otherwise. It also pays to remember, when we hear various claims of what is and what is not needed in navigation, that a lack of car wrecks is rarely proof of good driving.

The subject of celestial navigation, itself, and how it has evolved, has a certain fascination quite apart from its practical value. It is fascinating from a purely scientific point of view—and almost magic from a non-scientific one. The basic principles of mathematics and astronomy that make celestial navigation work are ancient—mostly discovered or invented (a philosophical question beyond this book) by Hipparchus around 200 B.C. The way celestial navigation is done today is essentially the same as the way it was done then, as far as the principles are concerned.

We do it, of course, much better now, but that does not mean we have better principles. We do it better because 2,000 years of technology have gone by. We now have better instruments (sextants and clocks), better star charts (almanacs), better ways to do the computations (sight reduction tables and computers), and better knowledge of some details, such as how light rays from the vacuum of outer space interact with the atmosphere of the earth. But we don't have better principles; the principles are the same as those understood 2,000 years ago.

This is not meant to downplay important developments in modern times; there have been many and they continue to appear. To highlight a few of the key points: In the mid-1400s, astronomy data was compiled specifically for global ocean navigation; in the 1700s, good sextants and seagoing clocks appeared; and the Sumner method of computation from about the time of the Civil War remains the standard way to solve the problem. But the Sumner method is just the computational practice in vogue during this narrow stage of history. Before Sumner it was done a different way, and now calculators and handheld computers are beginning to replace the Sumner method with direct numerical solutions of the ancient formulas.

The Sumner method, after all, is not as accurate as the numbers it uses. The fact that navigators can now carry a small computer in a shirt pocket (smartphone) quite simply out dates the Sumner method—although we indeed learn this Sumner method in this course (more precisely, a 1900 variation of it developed by Marc St. Hilaire), because it can be done without a computer of any kind. The most recent influence on the Sumner method itself occurred at the end of the Second World War, when big computers first became available for public projects. This allowed the government to calculate a new type of sight reduction table, which greatly simplified the application of this method. These appeared in the late 1930s, and the book and paperwork of celestial navigation have remained essentially identical since then.

The main changes during this latter period have been an improved availability of quality sextants starting in about 1960—not more accurate, but much easier to use—and the advent of inexpensive quartz watches in the late 1970s or so. In the late 1980s, the little computers appeared, and in 1989, the *Nautical Almanac* made a few noteworthy changes, which we will cover later. One thing they did was to start including the formulas for computer programmers to use.

1.3 Bird's-Eye View of a Celestial Fix

For some readers, it may prove useful to have a quick overview of what is physically involved in finding a position using celestial navigation. When learning celestial for the first time, it is easy to get caught up in the book work and still not yet know what the whole process looks like. This note is intended to remedy that. We will just imagine that we are a little bird on the boat watching a navigator do a fix, and describe what we see without going into details. This is not intended as an explanation of the steps, just a look at them. The rest of the course goes over each step in detail.

Let's say it is late afternoon and we know the navigator is getting ready to start preparations for a round of evening star sights. The first thing we would see is him sitting at the chart table looking at both the logbook and the plotting sheet that shows the navigational track of the boat. These are just blank charts with Lat-Lon grids. He would be reading the logbook and then using parallel rulers or some such device to lay out the individual legs of the recent record of the trip. His goal now is to figure out the present DR position.

Normally this does not come automatically. The logbook records only the course and course changes; the navigator must then translate these into lines on the chart using the latitude grid for miles and the compass rose to lay out the course direction. This process can take anywhere from five minutes to an hour or more. It depends on when it was done last and the conditions present. When reaching across the trade winds, for example, you might hold the same course for days, in which case this plotting is quick and easy. Or you might be sailing through variable weather, with course changes every few hours or so. With an approaching frontal system, for example, the winds back slowly around to the south over a period of half a day or so. In any event, he is sitting at the chart table doing reading and plotting for some length of time. Again, his goal is to figure out where he is now (as best he can by DR) and then to project ahead to figure out roughly where he will be at twilight, when it will be time to do the star sights.

Once he has this done, he will open the almanac and very quickly figure what the precise time of the sights will be. This depends on the estimated position at twilight and on the date. This takes just a minute, with only one piece of addition or subtraction. With this information in hand, he might double-check that he has the right estimated position for twilight, since he had to roughly guess the longitude in order to get the precise time. Now that he knows the time, he can fine-tune this, or at least check it. As we shall see later on, it does not matter for the sight taking itself if he happens to have an inaccurate DR position here. The preparation will still be useful even with large uncertainties in this estimated position.

With an estimated position and time of the sights, he goes back to the almanac and looks up another number needed for the preparation. With this done, he turns to another book (Pub. 249 Vol 1), and from it he finds the seven best stars to use for this evening's sights. The book lists the sextant settings and the directions of each of the stars, and also marks the three that will make the best fix. It will not matter one bit if the navigator happens to know these stars, or if he has never heard of them before. All stars are just points of light, and he knows where the points are located now from his perspective on the boat. Again, it only takes a minute to get this list.

He writes the list on a small notebook, which he will later take on deck to record the actual sights. At this point, he might set the alarm on his wrist watch to remind him of the time he should start the sights. And then the preparation is done. He might, however, use this time to check his watch. He would tune the SSB radio or SW receiver to WWV and listen to the time ticks as he watched his watch. When the time was announced (which it is each minute) followed by a distinct tone, he would note the time on his watch and then record in a navigational notebook the watch error he detected. He would not be setting the watch, just recording the error. This process usually takes 1 or 2 minutes.

Once he has in hand the estimate of his twilight time position, the total time it takes for the preparation, including watch check, is about 10 minutes. The books he has used so far are: the logbook; the plotting sheet; the *Nautical Almanac*; a large book called Pub. 249, Vol.1; a small notebook; and a navigational notebook. The latter is used for all nav notes in lieu of scrap paper, since nearly anything he might write down could prove to be important in tracking down some discrepancy later on if it should appear.

We fly around and do whatever until we hear the alarm go off. Then we see him go to the nav station, get out his small notebook and read and record the log reading along with his watch time. He is just making a note, for later use, of the precise time and corresponding log of when he started the sights. He also records the present course and speed. He then gets the sextant out and puts away the box, which is usually a hazard to leave lying about. (We notice that things were well organized in that he had a specific place to put the sextant box after he removed the instrument, which he could do with one hand, while the other hand held the sextant.) He then checks the mirrors to see if any salt spray has built up on them, and if so, he pours a cup of fresh water over them and cleans them off.

Thus, he goes on deck with his sextant, his watch on his arm, and a small notebook and pencil in his pocket. When he arrives on deck, the sun has already set, but the horizon is still essentially in daylight. No stars are yet visible. He quickly checks the compass so he can get the sky oriented with the boat.

We are in a bit of a seaway, so he positions himself next to the shrouds, and laces one leg through them and puts one arm around them. He sets the sextant to 0° 0' and then looks toward the horizon for a few seconds. He then reads the sextant and again checks the horizon. After that he makes a note in the small notebook. He has checked and recorded the index correction of the sextant, a procedure that is normally done at the beginning of each sight session. Then he reads from the notebook, to see what the sextant reading should be for the eastern most star since that part of the horizon is the darkest at this time. He then sets the sextant to that reading and points the sextant in the proper direction he had recorded. He does not have to worry about getting the direction precisely, because he can scan around the approximate direction and find the star since the sextant is already set to the proper reading.

The star will appear as a point of pure white light in a pale blue background. It is indeed a pretty thing to look at, and one of the quiet pleasures of being a navigator. For the first few times you do it, it is like a mini religious experience—to realize that you have found this little star in just the right place, from the middle of a big ocean, after looking up a few numbers in a table. Remember, too, at this stage of twilight, that if you take the sextant down, you won't see the star at all. Others around you won't see it either. Only you can see it, because you are looking in just the right place, and you are looking with a telescope.

When looking through the sextant telescope, the navigator will be seeing both the star and the horizon, and as he turns the micrometer drum of the sextant, the two will come together. When they just touch, he will gently rock the sextant to ensure that he has the proper vertical angle, as discussed later in Chapter 2, and then he will read his watch. He will then record the watch reading in the small notebook, and then read the sextant, record its reading, and that one sight is done. He will come back to this star for more sights later on, but first he takes sights of two other stars, roughly 120° apart in bearings, using the same procedures for each. There is rarely any reason to take sights of more than 3 stars. It is by far better to take 4 sights each of 3 well-positioned stars than it is to take 1 sight each of 12 different stars. The latter exercise is really a waste of time from an accuracy point of view (though it might be good practice); you would be better off with 6 sights each of 2 stars only. Also note that he is pointing the sextant telescope toward the horizon below the star, not at the star itself.

He will continue on with these sights until he has 3 or 4 sights of each star, or until it grows too dark to see the horizon. This usually takes between 20 and 40 minutes, depending on latitude and season. He then goes below, puts away the sextant, and again records the log reading, course, and corresponding watch time.

At this point, he could go to bed, knowing that he has the sights and tomorrow he can figure out where he was last night. More likely, though, he would follow through with the paperwork just after finishing the sights.

To do the paperwork (*sight reduction*), he will go back to the nav station and take out the same two books (*Nautical Almanac* and sight reduction tables) and probably a few work forms. The forms are outlines with blank spaces to be filled in, which guide the navigator through the various steps of the procedures. We will watch him filling out this form, turning back and forth between his two books and the forms. He may be using a small calculator to help with the arithmetic, or he could be doing it by hand on the forms. If he is just getting a routine fix, without special corrections for optimum accuracy, we might see him do this for about 30-45 minutes. At the end of the book and paperwork, we will see him drawing lines on the plotting sheet. He will have drawn three lines, corresponding to the three stars he took sights of. The intersection of these lines will

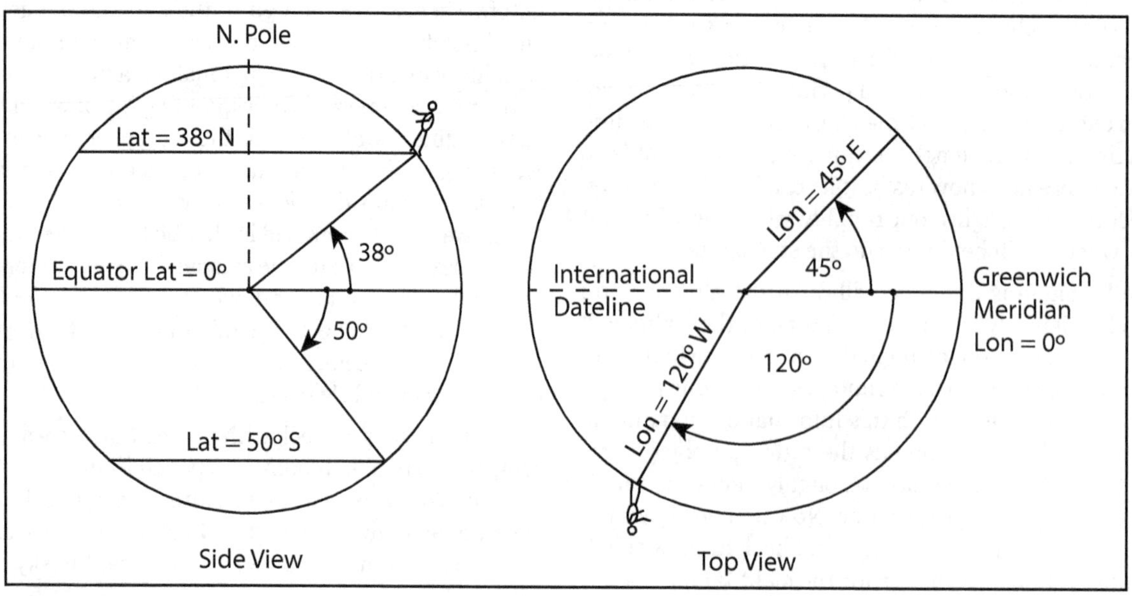

Figure 1.4-1 *The angles that define latitude and longitude..*

be the fix. The plotting part does not take long, maybe 5 or 10 minutes, once all the paperwork is done. One of the main tasks of this course—at least the part that takes the most pages of this book—is the explanation of what he is doing during these past 40 minutes or so.

After he has found the fix position, he will write it in the logbook and maybe plot it on a small-scale nautical chart that shows the progress of the voyage. Then we will see him sitting there for some time thinking about the results.

This story has referred to the navigator as "him", but we might add that some of the best ocean navigators in the Golden Age of Sail as well as the modern ocean racing circuit have been women. There is clearly no reason at all that one gender would do better than another at this skill, not to mention the great value of having both partners on a voyage be prepared to navigate.

1.4 Latitude, Longitude, and Nautical Miles

Latitude and longitude provide a grid on the surface of the earth that enables the navigator to give a precise label to every point on earth. The location of the light house at Cape Flattery, Washington, for example, is latitude 48° 23.5' North and longitude 124° 44.1' West. Latitude and longitude are given in degrees and minutes (1° = 60'), since both are defined in terms of angular distances on the globe.

Figure 1.4-1 shows the angles that lead to the definitions. Our latitude tells how far we are north or south of the equator, which is defined as latitude 0°. The North Pole is at latitude 90° North. Oregon and Washington lie between latitudes 42° N and 48° N. In other words, these states are about halfway between the equator and the North Pole. If we know our latitude we know how far we are up or down the earth relative to the equator; but we need to know our longitude to tell us how far we are around the earth. Figures 1.4-2 and 1.4-3 show how the Lat-Lon angles are angles displayed on a chart.

The reference line for longitude is the north–south line running through Greenwich, England. Longitude is measured relative to the Greenwich meridian, which is also called the Prime Meridian. This choice of reference is based on historical and political developments. The Greenwich meridian does not have special physical or geographical significance, as the equator does. To say where we are around the earth we say how far we are east or west of the Greenwich meridian. The longitude at the Greenwich meridian is 0°. The meridian at longitude 180°, the longitude line on the opposite side of the earth from the Greenwich meridian, is called the International Date Line. When one sails across this line from either direction, the local date changes by one day. Time and longitude are inseparably related in navigation, as we shall see in many examples throughout this course.

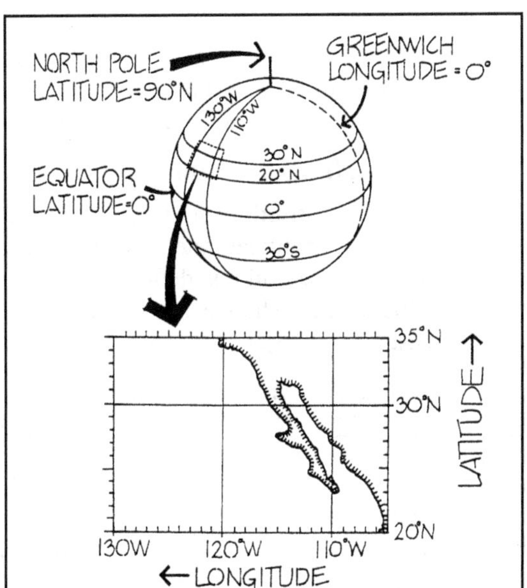

Figure 1.4-2 *Latitude and Longitude translated from the globe to a Mercator chart*

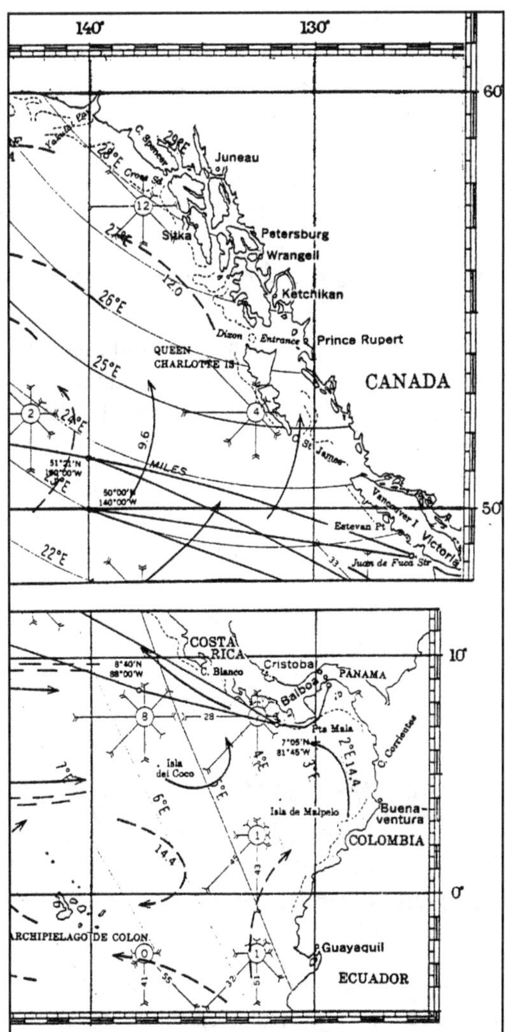

Figure 1.4-3 *Lat-Lon grids on a Mercator chart at different latitudes. The grids are square near the equator, but much narrower at high latitudes. The number of nautical miles per 1° of longitude = 60 × cos (Latitude). For details see Sections 11.4 and 11.10.*

An east–west line of constant latitude is called a *parallel* of latitude—along our northwestern boundary, the Canadian border is at the 49th parallel. A north–south line of constant longitude is called a *meridian* of longitude.

Besides describing the location of places, we can also use latitude and longitude to describe the location of heavenly bodies. The location of a star, for example, is the latitude and longitude of the point on earth directly below the object. A person standing at the location of the sun sees the sun directly overhead. Since the earth turns, and the sun and stars are fixed in space, the locations of the sun and stars circle the earth once a day. The sun or a star is said to be "on our meridian" or "crossing our meridian" when it bears due north or south, regardless of its height in the sky. To navigators, the meridian passage of the sun defines the time of local apparent noon.

This system of telling where the stars are located in terms of the latitude and longitude on earth that lies below them is the only logical way to do it. At any given time, this is a unique way to pin point its location that is valid for all people on earth. During a long-distance call to Hawaii, for example, we cannot meaningfully discuss the location of the star Arcturus in terms of bearings and heights above the horizon, since we would each see the star at different heights and bearings as we spoke. But we could talk about the location of the star as the point below it, because that point is unique. As the course proceeds, we shall see that by knowing the location of that point, we will be able to predict what the height and bearing of the star would be from any point on earth.

For several purposes in navigation and meteorology, it is convenient to divide the globe into latitude bands according to the relationship of the sun to the earth. The three regions are: the tropics, the latitudes, and the polar regions.

The tropics are defined as the central belt of the earth extending from latitude 23.4° S to 23.4° N. We write this latitude in this decimal form instead of the more common equivalent form of 23° 24' to draw your attention to the accidental numerical sequence (2-3-4) that makes this an easy number to remember. There are several emergency techniques in celestial navigation that are benefited by knowing this latitude precisely, although it is certainly not at all critical to know this for routine celestial. (23.44 would be a bit better, but the latter is easier to remember.)

The special latitude of 23.4° comes about because the earth's rotation axis is tilted 23.4° relative to the plane of its orbit around the sun. Because of this tilt, the sun can be viewed directly overhead only from within the tropics. During the winter, the sun is overhead at some latitude in the southern tropics; during the summer, the sun circles the earth over the northern tropics. (Throughout this book, we refer to summer and winter as they are defined in the Northern Hemisphere. In the Southern Hemisphere, these seasons are reversed. July and August are called summer months in the United States; in Australia, they are called winter months.)

The two polar regions are defined as latitudes greater than 66.6°, north or south. These regions are unique as the only places on earth where the sun can remain above or below the horizon for more than one day. In one sense the polar regions are the opposite of the tropics—the latitude 66.6° comes from 90° minus 23.4°.

Everywhere between the tropics and the polar regions, that is, between 23.4° and 66.6°, is called the temperate latitudes, or just the latitudes. In this book the phrase "northern latitudes" refers to the general region in the Northern Hemisphere north of the tropics and south of the polar region.

These latitude regions are of significance to navigation because we can navigate by the position of the sun. They are important to meteorology because the position of the sun, or at least the average position of the sun, causes the weather. There are no similar divisions of the earth according to longitude—because of the daily rotation of the earth, the earth is essentially symmetric in the east–west direction.

In modern ocean navigation, precise positions are usually recorded as degrees, minutes, and tenths of minutes (48° 39.7'), as opposed to degrees, minutes, and seconds (48° 39' 42"). You will see the latter notation in *USCG Light Lists*, but almost never in ocean navigation.

Nautical Miles

It is easy to think of latitude differences in terms of nautical miles, because the nautical mile was invented for just this purpose. One nautical mile is defined as the distance on earth equal to a latitude change of one arc minute. Or in terms of degrees:

Common Conversions	
1 nautical mile	= 1852 m
	≈ 1.15 statute miles
	≈ 6,000 ft
	≈ 1' of latitude
1 meter	≈ 3.28 ft

...In Depth

11.4 Mercator Charts.

Outside of the polar regions, nautical charts are based on a Mercator projection. This note explains the unique properties of these charts and why this is a good choice for navigators at sea and on land.

1° of latitude = 60 nautical miles.

This relationship is the key to the language of navigation. If my latitude is 10° N, I am 600 nautical miles north of the equator. If I am to sail from the Columbia River (46° N) due south to San Diego (33° N), then I must sail south for 13°, or a distance of 780 nautical miles (13 × 60 = 780). A nautical mile is just over 6,000 ft; it is 15% longer than a statute mile. In this book, the words mile and nautical mile are used interchangeably; any reference to miles means nautical miles. See Figure 1.4-4.

For longitude degrees, however, the conversion to miles is not as simple. The problem is the the meridians or longitude lines get closer together as you go north or south of the equator, so the number of miles between them decreases as the latitude increases. At the equator 1° of longitude does equal 60 nautical miles—in fact, this is very nearly true throughout the tropics. But as you go farther from the equator, this is no longer a good approximation. At latitude 48°, there are only 40 nautical miles to a degree of longitude. The precise number for any latitude can be read from a nautical chart or plotting sheet of the area.

1.5 Arithmetic of Angles and Time

Adding and subtracting angles and time is the only mathematics needed for celestial navigation. The problems we must solve are easy, but it will pay in the long run to stop and practice this before going on. As with all celestial navigation, it helps to have a systematic approach to the task.

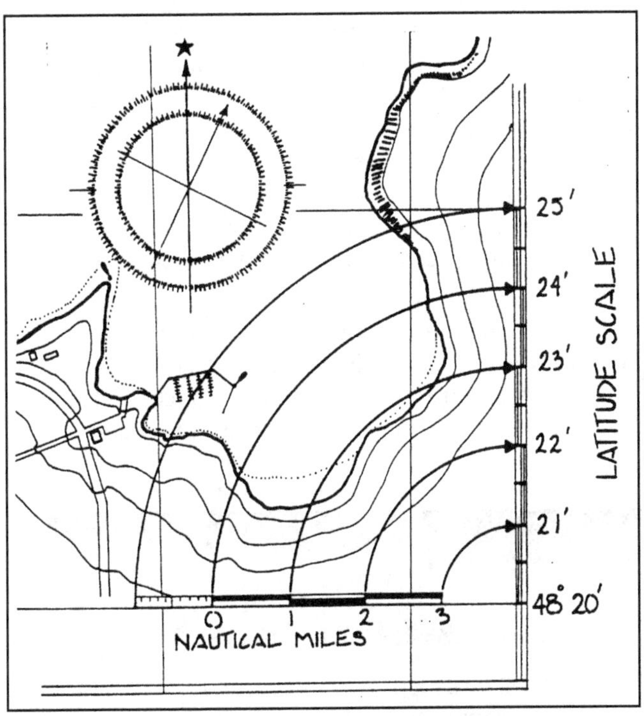

Figure 1.4-4 *Distances on a Mercator chart can be measured with the latitude scale, 1' of latitude = 1 nmi. Charts at scale of 1:40,000 or larger include a miles scale; on smaller scales we must use the latitude grid at about the same latitude we care about on the chart.*

The angles we must add and subtract will include degrees and minutes, and the minutes will usually be written in tenths. We do the minutes part and the degrees part of the problem separately, just as when adding feet and inches. Example:

$$\begin{array}{rr} 45^\circ & 20.6' \\ +\,13^\circ & 16.3' \\ \hline =58^\circ & 36.9' \end{array} \qquad \begin{array}{rr} 45^\circ & 20.6' \\ -\,13^\circ & 16.3' \\ \hline =32^\circ & 4.3' \end{array}$$

If the sum of the minutes is over 60', rewrite the result by subtracting 60' from it and adding 1° to the degrees part. Likewise, if the degrees part is over 360°, subtract 360° from it to get back to the primary angle. Example:

$$\begin{array}{rr} 114^\circ & 26.3' \\ +\,4^\circ & 51.5' \\ \hline 118^\circ & 77.8' \end{array} = 119^\circ \;\; 17.8'$$

$$\begin{array}{rr} 230^\circ & 12.0' \\ +\,155^\circ & 10.4' \\ \hline 385^\circ & 22.4' \end{array} = 25^\circ \;\; 22.4'$$

Sometimes we must subtract a large number from a smaller one. If this occurs in just the minutes part of the problem, we solve this by borrowing 1° from the degrees part. In other words, rewrite the angle by subtracting 1° from the degrees part and adding 60' to the minutes part. Example:

$$\begin{array}{rr} 120^\circ & 10.5' \\ -\,30^\circ & 25.4' \\ \hline & \end{array} \;⊠\; \begin{array}{rr} 119^\circ & 70.5' \\ -\,30^\circ & 25.4' \\ \hline =89^\circ & 45.1' \end{array}$$

If we must subtract a large angle from a smaller one, the first step is to add 360° to the small one. Then proceed as before. Example:

$$\begin{array}{rr} 18^\circ & 20.8' \\ -\,133^\circ & 15.2' \end{array} \;⊠\; \begin{array}{rr} +\,360^\circ & \\ 18^\circ & 20.8' \\ -\,133^\circ & 15.2' \end{array}$$

which is the same as:

$$\begin{array}{rr} 378^\circ & 20.8' \\ -\,133^\circ & 15.2' \\ \hline =245^\circ & 05.6' \end{array}$$

If both the degrees part and the minutes part are smaller, do the same, but write the 360° as 359° 60'. Example:

			+ 359°	60.0'
40°	27.8'	⊠	40°	27.8'
− 55°	42.3'		− 55°	42.3'

which is the same as:

399°	87.8'
− 55°	42.3'
= 344°	45.5'

If we must sum a column of angles with some positive and some negative, there are several ways to go about it. We could go down the list doing them two at a time, or we could add all the positive angles into one sum and then add all the negative angles into another sum, and then subtract the negative sum from the positive sum.

The easiest way to solve this problem, however, is to use a calculator that does accumulative sums. Most calculators, even the very inexpensive ones, can do this. With these you just go down the list entering the numbers (±) as they occur; the accumulated sum keeps track of the right sign. If you are summing the minutes part and the result is negative, just add 60' to it and subtract 1° from the degrees column. If the sum of the minutes is greater than 60', subtract 60' and add 1° to the degrees column. Calculator examples:

+ 330°	15.0'	+ 38°	55.3'
− 1°	2.2'		+ 1.3'
− 28°	53.4'		− 2.9'
+ 122°	20.0'		+ 15.5'
= 423°	-20.6'	= 38°	69.2'
− 1°	+ 60.0'	+ 1°	− 60.0'
= 422°	39.4'	= 39°	09.2'
− 360°			
= 62°	39.4'		

Practice problems are in the next section. Again, this is all the mathematics we need, but we are not allowed to make mistakes. We shall soon see that a 1' error in our arithmetic translates into a position error of about 1 nautical mile—and possibly more. If we look up a number in a table and it is 334° and we copy it to our work form as 343°, we are in for a 600-or-700-mile error.

Nearly all mistakes in celestial navigation are mistakes in arithmetic or in copying down a number—or copying a number from the wrong table page. Fortunately, most errors of this type result in a fix that is way off our known approximate position, and we catch the error. But usually we won't spot the mistake until near the end of our work, which may take 30 minutes or so. Thus going slow, checking and double-checking along the way always pays off.

Time and Timekeeping

We work with time and timekeeping all the time in celestial navigation. Ultimately, the time we care about is universal time, also called universal coordinated time, UTC. This is the reference time system used in all navigation and in most scientific work. This was formerly called Greenwich Mean Time (GMT), and we still see this name used in some applications.

Most watches use a 12-hour dial, with morning and afternoon times distinguished by a.m. and p.m., ante meridiem and post meridiem, before midday and after midday. We use a similar word, meridian, for the north–south line passing through our position. *Meridiem* is when the sun crosses our meridian.

In principle, the time of midday can be determined from either the bearing of the sun or the height of the sun. At meridian passage, the sun bears due south from northern latitudes or due north from southern latitudes. And viewed from any latitude, the sun reaches its highest point in the sky at midday (high noon). Another way to determine the time of midday would be to note the times of sunrise and sunset. Midday lies halfway between sunrise and sunset viewed from a stationary position. Regardless of how we do it, to tell the time we need to know the time of midday and the location of the sun. It is the location (the longitude) of the sun that ultimately determines the time of day.

In navigation, we do not use the a.m. and p.m. notation. We use a 24-hour dial, because it makes notation and arithmetic easier. Morning times are the same on both scales; afternoon times on the 24-hour scale are just the p.m. times plus 12 hours. In this course we navigate by watch time, and then correct it for any watch error and the time zone of the watch (called its zone description) to get UTC.

We use *watch time* to mean just what it says, namely the time you read from the watch on your arm. We recommend that you navigate from that watch, and do not change its time zone underway. It is also that watch whose

...In Depth

11.5 Timekeeping in Navigation

Practical timekeeping in navigation is easy if we keep it simple, but there are numerous ways to complicate the matter, so it is valuable to review the unnecessary options we are avoiding.

accuracy we monitor as explained in the In-Depth note on Timekeeping. If you ever have to navigate in an emergency, that watch will be the most important tool you have—you can find any port in the world if you have accurate UTC alone, without any other instrument—so having it at hand at all times is clearly prudent. Also any change to it such as changing time zone not only confuses the navigation, but also presents the greatest risk to losing the correct time. Just choose a convenient time zone for the voyage and stick with it. We do not gain anything by having UTC on the watch, because we have to make corrections to the time in any event.

Half the battle in all navigation is notation. It pays to be precise in the way we write down times. We recommend writing h, m, and s to label the hours, minutes, and seconds part of any time. It may seem awkward at first, but it will minimize mistakes. Any notation we can use that minimizes mistakes is beneficial. For example:

10:45 a.m. = 10h 45m,

10:45 p.m. = 22h 45m,

2:20:30 a.m. = 02h 20m 30s,

5:04:13 p.m. = 17h 04m 13s.

Adding and Subtracting Times

The arithmetic of time is just like the arithmetic of angles. The full circle of angles is 360°; the full circle of time is 24 hours. If we add angles and get a result bigger than 360°, we have gone around the circle. In angle addition, we don't care how many times we wrap around the circle; we only care about the final position on the primary circle. In adding times, however, we must be careful about going around the circle, because the date changes if we wrap around past 24 hours.

In adding and subtracting times, we must always end up with a positive time less than 24 hours. If the sum of two times is greater than 24 hours, subtract 24 and increase the date by one day. Likewise, if the answer to a subtraction problem is negative, add 24 hours and decrease the date by one day. Minutes and seconds should be written as less than 60, which means rewriting some answers, and in some problems, we must borrow from the hours to help the minutes and so forth, just as with angles. The following examples cover all cases we might run into. Examples:

5h 14m 32s	July 4th
+ 13h 20m 10s	
= 18h 34m 42s	July 4th

22h 16m 54s	July 4th
– 4h 04m 32s	
= 18h 12m 22s	July 4th

If you get stuck while working on your own, the following detailed rules should guide you through any type of angle or time problem.

Rules for Angle Addition

(AA-1) Add minutes column and then degrees column as two separate problems.

(AA-2) If minutes sum is greater than 60', subtract 60' and add 1° to the degrees sum.

(AA-3) If the degrees part is greater than 360°, subtract 360°. In rare cases you may have to subtract 360° twice to get back to the primary circle.

Rules for Angle Subtraction

First look at the problem, degrees part and minutes part, to determine what you must do. You will have one of four cases, and the rules here tell you what to do in each case to end up with the answer in the proper form.

(AS-1) Small degrees from large degrees; small minutes from large minutes. The simplest case. Just subtract them.

(AS-2) Small degrees from large degrees; large minutes from small minutes. Subtract 1° from the degrees part and add 60' to the minutes part. Now you are back to step (1).

(AS-3) Large degrees from small degrees; small minutes from large minutes. Add 360° to the degrees part, and you are back to step (1).

(AS-4) Large degrees from small degrees; large minutes from small minutes. Add 359° to the degrees part, and add 60' to the minutes part, and you are back to step (1).

Rules for Time Addition

(TA-1) Add the hours, minutes, and seconds parts as separate problems.

(TA-2) If seconds sum is greater than 60s, subtract 60s and add 1m to the minutes sum.

(TA-3) If minutes sum is greater than 60m, subtract 60m and add 1h to the hours sum.

(TA-4) If the hours sum is greater than 24h, subtract 24h and add 1 day to the date.

Rules for Time Subtraction

First look at the problem, hours part, minutes part, and seconds part, to determine what you must do. You will have one of eight cases; the rules here tell you what to do in each case to end up with an answer in the proper form.

(TS-1) Small hours from large hours; small minutes from large minutes; small seconds from large seconds. The simplest case; just subtract them.

(TS-2) Small hours from large hours; small minutes from large minutes; large seconds from small seconds. Subtract 1m from the minutes part and add 60s to the seconds part to get back to step (1).

(TS-3) Small hours from large hours; large minutes from small minutes; small seconds from large seconds. Subtract 1h from the hours part and add 60m to the minutes part to get back to step (1).

(TS-4) Small hours from large hours; large minutes from small minutes; large seconds from small seconds. Subtract 1h from the hours part, add 59m to the minutes part, and add 60s to the seconds part to get back to step (1).

(TS-5) Large hours from small hours; small minutes from large minutes; small seconds from large seconds. Add 24h to the hours part and subtract 1 day from the date, and you are back to step (1) with the proper date.

(TS-6) Large hours from small hours; large minutes from small minutes; small seconds from large seconds. Add 23h to the hours part, add 60m to the minutes part, and subtract 1 day from the date, and you are back to step (1) with the proper date.

(TS-7) Large hours from small hours; large minutes from small minutes; large seconds from small seconds. Add 23h to the hours part, add 59m to the minutes part, add 60s to the seconds part, and subtract 1 day from the date. This gets you back to step (1) with the proper date.

(TS-8) Large hours from small hours; small minutes from large minutes; large seconds from small seconds. Add 24h to the hours part, subtract 1m from the minutes part, add 60s to the seconds part, and subtract 1 day from the date. This gets you back to step (1) with the proper date. (Note that you could also work this one using rule TS-7, but then you might have to readjust the minutes answer when you finish.)

22h 15m 55s	May 3rd
+ 8h 28m 18s	
= 30h 43m 73s	May 3rd

30h 44m 13s	
− 24h 00m 00s	(+ 1 day)
= 06h 44m 13s	May 4th

To do a subtraction problem, first rewrite minutes and seconds such that you are subtracting a small number from a bigger one. Example:

18h 34m 21s	May 8th
− 10h 55m 33s	

which is the same as

18h	34m	21s	May 8th
− 1h			
	+ 59m		
		+ 60s	
= 17h	93m	81s	May 8th
− 10h	55m	33s	
= 7h	38m	48s	May 8th

which is now in a form that can be solved. If you notice that the hours are also too small—that is, you are going to get a negative time—then add on 24 hours to begin with. If you also notice that the minutes and seconds need help, take some from the 24 hours as you add it, that is, add 23h 59m 60s instead of 24h. Examples:

05h 52m 03s	May 5th
− 10h 32m 16s	

which is the same as

+ 23h 59m 60s	(−1 day)
05h 52m 03s	May 5th
− 10h 32m 16s	

which is the same as

28h 111m 63s	May 4th
− 10h 32m 16s	
= 18h 79m 47s	May 4th
= 19h 19m 47s	May 4th

Whenever you add 24 hours, you must subtract one day; when you subtract 24 hours, you add one day.

Without a doubt, the most important thing to learn about celestial navigation as soon as possible is the practice of continuously checking your work. When you get a number from a table, check and double-check that you are in the right place in the right table. And when you do your arithmetic, do it twice to check yourself. Mistakes in the minutes column may not stand out so clearly; you just get a bad fix.

1.6 Exercise on Adding and Subtracting Angles

The following are typical problems from celestial navigation. All answers (given at the back of the book) should be positive and less than 360°. If you get stuck, refer to the rules in the previous boxes.

Actually, these are not truly typical problems; most of these practice examples are the typical tricky ones, where you have to adjust the degrees and minutes and think about what is positive and what is negative. Most of the problems we run across are easier, with degrees and minutes working out nicely. This exercise just makes the hardest part of our work as hard as possible, so we don't have any surprises later on.

(a)	34° 34.9'	(g)	104° 26.6'
	+ 119° 23.5'		– 134° 26.6'
(b)	52° 46.8'	(h)	90° 00.0'
	+1° 30.3'		– 25° 16.5'
(c)	286° 45.2'	(i)	52° 16.8'
	– 122° 20.0'		– 52° 05.2'
(d)	147° 12.8'	(j)	38° 16.5'
	– 145° 30.1'		– 3.0'
			– 4.1'
(e)	50° 10.6'	(k)	54° 01.0'
	– 102° 05.2'		+ 1.5'
			– 3.9'
(f)	21° 15.6'	(l)	303° 23.4'
	– 65° 38.7'		+ 2° 35.6'
			+ 147° 19.7'

1.7 Exercise on Adding and Subtracting Times

Again, these practice problems cover all the tricks you might run across. The typical problems we run across are easier. Answers are at the back of the book.

(a)	5h	20m	43s	May 2
	+18h	02m		
(b)	11h	15m	30s	May 22
	+8h	22m	50s	
(c)	15h	59m	13s	May 1
	- 4h	13m	10s	
(d)	20h	11m	26s	May 2
	+ 7h	55m	12s	
(e)	5h	02m	19s	May 5
	– 6h	40m	05s	
(f)	18h	36m	28s	May 9
	– 7h	12m	40s	
(g)	10h	20m	19s	May 1
	– 23h	14m	08s	
(h)	6h	15m	33s	May 20
	– 17h	03m	48s	
(i)	16h	28m	02s	May 3
	– 16h	42m	10s	
			+ 06s	
(j)	18h	40m	51s	May 8
	+7h			
			+ 13s	
(k)	5h	35m	04s	May 29
			– 18s	
	– 8h			
(l)	12h	59m	54s	May 11
			+ 10s	
	– 8h			

1.8 New Terminology

celestial navigation (cel nav)
chronometer
dead reckoning (DR)
Greenwich meridian (G)
latitude (Lat)
longitude (Lon)
meridian
nautical mile (nmi)
parallel of latitude
tropics
universal time (UTC)
watch error (WE)
watch time (WT)
zone description

Chapter 2
Sextants

2.1 About Sextants

The raw data of celestial navigation is obtained from a handheld instrument called a sextant. Technical aspects of sextants are described in detail in *Bowditch*. A metal sextant, as opposed to a plastic one, should be considered when relying on celestial as a primary means of navigation. New metal sextants vary in price (in 2014) from about $660 to $2,500, and maybe more if you shop around. Plastic sextants are discussed in Section 11.8, which also includes notes on optimizing sights with metal sextants.

The more expensive ones are indeed better instruments, but they won't necessarily do a better job of what we want. In the vast majority of cases, ultimate accuracy in a position fix at sea depends on what we do with the sextant, not the actual specifications of the instrument. The more expensive ones are inherently more accurate, but we can rarely benefit from this extra accuracy. If we choose to sell apples by the pound, for example, we could quite successfully use a scale accurate to an ounce; we do not need an expensive scale that is accurate to a thousandth of an ounce. Furthermore, an apple weight accurate to a thousandth of an ounce does not have much validity anyway. This weight will vary with the relative humidity of the room, etc. There are similar uncertainties in sextant sights at sea that ultimately limit the obtainable accuracy of any single sight. And all metal sextants on the market surpass this limit.

On the other hand, if a bargain sextant falls apart a thousand miles from land, it wasn't such a good deal after all. Fortunately, we can do celestial without any sextant at all, so we don't have to be anxious about this unlikely event coming about.

Used models of high-quality instruments sell for about $700 to $1000. In most cases, if the instrument looks good and all parts move smoothly, chances are that it is OK. If you do not have experience with sextants, however, it is probably best to buy used sextants from a reputable sextant dealer or have one check it out for you.

Brass versus Aluminum

Just about any metal sextant that is not damaged will do the job and provide essentially the same level of accuracy in the final fix at sea. Sextants, do however, vary in their ease of use. Key factors are the size of the mirrors, style of mirrors, kinds of telescopes, and weight. Weights vary from about 2+ lbs (for aluminum alloy models) to as much as 4+ lbs for brass models. Light weight is a big advantage, because when the arms tire, we are not as careful as we should be. Do not believe the nonsense published in some catalogs that claim professionals prefer a heavy instrument because it has inertia, which makes it more stable. The same companies offer an unadvertised expensive custom model made of aluminum alloy, which they claim is the very top of the line because it is so light! (Should we hang a piece of lead on these when doing sights?) The advantage of brass is the metal itself, not its weight. More accurate gears can be cut in brass alloys than in aluminum alloys. Brass alloys withstand the sea air environment better than aluminum ones, but very little of the metal itself is exposed. With reasonable cleaning, either will last a lifetime. More important is the quality of the paint and primer that is protecting the bulk of the instrument.

Sextant Use

Sextant usage can be learned from a manual or textbook, but it is quickest to have it demonstrated by an experienced navigator. These days there are many videos online that show the process, but like much information online we must carefully evaluate what we see. Look at several not just one, and keep in mind what we say here about the process. We have seen some that are well made and indeed start out nicely, but then toward the end they spin out, and expose a limited experience in actually taking sights underway. Also check www.starpath.com/videos.

Sextant use is readily learned; exceptional skills and extensive training are not required. Don't worry if you have learned on land with shorelines or artificial horizons and not yet practiced at sea. Sights are often easier at sea than they are on land, even with some motion of the boat to contend with. Sextants do what they are supposed to—allow you to measure vertical angles precisely from a moving platform.

To do sextant sights, you go on deck with a sextant and your watch, along with paper and pencil to record the sights. A small notebook dedicated to this use is convenient. The sights are generally taken standing at some place with good visibility and some means of support. On a sailboat, this is often on the after deck or amidships next to the shrouds. In rougher seas, it is best to wrap an arm around shrouds or stays during the sights—or wrap the short tether of your safety harness around the shrouds and lean back. Some system is needed to free both hands to operate the sextant while still providing support against sudden boat motion. It is difficult to imagine any reason to go forward of the mast with a sextant. If sails block your view, alter course briefly for the sight.

Large sextant adjustments are made by squeezing the lever on the index arm and then moving the arm along the arc. Smaller adjustments are made by turning the micrometer drum. When reading a sextant, degrees are read from the arc opposite an index mark on the arm; minutes are read from the micrometer drum opposite an index mark on the arm. The index mark on the micrometer drum is often the zero point of a Vernier scale that is used to read tenths of minutes. In most cases, the tenths can be adequately estimated without use of a Vernier scale. A later section of this chapter covers sextant reading with practice problems.

2.2 How to Take a Sight

Before going on deck, record a log reading and corresponding watch time in your sight notebook. Also record the course and speed. This will be used later to correct the sights for boat motion during the sight session itself, which might take up to 45 minutes. Double check that no one has imminent plans to alter course significantly or to do major sail changes that might create havoc around you.

The sighting procedure begins with a check of the Index Correction (IC). Set the sextant to 0° 0' and look toward the horizon. If the direct and reflected views of the horizon form a smooth continuous line, there is no correction (IC = 0.0'). If not aligned, adjust the micrometer drum of the sextant to bring them into alignment, and then read the scale. After making the adjustment, if the micrometer scale reads a small number like 2.5', then record this number as IC = 2.5' "on the scale."

When the micrometer scale reads a large number when the horizon is aligned (back of 0') such as 58.4' then IC is found by subtracting this reading from 60.0'—in this case, record IC = 1.6' "off the scale."

Later on, we will apply this correction to the sextant reading. When doing this, the sign (±) of the correction is from the rule "If it's on, take it off; if off, put it on"—i.e., if a sextant reads 34° 23.5' and the IC is 1.6' off the scale, the corrected sextant reading is 34° 25.1'. Special care should be taken when measuring IC, and it should be checked at each sight session. This is usually done just before evening sights or just after morning sights, so that a sharp horizon is visible and you are not using up good twilight time. When taking a series of sun sights during the day, it could be done between the sights.

The terms *index error* and *index correction* are really the same thing. Some texts distinguish the error from the correction of the error, but this is not important. The "on take it off" rule handles this. We go back over the IC in the next chapter on noon sights.

After the IC has been checked, record the value in your notebook even if it has not changed. This is your proof that you did indeed check it if any question arises later on.

Next, face the object to be sighted and point the telescope of the sextant toward the horizon directly below the object. Adjust the index arm of the sextant to bring the reflected view of the object into simultaneous view with the horizon. This is done with an initial coarse movement of the arm made while squeezing the worm gear release, and then a fine adjustment with the micrometer or Vernier. The final adjustment must be made when the sextant is precisely vertical, or the angle you get will be too big. With the boat heeled, rolling, and pitching, this might seem at first an impossible challenge. A simple trick, however, solves the problem.

The final alignment is made while *rocking the sextant*—which means rotating it slightly to the right and then to the left (without moving the head) about an imaginary line drawn from your eye to the object as it appears on the horizon. The motion is equivalent to a gentle rolling of the sextant about its telescope axis without any yawing or pitching of the instrument as a whole. When the sextant is rocked the object viewed in the telescope will appear to swing in an arc. If the instrument begins to yaw during the roll, the object will begin to slip away from the center of the horizon glass; the job then is to adjust the heading of the sextant slightly as necessary to keep the object in view as you rock it. The sight is completed when the object just touches the horizon at the lowest point on the arc.

To find the lowest arc point in an actual sight, the sextant has to be rocked only some 10° to the right and left, but a good way to learn and master the motion is to greatly exaggerate the rocking angle when practicing. This will help develop your ability to keep the object in sight during unexpected boat motions. Hold your hand steady as you rock the instrument. The sextant telescope rotates against your stationary cheek as you do this.

Fine-tune the sextant angle until you feel you have the best possible alignment of object and horizon at the lowest point of its arc, and then stop further adjustments. Read your watch and record the time to the second. Don't worry about the sextant reading; it won't change. The first task is

...In Depth

11.6 Dip Short

The technique called *dip short* was developed long ago for doing sights from the high deck of a ship when the only option was a sun or moon over a nearby shoreline. It's not often such a circumstance shows up in small-craft navigation, but the method is ideal for doing practice sights using a shoreline for the horizon. Realistic sights can be taken on a lake as small as half a mile or so across...

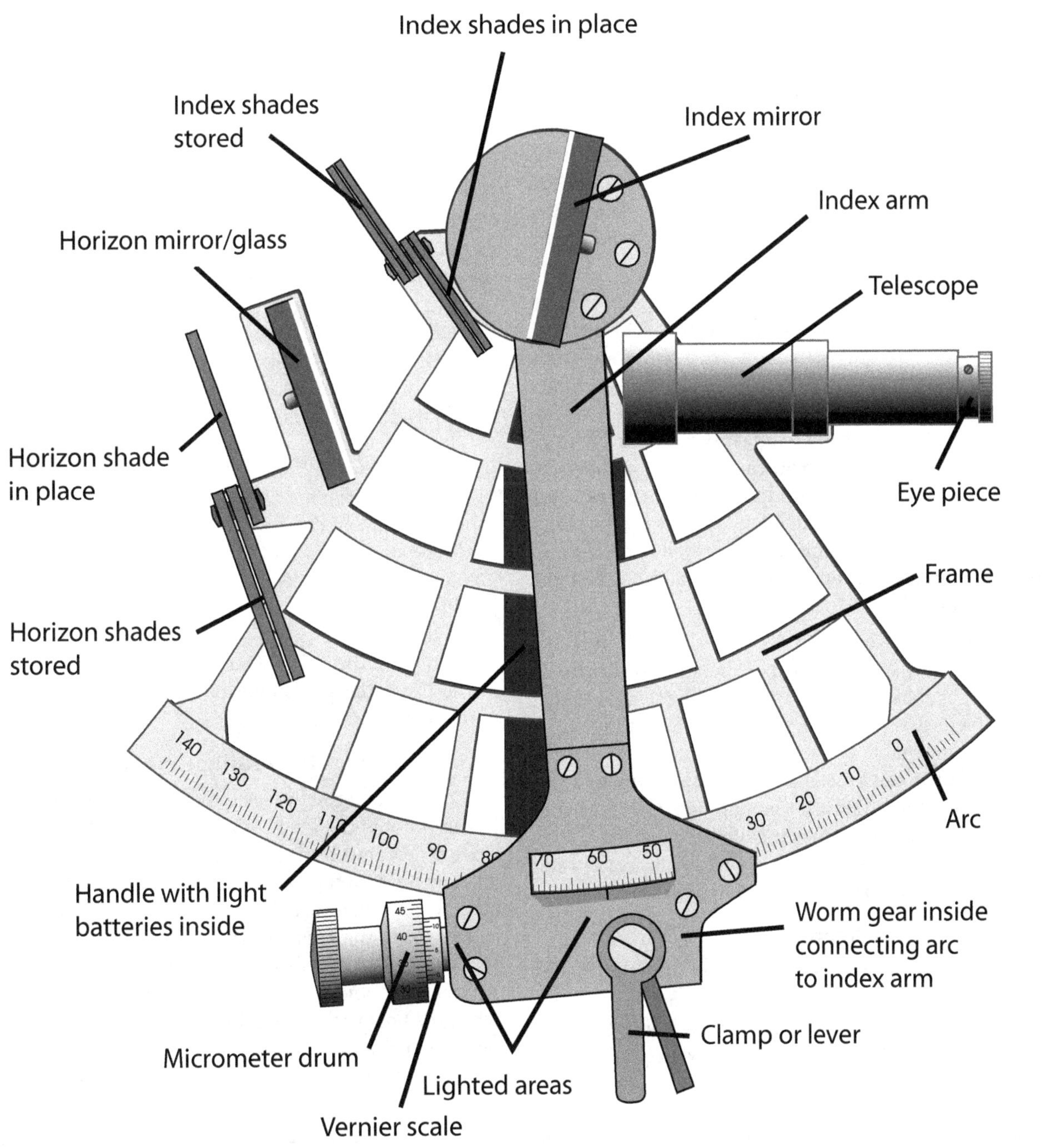

Figure 2.2-1 *Parts of a sextant. Remember when a shade is not in use, it should be rotated all the way into the stored position and not just rotated out of the line of sight.*

to get the time recorded before you forget it. If you pause or get delayed between releasing the drum and reading the watch, estimate the few seconds it cost, and adjust the time before recording it. That is, if it took you 3 seconds to read your watch (it was stuck under your cuff!), then record a time 3 seconds earlier than you read. Then read the sextant, double-check the reading, and then record it along with the name of the object sighted.

Complete the round of sights, store the sextant, and then make a final log and corresponding watch time entry into your notebook. Also confirm in your notebook that the course remained constant during the sights, although you would have known of any changes during the sight session as soon as anyone else, because you were watching the stars all this time. Recall that you recorded course *and* speed before starting, but now you can compute the actual average speed that you had. Just subtract the two log readings and subtract the two times and divide the distance run by that time interval to get your average speed.

Sight Notes

For sun or moon sights use the bottom edge (lower limb) when available. When the lower limb is obscured, use the upper limb, and adjust the sextant until the top edge just skims the horizon when rocked.

Shades are provided for sun sights to reduce the glare of the sun and horizon. Horizon shades are not often required, but index shades are nearly always needed for the sun. Choose any combination of shades that leaves the sun's disk prominent but not so bright as to distract your judgment of its alignment with the horizon.

Sun and moon sights can be taken any time of the day they are visible and well above the horizon. Star and planet sights must be taken during twilight when both the objects and the horizon are visible. Evening star sights begin when you can first see the stars (through the sextant telescope), and they end when you can no longer discern the horizon. Morning sights begin when you can first see the horizon, and they end when you can no longer see the stars. During specific periods of the year, Venus sights can be taken throughout the day. These are fairly rare sights that require good sextant optics and very clear skies in addition to a fortuitous location of the planet.

To bring the sun or moon down to the horizon in the view through the telescope, it can be helpful to estimate its angular height above the horizon and set the sextant to that value to begin with. Vertical angles can be estimated by hand at a comfortable outstretched arm's length. Thumb to forefinger of an outstretched hand is approximately 15°; thumb to tip of the little finger is more like 25°. Sitting at home with your sextant you can calibrate your hand span by noting what it spans on a nearby building or terrain and then use the sextant to measure what that is as an angle.

Precomputation

Star or planet sights are best prepared for with a process called *precomputation*. We have not yet covered how to do this, but it means using your cel nav books to determine what the height should be from what you think is your correct position. It generally takes just a few minutes. The answer won't be precisely right, but it does not have to be. You are effectively seeing a span of approximately 300 nmi (5°) vertically in the sextant telescope.

Precomputation gives us both the height and the bearing of the object, and again we do not care if the bearing is not precise. We pan the horizon in about the right direction and we find the body. Then, at the twilight time used for precomputation, set the sextant to the precomputed height, and look in the precomputed direction. The object will appear near the horizon, and the sight can be completed in the normal manner. Precomputation can be carried out by standard sight reductions using any sight reduction tables or, more readily, using Pub. 249 Vol. 1 or the 2102-D Star Finder, both of which are covered later in the book. Precomputed evening sights are easy and accurate because they can be taken early, in the brighter part of twilight while the horizon is still a sharp line. Precomputation of morning twilight sights facilitates the actual sight taking, but is not so crucial to star ID since you have as long as you wish to study the sky while waiting for the horizon to appear. Occasionally, daytime moon sights must also be precomputed to locate a faint moon in a bright or cloudy sky.

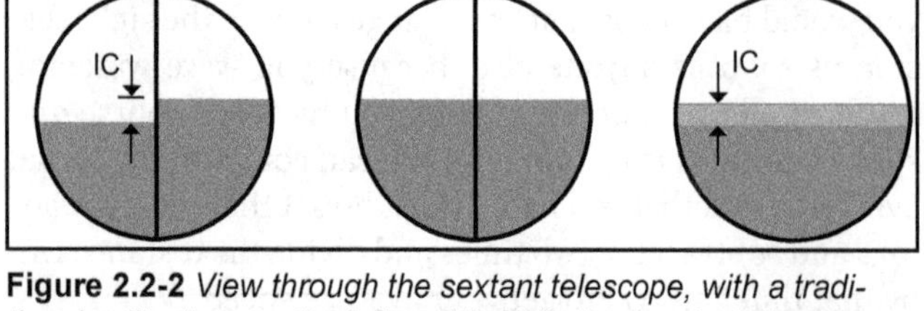

Figure 2.2-2 *View through the sextant telescope, with a traditional split mirror on the left and the full-view or whole horizon on the right.*

Inverting the Sextant

When star or planet sights must be taken without precomputation, you can use the special procedure of inverting the sextant. First set the scale to 0° 0', hold the sextant up-side-down in the left hand, and, while keeping the object in continuous view through the direct-view side of the glass, use the right hand to adjust the scale to bring the horizon up to the object. Once both object and horizon are in view, turn the sextant back over, and complete the sight in the normal manner.

Sights in Rough Weather

For sights in rough seas remember not to chase the object around as the boat swings around with passing seas. Once object and horizon are in view through the sextant, and you have found the best direction to face the object relative to your boat (usually the direction to the object when viewed from the crests of the bigger seas of a sequence), stay oriented in that direction. As the boat rocks (yaws and pitches) the object will go out of view, but it will return when the boat rocks back, since boat motion is typically repetitive in a seaway.

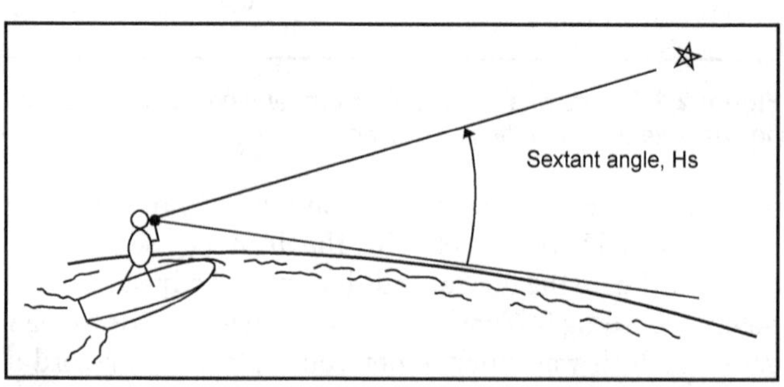

Figure 2.2-3 *The angle measured by the sextant is from the horizon up to the celestial body. The higher we are, the farther we see over the horizon, so the angle is slightly larger than it should be (way exaggerated in this sketch). This is corrected for with the dip correction, which is based on the height of the eye above the water.*

Do quick, minor adjustments while it is in view in the chosen direction, then stop when the object slips out of view but don't move, and wait for it to reappear before making further adjustments. The sights take longer—and they test your patience—but in the end, they can be just as good as those taken in calmer water.

Waves will occasionally block the horizon when you are ready to make an adjustment. When this happens, you might have to skip that cycle of boat motion and wait for the next. The true horizon will appear as a smooth steady straight line, whereas intervening waves are irregular and moving. If this approach of waiting out the motion is not followed and you try to keep the object in view as the boat bounces around, false adjustments are the usual result, and the process becomes quite frustrating.

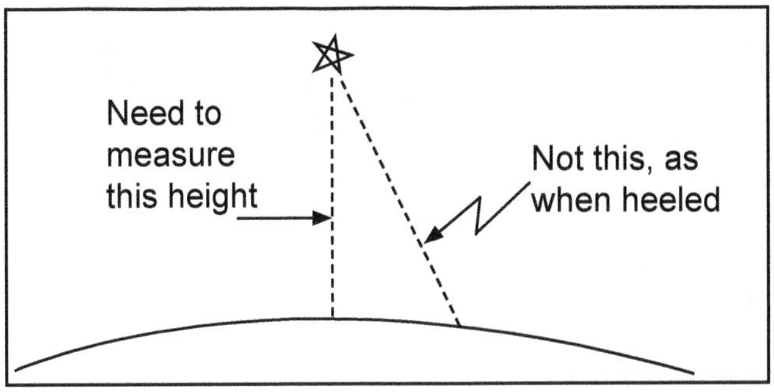

Figure 2.2-4 *Why we rock the sextant. If the sextant is not vertical to the horizon, we read a value that is too large. The simple process of rocking the instrument (rolling it without yawing). Various optical and mechanical gadgets have been proposed to help judge this alignment, but most just get in the way. Rocking is easy to learn and all that is needed to take professional sights.*

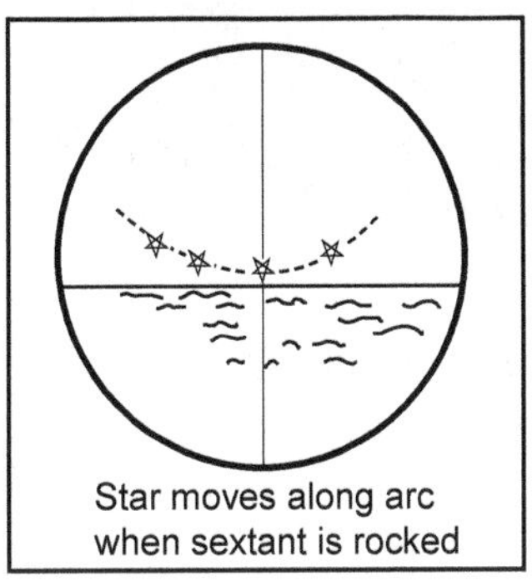

Star moves along arc
when sextant is rocked

Figure 2.2-5 *View though the sextant scope showing a star aligned with the horizon—very schematically. In practice a star will be a dot, and it will just touch the solid sea horizon when right.*

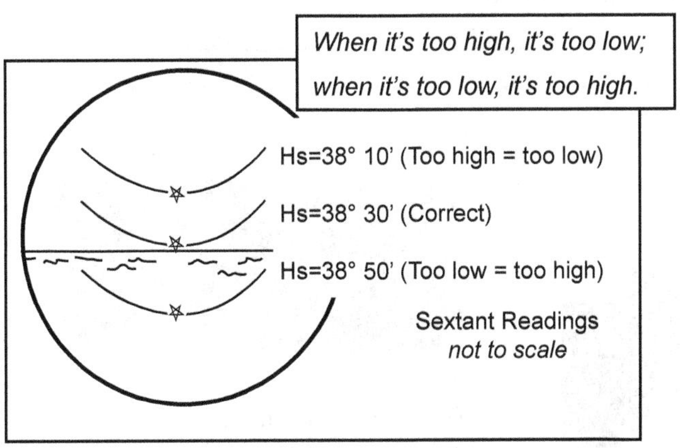

Figure 2.2-6 *View through the sextant telescope as you rock the sextant and adjust the micrometer to align the body with the horizon. Try setting the star or sun just above the horizon, read the dial, then right on the horizon, and read, then the same amount below and read. This gives a good feeling for the accuracy possible with the instrument. The diameter of the sun is about 32'*

Summary of a Sextant Sight

1. Record initial log, watch time, course, and speed
2. Check and record index correction
3. Face object, point sextant toward horizon below it
4. Adjust sextant to bring body and horizon together
5. Rock sextant and fine tune the alignment
6. Read watch time to the second and record it
7. Read sextant to 0.1' precision and record it
8. Record final log and watch time when finished

...In Depth

11.7 Solar Index Correction

Using the horizon is one way to measure the index correction and often the best choice underway, but if we really want to home in on accuracy, and get confidence that the values are right independent of subsequent sights, then reverting back to the methods of Lewis and Clark is the key to dependable results...

2.3 How to read a Sextant

Follow these steps for reading the sextant dials. The degrees are read from the arc, a section of which is on the right in each step, and the minutes from the micrometer drum. For now we just estimate the tenths of minutes. The next section explains the Vernier scale for the tenths.

Step 1

Notice that index marks align exactly with the numbers. The degrees increase when you move the index arm to the left, out away from you. The minutes increase as you "unscrew" the micrometer drum, counterclockwise.

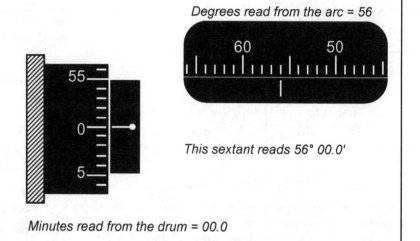

Degrees read from the arc = 56

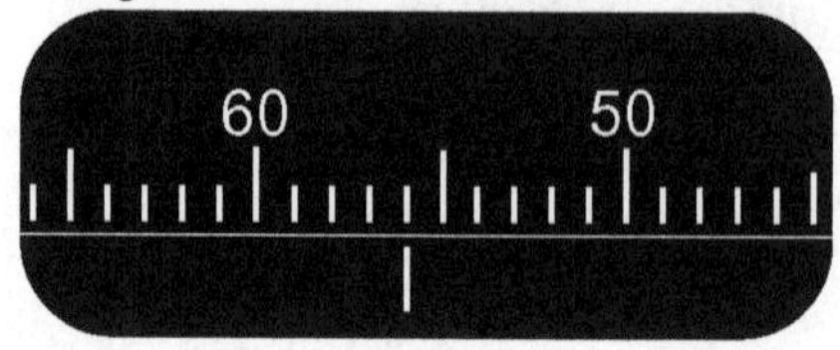

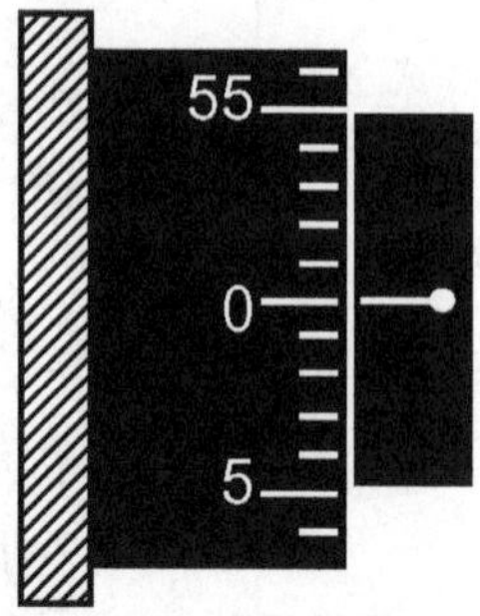

This sextant reads 56° 00.0'

Minutes read from the drum = 00.0

Step 2

Notice that the index mark on the arc is past the 56, about one third of the way to the 57. We can't tell that it is one third exactly, but we can tell that it is less than half. The minutes must be less than 30, as they are. The minutes align exactly with 19.0.

Caution: A possible mistake is to read the scales the wrong way and interpret this as 21'. Always check which direction is increasing before reading the dial. This type of error could be 2' (i.e., 19 vs 21) or as large as 8' (i.e., 16 vs 24). The smaller ones might be hard to detect later on.

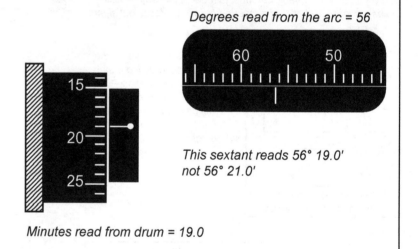

Degrees read from the arc = 56

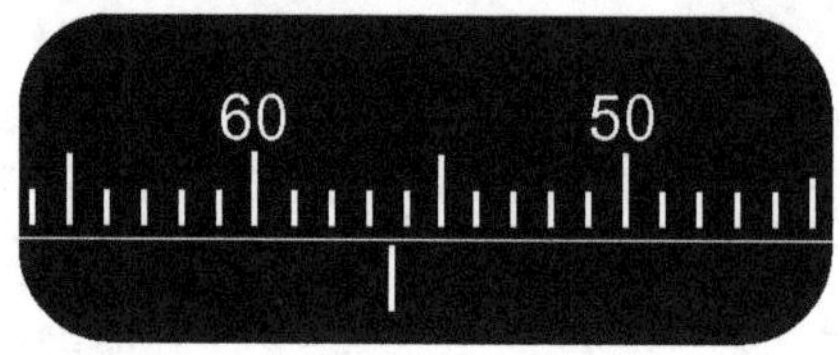

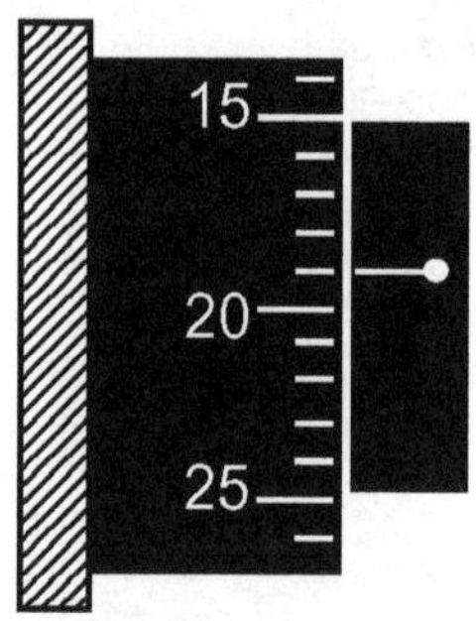

This sextant reads 56° 19.0'
not 56° 21.0'

Minutes read from drum = 19.0

Step 3

In cases like these, first check the minutes on the drum so you can interpret the degrees on the arc. After checking the direction, you see this is 58', or almost one full degree. So the degrees part of the angle must be just under 56, not just over it. Caution: Always double-check your readings, especially when the degrees marker is almost exactly lined up. This type of error, however, is a large one that will usually be apparent in a series of sights of the same object.

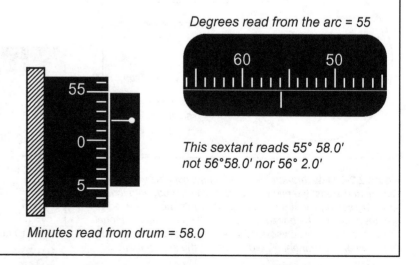

Degrees read from the arc = 55

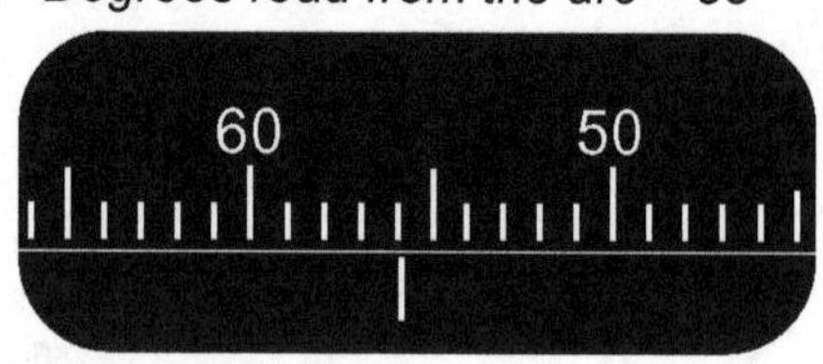

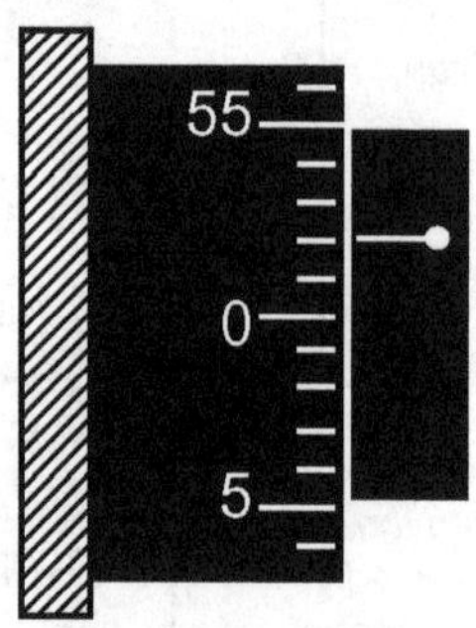

This sextant reads 55° 58.0'
not 56°58.0' nor 56° 2.0'

Minutes read from drum = 58.0

Step 4

If the sextant looked like this after aligning the reflected and direct views of the horizon, the instrument would have no index error. During actual sights, however, always record that you have checked it, even if it was zero.

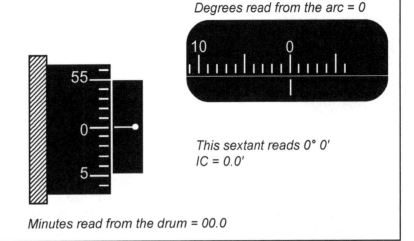

Degrees read from the arc = 0

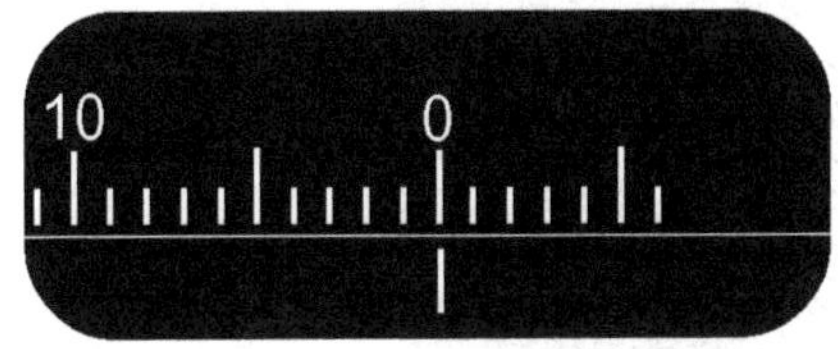

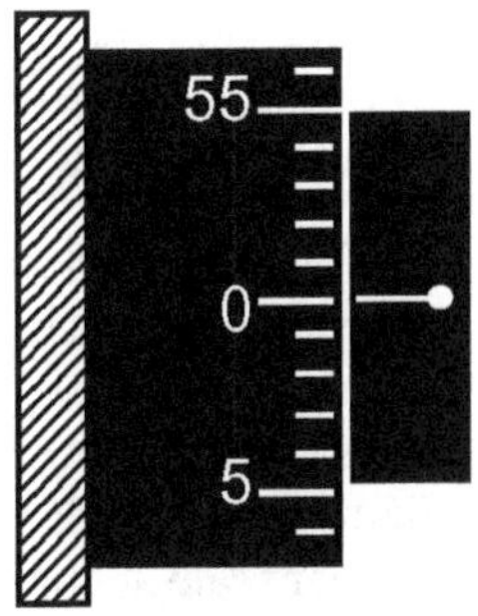

This sextant reads 0° 0'
IC = 0.0'

Minutes read from the drum = 00.0

Step 5

Notice that the index mark on the arc is barely past the 0° mark. In many cases you cannot tell if it is to the left (on the scale) or to the right (off the scale). The drum reading, however, will always clarify this.

In this example, the index mark is halfway between the second and third mark, so the IC would be 2.5' on the scale. Notice, however, that without a Vernier scale, we cannot really say if this is exactly 2.5. It could be 2.4 or 2.6.

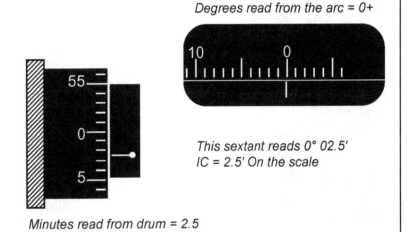

Degrees read from the arc = 0+

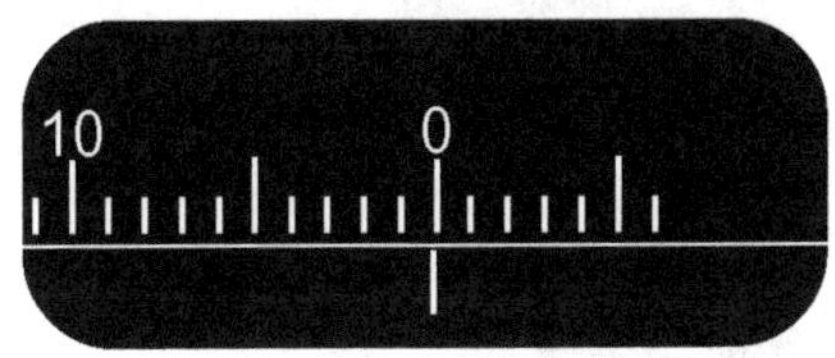

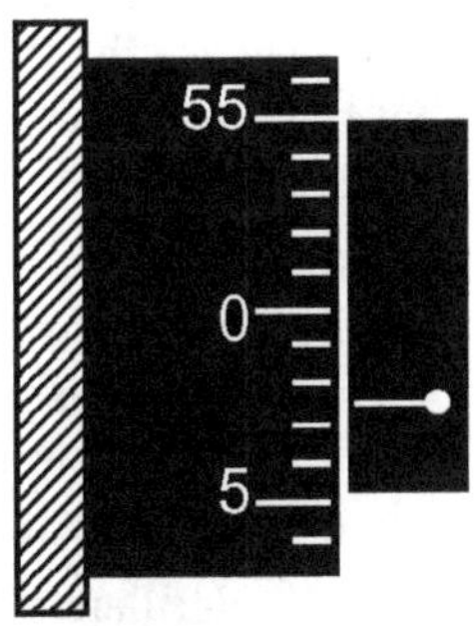

This sextant reads 0° 02.5'
IC = 2.5' On the scale

Minutes read from drum = 2.5

Step 6

For IC checks, you must nearly always tell from the minutes on the drum if you are off or on the scale. It will not be apparent on the arc for small corrections. Be careful to count in the right direction; this reads 58', not 2'. Alternatively, you can note that it is off the scale, and then count the IC backward. In this case, it reads 58 forward, which is the same as 2 backward. With fractional readings (such as 58.7'), however, one must be careful with this, as covered later on.

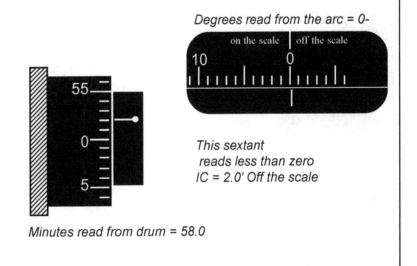

Degrees read from the arc = 0-

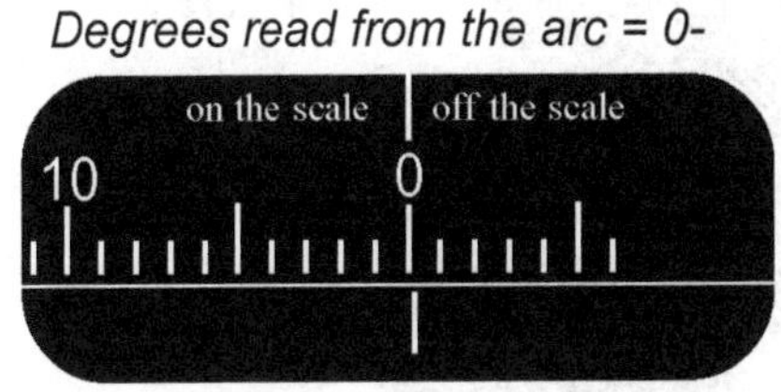

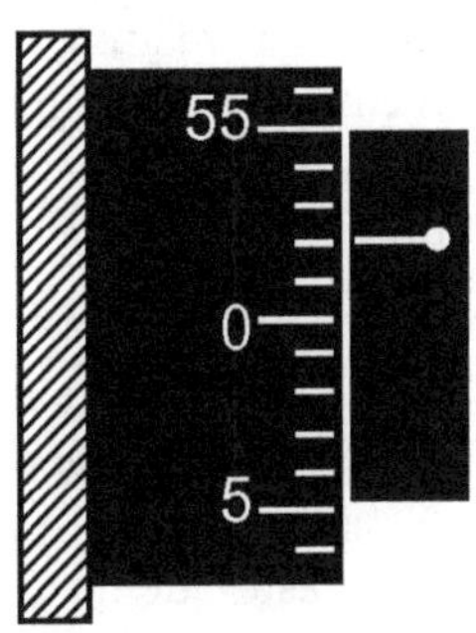

This sextant
reads less than zero
IC = 2.0' Off the scale

Minutes read from drum = 58.0

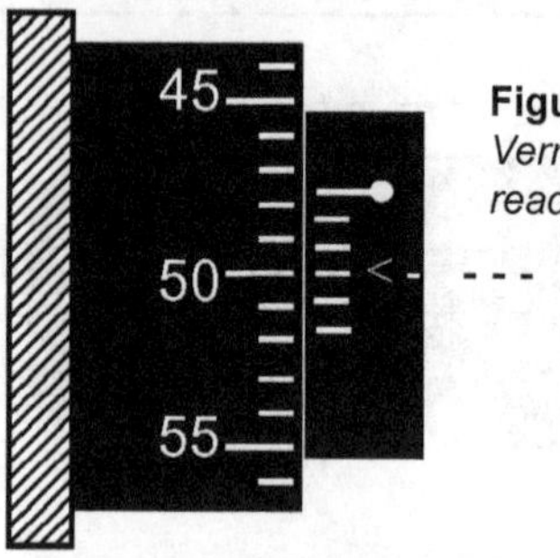

Figure 2.3-1 *Vernier reads 47.6'*

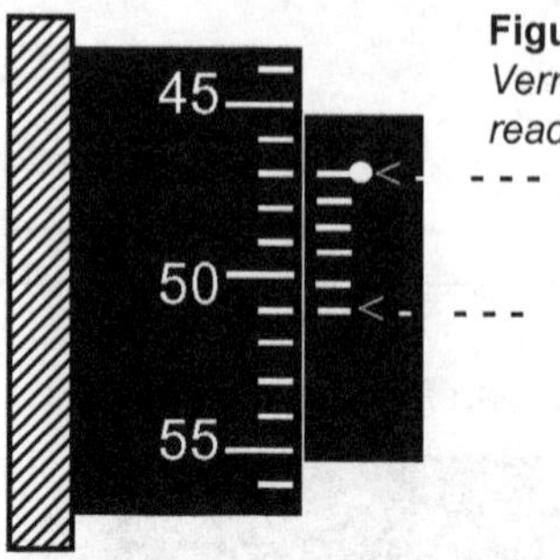

Figure 2.3-2 *Vernier reads 47.0'*

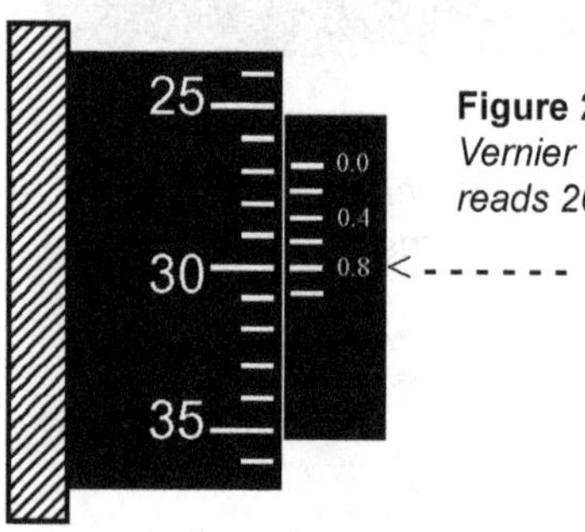

Figure 2.3-3 *Vernier reads 26.8'*

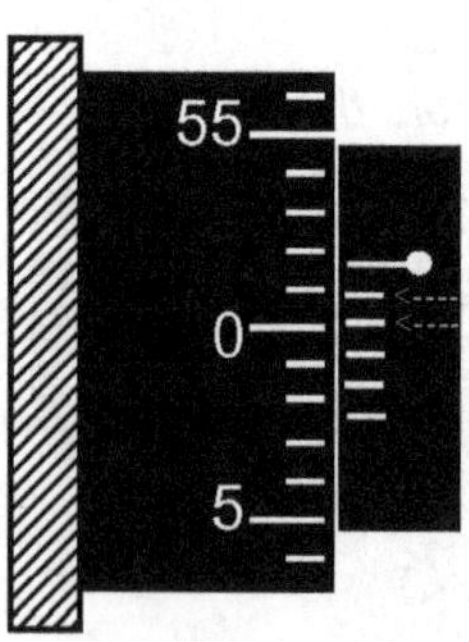

Figure 2.3-4 *Vernier reads 58.3'*

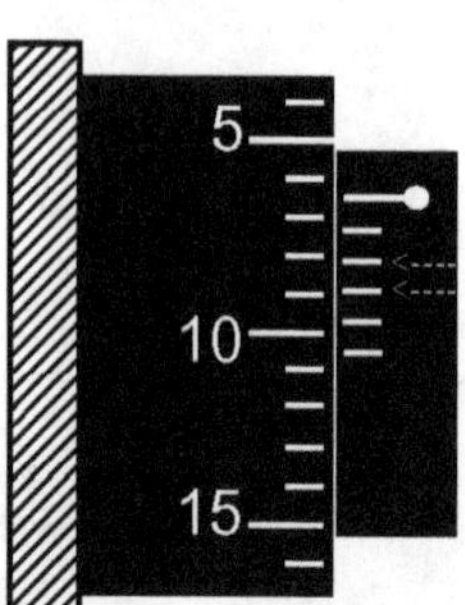

Figure 2.3-5 *Vernier reads 6.5'*

How to Read a Vernier Scale

Most sextants include a Vernier scale next to the drum scale. This extra scale is used to interpret the proportional parts of the drum scale reading. If the index mark, for example, lies about halfway between 47' and 48' (as shown in Figure 2.3-1), it is the Vernier reading that will tell us if this should be 47.4', 47.5', or 47.6'.

This clever arrangement of scales was an important invention from the early 1600's. Notice in Figure 2.3-2 that the parallel scales are similar, except that the divisions on the Vernier scale are smaller: five divisions on the Vernier span only four divisions on the drum. The scale in Figure 2.3-2 reads 47.0' because the index mark (or zero mark) of the Vernier scale aligns exactly with the 47 on the drum. Notice, in this case, that the last mark on the Vernier scale also aligns exactly with one of the drum marks (51 in this case). This is the way we tell that a drum reading is exact: the first and last Vernier marks align precisely with two marks on the drum scale.

When the drum reading is not exact, the index mark of the Vernier will not align with a drum mark, but one of the subsequent Vernier marks will. The Vernier mark that lines up is the one that tells us the tenths. Each Vernier mark is 0.2' In Figure 2.3-1, the proper reading is 47.6', because the third Vernier mark aligns with a drum mark. Notice that this third mark is the only one that lines up with a corresponding drum mark.

Some Vernier scales are marked with numbers to help with the reading (as in Figure 2.3-3), but most are not. Scales with a dot or arrow marking the zero point and no other labeling are common. Our job, then, is to check the alignment, count the marks, and figure the tenths—then double-check it.

Some Verniers are marked in individual tenths (showing ten divisions instead of just five; quite nice, if you find one), but most are in two-tenth intervals. When the Vernier is marked in two tenths, we have a problem with odd tenths. A 0.3 reading, for example, will not show a single exact alignment, but the 0.2 and 0.4 marks will be in closer alignment than any other, and these two will be equally unaligned in opposite directions, as shown in Figure 2.3-4. When there is no single mark aligned, look for two that are equally close. Always check the drum, however, to see that you are about right; that is, make a rough estimate from the drum reading alone, and then confirm the details with a Vernier reading. If the drum and Vernier read as shown in Figure 2.3-4 during an index error check, the index error would be 60 - 58.3, or IC = 1.7' off the scale.

An example of a 0.5' reading is shown in Figure 2.3-5.

Not all high-quality sextants have Verniers and in practice you won't really lose accuracy by estimating the tenths. Generally there are uncertainties in individual sights that cause uncertainties and fluctuations in measurements of approximately 0.2' to 0.3', even with good instruments, in good conditions, and in experienced hands. Nevertheless, if you have one, it is good practice to use it. On the other hand, there is no justification for using a Vernier reading on a Davis Mark 15 or 25 plastic sextant. These readings are not accurate enough to justify this extra precision. (The Davis Mark 3 model, on the other hand, relies on a Vernier to read the 2' precision it offers.)

2.4 Exercise on Sextant Reading

What do these sextants read? Find Hs in the first 6 and IC in the last 3. A good sextant is somewhat easier to read than these practice examples. Our scales are not precisely spaced and on a good sextant the tick marks are longer and not separated by the vertical white line shown here. Answers in the Answers section.

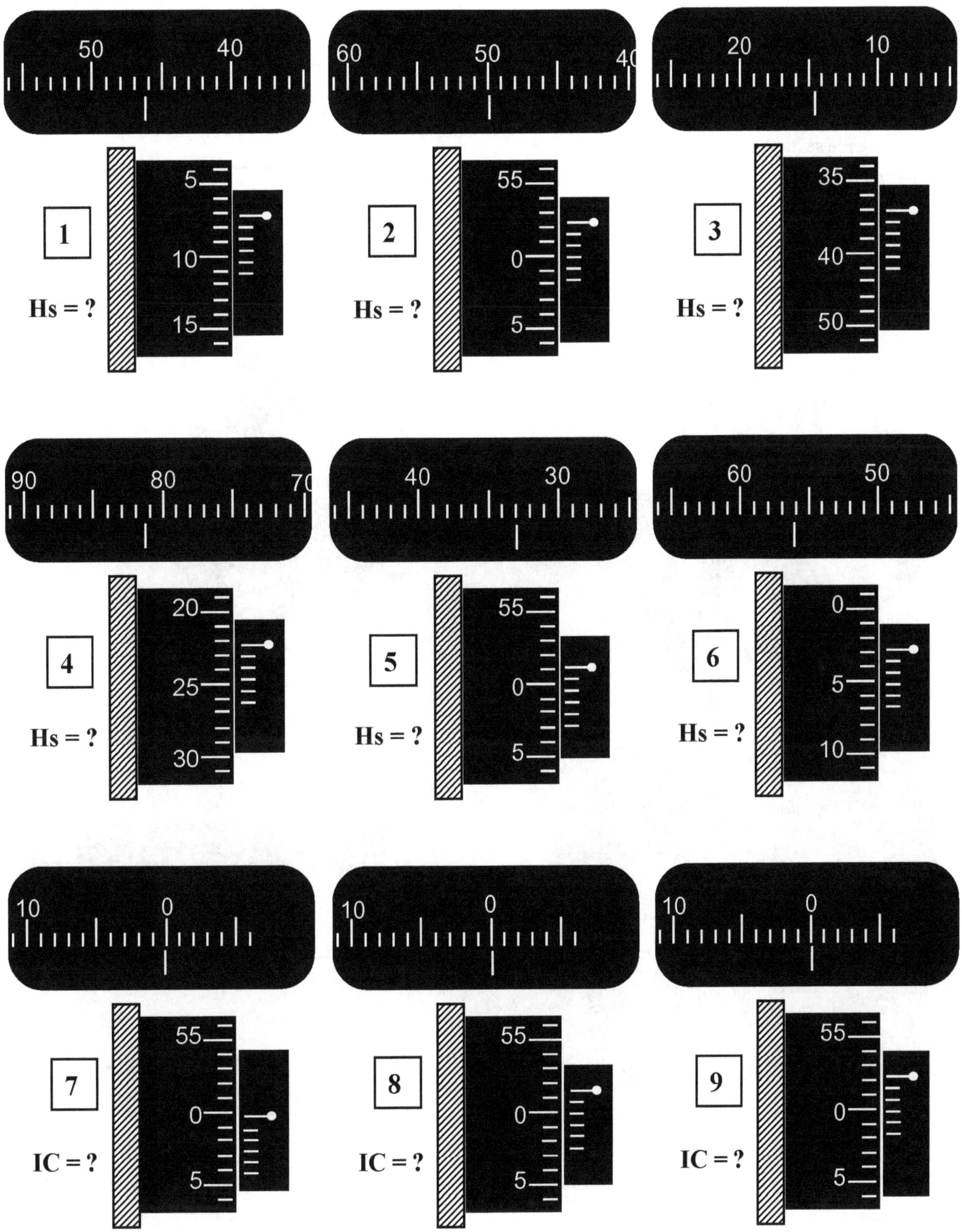

2.5 New Terminology

Bowditch
dip short
full-view horizon mirror
height of eye (HE)
horizon mirror
index arm
index correction (IC)
index mirror
inverting the sextant
micrometer drum
precomputation
sextant
Vernier

> ***...In Depth***
>
> **11.8 Optimizing Plastic and Metal Sextant Sights**
>
> Often disparaged by those who have not taken the time to learn how to use them, these light weight instruments can do the job well—and how we optimize sights with them is the same as we should do with metal sextants...

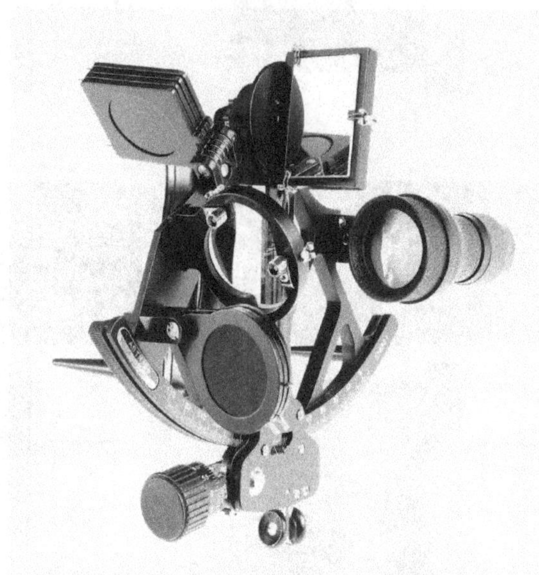

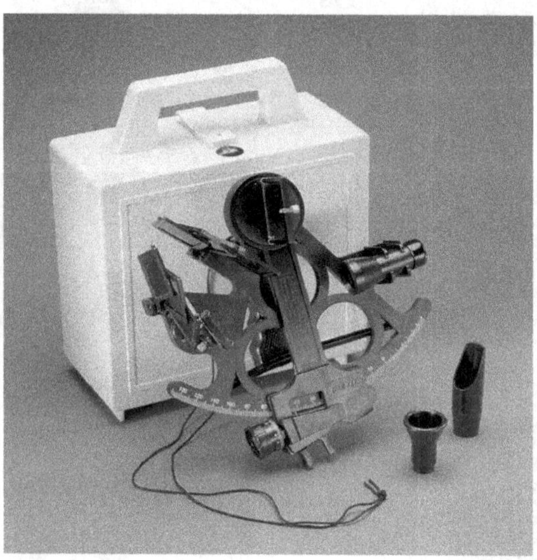

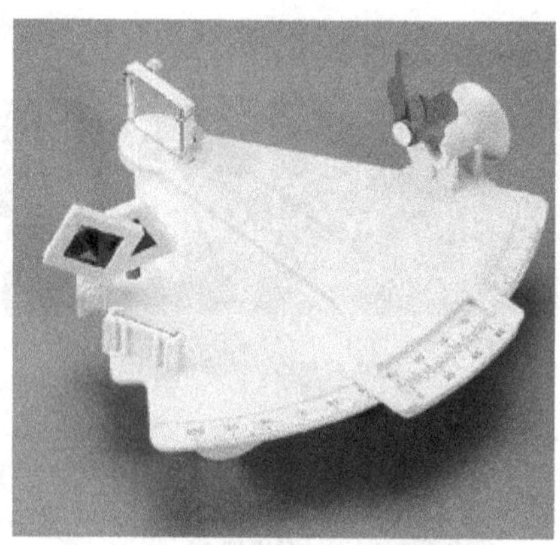

Figure 2.5-1 *Sample sextant pictures. Clockwise from top-left: Tamaya Jupiter, Astra 3b, Davis Mark 3, and Davis Mark 15.*

CHAPTER 3

NOON SIGHTS (LAN)

In this chapter, Section 3.1 gives an overview of the full noon sight process; then we back up in Section 3.2 and go step-by-step through the numerical procedures. When new terms appear, it might be useful to check the Glossary for more explanation. New terms are listed in Section 3.6.

This chapter introduces the use of several key tables and how to move around in the study materials from text, to tables, to answers, etc. By the end of this chapter you will have completed about 75% of the total learning process for celestial navigation.

3.1 Introduction to LAN

The first step in learning celestial navigation is the noon sight of the sun. It is a quick, easily learned process for finding your latitude at midday. It requires a sextant, a *Nautical Almanac*, and a watch. You can learn the process in an evening, practice next day, and master it the next. The latitude you find this way will be as accurate as your sextant sight—about 0.5 miles at best, more like 1 or 2 miles on the average.

The process is called a noon sight or LAN sight for latitude. LAN stands for local apparent noon; it is the time of day when the sun crosses your meridian, which means that it bears either due south or due north. North of the tropics you always see the noon sun to the south, and south of the tropics the noon sun always bears north. Within the tropics it can bear either direction depending on your latitude and the time of year. Hence another name for this process: Latitude by meridian passage of the sun.

When the sun crosses your meridian at LAN it has reached its maximum height in the sky for that day. To find latitude at LAN we need to catch the sun in the sextant at this moment. We need to know the precise maximum height of the sun. But this is not as hard to come by as you might guess, because the arc of the sun's path is fairly flat at the top. In other words, the sextant height (Hs) of the sun does not change much during the few minutes just before and after its maximum height. To ensure that we do indeed get the maximum value, however, the standard procedure is to start a series of sun sights just before LAN, continue them until the height starts to drop, and then take the maximum value of Hs from the list of heights recorded.

Once the maximum height (Hs-max) is measured, you make three numerical corrections to it, and subtract the result from 90°. The resulting number is called the *zenith distance* (z) of the sun. Then, use the *Nautical Almanac* to look up the declination of the sun. Your latitude is then the sum of the zenith distance you measured and the declination you looked up—or it could be the difference between these two numbers, but there is rarely any confusion between whether to add or subtract.

And that's all there is to it. With little practice and good procedure, the entire process takes about 30 minutes: a few minutes to predict the proper time to start taking the sights, 15 minutes or so for the sextant sights themselves, followed by another few minutes of arithmetic as outlined earlier and explained in detail in the following sections.

We now take a brief look at the principles behind this process with a numerical example, and then move on to the specifics of each step.

The point on earth directly underneath the sun at any moment is called the *Geographical Position* (GP) of the sun. If you were standing at the GP of the sun, the sun would be precisely overhead, at your zenith. The declination of the sun is defined as the latitude of the sun's GP. It varies slowly throughout the year from the Tropic of Cancer (overhead at 23° 26' N) on the Summer Solstice (June 21st) to the Tropic of Capricorn (overhead at 23° 26' S) on the Winter Solstice (December 21st), as shown in Figure 3.1-1. The declination of the sun is 0° 0' (overhead at the equator) on the two equinoxes (March 21st and September 23rd).

As the earth turns beneath the sun daily, the GP of the sun circles the earth at a constant latitude equal to its declination. If the sun passed directly over head at noon, you would find your latitude by simply looking up the declination of the sun on that date and time in the *Nautical Almanac*. If the sun passed exactly overhead you must, by definition, be at the latitude of the sun. Hence the main job of the *Nautical Almanac* is to tell us the precise latitudes (and longitudes) of the GPs of all celestial bodies (sun, moon, stars, and planets) at all times.

If we were not at the sun's latitude, the sun would not pass overhead. If you were 1° "north of the sun"—meaning your latitude was 1° north of the sun's declination—the sun would pass 1° south of overhead. This is the key to understanding the LAN latitude sight; it is true in every case: 30° north of the sun, the sun passes 30° south of overhead, and so forth.

Working this reasoning backward, if we know how far down from the zenith the sun passes at LAN, we know the latitude difference between us and the sun, and because the *Nautical Almanac* tells us the latitude of the sun at all times, we can figure out what our latitude must be.

In the terminology of celestial navigation, the angular distance measured from the point overhead down to the sun is called the *zenith distance*. This is what we want, but we have no reference point for measuring it directly—there is no marker at the zenith. So we use a sextant and the horizon. The full sextant angle from the horizon all the way up to the zenith is 90°. To find the zenith distance we measure the sextant height from the horizon up to the sun and then subtract that from 90°. What is left is what we want.

And so the process goes. We measure the maximum sextant height of the sun at LAN, make a few quick corrections to it (explained shortly for the sextant calibration, our height above the water, the atmosphere, and the angular width of the sun itself), then figure the zenith distance, look up the declination of the sun, and then add them together to get our latitude. The reason we must sometimes take the difference between the zenith distance and declination to get our latitude is simply because of the way latitudes and declinations are labeled North and South from the equator.

Now an example using one more special term: the height of the sun we get after making all corrections to Hs is called the *observed height* (Ho). Our DR (dead reckoning) position at noon is 48° 04.0' N, 135° 50.0' W on July 14th, 1982. The maximum value of the sun's height at LAN is found to be Ho-max = 63° 32.2', and we observed this height at a time of 21:09 UTC. Our actual navigation watch might have read something more like noon at this time, but when we converted its reading to UTC we got this late-evening universal time. So the zenith distance = 90° - Ho = 89° 60' - 63° 32.2' = 26° 27.8' (to make the subtraction, we rewrite 90° as 89° 60.0').

From the *Nautical Almanac* we find that at 21:09 UTC on July 14th, 1982 the declination of the sun is N 21° 37.8'. Now to get our latitude: Latitude = zenith distance + declination = 26° 27.8' + 21° 37.8' = 48° 05.6' N.

Finally we check that the latitude we found is reasonable; and it is—our actual latitude (the one we measured) is about 1.6' north of our DR latitude. The DR latitude is the latitude we thought we were at on the basis of our logbook and our most recent position fix. Since 1' of latitude is the same as 1 nautical mile, we are only 1.6 miles farther north than we thought. From that which we have done so far, we don't know anything about our longitude. Later we will discuss how we might use the observed UTC of LAN to tell us something about our longitude, but that's a longer story—longer even than many navigators want to admit. For now we stick with the latitude problem.

To complete this, let's look at a case where you have to subtract zenith distance and declination in order to find latitude. Suppose the Ho-max of our first example was observed at the same UTC but now from a DR position some 300 miles south of the equator at 4° 47.0' S, 135° 50.0' W, on our way to the Marquesas. In this example we would be looking north to the noon sun.

The direct sextant reading (Hs-max) and the corrected version (Ho-max) would be just the same, so the zenith distance would be the same; and we are saying that the UTC and date were the same also, so the declination of the sun was the same. But now if we added zenith distance and declination we would get what we got before, Lat = 48° 5.6', which we don't have to stare at very long to know can't be right—we are on the way to the Marquesas, not Cape Flattery. Therefore, we subtract them: Lat = zenith distance - declination = 26° 27.8' - 21° 37.8' = 4° 50.0' S, which is consistent with our DR latitude.

Note, however, that the principles are still the same. The zenith distance (of about 26° in this case) is the latitude difference between us and the sun. The sun was at about 21° N and we were looking north to see it. So we must be some 26° south of 21° N, which puts us at about 5° S. And so forth.

The circumstances that lead to adding versus subtracting to get Lat are illustrated in the next section when we go over the specific steps for doing the LAN sight, but we can propose this *Easy LAN Rule*: find the zenith distance and declination. Then add them to find your latitude. If the result does not make sense (i.e., far from your DR Lat), then adding must have been wrong, so subtract them. When subtracting you don't have to worry about which to subtract from which; always take the smaller from the larger.

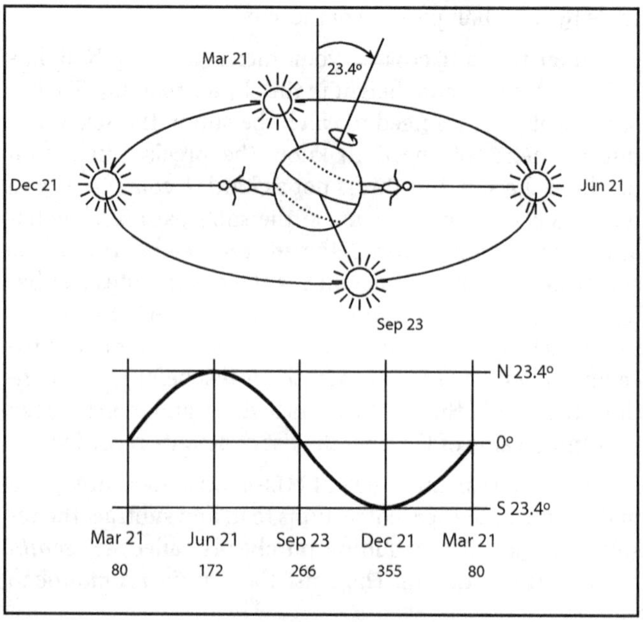

Figure 3.1-1. *Declination of the sun. The sun's declination varies from N 23.4° to S 23.4°. The turning points are at the solstices, June 21 and December 21, the longest and shortest days of the year. The sun crosses the equator on the equinoxes, March 21 and September 23, at which times the lengths of day and night are the same. The declination changes most rapidly near the equinoxes (about 24' per day) and most slowly near the solstices. The seasonal oscillation of the declination occurs because the tilt of the earth's axis remains constant as it circles the sun—here shown in reverse, with the sun circling the earth.*

Later for completeness we will list precise rules that tell what to do when, but it will be rare that you need them.

The next section covers procedural and practical details of the LAN latitude sight, including the sextant corrections mentioned earlier. Following that, we cover the topic of finding longitude from a noon sight, and then back to more general aspects of celestial navigation, like sextants and sextant use. If you have navigation questions, coastwise or ocean, you can get help from links at starpath.com/celnav-book.

Here is another example using what we have done so far. DR position is 30° 14.0' N, 135° 40.0' W, and we found Ho-max = 44° 39.6'. At the time of the sight the sun's declination = S 15° 10.5'. What was our latitude? Answer is 30° 9.9' N, about 4 miles south of the DR latitude.

		89° 60.0'
		- 44° 39.6'
z	=	45° 20.4'
Dec	=	15° 10.5'
Lat	=	30° 9.9' N

3.2 Step by Step LAN Procedure

Step (1) Predicting the Time of LAN

The noon latitude sight is popular because it is quick, easy, and accurate. It only takes a few minutes to figure your latitude once the sight is done. The sight itself, however, can take a long time if you are not prepared. If you don't know the time of LAN, it can take 30 minutes or more to watch the sun rise in the sextant, go through its maximum height, and then begin to descend. This takes a lot away from the beauty of the sight.

Furthermore, it's unnecessary. It is easy to predict the time of LAN for any location. If we know where we are to within 100 miles, we can predict the time to within 5 to 10 minutes, depending on our latitude. If we know our position better, we can predict the time more accurately.

The time of meridian passage of the sun is given in the *Nautical Almanac* (called mer pass) on the bottom right-hand side of the daily pages (T-1 through T-6 in the Table Selections). The time is listed accurate to the minute. See Figure 3.2-1.

The mer pass time listed in the *Nautical Almanac* is the UTC that the sun crosses the Greenwich meridian, longitude = 0°. Since the sun moves westward at a constant rate, it is easy for us to figure out when it will cross our meridian. If we are west of Greenwich (western longitudes) our UTC of mer pass will be later than the time listed. If we are east of Greenwich, the sun will pass us before reaching Greenwich, so the UTC of mer pass in east longitudes occurs earlier than the time listed.

The sun, or, if you like, the GP of the sun, moves westward at a rate of 15° of longitude per hour, because the earth rotates 360° in 24 hours, which is 15°/1h. If we are 30° west of Greenwich our mer pass time will be 2 hours later than the time listed. At longitude 60° East, the sun crosses the meridian exactly 4 hours before it reaches Greenwich. To get the UTC of mer pass for any longitude, convert your longitude to time at the rate of 15° per hour—there is a special table for this in the *Nautical Almanac*—and then add it to the mer pass time listed in the *Nautical Almanac* when you are in west longitudes, or subtract it when in east longitudes.

The following equations may help you remember this. Note that LAN is just another name for meridian passage, abbreviated Mer. Pass. Throughout this book, we often abbreviate *Nautical Almanac* as NA.

UTC of LAN =

Mer Pass time (NA) + Lon W (converted to time), or

Mer Pass time (NA) - Lon E (converted to time).

The longitude we use for this is always our DR-Lon at noon. This is just our best estimate of what our longitude will be at midday. We get it from our latest fix projected forward using estimated course and speed. If you do this LAN time prediction well before midday while you are traveling fast in the east-west direction it is valuable to find this projected DR-Lon and not just the present value.

The conversion from longitude degrees to time is done with the Conversion of Arc to Time table in the *Nautical Almanac*. It is the first page at the back of the almanac (T-7 in the Table Selections). First look up the degrees part of your DR-Lon and then add on the minutes part. Examples are shown later.

Usually you will just ignore or round off the seconds part of your predicted time. The seconds are not accurate unless your DR-Lon is very accurate. The accuracy of the time we figure will only be as accurate as our DR-Lon. If our DR-Lon is off by 15', the time we figure will be off by 1 minute. To figure uncertainties note: 15°/1 hour = 15'/1 minute. Two examples of the arc to time conversion are shown in Figure 3.2-2.

58	15 55	16 42	17 31	09 53	10 14	10 35	10 58
S 60	15 43	16 33	17 26	09 53	10 12	10 31	10 52

	SUN			MOON			
Day	Eqn. of Time 00ʰ	12ʰ	Mer. Pass.	Mer. Pass. Upper	Lower	Age	Phase
	m s	m s	h m	h m	h m	d	
24	06 25	06 26	12 06	03 41	16 06	19	
25	06 26	06 27	12 06	04 31	16 55	20	◑
26	06 27	06 27	12 06	05 19	17 43	21	

Figure 3.2-1. *Mer. Pass. time in the* Nautical Almanac *is given in the bottom right-hand corner of each daily page of data. This is a section of T-2 (July, 1978) in the Table Selections. The time listed (1206) is the UTC of the event observed from the Greenwich meridian. At your own meridian this will be midday and your watch will read near 1200, within an hour or so, depending on the time zone of your watch and your longitude. Here we see the same value for all 3 days listed, but on other dates these times may differ by a minute from day to day.*

Examples: Arc to Time

Find time for 122° 18.0'

122°	=	08h	08m	
+18.0'	=		01m	12s
	=	08h	09m	12s

Find time for 136° 10.5'

136°	=	09h	04m	
+10.5'	=			42s
	=	9h	04m	42s

CONVERSION OF ARC TO TIME

18.00' ↓ (0'.00 column) 10.50' ↓ (0'.50 column)

120°–179° °	h m	180°–239° °	h m	240°–299° °	h m	300°–359° °	h m	'	0'.00 m s	0'.25 m s	0'.50 m s	0'.75 m s
120	8 00	180	12 00	240	16 00	300	20 00	0	0 00	0 01	0 02	0 03
121	8 04	181	12 04	241	16 04	301	20 04	1	0 04	0 05	0 06	0 07
122	8 08	182	12 08	242	16 08	302	20 08	2	0 08	0 09	0 10	0 11
123	8 12	183	12 12	243	16 12	303	20 12	3	0 12	0 13	0 14	0 15
124	8 16	184	12 16	244	16 16	304	20 16	4	0 16	0 17	0 18	0 19
125	8 20	185	12 20	245	16 20	305	20 20	5	0 20	0 21	0 22	0 23
126	8 24	186	12 24	246	16 24	306	20 24	6	0 24	0 25	0 26	0 27
127	8 28	187	12 28	247	16 28	307	20 28	7	0 28	0 29	0 30	0 31
128	8 32	188	12 32	248	16 32	308	20 32	8	0 32	0 33	0 34	0 35
129	8 36	189	12 36	249	16 36	309	20 36	9	0 36	0 37	0 38	0 39
130	8 40	190	12 40	250	16 40	310	20 40	10	0 40	0 41	0 42	0 43
131	8 44	191	12 44	251	16 44	311	20 44	11	0 44	0 45	0 46	0 47
132	8 48	192	12 48	252	16 48	312	20 48	12	0 48	0 49	0 50	0 51
133	8 52	193	12 52	253	16 52	313	20 52	13	0 52	0 53	0 54	0 55
134	8 56	194	12 56	254	16 56	314	20 56	14	0 56	0 57	0 58	0 59
135	9 00	195	13 00	255	17 00	315	21 00	15	1 00	1 01	1 02	1 03
136	9 04	196	13 04	256	17 04	316	21 04	16	1 04	1 05	1 06	1 07
137	9 08	197	13 08	257	17 08	317	21 08	17	1 08	1 09	1 10	1 11
138	9 12	198	13 12	258	17 12	318	21 12	18	1 12	1 13	1 14	1 15
139	9 16	199	13 16	259	17 16	319	21 16	19	1 16	1 17	1 18	1 19

Figure 3.2-2. *Two examples of arc to time conversion. The inset table is a section of table T-7 from the Table Selections.*

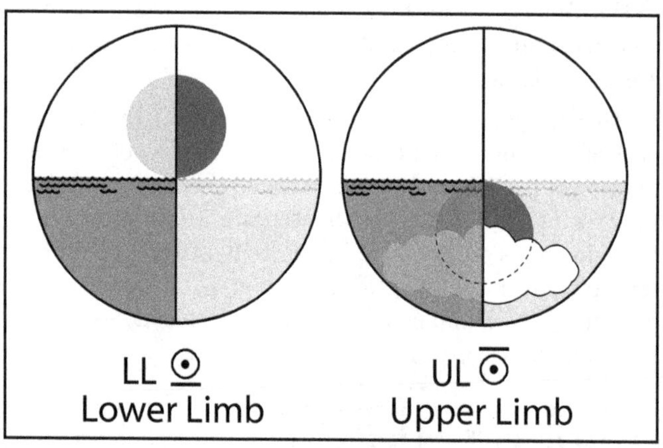

Figure 3.2-3. *Schematic views through a sextant telescope using a traditional split view horizon mirror—the left side is clear glass; the right side is a mirror. The sun is on the horizon at the time of these two independent sights. The left is a standard lower-limb sight; the right is an upper-limb sight. In each case the left side is looking direct to the horizon through clear glass, but this glass acts as a partial mirror so we often see a faint outline of what is on the mirror side, exaggerated in this schematic. Usually upper-limb sights are restricted to times when the lower limb is obscured by clouds, as indicated here.*

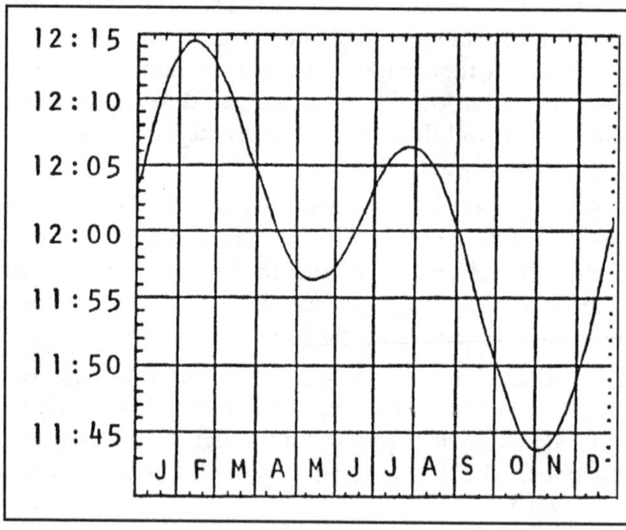

Figure 3.2-4 *UTC of LAN at Greenwich. The Equation of Time (EqT) is 12:00 minus these times. It is given accurate to the second in the Nautical Almanac. Generally we do not know our DR-Lon accurate enough to justify finding Mer Pass to the second, but this diagram shows how this time varies throughout the year. The tilt of the earth's axis relative to its orbit around the sun along with the elliptical shape of that orbit contributes to this unusual pattern.*

To get started, check the Table Selections to see where these times are listed.

July 25th, 1978: mer pass sun = 12h 06m

October 27th, 1978: mer pass sun = 11h 44m

Mar. 28th, 1981: mer pass sun = 12h 05m

If, for some reason, you want to know the exact time of LAN for an exact longitude, you can get the Mer Pass time to the second using the Equation of Time (Figure 3.2-4) The Equation of Time is the difference between the time of Mer Pass and 12h 00m 00s. The Equation of Time is listed next to the Mer Pass time in the *Nautical Almanac* (Figure 3.2-1). You would use the 12h value.

Example: Finding Time of LAN

(a) July 25th, 1978, DR-Lon = 122° 18.0' W
Find time UTC of LAN = ?
mer pass + DR-Lon(W) = UTC of LAN
12h 06m + 8h 09m 12s = 20h 15m 12s July 25th

(b) Oct. 27th, 1978, DR-Lon = 136° 10.5' E
Find UTC of LAN = ?
mer pass - DR-Lon(E) = UTC of LAN
11h 44m - 9h 04m 42s = 02h 39m 18s Oct. 27th

Once you've made your time prediction, set an alarm clock to go off about 10 minutes earlier, and then you can forget about it till noon.

Step (2) The Sextant Sight at LAN

Sextants and their use are discussed in Chapter 2. Here we just define or review a few of the special terms used. The angle you read from the sextant, after aligning the sun with the horizon, is called the sextant altitude or *sextant height*, Hs. On a good metal sextant you can read this angle to a precision of about 0.1'—although it is unlikely that the angle itself is actually that accurate. The degrees part of Hs is read at a pointer on the arc of the sextant, and the minutes part of the angle is read at a pointer on the micrometer drum that you turn to make the final fine adjustment of the sight.

A typical sextant height might read Hs = 46° 24.8'. In this case the sun was just over halfway up the sky. When doing the sun sights in clear skies, you have the choice of measuring the angle from the horizon up to the bottom edge of the sun (called its *lower limb* sometimes abbreviated LL), or up to the top edge of the sun (called the *upper limb* or UL). See Figure 3.2-3. It doesn't matter which you choose, although most navigators use lower limb when they can. The tables allow us to do upper limb because we must use the upper limb when the lower limb is covered by clouds. The difference in Hs between these two sights (though it's hard to think of any reason to do both) will always be about 32' since that is the typical angular width of the sun.

A circle with a dot in the center is the standard symbol of the sun—for your notes and so forth. A sun symbol with a line under it is used for a lower-limb sun sight, and a line above the sun symbol represents an upper-limb sight.

Before doing any sextant sight you should always check the index correction of the sextant. The index correction check tells you if the sextant angle is really zero when the pointers show 0° 0'. A sextant with an index correction—and most sextants have them—is like a speedometer that reads 5 mph when you are stopped. When this speedometer reads 35 mph, you are really only going 30 mph. This type of index correction is called *on the scale*, because you read something on the scale when you should read zero.

If the speedometer needle was below zero when you were stopped, say 3 mph behind the zero line, then the index correction is called *off the scale*. In this case you have

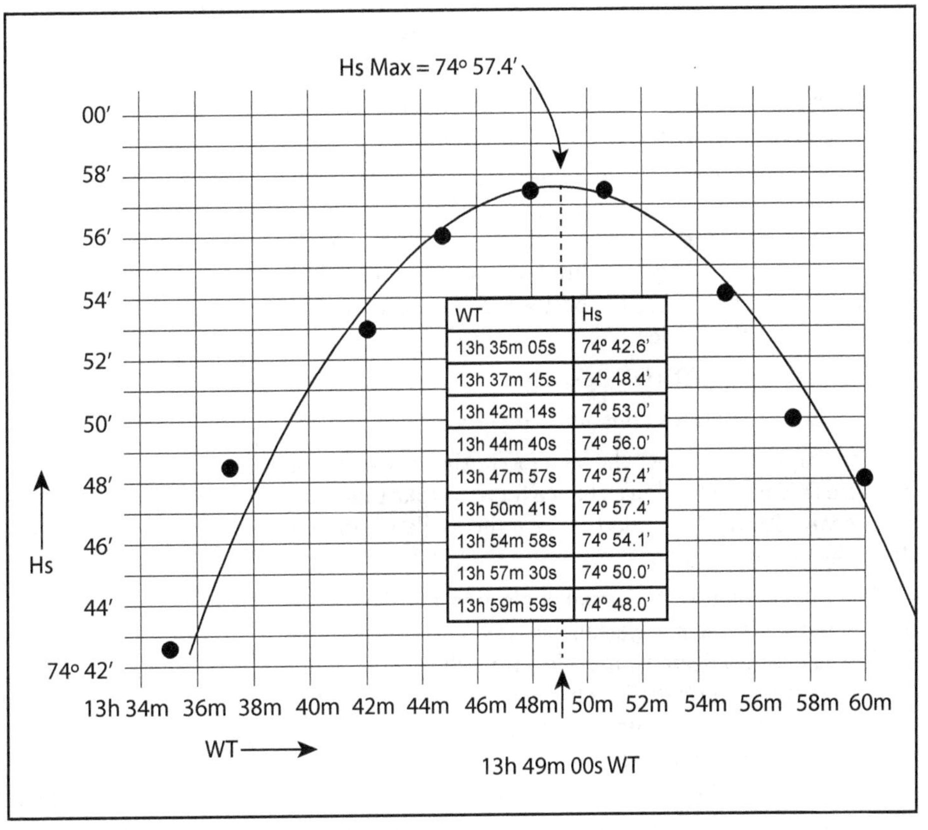

WT	Hs
13h 35m 05s	74° 42.6'
13h 37m 15s	74° 48.4'
13h 42m 14s	74° 53.0'
13h 44m 40s	74° 56.0'
13h 47m 57s	74° 57.4'
13h 50m 41s	74° 57.4'
13h 54m 58s	74° 54.1'
13h 57m 30s	74° 50.0'
13h 59m 59s	74° 48.0'

Figure 3.2-5 *An LAN sight plotted to show the rise and fall of Hs. In this case LAN occurred at 13h 49m 00s WT.*

to go 3 mph just to get the speedometer to read zero, and when your speedometer reads 35 mph, you are actually going 38 mph, and so on.

Referring back to Figure 2.2-2, to check the index correction of a sextant, you look at the horizon through the sextant with the instrument set to 0° 0', and then adjust the micrometer drum until the reflected view of the horizon aligns precisely with the direct view of the horizon. Then read the minutes scale on the drum to determine the correction and whether it is on or off the scale. If the mirrors are adjusted about right, on-scale values will read a small number of minutes (1, 2, or 3). Off-scale corrections are a few minutes below zero, but since the drum reads from 59' down on the back side of zero, the actual value you read will be in the high 50s. You have to subtract what you read from 60' to get the value of the off-scale IC.

After measuring the index correction, measure the height of the sun, note the time by your watch, and then write down Hs and the watch time in a notebook. (Refer back to the Section 1.3 for an overview.) Then repeat this process until you note that your list of heights has definitely gone through a maximum. You should be able to get a sight every few minutes. Then look at the list and pick the highest value of Hs. This is Hs-max, and it will tell us our latitude.

Sometimes it is valuable to plot Hs vs. WT if there is any doubt about where the peak is located. An example is shown in Figure 3.2-5.

Step (3) Correcting Hs to Get Ha

We must make three corrections to Hs-max before we can figure out our latitude. These are: the index correction, the dip correction, and the altitude correction.

The index correction is discussed in the previous step; we must either add it or subtract it, depending on whether IC is off the scale or on the scale. You can always go through the speedometer analogy to figure out if it's to be added or subtracted, but in practice the best way to take care of this is to remember the jingle:

If it's ON, take if off.

If it's OFF, put it on.

Don't try to remember the sign (±) of the IC when you measure it. There is too big a chance for a mistake this way. Just record ON or OFF, and then use the jingle when you start your paperwork.

The *dip correction* is a small correction that is always negative—that is, we always subtract it from Hs. This correction takes into account our elevation above the water level as we make the sight. The higher we are, the farther it is to the visible horizon (Figure 3.2-6). And the farther we see, the more the visible horizon dips below an imaginary plane at our feet. This makes the angles we measure slightly too big, because we are measuring Hs relative to the visible horizon. So we must correct Hs for the Dip using a table in the *Nautical Almanac*.

The dip correction depends only on the *height of your eye* (HE) above the water line as you stand doing the sight. This is something you typically only have to measure once, since elevations don't change much as you wander around a small boat. Besides, this correction does not change very fast with height. At HE = 9 ft the correction is about -3', and you have to go to an elevation of 16 ft to increase this to -4'. (Dip = 1' times the square root of HE, to within a decimal point or so, with HE given in feet.)

Dip corrections are in Table A2, on the inside of the front cover of the *Nautical Almanac* (our Table T-8). Go down the ft. column till you find your HE, or two values that bracket your HE, and the correction is to the left.

We will have more to say later about Dip and the Dip formula. As it turns out, this simple formula is very valuable to several aspects of navigation. It essentially gives you the distance to the horizon, so you can use it to predict the visible range of lights and land.

Once you have IC and the Dip, apply them to Hs to get what is called the *apparent height* (Ha). Ha is just Hs corrected for IC and Dip:

$$Ha = Hs + IC(off) - Dip$$

$$Ha = Hs - IC(on) - Dip$$

If we had a group of people standing at the same spot on earth, but at different heights using different sextants with various index errors, they would get different values of Hs for the height of the sun. But after they did their IC and Dip corrections, they should all end up with the same Ha. The height is called apparent because there is still another correction to make.

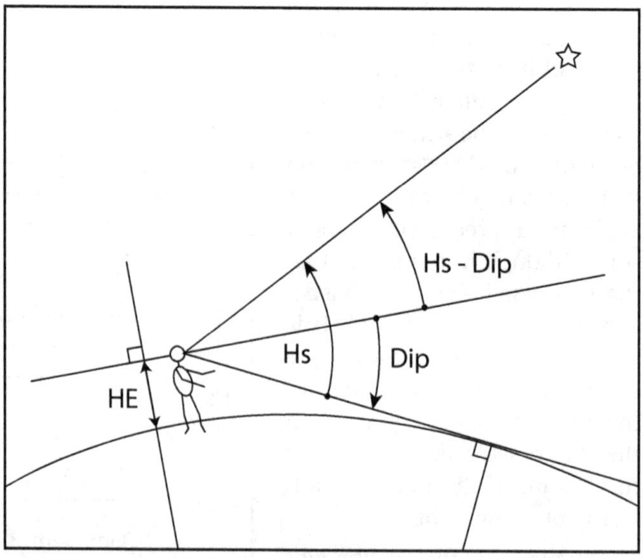

Figure 3.2-6 *The Dip angle makes all sextant sights (Hs) higher than they should be by a small amount that depends on the height of eye (HE) above the water. The scale here is* greatly distorted *in that we see the radius of the earth (about 4,000 miles) in the same picture with an HE, which is typically 6 to 100 ft on a vessel.*

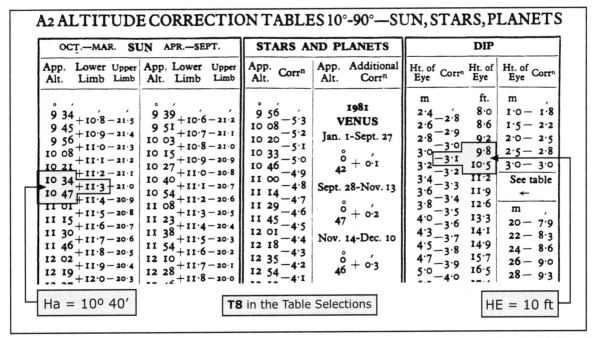

A2 ALTITUDE CORRECTION TABLES 10°-90°—SUN, STARS, PLANETS

OCT.—MAR. SUN App. Alt.	Lower Limb	Upper Limb	APR.—SEPT. SUN App. Alt.	Lower Limb	Upper Limb	STARS AND PLANETS App. Alt.	Corrⁿ
° ′	′	′	° ′	′	′	° ′	′
9 34			9 39			9 56	
	+10·8	−21·5		+10·6	−21·2		−5·3
9 45			9 51			10 08	
	+10·9	−21·4		+10·7	−21·1		−5·2
9 56			10 03			10 20	
	+11·0	−21·3		+10·8	−21·0		−5·1
10 08			10 15			10 33	
	+11·1	−21·2		+10·9	−20·9		−5·0
10 21			10 27			10 46	
	+11·2	−21·1		+11·0	−20·8		−4·9
10 34			10 40			11 00	
	+11·3	−21·0		+11·1	−20·7		−4·8
10 47			10 54			11 14	
	+11·4	−20·9		+11·2	−20·6		−4·7
11 01			11 08			11 29	
	+11·5	−20·8		+11·3	−20·5		−4·6
11 15			11 23			11 45	
	+11·6	−20·7		+11·4	−20·4		−4·5
11 30			11 38			12 01	
	+11·7	−20·6		+11·5	−20·3		−4·4
11 46			11 54			12 18	
	+11·8	−20·5		+11·6	−20·2		−4·3
12 02			12 10			12 35	
	+11·9	−20·4		+11·7	−20·1		−4·2
12 19			12 28			12 54	
	+12·0	−20·3		+11·8	−20·0		−4·1

App. Alt.	Additional Corrⁿ
1981 VENUS	
Jan. 1-Sept. 27	
0° 42°	+0·1′
Sept. 28-Nov. 13	
0° 47°	+0·2′
Nov. 14-Dec. 10	
0° 46°	+0·3′

DIP Ht. of Eye (m)	Corrⁿ	Ht. of Eye (ft.)
2·4		8·0
	−2·8	
2·6		8·6
	−2·9	
2·8		9·2
	−3·0	
3·0		9·8
	−3·1	
3·2		10·5
	−3·2	
3·4		11·2
	−3·3	
3·6		11·9
	−3·4	
3·8		12·6
	−3·5	
4·0		13·3
	−3·6	
4·3		14·1
	−3·7	
4·5		14·9
	−3·8	
4·7		15·7
	−3·9	
5·0		16·5
	−4·0	

Ht. of Eye (m)	Corrⁿ (′)
1·0	−1·8
1·5	−2·2
2·0	−2·5
2·5	−2·8
3·0	−3·0
See table ←	
20	−7·9
22	−8·3
24	−8·6
26	−9·0
28	−9·3

Ha = 10° 40′ | T8 in the Table Selections | HE = 10 ft

Figure 3.2-7 *Sample from Table T-8, showing the dip correction of -3.1′ for HE = 10 ft and an altitude correction of +11.3′ for a lower limb sun sight taken between October and March having an Ha of 10° 40′.*

Step (4) Correcting Ha to Get Ho, the Altitude Correction

This is the final step to correcting the sextant height. We must look up one number in the *Nautical Almanac*, and then add it or subtract it from Ha; the result we get is called Ho, the *observed height*.

Although we look up just one number, called the *altitude correction*, this one number actually includes three corrections (semidiameter, refraction, and parallax). First, it takes into account the angular width of the sun. We want the height to the precise center of the sun, but we must measure the height to the lower limb or upper limb—there's no easy way to align the center of the sun with the horizon. The width correction, therefore, depends on whether we did a lower limb or upper-limb sight; in the first case we must add half the width to get to the middle, and in the second case we must subtract it.

The altitude correction also depends on the month we did the sight. This is so because the distance from the earth to the sun changes slightly throughout the year, because our orbit around the sun is not a perfect circle. During the October-to-March half of the year, we are slightly closer to the sun than we are in the April-to-September half. When we are closer to the sun the apparent size of the sun is bigger, so the width correction is bigger. This width correction is called the *semidiameter* correction, but we don't ever have to make this correction separately. It is always included in the altitude correction.

You might wonder why half of the sun's width is called a semidiameter and not a radius, the usual name for half of a circle. The answer is that the visible sun is not a circle. If you looked at the sun's disk very carefully with a sextant you would find that it is an ellipse—especially when it's near the horizon. In some atmospheric conditions the setting sun can look very egg-like. The squashed look is caused by refraction—the second part of the correction we are now making. In geometry, half the width of an ellipse is called a semidiameter.

When light rays from the sun enter the earth's atmosphere they bend. And they always bend down, toward the earth, which means that when we see the light rays they are at a steeper angle than they should be (Figure 3.2-8). In other words, our sextant heights are always too big because of this refraction. *Refraction* is the technical name for bending light rays. It is the same effect that makes sticks look bent when they are half in the water and half out of the water.

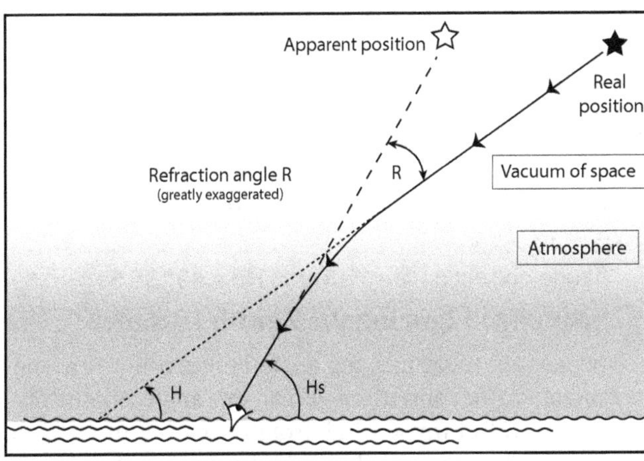

Figure 3.2-8. *Refraction. When light slows down entering the denser atmosphere it bends down toward the surface, causing sextant sights to appear too high.*

The amount that light rays from the sun bend depends on the angle they make with the horizon. When the sun is low on the horizon, the refraction is the greatest. It can be as large as half a degree or so when the sun is right on the horizon. But when the sun is straight overhead there is no refraction of the light rays—they can't bend down when they are already coming straight down on us. All light rays bend, not just those from the sun, so this correction will be needed for all celestial sights: sun, stars, moon, and planets.

There is also a third, very small correction buried in the sun's altitude correction. It is called *parallax*, but for the sun it never amounts to more than 0.1'. We will discuss this more when we get to the moon. Parallax is an important correction for the moon.

Now we see what all the sun's altitude correction depends on: it depends on Ha, the height of the sun, because the refraction depends on the height; it depends on whether we did a lower-limb or upper-limb sight, because it includes the semidiameter correction; and finally it depends on the month, because the semidiameter depends on the month.

With this information at hand, you can find the altitude correction in Table A2 on the inside of the front cover of the *Nautical Almanac* (Table T- 8 of the Table Selections, sample in Figure 3.2-7). Choose the appropriate side of the table for the season of your sight; choose the column for upper limb or lower limb; go down the column to find two values of Ha that bracket your value; and the correction will be to the side of it. The sign (±) of the correction tells you whether to add or subtract it from Ha to get Ho.

Example: Finding altitude correction

Refer to the Table Selections to check these.

(a) A November lower-limb sun sight.
Ha = 10° 40.0'
Altitude correction = + 11.3'
Ho = Ha + alt. corr.
Ho = 10° 40.0' + 11.3' = 10° 51.3'

(b) A July lower-limb sun sight.
Ha = 65° 17.6'.
Altitude correction is + 15.5' and Ho = 65° 33.1'.

(c) An October *upper*-limb sun sight.
Ha = 49° 52.4'.
Altitude correction is - 16.9' and Ho = 49° 35.5'.

Step (5) Figuring the Zenith Distance

The sextant measures the angle between the sun and the horizon. After corrections we call this angle Ho, the observed height. But if you recall from the earlier discussion of the principles of celestial navigation, it is not Ho that we want in the end; it is the zenith distance (z) since the angle z converted to miles is the distance between us and the GP of the sun. The *zenith distance* is the angle from the sun on up to the point directly overhead, the zenith. Since the angle between the horizon and the zenith is 90°, we can easily figure the zenith distance once we have Ho. We just subtract Ho from 90°—or to facilitate the subtraction, we replace 90° with 89° 60', which is the same thing.

So in this step do just that: subtract Ho from 89° 60' and call it z:

zenith distance (z) = 89° 60' - Ho

Step (6) Finding the Declination of the Sun

The *declination* (Dec) of the sun is the latitude of the GP of the sun. In other words, it is the latitude of the point on earth directly underneath the sun. This latitude will always be somewhere in the tropics; we can look it up in the *Nautical Almanac*, which is just what we do in this step.

The declination of the sun changes slowly throughout the year (recall Figure 3.1-1), so in this step you will use the date and the UTC of LAN. The time to use here is the time you recorded for the maximum value of Hs. We need UTC, so this usually means you must correct your watch time for the zone description of the watch and also correct it for watch error if it is fast or slow. Refer to the In-Depth section on Timekeeping (11.5) if you have questions about this.

The UTC that you observe for LAN will be close to the time you predicted in Step (1), but it may differ by a few minutes because your DR-Lon could have been off, and it is not so easy to tell to the minute what the actual time of maximum Hs was by just looking at a list of sextant heights and watch times. We will have more to say about this in the section on finding longitude at LAN (Section 11.9), which depends on the determination of this time.

The declination of the sun is listed on the daily pages of the *Nautical Almanac*. *Daily pages* is a common term in cel nav; it simply means the bulk of the book with daily data on them, as opposed to the corrections tables and other auxiliary data.

Go to the page for the right date—there are 3 days on each page—then to the column headed SUN, and then down that column till you are at the right date and the right hour of the UTC of LAN. (If your observed UTC was 20h 50m, go down to the 20-hour line.) You will find two numbers listed there. The first is the Greenwich Hour Angle (GHA), which is equivalent to the longitude of the GP—we don't need that now—and beside it is the declination (Dec). Record this value on the work form or in your notebook and don't forget the N or S. Declination is a latitude, so it always has to have a North or South label. Declination labels are usually written before the angle to distinguish them from latitudes.

That was the main job, but we aren't quite finished. What we have so far is the declination at the even hour; we

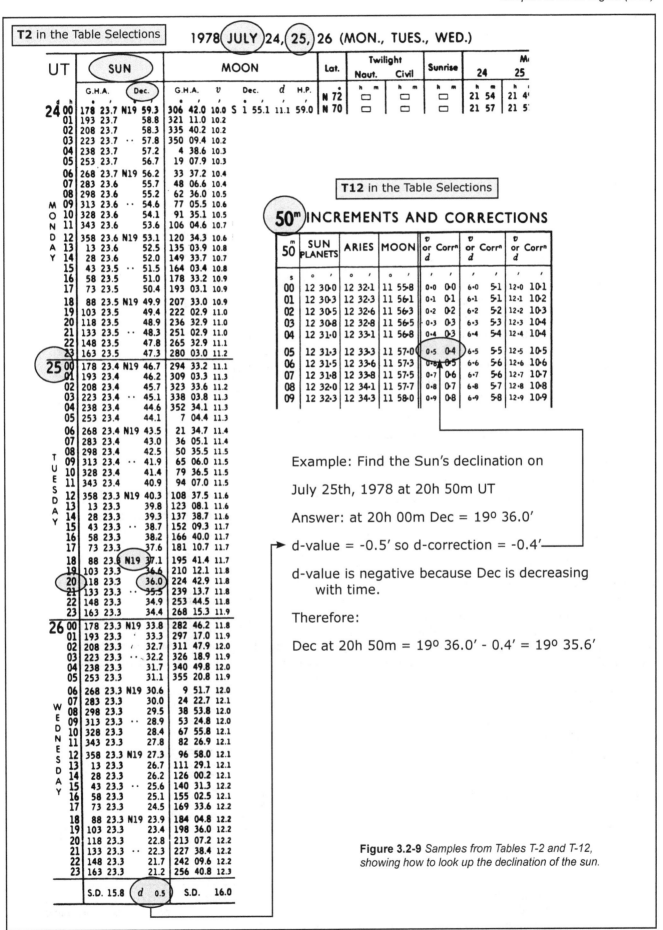

T2 in the Table Selections

1978 JULY 24, 25, 26 (MON., TUES., WED.)

UT	SUN G.H.A.	SUN Dec.	MOON G.H.A.	v	Dec.	d	H.P.
d h	° ′	° ′	° ′	′	° ′	′	′
24 00	178 23.7	N19 59.3	306 42.0	10.0	S 1 55.1	11.1	59.0
01	193 23.7	58.8	321 11.0	10.2			
02	208 23.7	58.3	335 40.2	10.2			
03	223 23.7	·· 57.8	350 09.4	10.2			
04	238 23.7	57.2	4 38.6	10.3			
05	253 23.7	56.7	19 07.9	10.3			
06	268 23.7	N19 56.2	33 37.2	10.4			
07	283 23.6	55.7	48 06.6	10.4			
08	298 23.6	55.2	62 36.0	10.5			
M 09	313 23.6	·· 54.6	77 05.5	10.6			
O 10	328 23.6	54.1	91 35.1	10.5			
N 11	343 23.6	53.6	106 04.6	10.7			
D 12	358 23.6	N19 53.1	120 34.3	10.6			
A 13	13 23.6	52.5	135 03.9	10.8			
Y 14	28 23.6	52.0	149 33.7	10.7			
15	43 23.5	·· 51.5	164 03.4	10.8			
16	58 23.5	51.0	178 33.2	10.9			
17	73 23.5	50.4	193 03.1	10.9			
18	88 23.5	N19 49.9	207 33.0	10.9			
19	103 23.5	49.4	222 02.9	11.0			
20	118 23.5	48.9	236 32.9	11.0			
21	133 23.5	·· 48.3	251 02.9	11.0			
22	148 23.5	47.8	265 32.9	11.1			
23	163 23.5	47.3	280 03.0	11.2			
25 00	178 23.4	N19 46.7	294 33.2	11.1			
01	193 23.4	46.2	309 03.3	11.3			
02	208 23.4	45.7	323 33.6	11.2			
03	223 23.4	·· 45.1	338 03.8	11.3			
04	238 23.4	44.6	352 34.1	11.3			
05	253 23.4	44.1	7 04.4	11.3			
06	268 23.4	N19 43.5	21 34.7	11.4			
07	283 23.4	43.0	36 05.1	11.4			
08	298 23.4	42.5	50 35.5	11.5			
T 09	313 23.4	·· 41.9	65 06.0	11.5			
U 10	328 23.4	41.4	79 36.5	11.5			
E 11	343 23.4	40.9	94 07.0	11.5			
S 12	358 23.3	N19 40.3	108 37.5	11.6			
D 13	13 23.3	39.8	123 08.1	11.6			
A 14	28 23.3	39.3	137 38.7	11.6			
Y 15	43 23.3	·· 38.7	152 09.3	11.7			
16	58 23.3	38.2	166 40.0	11.7			
17	73 23.3	37.6	181 10.7	11.7			
18	88 23.3	N19 37.1	195 41.4	11.7			
19	103 23.3	36.6	210 12.1	11.8			
20	118 23.3	36.0	224 42.9	11.8			
21	133 23.3	·· 35.5	239 13.7	11.8			
22	148 23.3	34.9	253 44.5	11.8			
23	163 23.3	34.4	268 15.3	11.9			
26 00	178 23.3	N19 33.8	282 46.2	11.8			
01	193 23.3	33.3	297 17.0	11.9			
02	208 23.3	32.7	311 47.9	12.0			
03	223 23.3	·· 32.2	326 18.9	11.9			
04	238 23.3	31.7	340 49.8	12.0			
05	253 23.3	31.1	355 20.8	11.9			
06	268 23.3	N19 30.6	9 51.7	12.0			
W 07	283 23.3	30.0	24 22.7	12.1			
E 08	298 23.3	29.5	38 53.8	12.0			
D 09	313 23.3	·· 28.9	53 24.8	12.0			
N 10	328 23.3	28.4	67 55.8	12.1			
E 11	343 23.3	27.8	82 26.9	12.1			
S 12	358 23.3	N19 27.3	96 58.0	12.1			
D 13	13 23.3	26.7	111 29.1	12.1			
A 14	28 23.3	26.2	126 00.2	12.1			
Y 15	43 23.3	·· 25.6	140 31.3	12.2			
16	58 23.3	25.1	155 02.5	12.1			
17	73 23.3	24.5	169 33.6	12.2			
18	88 23.3	N19 23.9	184 04.8	12.2			
19	103 23.3	23.4	198 36.0	12.2			
20	118 23.3	22.8	213 07.2	12.2			
21	133 23.3	·· 22.3	227 38.4	12.2			
22	148 23.3	21.7	242 09.6	12.2			
23	163 23.3	21.2	256 40.8	12.3			
	S.D. 15.8	d 0.5	S.D. 16.0				

Lat.	Twilight Naut.	Twilight Civil	Sunrise	Mo[onrise] 24	25
°	h m	h m	h m	h m	h m
N 72	▭	▭	▭	21 54	21 4
N 70	▭	▭	▭	21 57	21 5

T12 in the Table Selections

50m INCREMENTS AND CORRECTIONS

50m	SUN PLANETS	ARIES	MOON	v or d	Corrn	v or d	Corrn	v or d	Corrn
s	° ′	° ′	° ′	′	′	′	′	′	′
00	12 30·0	12 32·1	11 55·8	0·0	0·0	6·0	5·1	12·0	10·1
01	12 30·3	12 32·3	11 56·1	0·1	0·1	6·1	5·1	12·1	10·2
02	12 30·5	12 32·6	11 56·3	0·2	0·2	6·2	5·2	12·2	10·3
03	12 30·8	12 32·8	11 56·5	0·3	0·3	6·3	5·3	12·3	10·4
04	12 31·0	12 33·1	11 56·8	0·4	0·3	6·4	5·4	12·4	10·4
05	12 31·3	12 33·3	11 57·0	0·5	0·4	6·5	5·5	12·5	10·5
06	12 31·5	12 33·6	11 57·3	0·6	0·5	6·6	5·6	12·6	10·6
07	12 31·8	12 33·8	11 57·5	0·7	0·6	6·7	5·6	12·7	10·7
08	12 32·0	12 34·1	11 57·7	0·8	0·7	6·8	5·7	12·8	10·8
09	12 32·3	12 34·3	11 58·0	0·9	0·8	6·9	5·8	12·9	10·9

Example: Find the Sun's declination on July 25th, 1978 at 20h 50m UT

Answer: at 20h 00m Dec = 19° 36.0′

d-value = -0.5′ so d-correction = -0.4′

d-value is negative because Dec is decreasing with time.

Therefore:

Dec at 20h 50m = 19° 36.0′ - 0.4′ = 19° 35.6′

Figure 3.2-9 *Samples from Tables T-2 and T-12, showing how to look up the declination of the sun.*

want to know it at the actual time we observed, which will typically be some minutes later. The declination at this later time could be bigger or smaller than the value at the even hour, depending on whether the declination is moving toward the equator or away from it during that time of year (i.e., decreasing or increasing).

What we have left to do is an interpolation: we know, for example, the declination at 20h and at 21h from the daily pages, and from this we have to figure out what it should be at 20h 50m. It would be 50/60ths of the way between the two. However, as always in cel nav, this is done for us in a special table—we never have to multiply in cel nav!

IMPORTANT NOTE: When we do use these special tables (Increments and Corrections) we will not be using the seconds part of the UTC to find the declination. We use only the minutes part. During an LAN sight, this rarely offers any confusion since we won't know the time accurate to the second anyway. But later on when we are looking up the declination for sun lines and star lines we will know the time accurate to the second, and we will use it for some things, but not for the declination. If you do know the UTC accurate to the second, just forget the seconds when you do the declination.

To make the declination correction for the minutes part of the UTC we must first look to see if the declination is increasing or decreasing with time on the date of the sight. Look at the value of the declination at the next hour, or the next few hours, and that will tell you. If the declination is increasing, you will have to add the correction; if it's decreasing, you will subtract it. The sample table for July 24, 25, and 26 (Figure 3.2-9) shows an example of a decreasing declination.

The size of the correction depends on two things: on the minutes part of the UTC and on how much the declination changes each hour. The first we know; the second we find at the bottom of the sun column on the daily pages. This hourly change in the declination is called the "d-value." For the sun the d-value is the same all day for all 3 days listed on the daily page. So the next thing we do is record the d-value in our work form or notebook; call it (+) if the declination is increasing or (-) if the declination is decreasing. This is just a way to remind us that we are to add or subtract the correction.

The correction itself is found in the *Increments and Corrections* Tables. These are the pages at the back of the Almanac (T-9 to T-12 in our Table Selections). There is one table for each minute of the hour. Look now to the inserted table in Figure 3.2-9. Note that there are two parts to the table divided by a double line; these are completely separate tables used for different corrections. For the declination correction that we are doing now, we only use the right-hand part of the table. For now, completely forget about the left-hand side of the table.

On the right-hand table, go down the column headed "v or d" till you find your d-value; the correction you want will be listed beside it. There are three columns covering different ranges of d-values. The sun's correction will always be somewhere in the first column, since the d-value of the sun can never be bigger than 1.0'. The columns are headed "v or d" because we will use this same table later on to get a v-correction using a v-value.

There is an example worked out in Figure 3.2-9. Follow it through to see where each of the numbers comes from. For more practice looking up and correcting the sun's declination, you can work through the following practice exercises. The tables you need are in the Table Selections.

3.3 Exercise Looking up Sun's Dec

(a) On October 25th, 1978 at 10h 04m Sun's Dec =

(b) On March 28th, 1981 at 21h 51m Sun's Dec =

(c) On July 24th, 1978 at 12h 06m Sun's Dec =

(d) On October 27th, 1978 at 22h 49m Sun's Dec =

Answers are in the Answers section.

Step (7) Choosing the Rule

We now have all we need to find our latitude. We know the distance from us to the sun (the zenith distance), and

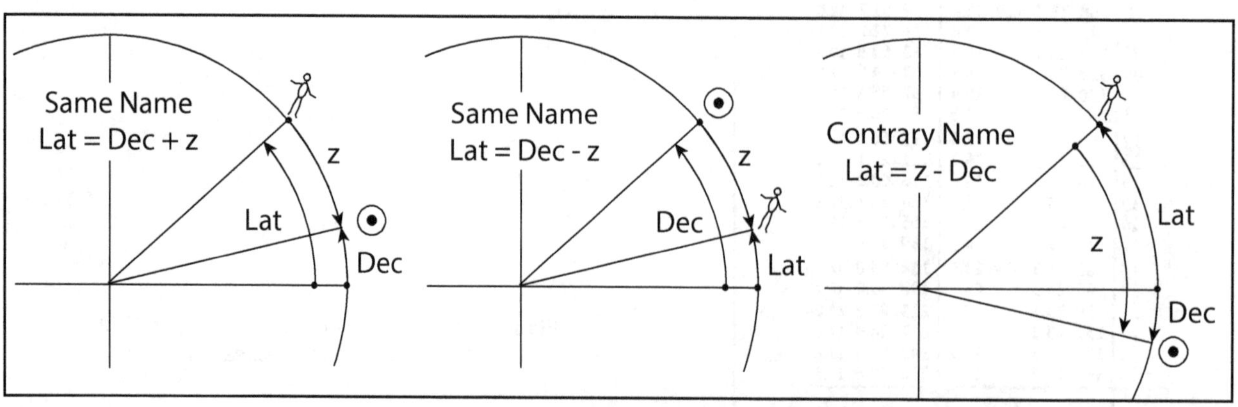

Figure 3.2-10. *The three cases for figuring Lat from the sun's declination (Dec) and the zenith distance (z). This applies to northern or southern hemisphere (just flip the pictures over). The only thing that matters is the name (N or S) of the Lat and Dec. Same name means both are on the same side of the equator; contrary means on opposite sides.*

we know where the sun is (the declination of the sun). If the zenith distance is 10° and the sun is at 20° N, then our latitude must be either 30° N or 10° N. These are the only two latitudes that are 10° distant from 20° N, which are the only latitudes that would give us the height of the sun that we observed. It is simple to decide which of these latitudes is correct, because in the one case we would have looked north to the sun at noon, and in the other case we would have looked south.

In this example, our latitude and the declination of the sun were in the same hemisphere. When this is true—Lat and Dec both North or both South—latitude and declination are said to have the *Same Name*. If we are in the opposite hemisphere from the sun (Lat N, Dec S; or Lat S, Dec N), latitude and declination have *Contrary Names*. The example in the last paragraph was a Same-Name case. In a Same-Name case your latitude will be either the sum of the zenith distance and the declination or the difference between them, depending on whether you are on the pole side or the equator side of the sun. (Look at the previous example again to see this, referring to Figure 3.2-10.) We will have an easy rule for choosing the right option, but you can see from the example how the reasoning goes.

For Contrary-Name cases you will always subtract declination from zenith distance to get latitude (Figure 3.2-10). Look at this example: you find the zenith distance = 42°, you know you are in the northern hemisphere (your DR-Lat is N), and the declination of the sun is 20° S. You are north; the sun is south. At noon the sun is due south of you by 42°. The sun is at 20° S, so you are 42° N of 20° S. In other words, you are at 22° N latitude—20° from the sun up to the equator plus your latitude of 22° N = 42°. For Contrary-Name cases you always subtract declination from zenith distance to get latitude.

These rules are summarized in Figure 3.2-11.

Notes on the Rules for LAN:

(1) If you get stuck without these rules and you are having trouble figuring out what they should be, just do this: remember that all you need is the zenith distance and the declination. Your latitude will always be either the sum or the difference of the two. So go ahead and add them, and compare the result with your DR-Lat. If this is way off, then you should have subtracted them. So subtract them, and compare this to your DR-Lat. The difference between the two solutions will be twice the declination of the sun, and for all but a few days of the year this will be many hundreds of miles. In other words, this last step of choosing the rule may look confusing at first, but in practice it never is.

(2) And typically you only have to figure out the rule once, or maybe twice, on an ocean voyage. You have to figure it out once when you first get started, and after that the rule remains the same every day until you either sail across the equator or under the sun. The rule could also change if you happen to be at sea on either equinox, March 21st or September 23rd, since the sun crosses the equator on about these dates.

(3) Once you have figured out your latitude, plot it on the plotting sheet you are using for your DR, and label it with: LAN, the date, the UTC, and the log reading at the time of Hs-max. This will be a straight horizontal line at the latitude you found. In other words, your LAN latitude is just like any other line of position (LOP) (that we will find later); it just happens to be parallel to the bottom of the page. We know we are somewhere on this line, but we won't know where on the line until we get another LOP that intersects the LAN line.

Figure 3.2-12 summarizes the full process for an LAN sight. Following that are three examples, and after that is an optional work form from the Appendix that can be used for these sights if you find that helpful. Later for sun lines at other times of the day the work forms are very useful, but after a few practice exercises, you may not need or want a work form for the LAN sights.

THE RULES FOR LAN

First have your DR-Lat, the Dec of the sun, and the zenith distance (z) at hand. Now look at the name of your DR-Lat and the Dec of the sun, and note if they are Same Name or Contrary Name. Then:

For Contrary Name, any DR-Lat, any Dec Lat = z - Dec

For Same Name, DR-Lat bigger than Dec Lat = z + Dec

For Same Name, DR-Lat less than Dec Lat = Dec - z.

But don't forget the *Easy LAN Rule*: Add them, and if that does not make sense, subtract them.

Figure 3.2-11. *Rules for figuring LAN Lat from DR-Lat, declination, and zenith distance.*

STEP-BY-STEP SUMMARY FOR A LAN SIGHT

This is an abbreviated work-guide for reference. Details of the individual steps are in the text

(1) Predict the UTC of LAN using the *Nautical Almanac* and your DR position:

UTC of LAN = Mer pass time from NA + DR-Lon (West)

UTC of LAN = Mer pass time from NA - DR-Lon (East)

(2) Using a sextant, measure the maximum height of the sun as it crosses your meridian at noon. This will occur near the time you predicted in step (1). The angle you read from the sextant is called Hs, the sextant height. Also measure IC, the index correction.

(3) Using the *Nautical Almanac*, correct Hs to get Ha, the apparent height:

Ha = Hs + IC(off) - Dip
Ha = Hs - IC(on) - Dip

(4) Using the *Nautical Almanac*, correct Ha to get Ho, the observed height:

Ho = Ha + altitude correction (lower limb)

Ho = Ha - altitude correction (upper limb)

(5) Subtract Ho from 90° to get z, the zenith distance:

89° 60' - Ho

Note: there is a work form for LAN sights (Form 107) in the Appendix, which you can use if you like. A sample is shown later in Figure 3.2-13.

(6) Using the *Nautical Almanac*, look up the declination of the sun (Dec) at the UTC of LAN:

Dec = Dec (Daily pages) + d-corr (Inc & Corr pages)

(7) Using DR-Lat and Dec, choose the proper rule, then add or subtract z and Dec to get Latitude:

Contrary Name, any DR-Lat, any Dec: Lat = z - Dec

Same Name, DR-Lat bigger than Dec: Lat = z + Dec

Same Name, DR-Lat less than Dec: Lat = Dec - z

Figure 3.2-12. *Rules for figuring LAN Lat from DR-Lat, declination, and zenith distance.*

Examples: Finding Latitude at LAN

Work through these three examples to verify that you understand where each of the numbers comes from. Refer to procedure above, and check the individual steps described earlier as needed. We will have more practice with LAN later on. For now, if you have control of this sight — the sequence, the tables, the arithmetic, and so forth — you might be relieved to know that you have completed about 75% of the work required to learn celestial navigation.

(A) DR position at noon on July 25th, 1978 was 44° 10' N, 131° 00' W. A series of noon sights were taken and Hs-max was found to be 65° 22.5' for a Lower Limb sight taken at 20h 50m UTC. The index error was 2.0' on the scale, and the height of eye was 9 feet. Find latitude at LAN.

(B) DR position at noon on Mar. 28th, 1981 was 16° 40' S, 146° 30' W. A series of noon sights were taken and Hs-max was found to be 69° 44.2' for a Lower Limb sight taken at 21h 51m UTC. The index error was 2.5' off the scale, and the height of eye was 12 feet. Find latitude at LAN.

(C) DR position at noon on Oct. 25th, 1978 was 34° 29' N, 025° 00' E. A series of noon sights were taken and Hs-max was found to be 43° 11.7' for a Lower Limb sight taken at 10h 04m UTC. The index error was 1.5' off the scale, and the height of eye was 14 feet. Find latitude at LAN.

A.

Hs-Max =	65°	22.5'
IC =		- 2.0'
Dip =		- 2.9'
Ha =	65°	17.6'
alt. corr. =		+ 15.5'
Ho =	65°	33.1'
90° =	89°	60.0'
- Ho	65°	33.1'
z =	24°	26.9'
Dec =	N 19°	36.0'
d-corr. =		- 0.4'
Dec =	N 19°	35.6'

Same name with Lat bigger than Dec, so:

z =	24°	26.9'
+ Dec	19°	35.6'
Lat =	43°	62.5'
or Lat =	44°	2.5' N

B.

Hs-Max =	69°	44.2'
IC =		+ 2.5'
Dip =		- 3.4'
Ha =	69°	43.3'
alt. corr. =		+ 15.8'
Ho =	69°	59.1'
90° =	89°	60.0'
- Ho	69°	59.1'
z =	20°	00.9'
Dec =	N 3°	12.5'
d-corr. =		+ 0.9'
Dec =	N 3°	13.4'

Contrary name, so:

z =	20°	00.9'
- Dec	3°	13.4'
Lat =	16°	47.5'
or Lat =	16°	47.5' S

C.

Hs-Max =	43°	11.7'
IC =		+ 1.5'
Dip =		- 3.6'
Ha =	43°	9.6'
alt. corr. =		+ 15.2'
Ho =	43°	24.8'
90° =	89°	60.0'
- Ho	43°	24.8'
z =	46°	35.2'
Dec =	S 12°	2.6'
d-corr. =		+ 0.1'
Dec =	S 12°	2.7'

Contrary name, so:

z =	46°	35.2'
- Dec	12°	2.7'
Lat =	34°	32.5'
or Lat =	34°	32.5' N

Step 1 Correct Hs to get Ho

1-1	Record Maximum Sextant Height (Hs = peak height of the sun at noon), and mark limb	Lower / Upper — Hs	65°	22.5'
1-2	Record Index Correction (mark sign + if off, - if on)	IC	Off + / On (–)	2.0'
1-3	Record eye height (HE) and Look up Dip Correction on the right-hand side of Table A2, front of the Almanac (T-8 in notes)	Dip; HE(ft) 9	(–)	2.9'
1-4	Sum the above three numbers to get Apparent Height	Ha	65°	17.6'
1-5	Look up altitude correction on lefthand side of Table A2, front of the Almanac (T-8 in notes) (correction depends on Ha, Limb, and month) (mark sign + for lower limb, - for upper limb)	Alt corr.	(+) / -	15.5
1-6	Sum the above two numbers to get Observed Height	Ho	65°	33.1'

Step 2 Determine the Zenith Distance

			89°	60.0'
2-1	Record Ho from Step 1, above, and then subtract it from 90° to get the zenith distance	Ho	-65°	33.1'
2-2	Zenith distance	z	24°	26.9'

Step 3 Use the Almanac to Find Sun's Declination GMT date = 25 July 1978

3-1	Record the date and GMT of the sight (the time the sun reached its peak height)	GMT (hr) = 20	GMT (min) = 50
3-2	Turn to the daily page of the Almanac for the date of the sight, and find the sun's declination (dec) for the hour of the sight (line 3-1) and record it here.	Dec (hr)	(N) / S 19° 36.0'
3-3	Record the d-value from the bottom of the dec column in the Almanac. Mark the signs of the d-value and d-corr + if the dec for the next hour is larger, or - if it is smaller.	d-value = + / (–) 0.5	d-corr = + / (–) 0.4'
3-4	Turn to the Increments and Corrections pages at the back of the Almanac (T-9 to 12, in the notes) and find the minutes table for the GMT minutes (line 3-1). On the right-hand side of the double line in the table, find the d-corr corresponding to the d-value of line 3-3	Declination =	(N) / S 19° 35.6'
3-5		Apply the d-corr to the dec(hr) and record it above.	

Step 4 Find Latitude from Zenith Distance and Declination

Record DR Latitude to use as a guide, and then take the sum or difference of zenith distance and declination to find your true Latitute at LAN.

Declination or Zenith distance	24°	26.9'
Zenith distance or Declination	19°	35.6'
Latitude =	43°	62.5'

DR-Lat = 44° 10' N

True Lat = 44° 02.5' N

Figure 3.2-13. *Left. Three worked LAN sights. Right. Work Form 107 for finding latitude at LAN. Example (A) is presented in the work form. Blank copies of these forms are in the Appendix. Many navigators find these useful at first, but then carry on later without them. The process used here for converting Hs to Ho will be used with every sight you do from now on, sun, moon, stars or planets. We will also be looking up the declination of each body, so your experience here will be reinforced throughout the remainder of the course.*

3.4 Exercise on LAN Sights for Latitude

The answers are in the Answers section. You should get the answer exact to the tenth of the minute—not that we can do navigation that accurately, but for practice. An error which might cause only a tenth or so on a sun sight might cause larger errors when doing other sights.

If you are off by just a few tenths of a minute, double-check that you got the altitude correction from the right season column, or that you did the d-correction properly. Off by 30' or so, might be a mix-up between upper and lower limb.

(1) DR position at noon on July 25th, 1978 was 56° 02' N, 164° 30' W. A series of noon sights were taken and Hs-max was found to be 54° 5.0' for a lower-limb sight taken at 23h 04m UTC. The index error was 2.0' on the scale, and the HE was 9 ft. Find latitude at LAN.

(2) DR position at noon on October 27th, 1978 was 10° 00' S, 166° 15' W. A series of noon sights were taken and Hs-max was found to be 87° 20' for a upper-limb sight taken at 22h 49m UTC. The index error was 2.0' off the scale, and the HE was 25 ft. Find latitude at LAN.

(3) DR position at noon on October 25th, 1978 was 35° 54' N, 074° 02' E. A series of noon sights were taken and Hs-max was found to be 41° 30.5' for a lower-limb sight taken at 06h 48m UTC. The index error was 4.0' off the scale, and the HE was 10 ft. Find latitude at LAN.

(4) DR position at noon on March 27th, 1981 was 37° 40' N, 15° 24' W. A series of noon sights were taken and Hs-max was found to be 54° 41.3' for a lower-limb sight taken at 13h 07m UTC. The index error was 2.0' off the scale, and the HE was 9 ft. Find latitude at LAN.

(5) DR position at noon on March 28th, 1981 was 22° 38' N, 64° 17' E. A series of noon sights were taken and Hs-max was found to be 71° 9.8' for a lower-limb sight taken at 07h 48m UTC. The index error was 2.2' on the scale, and the HE was 9 ft. Find latitude at LAN.

(6) DR position at noon on October 26th, 1978 was 27° 06' S, 163° 16' E. A series of noon sights were taken and Hs-max was found to be 74° 59.8' for a lower-limb sight taken at 00h 51m UTC. The index error was 1.4' off the scale, and the HE was 9 ft. Find latitude at LAN.

(7) DR position at noon on July 24th, 1978 was 28° 44' S, 85° 17' W. A series of noon sights were taken and Hs-max was found to be 42° 51.2' for a upper-limb sight taken at 17h 48m UTC. The index error was 1.5' on the scale, and the HE was 9 ft. Find latitude at LAN.

(8) DR position at noon on July 25th, 1978 was 44° 10' N, 131° 00' W. A series of noon sights were taken and Hs-max was found to be 65° 22.5' for a lower-limb sight taken at 20h 50m UTC. The index error was 2.0' on the scale, and the HE was 9 ft. Find latitude at LAN.

(9) DR position at noon on March 28th, 1981 was 16° 40' S, 146° 30' W. A series of noon sights were taken and Hs-max was found to be 69° 44.2' for a lower-limb sight taken at 21h 51m UTC. The index error was 2.5' off the scale, and the HE was 12 ft. Find latitude at LAN.

(10) DR position at noon on October 25th, 1978 was 34° 29' N, 025° 00' E. A series of noon sights were taken and Hs-max was found to be 43° 11.7' for a lower-limb sight taken at 10h 04m UTC. The index error was 1.5' off the scale, and the HE was 14 ft. Find latitude at LAN.

3.5 Review: LAN Virtues and Drawbacks

We have discussed the principles and procedures of noon sun sights for latitude. Now, after a brief review, we fill in a few details, virtues, and drawbacks.

To find your latitude this way, you first predict the time of LAN using the *Nautical Almanac* and your DR-Lon, then start a series of sun sights about 10 minutes or so before this time, and record Hs and WT of the sights as the sun rises, peaks, and begins to descend. At its peak the sun is just crossing your meridian—Good morning has changed to Good afternoon. You can typically take a sight every minute or so throughout this midday period. Next choose the peak height from your list, or plot a curve of Hs vs WT for the best estimate of the peak. With Hs-max in hand, apply the standard sextant corrections for index error, dip, and finally the altitude correction (a single correction that includes a correction for refraction and the width of the sun itself, called its semidiameter, and a small component for parallax). What you have then is called the observed height (Ho). We have taken a whole series of sights, but in this process we are using only one of them, which is our best estimation of the peak height.

We next figure the zenith distance (z) of the sun (z = 90° - Ho), and then we use the *Nautical Almanac* to find out what the declination (Dec) of the sun was at the time you observed the maximum height. Your WT must be converted to Universal Time (UTC) to do this step. Then figure your latitude from the reasoning given in the last section, which is always the sum or difference between z and Dec. Those standard rules work in all cases except the rare times you might be near the equator and not know if you are in fact north or south of it. That is, you do not know if Lat and Dec are Same Name or Contrary Name.

In this rare case, we give here another approach that does not depend on that knowledge, namely:

$$(\text{Lat}) = (\text{Dec}) - (z),$$

where the use of ( ) here means we now care about the sign (±) of each term. North latitudes and declinations are positive numbers, and southern values are negative. The sign (±) of z is determined by the direction of the noon sun. If you looked north to the noon sun, then z is positive; if you looked south, z is negative. The parentheses are used in the equation to emphasize that each term must be inserted with the proper algebraic sign (±). If your answer is positive you are north of the equator; if negative, you are south of the equator. With the sign rules given, this equation will work in all circumstances. Specifically, it will work when you are sailing near the equator, but don't know if you are north or south of it at the time of the sights. Standard textbook rules for LAN latitude listed earlier are ambiguous in this circumstance.

Once you find out what side of the equator you are on, later sights can generally revert back to using the *Easy LAN Rule* if your DR is kept up to date.

To expand, let's first look at validity of the *Easy LAN Rule* of first adding, then if necessary subtracting z and Dec. The *Easy Rule* will work whenever the difference between adding and subtracting is much larger than the uncertainty in your DR-Latitude. The difference between adding and subtracting will be either (2 × declination) or (2 × zenith distance), depending on your latitude and the time of the year. If the uncertainty in your DR-Lat is 4° or less—which it certainly should be since 4° = 240 miles—then the *Easy Rule* only has trouble whenever either the sun's Dec or z is less than 2°.

The sun's Dec is less than 2° for about a week either side of each equinox, for a total of about 4 weeks a year. The zenith distance, z, will be less than 2° whenever your DR-Lat is within 2° of the sun's declination. But in this latter case, the midday sun will be too high for a routine noon sight anyway so it doesn't count—very high sights can be done, but they are difficult, because with the sun near over head, you do not know which way to look to rock the sextant. In short, the *Easy Rule* will work from all locations, even straddling the equator if your DR is good, at all times but the equinoxes. Summary: use the Easy Rule, but record somewhere this rule using the direction of the sun to pull out for possible use when crossing the equator with poor DR—or just wait a day till your DR puts you safely on one side or the other.

The LAN latitude sight has two primary attractions: the sextant sights are easy (usually) and it only takes a few minutes to find your latitude once you have the maximum sextant height in hand. This latter attraction, however, goes away very quickly if it takes an hour to do the sights themselves—especially in lower latitude where it can be extremely hot at midday. To protect the attraction, you must know when to start the sights so you don't waste time waiting for the sun to peak out.

Furthermore, the longer you take, the heavier the sextant becomes, and a heavy sextant is not an accurate sextant. One tends to accept less than the very best sextant alignment of sun and horizon when your arm is throbbing with pain—hold a half-gallon of milk (the weight of a heavy sextant) in front of you for 20 seconds to get the point. So for accuracy and efficiency one should predict the starting time of the sights as close as possible.

To predict the time of LAN we need two numbers from the *Nautical Almanac* (mer pass sun and arc to time) and our DR-Lon at midday. The efficiency of the sight depends on the accuracy of our LAN time prediction, and the accuracy of our time prediction depends on the accuracy of our DR-Lon.

The *Nautical Almanac* tells us the time of LAN in a roundabout way. It tells us the UTC of LAN at Greenwich, and provides a table for us to correct this time for our particular longitude. The listed time is officially called the *local mean time* of meridian passage, but its meaning is important, not its name—one can navigate quite happily without the concept of local mean time beyond how we use it in this book. Indeed, if you want to see that cel nav can actually be funny, look up the official definition of local mean time in Bowditch... then quickly forget that experience and stick to our definition of what the times in the NA mean.

You might guess that the UTC of the sun's meridian passage (LAN) at Greenwich would always be at 12:00, or some other constant time, because the earth rotates daily on its axis beneath the sun at a very constant rate. But this is not the case; the situation is not quite so simple—the earth's rotation axis is tilted and the tilted, rotating earth is in annual motion around the sun in an orbit that is not a pure circle; it is an ellipse. As a result, the UTC that the sun crosses the Greenwich meridian oscillates back and forth, from one side of 12:00 to the other (11:44 to 12:14) throughout the year as was shown back in Figure 3.2-4.

Once you have this predicted time of LAN, set a digital alarm to go off 10 to 15 minutes earlier. When it goes off, unpack the sextant and start the sights. Take sights till the sextant height begins to drop, pack up the sextant, and figure your latitude.

If the sextant height is already dropping when you start taking your sights—the worst case from an LAN point of view, since you missed it—or it keeps going up well beyond the time you predicted for the peak, then, quite simply, there has been a mistake somewhere. You either copied the wrong number from the *Nautical Almanac*, or your arithmetic was wrong, or your DR-Lon was wrong. If you missed it, that's it; no LAN today—the process called *Reduction to the Meridian* designed to cover such cases is best left buried in *Bowditch*. As we learn in the next chapter, we still will get a perfectly good LOP from these sights, it just won't be parallel to the bottom of the chart when we plot it.

...In Depth

11.9 Longitude from LAN

Latitude from the peak height of the sun at noon is a routine and reliable technique. Finding longitude from the observed time of this peak height is possible in an emergency, but should not be considered a routine method. Here we show the technique and precautions that must be taken...

You might ask at this point "How accurate must my DR-Lon be to avoid missing LAN?" The answer is in the Arc to Time Table. The sun moves west at 15° of longitude each hour. Divide both by 60 to see that this is the same as 15' of longitude each minute of time. If my DR-Lon is wrong by 15', my time prediction will be wrong by 1 minute; if my DR-Lon is wrong by 1°, my time prediction will be off by 4 minutes. If I start 12 minutes early—which is conservative—my DR-Lon could be off by 3° or so and I should still catch LAN. A 3° longitude uncertainty corresponds to about 180 miles in the tropics or about 120 miles at 48° North. Rule of thumb: heading south from here, if you are confident you know your DR position to within 100 miles or so, you can start taking your LAN sights 15 minutes before your predicted LAN time and you won't miss it.

As for the magnitude of that level of uncertainty, think of a city 100 nmi from where you are now, and ask what you would have to do and for how long to not know which of these cities you were in.

Another, less obvious question might be "Do I want to bother with these sights at all?" The answer is: Yes, probably—at least at first. The sights are easy, they are good practice, and a good confidence builder. Headed straight south, down the coast they even tell you something of interest, how far south you are. But once the confidence is there, and once you head out, diagonally, across an ocean, the value and attraction of LAN sights fades rapidly.

The key point is the end result—your latitude. In the middle of the ocean, knowing the precise latitude line you are on is rarely more valuable than any other LOP; it just happens to be parallel to the bottom of your plotting sheet. You still don't know where you are, you only know you are somewhere along that LOP. To fix your position you need a second LOP to intersect with the first one. And the fix you get from two intersecting LOPs is just as accurate if they are both tilted. In short there is no virtue to having one of them be a latitude line.

And there is a notable disadvantage. You must take the LAN sights at a specific time of day, and very often at sea this is not convenient. You may well want to sleep at this specific time, or you may have to tend to the boat at this time, or you may want to eat at this time, or whatever... the sun could be behind a cloud at this time. Furthermore, no matter how well you predict the time and how fast you take the sights and do the paperwork, you can rarely complete the entire process faster than you can take and reduce a normal set of three or four sun lines (Chapter 5). You can take these anytime you please.

Even worse, if you do your sight reductions by a mobile app or computer program—not what we are learning at the moment—there is no virtue at all to the noon sight. Noon sights have gained notoriety because you can find something from the sun (i.e., your latitude) without learning how to do the rest of cel nav. If that is all you wanted, this would be as far as you needed to go in the training. But that is frankly negligent, and deprives you from learning the great joys and power of the full knowledge of the subject

3.6 New Terminology

altitude correction
apparent height (Ha)
daily pages
declination (Dec)
dip
dip correction
easy LAN rule
equation of time (EqT)
geographical position (GP)
local apparent noon (LAN)
meridian passage (mer. pas.)
noon sight
observed height (Ho)
parallax
refraction
semidiameter
sextant height (Hs)
upper and lower limb (UL, LL)
zenith
zenith distance (z)

Chapter 4
Plotting & Chart Work

4.1 Introduction

At this point, after finishing LAN work, with all its numbers and table look ups, we take a break from that type of study and just use our hands for some plotting practice. We will be doing what is actually the last step of a cel nav fix—plotting the lines of position (LOPs). At this stage you will not know where the data came from (we learn that in the next chapter); this is being treated as a pure plotting exercise, done in this order specifically to take a break from the number crunching.

We will cover basic plotting tools and procedures as well as the special types of plotting sheets used in open ocean navigation. We also introduce DR plotting from typical logbook entries.

After this plotting practice, we move on to sun lines (more table work) in Chapter 5, and after that take another break with more plotting in Chapter 6. At that point, we are essentially done, meaning the density of new information is much reduced and we start applying what we have learned so far, with simple extensions to the other bodies.

4.2 Universal Plotting Sheets

A universal plotting sheet is a way to make a small nautical chart for any region on earth. The chart covers a rectangular area of roughly 120 nautical miles around the mid-latitude and mid-longitude that you choose for the sheet. The first universal plotting sheets were invented by Capt. Fritz Uttmark, a navigation instructor in New York City, in 1918 (US Patent No. 1337168, 4/13/20). The design has changed somewhat over the years but the basic idea is the same. The Uttmark charts were a boon to navigation at the time.

Setting Up the Plotting Sheet

(1) Choose and label the mid-latitude on the center horizontal line, as shown in Figure 4.2-1. The horizontal lines are latitude lines; the vertical lines are longitude lines. Then label the latitudes above and below your mid-latitude. In northern latitudes, latitude increases to the north, that is, to the top of the page. South of the equator, the latitude lines increase to the south.

(2) Next, draw a horizontal line on the longitude diagram in the bottom right-hand corner at the position of your mid-latitude. This line is then the longitude scale you will use for reading and plotting the longitudes of points on the chart.

(3) Label the central vertical line with your mid-longitude. And now we draw in the other longitude lines, which is the main job in setting up these sheets.

(4) On the *outside scale* on the central compass rose, to the right of the mid-longitude line, go up from the mid-latitude line (0 on the curved scale) to your mid-latitude along the curved scale. If your mid-latitude is 42° N, go up 42°. Mark a point at this spot. Then go down from the center latitude line and mark another point in the same way. Draw a line between the two points to get the longitude line. You can do the same thing to the left of the center line to get another longitude line, but in this case the outer scale is not labeled, so you must just count off the degrees.

(5) Label the new longitude lines, remembering that west of Greenwich longitude increases to the west, or left. The chart is now set up and ready to go.

Using the Plotting Sheet

(1) The latitude of any point is read from the vertical center line. Each tick mark is equal to 1' of latitude. Each latitude line is separated by 60 marks, since 60' = 1°.

(2) The longitude of any point is read from the diagram in the bottom right hand corner. For example, to set your dividers on 34' of longitude, set one side of them on the 30' mark and the other side on the second mark to the right of 0'. Each division on the right side of the diagram is equal to 2' of longitude. This special diagram is taking into account how the longitude scale changes with latitude. The changes that apply for different latitudes on the same plotting sheet are so small that you can use the same mid-latitude line for reading any longitude on the page.

(3) For measuring distances between points, always use the central, vertical latitude scale. Each 1' of latitude equals 1 nmi. Recall that 1° of latitude always equals 60 nmi, but the number of miles per 1° of longitude changes with your latitude. At the equator 1° of longitude is 60 nmi, but as you go north, it gets smaller. Check the example page to see that at latitude 40°N the distance between each longitude line is 46 nmi. This takes into account the convergence of the longitude lines at the north pole.

Since the earth is symmetric about the equator, everything is the same for southern latitudes. The only thing that changes is the labels. In the south, latitude increases toward the bottom of the page.

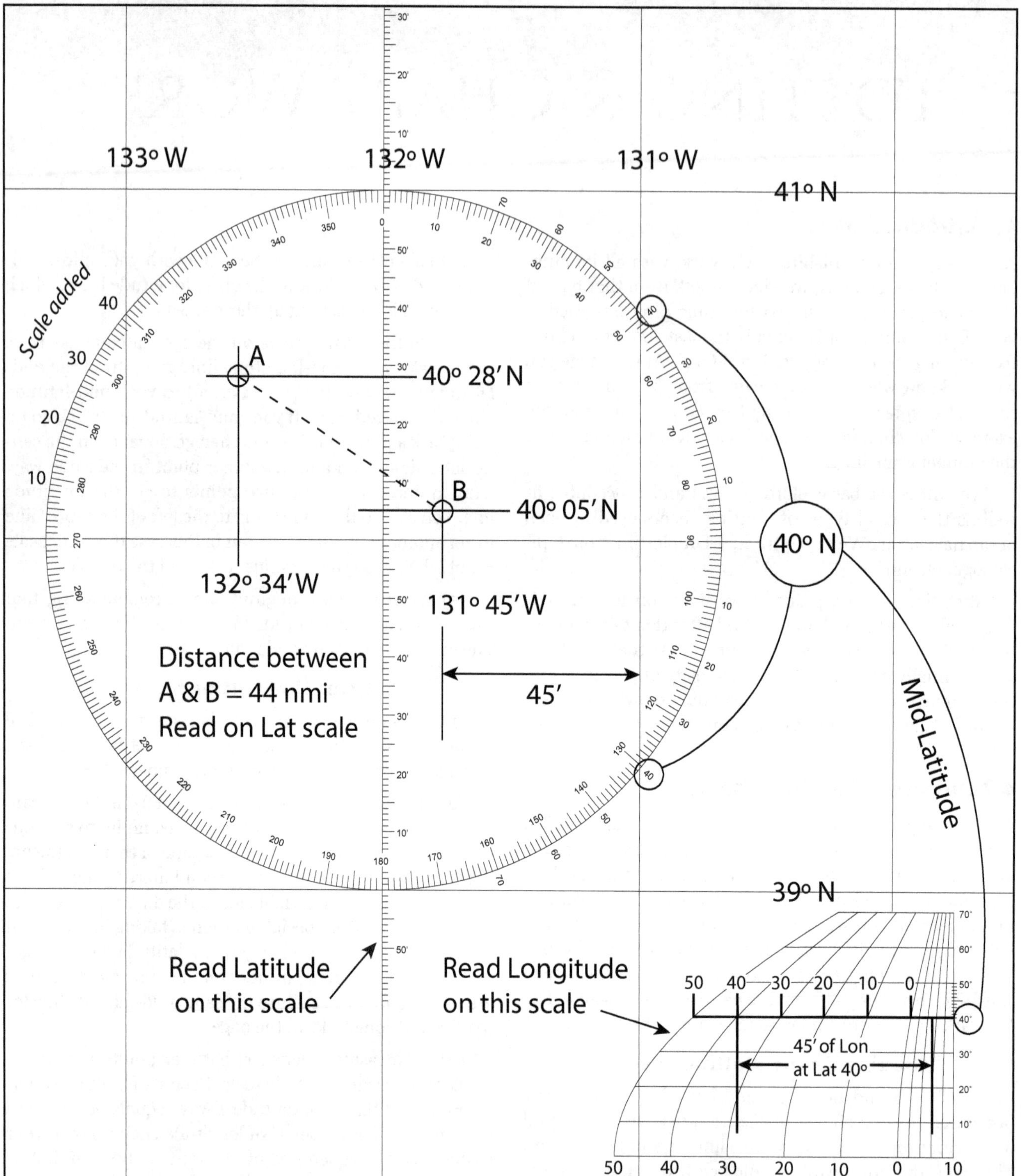

Figure 4.2-1. *A universal plotting sheet set up with a mid-latitude of 40 N. Once the meridians are drawn in as explained in the instructions in Section 4.2, longitude is read from the diagram in the bottom right. Latitude is read from the vertical scale in the center. For mid-latitudes such as 42° mentioned in the text, we must estimate where to draw in the line on the longitude scale diagram. The tick marks we show here are not on the standard sheets.*

High-Resolution pdf versions these plotting sheets can be downloaded at www.starpath.com/celnavbook

There are many examples of these plotting sheets set up in the book further on. You can refer to them for more examples.

4.3 Exercise on Universal Plotting Sheets

Using the plotting sheet in Figure 4.3-1, solve the following problems using only dividers and the scales on the sheets. Remember the distance or nautical miles scale is the same as the latitude scale.

1. What is the Lat-Lon of points A, B, C, and D?

2. Plot the following points on the sheet:

   (a) 45° 25' N, 122° 38' W,

   (b) 45° 09' N, 123° 16' W,

   (c) 44° 53' N, 122° 38' W.

Check that your answers are correct by noting that the results should form a triangle with each side 31' long.

3. What is the latitude difference between:

   (a) points A and B,

   (b) points B and C.

4. What is the longitude difference between:

   (a) points A and B,

   (b) points D and C.

5. What is the distance in nautical miles between:

   (a) points A and B,

   (b) points C and D.

6. Now, for practice reading azimuths or bearings from universal plotting sheets. What is the True bearing:

   (a) To point B from point A,

   (b) To point A from point B,

   (c) To point D from point A,

   (d) To point B from point C.

4.4 Plotting Lines of Position

Finding your position from sextant sights involves three steps: taking the timed sextant sights, the sight reduction of each of the sights, and the plotting of the lines of position (LOPs), one for each sight. In this section, we cover the last step of the process, the plotting. We treat it here purely as an exercise in plotting. For now we are just interested in learning the procedure; we will learn the principles behind this procedure very soon.

When doing the LAN sights in Chapter 3, we had an optional work form as a guide to the steps. When doing the full sight reductions for other types of celestial sights, which we start in Chapter 5, work forms are more valuable and we will focus the explanation around their use.

The end result of a sight reduction is Box 6 on the work form, and that is what we concentrate on in this chapter. See Figure 4.4-1. Box 6 contains four numbers. Two of them, the assumed latitude (a-Lat) and assumed longitude (a-Lon), define a position on the chart called the assumed position (AP). The third number (the azimuth, Zn) is a true bearing, and the fourth number (the altitude intercept, called "a-value") is a distance given in nautical miles.

Each sextant sight gives us one line on our chart (the plotting sheet). That sight and its sight reduction tell us we are located somewhere on that line. The line is called a Line of Position because we know we are on the line somewhere, but we don't know anything more about our position from that one sight. To find our actual position we need a second LOP from another sight. Our position is then the intersection of the two lines, since that is the only place that is on both of the lines at the same time.

Our task now is to see how the four numbers in Box 6 are used to plot this line on the chart. To do the plotting exercises you will need:

- Pencil (number 2 lead is recommended),
- Eraser (pencil type is recommended),
- Universal plotting sheets,
- Dividers (speed bow type is recommended),
- Nav protractor (5" or larger is recommended),
- Parallel rulers (15" clear is recommended),

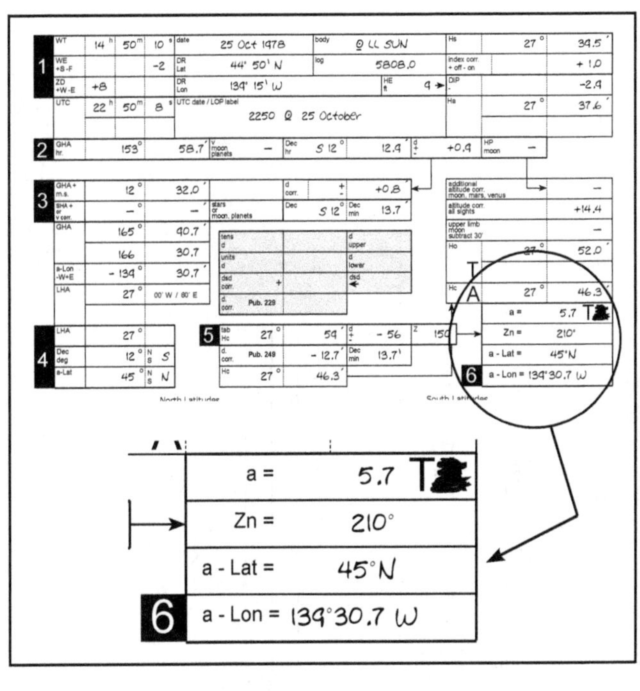

Figure 4.4-1. *Box 6 of the Starpath work form, which we learn to use in Chapter 5, includes all data needed to plot a celestial line of position. The a-value is a number of miles; the Zn is a true direction, and a-Lat and a-Lon define the position from which we start the plot.*

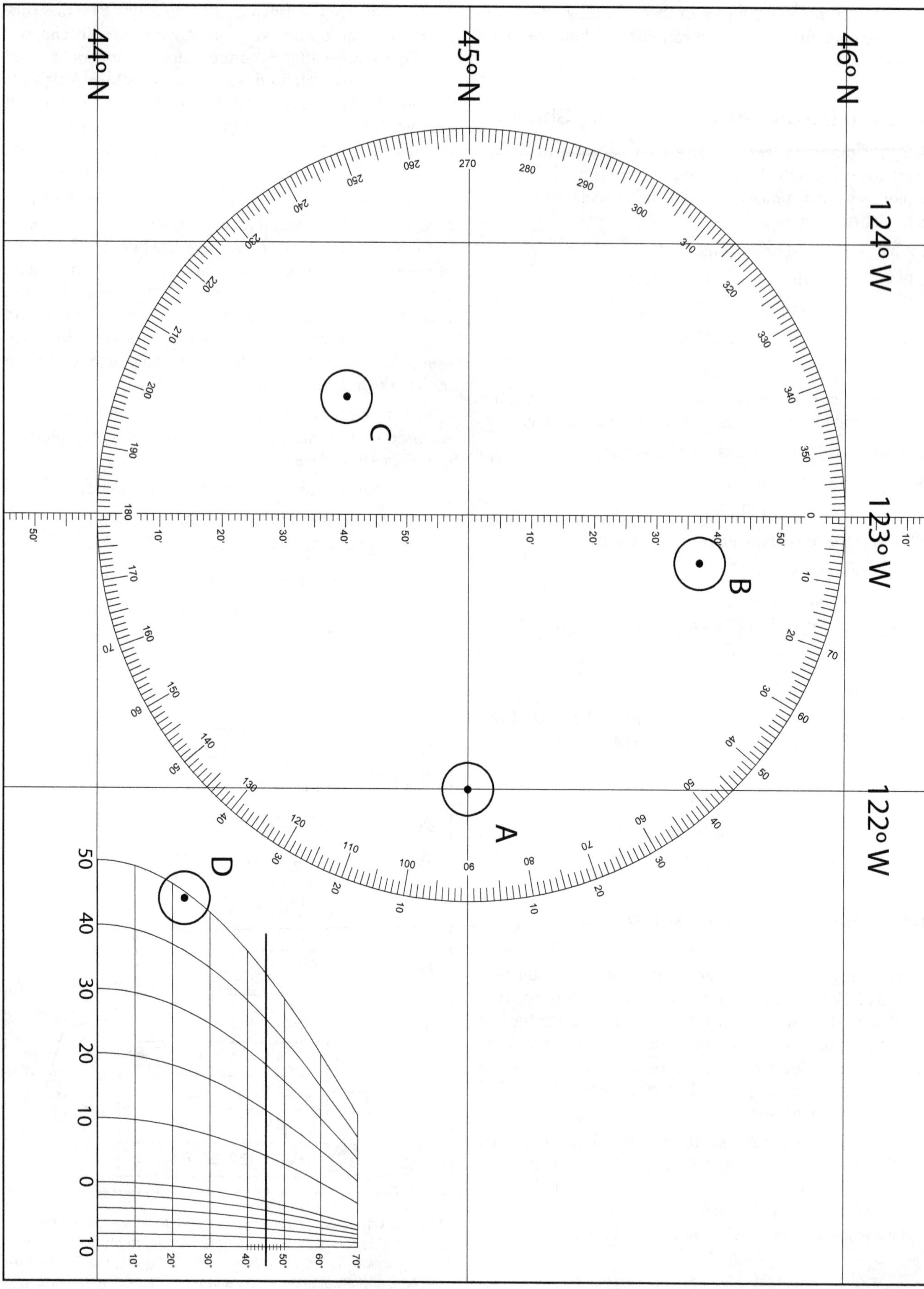

Figure 4.3-1 *Plotting sheet for Exercise on universal plotting sheets, Section 4.3. This can be worked right on the page.*

Procedure for Plotting LOPs

If you haven't done so already, review the earlier parts of the notes that describe universal plotting sheets and how to plot points and measure distances and bearings using these sheets.

Follow Figures 4.4-3 and 4.4-4 in the following pages.

(1) Set up a universal plotting sheet with mid-latitude equal to a-Lat, and mid-longitude equal to a-Lon rounded off to the nearest whole degree.

(2) Mark a point on the plotting sheet at the *assumed position* (a-Lat, a-Lon). The latitude we use here will always be in even degrees without minutes, so the assumed position will always lie on one of the main latitude lines of the plotting sheets. The longitude position is found from the diagram on the bottom right-hand side of the plotting sheet.

(3) Draw a line through the assumed position oriented in the direction of Zn. We call this line the *azimuth line.*

You can do this by placing a protractor directly on the assumed position, using the grid on it to assure it is aligned on the latitude line, and marking off the direction using the scale on the rim of the protractor (Figure 4.4-2). Alternatively, you can use parallel rulers to get the proper orientation from the compass rose printed on the plotting sheets, and then move this line over to the assumed position. When you are bouncing around at sea, it is easier and more accurate to use the protractor at the assumed position than it is to align and move the parallel rulers.

(4) Using the latitude scale on the plotting sheets for the nautical miles scale (1' of latitude = 1 nmi), set your dividers to a distance of "a" nmi. ("a" is given in Box 6.)

(5) Now look at the label of this a-value. It will be either T for Toward or A for Away. This means Toward or Away from the direction of Zn. We are now going to mark a point on the azimuth line a distance of "a" nautical miles from the assumed position.

The azimuth line runs in two directions from the assumed position, toward the direction Zn or away from the direction of Zn. If the label is T, mark the point on the azimuth line on the side of the line that heads toward Zn. If the label is A, mark the point on the azimuth line on the opposite side of the assumed position. Note that Away from Zn is the same as Toward (Zn + 180°).

(6) At the point just marked, draw a line perpendicular to the azimuth line. This perpendicular line is the LOP.

One way to construct this perpendicular line is to use the cross-hatch lines on square navigation protractor. Align one edge of the ruler with the point on the azimuth line, then shift the ruler until one of the thin cross lines overlaps the azimuth line precisely. This guarantees that the edge of the ruler is perpendicular to the azimuth line. You can also do this with the center line on the top edge of a square protractor, which is perpendicular to the bottom edge.

The square protractor is very handy for plotting celestial LOPs. It gives you the bearing (Zn), the straight edge for the azimuth line, and the perpendicular for the LOP. It also has the virtue of being essentially indestructible, which is a big asset at sea.

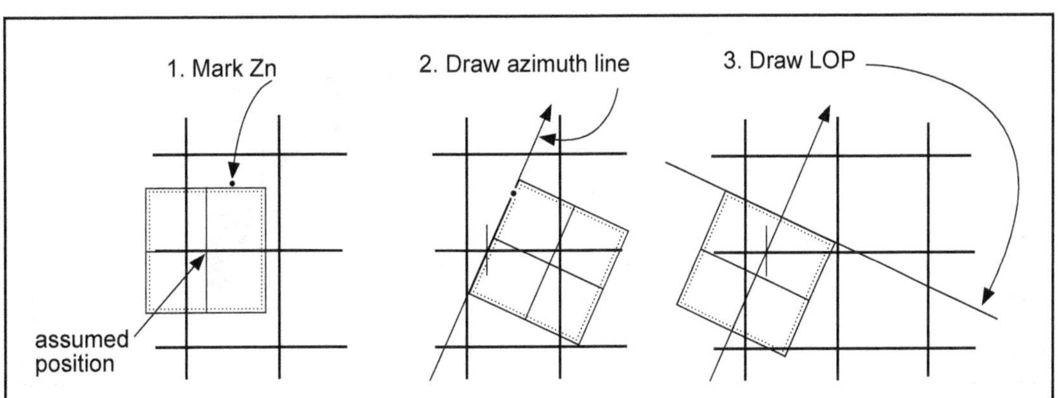

Figure 4.4-2 *Using a square protractor to draw LOPs. Any protractor that has a full 360° can be used for this application; the larger the better. Or you can plot using parallel rulers and the compass rose on the plotting sheets.*

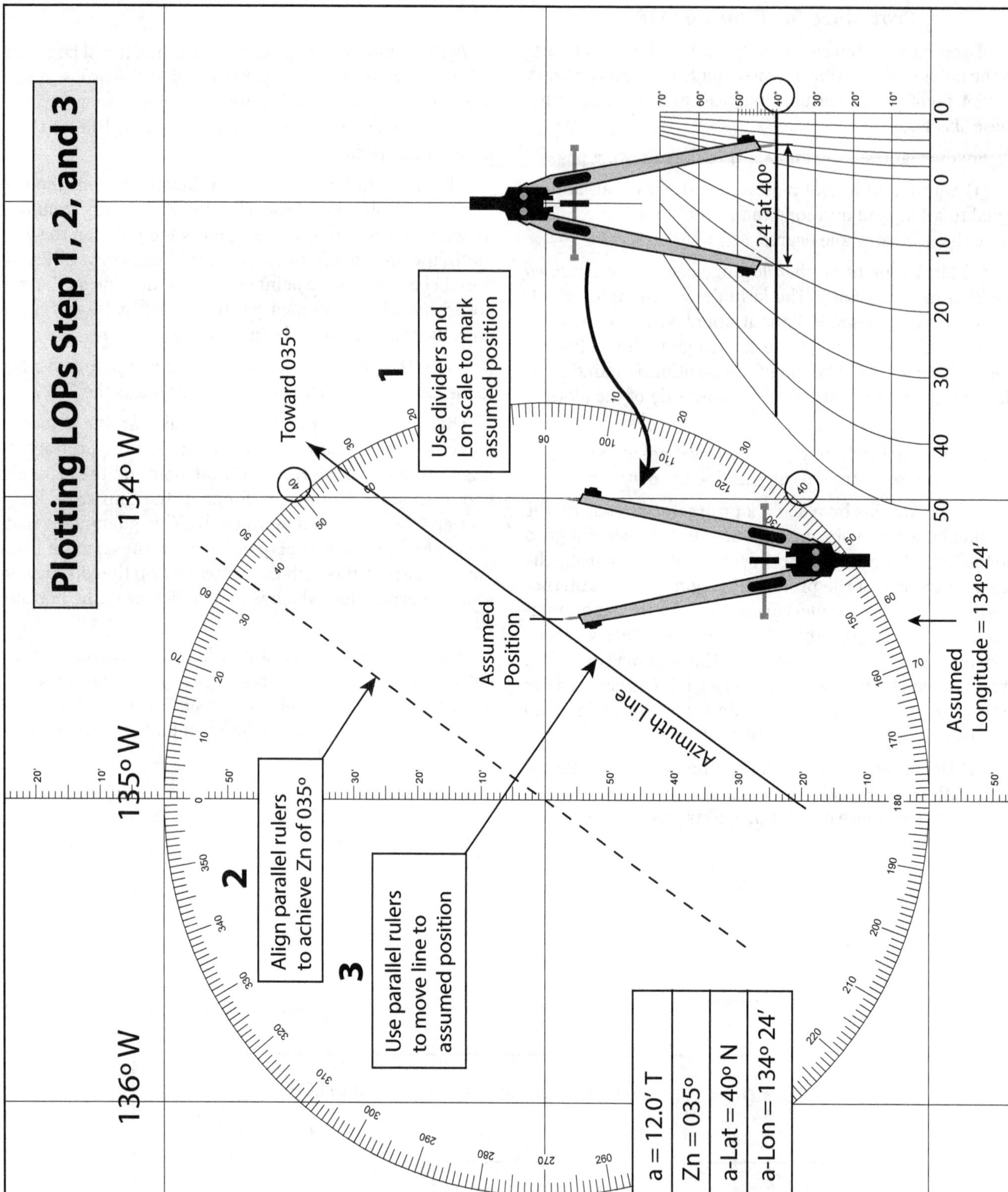

Figure 4.4-3 *The LOP plotting procedure, Part 1 (Section 4.4)*

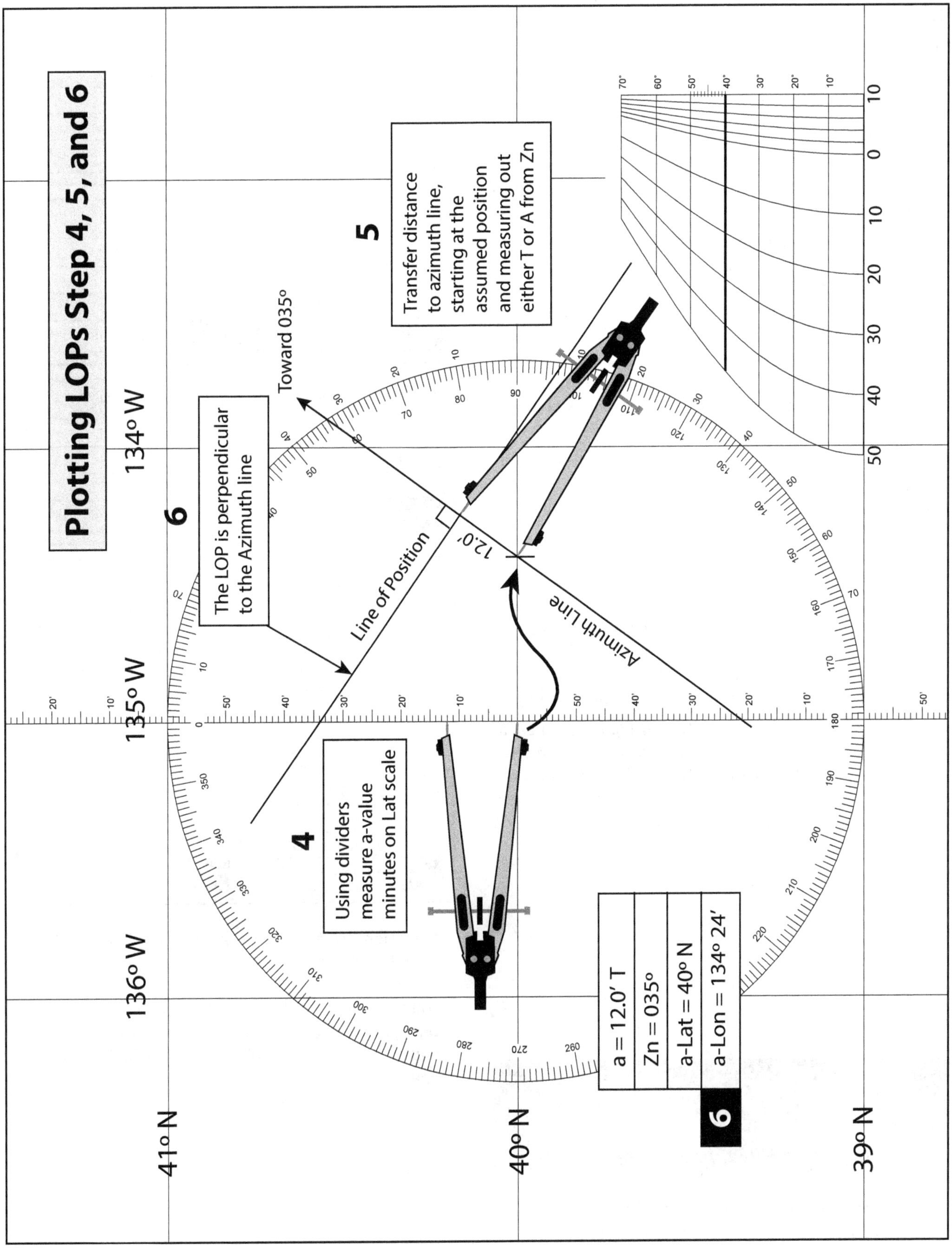

Figure 4.4-4 *The LOP plotting procedure, Part 2 (Section 4.4)*

4.5 Exercise on Plotting LOPs

This is an important exercise. It tests that you have learned how to do the plotting, and it shows you explicitly how careful you must be to get the most accuracy out of your celestial fix. If the plotting is not accurate, your fix will not be accurate. It is easy to lose 2 or 3 miles' accuracy in the plotting if you are not careful. This effectively throws away the accuracy of your sextant. A careless plotting turns a $2,000 sextant into a $49 sextant.

Here you are given five pairs of LOPs. The task is to plot each of the pairs and read the latitude and longitude of the fix you get from the intersection of the two lines. Then compare your result with the answers given. It is not difficult to get the right answers; just relax and follow the instructions. You don't have to be so precise that it makes you tense, but you can't be sloppy. When you can consistently get the answers to within 1' of the fix given, you have mastered this important stage of celestial navigation.

The answers are given accurate to the tenth of a minute to help you judge your results, but you can't read the plotting sheet that accurately using the printed scale of 60 miles per 3 inches.

Set up a universal plotting sheet for mid-latitude 35° N and mid-longitude 145° W. You can get all the problems on one sheet, but you will have lines crossing each other by the time you are done. Try both methods of drawing the azimuth line–with the protractor and with parallel rulers. Check your parallel ruler lines with the protractor to see if you are transferring the line accurately without slipping.

Part A, LOPs 1 and 2, are plotted in Figure 4.5-1 as an example. The others are not plotted out, but the intersection answers are in the Answers section. If you don't get the answer and are off just a little, then it is likely best to start all over again, rather than try to track down one or several very small discrepancies.

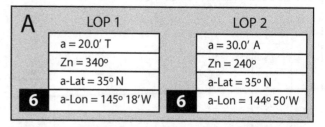

A	LOP 1		LOP 2
	a = 20.0′ T		a = 30.0′ A
	Zn = 340°		Zn = 240°
	a-Lat = 35° N		a-Lat = 35° N
6	a-Lon = 145° 18′W	6	a-Lon = 144° 50′W

B	LOP 3		LOP 4
	a = 37.0′ T		a = 21.0′ A
	Zn = 162°		Zn = 060°
	a-Lat = 35° N		a-Lat = 35° N
6	a-Lon = 146° 00′W	6	a-Lon = 146° 17′W

C	LOP 5		LOP 6
	a = 10.0′ T		a = 19.0′ T
	Zn = 020°		Zn = 290°
	a-Lat = 35° N		a-Lat = 35° N
6	a-Lon = 145° 00′W	6	a-Lon = 145° 20′W

D	LOP 7		LOP 8
	a = 25.0′ T		a = 6.0′ A
	Zn = 140°		Zn = 065°
	a-Lat = 35° N		a-Lat = 35° N
6	a-Lon = 146° 12′W	6	a-Lon = 146° 25′W

E	LOP 9		LOP 10
	a = 29.0′ A		a = 34.0′ A
	Zn = 173°		Zn = 092°
	a-Lat = 35° N		a-Lat = 35° N
6	a-Lon = 146° 04′W	6	a-Lon = 146° 08′W

Question: What do the a, Zn, a-Lat, a-Lon stand for in the above exercises?

Answer: We do not know yet! Treat this as a pure graphic exercise, and just follow the plotting instructions. It will all make sense in the next chapter.

...In Depth

11.10 *Ocean Plotting Sheets*

The standard universal sheets discussed here meet most needs underway, but there are options, that are outlined here, including pdf versions that could be convenient for practice...

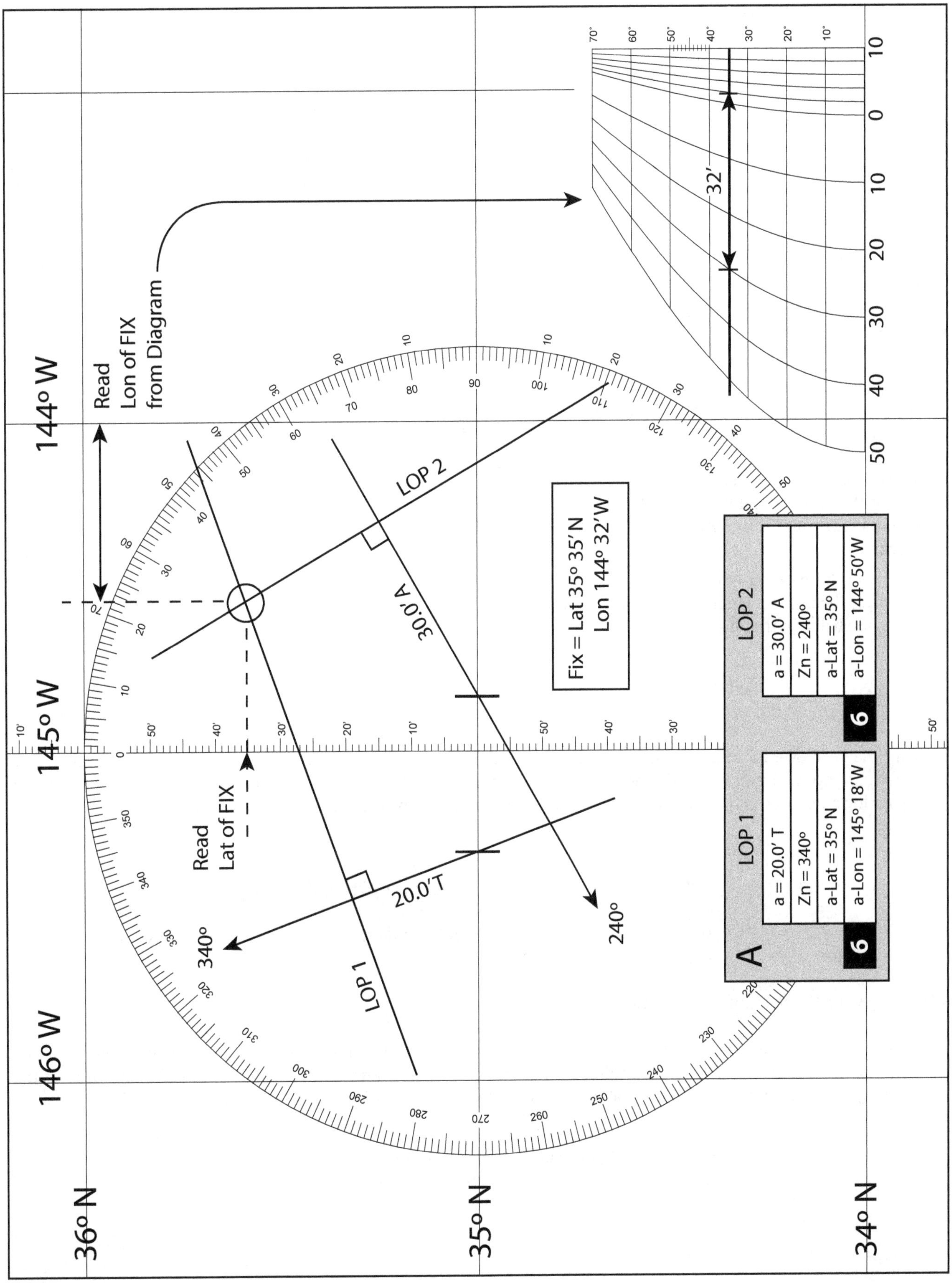

Figure 4.5-1 *Example plotting problem (A) in Exercise 4.6*

4.6 DR Plotting Exercise

If you are not caught up with the earlier parts of the course, then please go back to finish those parts before starting on this. *Accurate DR plotting is a crucial part of learning ocean navigation*, but you can add it in later as another break in the paperwork. We need to be sure that the LAN procedure of Chapter 3 is totally under control before moving on to Chapter 5.

When you can work on this DR plotting, the following exercises offer valuable practice plotting your DR track. You will need to do this type of plotting before doing the sight reduction of any celestial sight. To do these problems you should be familiar with the earlier section on Setting Up a Universal Plotting Sheet and the practice exercises using these sheets. For this practice, however, you do not need to be familiar with plotting LOPs.

In each case you start off from the position of your last fix, and then plot on a universal plotting sheet the course and course changes recorded in your logbook up to the log reading of your latest set of sights. Then read from the plotting sheet the latitude and longitude at the log reading of your new sights; this is the DR position that goes into the sight reduction.

All five of these exercises can be worked on one side of one plotting sheet as shown in Figure 4.6-1; final Lat-Lon positions are listed in the Answers section.

Set up the sheet for mid-latitude 25° N and mid-longitude 45° W, and draw in the meridian (longitude) lines for 43°, 44°, and 46° W. Remember to draw a line through the mid latitude 25° on the longitude scale at the bottom right hand side of the sheet.

These problems give the course as a true course to save you the step of converting from the magnetic course you actually steered. Even the logbook examples shown here record true course. But this is only for the purposes of this exercise. In practice, you will record compass courses in your logbook, and you must later make the conversion to true before plotting on the plotting sheets.

In each problem subtract successive log readings to find out how many miles you sailed on each heading. Then plot them out to find your DR position at the time of the sight. You may want to look ahead to the plotted answers (Figure 4.6-1) to see what is involved here if it is not clear. In each problem we start off from an even-degree latitude and longitude. This, of course, won't happen at sea. We do it here only to simplify the exercises.

(1) This one is an 89-mile run with no course changes. Last fix was at log reading = 202.0 and your position there was 24° 00' N, 45° 00' W. From this position you sailed off on course 075 T and did not alter course. When you took your sun lines your log read 291.0. What was your DR position at log reading 291.0? In your log book this leg might be recorded as:

Time	Log	Course (T)	Speed (kts)	Comments
	202.0	075	6.0	Fix at: 24° 00' N, 45° 00' W
	255.0	075	7.0	
	291.0	075	7.0	Sun line taken
	300.0	075	6.5	

What was your DR position at log 291.0?

(2) This one is a 96-mile run with one course change. Last fix was at log reading = 100.0 and your position there was 26° 00' N, 43° 00' W. From this position you sailed off on course 245 T and later changed course to 210 T, and while on this course did your sights. Find your position at log reading 196.0. In your log book this leg might be recorded as:

Time	Log	Course (T)	Speed (kts)	Comments
	100.0	245	5.5	Fix at: 26° 00' N, 43° 00' W
	130.0	210	6.0	
	145.0	210	7.0	
	196.0	210	7.0	Star sights taken

What was your DR position at log 196.0?

(3) This one is a 125-mile run with two course changes. Last fix was at log reading = 600.0 and your position there was 26° 00' N, 44° 00' W. From this position you sailed off on course 325 T and changed course twice before you did your sights. Find your position at log reading 725.0. In your log book this leg might be recorded as:

Time	Log	Course (T)	Speed (kts)	Comments
	600.0	325	6.0	Fix at: 26° 00' N, 44° 00' W
	638.0	227	7.0	
	693.0	315	7.0	
	725.0	315	7.0	Star sights taken

What was your DR position at log 725.0?

(4) This one is a 131-mile run with four course changes. Last fix was at log reading = 558.0 and your position there was 26° 00' N, 46° 00' W. From this position you sailed off on course 135 T but were gradually headed off to the south. You finally tacked at log = 662 to course 080, and while on this course you did your sights. What was your position at log reading 689.0? In your log book this leg might be recorded as:

Time	Log	Course (T)	Speed (kts)	Comments
	558.0	135	4.0	Fix at: 26° 00' N, 46° 00' W
	594.0	148	4.5	
	612.0	168	5.0	
	642.0	180	5.5	
	662.0	080	5.5	Tacked
	689.0	080	5.5	Star sights taken

What was your DR position at log 689.0?

(5) This one is a 111-mile run with three course changes. Last fix was at log reading = 666.0 and your position there was 24° 00' N, 46° 00' W. From this position you sailed off on course 115 T and, as in (4), were gradually headed to the south before you tacked. Find your position at log reading 777.0. In your log book this leg might be recorded as:

Time	Log	Course (T)	Speed (kts)	Comments
	666.0	115	7.5	Fix at: 24° 00' N, 46° 00' W
	690.0	115	6.0	
	704.0	130	5.5	
	718.0	140	5.0	
	741.0	055	6.0	Tacked
	777.0	055	7.0	Sun lines taken
	795.0	065	7.0	

What was your DR position at log 777.0?

4.7 More DR Plotting Practice

This exercise can be postponed till later, but if you would like more practice now on the important skill of DR plotting and wish to see a sample in actual use during an ocean passage, there is a segment of a logbook and the plotted DR track in Section 11.11 on Ocean Dead Reckoning. You can treat that as an exercise and plot this out on your own to see if you get the same positions recorded in the logbook. There is also a record of the DR errors at each fix.

> ***...In Depth***
>
> **11.11 *Ocean Dead Reckoning***
>
> In one sense, the most important goal of cel nav is to check our DR, because that might be all we have to go by. This note covers the procedures of good DR and how to use cel nav to monitor our progress with it.

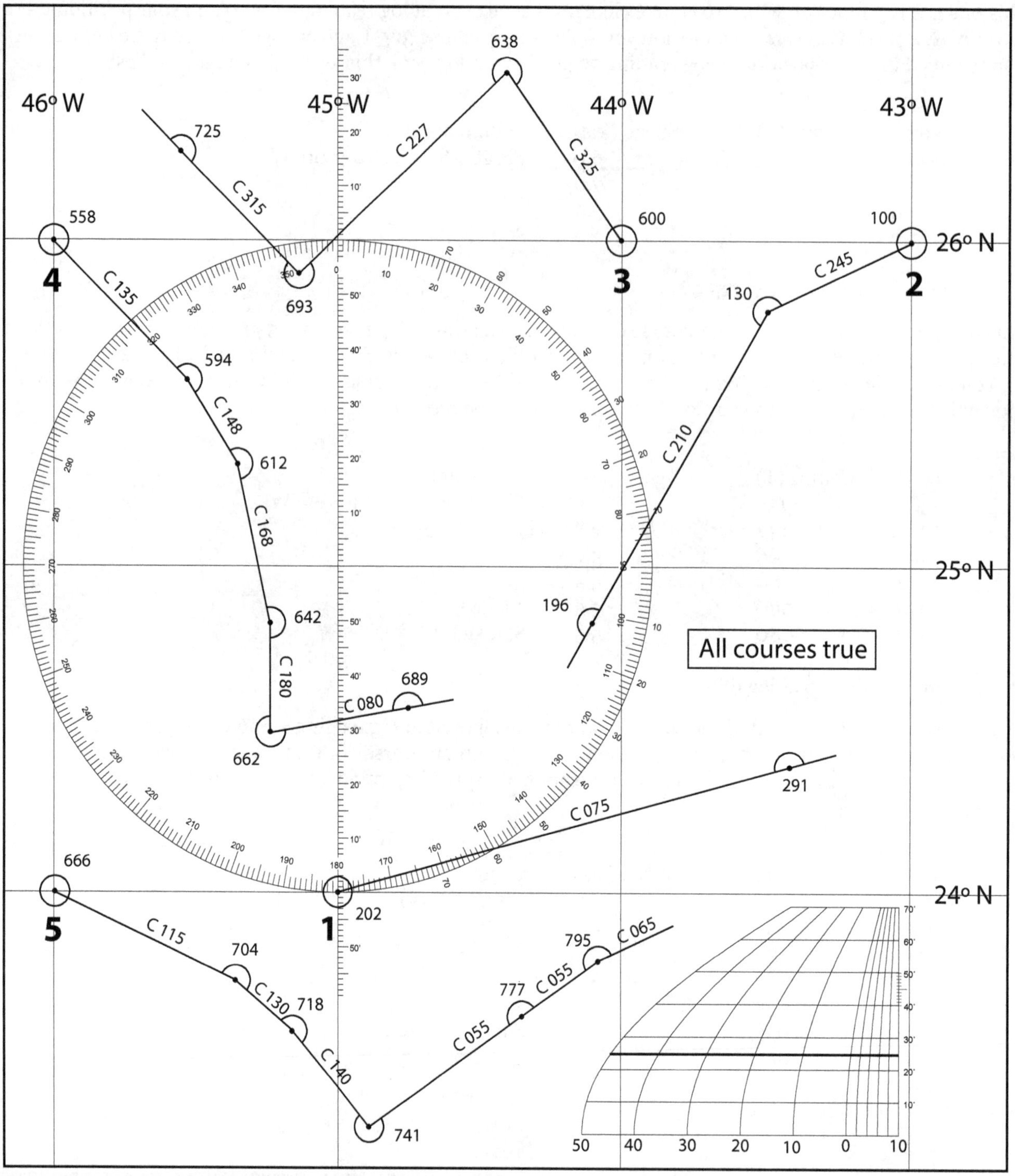

Figure 4.6-1 *Plots of DR plotting practice of Section 4.6. Numerical Lat and Lon of final positions are in the Answers.*

4.8 New Terminology

universal plotting sheet (UPS)

azimuth (Zn)

azimuth line

DR plotting, DR track

log

logbook

Chapter 5

Sun Sights

5.1 Introduction

We start with a discussion of sunrise and twilight, then move on to the main task of doing the full sight reduction of the sun for sun sights taken any time during the day—not just at noon as we did in Chapter 3. In the classroom course we say "roll up your sleeves and get an extra handful of M&Ms," after tonight's class it is all downhill. That is, once we learn the full process for sun sights at any time of day, the other bodies can all be added with just a note or two on the distinctions. You will also see that much of what we do with these we have learned in the LAN procedure.

We use the Starpath work forms, which will guide you through the process in a step-by-step manner. The forms themselves will then serve as instructions reminding you of the next step in the process.

Again, this is the main content of the course. After the sun lines are mastered, we can explain all the other bodies in half a page or so each. For the most part, the other bodies use the identical procedure; we just select the needed data from different columns in the tables.

5.2 Sunrise, Sunset, and Twilight Times

For both inland and ocean navigation we often like to know the time of sunset or sunrise—or, more generally, when it is going to get dark or light. On coastwise on inland routes, navigation at night is different than during the day—it is not necessarily harder, in some circumstances it is even easier, but it is different, and generally we like to know where we will be when it gets dark. In the ocean, on the other hand, we need these times accurately each day to prepare for celestial sights, because we can only take star sights during twilight, when we can see both stars and horizon.

Several factors enter into these time predictions. Rarely can we get, even on inland or coastal waters, what we want by simply looking these times up in the current issue of a newspaper the day before a sail. Obviously in the ocean we can't do that, nor can we get them from a radio broadcast. We may get the time of sunrise or sunset that way, but we would still have to make some guess at the length of twilight. If we are a long way from the city that prepared the newspaper or broadcast, even the times of sunrise and sunset could be way off. Likewise, sunrise and sunset times on calendars and commercial tide tables are only applicable to their city of origin.

The times of sunset and twilight (and the length of twilight) depend on the date, our latitude, and our longitude. The seasonal changes are well known: in the summer the sun rises early, sets late, and the days are long; in the winter the sun rises late, sets early, and the days are short. In the Northern Hemisphere summer, if you head south you are headed toward the Southern winter, so you are headed toward shorter days, earlier sunsets, and so on. With this reasoning you can always figure what will happen to these times if you head north or south, in the summer or winter, in either hemisphere.

Accurate sunrise and set times change with longitude even within the same time zone, because everyone in a particular time zone keeps the same time on their watch, even though one may be as much as 900 miles to the east of the other. Since the sun comes from the east as its GP circles the earth, an observer to the east sees it first. If you live in Seattle and are on the phone to a friend in Spokane (about 5° of longitude to the east), and your friend tells you the sunrise is beautiful, you will have to take their word for it. You won't see the sunrise in Seattle for another 20 minutes or so. Sunset is officially defined as the moment the top edge (upper limb) of the sun drops below the visible horizon. The assumption here is that we are at sea or some such place where we can indeed see the true horizon. Nevertheless, the times we figure always apply to that definition, even if we can't see the horizon. If there are mountains between us and the true horizon, the sun will set over the mountain horizon earlier than the sunset time we figured.

This might make us realize that the time of sunrise also depends on the height of eye (HE). At higher heights, you see a horizon that is farther off, and thus see the sunrise earlier than someone viewing from a lower perspective. But for practical work on using this data for navigation from the deck of a vessel this correction is rarely used.

...In Depth

11.12 Practice with Time Prediction

The procedure for predicting sunrise, sunset, and twilight times is the same as given in Section 3.2 for LAN. We include a few practice exercises here...

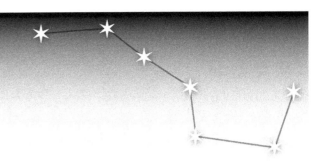

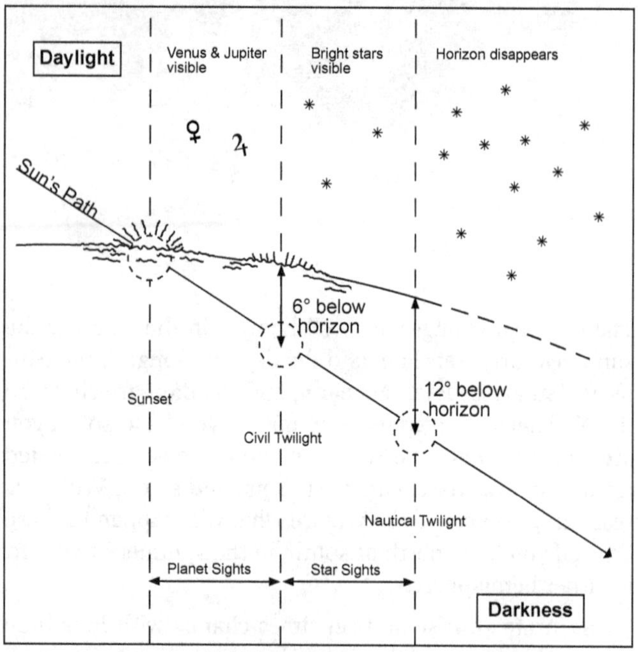

Figure 5.2-1 *Twilight times defined.*

The times of sunrise and sunset (as well as moonrise and moonset) are listed in the *Nautical Almanac*. The times are listed by date and latitude. The times are given in *local mean times*, which as noted in the LAN time discussion of Chapter 3, we can interpret as the UTC of the event, observed from Greenwich (Lon = 0). To figure the UTC of sunset for your longitude you must add to the tabulated times your West longitude converted to time with the Arc to Time table. In east longitudes, you subtract your longitude from the tabulated times. Once you have the UTC of the event, you can convert it back to watch time using the zone description of the watch. For more discussion of timekeeping, see Section 11.5 and for practice making numerical predictions, see Section 11.12.

In common usage twilight is the time period between sunset and darkness (or darkness and sunrise). For the purposes of navigation, twilight is defined more precisely. There are two twilight times, *civil twilight* and *nautical twilight*. These names refer to precise times, not time periods. Civil twilight is the time the sun is about 6° below the horizon. For reference, the sun is 6° above the horizon when it is about 12 sun widths above the horizon, which will be about 3 finger widths as you hold your arm out stretched in front of you.

At civil twilight under normal atmospheric conditions it is typically dark enough to see the brightest stars. This is the motivation for defining it as it is. This is the time celestial navigators can start their star sights.

Nautical twilight is meant to be the dividing time between darkness and light. It is defined as the time the sun is about 12° below the horizon. At nautical twilight, under normal atmospheric conditions, it is typically too dark to see the horizon. Again the definition comes from celestial navigation—if you can't see the horizon you can't do star sights with a conventional sextant.

These times are illustrated in Figure 5.2-1 for the evening case. In the evening the time sequence is: sunset, civil twilight, then nautical twilight. In the morning, however, the sequence is reversed. From darkness you first see the horizon at nautical twilight, the stars fade at civil twilight, then the sun comes up at sunrise—the moment of sunrise is when the upper limb first appears on the horizon.

Celestial star sights are typically done between civil and nautical twilight—evening sights begin at civil and end at nautical twilight; morning sights begin at nautical and end at civil twilight. The bright planets Venus and Jupiter, however, can typically be seen with the naked eye—or at least through the small telescope of a sextant—during the brightest part of twilight when the sun is just below the horizon. The horizon is sharpest then, so these planet sights are best reserved for this period. The accuracy of sextant sights is often determined by the sharpness of the horizon.

For celestial sights, we must predict the times of twilight as accurately as possible, but for inland navigation we only need an estimate of the length of twilight—to let us know, for example, when we won't be able to see land.

Time Interval, Sunset to Civil Twilight (= Civil Twilight to Sunrise)

	0° N	*20° N*	*40° N*	*50° N*	
Jun 21	22 min	25 min	33 min	45 min	Jun 21
Sept 23	20 min	22 min	27 min	32 min	Mar 21
Dec 21	23 min	24 min	31 min	38 min	Dec 21

Time Interval, Civil to Nautical Twilight (= Nautical to Civil Twilight)

	0° N	*20° N*	*40° N*	*50° N*	
Jun 21	26 min	29 min	42 min	66 min	Jun 21
Sept 23	24 min	26 min	32 min	39 min	Mar 21
Dec 21	26 min	28 min	34 min	42 min	Dec 21

Figure 5.2-2 *Twilight related time intervals for various latitudes and dates*

The times and length of twilight are given in the *Nautical Almanac*, but not in the Tide Tables, where you can find sunrise and sunset times. Figure 5.2-2 shows how twilight times and lengths vary with latitude and date—the times are relative to sunrise or sunset. This much information should be adequate for applications inland. For example, in mid-June at 48° North, you will first see stars—if we might use this as a measure of darkness—about 45 minutes after sunset, and in another 66 minutes or so from then, it will be too dark to see unlit land. In short, you have some 111 minutes, or about 2 hours of usable twilight after sunset for visual navigation. Near either equinox (mid-September or mid-March), on the other hand, you would only have about an hour of light without the sun at this latitude.

Note that in the tropics, latitudes less than 23.45°, these times do not change much throughout the year. And at any latitude, the length of twilight is shortest at the equinoxes, even though the days are shortest on the winter solstice. And a final note on the rules of the nautical road, versus the rules of the roads we drive on: by law, your boat lights must go on at sunset; but your car lights must go on at civil twilight. In both cases, however, it is not illegal to run your lights over longer periods, or even always.

5.3 Sun Lines Using Starpath Work Forms

The work form is divided into six boxes, numbered in bold blocks on the left of each box. The task of the sight reduction is to start with the information in Box 1 and end up with the information in Box 6. This process requires a *Nautical Almanac* (abbreviated here as NA) and a set of Sight Reduction Tables. There are several types of Sight Reduction Tables available; Pub. 229 and Pub. 249 are the two most popular. The Starpath work forms can be used with either of these tables.

These instructions are fairly long since these are used as an introduction to the sight reduction process. After some practice, however, you should find that the work forms alone are enough to guide you through the process.

Once you have learned to do sun lines, the sight reduction for stars, planets, and the moon will be very easy. With these detailed instructions for the sun, the notes on how to do the other bodies can be brief. In short, these are essentially instructions for doing any type of sight reduction. Instructions for filling out the work form and explanations of what goes in each of the individual spaces are mixed together. When an individual space is explained for the first time, the name of the space is shown in bold face.

Step 1. Box 1–Sight Data

Fill in Box 1, which contains the basic starting information of the sight. Figure 5.3-1. These are numbers we measure or know from other work. They are not looked up in any tables. The individual spaces in Box 1 are for the following:

WT - is the Watch Time of the sight—the time you read directly from your watch when the sight was taken, without any corrections applied.

date - is the date of the sight according to the watch used for WT.

body - is the celestial body that was sighted. In this example it is the sun. Remember to indicate upper or lower limb for sun and moon sights. You can use symbols here. The standard symbol for a lower limb sun sight is an underlined circle with a dot in the center.

Hs - is the angular sextant height of the sun exactly as you read it from the sextant. Using a good metal sextant, this number should be read and recorded accurate to the tenth of a minute. With plastic sextants, the precision will not be as dependable or even achievable, but we do the best we can.

WE - is the Watch Error. Determine the Watch Error from WWV radio broadcasts, GPS, or your chronometer logbook. WE will increase daily throughout your voyage, but the rate of increase will rarely be more than about 10 to 15 seconds a month for quartz watches. If, for example, the watch is 10 seconds slow on the day of your sight, the WE is 10s and you must add this error; if the watch is fast you subtract WE.

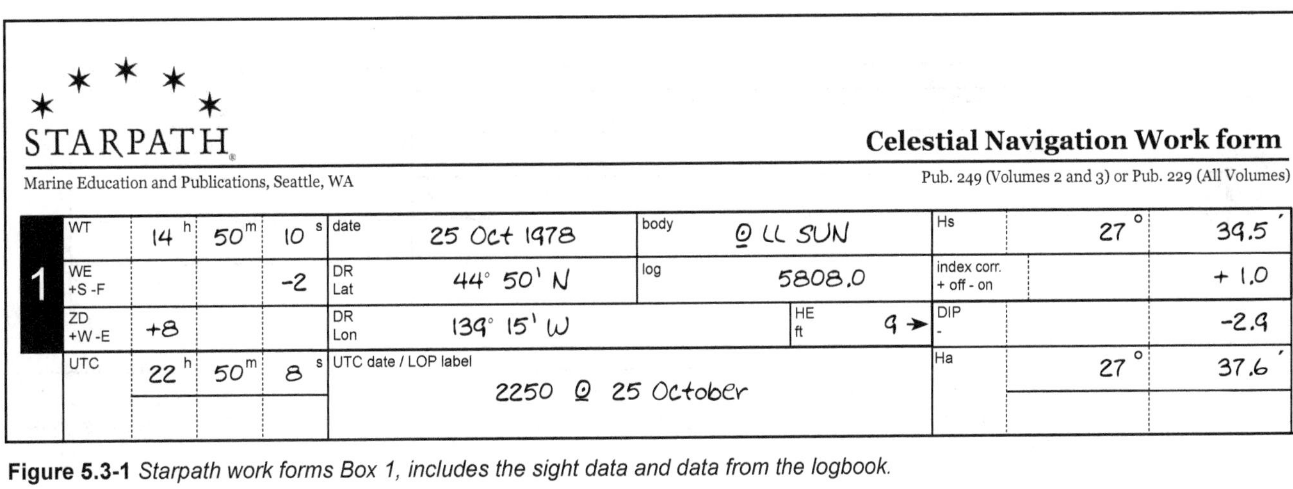

Figure 5.3-1 *Starpath work forms Box 1, includes the sight data and data from the logbook.*

DR-Lat - is your dead reckoning latitude. This should be your best estimate of your latitude at the time of the sight. Figure it from the DR plot of your course changes since your last fix.

Log - is your log (odometer) reading at the time of the sight. We need this if we are to advance this sun line to a later sun line or LAN latitude line for a running fix. Record your log reading before and after your sight session, and from these you can figure the approximate log reading for each of the individual sights taken during that session.

IC - is the Index Correction of your sextant, which you must measure at each sight. The correction is (+) when the index mark is off the scale when the horizon is aligned; it is (-) when the index correction is on the scale. The form reminds you of this; or use the jingle "When it's on, take it off."

ZD - is the Zone Description (time zone) of the watch. This is the number of hours you must add to the Watch Time to get UTC. Remember it is the ZD of the watch we need here, not the ZD of the time zone we happen to be in at the time of the sight. We could be in time zone +9 with our watch set to time zone +7. You find the ZD of the watch from WWV broadcasts. If your watch reads 13:40:05 when WWV says the time is 20:40:00, then your ZD is +7 and your WE is 5s fast.

DR-Lon - is your dead reckoning longitude—the longitude of your DR position at the time of the sight.

HE - is the Height of your Eye in feet at the time of the sight. In practice this will be the same for all sights.

Add WT, WE, and ZD to get UTC. Use the extra space provided to adjust minutes and seconds to less than 60 if necessary. If the result is greater than 24h, subtract 24h and increase the date by 1 day. If the result is negative—which is only possible when your watch is set on an east-longitude (negative) time zone—then add 24h and decrease the date by 1 day.

Record the proper UTC and date in the large space provided.

UTC date / LOP label - is a large space provided for recording the UTC and the label you wish to use for this sight. With this label prominent it is easy to find a particular sight if we must leaf through a series of them at a later time.

Step 2. Box 2–Almanac Daily Pages

Fill in Box 2 using the *Nautical Almanac* (NA). See Figures 5.3-2 and 5.3-3. First look at Box 2 and draw a line through the spaces labeled "v" and "HP-moon." We do not use these for sun lines. As shown on the form, v is only used for moon and planets and HP is only used for moon sights. Now turn to the daily pages of the NA for the appropriate UTC date. (The pages you need for the practice problems are included in the Tables Selections.)

Under the column headed SUN, go down the list of UTCs to the hour of the sight. (Recall the NA uses the abbreviation UT for UTC, Section 11.5.) You will find two numbers listed to the right of this hour; one is the GHA of the sun and beside it is the declination of the sun. Check the top of the column to see which is which. Record these in the spaces provided in Box 2.

GHA-hr - is the Greenwich Hour Angle of the sun at the exact hour of the UTC of the sight. If, for example, the UTC of the sight is 13h 48m 13s, record in this space the GHA of the sun at 13h.

v/moon/planets - is not used for sun lines, only moon and planet lines.

Dec-hr - is the declination of the sun at the exact UTC hour of your sight. It is listed beside the GHA in the NA. Remember to record the label (name) of the declination, i.e., North or South—it is usually recorded preceding the number as N 20° 15.2' to distinguish it from a latitude that has the label at the end.

Now look to the bottom of the sun column in the NA to find the "d-value," and record it in the space provided in Box 2. Label the d-value (+) if the declination is increasing with time or (-) if the declination is decreasing. This procedure is the exactly the same as we did finding the declination of the sun for LAN sights.

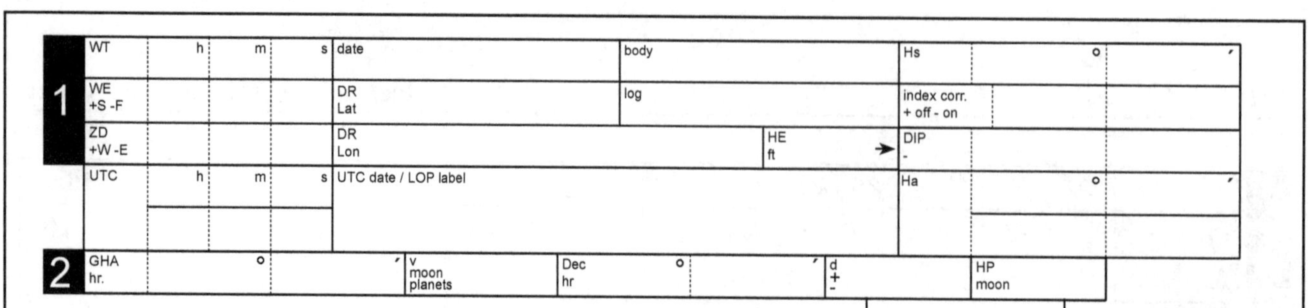

1
WT
h
m
s
date
body
Hs
WE +S -F
DR Lat
log
index corr. + off - on
ZD +W -E
DR Lon
HE ft
DIP
UTC
UTC date / LOP label
Ha
2
GHA hr.
v moon planets
Dec hr
d + -
HP moon

Figure 5.3-2 *Starpath work forms Box 2, in which we will enter data from the daily pages of the* Nautical Almanac. *We use the UTC we figured below Box 1. Box 2, together with the results of Box 3, tell us where the body was over the earth at the time of the sight—its geographical position (GP).*

d - is the declination d-value. It is the hourly change in the declination, listed at the bottom of the sun column on the NA daily pages. Remember to record the sign of d, + or -.

HP-moon - is not used for sun lines, only moon lines.

You are now done with the daily pages of the *Nautical Almanac.*

Step 3. Box 3– Increments and Corrections

Next fill in Box 3 (Figure 5.3-4), but first draw a line through the space in Box 3 labeled "SHA or v-corr"; we do not use this space for sun lines.

SHA or v-corr - are not used for sun lines. SHA is used for star sights; v-corr is used for moon and planet sights.

Turn to the Increments and Corrections pages at the back of the NA (or our Table Selections). There is one table for each minute of the hour. Pick the one corresponding to the minutes part of the UTC of the sight, i.e., if the UTC is 13h 48m 13s, turn to the table labeled 48 min.

There are two tables on each page of the NA (48 min and 49 min, for example). Each table is divided into two parts (left part and right part) separated by a vertical double line. The GHA correction is taken from the left part of the table; the declination correction is from the table on the right side. Please note this distinction clearly; it can be a source of error when first learning these tables.

GHA-m,s - is the increase in the GHA for the minutes and seconds part of the UTC. To find this correction, go to the left-hand part of the table to the column headed SUN, then go down the column until you are opposite the seconds part of your UTC. The seconds are listed on the far left. Record this value in the space provided. This correction is always positive.

d-corr - is the change in the declination during the minutes and seconds part of the UTC. For the sun this correction is always small (1' or less). The size of the d-correction depends on the d-value that is recorded in Box 2. Find the d-correction just as you did for LAN sights on the right-hand side of the table. Go down the column headed "v or d" till you reach the value of d; the correction is listed beside it. Note that there are three "v or d" columns for different values of v or d. For the sun you will always use the first one because the maximum value of d for the sun is 1.0'. (The columns are headed "v or d" because for moon and planet sights we will use this same table for a v-correction.)

Recall that the d-corr does not depend on seconds, only on the d-value. Do not be confused by the seconds column

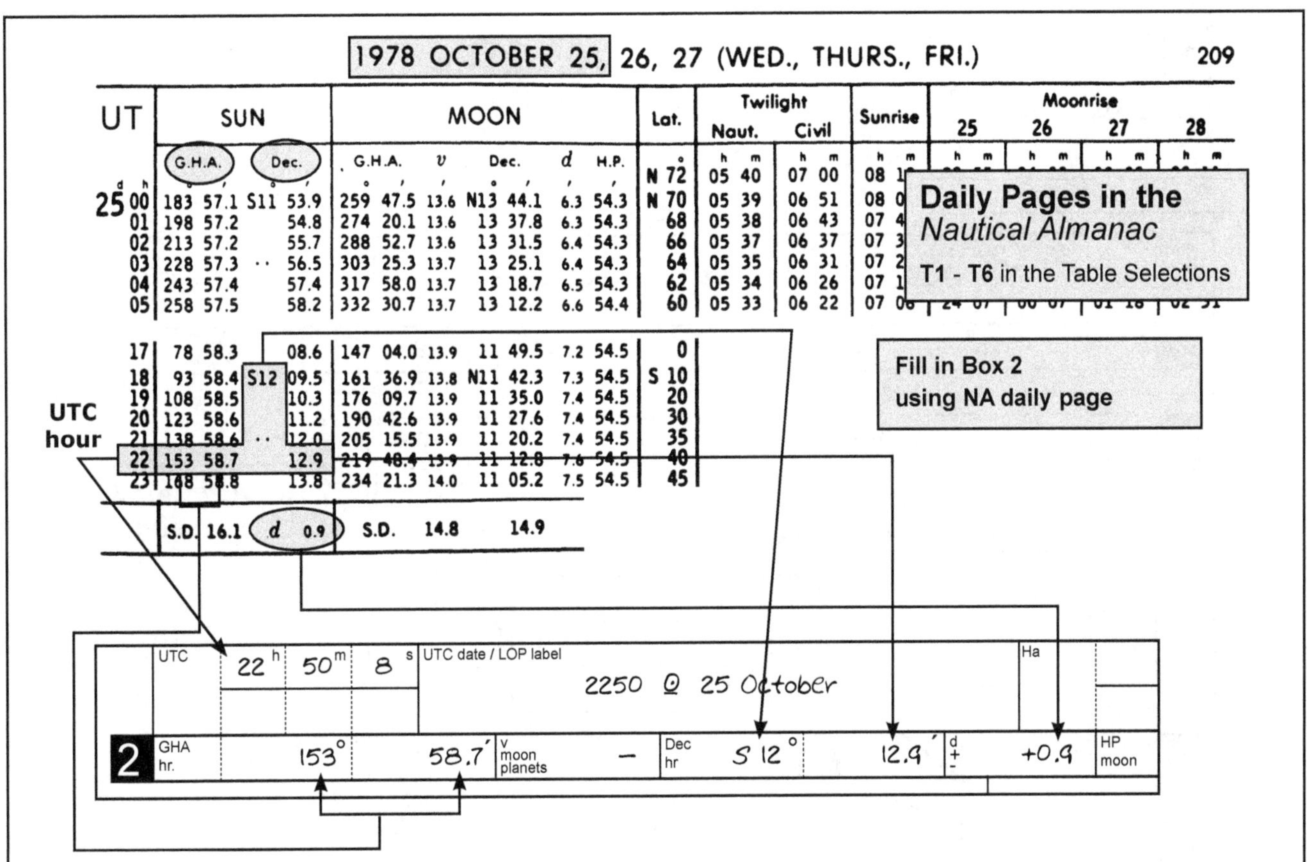

Figure 5.3-3 *Fill in Box 2 from daily* Nautical Almanac *pages. The data enters the form in the same order as presented in the NA.*

along the far left side of the table. These seconds are only used for the GHA corr.

Record the d-correction in the space provided and give it the same sign (±) as the d-value in Box 2. In other words, if d is (+) the d-correction is added; if d is (-) the correction is subtracted. This step is the same as was done in LAN sights.

Add d-corr to Dec-hr just above it to get the declination, and record it in the space provided. And then, for future convenience, record the degrees part of the corrected declination in the space labeled Dec-deg in the center of Box 4—together with a big N or S for north or south declination. Likewise, record the minutes part of the declination in the space labeled "Dec-min" near the center of Box 5.

Add GHA-m,s to GHA-hr to get GHA and record it in the space provided. Adjust the minutes part of GHA to be less than 60, if necessary, using the extra space provided. (It does not matter for now if the degrees part of GHA is greater than 360; we will correct this later if necessary.)

GHA - is the Greenwich Hour Angle of the sun at the time of the sight. It comes from the sum of GHA-hr and GHA-m,s.

Dec - is the corrected declination of the sun at the time of the sight. It comes from Dec-hr corrected by d-corr.

You now know exactly where the GP of the sun was at the time of the sight. The GHA corresponds to the longitude of the GP; the declination is the latitude of the GP.

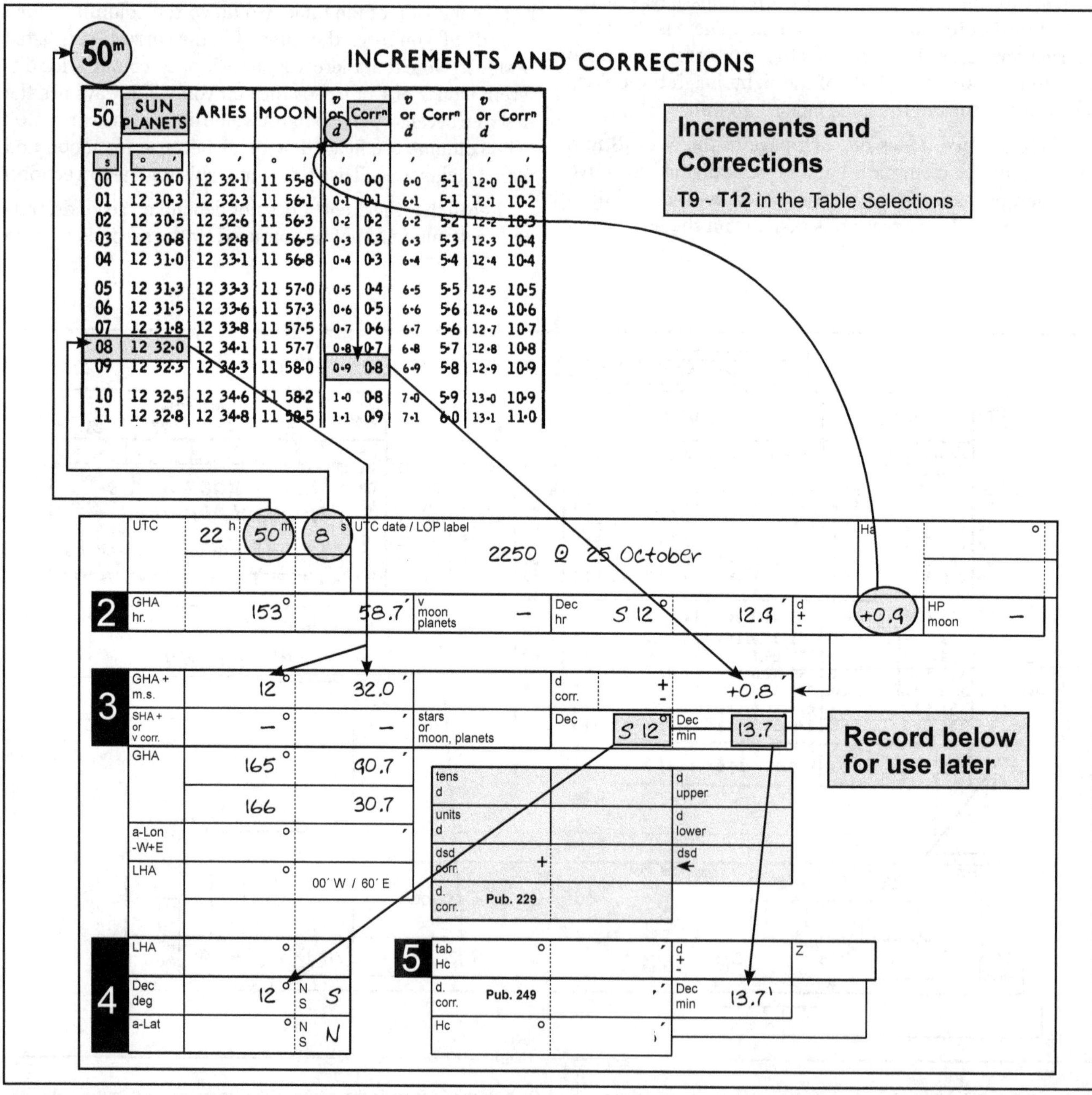

Figure 5.3-4 *Fill in Box 3 using Tables T-9 through T-12*

Referring to the example, at 22h 50m 08s on October 25th, 1978, the GP of the sun was at declination S 12° 13.7' and GHA 166° 30.7'. A person standing at latitude 12° 13.7' S and longitude 166° 30.7 W would have observed the sun precisely overhead at that moment.

Step 4. Box 4–Choosing the Assumed Position

In this step we choose the *assumed position* (a-Lat, a-Lon; abbreviated AP). This step does not require tables. It is part of a standard trick that simplifies the later use of the Sight Reduction Tables. See Figure 5.3-5.

The name "assumed position" might be misleading. We are not in any way assuming we are at that position. It is an artifact we use to facilitate the use of the tables. Later we will come back to discuss the background to this method of sight reduction.

a-Lat - is the assumed latitude. To find the assumed latitude, simply round off your DR latitude (recorded in Box 1) to the nearest whole degree. For example, if your DR-Lat is 35° 20' N, the a-Lat should be 35° N. If the DR-Lat is 35° 40' N, choose 36° N for the a-Lat. If the minutes part of DR-Lat happen to be exactly 30' it doesn't matter if you round up or down to get a-Lat. Record the assumed latitude in Box 4, with a big N or S—also record this same number in Box 6 for later use.

a-Lon - is the assumed longitude. The space for this is just below the GHA. Choosing the assumed longitude requires a little more thought than choosing the assumed latitude, but not much more. (The logic behind why we do this step the way we do will be clear shortly.)

We choose the minutes part of a-Lon first and then the degrees part. Look at your DR-Lon recorded in Box 1 and the GHA recorded just below Box 3. If your DR-Lon is West, choose the minutes part of a-Lon equal to the minutes part of the GHA of the sun.

The degrees part of the assumed longitude will be the same as those of the DR-Lon, or, at most, they will differ by 1°. The task here is to choose the degrees part of a-Lon so that a-Lon differs from your DR-Lon by at most 30'. For example, if the GHA of the sun is 200° 10' and your DR-Lon is 135° 15' W, the proper choice of a-Lon would be 135° 10' W; but if your DR-Lon were 135° 45' W, the proper choice would be 136° 10' W. The W. Lon rule is: Choose a-Lon within 30' of DR-Lon with the same minutes as the GHA.

If your DR-Lon is east, the rule is slightly different. For east longitudes still choose a-Lon within 30' of your DR-Lon, but choose the minutes part of a-Lon equal to 60' - (the minutes part of the GHA). For example, if the GHA is 200° 10' and your DR-Lon is 75° 45' E, choose a-Lon equal to 75° 50' E, but if your DR-Lon is 75° 15' E, the proper choice of a-Lon is 74° 50'. The E. Lon rule is: Choose a-Lon within 30' of DR-Lon with a-Lon minutes equal (60 - GHA minutes).

Record a-Lon in the space provided below GHA, and also record it in Box 6 for future use.

LHA - is the Local Hour Angle. To find the local hour angle (LHA), you will either add or subtract a-Lon and GHA. If a-Lon is West, subtract a-Lon from GHA to get the LHA. If a-Lon is East, add a-Lon to GHA to get LHA. The form reminds you of this difference with a "-W,+E."

Record the LHA in the space provided below a-Lon. If LHA is greater than 360° subtract 360° using the extra space provided. If LHA is negative, add 360°. The corrected value of LHA should be a whole number of degrees (the minutes should cancel if we chose a-Lon correctly), and it should be a positive number less than 360°. Record the corrected value of LHA in Box 4.

(The next tables we use have LHA only listed as whole degrees, so that is why we chose a-Lon the way we did.)

Box 4 now contains all the information you need to use the Sight Reduction Tables (Pub. 249, Pub. 229, or any other version).

In the next step we need to know if a-Lat and Dec have the same labels, both North or both South (called Same Name) or whether one is North and the other South (called Contrary Name). You can tell this at a glance from Box 4.

Step 5. Box 5–Sight Reduction Tables, Pub. 249

Only this step and the next depend on the type of Sight Reduction Tables used. We cover Pub. 249 here, but the difference between this one and Pub. 229 is not much. Use of Pub. 229 is covered in the work form instructions in the Appendix. You should get the same answer (within a few tenths of a minute) regardless of the tables you use. The box without a number in the center of the form is only used with Pub. 229. Later, we also cover sight reduction with the NAO tables in Chapter 11.

Pub. 249 (Sight Reduction Tables) comes in three volumes. Volume 1 is used for stars only; Volumes 2 and 3 are for the sun, moon, and planets—and some stars. Volume 2 is for assumed latitudes between 0° and 40° (North or South), and Volume 3 is for assumed latitudes between 39° and 89°.

Box 4 contains all the information needed to use the Sight Reduction Tables. Box 5 contains all the information we will get from the Sight Reduction Tables.

> **...In Depth**
>
> **11.13 Practice Choosing the AP**
>
> Because this step is sometimes elusive on the first pass through it, we include here more practice and another way of explaining the process...

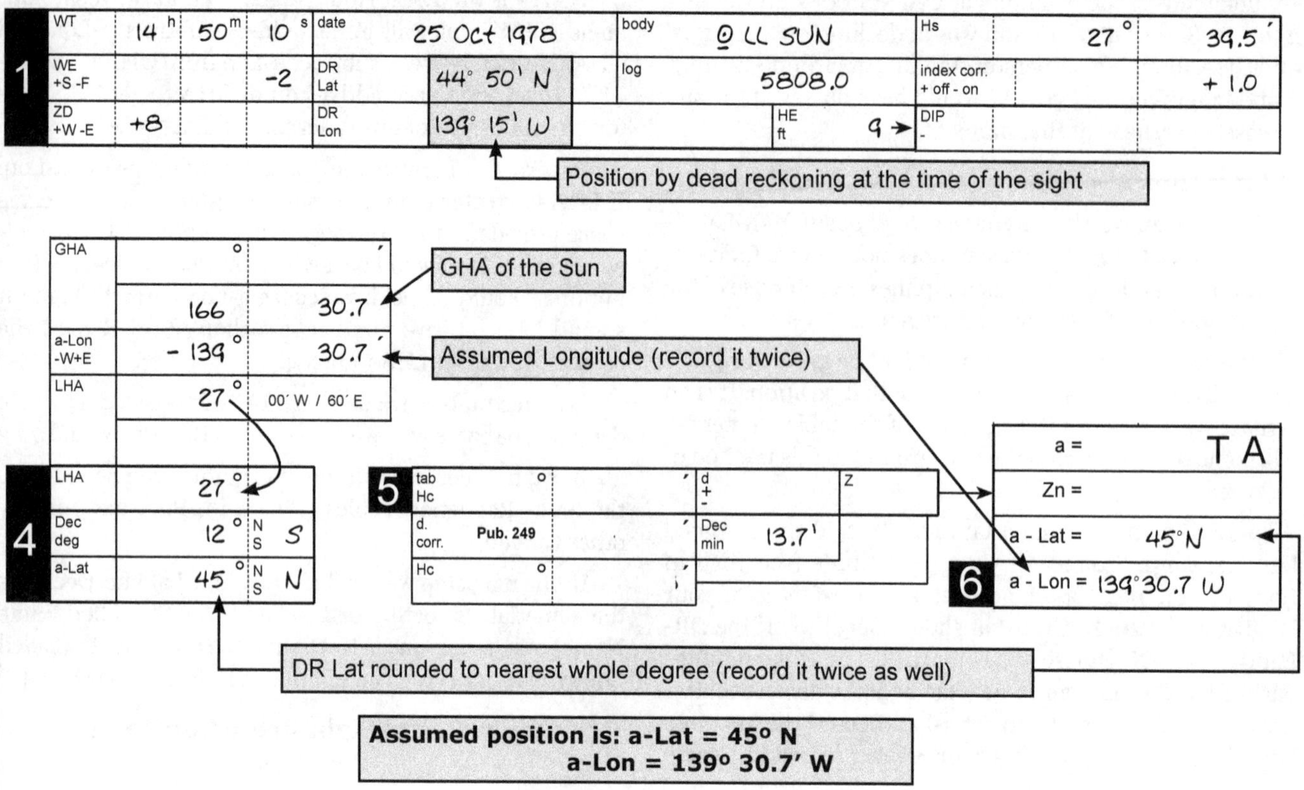

Box 4 now contains all the information you need to use the Sight Reduction Tables (Pub. 249, Pub.229, or any other version). In the next step we need to know if the assumed latitude and the declination of the Sun are both North or both South (called SAME NAME) or whether one is North and the other is South (called CONTRARY NAME). You can Tell this at a glance from Box 4.

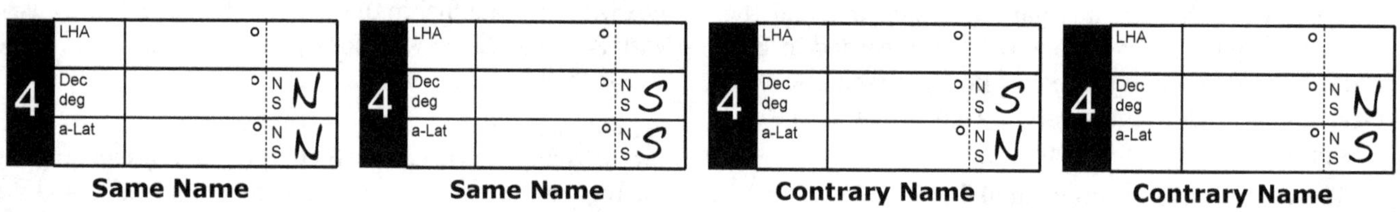

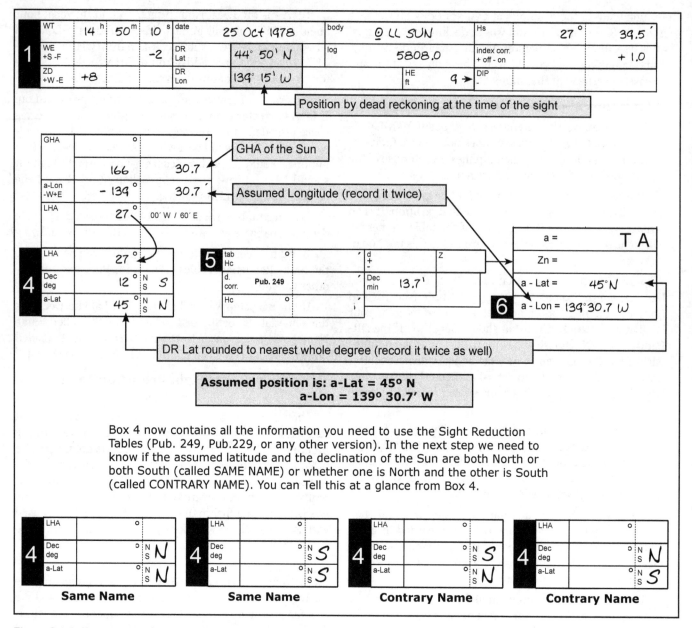

Figure 5.3-5 *Step 4, choosing an assumed position. The bottom is just a graphic reminder of the definition of same name and contrary name.*

Turn to the appropriate volume and page of Pub. 249 (we have several in the Tables Selections). Each page is labeled with an assumed latitude; find the pages labeled with the a-Lat recorded in Box 4. There is no distinction between north and south latitudes in these tables. Each of these pages is further labeled with a range of declinations (0° to 14° or 15° to 29°) and a name, Same Name or Contrary Name. Find the page that includes the Dec and Name given in Box 4. In each case there should be two pages that meet these conditions, but only one of them will include the LHA of Box 4.

After finding the proper page, go down the appropriate Dec column till you are opposite the appropriate LHA listed to the left *or* right of each page. You find three numbers listed there; copy these into Box 5. (Figure 5.3-6).

tab Hc - is the tabulated value of Hc, the calculated altitude.

d - is another d-value, but in this case it represents the change in Hc for a 1° change in the declination. The sign (±) of this d-value is listed with it, or just above it with an earlier entry.

Z - is the Azimuth Angle, the relative bearing of the sun. It is relative in the sense that if Z = 100°, the true bearing of the sun is either 100° to the east or west of north or south, depending on our latitude and the LHA. We will immediately convert Z to a true bearing in the next step.

Zn - is the true Azimuth of the sighted body. Convert Z (relative bearing) to Zn (true bearing) using the rules given on each page of the Sight Reduction Tables and also reproduced in the center of the work forms. The conversion rule depends on the size of LHA relative to 180°; there are separate rules for north and south assumed latitudes. Record Zn in Box 6.

There is a set of practice problems covering Step 5 alone in the Section 11.14. Please check those to be sure that this step is under control on its own before putting all the pieces together.

Step 6. Correction to Hc Using Pub. 249

Now find the d-correction to Hc. This correction depends on the d-value recorded in Box 5 and on Dec-min, which are the minutes part of the declination recorded just below it on the work form.

Turn to the back of Pub. 249 to find Table 5. A section is shown in Figure 5.3-7. The top of the table lists the d-values, the sides are the Dec-min. Go across the top till you reach the d-value you have (56 in this example), then down that column to the whole number of Dec-min (13 in

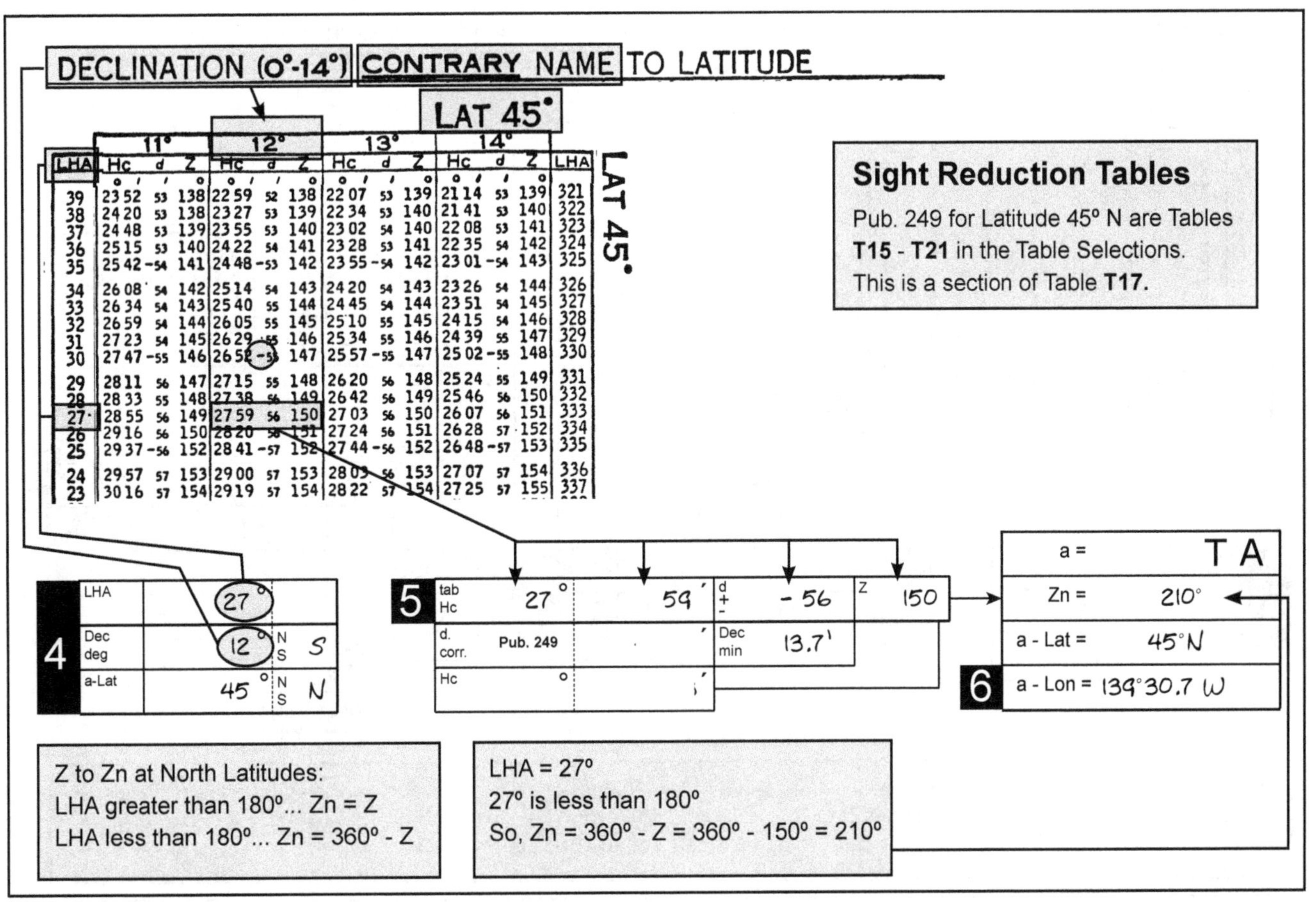

Figure 5.3-6 *Fill in Box 5 using* Pub. 249 Sight Reduction Tables.

this example). Then note the d-correction given (12 in this example). But our full Dec-min is 13.7, so we look at the correction given for the next Dec-min (14) and see that that correction is 13. So the interpolated d-correction is just 12.7'.

In all cases, the d-corr increases at most 1' with each 1' increase in the Dec-min. Therefore this interpolation is done by just using the same tenths we have in the Dec-min for the d-corr. In some cases, the next correction will be the same as the previous one. In this case, there are no tenths to the correction. An example of this is seen when d-value = 54 and Dec-min = 4 or 5. In both cases the correction is 4. You can see a few other cases like this in Table 5, but most corrections are 1' apart. (There is extra practice on this step in Section 11.14.)

Record the d-correction in the space provided below Box 5, and then add it or subtract it to "tab Hc" to get the final value of Hc. The sign (+ or -) of the correction is the same as that of the d-value.

Note that Pub. 249 lists numbers accurate only to the minute; they do not use tenths of minutes. When you look up your d-correction, just round off Dec(') to the nearest whole minute.

Hc - is the corrected value of the calculated height of the body—also called calculated altitude.

This finishes the Hc part of the sight reduction. We turn now to correcting Hs to get Ho. This is Step 7, which is identical to that which you have done in the LAN latitude sights.

Step 7. Sextant Altitude Corrections (Hs to Ho)

Looking to the right-hand side of the work form (Figure 5.3-8), first draw a line through the spaces labeled "additional altitude corrections, moon, Mars, and Venus" and "upper limb moon, subtract 30'"; we do not use these for sun lines.

What you have left to do are the IC, dip, and altitude corrections just as you did with LAN sights. Refer to those instructions for a more detailed explanation.

Look up the dip correction in the front cover of the NA and record it in the space provided. The size of the dip correction depends only on HE; the sign of the correction is always (-).

Add IC and Dip to Hs to get Ha, the apparent altitude, and record it in the space provided.

Dip - is the dip correction.

Ha - is the apparent altitude (apparent height).

altitude correction, all sights - is the altitude correction to Ha that applies to all sights. It includes refraction, semidiameter, and so on.

TABLE 5.—Correction to Tabulated Altitude for Minutes of Declination

d / '	1	2	3	4	5	6	49	50	51	52	53	54	55	56	57	58	59	60	d / '
0	0	0	0	0	0	0	0	0	0	0	0	0	0	0	0	0	0	0	0
1	0	0	0	0	0	0	1	1	1	1	1	1	1	1	1	1	1	1	1
2	0	0	0	0	0	0	2	2	2	2	2	2	2	2	2	2	2	2	2
3	0	0	0	0	0	0	2	2	3	3	3	3	3	3	3	3	3	3	3
4	0	0	0	0	0	0	3	3	3	3	4	4	4	4	4	4	4	4	4
5	0	0	0	0	0	0	4	4	4	4	4	4	5	5	5	5	5	5	5
6	0	0	0	0	0	1	5	5	5	5	5	5	6	6	6	6	6	6	6
7	0	0	0	0	1	1	6	6	6	6	6	6	6	7	7	7	7	7	7
8	0	0	0	1	1	1	7	7	7	7	7	7	7	7	8	8	8	8	8
9	0	0	0	1	1	1	7	8	8	8	8	8	8	8	9	9	9	9	9
10	0	0	0	1	1	1	8	8	8	9	9	9	9	9	10	10	10	10	10
11	0	0	1	1	1	1	9	9	9	10	10	10	10	10	10	11	11	11	11
12	0	0	1	1	1	1	10	10	10	10	11	11	11	11	11	12	12	12	12
13	0	0	1	1	1	1	11	11	11	11	11	12	12	12	12	13	13	13	13
14	0	0	1	1	1	1	11	12	12	12	12	13	13	13	13	14	14	14	14

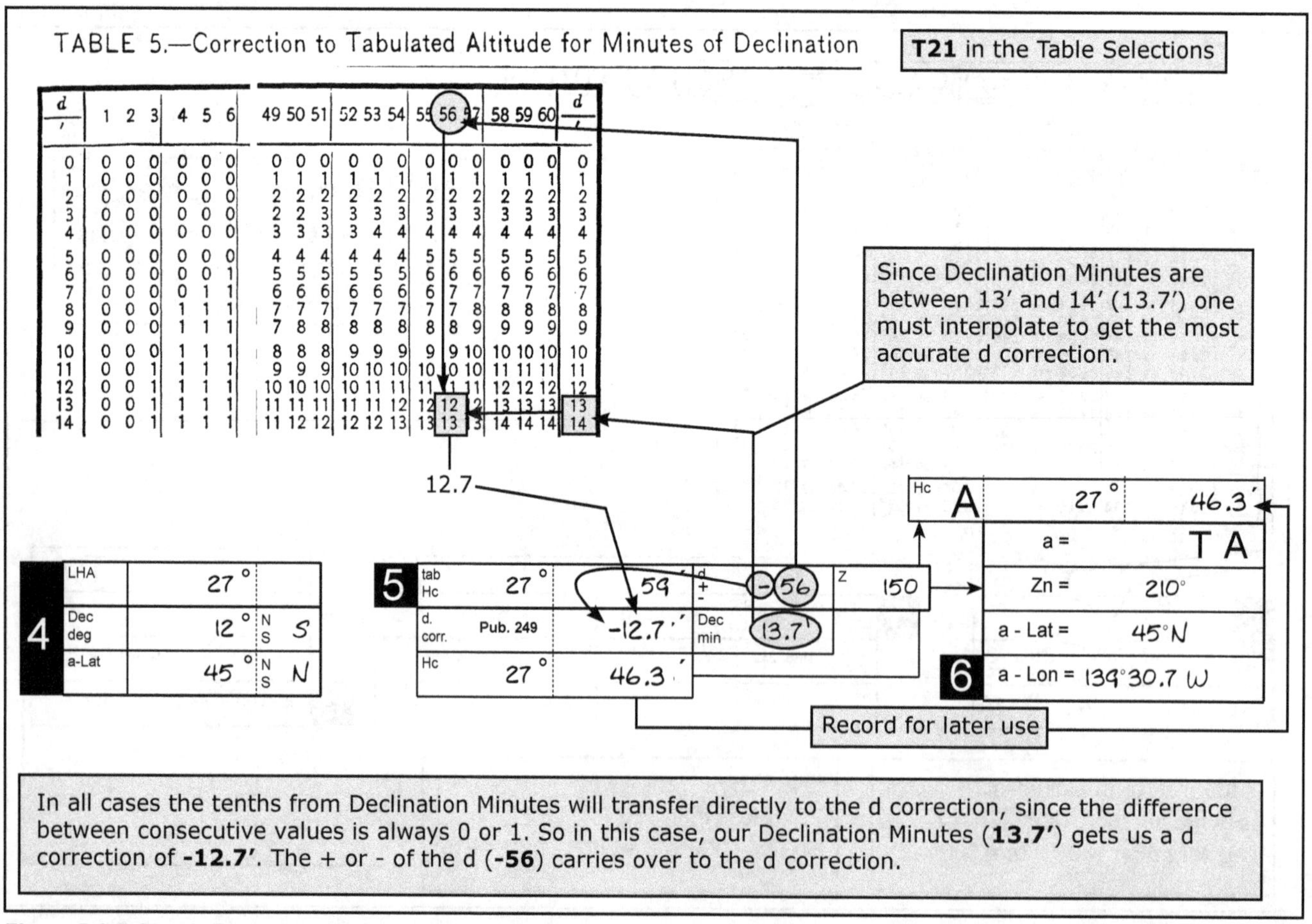

Figure 5.3-7 *Step 6, Correction to Hc.*

Look up the altitude correction for the sun on the front cover of the NA. The altitude correction of the sun depends on the month, the size of Ha, and on whether the sight was upper or lower limb. Note that there are two altitude correction tables for the sun. One is for Ha less than 10° and the other is for Ha greater than 10°.

Add the altitude correction to Ha to get Ho, the observed altitude, and record it in the space provided.

Ho - is the observed height of the sun. Note that all of Step 7 is the same as we did for LAN sights.

Step 8. Box 6–Figuring the a-value

The final step in the sight reduction is to compare Hc to Ho, and subtract the smaller from the larger to get the altitude intercept, which is called the "a-value."

There are extra spaces provided on the work form to make this comparison and subtraction easier. If the degrees part of Ho and Hc are the same, you can just recopy Hc to the space under Ho and make the subtraction. The space for "a" is in Box 6.

If the degrees part of Hc and Ho are not the same, rewrite the larger of the two so that it has the same degrees as the smaller. Use the space under Ho to rewrite it, if necessary. If you must rewrite Hc, you can do it as you transfer it to the space under Ho. Then subtract the minutes parts to get the a-value.

Now label the a-value in Box 6 as "T" for Toward or "A" for Away. The rule is: If Hc is greater than Ho, the label is Away; otherwise it is Toward. The jingle is: "Calculated Greater Away" where the first letters of Coast Guard Academy help you remember this. There are also T and A labels next to Hc and Ho on the forms. Choose the label that is next to the larger of the two.

The sight reduction is now completed; Box 6 contains all that is needed to plot the Line of Position for this sight—which you have already done in Chapter 4.

There is a summary of the example we have just done on the next page along with a schematic description of the work form. After that, we review the plotting procedure in Step 9, and then give some practice exercises.

Step 9. Plotting the LOP

Here is a summary of the procedure. An example of the sight reduction just completed is in Figure 5.3-9. The procedure was given in more detail in Section 4.4, on Plotting.

(1) Set up a universal plotting sheet centered near your AP. Plot a point at your AP (a-Lat, a-Lon).

(2) Draw a line through this point in the true direction of Zn. We will call this line the azimuth line.

(3) Put a mark on the azimuth line at a distance of "a" nautical miles from the AP, where "a" is the a-value in Box 6 expressed in minutes of arc. Mark the azimuth line in the direction toward Zn, when "a" is labeled Toward; go the op-

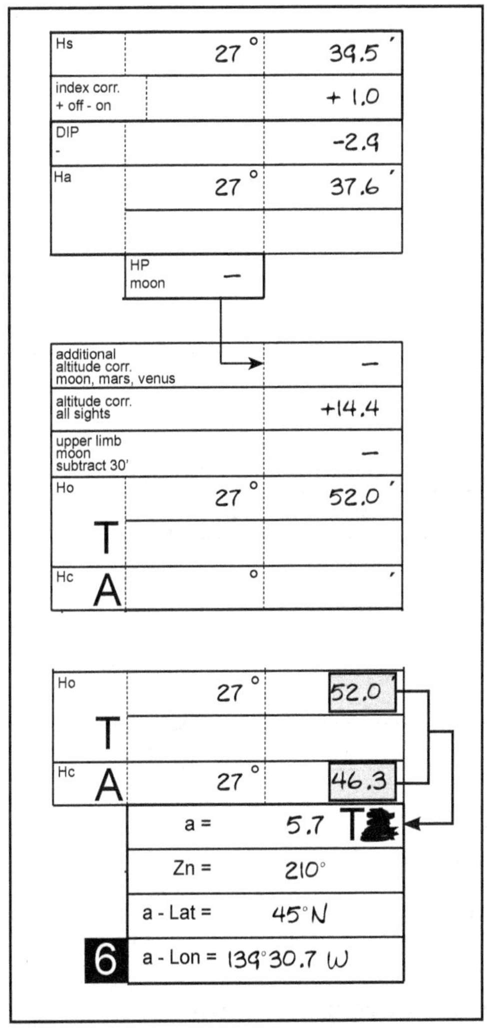

Figure 5.3-8 *The altitude intercept (a-value) is the difference between Hc and Ho. To choose the label of a: if Hc is greater than Ho, then a is "Calculated Greater Away" or just Away. Else it is Toward. Some navigators like the jingle given to us by the Japanese Admiral Homoto. If Ho is Mo, it is To.*

...In Depth

11.14 Practice with Pub. 249 Vol. 2, 3

For practice with these last two steps (finding Hc and Zn), we have here a few more examples and practice exercises on going from Box 4 to Box 5 and 6...

Summary of the Sun Sight Sample, Sun #1

1

	h	m	s						
WT	14 h	50 m	10 s	date	25 Oct 1978	body	☉ LL SUN	Hs	27° 39.5′
WE +S -F			-2	DR Lat	44° 50′ N	log	5808.0	index corr. + off - on	+ 1.0
ZD +W -E	+8			DR Lon	139° 15′ W	HE ft	9 →	DIP -	-2.9
UTC	22 h	50 m	8 s	UTC date / LOP label	2250 ☉ 25 October			Ha	27° 37.6′

2

GHA hr.	153° 58.7′	v moon planets	—	Dec hr	S 12° 12.9′	d + -	+0.9	HP moon	—

3

GHA + m.s.	12° 32.0′	d corr. + -	+0.8′
SHA + or v corr.	—° —′ (stars or moon, planets)	Dec	S 12° Dec min 13.7′
GHA	165° 90.7′		
	166 30.7		
a-Lon -W+E	- 139° 30.7′		
LHA	27° 00′ W / 60′ E		

tens d		d upper
units d		d lower
dsd corr. +		dsd ←
d. corr. Pub. 229		

additional altitude corr. moon, mars, venus	—
altitude corr. all sights	+14.4
upper limb moon subtract 30′	—
Ho	27° 52.0′
T	
Hc A	27° 46.3′

4

LHA	27°
Dec deg	12° N S — S
a-Lat	45° N S — N

5

tab Hc	27° 59′	d + -	- 56	Z 150
d. corr. Pub. 249	-12.7′	Dec min	13.7′
Hc	27° 46.3′		

6

a =	5.7 T
Zn =	210°
a - Lat =	45° N
a - Lon =	139° 30.7 W

North Latitudes
LHA greater than 180° .... Zn = Z
LHA less than 180° .... Zn = 360° - Z

South Latitudes
LHA greater than 180° .... Zn = 180° - Z
LHA less than 180° .... Zn = 180° + Z

Summary of form content

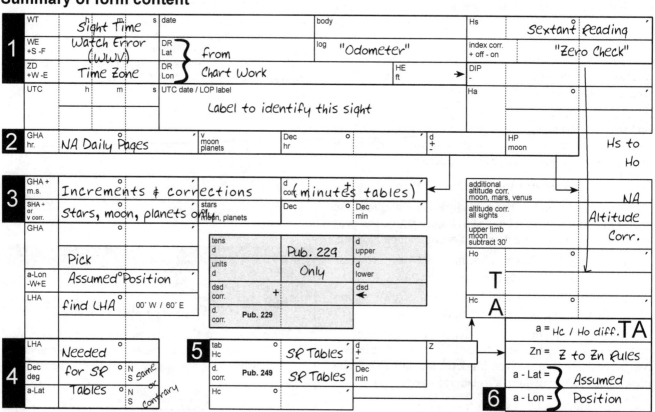

1

WT h m s	Sight Time	date		body		Hs	Sextant Reading
WE +S -F	Watch Error (WWV)	DR Lat	from	log	"Odometer"	index corr. + off - on	"Zero Check"
ZD +W -E	Time Zone	DR Lon	Chart Work	HE ft	→	DIP -	
UTC h m s		UTC date / LOP label	Label to identify this sight			Ha ° ′	

2

GHA hr.	NA Daily Pages	v moon planets		Dec hr		d + -		HP moon	

Hs to Ho

3

GHA + m.s.	Increments & corrections	d corr.	(minutes tables)
SHA + or v corr.	Stars, moon, planets only (stars or moon, planets)	Dec	Dec min
GHA			
	Pick		
a-Lon -W+E	Assumed Position		
LHA	find LHA 00′ W / 60′ E		

tens d	Pub. 229	d upper
units d	Only	d lower
dsd corr. +		dsd ←
d. corr. Pub. 229		

additional altitude corr. moon, mars, venus	NA
altitude corr. all sights	Altitude
upper limb moon subtract 30′	Corr.
Ho	
T	
Hc A	

4

LHA	Needed
Dec deg	for SR (N S — same or contrary)
a-Lat	Tables

5

tab Hc	SR Tables	d + -	Z
d. corr. Pub. 249	SR Tables	Dec min	
Hc			

6

a =	Hc / Ho diff. TA
Zn =	Z to Zn Rules
a - Lat =	Assumed
a - Lon =	Position

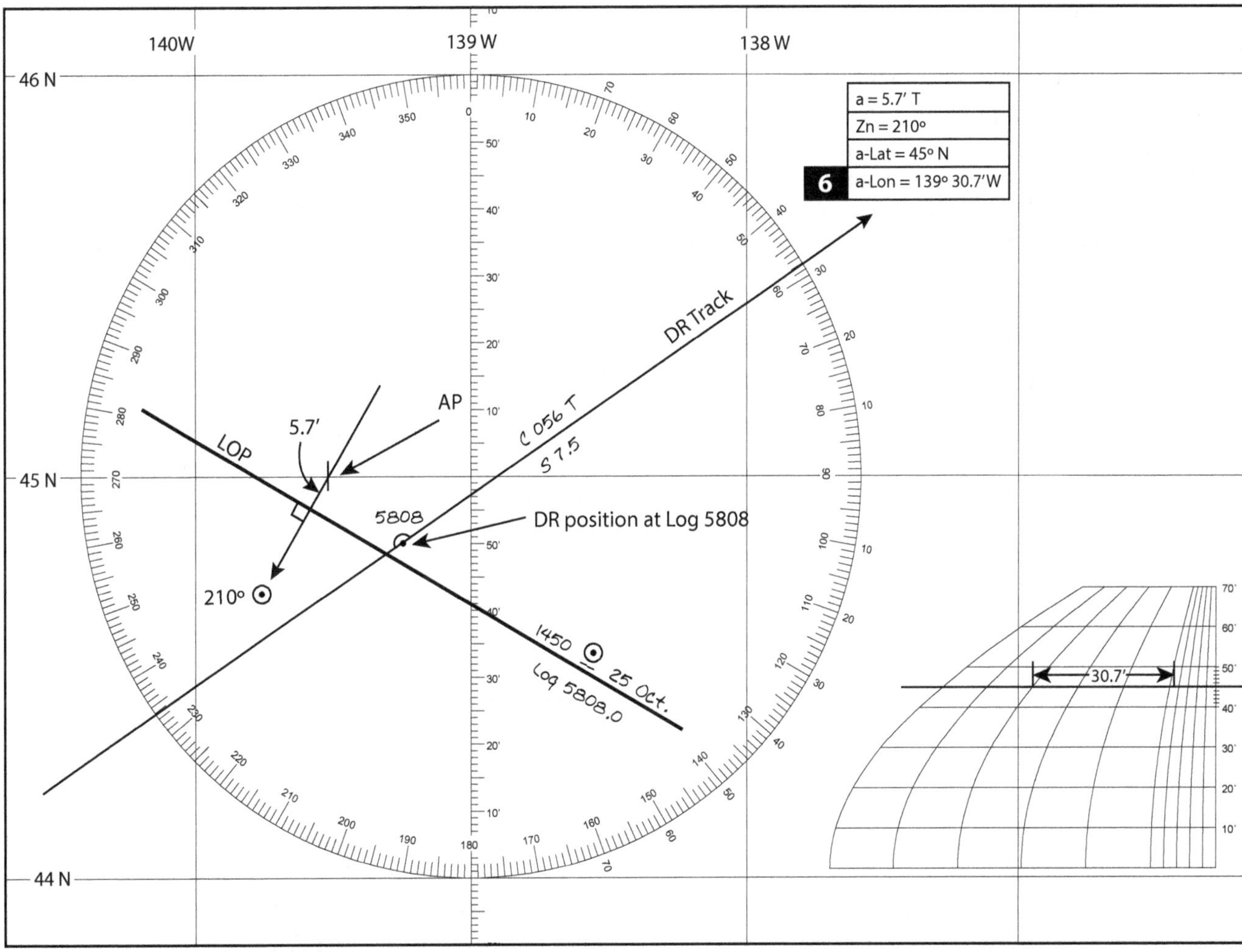

Figure 5.3-9 *Plotting the LOP for Sun Sight #1 on the same sheet that we plot the DR track. The label AP (assumed position) is a-Lat, a-Lon. We know from this one sun sight that we are somewhere on that line, but we must be careful to go beyond that.*

With just this one LOP, we know only two things. We are somewhere on this LOP, and we know that our present DR position for log 5808 is not right. If the LOP had crossed right through our DR position, then we also know that our DR might be right. *But one LOP only does not assure that.*

If we are lucky, and happen to be at the closest possible place on the LOP, then we are only off by 3 or 4 miles. The closest place on the LOP to the DR (drop a perpendicular from DR to LOP) is called by some the "estimated position," but this is not a very useful concept defined this way. It is more wishful thinking than practical use. If this vessel had been sailing to weather in a fresh easterly, for example, you are almost certainly downwind of your DR position, which would put you on the other side of the DR track.

In this course we reserve the term estimated position (EP) *to be equivalent to a DR position that has been determined using all knowledge available short of a measurement of any kind. This other EP (closest point on an LOP to the corresponding DR) is based on a measurement, i.e., the one LOP, but sailing in the ocean this is not a useful concept, and it is indeed wrong in some circumstances, as in the example cited.*

posite direction along the azimuth line when "a" is labeled Away. Remember that nautical miles are measured along the latitude scale: 1' of latitude = 1 nmi.

(4) Finally, draw a line perpendicular to the azimuth line passing through the point just marked. This line is your Line of Position. This sight and sight reduction have told you that you are located somewhere on this line. Label the line with the name of the celestial body, your log reading, and the UTC.

— DONE! —

That is the full sight reduction process for sun sights—how to go from a timed sextant height of the sun to an LOP on your chart.

To follow are four exercises for practice, followed by the opportunity to work through the original LAN sights from Chapter 3 as normal sun lines. All the answers are provided. Do not hesitate to check your work as you proceed to save time.

Sights #2 and #3 are completely independent of each other (we only practice the paperwork with these), but you can plot the fix from sun #4 and #5, which were taken from the same (dead in the water) position, several hours apart. The answer to that is shown in Figure 5.3-10. In the next chapter we see how to correct these LOPs when we are moving. It takes us back to more chart work.

The main task now is to learn the procedure for filling out the form, and noting whenever possible how the form itself reminds you what to do next.

Again, after you have mastered the actual practice of finding a fix, we will come back and look more into the mathematical principles behind the process, or if you are more comfortable knowing the background before getting into these practical matters, skim through the In Depth topics of Chapter 11 to see several related articles.

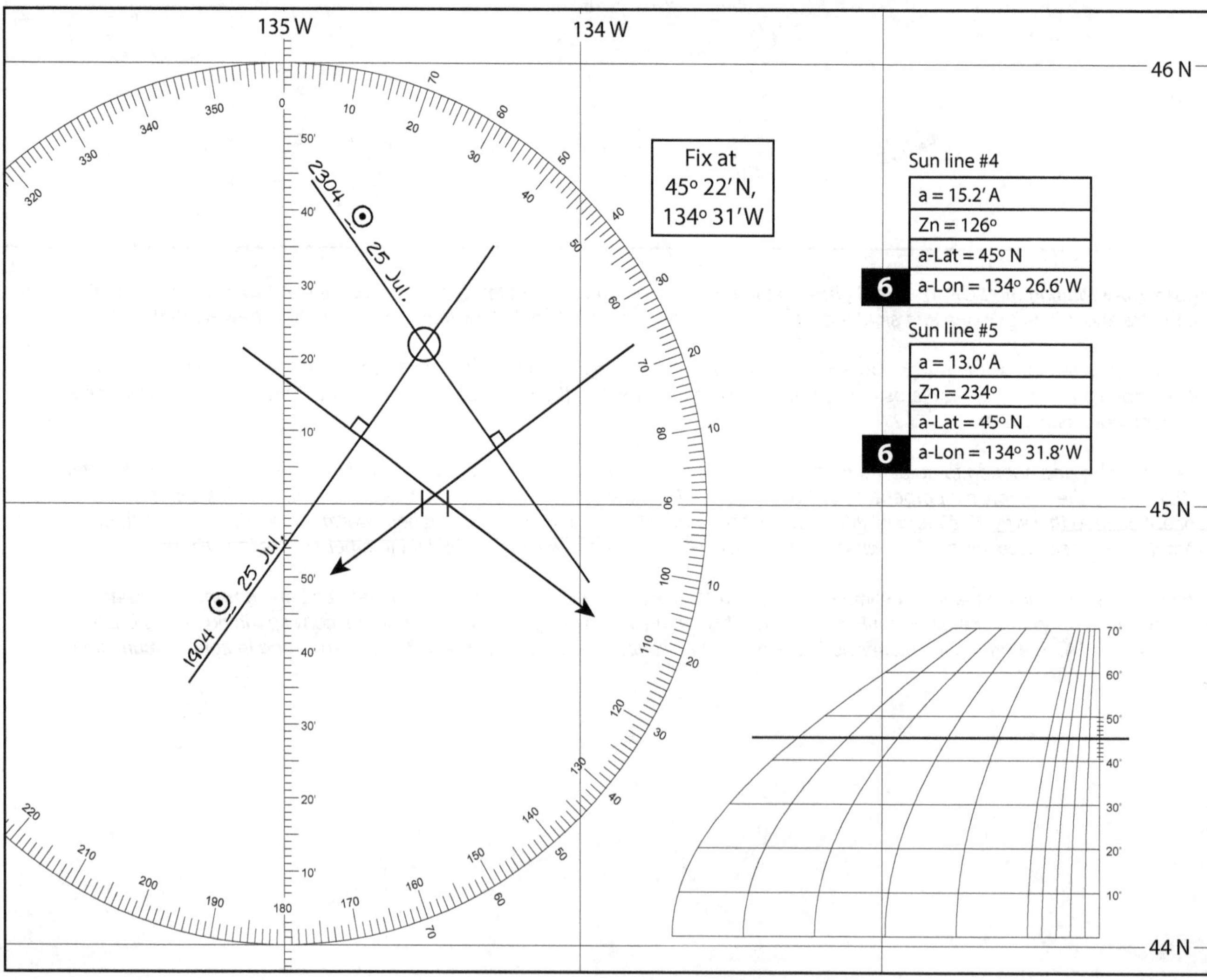

Figure 5.3-10 *Plotting a fix between morning and afternoon sun lines (#4 and #5). In this case there is no motion of the boat between sights.*

5.4 Sun Sight Exercise, Sun #2

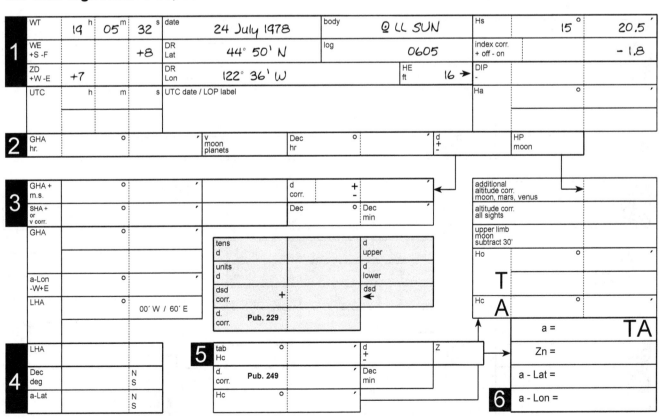

1

WT	14 h	49 m	10 s	date: 26 July 1978	body: ☉ LL SUN
WE +S -F			-13	DR Lat: 44° 40' N	log: 882.0
ZD +W -E	+7			DR Lon: 123° 0' W	HE ft: 16 →
UTC	h	m	s	UTC date / LOP label	

	°	′
Hs	58	24.8
index corr. + off - on		0.0
DIP -		
Ha		

2

GHA hr. ° ′	v moon planets	Dec hr ° ′
d + -	HP moon	

3

GHA + m.s. ° ′		d corr. + - ′
SHA + or v corr. ° ′	stars or moon, planets	Dec ° Dec min ′
GHA ° ′		
a-Lon -W+E ° ′		
LHA °	00′ W / 60′ E	

tens d		d upper
units d		d lower
dsd corr. +		dsd ←
d. corr. **Pub. 229**		

additional altitude corr. moon, mars, venus	
altitude corr. all sights	
upper limb moon subtract 30′	
Ho ° ′	T
Hc ° ′	A

4

LHA	°	
Dec deg	°	N S
a-Lat	°	N S

5

tab Hc ° ′		d + -	Z
d. corr. **Pub. 249** ′		Dec min	
Hc ° ′			

6

a =	TA
Zn =	
a - Lat =	
a - Lon =	

North Latitudes	
LHA greater than 180°	Zn = Z
LHA less than 180°	Zn = 360° - Z

South Latitudes	
LHA greater than 180°	Zn = 180° - Z
LHA less than 180°	Zn = 180° + Z

5.5 Sun Sight Exercise, Sun #3

1

WT	19 h	05 m	32 s	date: 24 July 1978	body: ☉ LL SUN
WE +S -F			+8	DR Lat: 44° 50' N	log: 0605
ZD +W -E	+7			DR Lon: 122° 36' W	HE ft: 16 →
UTC	h	m	s	UTC date / LOP label	

	°	′
Hs	15	20.5
index corr. + off - on		- 1.8
DIP -		
Ha		

2

GHA hr. ° ′	v moon planets	Dec hr ° ′
d + -	HP moon	

3

GHA + m.s. ° ′		d corr. + - ′
SHA + or v corr. ° ′		Dec ° Dec min ′
GHA ° ′		
a-Lon -W+E ° ′		
LHA °	00′ W / 60′ E	

tens d		d upper
units d		d lower
dsd corr. +		dsd ←
d. corr. **Pub. 229**		

additional altitude corr. moon, mars, venus	
altitude corr. all sights	
upper limb moon subtract 30′	
Ho ° ′	T
Hc ° ′	A

4

LHA	
Dec deg	N S
a-Lat	N S

5

tab Hc ° ′		d + -	Z
d. corr. **Pub. 249** ′		Dec min	
Hc ° ′			

6

a =	TA
Zn =	
a - Lat =	
a - Lon =	

5.6 Sun Sight Fix Exercise, Sun #4

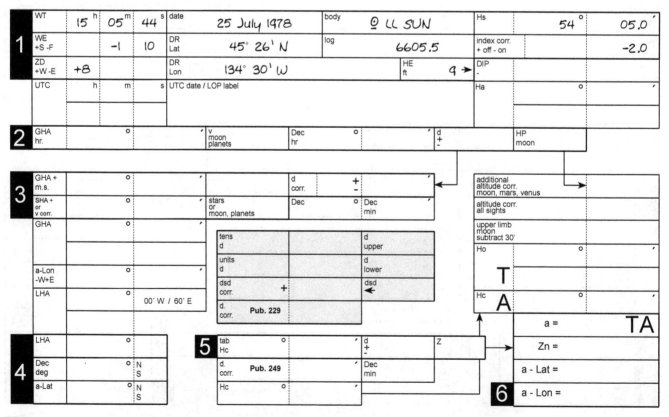

1

	h	m	s							
WT	11 h	05 m	23 s	date	25 July 1978	body	⊙ LL SUN	Hs	54 °	05.0 ′
WE +S -F		-1	10	DR Lat	45° 26' N	log	6605.5	index corr. + off - on		-2.0
ZD +W -E	+8			DR Lon	134° 30' W	HE ft	9 →	DIP -		
UTC	h	m	s	UTC date / LOP label				Ha	°	′

2

GHA hr.	°	′	v moon planets	Dec hr	°	′	d + -	HP moon

3

GHA + m.s.	°	′		d corr.	+ -	′
SHA + or v corr.	°	′	stars or moon, planets	Dec	°	Dec min ′
GHA	°	′				
a-Lon -W+E	°	′				
LHA	°	00′ W / 60′ E				

tens d		d upper
units d		d lower
dsd corr. +		dsd ←
d. corr. Pub. 229		

additional altitude corr. moon, mars, venus		
altitude corr. all sights		
upper limb moon subtract 30'		
Ho	°	′
T		
Hc A	°	′

4

LHA	°	
Dec deg	°	N S
a-Lat	°	N S

5

tab Hc	°	′	d + -	Z
d. corr. Pub. 249		′	Dec min	
Hc	°	′		

6

TA
a =
Zn =
a - Lat =
a - Lon =

<u>North Latitudes</u>
LHA greater than 180° .... Zn = Z
LHA less than 180° .... Zn = 360° - Z

<u>South Latitudes</u>
LHA greater than 180° .... Zn = 180° - Z
LHA less than 180° .... Zn = 180° + Z

5.7 Sun Sight Fix Exercise, Sun #5

1

	h	m	s							
WT	15 h	05 m	44 s	date	25 July 1978	body	⊙ LL SUN	Hs	54 °	05.0 ′
WE +S -F		-1	10	DR Lat	45° 26' N	log	6605.5	index corr. + off - on		-2.0
ZD +W -E	+8			DR Lon	134° 30' W	HE ft	9 →	DIP -		
UTC	h	m	s	UTC date / LOP label				Ha	°	′

2

GHA hr.	°	′	v moon planets	Dec hr	°	′	d + -	HP moon

3

GHA + m.s.	°	′		d corr.	+ -	′
SHA + or v corr.	°	′	stars or moon, planets	Dec	°	Dec min ′
GHA	°	′				
a-Lon -W+E	°	′				
LHA	°	00′ W / 60′ E				

tens d		d upper
units d		d lower
dsd corr. +		dsd ←
d. corr. Pub. 229		

additional altitude corr. moon, mars, venus		
altitude corr. all sights		
upper limb moon subtract 30'		
Ho	°	′
T		
Hc A	°	′

4

LHA	°	
Dec deg	°	N S
a-Lat	°	N S

5

tab Hc	°	′	d + -	Z
d. corr. Pub. 249		′	Dec min	
Hc	°	′		

6

TA
a =
Zn =
a - Lat =
a - Lon =

5.8 Exercise—More Sun Sight Practice

In Exercise 3.4 of Chapter 3, we did 10 noon sights that were analyzed in the LAN procedure to find latitude. For these special sights of the peak height of the sun, the sight reduction reduces to just arithmetic of the declination and zenith distance. These are perfectly good sun sights, however, and they can be reduced by the conventional means using a work form as we have just been practicing. This exercise does just that. There are special sight reduction tables for these in the Tables Selection, and there is a table of intermediate step results in the Answers section.

These exercises will also introduce you to sight reductions from eastern longitudes, where the LHA is found from LHA = GHA + a-Lon(E). To make the minutes part of LHA vanish in this case, the assumed longitude must be chosen so that the sum of GHA and a-Lon has no minutes part, which you achieve by choosing the minutes to add up to 60' exactly.

Because we know that these are noon sights with the sun crossing your meridian, in these exercises, you should end up with an azimuth (Zn) of nearly 180° or 0°, depending on whether you were looking south or north to the sun. In either case, the LOP is in fact a latitude line, whose latitude is just the assumed latitude corrected for the a-value. For example, if the a-Lat was 48° N and the a = 10.0' Toward 180, then your latitude must be 10' south of 48°, or 47° 50.0' N.

Figure out the latitude from each of these LOPs by doing a regular sight reduction using the work form and then adjusting the a-Lat for the a-value. Your answers should come out within a few tenths of a minute—they could be off by this little amount if the Zn is not precisely on the meridian.

(1) DR position at sight time on July 25th, 1978 was 56° 02' N, 164° 30' W. A sight of the sun was taken and Hs was found to be 54° 5.0' for a Lower-limb sight taken at 23h 04m 00s UTC. The index error was 2.0' on the scale, and the HE was 9 ft. Find a-value, Zn, and latitude.

(2) DR position at sight time on October 27th, 1978 was 10° 00' S, 166° 15' W. A sight of the sun was taken and Hs was found to be 87° 20' for a upper-limb sight taken at 22h 49m 00s UTC. The index error was 2.0' off the scale, and the HE was 25 ft. Find a-value, Zn, and latitude.

(3) DR position at sight time on October 25th, 1978 was 35° 54' N, 074° 02' E. A sight of the sun was taken and Hs was found to be 41° 30.5' for a lower-limb sight taken at 06h 48m 00s UTC. The index error was 4.0' off the scale, and the HE was 10 ft. Find a-value, Zn, and latitude.

(4) DR position at sight time on Mar. 27th, 1981 was 37° 40' N, 15° 24' W. A sight of the sun was taken and Hs was found to be 54° 41.3' for a lower-limb sight taken at 13h 07m 00s UTC. The index error was 2.0' off the scale, and the HE was 9 ft. Find a-value, Zn, and latitude.

(5) DR position at sight time on Mar. 28th, 1981 was 22° 38' N, 64° 17' E. A sight of the sun was taken and Hs was found to be 71° 9.8' for a lower-limb sight taken at 07h 48m 00s UTC. The index error was 2.2' on the scale, and the HE was 9 ft. Find a-value, Zn, and latitude.

(6) DR position at sight time on Oct. 26th, 1978 was 27° 06' S, 163° 16' E. A sight of the sun was taken and Hs was found to be 74° 59.8' for a lower-limb sight taken at 00h 51m 00s UTC. The index error was 1.4' off the scale, and the HE was 9 ft. Find a-value, Zn, and latitude.

(7) DR position at sight time on July 24th, 1978 was 28° 44' S, 85° 17' W. A sight of the sun was taken and Hs was found to be 42° 51.2' for a upper-limb sight taken at 17h 48m 00s UTC. The index error was 1.5' on the scale, and the HE was 9 ft. Find a-value, Zn, and latitude.

(8) DR position at sight time on July 25th, 1978 was 44° 10' N, 131° 00' W. A sight of the sun was taken and Hs was found to be 65° 22.5' for a lower-limb sight taken at 20h 50m 00s UTC. The index error was 2.0' on the scale, and the HE was 9 ft. Find a-value, Zn, and latitude.

(9) DR position at sight time on Mar. 28th, 1981 was 16° 40' S, 146° 30' W. A sight of the sun was taken and Hs was found to be 69° 44.2' for a lower-limb sight taken at 21h 51m 00s UTC. The index error was 2.5' off the scale, and the HE was 12 ft. Find a-value, Zn, and latitude.

(10) DR position at sight time on Oct. 25th, 1978 was 34° 29' N, 025° 00' E. A sight of the sun was taken and Hs was found to be 43° 11.7' for a lower-limb sight taken at 10h 04m 00s UTC. The index error was 1.5' off the scale, and the HE was 14 ft. Find a-value, Zn, and latitude.

5.9 Progress Report

The contents of Chapter 5 are the peak of the course; please do not be discouraged if this one takes some extra time. It is essentially all of celestial navigation practice, in that all the other sights are essentially the same. We learn here the process of doing sight reductions, and we have now used all of the standard tables and have been through the plotting earlier.

From this point on, we just add more examples for practice, and it won't really matter if they are stars or planets, or the moon. With our work forms, the other bodies are all done in a very similar way. With the extra practice we can catch and resolve common mistakes while we are still in the learning process, and not have to find them when we are underway.

As we proceed we will fine tune the process to make it more accurate and versatile. The challenge of real world reliance on cel nav is much better met when we have a bag of tricks we can reach into as needed.

Also after just a bit more practice we can bounce back and look into the foundations of the procedures we are using. It will help the process jell and indeed show why some of the tricks we shall cover are valuable.

5.10 New Terminology

altitude intercept (a-value)
assumed position (AP)
azimuth angle (Z)
calculated height (Hc)
civil twilight
Greenwich hour angle (GHA)
local hour angle (LHA)
nautical twilight
sight reduction tables
sunrise
sunset
work form

...In Depth

11.24 Optimizing Celestial Fixes

This section has details of more interest toward the end of the course, but see the short subsection on checking assumed positions when plotting LOPs for a fix, which answers the question, "Are the a-values too large?"

Chapter 6

Running Fixes

6.1 Introduction

We often say in class that the transition from prudent skipper to navigator takes place with the mastering of the running fix. Most basic navigation prior to that involves finding a fix from two separate objects, whereas the running fix lets you find a fix from a single object. We can also do the same by finding distance off and a bearing, but those piloting methods are not as universally applicable as is the running fix.

The technique is not so often learned because it is not so often needed on inland waters, but when it is needed, you need a navigator. Now in the age of GPS, it is even less needed, and such skills are almost doomed in the eyes of many skippers. On the other hand, when it is needed now, the need for a navigator is even more pronounced.

One of the benefits of learning celestial navigation is the necessity of learning the running fix. Although it is rare to need a running fix in sight of land, it is a crucial daily chore of routine celestial navigation.

In this chapter, we discuss the process and then offer practice problems, starting with the simplest and leading up to a specially constructed set of exercises that can be used to master sun line navigation in all hemispheres.

For anyone behind in the sun line sight reduction processes from Chapter 5, however, we recommend that you complete some of the sun line sight reduction exercises before starting these plotting exercises.

6.2 Running Fixes in Coastal Nav

One of the important challenges a navigator faces is finding position from a single landmark or celestial body. On inshore waters, the problem occurs in the fog whenever a single light is the only reference; it also occurs on clear days whenever only one coastal feature (peak, tower, islet) can be identified. When relying on celestial navigation offshore, the problem arises daily when navigating by the sun alone—the moon is well positioned for simultaneous fixes with the sun for only about a week or so each month. Depending on the circumstances, there are several ways to find position from a single reference (both inshore and offshore), but a running fix is the most reliable and versatile method. It is a plotting technique that combines piloting and dead reckoning.

When done with compass bearings, the procedure boils down to taking one bearing, moving far enough that this bearing changes by 30° or more, and then figuring out where you must be in order to see what you saw after doing what you did. With the two lines of position (LOPs) plotted on the chart, the chart work is equivalent to finding the one place along the first LOP that you could leave from, sail the distance you did in the direction you did, and end up on the second LOP (see Figure 6.2-1).

Running-fix Procedure

(1) Take a magnetic bearing to the light and plot the LOP on the chart labeled with the log reading and watch time of the sight.

(2) Hold a steady course and speed until the magnetic bearing to the light has changed by at least 30°, preferably more. Smaller bearing changes give weaker fixes, but there is little to be gained by waiting beyond a bearing change of 60°. With a log available to count miles run, it is not necessary to keep a constant boat speed.

(3) Take a second magnetic bearing to the light and plot this LOP, labeled with the second watch time and second log reading. Subtract the two log readings to find the distance run between sights; without a log, figure the distance run from average speed and time between sights.

(4) Starting from any point A on the first LOP, draw a line in the direction sailed between sights and mark off the distance run between sights along that line. Then use parallel rules to *advance* the first LOP to the point B, which marks the distance run between sights. Label the advanced LOP with both log readings (or times) joined by an arrow. Your position at the time of the second LOP is the place where the advanced LOP crosses the second LOP.

Advancing an LOP means moving it without rotating it. This can be achieved with parallel rules or a roller plotter.

A running fix is as accurate as a conventional bearing fix from near-simultaneous bearings to two separated objects provided the DR between the two sights of the running fix is accurate. This requires a calibrated log or knotmeter, a corrected compass, and careful records between sights. It also requires that you know the currents present—so far we have assumed they do not exist. Leeway should also be included when sailing to windward in very strong or very light air–also not added yet.

On coastal waters, the object of the sights must be close enough that its bearing changes significantly in a reasonable time. If the object is too far away, or too near the bow

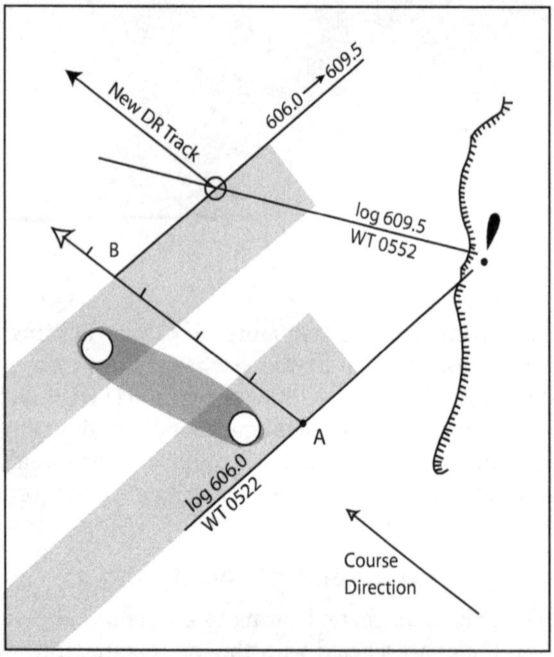

Figure 6.2-1 *A running fix without current or course changes. The distance between points A and B is the difference in log readings at the bearing times; the direction A to B is the course steered between bearings.*

or stern, the time required to see a bearing change between sights will be so long that small uncertainties in the DR will accumulate and the accuracy of the fix will suffer. As a rule of thumb, consider that the uncertainty in the final running fix will be slightly larger than the uncertainty in the DR between sights.

How to compensate for current and leeway in a running fix is discussed in detail in our textbook *Inland and Coastal Navigation*, but here is an overview. Start the DR plot from point A, but now plot a corrected DR track between the two sight times. In other words, assume that point A was your DR position at the time of the first sight, plot your best guess of where you should have been at the time of the second sight taking into account current and leeway, and then advance the first LOP to that point, as shown in Figure 6.2-2.

The same procedure is used for running fixes between two sun lines, although in this application the time between sights is likely to be longer (1 to 4 hours) and consequently it is likely that there will be course changes between sights. In any event, the method is the same as when correcting for current. Forget where your actual DR position is, choose any point A on the first sun line and assume that it is your DR position at that time. From point A, DR to the time of the second sight, and advance the first sun line to that point, as shown in Figure 6.2-2. In other words, when you advance an LOP, you simply move it exactly as you think your boat moved between sights.

It is possible to sail many miles on inshore waters and never need a running fix, but if you sail long enough in varied conditions, eventually you will run across a situation where a running fix is the only way to find out where you are. A navigator should be prepared for all conditions, so practice with running fixes is fundamental to good navigation preparation. For ocean sailing, it is mandatory.

Correcting DR for Leeway and Current

We review this procedure here for completeness, but in our ocean cel nav exercises that follow we will not be making these corrections. We do need basic running fixes and have important exercises on them, but not more on current and leeway than the following review. If you happen to be sailing in an area with strong current or conditions with known leeway, then it is important to review these corrections and include those in the running fix.

In Figure 6.2-3, the black line A, B, C, D is the DR plot without corrections. To correct for leeway, use the same distance run for each leg, but plot each course leg to leeward of the actual course steered by an amount equal to the estimated or measured leeway angle. This is the gray line. Note length AB = AB, BC = BC, etc; it is just the course angles that are offset.

Then correct for the current set at the end of the plot by moving the final position by the amount set during the time of the run. In this example, the line DE is the net drift that

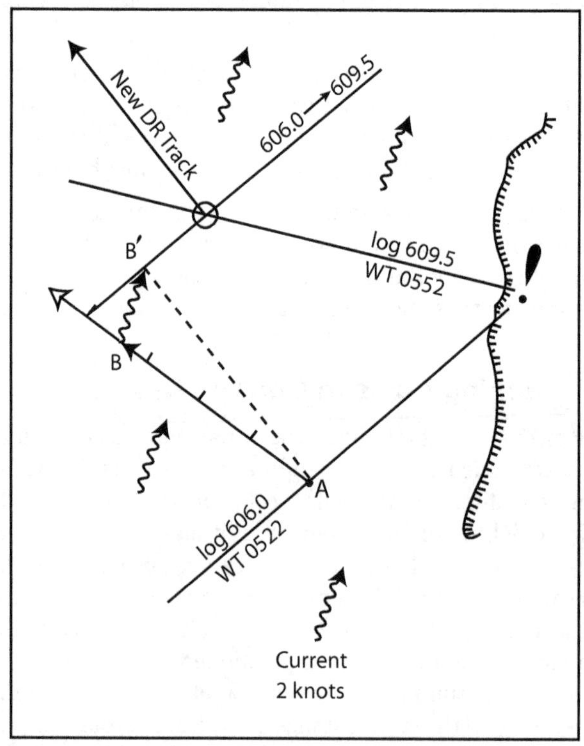

Figure 6.2-2 *A running fix corrected for current. This is the same situation shown in Figure 6.2-1, but now in a northerly current of 2 kts. The time between sights was 30 minutes, so point B must be advanced 1 mile (2 kts × 0.5h) to B' in the direction of the current set. The new DR track runs parallel to the A to B' line (course made good) to account for the current set in subsequent dead reckoning—if we assume the current will be the same then.*

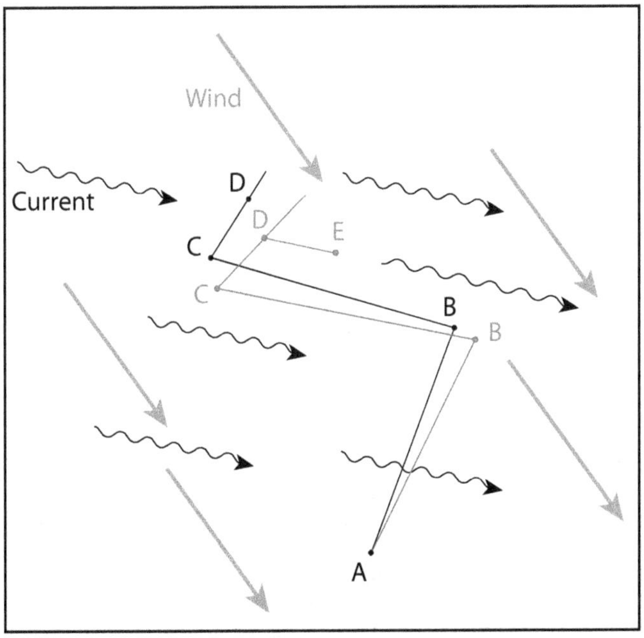

Figure 6.2-3 *Correcting DR for leeway and current. Same as regular plot, but rotate each course leg downwind by the leeway angle on each leg, then off set the result (D to E) with the net drift during the full run time (A to D).*

we move in the direction of the set. If T is the total time in decimal hours from A to D and Sc is the current speed in kts, then this total drift in nmi DE = T × Sc.

This analysis makes these two assumptions: (1) The wind speed and direction are constant over the plot and we are on the same point of sail on each leg (else the leeway changes), and (2) the set and drift of the current are constant over the region of the plot. For more details and nuances of DR in various conditions, see *Inland and Coastal Navigation* (Starpath Publications, 2014).

6.3 Running Fixes in Celestial Nav

The running fix is the best way to find both latitude and longitude from sun sights alone. In principle, there is a way to Lon from the time of LAN, but as we shall see later, this is not a dependable method. To navigate by the sun throughout the day, the best solution is a running fix from the sun.

To do it you need two sun lines or a sun line and LAN latitude line. In either case, the bearing to the sun must have changed by at least 30° between sights—90° is a theoretical ideal, but 30° is good enough, and indeed one does not get any improved accuracy beyond about 60°. To get a 30° bearing change typically means that the lines must be taken roughly 2 or 3 hours apart, depending on the circumstances—in particular, your latitude and the time of year. In planning the times of the sights, the sun's shadow on your compass card is one way to note the bearing of the sun.

Figure 6.3-1 shows the procedure plotted out. An LAN sight gave the boat's latitude at log reading 556. This LAN latitude line is plotted and labeled. The label also includes the time of the sight, but we do not need this time for the running fix when we have log readings (because we are not correcting for current).

The half-circles on the DR track are the DR positions at the log readings indicated. Note that the 556 DR position does not fall on the 556 LAN line. This means the DR is wrong—your DR will always accumulate error with time, which is the reason we need celestial fixes.

After the LAN sight, the boat sailed on and later that afternoon took a regular sun line sight. The LOP from this sight, labeled sun line #3, is plotted in the regular way us-

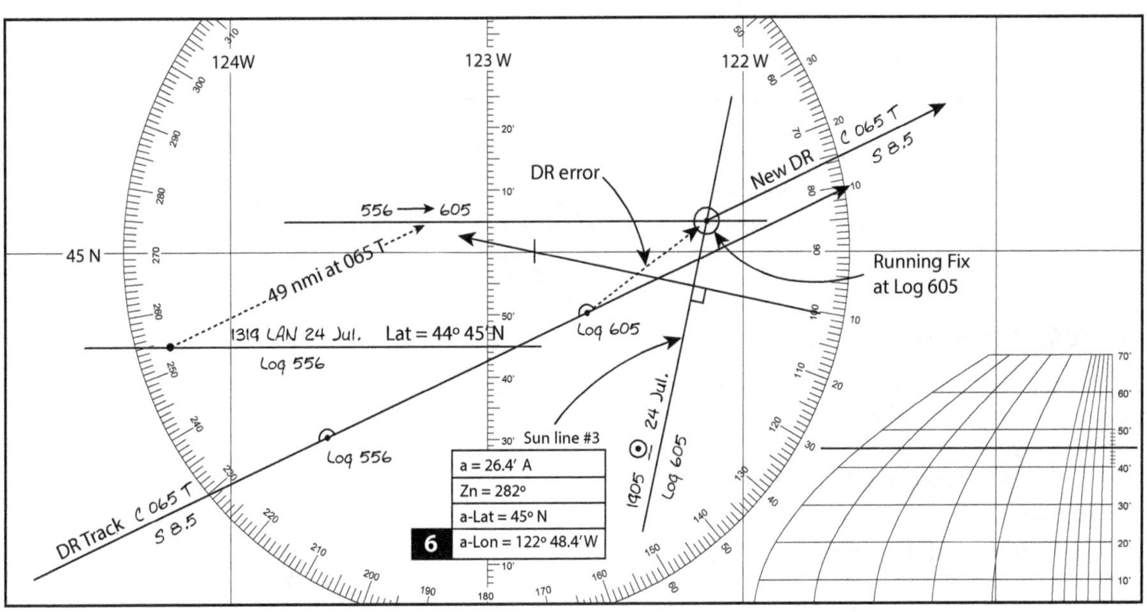

Figure 6.3-1 *Running fix between an LAN latitude line and a sun line.*

ing the data given in Box 6. The log read 605 at the time of this sight, so the line is labeled accordingly.

The DR position of the boat at log 605 is also shown on the DR track. This point is 49 miles (605-556) up the track from the 556 position. (Remember the miles scale is always the latitude scale.)

The task now is to advance the 556 line to the 605 line to take into account your motion between sights, and in this way find both latitude and longitude. Note that the angle between the 556 line and the 605 line is greater than 30°, meaning the bearing of the sun had changed sufficiently. The angle between successive sun lines equals the change in the sun's bearing, and for a good fix this angle should be 30° or greater.

To do the chart work, mark off 49 miles on the DR track starting at the point where the 556 LAN line crosses the DR track. Then use parallel rulers to move the 556 line up the DR track to this point, and re-draw the advanced 556 line. The advanced line is labeled 556 —> 605.

Your position at log 605 is then the intersection of the advanced line with the 605 sun line. At this point you abandon your old DR track and start a new one.

It is also good practice to record in your logbook how far and in what direction your DR was off. In this example, the boat had sailed off its DR by 24 miles in direction 053. The significance of this error depends on the time of the last fix. If the last fix was 1 day and 100 miles earlier, this error is not so large. In 24 hours this amounts to an effective current of 1 kt. It could also be accounted for in this 1-day run of 100 miles by a smaller, more typical, current of 0.5 kts (a 12-mile error) together with a combined error in both sun lines of about 3 miles, an average helmsmanship error of 3° (a 5-mile error), a leeway of 3° (a 5-mile error), and a log error of 5% (another 5-mile error).

These errors add up to about 30 miles. If these errors were unrelated to each other, it would be statistically very unlikely that they would all be in the same direction. The net error would be less than 30 miles. However, sailing to weather in strong winds and big seas these errors of navigation are not unrelated; they do, in fact, tend to be in the same direction. Figure 6.3-2 shows how you can extend this process when you have courses changes between sights.

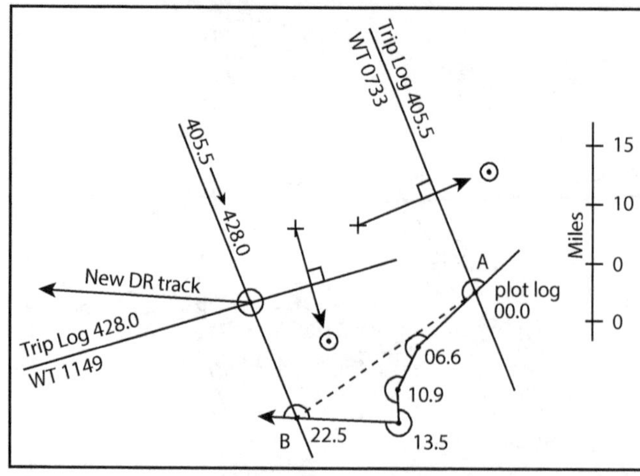

Figure 6.3-2 *A running fix between two sun lines corrected for course changes between sights. The total distance run between sights was 22.5 miles with three course changes, so we have to figure the course made good to do the advancement. Sometimes you can read the course and distance made good between sights from the ongoing DR plot, but It is often best to construct a special DR plot as shown. Then we advance from A to B as if that is what we sailed. In other words, we always advance along the course made good between sights (dotted line). This plot could then be corrected for current as shown in Figure 6.2-2.*

6.4 Exercises on Running Fixes

Set up a universal plotting sheet with mid Lat = 30° N and mid Lon = 145° W. Also draw in the meridians 143° through 147° W. The notation "AP" means assumed position (a-Lat, a-Lon). All problems will fit on this sheet.

(1) Example with solution: Morning sun line taken at log 606 is: AP(31° N, 143° 12' W); Zn = 130°; a = 8' A. Your course is 260° T. Later on your latitude is found from an LAN sight to be 31° 15' N, and the log read 632 at LAN. Do a running fix to find your Lat and Lon at log 632.

Example (1) solution: As shown in Figure 6.4-1, plot the 606 sun line LOP in the regular way. Plot the 632 LAN lat line—a straight line across the chart at the measured latitude. At any point "A" on the 606 LOP draw in your course line at 260° T. Subtract log readings to find the distance run between sights: 632 - 606 = 26 miles. Mark off this distance on your course line starting at the point A. Use parallel rulers to move the 606 line to this end point, and

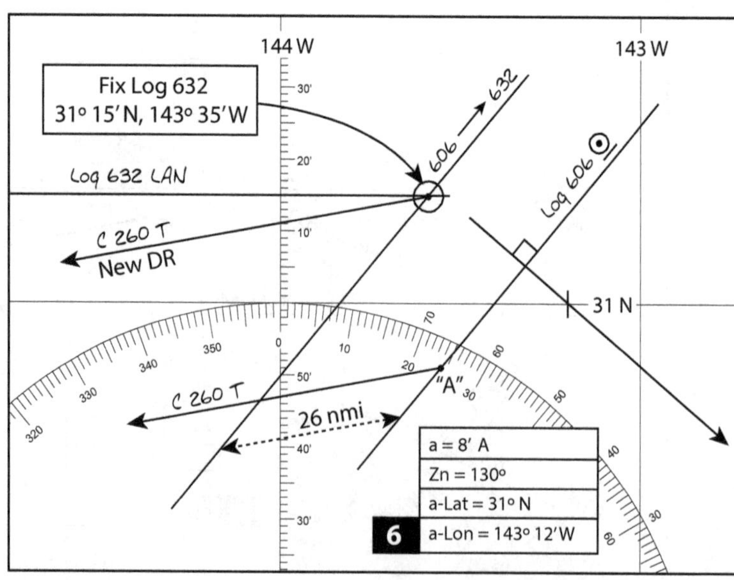

Figure 6.4-1 *Running fix between sun line and LAN, from Ex. 6.4 (1).*

re-draw the advanced 606 line. Label it 606 —> 632. Your running fix (shown in Figure 6.4-1) is the intersection of this advanced line and the 632 LAN line.

(2) Morning sun line at log 414: AP(30° N, 144° 20' W); Zn = 146°; a = 3' T. Afternoon sun line at log 450: AP(29° N, 144° 39' W); Zn = 190°; a = 10' A. Your course between sights was 200 T. What is your position at log 450?

(3) Early afternoon sun line at log 863: AP(30° N, 145° 50' W); Zn = 212°; a = 18' T. Later afternoon sun line at log 878: AP(30° N, 146° 23' W); Zn = 274; a = 13' T. Your course between sights was 320 T. What is your position at log 878?

(4) First sun line at log 955: AP(31° N, 145° 08' W); Zn = 113°; a = 7' T. Second sun line at log 983: AP(31° N, 145° 48' W); Zn = 164°; a = 12' A. The course between sights was 310° T. What is your position at log 983?

6.5 Running Fix with Sun lines #6 and #7

Description

This is a realistic running fix problem from two sets of sun lines that we will use to illustrate several things. It can be worked in the standard way and full solutions are provided for sight reduction by Pub. 249. All necessary tables are included in the Table Selections.

The first thing this problem will illustrate about running fixes is that the plotting can get messy at times; that is, there will be many lines on the plotting sheet, so you must label lines carefully to keep track of which line is which. Often previously placed labels must be erased and relocated to clean up the region of interest. Without careful labels, it is sometimes even difficult to tell which intersection is the fix.

The Exercise

On October 27th, 1978 you are sailing on course 195 True at a speed of 8.0 kts. Your DR position at 0630 WT is 45° 53' N, 131° 24' W, at which time the log read 596.0 miles. You desire to find an afternoon position by sun alone using a running fix. The running fix will be between two sun lines, one at mid morning and the other just after midday. Your course and speed remain constant throughout the day. For this problem: HE = 10 ft., IC = 1.8' on the scale, ZD = +8h and WE = 6s Fast (i.e., UTC = WT + 8h - 6s).

Between 0945 and 0955 WT, you take a series of five sun lines a minute or two apart. After analyzing them in a method we cover later, you decide the following is the best representative of a sun line at that time: Hs = 21° 18.3' LL at WT 09h 51m 20s. The corresponding log reading was 622.8.

You carry on until 1300 and then take another series of sun lines and decide that the best average for this set of sights was: Hs = 31° 10.4' LL at WT 13h 06m 55s, with a corresponding log reading of 648.9.

Find your position at 1307 WT by doing a running fix between the two sun lines. Try this first on your own without checking details of the solution. The answer is on the plot following the completed work forms. We call the first Sun #6 and the second Sun #7.

Procedure

(1) Set up a plotting sheet; plot the 0630 position; lay out the course; and find the DR positions for 0951 and 1307 WT by marking off the course DR track with the logged runs. (Take a peek at the solution work forms in the Answers section to check your answers, as it will cost much in time if these are off to begin with.)

(2) Do the sight reductions of the two sun lines and then plot them. (Again, check the solutions before going on.)

(3) Figure the distance run between sights by subtracting log readings (26.1 miles), and then advance the first line to the second by this amount in direction 195 T. The advanced line should cross the 1307 line at the position marked on the answer plot.

Filled-out forms and plots for the intersection fix are in the Answers section.

Note on the Time of Running Fixes

The time you must wait between sights to get a bearing separation of 30° or more depends on how fast the bearing of the sun changes with time. If the noon height of the sun is less than halfway up the sky (Hs less than about 45°), then the sun's bearing throughout the day changes at about 15° per hour. If the noon sun is higher than this, then its bearing changes more slowly than this in the mornings and afternoons, and faster near midday. As a general rule, the time required is about 2 hours.

To see numerically how long you must wait in specific conditions, you can do two sight reductions, one for the present time and one for 2 hours later, and note the change in Zn, the sun's azimuth. The change in Zn is the change in bearing. From this you can estimate how long to wait.

In fact, you do not need to do the full sight reductions. From your DR position figure a-Lat, LHA, Dec, and using Pub. 249 look up the azimuth angle Z. Then recall that LHA increases at 15° per hour, so then with these same values of a-Lat and Dec look up Z for LHA + 30°. The difference

...In Depth

11.15 AM to PM Running Fixes

In the old days when navigators relied on celestial navigation they spent more time on optimizing the procedures. From an old text, we adopt this method of getting the most accurate running fix in the shortest amount of time...

between the two Zs is how much the sun bearing is changing in 2 hours. Z is only the relative bearing, but the change in Zn will be the same as the change in Z.

6.6 More Practice on Running Fixes

Exercise 6.6 contains special practice problems, in an unusual format. Please read through this entire section before starting. These exercises are worked with tables T-23 to T-25. If you are behind in the earlier course work, please skip these and use the time to get caught up. These are more for review and practice.

These exercises give you more practice with the sight reduction tables and choice of assumed position, but they don't provide almanac practice, because all almanac data are all given. These problems also remind you of the differences that apply to sight reductions and plotting when in east longitudes and south latitudes since all combinations are included.

Also, since Ho (not Hs) is given, there is no need for sextant height corrections. Consequently, the UTCs given are not needed. You only need the WTs of the sights to know how much to advance each of the lines—we don't need to know our distance run figured to the second since our speed and course won't be that accurate to begin with.

In each case, we are given three sun lines but you only need two for a fix. In general the first and the last will intersect at the best angle, so you could omit the middle one. It is there for more practice if you want it, or as a double-check on your answer—in fact, the real reason the third is there is because these are modeled after a type of USCG exam question, and that is the way they are provided! This explains why the speeds in these problems are faster than typical sailboat speeds, but this has no effect of the value of these for practice; a navy destroyer and a 30-ft sailboat do running fixes at sea in precisely the same manner.

We use times in these problems to mark DR positions instead of log readings. Generally log readings are a better way to do it, but this gives you practice with speed, time, and distance, which you will need if your log quits working.

Assuming you know how to look up Dec and GHA in the almanac, these problems are your graduation test for sun lines. Do as many as you have time for. Note that these are for latitudes that are not covered in the standard tables we use elsewhere in the book, so special sections of Pub. 249 are included for these problems. If you have your own tables, you can use them. These tables are also available in full as free downloads online (www.starpath.com/navpubs). Follow the example in Figure 6.6-1 as you work through the procedure.

Procedure

STEP (1). Set up a universal plotting sheet centered near the given DR position. Remember, in south latitudes that latitude increases down the page, opposite to the printed scale. Also double-check that you have eastern longitudes increasing toward the east, to the right, and so forth. If this is done wrong to begin with, much time is lost in the practice.

Plot the given initial position and lay off the given course from that point. Double check it. Using the speed and WTs given, figure the distance run from the given position to each of the other three WTs. Using dividers lay off these distances to mark the three DR positions. The proper DR positions for each line are given in the answers, so you can check yourself at this point if you like. At the end of STEP (1) you should have a course line drawn across your plotting sheet with four DR positions marked on it (the initial position and then the positions at each of the sights. Label these positions with the appropriate WTs).

STEP (2). We will do the last LOP first, which can save time in this practice exercise because we know the answers. Normally you would plot first sights first. Now do the sight reduction for the last sight and plot this LOP: Look at the last DR position and compare it with the given GHA of the sun to pick your Assumed Longitude, and from these figure the LHA. Then round off the DR-Lat to the nearest whole degree for the Assumed Latitude. With LHA, Dec (given), and Lat, go to the special section of Sight Reduction Tables (T-23, Tables Selections) to find Hc, d, and Z. Convert Z to Zn (remember there are different rules for N and S latitudes), correct Hc for the d-correction, and then figure the a-value by comparing Hc with the Ho that is given. Plot the LOP neatly and carefully, and label it with its WT.

STEP (3). To save time on your practice, you might crib a bit here and check that the answer does lie along this last LOP. Since we want position at the last WT, the answer must be along this line, we just don't know where until we advance an earlier line. (Of course you won't have this luxury in the ocean). If your LOP does not go through the answer, then the LOP or plotting is wrong and we might as well stop here to look for the problem. The proper a-Lat and a-Lon are listed in the answers to check that stage.

STEP (4). Now do the sight reduction for the first or second line just as you did for the last one. Then plot it and advance it to get the running fix. For more practice you can reduce, plot, and advance both of the earlier lines. They should give the same answer.

The problems in Exercise 6.6 require careful plotting, so a quick look to the answers might help at each stage to be sure you are advancing the correct amount. Again, start with just first and third sights, and then add the middle one if you want still more practice.

DR position at 0900 WT, Aug. 13, 1982 is 28° 30.4' S, 62° 33.2' E, Course 010° T, Speed 15 kts. While on this course, the 3 sun lines listed below were taken. Find your latitude and longitude at 1620 WT by plotting all 3 lines and advancing the first two to the time of the last one.

WT	UTC	GHA sun	Ho	Dec
1016	06h 16m 10s	272° 48.9'	40° 59.9'	N 14° 45.4'
1230	08h 30m 05s	306° 18.1'	46° 47.1'	N 14° 43.9'
1620	12h 20m 13s	003° 50.3'	13° 06.0'	N 14° 40.8'

Answer: 26° 38.7' S, 62° 58.9' E.

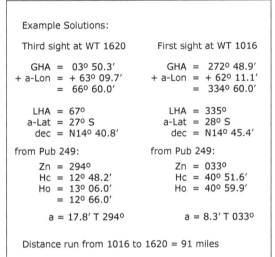

Example Solutions:

Third sight at WT 1620

GHA = 03° 50.3'
+ a-Lon = + 63° 09.7'
= 66° 60.0'

LHA = 67°
a-Lat = 27° S
dec = N14° 40.8'

from Pub 249:

Zn = 294°
Hc = 12° 48.2'
Ho = 13° 06.0'
= 12° 66.0'

a = 17.8' T 294°

First sight at WT 1016

GHA = 272° 48.9'
+ a-Lon = + 62° 11.1'
= 334° 60.0'

LHA = 335°
a-Lat = 28° S
dec = N14° 45.4'

from Pub 249:

Zn = 033°
Hc = 40° 51.6'
Ho = 40° 59.9'

a = 8.3' T 033°

Distance run from 1016 to 1620 = 91 miles

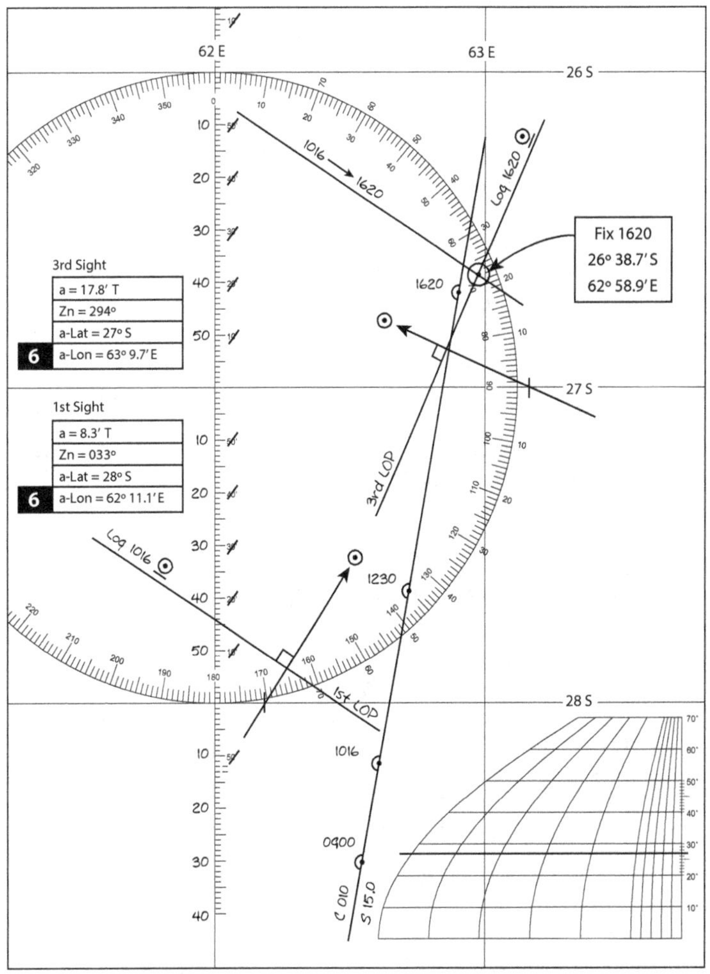

Figure 6.6-1 *A worked example of the type of problem given in Exercise 6.6. There are details for each step given in the Answers for each one.*

...In Depth

11.16 An Ocean-going Nav Station

Sometimes where we do our work and the tools we use are crucial to the work we do. Here we list a few conclusions we have come to about these matters...

...In Depth

11.17 Offshore Navigation Checklist

Sailors are renown for having a list of lists as the departure approaches, so looking ahead here are a few things to consider for the nav station...

Exercise 6.6 Practice With Running Fixes

Please check the Answers Section as you work each of these problems. All the intermediate steps are provided. Remember, you must DR from the given initial time to the time of the first sight to start off.

(1) DR position at 0900 WT, Aug. 12, 1982 was 21° 56.4' N, 124° 10.4' W. Course 250° T, Speed 13 kts. Find 1425 position from the three sun lines listed.

WT	UTC	GHA sun	Ho	Dec
1015	18h 16m 08s	092° 47.1'	59° 09.7'	N 14° 54.5'
1156	19h 57m 15s	118° 04.1'	80° 38.0'	N 14° 53.2'
1425	22h 26m 10s	155° 18.1'	60° 54.9'	N 14° 51.3'

(2) DR position at 0840 WT, Dec. 22, 1982 was 28° 24.2' N, 06° 18.2' W. Course 120° T, Speed 9 kts. Find 1420 position from the 3 sun lines listed.

WT	UTC	GHA sun	Ho	Dec
1015	10h 14m 30s	334° 00.4'	29° 50.8'	S 23° 26.5'
1200	11h 59m 40s	000° 17.4'	38° 12.6'	S 23° 26.4'
1420	14h 19m 07s	035° 08.4'	31° 10.7'	S 23° 26.4'

(3) DR position at 0800 WT, July 13, 1982 was 28° 14.1' N, 135° 37.3'E.
Course 190° T, Speed 11 kts. Find 1646 position from the 3 sun lines listed.

WT	UTC	GHA sun	Ho	Dec
1013	01h 12m 15s	196° 39.9'	64° 04.5'	N 21° 54.1'
1255	03h 54m 28s	237° 12.9'	77° 18.6'	N 21° 53.1'
1646	05h 45m 10s	264° 53.3'	53° 16.2'	N 21° 52.5'

(4) DR position at 0815 WT, July 12, 1982 was 20° 05.8' S, 32° 13.0' W. Course 220° T, Speed 10 kts. Find 1404 position from the 3 sun lines listed.

WT	UTC	GHA sun	Ho	Dec
1018	12h 18m 20s	003° 12.0'	38° 49.9'	N 21° 58.6'
1255	14h 55m 36s	042° 30.8'	46° 14.4'	N 21° 57.7'
1404	16h 04m 22s	059° 42.2'	39° 48.7'	N 21° 57.3'

(5) DR position at 0815 WT, Mar. 30, 1982 was 29° 46.7' S, 36° 25.9' E. Course 295° T, Speed 12 kts. Find 1455 position from the 3 sun lines listed.

WT	UTC	GHA sun	Ho	Dec
1000	08h 01m 05s	299° 06.8'	49° 04.8'	N 3° 41.2'
1235	10h 36m 00s	337° 51.1'	54° 33.3'	N 3° 43.7'
1455	12h 56m 20s	012° 56.5'	33° 31.2'	N 3° 46.0'

6.7 New Terminology

running fix

advanced LOP

retired LOP

leeway

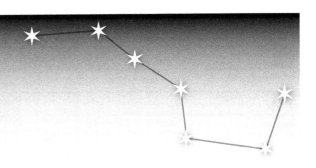

CHAPTER 7
STAR SIGHTS

7.1 Introduction

The true power of celestial navigation for position fixing comes with the use of the stars. Sun sights are often considered easier, in the sense that they can be taken anytime of day, and the sun is usually perceived as easier to find in the sky than is some specific star in its background of myriads—but these are, for the most part, uninformed biases.

The disadvantage of the sun is that it gives only one LOP, and after completing the running fix some time later, the accuracy of the final fix is limited by the accuracy of the DR between the two sights. In actual practice, the total time devoted to getting a fix from star sights will be shorter than from sun sights, and the star results will be more accurate.

Also, as we shall see, when done right, it is actually easier and usually faster to set up the sextant for a particular star sight and have it ready to be measured than it is to get the sun set up in the sextant with the proper shades in place. The special preparation needed for the star sights takes just minutes. The process is called precomputing star sights. We postpone this process till Chapter 10 on Star Identification purely so we can complete the learning of sight reductions for all bodies first—while we are warmed up and in the process of mastering these procedures.

The main goal of this chapter is just to learn and practice the sight reduction of stars, but before leaving the chapter, please review Sections 1.2 and 1.3 on the overall picture of taking a star sight, along with Section 5.2 on twilight times—we usually take star sights between nautical and civil twilight.

The most basic star sight, in a sense, is a sight of Polaris, the North Star. A sight of this special star, which is essentially on our meridian at all times, is analogous to the LAN sight of the sun on our meridian. The full sight reduction collapses to the adding and subtracting of a few numbers. Latitude by Polaris alone is covered at end of this chapter, as it is a special case.

The Star Finder Book includes much information on star motions, colors, terminology, names, etc. along with notes on preparing the sights. If questions arise about terminology or star motions, please refer to Section 3.1 of that book along with the Glossary of this one.

New terms used for specifying star locations are Aries (♈), which is the "Greenwich meridian" of a star globe, and sidereal hour angle (SHA), which is the longitude of a star on the star globe relative to Aries, as shown in Figure 7.7-1.

The process of preparing for star sights and the general subject of star and planet identification is presented in Chapter 10, along with the option to use Pub. 249 Vol. 1 for selected stars. Here we are sticking with Vols. 2 and 3, which cover stars with declinations less than 29°. Other options will be clear shortly.

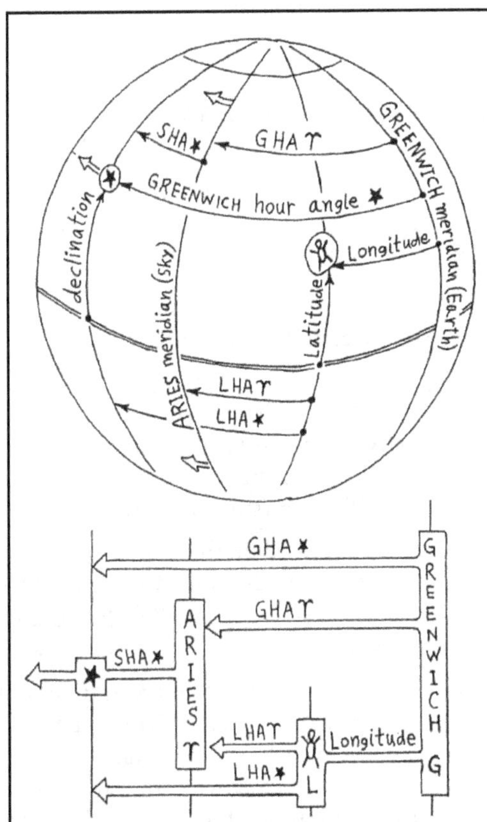

Figure 7.1-1 *Star coordinates. Aries is a specific line through the stars that serves as the Greenwich meridian of the sky. The almanac tells where it is relative to Greenwich at all times. The Sidereal Hour Angle (SHA) is the longitude of the star relative to Aries. It is a permanent property of the star, just as its declination is. GHA of Aries is how far Aries is west of Greenwich; The SHA of a star is how far it is west of Aries. Thus the GHA of star, which is how far it is west of Greenwich, is just the GHA of Aries plus the SHA of the star. Coordinates relative to us are called Local. The Local Hour Angle (LHA) of Aries is how far Aries is west of us. The LHA of the star is how far the star is west of us.*

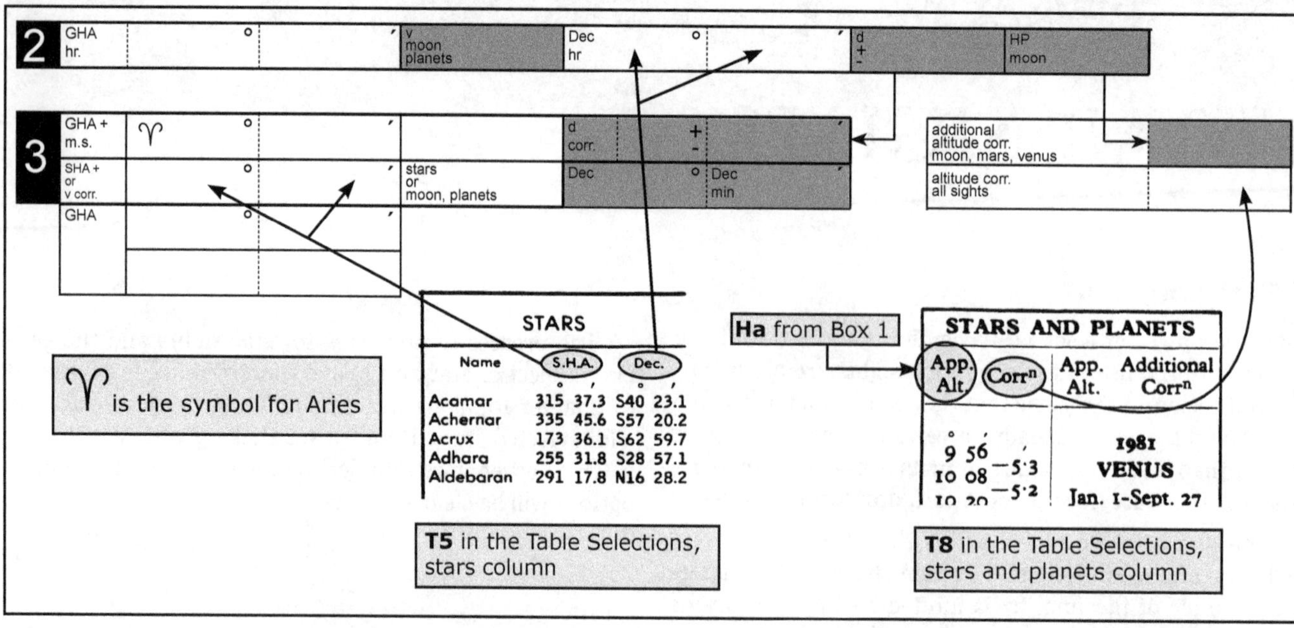

Figure 7.2-1 *Section of a star sight reduction. Except for this special way of getting the GHA of a star, all the rest of the sight reduction is the same. There are also no declination corrections for stars. The LOP plotting is also the same.*

7.2 Sight Reduction of Stars

The sight reduction of stars is nearly identical to that of the sun. If a step here might be unclear, please review the corresponding step use for sun lines. The only differences in the procedures are listed in the following sections.

Differences Between Sun Sights and Star Sights

(1) In filling out BOX 2 from the Daily Pages of the *Nautical Almanac* record the declination of the star, and in the space marked GHA record the GHA of Aries. We will also get one extra number at this point that we did not use for the sun—the SHA of the star (sidereal hour angle).

The GHA of Aries is listed on the Daily Pages, first column to the left of the page. You might want to mark the GHA box with a small Aries symbol (♈) when doing star sights to remind you of that.

Find the declination of the star in the star column on the Daily Pages. The stars are listed alphabetically with the declination given beside each star. For stars there is no d value or d-correction—on a daily scale, the stars do change location in the sky, even though the sky as a whole is rotating above us. Star declinations do not depend on time or date. For any of the three days on each Daily Page, you use the same star column for declination.

Beside the declination in the star column you will find the SHA of the star. Record this in the space provided in BOX 3.

(2) When filling out BOX 3, get the minutes and seconds part of the GHA from the Aries column.

(3) Find the GHA of the star by adding GHA (hr), GHA (m,s), and SHA. Mark GHA with a star if you like to remind yourself that this is the star value.

(4) The final difference between sun and star lines comes when correcting Ha to get Ho for the star. Here you get the altitude correction from the Stars and Planets Table. Altitude corrections for stars are listed right beside the corresponding altitude corrections for the sun.

A completed star sight form (Star # 1) is shown on the next page. Using the *Almanac* data, check that these values all make sense.

The first two star practice sights are shown as taken at the same precise time. It is impossible to actually take sights this way, but there is a good trick for taking a series of sights and then averaging them and assigning them the same sight time. We cover the technique in Chapter 11. Assume that this has been done for these two sights, then fill out the forms and plot the LOPs for a fix. The full forms and plot are in the Answers section.

...In Depth

11.20 Star and Planet Brightness

Notes on the complex system used to specify brightness and tables to make it easier...

Altair Sight Sample, Star #1

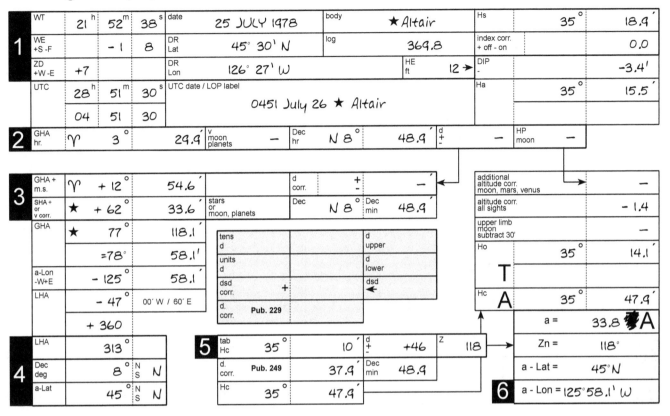

1

WT	21 h	52 m	38 s	date	25 JULY 1978	body	★Altair	Hs	35°	18.9′
WE +S -F		- 1	8	DR Lat	45° 30′ N	log	369.8	index corr. + off - on		0.0
ZD +W -E	+7			DR Lon	126° 27′ W	HE ft	12 →	DIP -		-3.4′
UTC	28 h	51 m	30 s	UTC date / LOP label	0451 July 26 ★ Altair			Ha	35°	15.5′
	04	51	30							

2

GHA hr.	♈ 3°	29.9′	v moon planets	—	Dec hr	N 8°	48.9′	d + -	—	HP moon —

3

GHA + m.s.	♈ + 12°	54.6′		d corr.	+ -	—
SHA + or v corr.	★ + 62°	33.6′	stars or moon, planets	Dec	N 8°	Dec min 48.9′
GHA	★ 77°	118.1′				
	=78°	58.1′				
a-Lon -W+E	- 125°	58.1′				
LHA	- 47°	00′ W / 60′ E				
	+ 360					

tens d		d upper
units d		d lower
dsd corr. +		dsd ←
d. corr. Pub. 229		

additional altitude corr. moon, mars, venus	→	—
altitude corr. all sights		- 1.4
upper limb moon subtract 30'		—
Ho	35°	14.1′
T		
Hc A	35°	47.9′

4

LHA	313°	
Dec deg	8°	N S — N
a-Lat	45°	N S — N

5

tab Hc	35°	10′	d + - +46	Z 118
d. corr. Pub. 249		37.9′	Dec min 48.9	
Hc	35°	47.9′		

6

a =	33.8 A
Zn =	118°
a - Lat =	45° N
a - Lon =	125° 58.1′ W

Z to Zn rules same for all sights

♈ ★ For the first couple sights we added aries and star symbols as a reminder, but these should be added by hand when doing the sights and are skipped later.

7.3 Arcturus Sight Exercise, Star #2

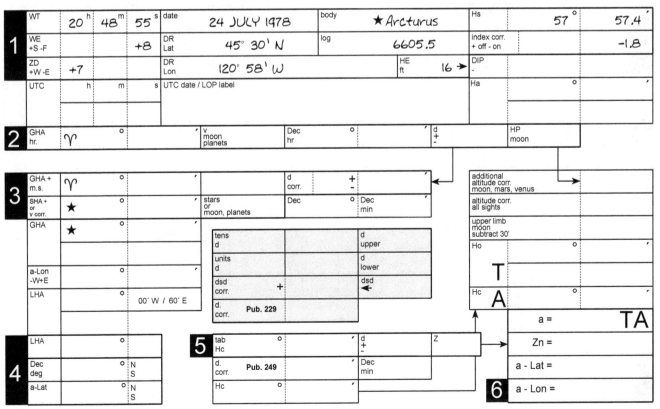

1

WT	20 h	48 m	55 s	date	24 JULY 1978	body	★Arcturus	Hs	57°	57.4′
WE +S -F			+8	DR Lat	45° 30′ N	log	6605.5	index corr. + off - on		-1.8
ZD +W -E	+7			DR Lon	120° 58′ W	HE ft	16 →	DIP -		
UTC	h	m	s	UTC date / LOP label				Ha	°	′

2

GHA hr.	♈ °	′	v moon planets		Dec hr	°	′	d + -		HP moon

3

GHA + m.s.	♈ °	′		d corr.	+ -	′
SHA + or v corr.	★ °	′	stars or moon, planets	Dec	°	Dec min ′
GHA	★ °	′				
a-Lon -W+E	°	′				
LHA	°	00′ W / 60′ E				

tens d		d upper
units d		d lower
dsd corr. +		dsd ←
d. corr. Pub. 229		

additional altitude corr. moon, mars, venus	→	
altitude corr. all sights		
upper limb moon subtract 30'		
Ho	°	′
T		
Hc A	°	′

4

LHA	°	
Dec deg	°	N S
a-Lat	°	N S

5

tab Hc	°	′	d + -	Z
d. corr. Pub. 249		′	Dec min	
Hc	°	′		

6

a =	TA
Zn =	
a - Lat =	
a - Lon =	

7.4 Altair Sight Exercise, Star #3

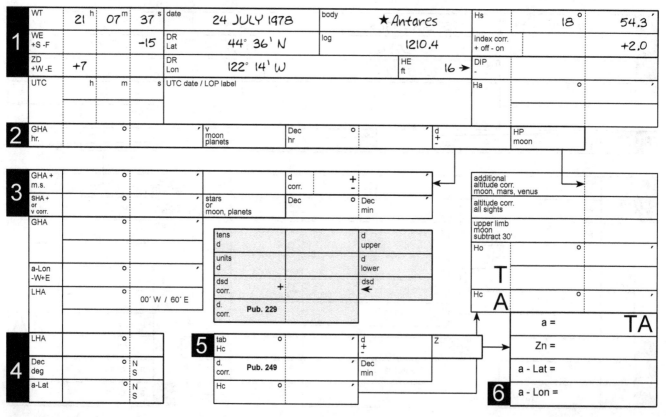

1

WT	21 h	07 m	37 s	date	24 JULY 1978	body	★Altair	Hs	30 °	35.4 ′
WE +S -F			-15	DR Lat	44° 36′ N	log	1210.4	index corr. + off - on		+2.0
ZD +W -E	+7			DR Lon	122° 14′ W	HE ft	16 →	DIP -		
UTC	h	m	s	UTC date / LOP label				Ha	°	′

2

GHA hr.	°	′	v moon planets	Dec hr	°	′	d + -	HP moon

3

GHA + m.s.	°	′		d corr.	+ -	′
SHA + or v corr.	°	′	stars or moon, planets	Dec	°	Dec min ′
GHA	°	′				
a-Lon -W+E	°	′				
LHA	°	00′ W / 60′ E				

tens d		d upper
units d		d lower
dsd corr. +		dsd ←
d. corr. Pub. 229		

additional altitude corr. moon, mars, venus	
altitude corr. all sights	
upper limb moon subtract 30′	
Ho	° ′
Hc	° ′

T A

4

LHA	°	
Dec deg	°	N S
a-Lat	°	N S

5

tab Hc	°	′	d + -	Z
d. corr. Pub. 249		′	Dec min	
Hc	°	′		

6

a =	TA
Zn =	
a - Lat =	
a - Lon =	

7.5 Antares Sight Exercise, Star #4

1

WT	21 h	07 m	37 s	date	24 JULY 1978	body	★Antares	Hs	18 °	54.3 ′
WE +S -F			-15	DR Lat	44° 36′ N	log	1210.4	index corr. + off - on		+2.0
ZD +W -E	+7			DR Lon	122° 14′ W	HE ft	16 →	DIP -		
UTC	h	m	s	UTC date / LOP label				Ha	°	′

2

GHA hr.	°	′	v moon planets	Dec hr	°	′	d + -	HP moon

3

GHA + m.s.	°	′		d corr.	+ -	′
SHA + or v corr.	°	′	stars or moon, planets	Dec	°	Dec min ′
GHA	°	′				
a-Lon -W+E	°	′				
LHA	°	00′ W / 60′ E				

tens d		d upper
units d		d lower
dsd corr. +		dsd ←
d. corr. Pub. 229		

additional altitude corr. moon, mars, venus	
altitude corr. all sights	
upper limb moon subtract 30′	
Ho	° ′
Hc	° ′

T A

4

LHA	°	
Dec deg	°	N S
a-Lat	°	N S

5

tab Hc	°	′	d + -	Z
d. corr. Pub. 249		′	Dec min	
Hc	°	′		

6

a =	TA
Zn =	
a - Lat =	
a - Lon =	

7.6 Arcturus Sight, Star #5

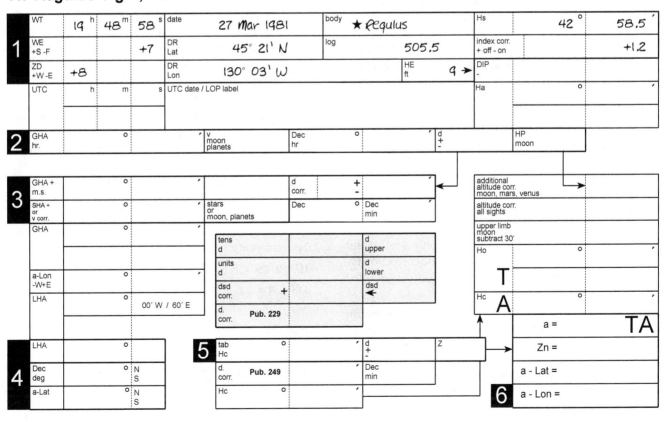

1						
WT	21 h	49 m	25 s	date: 25 JULY 1978	body: ★ Arcturus	Hs: 50° 50.9′
WE +S -F		- 1	08	DR Lat: 45° 30′ N	log: 369.8	index corr. + off - on: 0.0
ZD +W -E	+7			DR Lon: 126° 27′ W	HE ft: 12 →	DIP -
UTC	h	m	s	UTC date / LOP label		Ha ° ′

2						
GHA hr.	° ′	v moon planets	Dec hr	° ′	d + -	HP moon

3					
GHA + m.s.	° ′		d corr.	+ -	′
SHA + or v corr.	° ′	stars or moon, planets	Dec	°	Dec min ′
GHA	° ′				
a-Lon -W+E	° ′				
LHA	° 00′ W / 60′ E				

Pub. 229		
tens d		d upper
units d		d lower
dsd corr. +		dsd ←
d. corr.		

additional altitude corr. moon, mars, venus	
altitude corr. all sights	
upper limb moon subtract 30′	
Ho	° ′
Hc	° ′

4		
LHA	°	
Dec deg	°	N S
a-Lat	°	N S

5				
tab Hc	° ′		d + -	Z
d. corr.	Pub. 249 ′		Dec min	
Hc	° ′			

6 TA
a =
Zn =
a - Lat =
a - Lon =

7.7 Regulus Sight, Star #6

1						
WT	19 h	48 m	58 s	date: 27 Mar 1981	body: ★ Regulus	Hs: 42° 58.5′
WE +S -F			+7	DR Lat: 45° 21′ N	log: 505.5	index corr. + off - on: +1.2
ZD +W -E	+8			DR Lon: 130° 03′ W	HE ft: 9 →	DIP -
UTC	h	m	s	UTC date / LOP label		Ha ° ′

2						
GHA hr.	° ′	v moon planets	Dec hr	° ′	d + -	HP moon

3					
GHA + m.s.	° ′		d corr.	+ -	′
SHA + or v corr.	° ′	stars or moon, planets	Dec	°	Dec min ′
GHA	° ′				
a-Lon -W+E	° ′				
LHA	° 00′ W / 60′ E				

Pub. 229		
tens d		d upper
units d		d lower
dsd corr. +		dsd ←
d. corr.		

additional altitude corr. moon, mars, venus	
altitude corr. all sights	
upper limb moon subtract 30′	
Ho	° ′
Hc	° ′

4		
LHA	°	
Dec deg	°	N S
a-Lat	°	N S

5				
tab Hc	° ′		d + -	Z
d. corr.	Pub. 249 ′		Dec min	
Hc	° ′			

6 TA
a =
Zn =
a - Lat =
a - Lon =

7.8 Latitude by Polaris

When sailing in the Northern Hemisphere at latitudes above 5° or so, there is an especially easy way to find your latitude at twilight using the North Star, Polaris. The sight is easy to prepare for and quick to analyze for latitude.

Taking the Sight

At twilight, with watch at hand, set your sextant to Hs = DR-Lat. Using the steering compass as a guide, face due north and scan the horizon with the sextant. You will see Polaris in the sextant not far from the horizon seen in the sextant. Using the micrometer drum, bring the star to the horizon so that it just touches the horizon at its lowest point as you rock the sextant. When this is achieved, record the WT and Hs, and also record your log reading.

With the sextant preset this way to the right height, looking in the right direction, you can often see this star very early in twilight, usually before it can be seen with the naked eye. This is especially true if your sextant has a 4x40 telescope and the sky is clear. This technique of presetting the sextant is very valuable for star sights because it extends the useful length of twilight, and it makes finding the right star very easy. Also, the earlier in evening twilight that you can take the sight, the sharper the horizon will be, and it is the sharpness of the horizon that usually determines the accuracy of celestial sights.

Polaris is not a bright star, so this advantage is not as great here as it is with bright stars like Vega and Capella, which you can almost always see through the telescope of a preset sextant before you can with your naked eye. For stars other than Polaris, however, precomputing star heights is slightly more involved than just setting your sextant at your DR-Lat. It takes a few minutes of computation to figure out the right heights and directions. Polaris is simple to figure because it is always due north at a height equal to your DR-Lat.

Finding Latitude

(1) The first step in the short sight reduction of Polaris sights is the same as it is for any sight; we convert Hs, the sextant height, to Ho, the observed height. This is done the same way for all sights: Ha = Hs ± IC - Dip, and then Ho = Ha - altitude correction.

As noted earlier, the only difference between sun and stars at this stage is the table we get the altitude correction from. For stars this correction (which is only a refraction correction) is listed next to the sun's altitude correction table on the inside of the front cover of the *Nautical Almanac* (T-8 in the Table Selections).

(2) Once we have Ho of Polaris, we must make several small corrections to it to take into account the motion of Polaris around the true north pole of the sky. Start by converting the WT of the sight to UTC by removing the Watch Error and adding the Zone Description of the watch.

(3) Following a sample in Figure 7.8-1, turn to the proper Daily Page of the *Nautical Almanac* (T-1 through T-6) and look up the GHA of Aries at the hour of the sight. Then turn to the Increments and Corrections pages (T-9 through T-12) to find the minutes and seconds part of the GHA of Aries. Add this correction to the hours part to get the GHA of Aries at the time of the sight.

(4) Now find the LHA of Aries, which is as before, when sailing in western longitudes the GHA of Aries minus your DR-Lon (West). In eastern longitudes you find the LHA by adding your DR-Lon (East) to the GHA of Aries. Then round off the LHA to the nearest whole degree. If the result is greater than 360°, subtract 360°, and if the result is negative, add 360°.

Aries is the Greenwich Meridian of the sky. In this step we are finding how far west of us this reference line lies. When we know this we know which part of the sky is overhead, and from this the tables can tell us where Polaris is on its daily trip around the pole.

(5) Now turn to the Polaris Tables at the back of the *Nautical Almanac* (Table T-22). Here we will find three corrections; the largest depends on LHA Aries, the two smaller ones depend on the month of the sight and the DR-Lat. Note that at the bottom of the Polaris corrections pages in the *Nautical Almanac* they give full instructions for finding latitude from Polaris. After a little practice, those will probably be the only instructions you need for this process.

$$\text{Latitude} = \text{Ho} - 1^\circ + a0 + a1 + a2$$

Note that in the Polaris instructions the Almanac calls Ho the "Apparent altitude (corrected for refraction)." They know this is the same as Ho, and they know that nowhere in the *Almanac* is the altitude correction of a star called a refraction correction, but they do this nevertheless. They do things like this to help support navigation schools.

Here is an example that is worked out on the next several pages. You can follow the time conversions and Hs to Ho corrections using the work form, as shown. Sample tables show where the corrections come from.

Starting with this information:

WT = 18h 50m 30s, WE = 25s Fast, ZD = +9h

Date = 24 October 1978

Hs Polaris = 29° 15.5'

IC = 2' on, HE = 9 ft

DR-Lat = 29° 5' N DR-Lon = 148° 30' W

Find your Latitude.

The answer, displayed in Figure 7.8-2 is,

Lat = 29° 10.1' N.

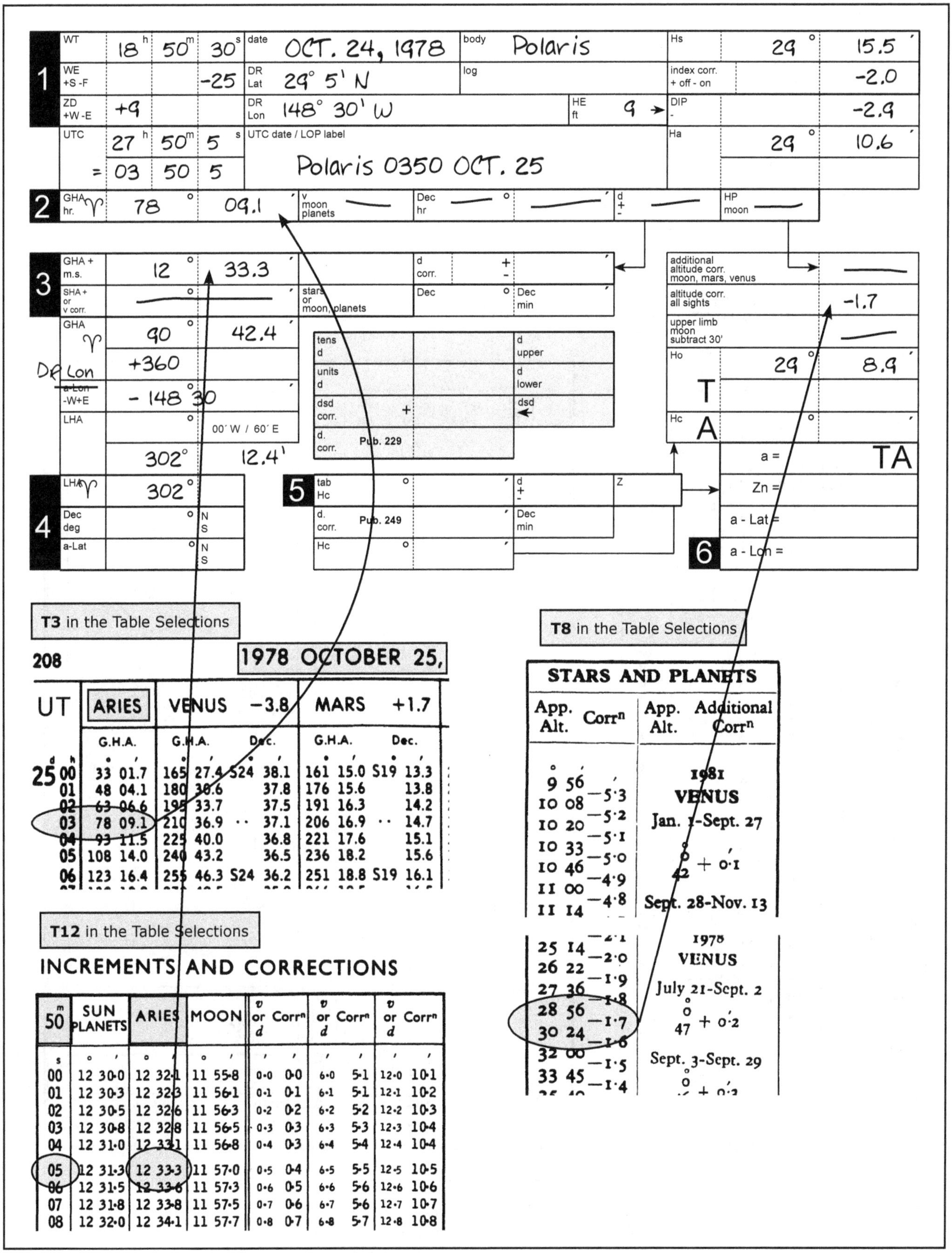

Figure 7.8-1 *Section of a work form used to figure LHA Aries and the observed height of Polaris, along with related pages from the Nautical Almanac.*

Latitude = Apparent altitude (corrected for refraction) $- 1° + a_0 + a_1 + a_2$

The table is entered with L.H.A. Aries to determine the column to be used; each column refers to a range of 10°. a_0 is taken, with mental interpolation, from the upper table with the units of L.H.A. Aries in degrees as argument; a_1, a_2 are taken, without interpolation, from the second and third tables with arguments latitude and month respectively. a_0, a_1, a_2 are always positive. The final table gives the azimuth of *Polaris*.

Almanac Instructions

ILLUSTRATION
On 1978 April 21 at G.M.T. $23^h 18^m 56^s$ in longitude W. 37° 14′ the apparent altitude (corrected for refraction), *Ho*, of *Polaris* was 49° 31′·6.

DR-Lat = 50° N

From the daily pages:	° ′
G.H.A. Aries (23^h)	194 39·4
Increment ($18^m 56^s$)	4 44·8
Longitude (west)	−37 14
L.H.A. Aries	162 10

	° ′
Ho	49 31·6
a_0 (argument 162° 10′)	1 30·8
a_1 (lat. 50° approx.)	0·6
a_2 (April)	0·9
Sum − 1° = Lat. =	50 03·9

Almanac Example

POLARIS (POLE STAR) TABLES, 1978

FOR DETERMINING LATITUDE FROM SEXTANT ALTITUDE AND FOR AZIMUTH

275

L.H.A. ARIES	120°–129°	130°–139°	140°–149°	150°–159°	160°–169°
	a_0	a_0	a_0	a_0	a_0
°	° ′	° ′	° ′	° ′	° ′
0	0 56·8	1 05·5	1 14·0	1 22·0	1 29·3
1	57·7	06·4	14·8	22·8	30·0
2	58·6	07·2	15·7	23·5	30·7
3	0 59·4	08·1	16·5	24·3	31·3
4	1 00·3	09·0	17·3	25·0	32·0
5	1 01·2	1 09·8	1 18·1	1 25·8	1 32·6
6	02·1	10·7	18·9	26·5	33·3
7	02·9	11·5	19·7	27·2	33·9
8	03·8	12·3	20·5	27·9	34·5
9	04·7	13·2	21·3	28·6	35·1
10	1 05·5	1 14·0	1 22·0	1 29·3	1 35·7
Lat.	a_1	a_1	a_1	a_1	a_1
°	′	′	′	′	′
0	0·2	0·2	0·2	0·3	0·4
10	·2	·2	·3	·3	·4
20	·3	·3	·3	·4	·4
30	·4	·4	·4	·4	·5
40	0·5	0·5	0·5	0·5	0·5
45	·5	·5	·5	·6	·6
50	·6	·6	·6	·6	·6
55	·7	·7	·7	·7	·6
60	·8	·8	·8	·7	·7
62	0·9	0·8	0·8	0·8	0·7
64	0·9	0·9	·9	·8	·8
66	1·0	1·0	0·9	·9	·8
68	1·1	1·0	1·0	0·9	0·9
Month	a_2	a_2	a_2	a_2	a_2
	′	′	′	′	′
Jan.	0·6	0·6	0·6	0·6	0·5
Feb.	·8	·7	·7	·7	·7
Mar.	0·9	0·9	0·9	0·8	·8
Apr.	1·0	1·0	1·0	1·0	0·9
May	0·9	1·0	1·0	1·0	1·0
June	·8	0·9	0·9	1·0	1·0
July	0·7	0·7	0·8	0·9	0·9
Aug.	·5	·6	·6	·7	·8
Sept.	·4	·4	·5	·5	·6
Oct.	0·3	0·3	0·3	0·3	0·4
Nov.	·2	·2	·2	·2	·3
Dec.	0·3	0·3	0·2	0·2	0·2

Almanac Example

Textbook Example

L.H.A. ARIES	290°–299°	300°–309°	310°–319°
	a_0	a_0	a_0
°	° ′	° ′	° ′
0	1 10·3	1 01·6	0 52·9
1	09·4	1 00·8	52·1
2	08·6	0 59.9	51·2
3	07·7	59·0	50·3
4	06·8	58·2	49·5
5	1 06·0	0 57·3	0 48·6
6	05·1	56·4	47·8
7	04·3	55·5	46·9
8	03·4	54·7	46·1
9	02·5	53·8	45·2
10	1 01·6	0 52·9	0 44·4
Lat.	a_1	a_1	a_1
°	′	′	′
0	0·2	0·2	0·2
10	·2	·2	·2
20	·3	·3	·3
30	·4	·4	·4
40	0·5	0·5	0·5
45	·5	·5	·5
50	·6	·6	·6
55	·7	·7	·7
60	·8	·8	·8
62	0·8	0·9	0·8
64	0·9	0·9	0·9
66	1·0	1·0	1·0
68	1·1	1·1	1·0
Month	a_2	a_2	a_2
	′	′	′
Jan.	0·6	0·6	0·6
Feb.	·4	·4	·5
Mar.	·3	·3	·3
Apr.	0·3	0·2	0·2
May	·3	·3	·2
June	·4	·4	·3
July	0·6	0·5	0·5
Aug.	·8	·7	·6
Sept.	·9	·8	·8
Oct.	0·9	0·9	0·9
Nov.	·9	1·0	1·0
Dec.	0·8	0·9	0·9

T22 in the Table Selections

LHA ♈ = 302°
a_0 = 59.7′

DR Lat = 29° 5′
a_1 = 0.4′

month = Oct.
a_2 = 0.9′

Ho	29° 8.9′
−1°	− 1°
+ a_0	+ 59.7′
+ a_1	+ 0.4′
+ a_2	+ 0.9′

Lat = 29° 9.9′

Figure 7.8-2 *Top shows instructions and example from the* Nautical Almanac *on how to do Latitude by Polaris. Left column shows the required tables from the almanac, with the values marked for the example given in the almanac at the top of the page. On the right are the corresponding tables marked for the example we use in this text from previous few pages. Notice in the almanac example, they interpolated for the 10′ of LHA, and used a0= 30.8′ and not just the 30.7′ for 162° 00′. In our example we do the same, interpolating for the 12.4′ of LHA Aries, namely: 59.9 - (12.4/60) x (59.9 - 59.0) = 59.7′.*

Notice that when finding the ao correction (Figure 7.8-2) there can sometimes be a notable difference between successive whole degrees of LHA. As a first step we just rounded LHA off as we have done for all sights so far, but in this case if you do notice a large difference you might keep the minutes part of the LHA and then interpolate for ao. In rare cases this could improve your result by up to 0.4'.

7.9 Practice with Latitude by Polaris

For each of these exercises the Index Correction is 2.0' on the scale, and the Height of Eye is 9 ft. This means that Ha = Hs - 2.0' - 2.9' = Hs - 4.9'. You must look up the altitude correction for each one to get Ho from the Ha.

Work (1) on your own now (the sample just given), and then check the sample as needed. The solutions for (2) are outlined in the Answers, and the final answers for last two are given.

(1) Hs = 29° 15.5', UTC = 03h 50m 05s, October 25th, 1978
DR position is 29° 05' N, 148° 30' W. Latitude = ?

(2) Hs = 25° 02.0', UTC = 03h 49m 20s, July 24th, 1978
DR position is 25° 00' N, 60° 13' W. Latitude = ?

(3) Hs = 42° 31.2', UTC = 20h 04m 10s, July 25th, 1978
DR position is 42° 40' N, 30° 10' E. Latitude = ?

(4) Hs = 44° 55.6', UTC = 05h 04m 00s, July 26th, 1978
DR position is 45° 28' N, 126° 30' W. Latitude = ?

(5) Are the latitudes you get North or South, and why?

7.10 Star Names

For navigational purposes, stars have two naming conventions: proper names such as Canopus or a Greek letter designation, called the Bayer system, such as Alpha Carinae, meaning the alpha star of the constellation Carina. The alpha star means most dominate, or if all are about the same brightness, the first one in a logical sequence of numbering, as in the Big Dipper, which goes alphabetically from Alpha Ursa Majoris (Dubhe) at tip of the cup to Eta Ursa Majoris (Alkaid) at the end of the handle. Officially the constellation name in this system is in the Latin genitive form (belonging to), but Alpha Ursa Major would be adequate for record keeping and communications. All magnitude-1 stars (see Section 11.20 on brightness and magnitude) and most magnitude-2 stars have proper names. Less bright stars typically do not.

The 57 stars listed on the daily pages are called *navigational stars*. They are also on the Index to Selected Stars in the back of the Almanac (page xxxiii), listed both alphabetically and by their unique permanent number. These are bright stars, magnitude 1 or 2, but they are not chosen by brightness alone, but rather selected uniformly around the sky so that several of them will be in view at all times from any location. Polaris is notably not on that list, though it is used routinely for navigation.

There are another 116 stars listed in the back of the Almanac that do not show up on the daily pages. That full list (174 stars) includes the navigational stars, and is presented in a unique manner. The first half of the year (January to June) lists the stars by their Bayer designation, whereas from July to December they are listed by their proper names. This can be an important nuance to know when it comes to some star ID questions. All navigational stars have a proper name. For more info see the classic Victorian text *Star Names Their Lore and Meaning* by Richard Hinckley Allen, which is online.

7.11 New Terminology

2102-D Star Finder

Aries

GHA Aries

LHA Aries

magnitude

navigational stars

Polaris sight

sidereal hour angle (SHA)

...In Depth

11.18 Checking a Sextant with Stars

We have many ways to check the index correction of a sextant, but that is just an offset; it does not tell us if the actual angles being measured are correct. This note—definitely in the special topics category—tells how we can check the reading by measuring the diagonal angle *between* two stars...

...In Depth

11.19 Artificial Horizons

Usually if we have any water at all near by we get the best sextant practice using the Dip Short method. With no convenient water nearby, we can always take sights using an artificial horizon from any location. This note explains the procedure and some options...

Star charts from the *Nautical Almanac*.

STAR CHARTS

Southern Hemisphere and more equatorial stars are at the end of Chapter 8.

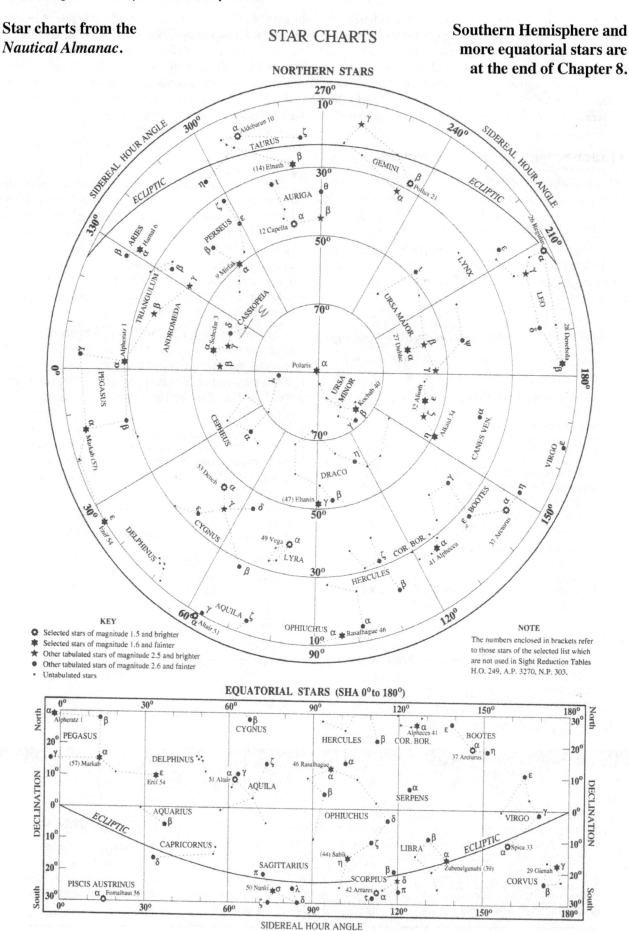

NORTHERN STARS

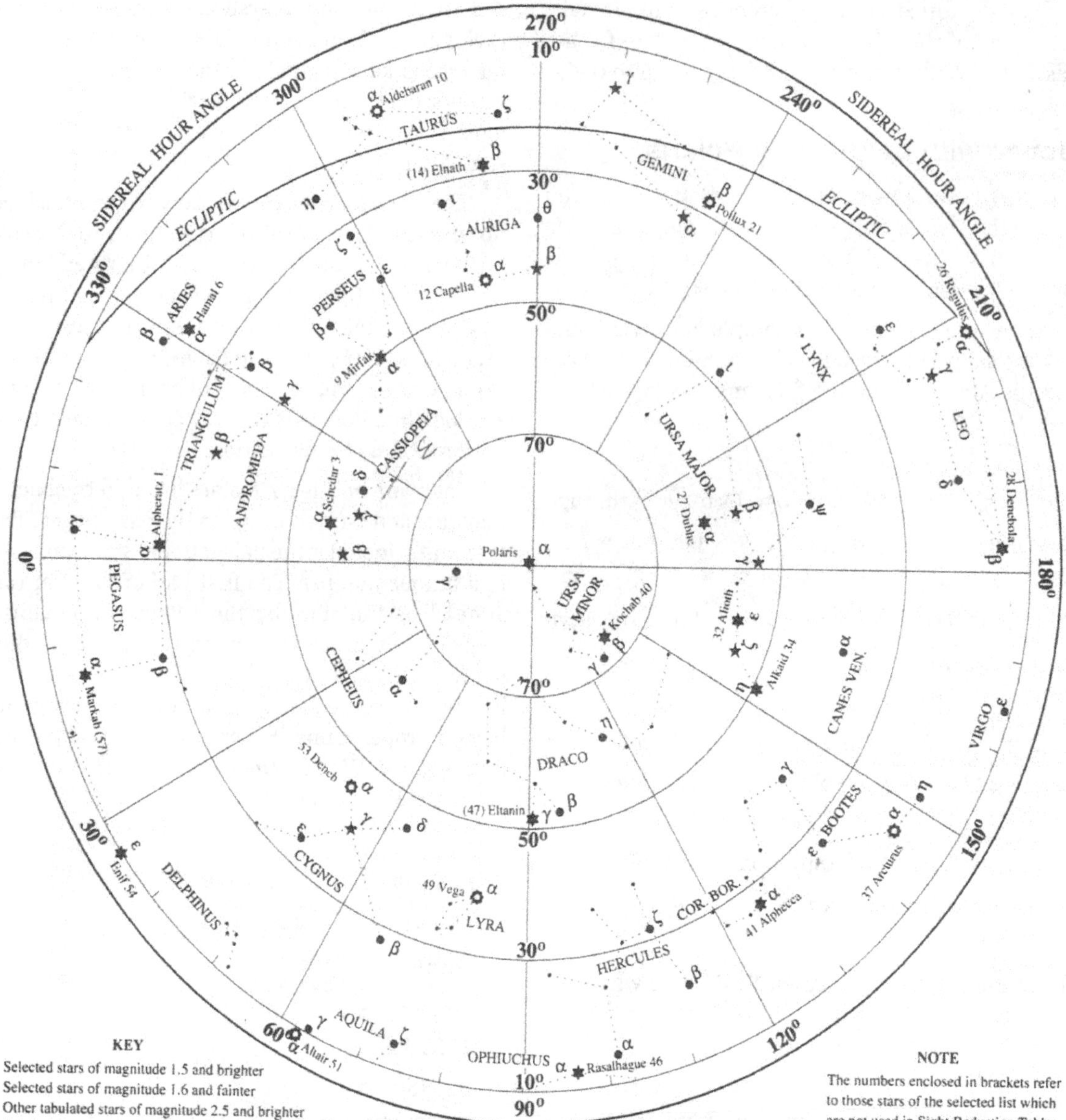

KEY

- Selected stars of magnitude 1.5 and brighter
- Selected stars of magnitude 1.6 and fainter
- Other tabulated stars of magnitude 2.5 and brighter
- Other tabulated stars of magnitude 2.6 and fainter
- Untabulated stars

NOTE

The numbers enclosed in brackets refer to those stars of the selected list which are not used in Sight Reduction Tables H.O. 249, A.P. 3270, N.P. 303.

EQUATORIAL STARS (SHA 0° to 180°)

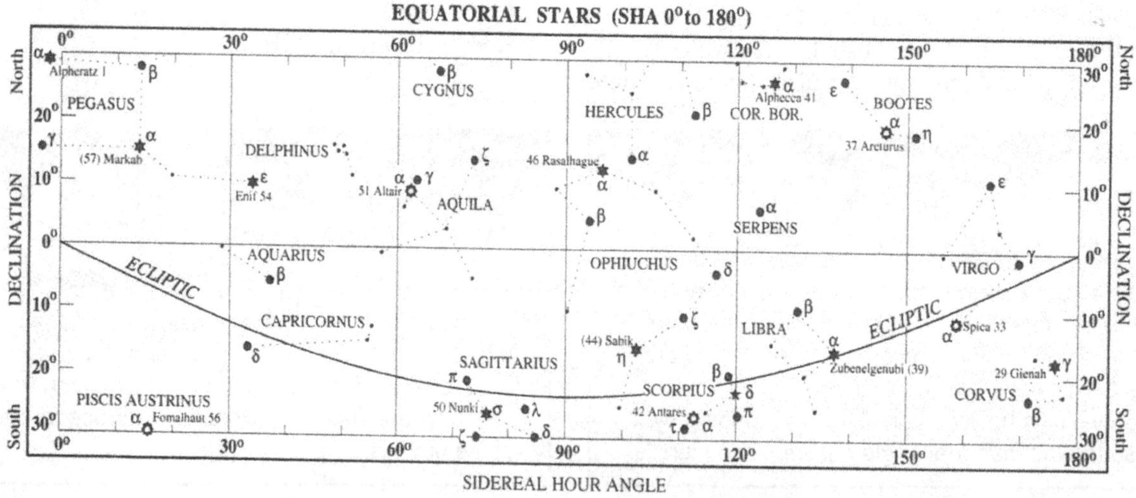

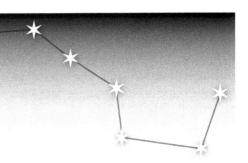

CHAPTER 8
PLANET SIGHTS

8.1 Introduction

There are five planets visible to the naked eye that might be used for navigation: Mercury, Mars, Venus, Jupiter, and Saturn. Of these, only Mercury is not cataloged in the *Nautical Almanac* for use in celestial navigation. This is because it is so close to the sun that it can only be seen rarely and then just before sunrise or after sunset and its altitude will always be very low. As a rule, one tries to avoid sights below some 10°, because refraction uncertainties are largest at low angles. The appearances of Mercury throughout the year are discussed in the *Almanac* so we do not confuse it with Venus or a bright star.

Of the four other planets, only Venus and Jupiter are special, because of their exceptional brightness. If either of these is in the sky, it will be brighter than any of the stars. Mars does periodically go through periods of being very bright, but as a rule, Mars and Saturn are just there to confuse us as bright or medium bright stars sitting at places where no star should be. If well positioned and adequately bright, they can be combined with stars for routine sights, but they have no special significance other than that. The Planet Diagram (Figure 8.1-1) is a quick way to estimate what planets are in view.

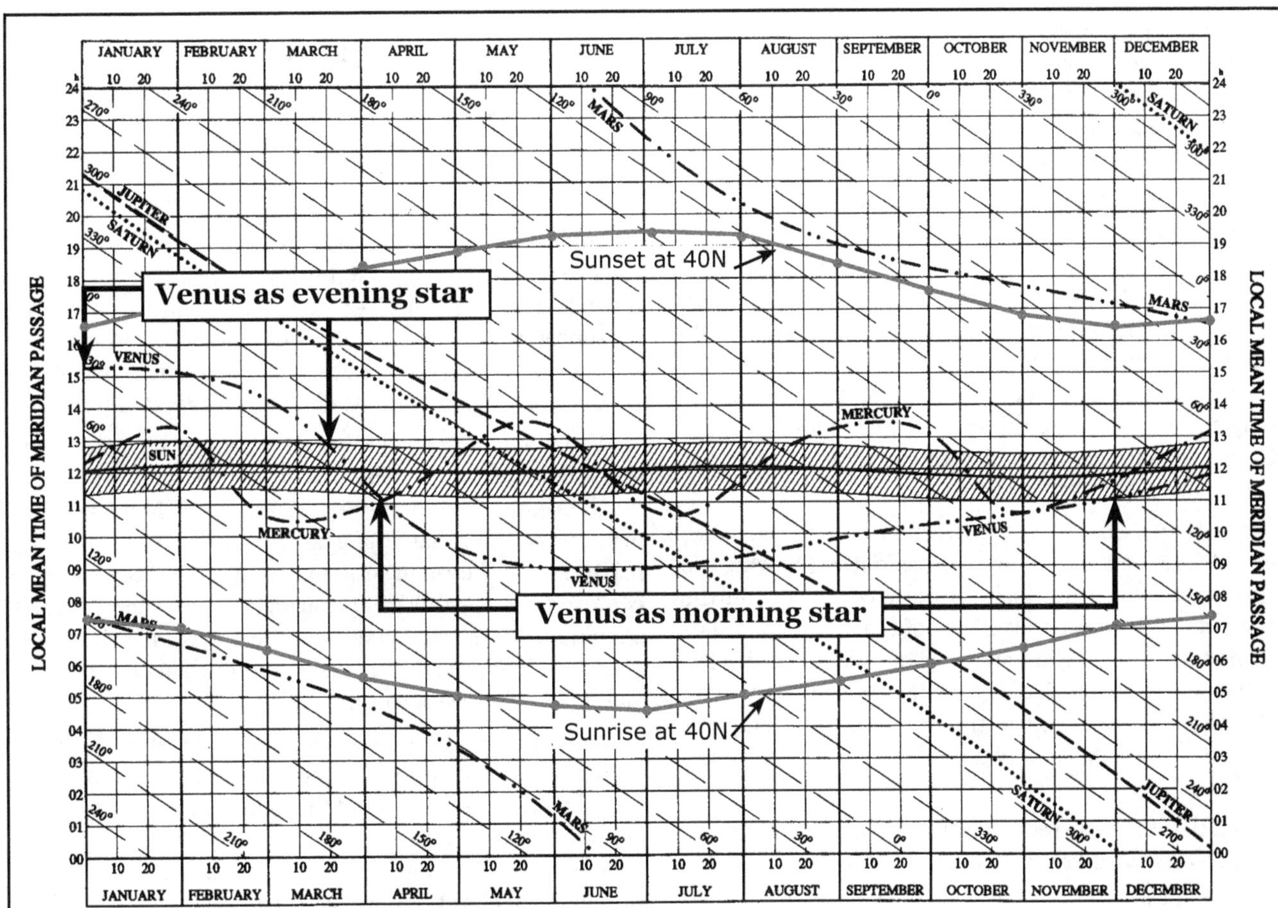

Figure 8.1-1 *A sample Planet Diagram from the* Nautical Almanac, *to which we have added sun rise and set times. Mer pass of stars can be estimated from the SHA lines shown. On February 1, Venus is 3h behind the sun, so it will be well to the east (left) of the sunset. At the end of March it passes behind the sun and emerges as a morning star. At 40 N we see Mars is visible most of the night, throughout the year. More generally, any body crossing the meridian near midnight will be visible all night during that day. Shaded areas means bodies too close to the sun to see. We would see Mercury as an evening star in September. A study of this diagram with a 2102D Star Finder in hand is a good way to learn what all it tells us. The planet curves change each year. Always check the Planet Diagram notes in a new* Almanac.

Venus and Jupiter, on the other hand, can often be used to extend the sight taking time periods because they can be seen almost immediately after sunset in the evening, before the other stars appear, or taken last in the morning after the stars begin to fade.

8.2 Sight Reduction of Planets

The sight reduction of planet sights (Venus, Jupiter, Mars, and Saturn) are very similar to a sun line sight reduction. The difference from sun lines occurs in Steps (2) and (3), looking up the GP. Follow the examples shown in Figures 8.2-1 and 8.2-2.

In Step (2), Box 2, after finding the hours part of the GHA of the planets on the Daily Pages, you must also record one extra number on the work form that we did not use for the sun, namely the v-value. For each planet this is listed on the Daily Pages at the bottom of the planet's column. For planets we do not use the space marked HP-moon, so you can draw a line through this space.

We use the v-value in Step (3) to find a small correction to the GHA of the planet. This extra correction is needed for the moon and planets to take into account their motion relative to the earth as we all circle the sun. The relative motion of the moon and planets causes their GPs to circle the earth at slightly different rates throughout the year. The size of "v" tells us how much their present rate varies from the average rate tabulated on the Daily Pages.

The d-value for the moon and planets means the same thing it does for the sun; it tells us how much their declination changes each hour. We also look up the d-correction to the declination in the same way as for the sun. The only difference here is the d-values, and hence d-corrections for moon and planets can be much larger than they are for the sun. Again, the reason for this is the relative motions of the earth, moon, and planets, which causes their declinations to change at a faster rate in some cases.

In Step (3), Box 3, the v-correction goes in the space marked "SHA or v-correction." Cross out SHA, which is used only for stars, and look up the v-correction on the Increments and Corrections Pages of the *Nautical Almanac*. The v-correction is found in the table labeled with the minutes part of the UTC of the sight—the same table you use for the d-correction, and the procedure for using the table is the same. This is why the columns in this table are headed "v or d."

Note that the v-correction, with one occasional exception, is always positive, so it must be added to the GHA. The occasional exception is Venus, and only Venus, which can have a negative v-correction. If this case applies, the v-value of Venus is tabulated on the Daily Pages as a negative number. To summarize: the v-correction is added unless the v-value is listed as negative, and only Venus can have a negative v-value.

The GHA of the planet is found by adding the v-correction to the hours and minutes part of the GHA.

The final difference in the sight reduction comes when finding the altitude correction to Ha. The altitude correction for planets is in the same table used for the altitude corrections of stars (T-8). All planets get their main altitude correction from this table. This correction for stars and planets is always negative.

For MARS or VENUS sights there is occasionally one further correction that you also find in the altitude correction tables. This correction is always small and always positive; the size of the correction depends on Ha and the season. This correction is primarily a parallax correction needed occasionally because these two planets, our nearest neighbors, are much closer to the earth than the stars, sun, and outer planets. (This correction is larger for the moon, since it is even closer.)

This parallax correction goes in the work form space marked "additional altitude correction," below Ha. The names "moon," "Mars", and "Venus" are printed in this space to remind you that this correction applies only to these sights.

Now to find Ho, apply the altitude correction and the additional altitude correction to Ha. The rest of the sight reduction of planets is the same as for the sun.

Tips on Planet Identification

The planet Mercury can be seen with the naked eye, and it can even be quite bright. But it is only rarely visible, when it will be low on the horizon, just before sunrise or just after sunset, very near the sun. Since it is rare to be seen and always very low on the horizon it is not used for navigation. Its Dec and SHA are not listed in the *Nautical Almanac*.

Venus and Jupiter always stand out nicely among the stars. When either of these two are visible, they are always much brighter than any stars around them. Mars and Saturn, on the other hand, appear only as bright or medium bright stars. The main function of Mars and Saturn is to confuse the navigator by appearing as stars where no stars should be. Mars can sometimes appear reddish, and most planets will appear as tiny disks, rather than points, when viewed through 10-power binoculars.

Another identifying characteristic of planets is their lack of twinkle. Stars twinkle, planets do not. The reason can be traced to the apparent size of the light source—distant stars are point sources of light; the much closer planets are disk sources. A patch of warm air can momentarily refract all of the star light out of our eye, causing it to twinkle; but such transient refraction cannot remove all of the light from a planet since it comes from slightly different angles depending on its origin on the disk.

The relative location of the planets can also sometimes confirm or assist in their identification. The sun, moon, and all planets always lie along the same arc across the sky.

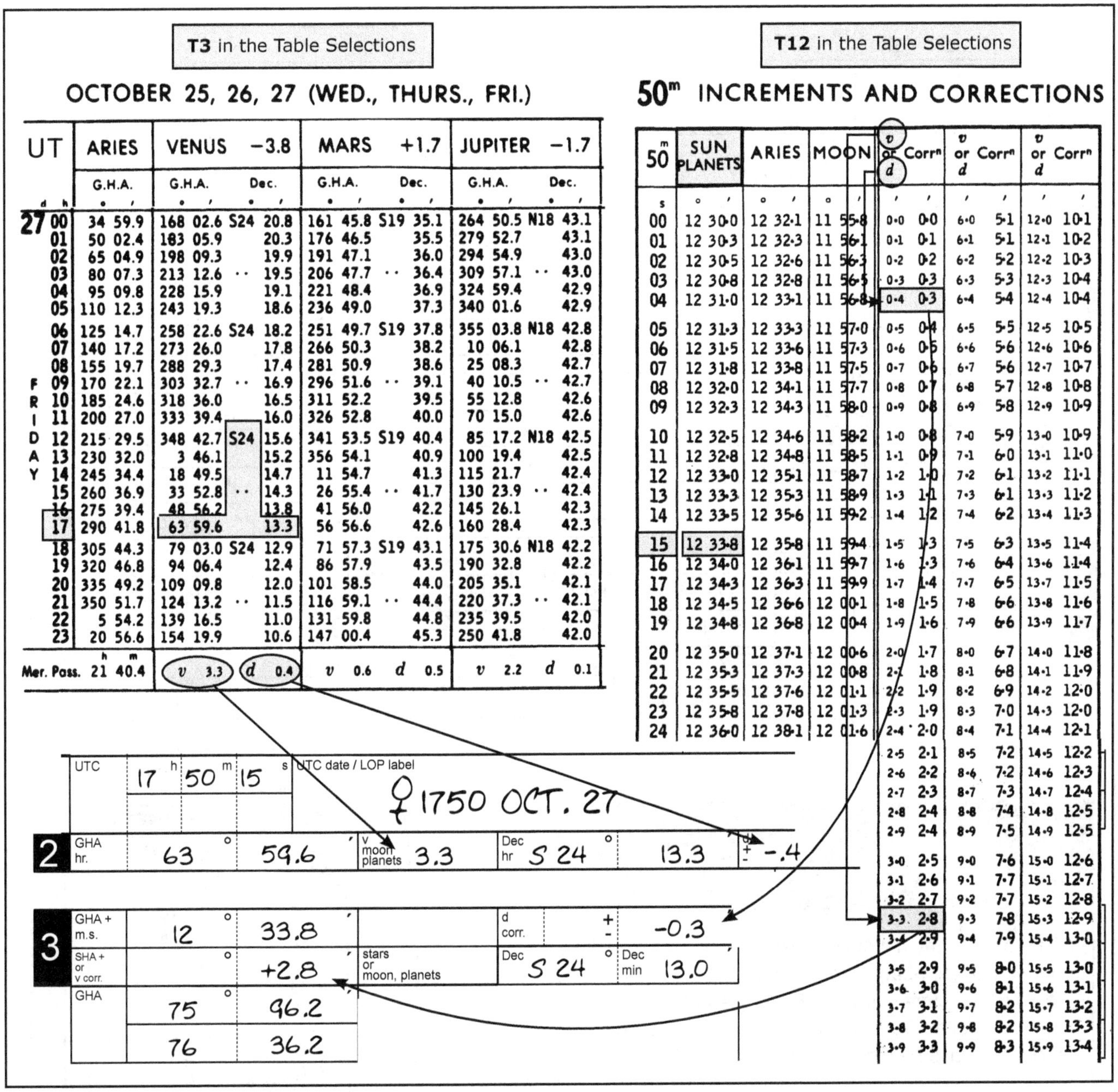

OCTOBER 25, 26, 27 (WED., THURS., FRI.)

UT d h	ARIES G.H.A.	VENUS −3.8 G.H.A.	VENUS Dec.	MARS +1.7 G.H.A.	MARS Dec.	JUPITER −1.7 G.H.A.	JUPITER Dec.
	° ′	° ′	° ′	° ′	° ′	° ′	° ′
27 00	34 59.9	168 02.6	S24 20.8	161 45.8	S19 35.1	264 50.5	N18 43.1
01	50 02.4	183 05.9	20.3	176 46.5	35.5	279 52.7	43.1
02	65 04.9	198 09.3	19.9	191 47.1	36.0	294 54.9	43.0
03	80 07.3	213 12.6	·· 19.5	206 47.7	·· 36.4	309 57.1	·· 43.0
04	95 09.8	228 15.9	19.1	221 48.4	36.9	324 59.4	42.9
05	110 12.3	243 19.3	18.6	236 49.0	37.3	340 01.6	42.9
06	125 14.7	258 22.6	S24 18.2	251 49.7	S19 37.8	355 03.8	N18 42.8
07	140 17.2	273 26.0	17.8	266 50.3	38.2	10 06.1	42.8
08	155 19.7	288 29.3	17.4	281 50.9	38.6	25 08.3	42.7
F 09	170 22.1	303 32.7	·· 16.9	296 51.6	·· 39.1	40 10.5	·· 42.7
R 10	185 24.6	318 36.0	16.5	311 52.2	39.5	55 12.8	42.6
I 11	200 27.0	333 39.4	16.0	326 52.8	40.0	70 15.0	42.6
D 12	215 29.5	348 42.7	S24 15.6	341 53.5	S19 40.4	85 17.2	N18 42.5
A 13	230 32.0	3 46.1	15.2	356 54.1	40.9	100 19.4	42.5
Y 14	245 34.4	18 49.5	14.7	11 54.7	41.3	115 21.7	42.4
15	260 36.9	33 52.8	·· 14.3	26 55.4	·· 41.7	130 23.9	·· 42.4
16	275 39.4	48 56.2	13.8	41 56.0	42.2	145 26.1	42.3
17	290 41.8	63 59.6	13.3	56 56.6	42.6	160 28.4	42.3
18	305 44.3	79 03.0	S24 12.9	71 57.3	S19 43.1	175 30.6	N18 42.2
19	320 46.8	94 06.4	12.4	86 57.9	43.5	190 32.8	42.2
20	335 49.2	109 09.8	12.0	101 58.5	44.0	205 35.1	42.1
21	350 51.7	124 13.2	·· 11.5	116 59.1	·· 44.4	220 37.3	·· 42.1
22	5 54.2	139 16.5	11.0	131 59.8	44.8	235 39.5	42.0
23	20 56.6	154 19.9	10.6	147 00.4	45.3	250 41.8	42.0
Mer. Pass.	h m 21 40.4	v 3.3	d 0.4	v 0.6	d 0.5	v 2.2	d 0.1

50^m INCREMENTS AND CORRECTIONS

50^m s	SUN PLANETS ° ′	ARIES ° ′	MOON ° ′	v or d ′	Corr^n ′	v or d ′	Corr^n ′	v or d ′	Corr^n ′
00	12 30·0	12 32·1	11 55·8	0·0	0·0	6·0	5·1	12·0	10·1
01	12 30·3	12 32·3	11 56·1	0·1	0·1	6·1	5·1	12·1	10·2
02	12 30·5	12 32·6	11 56·3	0·2	0·2	6·2	5·2	12·2	10·3
03	12 30·8	12 32·8	11 56·5	0·3	0·3	6·3	5·3	12·3	10·4
04	12 31·0	12 33·1	11 56·8	0·4	0·3	6·4	5·4	12·4	10·4
05	12 31·3	12 33·3	11 57·0	0·5	0·4	6·5	5·5	12·5	10·5
06	12 31·5	12 33·6	11 57·3	0·6	0·5	6·6	5·6	12·6	10·6
07	12 31·8	12 33·8	11 57·5	0·7	0·6	6·7	5·6	12·7	10·7
08	12 32·0	12 34·1	11 57·7	0·8	0·7	6·8	5·7	12·8	10·8
09	12 32·3	12 34·3	11 58·0	0·9	0·8	6·9	5·8	12·9	10·9
10	12 32·5	12 34·6	11 58·2	1·0	0·8	7·0	5·9	13·0	10·9
11	12 32·8	12 34·8	11 58·5	1·1	0·9	7·1	6·0	13·1	11·0
12	12 33·0	12 35·1	11 58·7	1·2	1·0	7·2	6·1	13·2	11·1
13	12 33·3	12 35·3	11 58·9	1·3	1·1	7·3	6·1	13·3	11·2
14	12 33·5	12 35·6	11 59·2	1·4	1·2	7·4	6·2	13·4	11·3
15	12 33·8	12 35·8	11 59·4	1·5	1·3	7·5	6·3	13·5	11·4
16	12 34·0	12 36·1	11 59·7	1·6	1·3	7·6	6·4	13·6	11·4
17	12 34·3	12 36·3	11 59·9	1·7	1·4	7·7	6·5	13·7	11·5
18	12 34·5	12 36·6	12 00·1	1·8	1·5	7·8	6·6	13·8	11·6
19	12 34·8	12 36·8	12 00·4	1·9	1·6	7·9	6·6	13·9	11·7
20	12 35·0	12 37·1	12 00·6	2·0	1·7	8·0	6·7	14·0	11·8
21	12 35·3	12 37·3	12 00·8	2·1	1·8	8·1	6·8	14·1	11·9
22	12 35·5	12 37·6	12 01·1	2·2	1·9	8·2	6·9	14·2	12·0
23	12 35·8	12 37·8	12 01·3	2·3	1·9	8·3	7·0	14·3	12·0
24	12 36·0	12 38·1	12 01·6	2·4	2·0	8·4	7·1	14·4	12·1
				2·5	2·1	8·5	7·2	14·5	12·2
				2·6	2·2	8·6	7·2	14·6	12·3
				2·7	2·3	8·7	7·3	14·7	12·4
				2·8	2·4	8·8	7·4	14·8	12·5
				2·9	2·4	8·9	7·5	14·9	12·5
				3·0	2·5	9·0	7·6	15·0	12·6
				3·1	2·6	9·1	7·7	15·1	12·7
				3·2	2·7	9·2	7·7	15·2	12·8
				3·3	2·8	9·3	7·8	15·3	12·9
				3·4	2·9	9·4	7·9	15·4	13·0
				3·5	2·9	9·5	8·0	15·5	13·0
				3·6	3·0	9·6	8·1	15·6	13·1
				3·7	3·1	9·7	8·2	15·7	13·2
				3·8	3·2	9·8	8·2	15·8	13·3
				3·9	3·3	9·9	8·3	15·9	13·4

Figure 8.2-1 *Filling out Box 2 and 3 in the work form. The number next to each planet is its brightness, expressed as a magnitude. See Section 11.20.*

On those occasions when 3 or more of these objects are visible (say, moon and two planets), this alignment can sometimes aid in their identification.

A consequence of the above, which comes about because the orbits of all of these bodies lie within the same plane (± 9° or so), is that planets are always found within a Zodiac constellation. With that said, the concept of constellation, let alone the Zodiac, does not come up much in cel nav as we do not need it for anything. We do refer to groups of stars, but these are groups we make up from stars of neighboring constellations, such as the *Summer Triangle*.

...In Depth

11.21 Compass Checks at Sea

In modern times we may not be often called upon to rely on celestial navigation, but it is almost certain that at some point we will need to check a compass at sea, and our knowledge of cel nav makes this an easy operation...

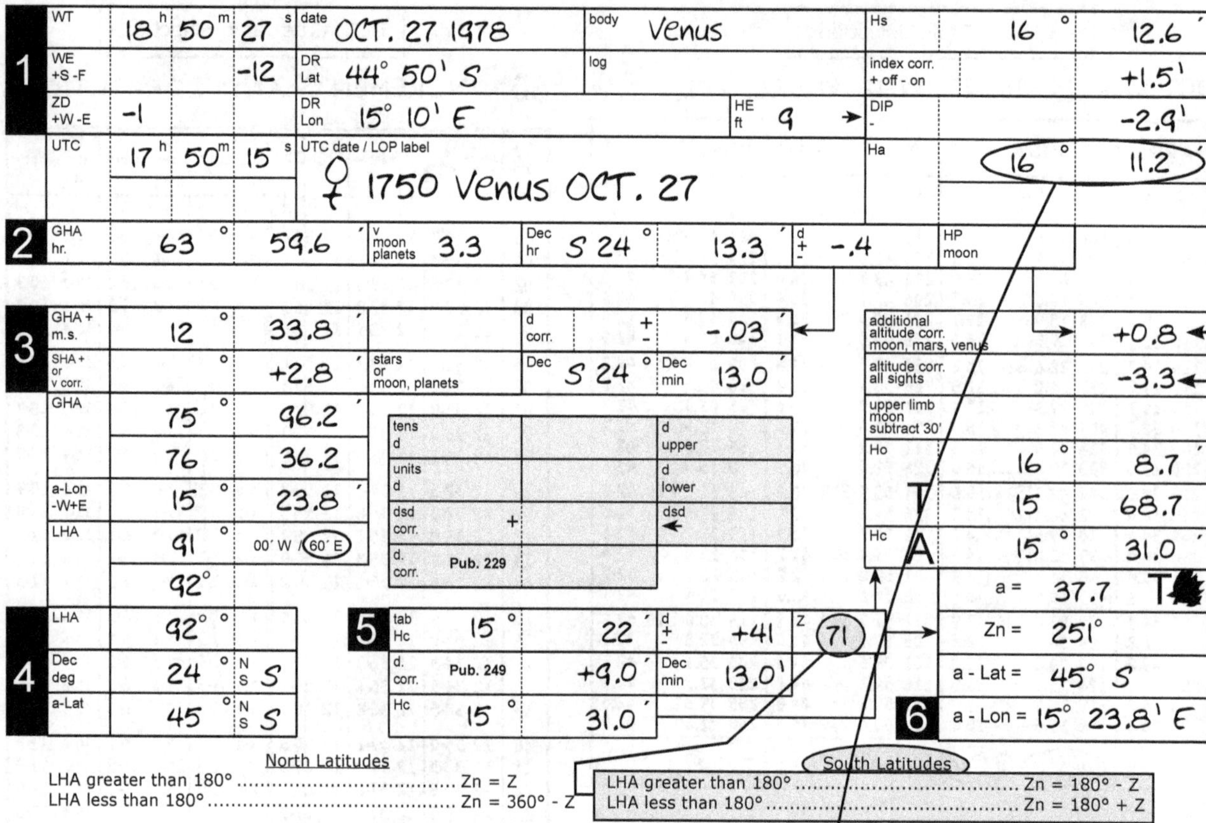

T8 in the Table Selections

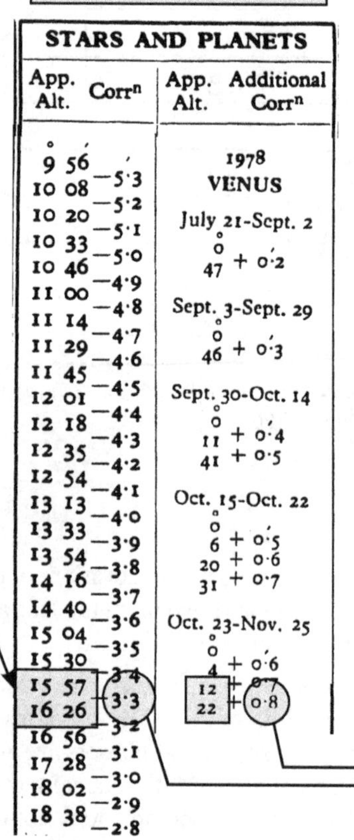

STARS AND PLANETS
App. Alt.
Corrn
App. Alt.
Additional Corrn
9 56
10 08 -5·3
10 20 -5·2
10 33 -5·1
10 46 -5·0
11 00 -4·9
11 14 -4·8
11 29 -4·7
11 45 -4·6
12 01 -4·5
12 18 -4·4
12 35 -4·3
12 54 -4·2
13 13 -4·1
13 33 -4·0
13 54 -3·9
14 16 -3·8
14 40 -3·7
15 04 -3·6
15 30 -3·5
15 57 -3·4
16 26 -3·3
16 56 -3·2
17 28 -3·1
18 02 -3·0
18 38 -2·9
-2·8
1978
VENUS
July 21-Sept. 2
47 + 0·2
Sept. 3-Sept. 29
46 + 0·3
Sept. 30-Oct. 14
11 + 0·4
41 + 0·5
Oct. 15-Oct. 22
6 + 0·5
20 + 0·6
31 + 0·7
Oct. 23-Nov. 25
4 + 0·6
12 + 0·7
22 + 0·8

...In Depth

11.22 Great Circle Sailing

Though we may not often follow a great circle route under sail, the heading toward this shortest way to go is sometimes of value to our planning. The solutions follow from standard cel nav procedures, though always best done by direct computation...

...In Depth

11.23 Rhumb-line Sailing

Generally we solve this problem by just drawing a line on a Mercator chart, but the task of actually computing the heading and the precise rhumb-line distance is more involved than a simple great circle route. Here we explain the standard tables that solve this for us...

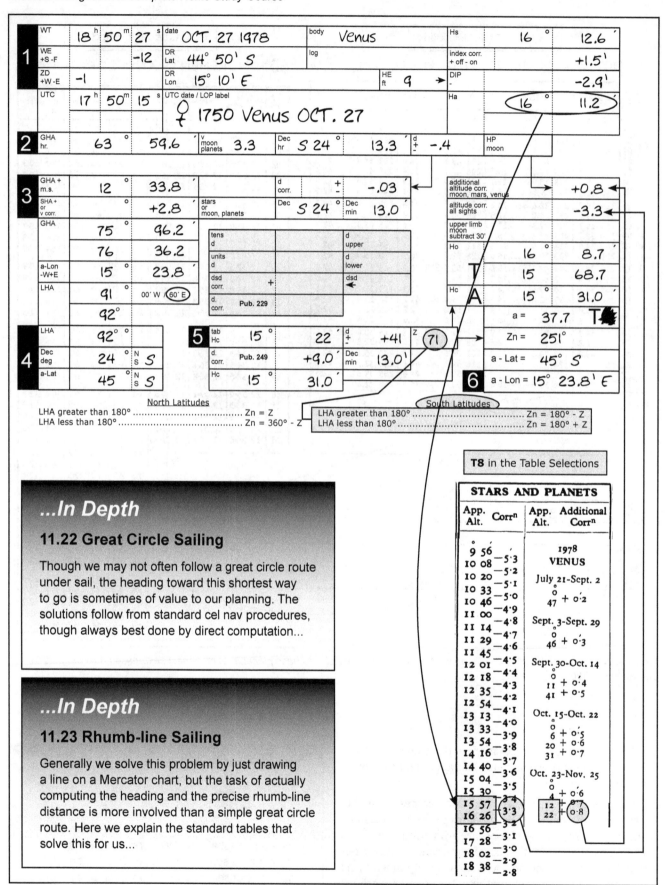

Figure 8.2-2 *Sample sight reduction of Venus. Note South Lat and East Lon. Complete planet form used in the examples, Planet #1*

8.3 Jupiter Sight Exercise, Planet #2

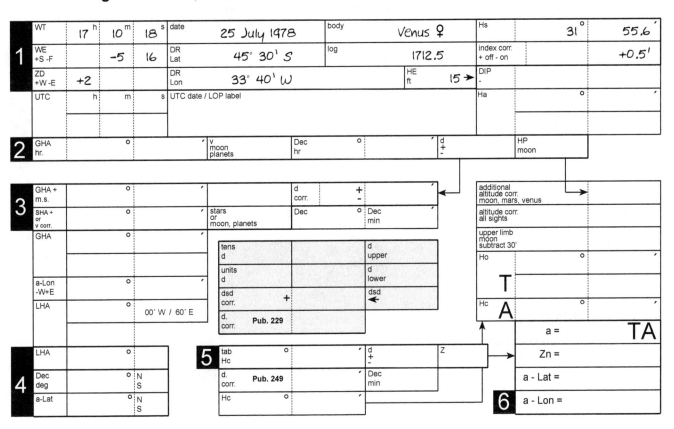

1

	h	m	s							
WT	5 h	56 m	58 s	date	26 OCT 1978	body	Jupiter ♃	Hs	62 °	51.9 ′
WE +S -F		+ 7	30	DR Lat	45° 05′ N	log	1344.2	index corr. + off - on		-2.5′
ZD +W -E	-11			DR Lon	160° 25′ E	HE ft	19 →	DIP -		
UTC	h	m	s	UTC date / LOP label				Ha	°	′

2

GHA hr.	°	′	v moon planets	Dec hr	°	′	d + -
HP moon							

3

GHA + m.s.	°	′		d corr.	+ - ′
SHA + or v corr.	°	′	stars or moon, planets	Dec °	Dec min ′
GHA	°	′			
a-Lon -W+E	°	′			
LHA	°	00′ W / 60′ E			

tens d		d upper	
units d		d lower	
dsd corr.	+	dsd ←	
d. corr.	Pub. 229		

additional altitude corr. moon, mars, venus	
altitude corr. all sights	
upper limb moon subtract 30′	
Ho	° ′
T	
Hc	° ′
A	

4

LHA	°	
Dec deg	°	N S
a-Lat	°	N S

5

tab Hc	°	′	d + -	Z
d. corr.	Pub. 249	′	Dec min	
Hc	°	′		

6

a = TA
Zn =
a - Lat =
a - Lon =

8.4 Venus Sight Exercise, Planet #3

1

	h	m	s							
WT	17 h	10 m	18 s	date	25 July 1978	body	Venus ♀	Hs	31 °	55.6 ′
WE +S -F		-5	16	DR Lat	45° 30′ S	log	1712.5	index corr. + off - on		+0.5′
ZD +W -E	+2			DR Lon	33° 40′ W	HE ft	15 →	DIP -		
UTC	h	m	s	UTC date / LOP label				Ha	°	′

2

GHA hr.	°	′	v moon planets	Dec hr	°	′	d + -
HP moon							

3

GHA + m.s.	°	′		d corr.	+ - ′
SHA + or v corr.	°	′	stars or moon, planets	Dec °	Dec min ′
GHA	°	′			
a-Lon -W+E	°	′			
LHA	°	00′ W / 60′ E			

tens d		d upper	
units d		d lower	
dsd corr.	+	dsd ←	
d. corr.	Pub. 229		

additional altitude corr. moon, mars, venus	
altitude corr. all sights	
upper limb moon subtract 30′	
Ho	° ′
T	
Hc	° ′
A	

4

LHA	°	
Dec deg	°	N S
a-Lat	°	N S

5

tab Hc	°	′	d + -	Z
d. corr.	Pub. 249	′	Dec min	
Hc	°	′		

6

a = TA
Zn =
a - Lat =
a - Lon =

8.5 Jupiter-Hamal, Plot Exercise, Planet #2, Star #7

We are dead in the water at a DR position of 45° 05' N, 160° 25' E. It is October 26, 1978 WT. ZD of the watch is -11. WE = 7m 30s Slow, HE = 19 ft. IC = 2.5' On the scale. We take several sights of Hamal and the average is: Hs = 19° 58.3' at WT = 5h 41m 9s and then take a series of Jupiter sights and the average is: Hs = 62° 51.9' at WT = 5h 56m 58s. Do the sight reduction of both sights using your own work forms and then plot the LOPs for a fix. The full work forms are given in the Answers section, the plot is below. *Note this is an East longitude problem—also these watch errors are very large; usually the WE will be in the seconds, unless it has not been set for a long time.*

8.6 Venus-Sirius, Plot Exercise, Planet #3, Star #8

We are dead in the water at a DR position of 45° 30' S, 33° 40' W. It is July 25, 1978 WT. ZD of the watch is +2. WE = 5m 16s Fast, HE = 15 ft. IC = 0.5' Off. We take several sights of Sirius and the average is: Hs = 11° 5.2' at WT = 16h 54m 37s and then take a series of Venus sights and the average is: Hs = 31° 55.6' at WT = 17h 10m 18s. Do the sight reduction of both sights using your own work forms and then plot the LOPs for a fix. The full work forms and plot are given in the Answers section. *Note this is a South Latitude problem*

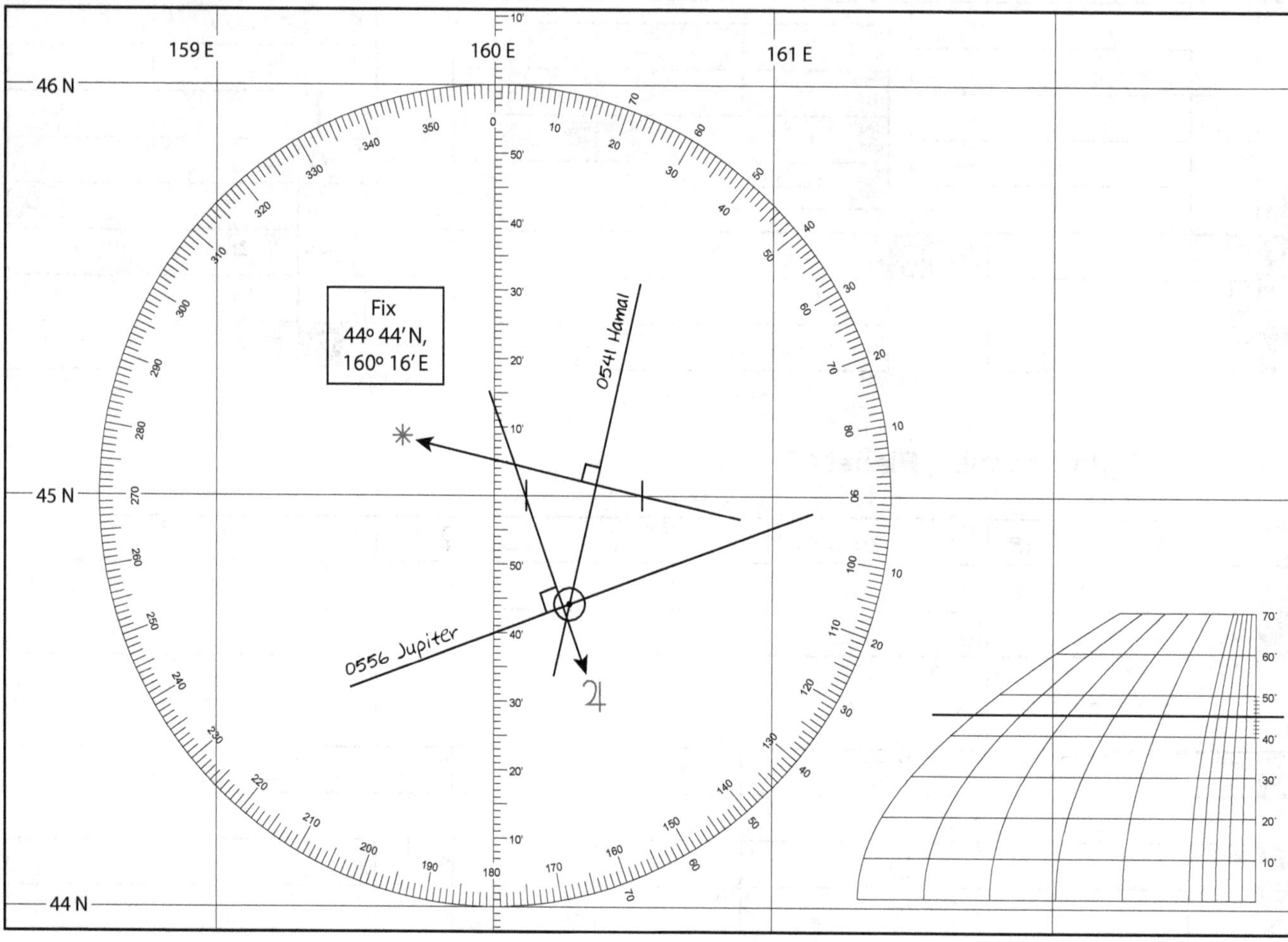

Figure 8.5-1 *Plot for Exercise 8.5*

8.7 New Terminology

additional altitude correction

planet diagram

visible planets

v correction

Star charts from the *Nautical Almanac*.

STAR CHARTS

Northern Hemisphere and more equatorial stars are at the end of Chapter 7.

SOUTHERN STARS

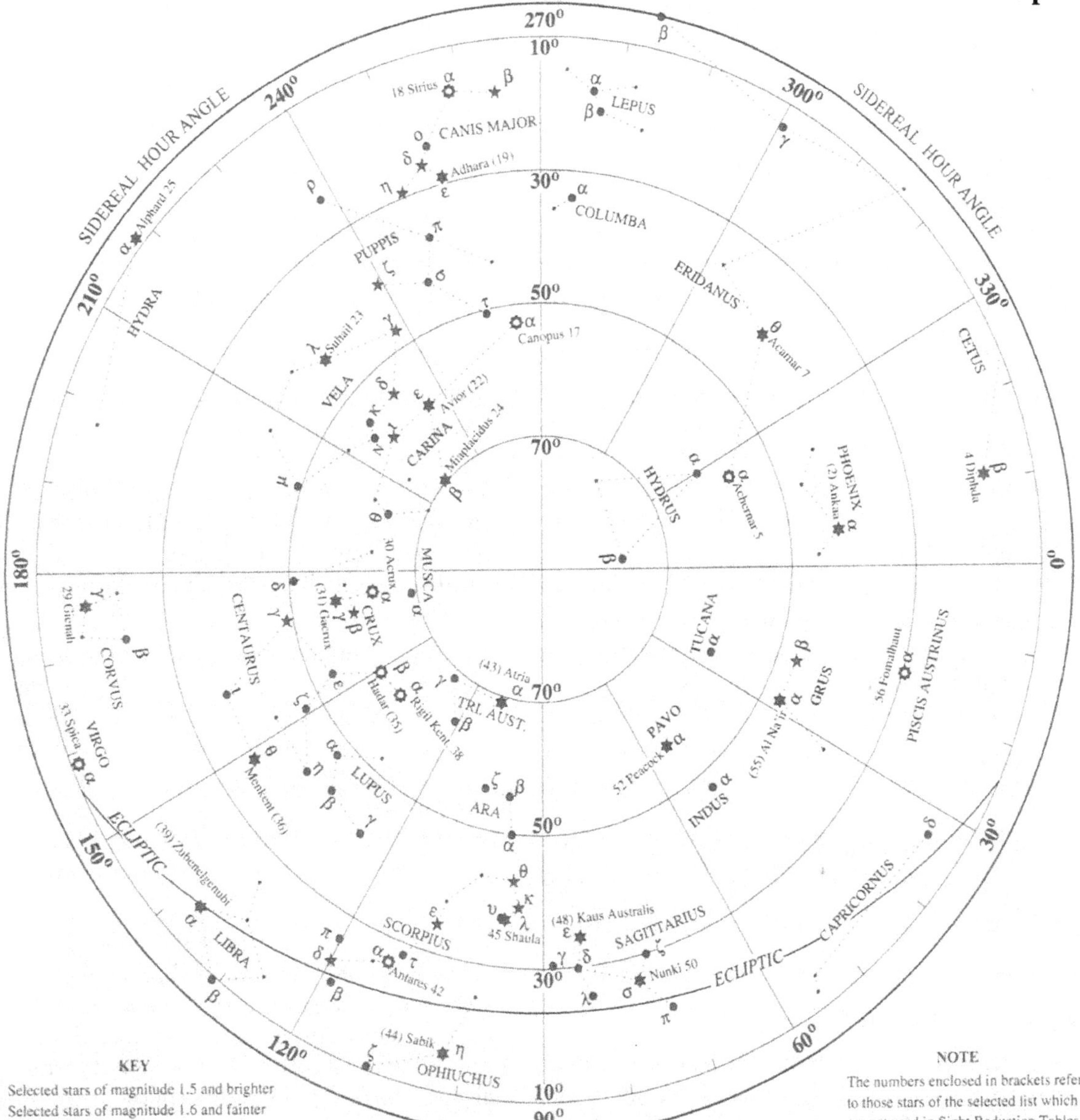

KEY

- Selected stars of magnitude 1.5 and brighter
- Selected stars of magnitude 1.6 and fainter
- Other tabulated stars of magnitude 2.5 and brighter
- Other tabulated stars of magnitude 2.6 and fainter
- Untabulated stars

NOTE

The numbers enclosed in brackets refer to those stars of the selected list which are not used in Sight Reduction Tables H.O. 249, A.P. 3270, N.P. 303.

EQUATORIAL STARS (SHA 180° to 360°)

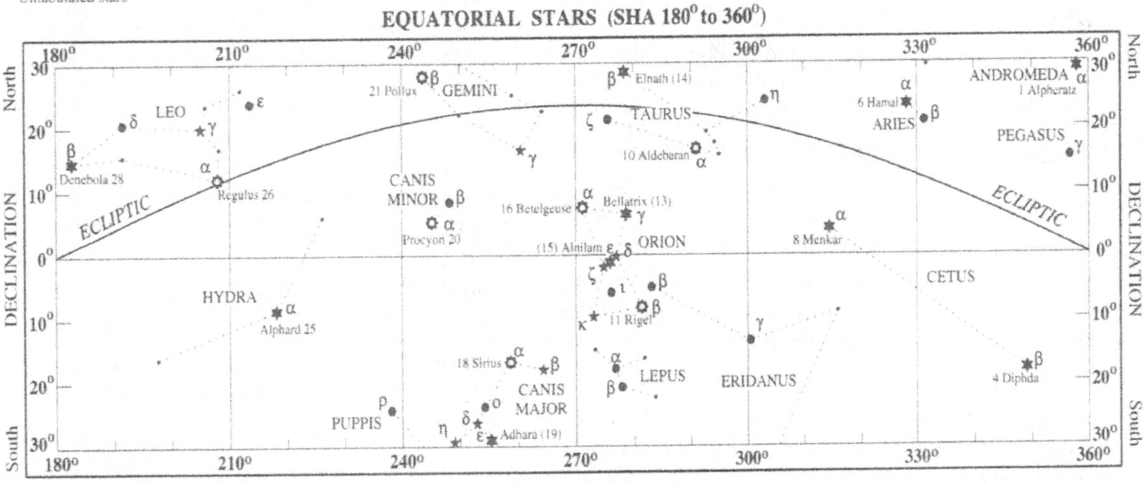

Chapter 9
Moon Sights

9.1 Introduction

The moon is a mixed blessing in celestial navigation because when it is very prominent in the night sky, its glare on the water can distort the horizon below it. Crescent moons, however, can be an asset in some circumstances.

The moon is most useful in routine navigation for daylight fixes with the sun, which can be done periodically throughout the month, as explained in Section 9.10. For now, the task is how to do the sight reductions, which is the same regardless of the phase of the moon. You will soon note that our work forms make doing moon sights as easy as any other sight, despite the fact that the moon has a few extra steps to its sight reduction.

In the *Emergency Navigation* book, we show the real power of the moon—its ability to tell us UTC if we happen to lose that crucial component of celestial navigation. The moon is the only body in the sky that moves relative to the stars fast enough to tell time from its position. The procedures for extracting that data from moon sights, however, is not at all routine and takes special instruction and resources.

We first get right to the sight reduction process, which is the last body to cover, and following that there is discussion of how to optimize the use of the moon in daily procedures.

9.2 Sight Reduction of the Moon

Moon sight reductions are similar to planets—meaning they are done the same as a sun line with the addition of a v-correction to the GHA and an additional altitude correction to Ha. The work forms are designed specifically to make moon sights easy.

The steps listed here are illustrated in Figure 9.2-1. In Step (2), to fill out Box 2 from the Daily Pages, you simply copy everything down on the work form exactly as it is listed in the Moon column of the Daily Pages of the *Nautical Almanac*. This will include the GHA, v-value, declination, d-value, and something new called HP, the horizontal parallax. These are listed in this order on the Daily Pages at the hour of the sight. This new parameter, HP, is a measure of the distance to the moon, which changes throughout the month. HP is used to find the additional altitude correction to Ha, which depends on the distance to the moon.

In Step (3), Box 3, find the v-correction to the GHA in the Increments and Corrections pages. The procedure is exactly the same as it is with planet sights.

The altitude corrections for the moon are listed in a special table on the back inside cover of the *Nautical Almanac*. There are two tables–one for Ha in the range of 0° to 35°, and one for 35° to 90°. These are Tables T-13 and T-14 in the Tables Selections.

We find both the regular altitude correction and the additional altitude correction in this table. The altitude correction depends on Ha. Go across the top of the table to the correct range of Ha, and then down the column to the degrees part of Ha, and then farther on down till you are opposite the minutes part of Ha, which are listed at the sides of the table. The correction you find there is called the altitude correction; record it in the corresponding space on the work form.

Now to find the additional altitude correction: stay in the same column and continue on down to the bottom part of the table, and stop when you are opposite the value of HP recorded in Box 2. At that location in the table there are two corrections; one is for upper limb sights (U), the other is for lower limb sights (L). Choose the appropriate one and record it in the space marked "additional altitude correction." Both altitude corrections are always positive for the moon.

If the moon sight is of the upper limb, enter a -30' in the space marked "upper limb moon." For lower limb sights we just ignore this space on the work form. This step is simply a trick the almanac does that allows the other two corrections to always be positive. For upper limb sights you always subtract 30' regardless of the size of Ha.

To get Ho, add to Ha all corrections listed below it. For lower limb sights, these are the altitude correction and the additional altitude correction; and for upper limb, it is these two and an additional -30'.

The rest of the moon's sight reduction is the same as any other sight reduction. The d-value for the moon is listed every hour, but we use it the same way we do for sun and planet sights. Select the sign of d (±) the same as with the sun or planets by noting if the declination is increasing (+) or decreasing (-) with time. *Don't make the mistake of using the d-value itself for this.* The d-value can go up with time when the declination is going down, and vice versa.

Form sections that are different for the moon are shown in Figure 9.2-2, i.e., only Boxes 2 and 3.

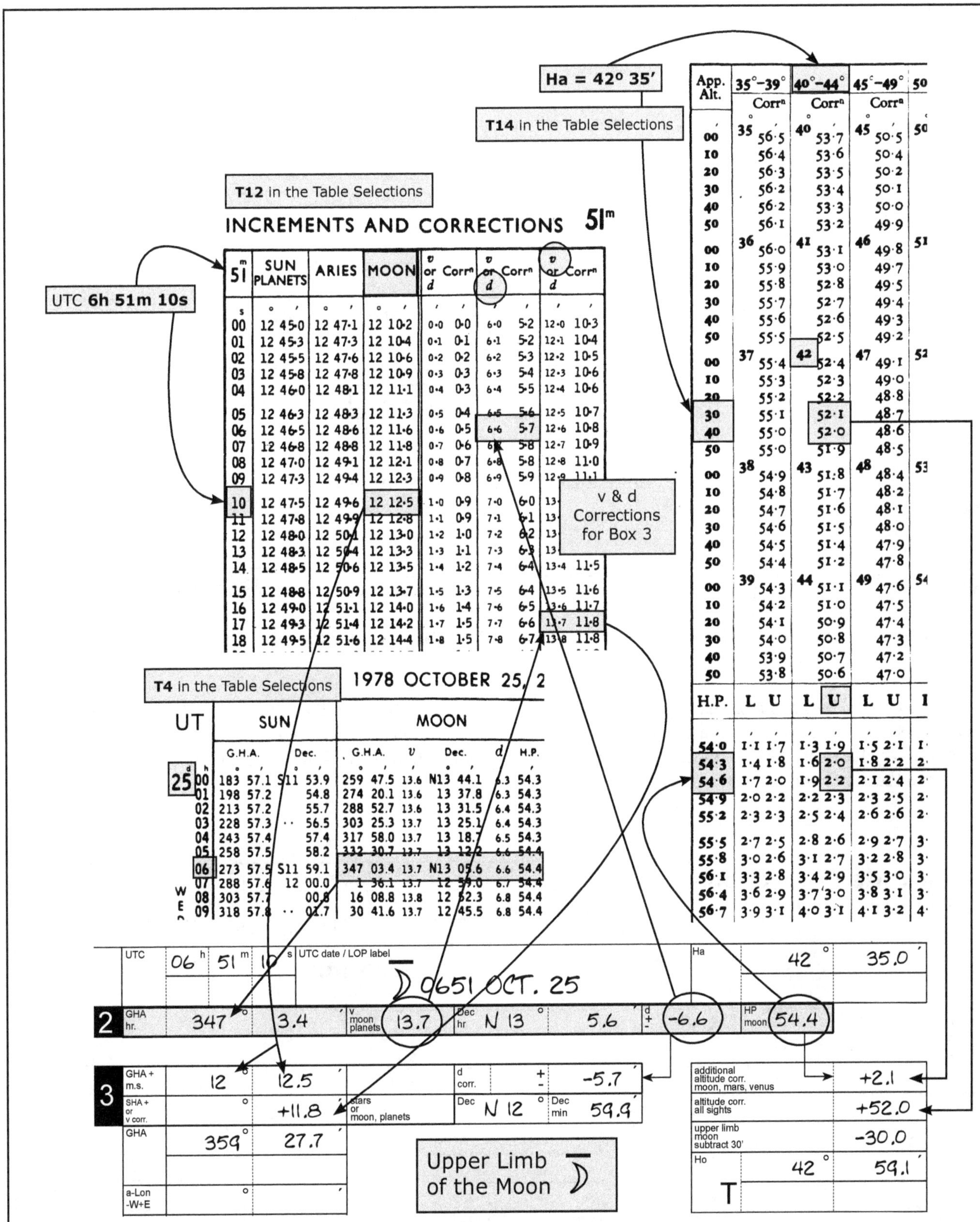

Figure 9.2-1 *Moon sight reduction. Starpath forms are designed to make moon sights easy, even though they have a few extra steps. Moon data are copied, item for item, from Almanac to form as shown in Box 2. The v and d corrections are tabulated and recorded just like planets, but the corrections can be larger and the d and v values themselves are changing hourly, not just daily as with planets. Then after recording the altitude correction, there is one* additional altitude correction *that depends on the HP-moon value, which can sometimes call for an interpolation, as shown. Last step is subtract 30' for upper limb sights. That is it, then all else is the same as other sights.*

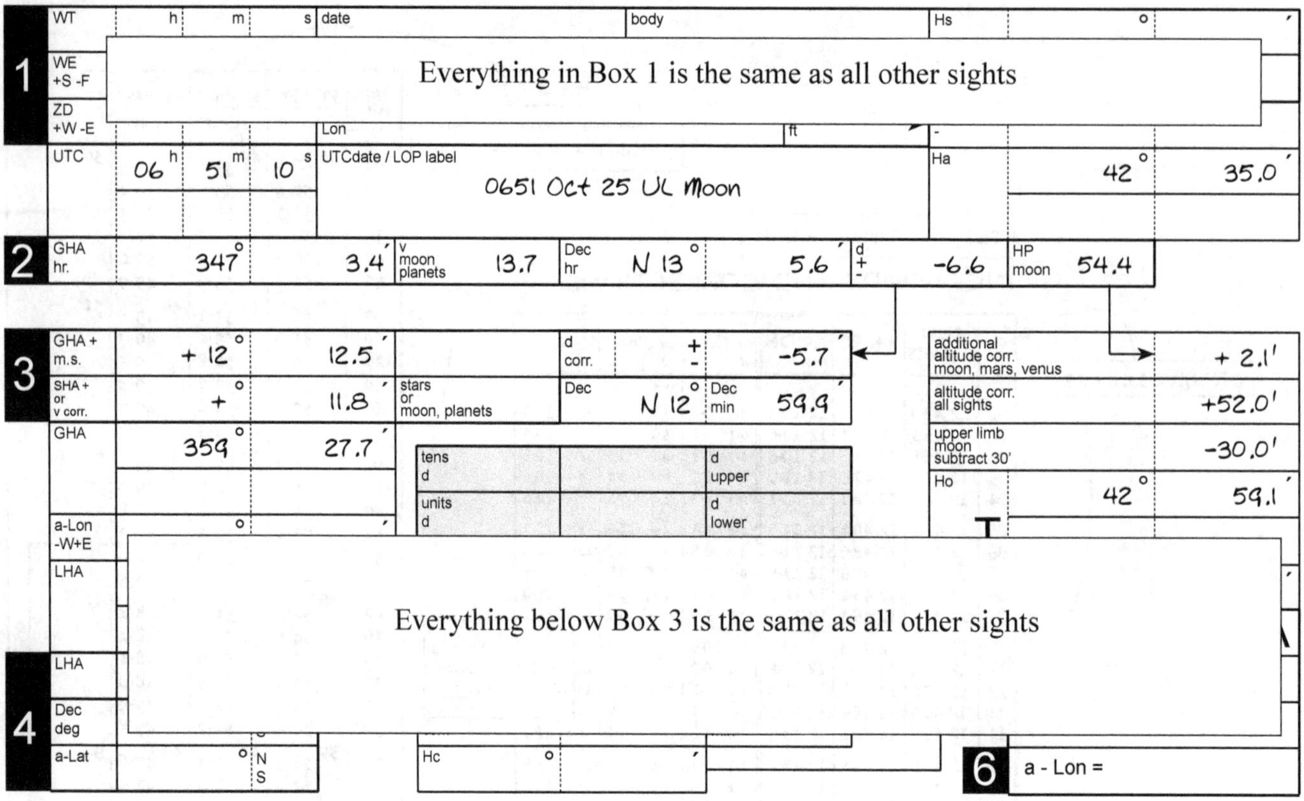

Everything in Box 1 is the same as all other sights
UTC 06 h 51 m 10 s
0651 Oct 25 UL Moon
Ha 42° 35.0'
GHA hr. 347° 3.4'
v moon planets 13.7
Dec hr N 13° 5.6'
d +/- -6.6
HP moon 54.4
GHA + m.s. + 12° 12.5'
d corr. -5.7'
additional altitude corr. moon, mars, venus + 2.1'
SHA + or v corr. + 11.8'
Dec N 12°
Dec min 59.9
altitude corr. all sights +52.0'
GHA 359° 27.7'
upper limb moon subtract 30' -30.0'
Ho 42° 59.1'
Everything below Box 3 is the same as all other sights
a - Lon =

Figure 9.2-2 *Differences between Moon and other sights, Moon #1. Box 2 data and the additional altitude correction is the main difference.*

Figure 9.2-3 shows two more examples of the altitude correction for the moon, and after that there are two exercises on just this step. Following that is a chance to work though this first example from beginning to end on your own (called Moon#1), which can be checked underway using the example given. Then we work several more moon sights and discuss the role of the moon and planets in daily work.

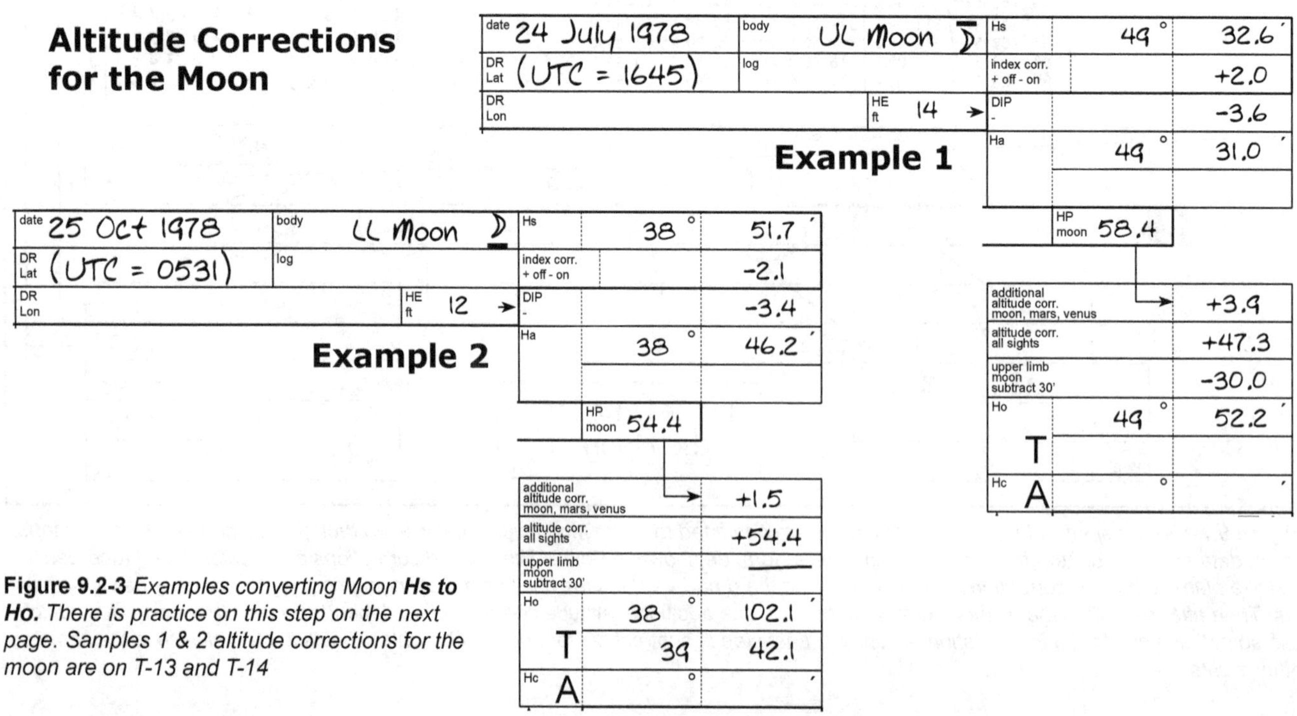

Altitude Corrections for the Moon
Example 1
date 24 July 1978
body UL Moon
(UTC = 1645)
HE 14
Hs 49° 32.6'
index corr. +2.0
DIP -3.6
Ha 49° 31.0'
HP moon 58.4
additional altitude corr. +3.9
altitude corr. all sights +47.3
upper limb moon subtract 30' -30.0
Ho 49° 52.2'
Example 2
date 25 Oct 1978
body LL Moon
(UTC = 0531)
HE 12
Hs 38° 51.7'
index corr. -2.1
DIP -3.4
Ha 38° 46.2'
HP moon 54.4
additional altitude corr. +1.5
altitude corr. all sights +54.4
Ho 38° 102.1'
39 42.1

Figure 9.2-3 *Examples converting Moon **Hs** to **Ho**. There is practice on this step on the next page. Samples 1 & 2 altitude corrections for the moon are on T-13 and T-14*

9.3 Exercise Converting Moon's Hs to Ho

Exercise 9.3a

date 26 July 1978	body LL Moon	Hs	58° 16.6′
DR Lat (UTC = 1736)	log	index corr. + off - on	+2.0
DR Lon	HE ft 16 →	DIP -	
		Ha	° ′
		HP moon	
		additional altitude corr. moon, mars, venus	
		altitude corr. all sights	
		upper limb moon subtract 30′	
		Ho T	° ′
		Hc A	° ′

Exercise 9.3b

date 26 Oct 1978	body UL Moon	Hs	24° 36.5′
DR Lat (UTC = 1350)	log	index corr. + off - on	+2.0
DR Lon	HE ft 13 →	DIP -	
		Ha	° ′
		HP moon	
		additional altitude corr. moon, mars, venus	
		altitude corr. all sights	
		upper limb moon subtract 30′	
		Ho T	° ′
		Hc A	° ′

*Practice converting Moon **Hs to Ho**. Examples are shown in Figure 9.2-3. Altitude corrections for the moon are on T-13 and T-14 in the Tables Selections. Results in the Answers.*

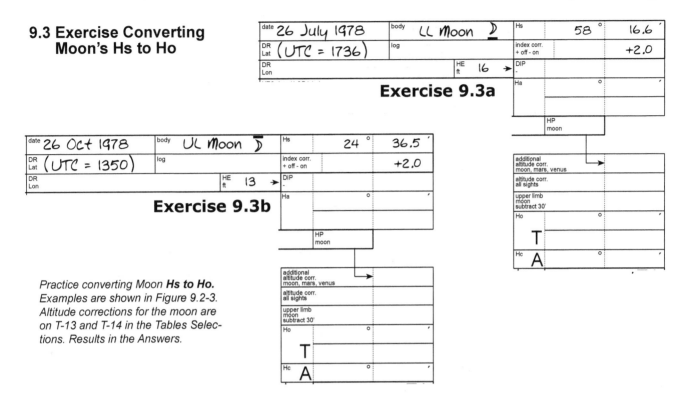

9.4 Moon Sight Reduction, Moon #1

This is the same sight used in the instructions, to be repeated for practice.

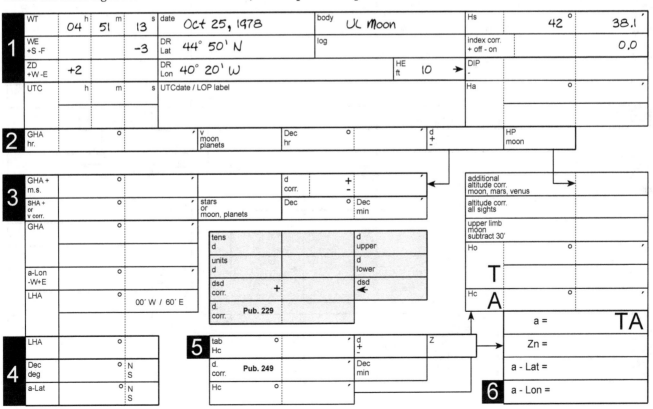

1

	h	m	s				
WT	04	51	13	date Oct 25, 1978	body UL Moon	Hs	42° 38.1′
WE +S -F			-3	DR Lat 44° 50′ N	log	index corr. + off - on	0.0
ZD +W -E	+2			DR Lon 40° 20′ W	HE ft 10 →	DIP -	
UTC	h	m	s	UTCdate / LOP label		Ha	° ′

2

GHA hr.	° ′	v moon planets	Dec hr ° ′	d + -	HP moon

3

GHA + m.s.	° ′		d corr. + -	
SHA + or v corr.	° ′	stars or moon, planets	Dec °	Dec min ′
GHA	° ′			
a-Lon -W+E	° ′			
LHA	° 00′ W / 60′ E			

tens d		d upper	
units d		d lower	
dsd corr.	+	dsd ←	
d. corr.	Pub. 229		

additional altitude corr. moon, mars, venus	
altitude corr. all sights	
upper limb moon subtract 30′	
Ho T	° ′
Hc A	° ′

4

LHA	°	
Dec deg	°	N S
a-Lat	°	N S

5

tab Hc	° ′	d + -		Z
d. corr.	Pub. 249 ′	Dec min		
Hc	° ′			

6

a =	TA
Zn =	
a - Lat =	
a - Lon =	

9.5 Moon-Sun Running Fix Exercise, Moon #2

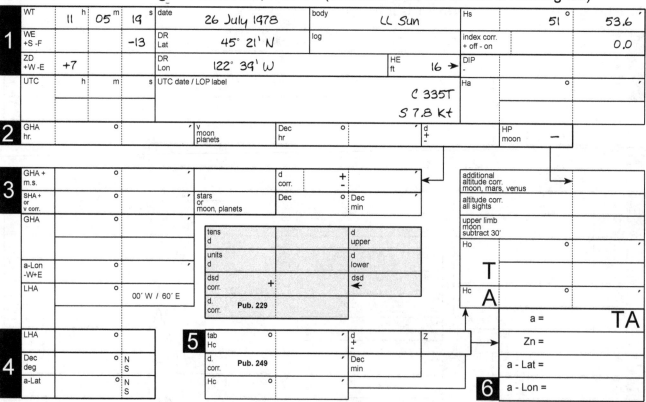

1						
WT	7 h	50 m	07 s	date: 26 July 1978	body: UL Moon	Hs: 51 ° 25.2 ′
WE +S -F			-13	DR Lat: 44° 58' N	log: 852.0	index corr. + off - on: 0.0
ZD +W -E	+7			DR Lon: 122° 24' W	HE ft: 16 →	DIP -
UTC	h	m	s	UTC date / LOP label: C 335T S 7.8 Kt		Ha ° ′

2					
GHA hr. ° ′	v moon planets	Dec hr ° ′	d + -	HP moon	

3				
GHA + m.s. ° ′		d corr. + - ′		additional altitude corr. moon, mars, venus
SHA + or v corr. ° ′	stars or moon, planets	Dec °	Dec min ′	altitude corr. all sights
GHA ° ′				upper limb moon subtract 30′
a-Lon -W+E ° ′				Ho ° ′
LHA ° 00′ W / 60′ E				T
				Hc ° ′ A

tens d		d upper
units d		d lower
dsd corr. +		dsd ←
d. corr. Pub. 229		

4	
LHA °	
Dec deg °	N S
a-Lat °	N S

5			
tab Hc ° ′		d + -	Z
d. corr. Pub. 249 ′		Dec min	
Hc ° ′			

6	
a =	TA
Zn =	
a - Lat =	
a - Lon =	

9.6 Moon-Sun Running Fix Exercise, Sun #8 (combine with 9.5 to find a running fix.)

1						
WT	11 h	05 m	19 s	date: 26 July 1978	body: LL Sun	Hs: 51 ° 53.6 ′
WE +S -F			-13	DR Lat: 45° 21' N	log	index corr. + off - on: 0.0
ZD +W -E	+7			DR Lon: 122° 39' W	HE ft: 16 →	DIP -
UTC	h	m	s	UTC date / LOP label: C 335T S 7.8 Kt		Ha ° ′

2					
GHA hr. ° ′	v moon planets	Dec hr ° ′	d + -	HP moon —	

3				
GHA + m.s. ° ′		d corr. + - ′		additional altitude corr. moon, mars, venus
SHA + or v corr. ° ′	stars or moon, planets	Dec °	Dec min ′	altitude corr. all sights
GHA ° ′				upper limb moon subtract 30′
a-Lon -W+E ° ′				Ho ° ′
LHA ° 00′ W / 60′ E				T
				Hc ° ′ A

tens d		d upper
units d		d lower
dsd corr. +		dsd ←
d. corr. Pub. 229		

4	
LHA °	
Dec deg °	N S
a-Lat °	N S

5			
tab Hc ° ′		d + -	Z
d. corr. Pub. 249 ′		Dec min	
Hc ° ′			

6	
a =	TA
Zn =	
a - Lat =	
a - Lon =	

9.7 Moon-Arcturus Fix Exercise, Moon #3

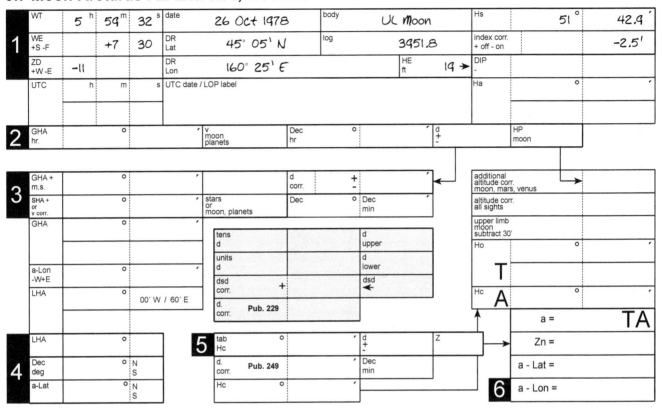

1

	h	m	s							
WT	5 h	59 m	32 s	date	26 Oct 1978	body	UL Moon	Hs	51 °	42.9 ′
WE +S -F		+7	30	DR Lat	45° 05′ N	log	3951.8	index corr. + off - on		-2.5′
ZD +W -E	-11			DR Lon	160° 25′ E	HE ft	19 →	DIP -		
UTC	h	m	s	UTC date / LOP label				Ha	°	′

2

GHA hr.	°	′	v moon planets	Dec hr	° ′	d + -	HP moon

3

GHA + m.s.	°	′		d corr.	+ - ′
SHA + or v corr.	°	′	stars or moon, planets	Dec °	Dec min ′
GHA	°	′			
a-Lon -W+E	°	′			
LHA	°	00′ W / 60′ E			

tens d		d upper
units d		d lower
dsd corr.	+	dsd ←
d. corr.	Pub. 229	

additional altitude corr. moon, mars, venus	
altitude corr. all sights	
upper limb moon subtract 30′	
Ho	° ′
T	
Hc	A ° ′

4

LHA	°	
Dec deg	°	N S
a-Lat	°	N S

5

tab Hc	°	′	d + -	Z
d. corr.	Pub. 249	′	Dec min	
Hc	°	′		

6

a =	TA
Zn =	
a - Lat =	
a - Lon =	

9.8 Moon-Arcturus Fix Exercise, Star #9. *(See starpath.com/celnavbook for Ha <10° tables.)*

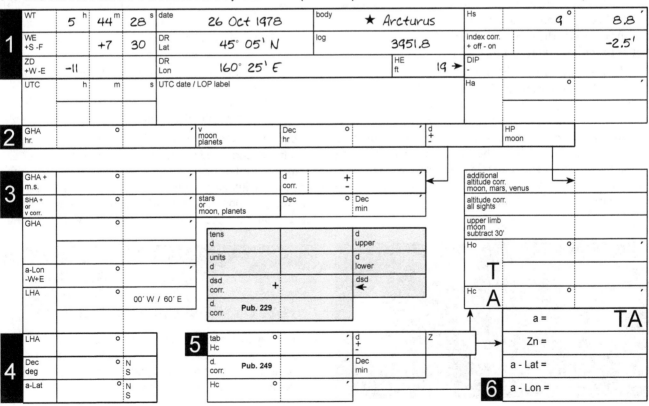

1

	h	m	s							
WT	5 h	44 m	28 s	date	26 Oct 1978	body	★ Arcturus	Hs	9 °	8.8 ′
WE +S -F		+7	30	DR Lat	45° 05′ N	log	3951.8	index corr. + off - on		-2.5′
ZD +W -E	-11			DR Lon	160° 25′ E	HE ft	19 →	DIP -		
UTC	h	m	s	UTC date / LOP label				Ha	°	′

2

GHA hr.	°	′	v moon planets	Dec hr	° ′	d + -	HP moon

3

GHA + m.s.	°	′		d corr.	+ - ′
SHA + or v corr.	°	′	stars or moon, planets	Dec °	Dec min ′
GHA	°	′			
a-Lon -W+E	°	′			
LHA	°	00′ W / 60′ E			

tens d		d upper
units d		d lower
dsd corr.	+	dsd ←
d. corr.	Pub. 229	

additional altitude corr. moon, mars, venus	
altitude corr. all sights	
upper limb moon subtract 30′	
Ho	° ′
T	
Hc	A ° ′

4

LHA	°	
Dec deg	°	N S
a-Lat	°	N S

5

tab Hc	°	′	d + -	Z
d. corr.	Pub. 249	′	Dec min	
Hc	°	′		

6

a =	TA
Zn =	
a - Lat =	
a - Lon =	

9.9 Moon Exercise, Moon #4

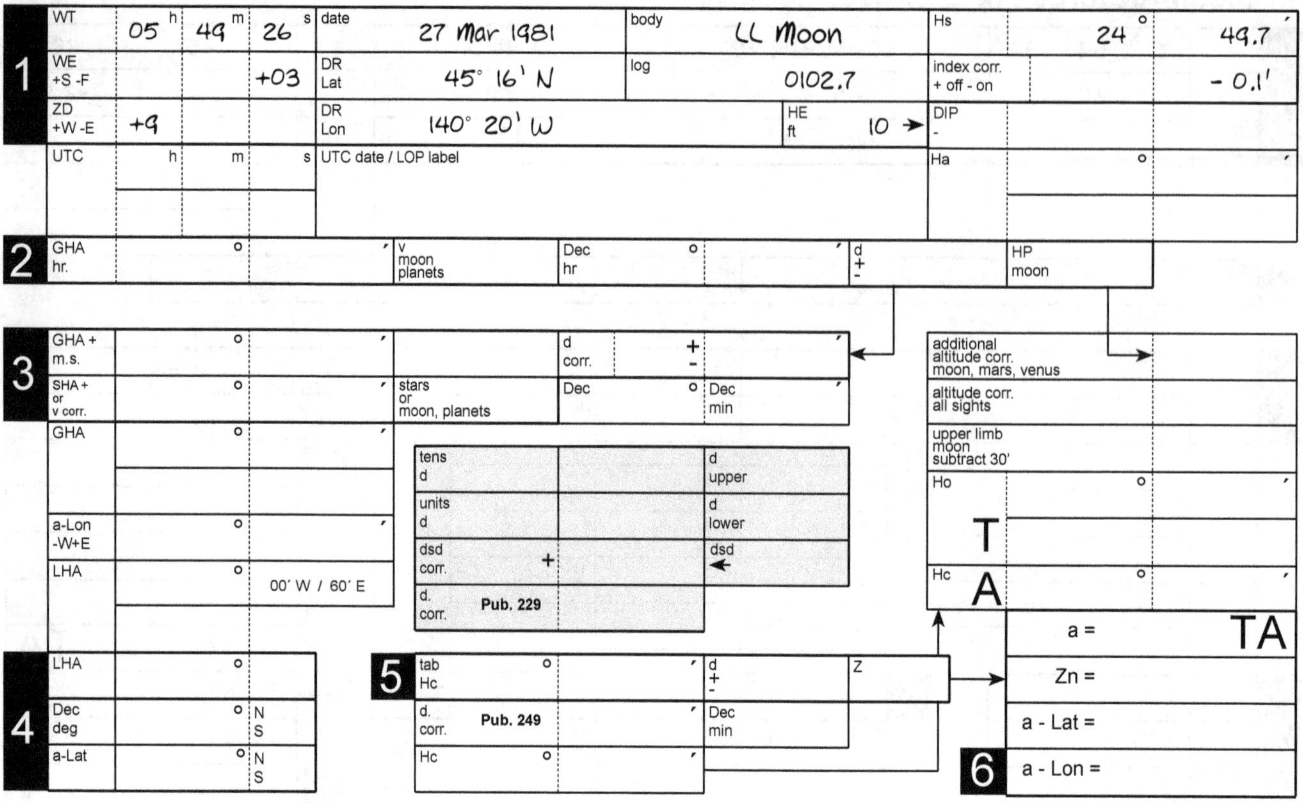

WT 05 h 49 m 26 s
date 27 Mar 1981
body LL Moon
Hs 24° 49.7′
WE +S -F +03
DR Lat 45° 16′ N
log 0102.7
index corr. + off - on -0.1′
ZD +W -E +9
DR Lon 140° 20′ W
HE ft 10
DIP -
UTC h m s
UTC date / LOP label
Ha
GHA hr.
v moon planets
Dec hr
d + -
HP moon
GHA + m.s.
d corr. + -
additional altitude corr. moon, mars, venus
SHA + or v corr.
stars or moon, planets
Dec
Dec min
altitude corr. all sights
GHA
tens d
d upper
upper limb moon subtract 30′
units d
d lower
Ho
a-Lon -W+E
dsd corr. +
dsd
T
LHA
00′ W / 60′ E
d. corr.
Pub. 229
Hc
A
a =
TA
LHA
tab Hc
d + -
Z
Zn =
Dec deg
N S
d. corr.
Pub. 249
Dec min
a - Lat =
a-Lat
N S
Hc
a - Lon =
1
2
3
4
5
6

9.10 Use of the Moon and Planets

Although it is rare to do an upper limb of the sun, which we would do only when the lower limb is in the clouds, this is not the case with the moon, which could just as well be upper as lower limb (Figure 9.10-1).

The accuracy of twilight sextant sights is typically determined by the sharpness of the horizon. If the horizon is a sharp line we get good sights because we know precisely where to align the stars in the sextant. When the horizon is obscure, with the sky blending almost imperceptibly into the sea, we must resort to our best judgment when aligning the star with the horizon—and this will vary from person to person, and from one star to another for the same person looking in different directions.

Evening sights start with a good horizon and end with a poor one. The reverse is true for morning twilight sights: we start in the dark with a weak horizon, which then slowly sharpens as daylight approaches. Any sights we can take during the brighter part of twilight, morning or evening, will improve the accuracy of our fixes. The moon, Venus, and Jupiter are the three bodies that can be seen during the brightest part of twilight when the stars are not visible.

Since we need a triangle of three well positioned bodies for a fix (Section 11.24), the standard procedure is to take Venus or Jupiter, or possibly the moon and then pick the best stars available to complete the triangle. Most navigators would probably agree with this use of Venus or Jupiter, but all may not extend this philosophy to the moon,

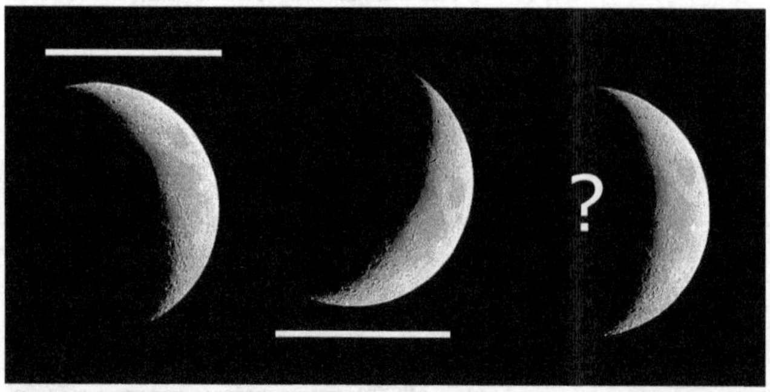

Figure 9.10-1 *Choosing the limb for moon sights.*

> ### *...In Depth*
>
> **11.24 Choosing Optimum Sights**
>
> The key to a good fix is starting with the right bodies and then evaluating the sights once taken. Here we review the basics that lead to an optimum fix using the fit-slope method...

because sights of a bright moon might not be as accurate as those of a well-positioned crescent moon or a planet—the reason is the bright moon lights up the horizon below it, which effectively moves it closer to you, so your sights could end up too high.

Sometimes none of these bright bodies will be available, or the moon will be there but not in a usable phase or location. In that case we go by stars alone, but even then it is productive to figure ahead of time the best three stars to use and precompute their heights and bearings. In the evening, this procedure still gives you a good head start on the brighter stars before the horizon begins to fade; in the morning, it lets you postpone brighter stars till the end of twilight when the horizon has improved.

In summary, if Venus or Jupiter is available it is good practice to use them. They are bright enough to spot by just looking around as you start your voyage. To find out where they will be and when they might be useful for a later cruise, check the *Nautical Almanac's* Planet Notes and Diagram. As a general rule, Mars and Saturn offer no special aid to your sights, and they would only be chosen if they happen to be bright and make up the best triangle with the available bright stars.

The usefulness of the moon cannot be specified precisely because it is difficult to make reliable generalizations about where the moon is. It simply moves around too much in the sky, and as a result its location in your sky depends on where you are and when. But we can provide guidelines we have found are valuable for getting started at more precise predictions. These guidelines are presented in Table 9.10-1. They are given according to the age of the moon that is listed for each day on the daily pages of the *Nautical Almanac*.

Besides these guidelines you also have the moonrise and moonset times given in the *Nautical Almanac*. When considering moon sights, first check Table 9.10-1, then double-check the moon's rising and setting times to be sure the moon is above the horizon at the time you plan the sights. The meridian passage time of the moon is also listed. Use the time of upper transit to tell when the moon will cross your meridian at its maximum height in the sky, bearing either due north or due south depending on your latitude and the declination of the moon. All times listed in the Almanac have to be converted to Watch Time, but for judging roughly where the moon is relative to the sun, recall that the tabulated mer. pass. time of the sun is midday, regardless of what WT it translates to. If the moon's tabulated meridian passage time is earlier than that listed for the sun, the moon is ahead of the sun, meaning to the west of it. With practice, the rising, meridian passage, and setting times of the moon relative to the sun will give you a fairly good idea of the moon's location.

Referring to Table 9.10-1, we see that the moon is typically best positioned for daytime sights with the sun during moon ages 6 to 8 and 21 to 23, or about 1 week of each month. In practice, however, these sights might be available for longer periods, up to almost 2 weeks in some cases (ages 4 to 10 and 19 to 25), depending on your latitude and the moon's declination. In some of these extended cases, however, the optimum sight times might be so close to twilight that there is no virtue in the sun-moon fix when you have a star fix available within a couple of hours.

Table 9.10-1 also tells when you might combine the moon with star sights. Again, just use it as a guide and then make more specific choices from your specific circumstances. It could be, for example, that the moon is indeed

Table 9.10-1. Guidelines for the Use of the Moon*

Age (days)	Phase and Location	Sight Time	Special Value
1-3	Waxing crescent, setting near western horizon at sunset	Just after sunset, before evening stars appear	Combine with evening star sights
6-8	Waxing half moon, near the meridian at sunset	Mid afternoon	Combine with sun for daytime fix
12-14	Waxing full moon, rising near eastern horizon at sunset	Just after sunset, before evening stars appear	Combine with evening star sights
15-17	Waning full moon, setting near western horizon at sunrise	Just before sunrise, after morning stars fade	Combine with morning star sights
21-23	Waning half moon, near the meridian at sunrise	Mid morning	Combine with sun for daytime fix
26-28	Waning crescent, rising near eastern horizon at sunrise	Just before sunrise, after morning stars fade	Combine with morning star sights

* *The range of ages might be off a day or so in some circumstances — the predictions are least dependable when either sun or moon pass overhead during the days in question. The best use of the moon depends on your latitude and the declination of the moon. The moon's age is listed on the daily pages of the* Nautical Almanac.

visible for evening twilight sights on the day (age) that the Table predicts, but for your location and date it is too low for an accurate sight.

In some circumstances you can take star sights at night by a moonlit horizon. The accuracy will not be the best, but it is possible when you have a bright moon that is *fairly high in the sky*. The trick is to pick the three optimum bodies (Section 11.24) and then hope that the errors will be about the same in each of the sights. Any one sight will not be very accurate, but if the errors for each star are roughly the same your fix will be a good one. The errors are more likely to be similar if the horizon is similar in all directions. Your three LOPs will make a fairly large triangle, but its center might be a reasonable fix. The procedure is not recommended for routine usage.

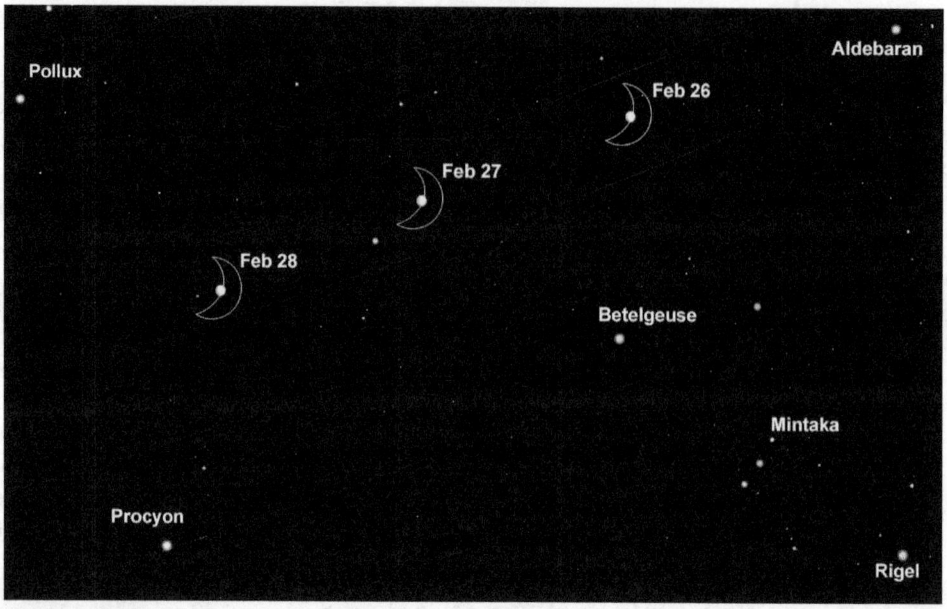

Figure 9.10-2 *Motion of the moon, eastward through the stars. The moon circles the earth (full moon to full moon) at a rate of about 12° per day relative to the fixed stars behind it (360°/29.5 days). To see this, look at the moon relative to a prominent star* at the same time *on consecutive nights. Recall that the diameter of the full moon is about 0.5°, so 12° is 24 moon diameters, about half a hand span. This graphic was created from the wonderful free program Stellarium (www.stellarium.org), with the exaggerated moon sketches added. We leave it as an advanced exercise, but in principle you can find the Lat and Lon of the observer from this picture and a* Nautical Almanac *alone.*

Figure 9.10-2 is a reminder of how the moon moves eastward through the stars each night, as it progresses through the lunar cycle. The *Emergency Navigation* book has an extended discussion of how the moon moves across the sky. That book emphasizes how to determine the direction of the moon based on its phase and the time of night. It all ties in to a better understanding of what we see in the sky and how this helps us stay oriented.

9.11 New Terminology

horizontal parallax

moon age

Stellarium

waning

waxing

...In Depth

11.25 Star and Planet ID

We do not need to know how to identify stars by just looking at the sky if we do our homework properly, but when there is not time for that or, we are in an emergency without our standard tools, then the more we know about star ID the better...

...In Depth

11.26 Emergency Procedures

Several methods of standard cel nav can be adapted to use with limited resources, and basic principles lead to even further backup methods. We review some of these here...

...In Depth

11.27 Pub. 249 Vol. 1, Selected Stars

The sun, moon, and all planets can be sight reduced with Pub. 249 Vols. 2 and 3, as well as stars with Dec less than 29°. Vol 1 is intended for sight reduction of other selected stars. The procedure is different, but shorter, as explained in this note. You can also use Pub. 249 Vol. 1 to predict the best three stars to use...

CHAPTER 10
PRINCIPLES OF CEL NAV

10.1 A One-Hour Course in Cel Nav

If we understand just a few principles of celestial navigation, we can begin to use it immediately. To punctuate that thought, with just this Section 10.1 alone you should be able to find your way to any port in the world, from any place at sea, with nothing more than a *Nautical Almanac* and a watch. The rest of this chapter fills in other details we have relied upon in earlier parts of the book.

To begin with, the only reason we need a full book on celestial navigation—as opposed to knowing it intuitively since birth—is the fact that the earth turns on its axis, once every 24 hours. To prove this point, we look at the consequences of stopping this motion.

The visible stars around us are more or less evenly distributed across the hemisphere of the sky we see, regardless of whether we are in Seattle or in Auckland. In the real world, if we watch these stars throughout the night we see them rise from the eastern horizon, reach peak heights in the sky when bearing north or south, and then set somewhere on the western horizon. But if we stop the earth, all that motion stops. At the moment we stop the earth from rotating, every star we see in the sky freezes in position, right where it is, and it stays there, night after night, year after year. And that situation would have a dramatic influence on celestial navigation.

Imagine that each of these stars distributed across the stationary sky sent out a laser beam that went straight through the center of the earth (Figure 10.1-1). And as this beam burned through the surface of the earth it made a mark. That mark is called the *geographical position* of that star, usually abbreviated GP.

This is the concept underlying the construction of star globes seen in astronomy displays or book stores periodically. It is a static projection of the stars down onto the globe of the earth, although they don't usually show the map of the earth, but rather just a blue background. All the relative positions of the stars within the constellations are laid out on a sphere (Figure 10.1-2). Just imagine now that that sphere is a globe of the earth.

If you happened to be located at the GP of a star, you would observe that star precisely overhead *at your zenith*—the laser beam going right through the top of your head. If you had a sextant, you would measure its height above the horizon as exactly 90°, (i.e., overhead). If you were not at the GP of a star, that star would not appear overhead but rather off of your zenith, at a lower altitude in the sky. How much lower would depend on how far off you were from it.

There is a direct and simple correlation, which we will prove a bit later on. If you move 1° away from the GP, the star will move down 1° from the zenith—it will be 89° high in the sky. Move 10° away from the GP and the star will now be 80° high in the sky. We also clarify later that a distance of 1° of latitude on the surface of the earth is equal to 60 nmi, but do not be distracted by these details at this point. The summary is all that matters: if you are at the GP, the star is overhead; if you are away from the GP, the star is lower. As you move toward the GP, the star gets higher, until you are precisely at the GP, at which point it is overhead on your zenith. And remember, too, our model: the earth is not rotating, so the sky is permanent.

If we happened to be about half way up Vancouver Island, BC, when we stopped the earth, then one star that might have stopped right overhead is Alkaid, on the tip of

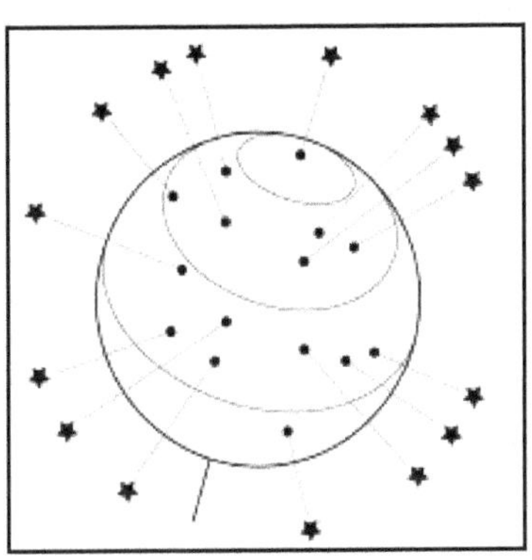

Figure 10.1-1 *Stars marking geographical positions on the earth.*

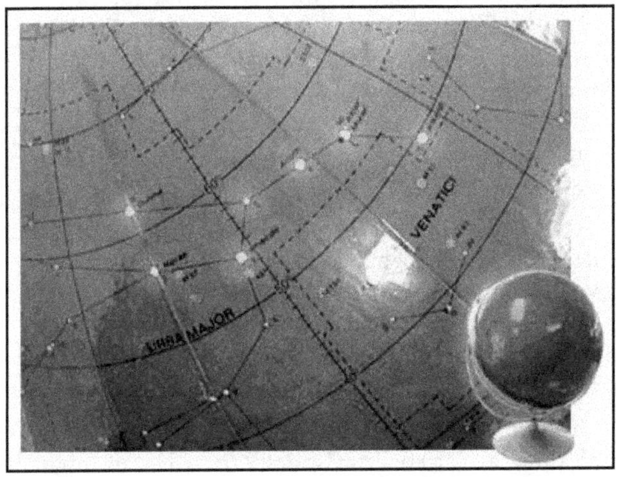

Figure 10.1-2 *Section of a star globe showing Big Dipper.*

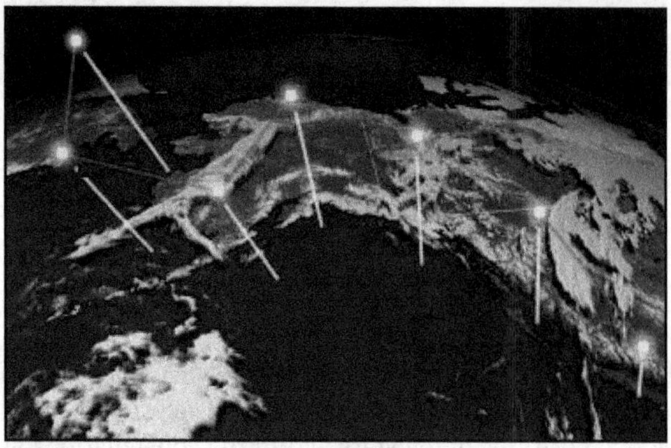

Figure 10.1-3 *Dipper as it might appear stopping in the sky over Alaska and British Columbia.*

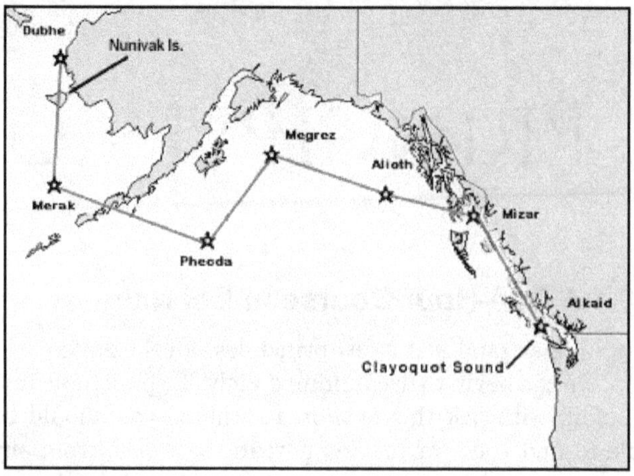

Figure 10.1-4 *The Land of Ursa Major, in what we now call the Pacific Northwest.*

the handle of the Big Dipper in Ursa Major. For everyone living in that region (Clayoquot Sound), Alkaid would be a zenith star, overhead all night, every night of the year—let us simply forget for the moment that if we did stop the earth rotating it would be night all the time; that detail does not concern us now.

Ursa Major itself would stretch all the way to Nunivak Island in the Bering Strait, with Dubhe (tip of the cup) just north of you (Figure 10.1-3 and 10.1-4). And if that had been the case since the beginning of time (i.e., the earth never had rotated) then almost certainly, people in that region would have described where they lived something like, "I live in the Land of Ursa Major, near Alkaid." And this would be so because everyone could see an entire map of the globe reflected in the sky. From Clayoquot Sound (Alkaid), I could see Nunivak (Dubhe). Furthermore, I would know how to get there. Just head toward Dubhe.

Now imagine we are sitting in Clayoquot Sound (in the cold wet Pacific Northwest) and a sailing vessel comes in from the Pacific Ocean with the report that they have just come from the Land of Arcturus, in the middle of the ocean. And they found there a paradise of white sand beaches, clear warm water, palm trees, mahi mahi, hula hula, etc. And you would like to go there. Well, the navigation part is done. They have told you where it is, *and you can see it in the sky*—follow the arc of the handle of the Big Dipper, away from the cup for a distance about equal to the breadth of the dipper to an isolated (yellowish) bright star. That is Arcturus—sailors say "Arc to Arcturus" to remember how to find it from the Big Dipper.

Now sail off toward Arcturus. Each night as you get closer, it will be higher in the sky (Figure 10.1-5), and then when Hawaii is in sight, Arcturus will be overhead. If you have a sextant, you can measure its height every 24 hours or so during the voyage to monitor your progress. If it is 2° higher today than it was yesterday at this time, then you have made good 120 nmi.

In short, if the earth did not rotate, there would be no such thing as celestial navigation—or at best it might be called "sky pilotage." This concept of a GP and how the height of a star in the sky depends on how far you are from its GP is the very basis of celestial navigation. These principles have been known on various levels since ancient times.

But we have more to do to meet our practical goal because we know the earth does in fact rotate once a day. If we were to head off toward Arcturus in the real world, we would be chasing a moving target all over the ocean, and we would not likely find our way to Hawaii.

We need to solve our real-world problem in two steps: latitude first, then longitude.

Latitude

We know the key to the latitude part, however, right from the beginning. Arcturus does indeed travel over the top of Hawaii. Unfortunately, it is not locked overhead there, it just passes overhead in Hawaii once a day—over the southern tip of the Big Island. To understand why this is the key to latitude, we must go back to our star globe and the laser beams.

Imagine our star globe fixed in space with all the laser beams lit up and penetrating the surface. The axis of the earth is pointed to the North Star, Polaris. The North Pole is the GP of Polaris. The orientation of the axis is fixed in space and not moving. Now with the laser beams burning holes in the earth, and the axis not moving, start rotating

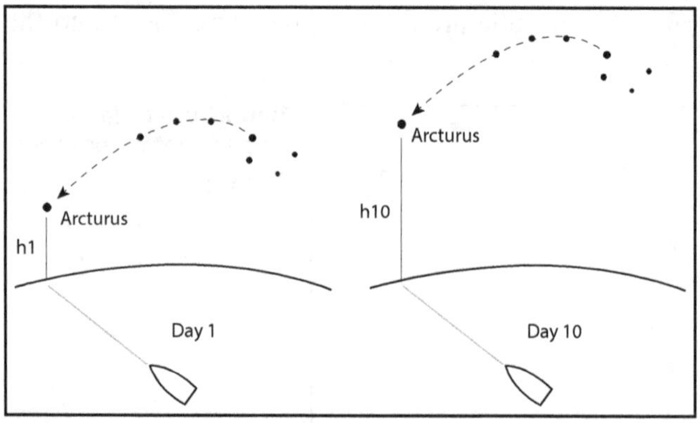

Figure 10.1-5 *With the earth not rotating, Arcturus would not move across the sky, it would just get higher as you got closer to it.*

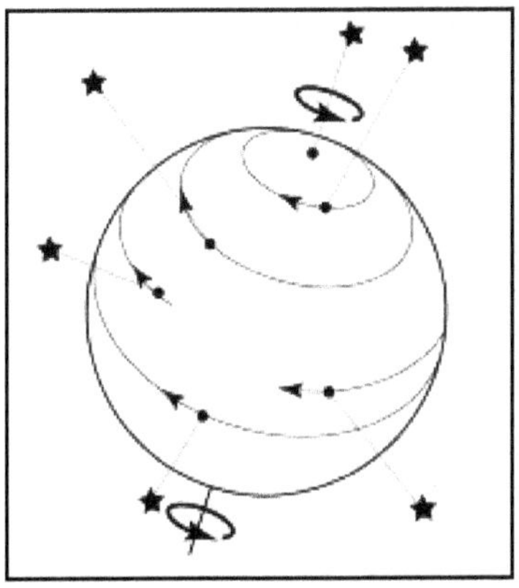

Figure 10.1-6 *As the earth rotates to the east, the GPs of all the stars move westward around the globe, locked in on fixed latitudes called the declinations of the stars. They circle the globe once every 24 hours.*

the earth to the east in your mind. You will see that the stars burn trails on the globe as the GPs move westward, and these lines do not cross each other because the axis of the rotation is not moving. That is, as the earth rotates, any given laser beam does not get any farther from the North Pole. And a line around the earth that is the same distance from the North Pole all the way around, is called a *latitude* line. (Figure 10.1-6).

In other words, every star in the sky is locked onto a specific latitude. Stars are on railroad tracks. They do not deviate. Once a day, the GP of a star circles the earth on its own track, passing over every point on earth that has that latitude. This is another fundamental concept. Every star has a unique latitude over which it circles the earth daily. The latitude of a star is called the star's *declination.* (We should not confuse this term with the one land lubbers use when they mean magnetic variation.) The declination of a star is the latitude of the star's GP. To avoid confusion, we label the declination with the N or S before the value and we label the latitude of a place with the N or S after the value. Thus, the latitude of the southern tip of the Big Island of Hawaii is 19° 6' N, whereas the declination of the star Arcturus is N 19° 6'.

Here now is the significance of this. No matter where I am on the globe, and no matter what time of year it is, or

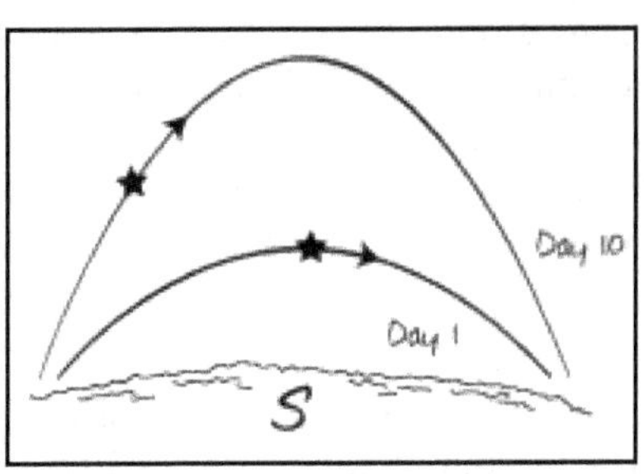

Figure 10.1-7 *In the real sky, above a rotating earth, the peak height of Arcturus at meridian passage will get higher every night as you proceed south toward latitude 19° N.*

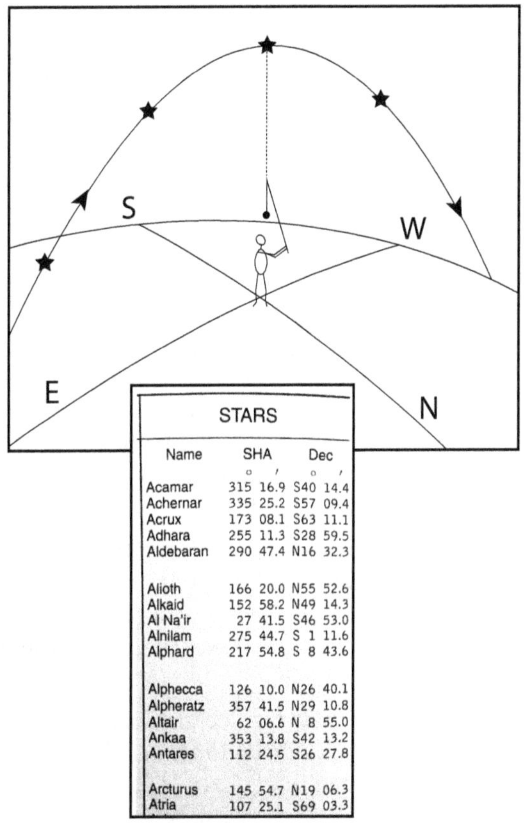

Name	SHA	Dec
	° ′	° ′
Acamar	315 16.9	S40 14.4
Achernar	335 25.2	S57 09.4
Acrux	173 08.1	S63 11.1
Adhara	255 11.3	S28 59.5
Aldebaran	290 47.4	N16 32.3
Alioth	166 20.0	N55 52.6
Alkaid	152 58.2	N49 14.3
Al Na'ir	27 41.5	S46 53.0
Alnilam	275 44.7	S 1 11.6
Alphard	217 54.8	S 8 43.6
Alphecca	126 10.0	N26 40.1
Alpheratz	357 41.5	N29 10.8
Altair	62 06.6	N 8 55.0
Ankaa	353 13.8	S42 13.2
Antares	112 24.5	S26 27.8
Arcturus	145 54.7	N19 06.3
Atria	107 25.1	S69 03.3

Figure 10.1-8 *Schematic of a star rising, crossing the meridian at peak height bearing due south, and setting. The insert shows a section of the list of star declinations from the 2015 Nautical Almanac. The SHA listed beside it is equivalent to the longitude of a star on the star globe, but we do not get into that till later in the course.*

what time of night it is, if I see Arcturus pass overhead, I know I am at latitude 19° 6' N. In a real voyage at sea, however, I only get to make this evaluation once a night. The star will rise in the east, move toward the south throughout the night as it rises, reach a peak height in the sky bearing due south as it crosses my meridian, and then descend as it heads toward the western horizon.

We assume for now that the star we chose does indeed cross our meridian at night. If it does not, then we must choose another star to mark the latitude we want. If we were sailing north from Tahiti (17° S) to Hawaii, we would see this star reach its peak height bearing north as it crossed our meridian.

So now, for the real world solution of sailing to Hawaii from Clayoquot Sound. First, I know my destination is at the latitude of Arcturus and that it is in the middle of the ocean, well to the west of North America. Later when we learn the longitude part, we can make our route more efficient, but for now we are going purely by latitude. So I first head due west for some miles to get safely offshore. I do not want to run into Cape Alava, WA, the most western point of the continental US—or more specifically, Umatilla Reef, which is rather farther offshore than the Cape itself. Then I turn left, and head south.

Each night I watch Arcturus rise and cross my meridian. Early in the voyage it will be low in the sky at peak height, but as I proceed south, it will be higher at peak height each night as my latitude decreases. Clayoquot Sound was at 49° 17' N. I am headed toward 19° 6' N, a distance south of 49 - 19 = 30°, and each degree is 60 nmi, so we must go some 1800 nmi to the south. This is not the shortest route to Hawaii! Eventually I will see Arcturus cross my meridian directly overhead. I know then I am at the desired latitude, so I turn right and head west.

Now that I know I am at the right latitude, my job is to watch each night to see that I have not slipped north or south of where I want to be. If Arcturus is not overhead any longer, but a bit north of my zenith, then I know I have slipped south and I correct my course to the north. And so on, until the islands are in sight.

This is a long, roundabout way of getting places. It is called latitude or parallel sailing. It was indeed the way early explorers, including the Vikings, got around the world, place to place. It is the only safe way to travel if you do not know how to find longitude.

A list of navigational star declinations is included on each daily page of the *Nautical Almanac.* There are another 100 or so stars listed in the back of the almanac, along with several star maps that might help identify the stars relative to prominent configurations.

Recalling our original promise, here is how you might get from one place to another with this technique. Use the *Nautical Almanac* to look up a star with declination near the latitude of where you want to go. You can identify the star using the star maps from the back of the almanac. Then sail to the latitude of the star as described, making certain you know if you are well east or west of your destination. Once at the latitude, turn to your destination and monitor your course each night.

Without a sextant, you will need some method to determine more or less precisely when a star passes overhead, but there are several tricks. We leave those to the book *Emergency Navigation*; for now we just want to understand the principles. Other parts of that book explain how we would actually get to Hawaii, but it never hurts to keep these principles in mind, and watch the stars ahead of you rise each night as you proceed south.

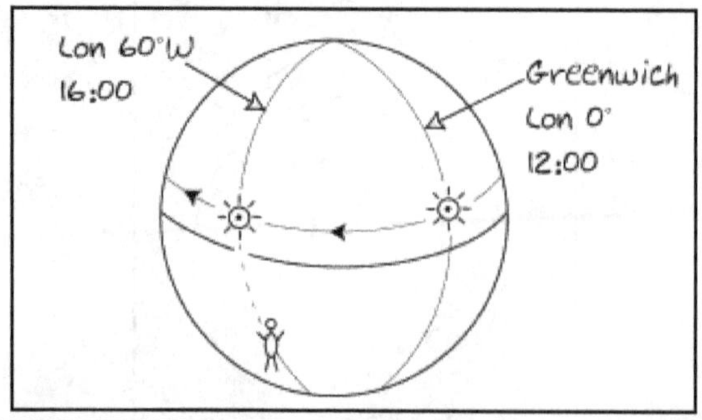

S 50	16 12	16 50	17 31	08 05	08 49	09 27	09 58
52	16 03	16 43	17 27	08 15	08 59	09 35	10 05
54	15 53	16 36	17 21	08 27	09 10	09 45	10 13
56	15 41	16 27	17 16	08 40	09 22	09 56	10 21
58	15 27	16 17	17 09	08 55	09 37	10 08	10 31
S 60	15 11	16 07	17 02	09 13	09 53	10 22	10 42

Day	SUN			MOON			
	Eqn. of Time 00h	12h	Mer. Pass.	Mer. Pass. Upper	Lower	Age	Phase
	m s	m s	h m	h m	h m	d	
6	04 33	04 38	12 05	24 39	12 14	15	
7	04 43	04 48	12 05	00 39	13 03	16	○
8	04 53	04 58	12 05	01 27	13 51	17	

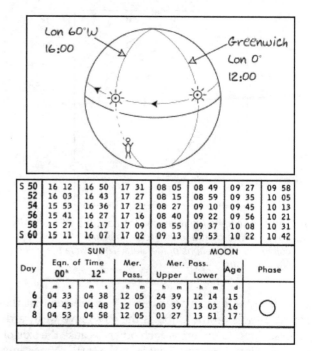

Figure 10.1-9 Top *Meridian passage facing North.*
Bottom *Meridian passage found in the* Nautical Almanac.

Longitude

When you travel north or south along the globe of the earth the stars change in unique ways, as we have just discussed. New stars are seen overhead, new ones appear on the horizon, and so on. From any place on earth, I can always look at the sky and figure out my latitude. It does not matter what part of the globe I am on, or what time of year I look at the sky, or what time of night I look at the sky. I do not need to know time to find my latitude.

Longitude, on the other hand, is a totally different matter because the stars are locked onto specific latitudes as we discussed earlier. Because the earth rotates 360° around its axis once every 24 hours, the GPs of all the stars move west along the surface of the earth at a rate of 15° of longitude each hour (360°/24 hours = 15°/hour). Looking up, when viewed from any specific latitude, the sky as a whole rotates westward at this same rate, 15° of longitude per hour.

This means that the sky I see right now will look *identical* to the sky that is seen by someone at my same latitude, who is located 15° of longitude west of me, 1 hour later. If I write down the heights and bearings of numerous stars and then call this person on the radio 1 hour later, he will measure precisely the same heights and bearings for these stars. In other words, without knowing the time of night, I could not differentiate my longitude from his longitude based on what we see in the sky. (Someone who is 15° of latitude south of me, on the other hand, will see a different sky no matter what time they look at it.)

One way this is often summarized is to say, "You need time to find longitude." But the relationship is stronger than that. Longitude and time are completely equivalent in celestial navigation. If I know the correct time, I can find my longitude, and equally, if I know my longitude, I can find the correct time. Longitude and time are essentially identical. Without pursuing the specifics for the moment, this is why we split the day into AM and PM and why we split the circumference of the globe into West longitude and East longitude.

To clarify the relationship with a practical example, consider this situation. Suppose I have a watch, and from wherever I happen to be, I call up the Greenwich Observatory in the UK, which is located precisely on the longitude 0° line, and ask them to help me with this illustration. I ask them to keep an eye on the direction to the sun, and to please tell me when the sun bears precisely due south from their location. The sun will also be at its peak height in their mid-day sky at this time, but for now I just need to know when it crosses due south at Greenwich. For now, I do not care how they do this—they could have a tall rod and just watch when its shadow crosses over a thin line running north-south.

The moment they tell me the sun is due south, I set my watch to 12:00 and thank them. That is all I need to keep track of my own longitude for now. This is, of course, just an example; we will have much easier ways to do this!

Now, to dramatize the point I want to make, I get into a box, and have this large box put into an airplane, and let it take off at high speeds to any place in the world. The crew is testing me to see if I can indeed find longitude—and I must say, I don't know where the box idea came from; the lecture has always been presented this way, but a blindfold would be a more comfortable choice!

After many hours of travel, maybe circling back, the plane lands. I get out of the box and have no idea whatsoever (at least for the time being) where we are. And someone asks, what is our longitude? Preparation for the answer depends on a couple of things. Will they tell me which way is south or north right now or won't they. If they tell me, then I can answer "Give me till noon," presuming it is before noon wherever we are, or "Give me till the next noon," if noon is already past. I need to watch the sun cross the north-south line, our local meridian.

If they won't tell me directions, then I have to wait one full day to use the sun or stars to find a precise N-S line, but that is easy, by various methods.

So let's say it is before noon and I know a true north-south line. As I watch the sun, I note that it will be crossing north, rather low in the sky—which means I must be fairly far into the Southern Hemisphere, but latitude is not the issue at hand. As the sun crosses the local meridian, I simply look at my watch and it reads 16:00 (4 pm) (Figure 10.1-9 Top). And with that simple, single observation, I can make the statement that our longitude is 4 hours west of Greenwich, which means our longitude is 4 hours × 15°/hour = 60° west of Greenwich. Recall that whenever we say our longitude is, for example, 120° West, we always mean 120° west of the Greenwich meridian. We just usually omit the last phrase. It is like saying our latitude is 37° North, rather than 37° north of the equator. The reference line is understood.

To review this reasoning: we know the sun crossed the Greenwich meridian at 12:00 according to this watch, and we know that all celestial bodies move west around the globe at 15° of longitude per hour. You can think of the bodies moving across the sky at this rate, or think of their GPs moving along the surface of the earth at this rate. It does not matter. The time we observed the meridian passage of the sun (a phrase we use often in cel nav) at the unknown location was later than 12:00, so we had to be west of Greenwich. And from the time difference, we can compute the longitude difference. This is an exact solution. If we know all the numbers precisely (i.e., the time the sun passed Greenwich and the time the sun passed us), we can figure out our longitude precisely. That is always a true statement, not just part of the exercise we are working on now.

If we had observed the meridian passage at 03:00 (3 am) at our unknown position, then we would say: "the sun passes us at 03:00 and we know it is heading west and will pass Greenwich at 12:00, so we must be 9 hours east of Greenwich, so our longitude must be 9 hours × 15°/hour = 135° East".

In other words, once you know the right time, you can always find your longitude from the sun in this manner. In this example, we don't really know what time system or time zone we are using, but hopefully you see it does not matter. We only need to know what time the sun passed Greenwich according to our watch. The method used here is obviously not very practical unless you have a satellite telephone, but that is not the point. It is the principle we want to clarify.

We can make this a practical exercise that you can do immediately (i.e., at the end of this "1-hour course", as promised) by cleaning up some details. What do we need? We need to know the time the sun passed Greenwich and the time the sun passed us. The first we get from the *Nautical Almanac*, and the second relies on a measurement of our own, and we need a watch set to the correct UTC (same as what used to be called GMT).

First you need to know what time the sun crossed the Greenwich meridian on the date you are observing it cross your own meridian. In other words, this is not a constant time from day to day. It will always be within 16 minutes or so of 12:00 UTC, but you need to know it precisely. You get this daily time of meridian passage at Greenwich from the *Nautical Almanac*. It is on each Daily Page as "Mer. Pass." in the Sun box. In Figure 10.1-9 for day 7 of the month selected, this time is 12:05 UTC, rounded to the nearest minute.

Next we need to determine when the sun crosses our meridian. If you had an unobscured view to both the east and west sea horizons, one easy way to find the time of local noon is to time the sunrise and then sunset and take the average of the two (i.e., half way between them). That will be an accurate time, if you have accurate rise and set times. Otherwise you could hold a credit card at arm's length with the bottom edge aligned with the sea horizon and time when the sun peaks over the card while rising and then when it drops below the card while setting, and take the average of those two times. With a real sextant, we have even better ways.

The reason this is not a good *routine* method of finding longitude is that it is not so easy to determine a precise time of meridian passage of the sun (also called *Local Apparent Noon*) no matter how you do it. We have better ways to navigate covered elsewhere in this book. This method, however, is indeed useful in an emergency, and we also hope that it is useful for illustrating the principle of finding longitude.

10.2 Distant Light Rays

The key to understanding how cel nav works has to start with the geometry of the light rays that we are looking at and the concept of *parallax*. Parallax is the difference in apparent position of an object when viewed from two different lines of sight. We face this issue daily (on a much smaller scale) when reading the dial on an instrument, such as an aneroid barometer. If we do not view it straight on, we get the wrong reading. In cel nav the issue underlies what we do on a much grander scale.

In Figure 10.2-1 we see an illustration of this. A person at point A sees the light of an aircraft a distance h1 away at angle α, whereas at the same moment a person at B sees the same light at an angle β. Then they look at a plane a distance h2 away, and again one at h3 away. You see from the figure that the farther away the light is, the closer β becomes to α. In other words, the farther away the light source, the closer to parallel the light rays become. In cel nav sights, the light is from a star and the distance away is immense, so the light is parallel not only over earthly separations like thousands of miles, but indeed over the full plane of the earth's orbit around the sun (Figure 10.2-2).

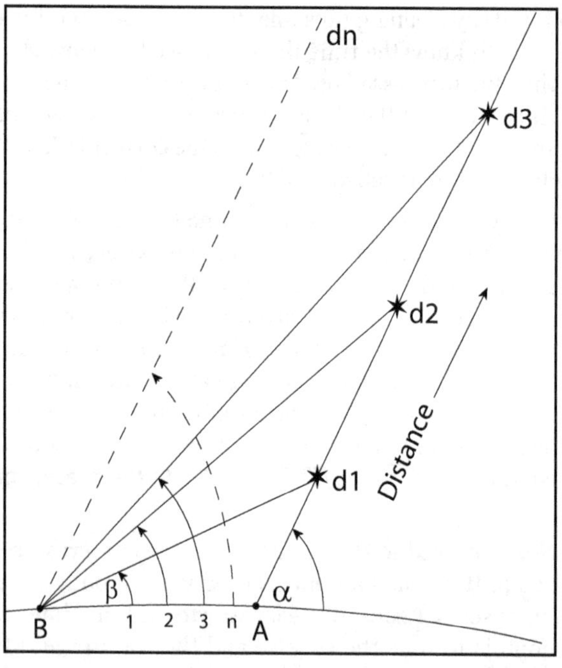

Figure 10.2-1 *Angular height of an aircraft light as a function of distance to the observer. When the light is low, a person at point A measures a higher angle (α) than a person at point B (β). But as the light is moved farther and farther away, the two angles become the same, since the light rays become parallel. You can see this already in this picture. By the time you get to about d10 or so these lines would be nearly parallel. But these are still earthly scales. The distance between A and B could be at most some 8,000 miles (the earth's diameter), so at the scale shown, this would only be about 80,000 miles away. The closest stars are some 6 million-million miles away, so their light is not only parallel across the earth, but across the entire orbit of the earth.*

Because the light from a single star hits the spherical earth in parallel rays, we can develop the geometry upon which cel nav principles are based. The angle we observe for the star can be related to our distance from the point where the star appears overhead, as shown in the next section.

10.3 Zenith Distance = Distance to the GP

When the parallel light from a single star illuminates the earth, observers at different locations see its height above the flat horizon at different angles, as shown in Figure 10.3-1. The key here is the definition of the *horizon*, being the plane that is perpendicular to the radius of the earth at that point. Observers at the geographical position (GP) of the star see it overhead, but those at A (in this schematic) see it 80° above the horizon and those farther away at B see it at the same time at 40° above the horizon. This general behavior was discussed in Section 10.1.

But now with a little basic geometry, we can be much more specific. We only need two intuitive rules: first when two straight lines intersect, the angles they make are the

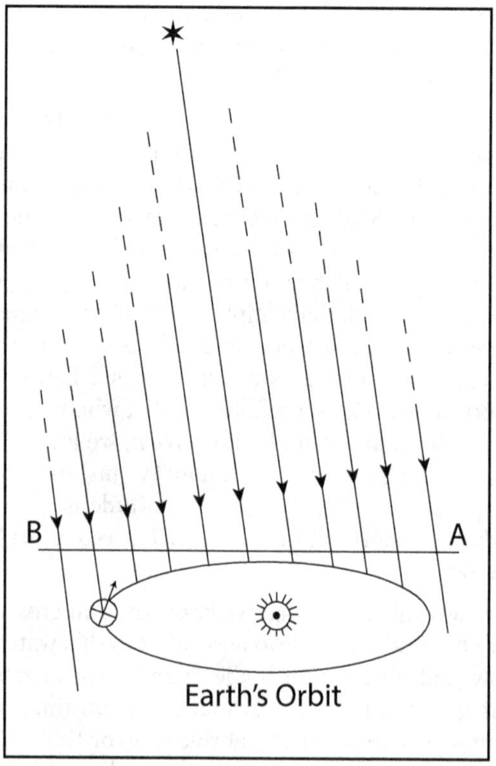

Figure 10.2-2 *Stars are so distant (10 million million miles) that the light we see is parallel over the full span of the earth's orbit, only about 2 x 93 million miles.*

same on each side, and secondly we need the rule that when two parallel lines intersect with another straight line they cross at the same angle. These rules are shown in the inset to Figure 10.3-2.

As we learn elsewhere in this book, the angle a star makes with the true, flat horizon is called Ho (observed height). We get this in the normal procedures after removing complicating factors such as refraction in the atmosphere, which bends the light rays, and our own height above the water, which exaggerates this angle; but these details do not matter at this point.

We also define the angle between the star and the zenith above us as the *zenith distance*, z. So we have Ho, as the angular height of the star above the horizon, and z as the remaining angle on up to the zenith. And since our zenith is always perpendicular to our horizon, by definition Ho + z is always equal to 90°.

Now we can look at two specific light rays from this one star; the one going through the GP and the one we see in our sextant. On Figure 10.3-2, follow the light ray through the GP to the center of the earth and see where it intersects the line projected down from our zenith. It is to this angle that we apply our geometry theorem. The two light rays are parallel, so the angle must equal z, the zenith distance.

Now we return to the definition of a nautical mile, and in doing so, we actually learn why a nautical mile is defined the way it is. In much of navigation we just refer to a latitude difference in terms of nautical miles, such as 38° N is 10° south of 48° N, so we know it is 600 nmi south, because 1° of latitude equals 60 nmi. But the definition is actually much more general than that.

The general rule is that any two points on earth have a great circle distance between them, and that distance along the surface of the earth is equal in nautical miles to the angle subtended by a line from each of the two points on earth to the center of the earth. We start with a three-dimensional picture of two points on a globe, then we draw a line from the center of the globe to each of these points, and imagine the angle between those two lines. The distance between those two points on the surface will equal in nautical miles the number of arc minutes in that angle. We do this reckoning with latitude routinely, but that is just a special case where one of the points happens to be due north or south of the other. The definition is true for any two points on the globe.

Thus we have the fundamental rule of celestial navigation that the zenith distance is the distance from us to the GP. If we measure the height of a star to be 30°, then the GP of that star at that moment is located 60° or 3600 nmi away from us—because Ho + z is always 90°.

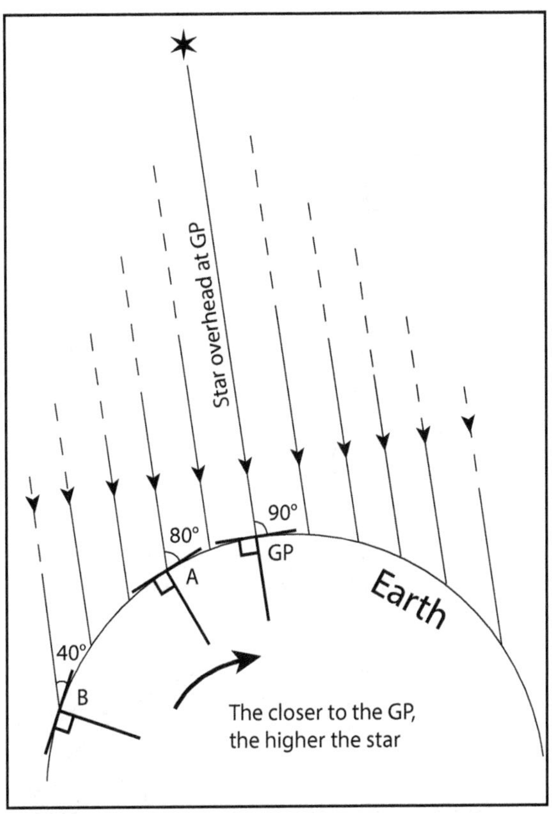

Figure 10.3-1 *Light rays from a single distant star are parallel across the surface of the earth. The one at the GP goes through the center of the earth. At the GP, the star is overhead. As you move away from the GP the star descends in the sky.*

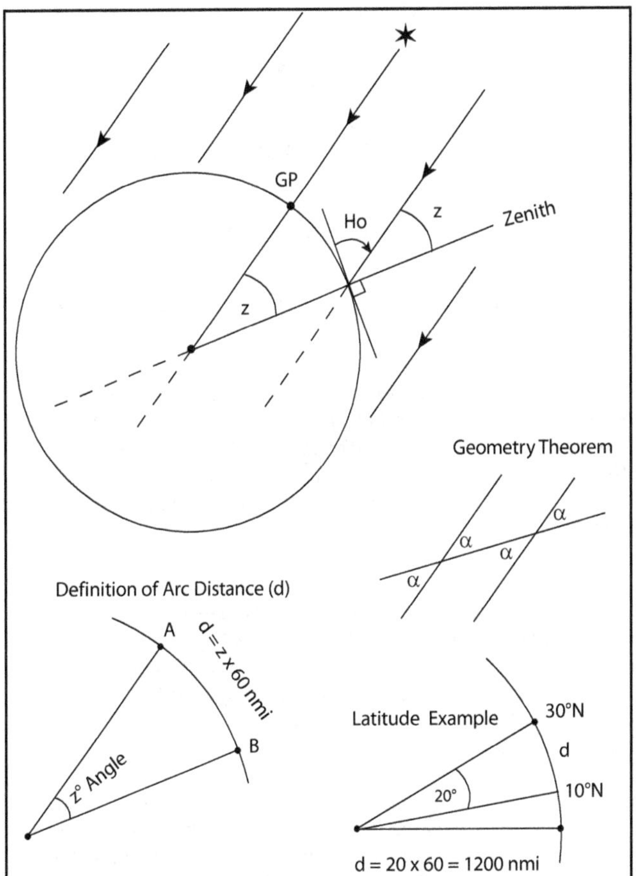

Figure 10.3-2 *Geometry of a sextant sight, showing that the zenith distance z is equal to the distance from the observer to the GP.*

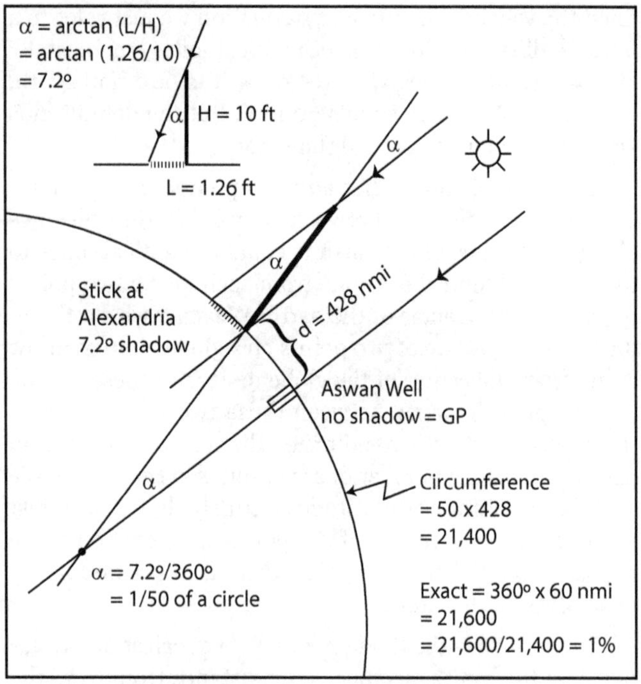

Figure 10.3-3 *How Eratosthenes measured the circumference of the earth in about 250 BC. On the solstice he knew the sun was overhead in Syene (Aswan, 24° 4'N, 53° 7'E), as the sun was known to shine directly down deep wells. It was also known that in Alexandria, 428 nmi to the north, on the same day at noon there were indeed shadows cast by the midday sun. He measured the sun's zenith distance of 7.2° there at that time, probably from the length of a shadow as shown. The distance between these two cities was well known at the time. Since the measured angle turned out to be 1/50th of a full circle, the full circle must be 50 × the distance between the cities.*

We are not sure exactly how well he knew it at the time, but we now know there is 428 nmi of latitude between these two cities. This gives a result that is almost spot on the right circumference. Celestial navigators know the circumference of the earth automatically, because of the definition of a nautical mile, namely: 360° × 60 nmi/1°, or 21,600 nmi.

The main uncertainty in figuring his exact accuracy stems from not knowing the exact definition of his unit of length. Using all variations of this and accounting for the offset to the west of Alexandria, his error was somewhere between 0.1% and 16%. In any case, very good. The factor of exactly 1/50th is just a numerical accident from the geometry of the measurement.

What is rather more curious than the greatness of his achievement—he had so many, in various sciences—is that Columbus was totally oblivious to this information 1240 years later. Other navigators before Columbus and after him were well aware of the dimensions of the earth. It was not long after Columbus's voyages that this knowledge all resurfaced and world charts proliferated.

Syene had been a famous city in Egypt, long before the Aswan dam. Since ancient times it was the southern frontier, located at the first cataracts that blocked farther navigation of the Nile to the south. It was a 3 to 4 week sail from Syene to Alexandria. The stones of the pyramids were quarried near there and shipped north.

So we are sneaking up on the principles of cel nav. We have learned, for example, that it is the zenith distance that is the most primary number, not the sextant height above the horizon. We only measure that because we have a good reference for it (the horizon), whereas we have no usable reference for the point overhead. Thus with the sextant we in effect measure our distance to the GP, and then the *Nautical Almanac* tells us where the GP was at that moment.

To put things in a historical perspective, compare what we are discussing here in 2015 (Figure 10.3-2) with Figure 10.3-3, which illustrates how Eratosthenes measured the circumference of the earth in 250 BC.

10.4 Why the Sun Rises and Sets

With apologies for using such a provocative title, we are going to have to leave the real answer to the philosophers and preachers, and instead simply explain why we observe celestial bodies rise in the east, reach a peak height as they cross our meridian, and then set in the west.

This would have to be considered one of the basic observations of celestial navigation, and we now have all the tools we need to understand it. The answer is all in one picture shown here in Figure 10.4-1. If you know celestial

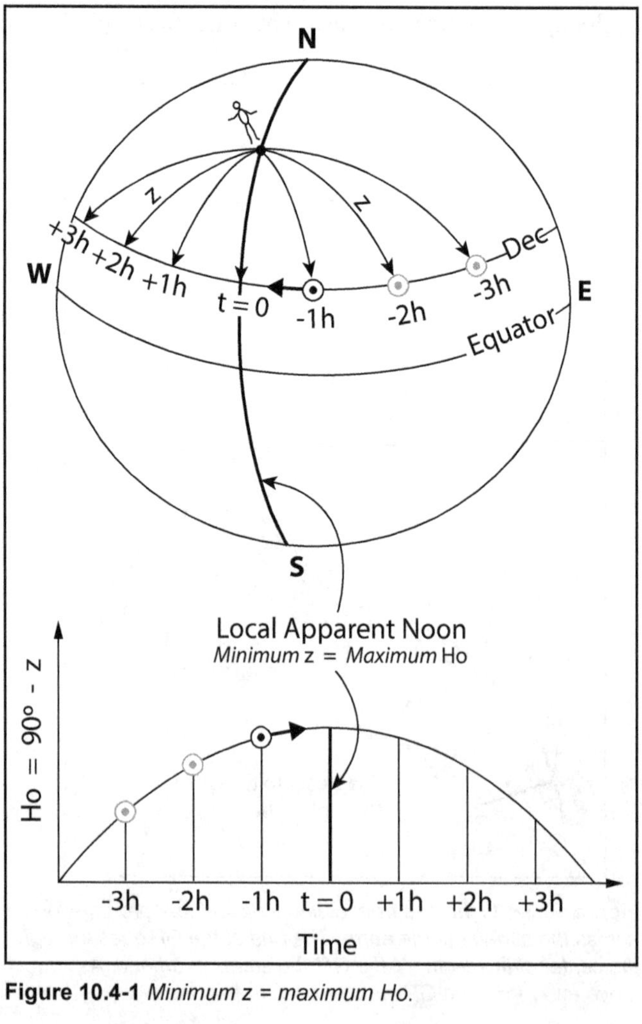

Figure 10.4-1 *Minimum z = maximum Ho.*

navigation, you may have friends who expect you to be able to explain that to them!

First recall from Section 10.1, that the GPs of all cel nav bodies circle the earth from east to west at a constant rate of 15° of longitude per hour, and each body is locked in on its own unique latitude called the declination of the body. In Figure 10.4-1 we show the sun moving westward along a northern declination.

z is the zenith distance to the sun. The sun first comes over the eastern horizon when z is just less than 90°, and as the sun moves toward our meridian, the zenith distance gets progressively smaller. z is at a minimum when the sun crosses our meridian (local apparent noon), and then it starts to increase again as the sun moves to the west of us.

But we know that $z + Ho = 90°$, so the height of a body in the sky at any time is $90° - z$. That means that when z gets smaller, Ho gets larger and vice versa. So bodies rise and peak out in height and then descend as they move west because they are tracking along a fixed latitude line as we watch them. When they cross our meridian, they are at their peak height in the sky.

10.5 Lat and Lon without Math

Now that we know the basics, we can use them to get our actual latitude and longitude from a sextant, watch, and almanac *without* what we call in earlier chapters the *sight reduction* process, which is frankly what the bulk of the earlier chapters is about! This will not be an accurate solution, but this procedure illustrates an important step in piecing together the full picture of how celestial navigation works.

Recall what we know from Section 10.3. The sextant measures our distance to the GP and the almanac tells us where the GP is located at the time we measured the height of the body. We do not know any more than that. There is a specific point on earth (the GP of the body at that moment) and we know how far we are from it. This information defines a circle on the face of the globe marking all points equidistant from the GP, as shown in the top of Figure 10.5-1. This circle is called the *circle of equal altitude.* There could be two other navigators at the same moment who would also measure this same distance to the GP. We would just be looking in different directions at the time.

That one sextant sight has established what is called a circle of position. Everyone on that circle at that time would have measured exactly the same angular height of that body. We know we are on that circle, but we do not know where. It is analogous to measuring the compass bearing to a lighthouse, from which we establish a line of position. We know we are on it, but we do not know where.

From one body we get one circle of position. Now do the same thing for another body and you see how it works. These two circles of position will intersect and we are located at the intersection of the two. The fact that there are two intersections does not matter; we can rule one out by just recalling very roughly what directions we were looking, or by taking a sight to a third body (Figure 10.5-1.)

Now, how do you do this from your back porch? We will need a current almanac, or look up the data online at www.starpath.com/usno. First we need to identify two navigational stars that we can see in the sky at the same time, any time of night, that happen to be 40 to 100° apart in bearing. You can learn that from the almanac or from the link provided. A navigational star simply means one from the list given in the almanac's daily pages. Or if there is a nice bright planet in the sky, use it along with a star off to the side of it.

Then make a simple device as shown in Figure 10.5-2 that we can use to measure the height of a star or planet from land. With this tool we do not need a sea horizon to measure the height above the flat horizon we care about (Section 10.3). Measure the angular height of the two bodies you chose and note the time of each observation, then convert those times to UTC.

Now use the almanac or link provided to look up the declination and GHA of the first body sighted. The Lat of

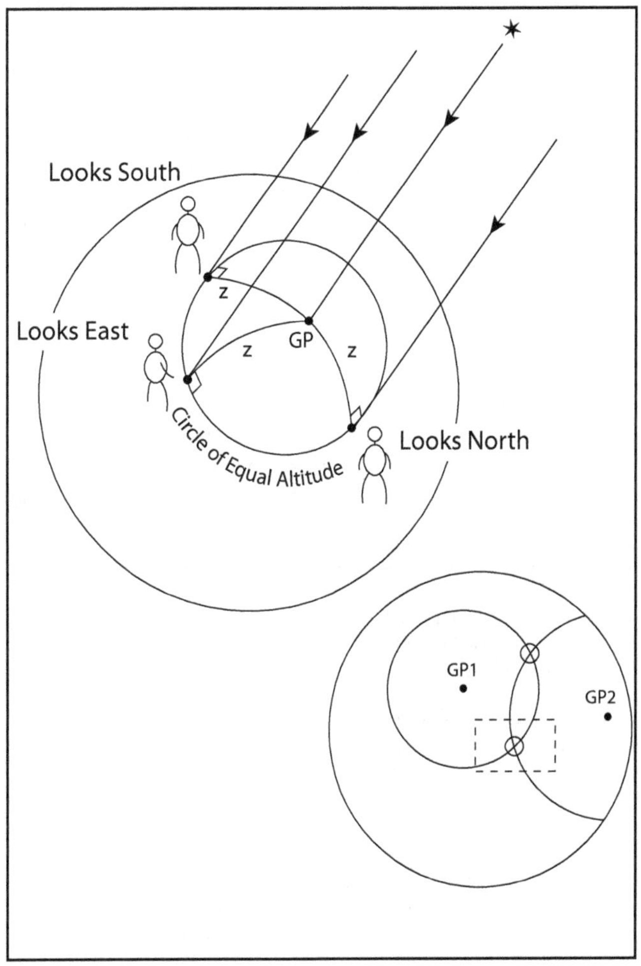

Figure 10.5-1 Top. *Circles of Equal Altitude.* **Bottom**. *The intersection of two circles forms a fix. We resolve the ambiguity by recalling the directions to the stars we observed, or by taking a third star sight. In the next section we come back to the region in the dashed box.*

the GP is the same as this declination, and the Lon W of the GP is the GHA of the GP if the GHA is less than 180. If the GHA is greater than 180°, then subtract it from 360° and label the result Lon E.

Next figure the zenith distance, z = 90° - Ho. We will just assume for this example that what we measure with the plumb bob is the same as Ho. Then convert z to nmi by multiplying by 60.

We have all the data we need; now we need a trick to avoid the math. There are two solutions. If you have a globe you can use it. Just plot the GP on the globe and then use the latitude scale on the globe for your miles scale and with a drawing compass draw a circle around that point with a radius equal to the zenith distance. Your first sight has told you that you are somewhere on that circle. It should run through your location, keeping in mind that it is not easy to do all this drawing very precisely and we only know the radius to about 60 nmi at best.

Then follow the same procedure for the second star, and these two circles will intersect at your back yard! Or at least within the errors of the method. The main goal is to convince yourself that this is all there is to the principle of cel nav.

Plotting on a globe is likely the easiest approach if you have one. An alternative is to use a great circle (GC) chart for the plotting. You can buy full size versions of these as print on demand products from many NOAA chart dealers online. There are two classes of these charts, called sailing and tracking. You can practice with the two free downloads we have of the tracking charts at www.starpath.com/celnavbook. The sailing versions have better resolution, but you will have to choose your stars more carefully to be sure that their GPs fit on the chart.

Do this exercise just once and you will have the principles of cel nav in hand. Note that measuring accurate distances on GC charts can be tricky. An alternative is to use an echart program and draw a large range ring about the GP.

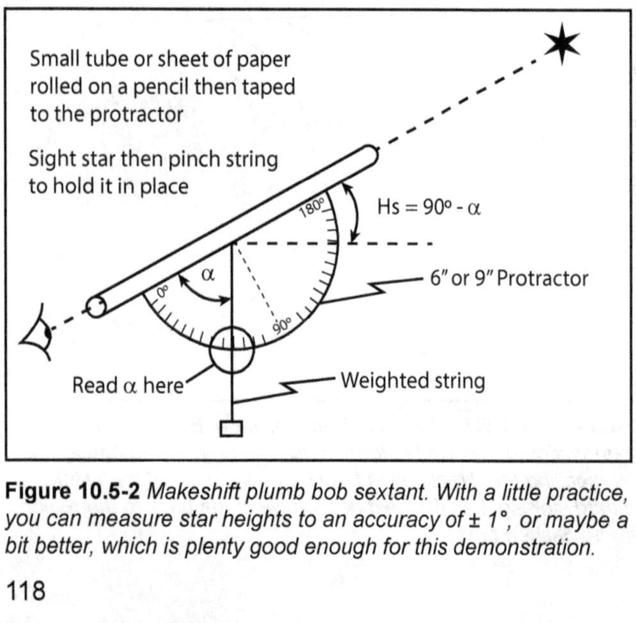

Figure 10.5-2 *Makeshift plumb bob sextant. With a little practice, you can measure star heights to an accuracy of ± 1°, or maybe a bit better, which is plenty good enough for this demonstration.*

10.6 How Sight Reduction Works

Frankly, at this point we know all of the important principles of celestial navigation (Sections 10.1 to 10.4). The sextant measures the height of the body and equivalently our distance to its GP. The almanac says where the GP is. Then we can plot the circle of equal altitude on a globe or great circle chart to get a circle of position. Do the same with another star and the intersection of the two circles is the fix.

The only thing left is figuring out a way to do that last plotting on a large-scale Mercator chart—the kind we sail with daily—so we can achieve higher accuracy. Our sextant sights are good to below 1 mile, and our clocks are good to a second, but we have not taken advantage of that accuracy yet in these principles. In short, we want to expand that small region around the fix that is marked in Figure 10.5-1. We need to plot our fix without having to plot the GP on the same chart, because it is so far away.

From earlier parts of the book, we know how we do this in practice. We did it in Chapters 4 and 5 (see Figure 10.6-1.) We choose an assumed position within 30' of our DR latitude and longitude, and we use Sight Reduction Tables to compute the Hc and Zn of the body from that location. Then we compare the Ho we observed to this computed Hc to learn if our circle of equal altitude is closer or farther from the GP than we assumed. We know that the circle of equal altitude is perpendicular to any azimuth line that points to the GP, so we can move the short, straight-line approximation of a segment of the circle of equal altitude (what we call the line of position) to the proper location without having to plot the GP itself. The amount we shift the line is the a-value, which is the difference between Hc and Ho.

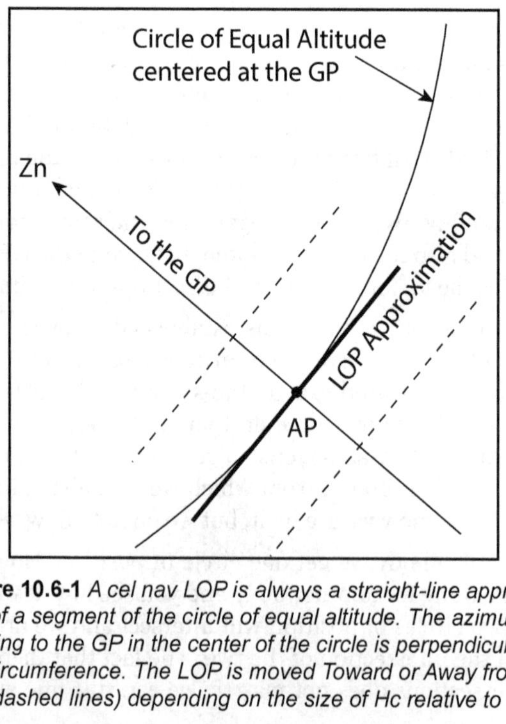

Figure 10.6-1 *A cel nav LOP is always a straight-line approximation of a segment of the circle of equal altitude. The azimuth line pointing to the GP in the center of the circle is perpendicular to the circumference. The LOP is moved Toward or Away from the GP (dashed lines) depending on the size of Hc relative to Ho.*

One can accept that such a computation is doable and just quit there. To learn more about how this takes place, we need to back up to review some trigonometry, starting from basics that are more commonly known.

Plane Trigonometry

Figure 10.6-2 shows a flat triangle along with one of several equations than can be used to relate its sides. The phrase "solving the triangle" means that if we know parts of it, we can determine the other parts. Just looking at it we can tell that knowing the length of the three sides determines uniquely the angles between the sides. (The reverse is not true; the three angles alone could define any number of triangles of different sizes.) More specifically, knowing any sequence of side-angle-side or angle-side-angle also uniquely determines the triangle.

Mathematicians have worked out the equations that solve the triangle based on these observations, and on the fact that the sum of the angles in a plane triangle must equal 180°. The most famous of these solutions is side-angle-side when the angle is 90° forming a right triangle. The general equation then reduces to the Pythagorean theorem: $a^2 + b^2 = c^2$.

In plane trigonometry, it is easy to prove any of these results for an arbitrary triangle by drawing the triangle to scale and measuring the results with ruler and protractor.

Spherical Trigonometry and the Navigational Triangle

The formulas for solving the triangle get a bit longer when you draw the triangle on the surface of a sphere, but the principles and procedures are the same. We also have new definitions for the *sides* of a spherical triangle. They are now angles as well, equal to the angle the two endpoints subtend from the center of the sphere. In other words, it is the same concept Eratosthenes used and we all use to define a nautical mile. Five degrees of arc along any great circle subtends 5° viewed from the center of the earth. We can think of this segment as 300 nmi or we can think of it as 5° of arc.

Figure 10.6-3 shows the navigational triangle that forms the basis for all celestial navigation sight reduction. The three corners are the pole (N or S), the GP and the AP. We know side-angle-side (namely 90 - dec, LHA, and 90-aLat), so we know we can solve for all other parts. The parts we want are, the zenith distance (z) between AP and GP which is 90 - Hc and the azimuth angle (Z), which is the bearing from AP to GP relative to the elevated pole. We use the North Pole in north latitudes and South Pole in southern latitudes. We then find Hc = 90 - z, and we use standard formulas to convert Z to azimuth (Zn).

The triangle can be solved in two ways. We can use formulas or we can use tables. There are multiple formulas that will solve this triangle, but in a sense the easiest and most reliable equations are:

Sin(Hc) =

Sin(dec) × Sin(aLat) + Cos(dec) × Cos(aLat) × Cos(LHA).

And once we have found Hc,

Cos(Z) =

[Sin(dec) - Sin(aLat) × Sin(Hc)] / [Cos(aLat) × Cos(Hc)].

Sign rules: (1) All angles are treated as positive, regardless of hemisphere, except for contrary name, make declination negative, regardless of hemisphere. (2) If the final Z is negative, then Z = Z + 180, regardless of hemisphere.

Alternatively, we can solve the triangle with Sight Reduction Tables. There are several styles of these tables (Pub. 249, 229, NAO, and others), but they all do the same thing. You tell them dec, aLat, and LHA and they tell you Hc and Zn. Chapter 5 explains how to use these tables.

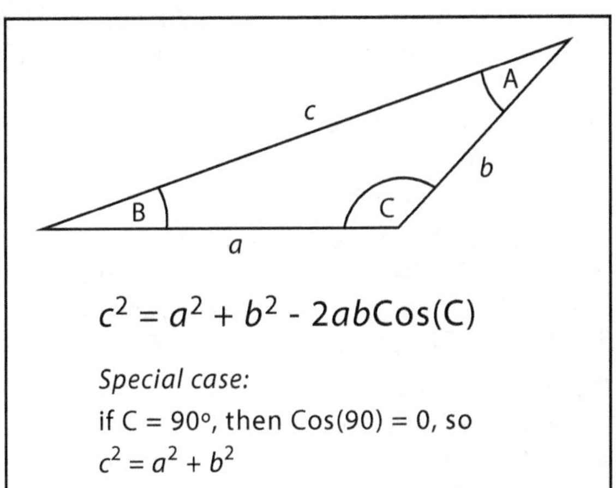

Figure 10.6-2 *An arbitrary plane triangle showing one of several equations that can be used to solve for all parts given side-angle-side (a-C-b). There are wonderful resources online that offer a quick review of trigonometry, or an easy introduction.*

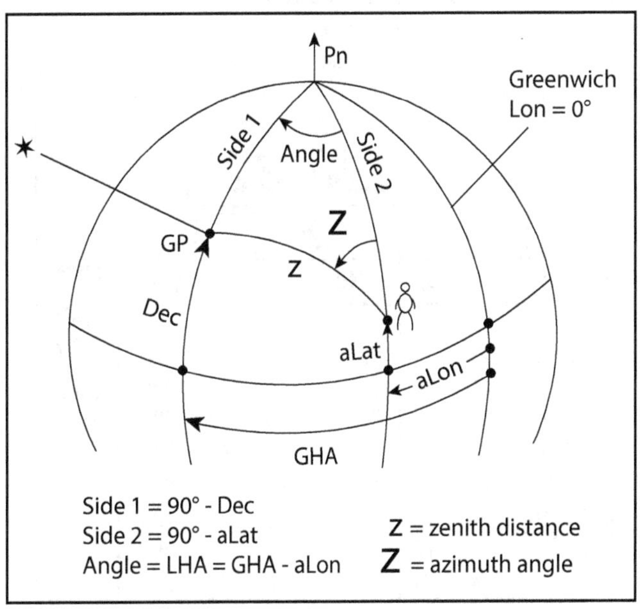

Figure 10.6-3 *The special spherical triangle called the navigational triangle that forms the basis of celestial navigation. Knowing side-angle-side we can solve for azimuth angle (uppercase Z) and zenith distance (lowercase z), either with equations or using Sight Reduction Tables.*

The traditional method of cel nav uses these tables to find Hc and Zn. Computed solutions (using computers, calculators, or mobile apps) use the formulas.

A sample Pub. 249 solution is shown in Figure 10.6-4. We can get the same result by direct computation:

Sin (Hc)=Sin(28)xSin(32)+Cos(28)xCos(32)xCos(285)

Sin (Hc) = 0.44258, and

Hc = Arcsin(0.44258) = 26.2686° = 26° 16.1’

Cos(Z)=(Sin(28)-Sin(32)xSin(26.2686))/Cos(32) xCos(26.2686)

Cos(Z) = 0.30894, and

Z = Arccos(0.30894) = 72.0°

Summary of Sight Reduction

We measure Ho, then we choose an AP near our DR position and then compute Hc and Zn from that position. We now know the direction to the GP and we know we are on a line (segment of the circle of equal altitude) that is perpendicular to that direction. If Hc turned out to be exactly Ho (a=0) then we are done. But if the Ho we measured is higher (larger) than Hc, then we know we must be closer to the GP, so we move that line toward the GP by the value of a. Likewise if Ho were smaller, we would move it away.

Fix from Ho and Zn Alone

As you study the procedures and principles used, you will eventually run across this observation: If I measure distance to the GP of a star with the sextant, and then take a precise compass bearing to the star, I can get a fix from that one star using a great circle chart. Just plot the GP from the almanac, draw in the bearing line to it, and mark off the measured distance. It would be rather like measuring the height and bearing to a peak on the shoreline, which is a standard piloting technique to find a fix from one target. The same procedure is used frequently in radar navigation.

LAT 32°

28°			29°			
Hc	d	Z	Hc	d	Z	LHA
° ′	′	°	° ′	′	°	
30 19	23	74	30 42	22	73	290
29 31	23	74	29 54	22	73	289
28 42	23	73	29 05	23	72	288
27 53	24	73	28 17	23	72	287
27 05	23	72	27 28	24	71	286
26 16	24	72	26 40	24	71	285
25 28	24	72	25 52	24	71	284
24 40	24	71	25 04	25	70	283

LAT 32°

Figure 10.6-4 *Sample of Pub. 249 solution to the navigational triangle. When you are at latitude 32° looking at a star in the same hemisphere that has a declination of 28° that is 285° west of you, you will see that star at a height of 26° 16’ above the horizon in a direction of 072° true.*

And that is in fact the case. You can in principle get a celestial fix that way. This is, however, an example of where practical limits way override theoretical principles. With the best bearing instruments and special care you might hope for a bearing to the star accurate to ±1°.

Recall our Small Angle Rule that a 6° error in bearing corresponds to a 10% error in displacement. So a 1° error is 10/6 percent, which is a factor of 0.017. So for a star 40° high, the GP is (90 - 40) x 60 = 3000 miles off, and your error would be 0.017 x 3000 = 51 nmi. That is, if you had any hope of measuring to a 1° accuracy and then plotting a line to a 1° accuracy on a large globe or great circle chart, neither of which is possible, frankly. So although it is valuable to appreciate this principle of cel nav, we just cannot use it in any practical manner.

Short History of Sight Reduction

Sight reduction as we do it now was essentially discovered underway in 1837 by US Navy Capt. Thomas H. Sumner, and consequently it was at the time and often still is called the *Sumner Method.*

Prior to Sumner, standard cel nav procedure was to measure a latitude at LAN, and then sometime later measure the Hs of the sun at a known time and convert it to Ho with the same corrections we do now. They had good almanacs so they could look up Dec and GHA. With a known Lat (using DR from LAN to sight time) they could then solve the navigational triangle equation given earlier replacing Hc with measured Ho and their known Lat to solve for the LHA of the sun at the time of the sight. From LHA and a known GHA they got their longitude.

In other words, they did not use a line of position concept at all, but just measured individual Lat-Lon positions as described. They solved the equations using custom tables based on logarithmic solutions to the equation.

On one particular voyage Sumner found himself in a difficult situation but did not know his Lat. So he just guessed his highest possible Lat and found a Lon for that and plotted that position. Then he did the same thing for a guess at his lowest possible Lat and found a new position and plotted it. Then doing this again for a couple other Lat guesses he noticed that the possible positions all fell upon one straight line, and he rightfully concluded that he must be somewhere on that line.

He published the procedure in 1843 as *A New Method of Finding a Ship's Position at Sea*. Early editions are available online. It became an instant success, and was adopted by the US Navy the same year (Figure 10.6-5).

The Sumner line of position required two lengthy computations and led to an LOP that was a chord of the circle of equal altitude—two points on the circle with a line drawn between them. Then 30 years later in 1873, the French sea captain Marc St. Hilaire published another way to obtain this LOP (by then known as a Sumner line) that took only one computation based on an assumed position. They still had to use complex log tables to solve the triangle in those days, but the single computation was so much preferred that this method in turn quickly became the standard used throughout the world. It is identical to what we do today, although we use different tables to solve the equations.

Today, in some textbooks you see the method we use referred to as the "Sumner Method" and in others as the "Marc St. Hilaire Method," and in still others the "Sumner-Marc St. Hilaire Method." It really does not matter. Sumner invented the concept of using a straight line segment of the circle of equal altitude as a celestial LOP (a Sumner line, being a chord of the circle), and Marc St. Hilaire discovered a simpler way to compute the Sumner line as a tangent to the circle using just one computation.

St. Hilaire also introduced the concept of *assumed position*, which was a more logical name at the time as they did indeed use the DR position for the computations. The DR position in those days (as it should be today) was always considered to be your best estimate of your position, taking all information into account, and as such it was fair to assume you were there till you learned otherwise. Using the tables we do today, the assumed position is not the DR position, so the name can be troublesome to some.

As time went by it was shown that this method could be applied to any two bodies and combined for a fix. In the early 1900s, the universal plotting sheets were invented by navigation instructor Capt Fritz Uttmark, which pinned down the system that we use to this day. (Figure 10.6-6).

As for historic credit, it would seem best to consider this a joint contribution rather than two independent discoveries in that, every English speaking ship in the world had been using the Sumner method for 30 years before St. Hilaire published his method.

The main change in sight reduction since then was the appearance of computers (on some level), which led to *inspection tables*, meaning we could put away the log tables and just look up Hc and Zn from aLat, Dec, and LHA. This took place sometime in the 1930s, with the first set of popular inspection type tables being Pub. 214 issued in 1936. Pub. 249 was introduced in 1951 for use with aircraft navigation, and remains in use today. Pub. 214 was replaced with Pub. 229 in 1970. Pub. 229 offers more precision than does Pub. 249 and it can be used for all declinations.

The Nautical Almanac Office (NAO) Sight Reduction Tables that appear in the *Nautical Almanac* were developed by Admiral Thomas Davies together with Paul Janiczek of the US Naval Observatory (USNO). They were first published in the 1989 edition of the *Nautical Almanac* and remain there today. They are in a sense, a practicable step backward, reverting to log solutions in a convenient format that saves much space and weight on board at the expense of a few extra steps in the sight reduction. They are an excellent backup to a computed solution.

A key step in the evolution of sight reduction was the introduction of programmable calculators in the mid-1970's, and in particular the HP-41C in 1980, which had a dedicated celestial navigation program that did both almanac data predictions as well as sight reduction. There are now numerous computer programs and mobile apps to assist with celestial navigation.

The advent of the Internet has also brought with it several wonderful resources, notably the online data from the USNO (see www.starpath.com/usno).

...In Depth

11.28 Computed Solutions

Once we are confident that we know the traditional method of cel nav using tables, it is worth looking into a computed solution. It is not just faster; it will also lead to more accurate navigation...

10.7 New Terminology

computed solution
solving a triangle
Marc St. Hilaire method
NAO Sight Reduction Tables
navigational triangle
parallax
Sumner method
USNO

"Capt. Sumner's *New Method of Finding a Ship's Position at Sea...* may be considered as the commencement of a new era in practical navigation. An order has been given to supply every ship in the Navy with it."

—M. F. Maury, Lt. U.S. Navy, Oct 9, 1843

Maury, the Father of Oceanography, later became head of the USNO.

"The Marc St. Hilaire method of finding a ship's position at sea is one of the best in existence by employing the intersection of the Sumner lines, and is exclusively used in the US Navy and gaining popularity in the merchant marine." **—US Naval Institute Proceedings, June 1918.**

Reprinted in Marc St. Hilaire Method for Finding a Ship's Position at Sea *by Capt. F.E. Uttmark, inventor of the first universal plotting sheets.*

Figure 10.6-5 *News items from the past showing one navigation system replacing the other as the "New" navigation.*

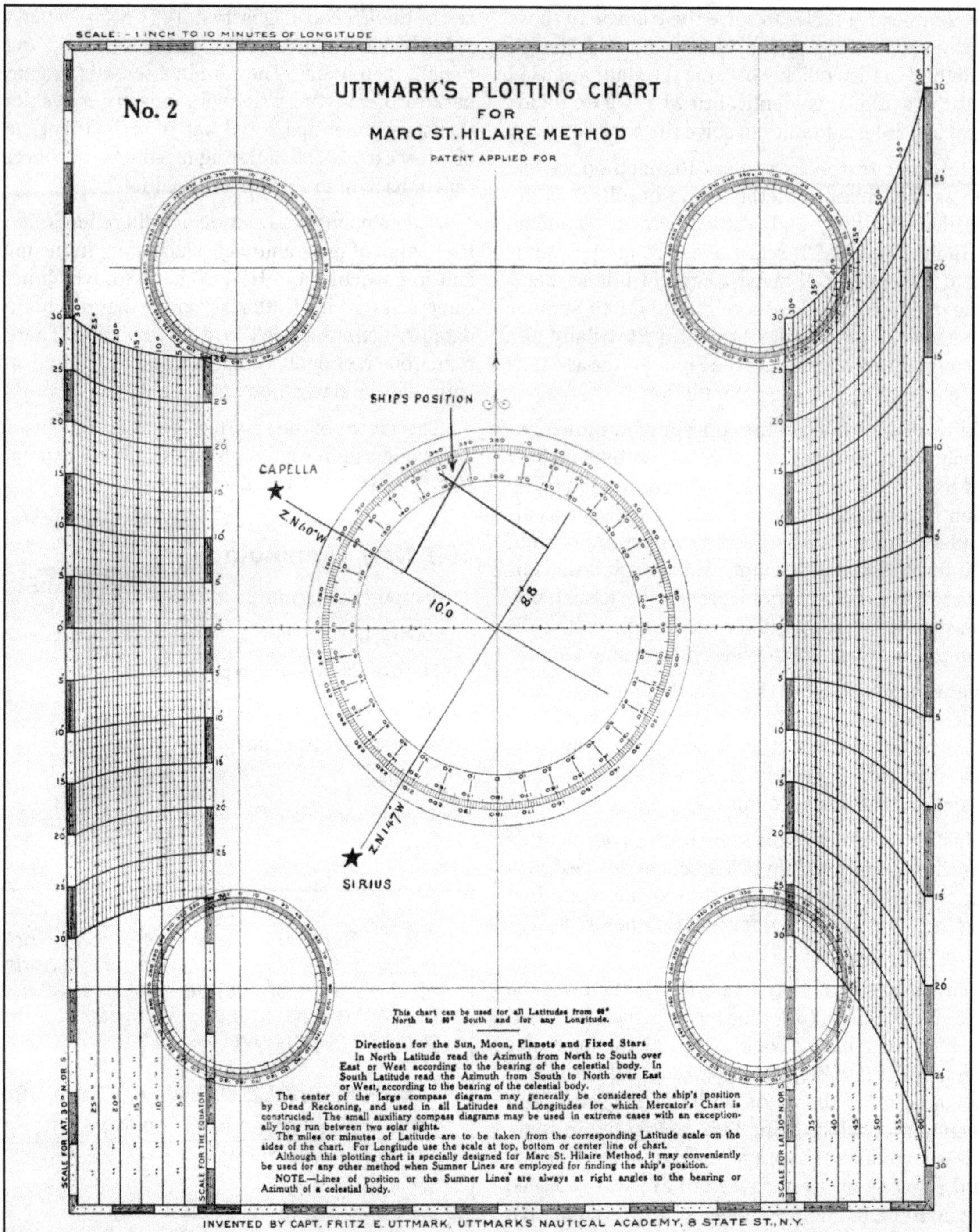

Figure 10.6-6 *The first universal plotting sheet from 1918.*

...In Depth

11.29 NAO Sight Reduction Tables

If we do choose a computer solution, then a logical backup are the NAO tables included in every *Nautical Almanac*. They are also a reasonable choice as the primary means of sight reduction, in that cel nav itself is a backup these days...

...In Depth

11.30 N(x) Table

Once we understand what sight reduction tables do for us, we might wonder what the bare minimum table might be do to the job. This method is likely that answer. It can be viewed as a backup or just a novelty...

CHAPTER 11

IN DEPTH...

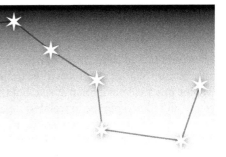

This chapter gathers special topics so they do not distract from the basics. There is no particular order to the topics. All are related to successful ocean navigation on some level. Some are fine points not covered earlier, others are just more practice or expanded coverage of earlier topics.

New Terminology

Air Almanac
artificial horizon (AH)
departure
fit slope method
GPS, WAAS, COG, SOG, VMG
great circle sailing (GC)
International Date Line
local mean time (LMT)
Mercator chart
Mercator sailing
mid-latitude sailing
parallel sailing
rhumb line (RL)
set and wait method
Sky Diagrams
small angle rule
solar index correction
standard time
WWV and WWVH
zone time (ZT)

11.1 Bowditch and Other References

We would like to think that your text here contains all the information you need to learn accurate and versatile cel nav for practical navigation at sea, but there may be details you would like to pursue, or related topics we do not cover. Sometimes we simplify a concept to make it more practical, but you may want to compare with more standard formalism. We also refer to various navigation tables that appear in other books.

A main reference for such matter will typically be *The American Practical Navigator, NGA Pub. No. 9*, originally (1802) by Nathaniel Bowditch, now referred to simply as *Bowditch*. There is a free download of the latest edition online (www.starpath.com/navpubs), but for cel nav you might want to check older editions—1938 or 1980 editions are good resources; in later editions, the cel nav content has gradually diminished. For lunar solutions (Section 11.26) you have to go back to before about 1900. Old editions of Bowditch are also available online as scanned downloads or in print in used book outlets, such as used.addall.com.

A comparable book that some readers prefer for its plainer language is called *Dutton's*. The original edition *Navigation and Nautical Astronomy* (1926) was by Benjamin Dutton. The 15th edition from 2003 is by Thomas J Cutler is called *Dutton's Nautical Navigation,* based on Elbert S. Maloney's editions called *Dutton's Navigation and Piloting*. There are no ebooks, but used editions are readily available online.

In 2002 Starpath, working with the Navigation Foundation, compiled a complete set of all articles on celestial navigation and closely related topics published by the Institute of Navigation (ION) in their professional Journal. A CD of these 279 articles is available from the ION. The index to these can be found at www.starpath.com/celnavbook.

A similar but less formal collection of very many articles on celestial navigation topics have recently been made available to the public at no charge from the Navigation Foundation. The full index to all of these articles and a link to download them is at the same link above.

For online almanac data and other valuable resources see the United States Naval Observatory (USNO) Astronomical Applications Department, to which we have a portal link at www.starpath.com/usno and for marine navigation computations including sight reduction, sailings, and DR, see www.starpath.com/calc.

Other often-cited historical texts on celestial navigation are available online. After the basic procedures of cel nav have been mastered from the material in this book, a next step in mastering the practical application of this knowledge would be to put it to work by analyzing the exercises in the book *Hawaii by Sextant* (Starpath Publications, 2014). This book presents a full ocean voyage carried out by cel nav alone. All the sights are provided along with the logbook of DR information. The solutions for all sights are presented, as well as an ongoing DR track of the voyage, updated daily with celestial fixes. Short of a voyage of your own, there is no better way to gain the confidence that these methods are in place and ready for use as needed.

We do not cover it in this text, but there is another annual source of official almanac data that can be used for celestial navigation called the *Air Almanac*. See the author's book *How to Use the Air Almanac for Marine Navigation: With a Comparison to the Nautical Almanac and an Extended Discussion of the Sky Diagrams*. This extended discussion is primarily about using the Sky Diagrams for predicting the best celestial bodies to use for a fix. It is a very convenient method that competes favorably with the alternatives of *Pub 249, Vol. 1* or the use of the Star Finder covered in this Chapter. See www.starpath.com/celnavbook for the latest copy of the annual sky diagrams along with a link to an article on using them.

For matters of practical small-craft navigation on inland and coastal waters see *Inland and Coastal Navigation*, and for matters of marine weather routing, see *Modern Marine Weather* (both from Starpath Publications).

LAS TRES MARIAS.
The Western Point of the Northern Island, bearing N. 50° E., three leagues.

11.2 Taking Your Departure

One of the long-established traditions of ocean navigation that has slipped away somewhat from standard modern procedures is the practice of taking and recording your *departure*. This simply means noting the last visible landmark as it slips out of sight and recording in the logbook the bearing to the landmark, time of departure, and your estimate of distance off.

This was absolutely standard rigorous practice throughout the 1800s and into the early 1900s, but at some point reference to it fell out of the textbooks. Our job now is to get it back into the textbooks, simply because the significance of it has not really changed over these years. As you sail into the ocean, out of sight of land, your departure is in fact the last thing you know for certain until you get a proper celestial fix, or reach your destination. If the weather socks in for two or three weeks, it may be the last thing you know for certain till you see your arrival point, whether or not it is the one you intended to make.

With GPS on board, folks tend to forget that the above reasoning is still true on some level. If all you have to go by is GPS, you truly do not know for certain that it is right till you arrive. Chances are it is right if functioning normally, but that is not guaranteed. Not to mention that it is, no matter how guarded and backed up, a vulnerable piece of electronics that requires a source of power. It also assumes that there are no intervening political events that end up shutting down these signals you depend on.

The nature of your departure depends on many factors—the height of the nearest land, day or night, clear or socked in, but regardless of conditions, there is always a unique moment when you make your departure, and it pays to be aware of this event and prepare to record it. The distance could be a mile or two, or it could be 100 miles.

JOURNAL

OF A VOYAGE FROM BOSTON TO MADEIRA.

H.	K.	F.	*Courses.*	*Winds.*	*Lee-way.*	REMARKS *on board, Friday, March* 25, 1836.
1						At noon, got under way, with a fine breeze from the N. W.
2						
3						
4						
5						
6						
7						
8						
9	6	5	E. by S.	N. W.		At 8 P. M., Cape Cod light-house bore S. by E. ¾ E., distant 14 miles; from which I take my departure.
10	6	5				
11	6	5				
12	6	5				
1	6					
2	6					
3	6					
4	6					
5	6	5				
6	6	5				
7	6			North.		
8	6					
9	6					
10	6					
11	7					
12	7					Variation ¾ of a point westerly.

Course.	*Dist.*	*Diff. Lat.*	*Dep.*	*Lat. by D. R.*	*Lat. by Obs.*	*Diff. Long.*	*Longitude in, by D. R.*	*Lun. Obs.*	*Chron.*
N.85° 34′E.	95	N. 7	E. 94	N. 42° 10′		E. 2° 7′	W. 67° 57′	.	

Figure 11.2-1 *(Top) From an 1853 US Coast Pilot of the West Coast of North America. You can find it online in Google Books. A league is about 3 nmi. Nav texts in those days used miles (nautical miles), leagues, and Spanish leagues, which are probably slightly different. This picture is not a departure. The text points out that this land can be seen in good conditions out to 18 leagues.* **11.2-2** *(Bottom) section of page 1 of the daily logbook for this voyage included in full in the 1851 edition of Bowditch. If you wish to brush up on compass directions used in those days, see http://davidburchnavigation.blogspot.com/2015/02/boxing-compass.html*

11.3 Electronic Navigation

GPS is not a subject of this book, but some readers may be new to cel nav *and* GPS nav so we include this optional background and application notes.

Overview of GPS

The Global Positioning System, known universally now as GPS, is an extensive satellite-based navigation system developed through Department of Defense contracts during the early 1980s. It was conceived as a military system and remains under military control. The loss of the Korean airliner that was destroyed when it wandered into Soviet air space in 1983 was influential in making the system accessible to civilian use to prevent similar disasters. As of about 1989, it was available for public use on a limited basis; today it is the primary electronic navigation system for all vessels, vehicles, and individuals, commercial and recreational. This system can tell you where you are (in terms of latitude and longitude) to an astonishing precision, anywhere on earth in any weather, along with the direction you are moving and the speed of your motion, accurate to a tenth of a knot. The associated software in most devices also provides course and distance to any other location along with other navigational data. Reasonably accurate elevation requires connection to a WAAS satellite.

Before getting to the practical use of this tool, I will share the personal conviction that GPS is one of the most dramatic technological developments in modern history. It is the first example of space science technology that has had significant influence on several aspects of the lives of everyone living in a modern environment. Its application to guiding boats around the waters of the world was just the beginning of its public use. It has revolutionized the fields of surveying, mapping, and exploration. GPS instrumentation mounted near geological faults and volcanoes are being used to measure otherwise imperceptible motions of the earth's surface for forecasting earthquakes and eruptions.

Combined with automated position broadcasts from moving GPS-equipped vehicles or vessels, tracking systems will eventually be developed to warn of collision courses between cars, planes, or boats. Automatic Identification System (AIS) technology is the key to using GPS for this application. Right now there are GPS units available that have stored in their memories the precise location of most navigational lights and buoys in the United States and Canada. New applications are being developed or dreamed of hourly.

On the down side, the more efficient any tracking capability becomes, the more the question of privacy arises, not to mention security issues of automated precision navigation. Or who is liable for the oil clean-up when a Japanese freighter collides with a Norwegian tanker carrying Brazilian oil to France when both were navigated by American satellites that failed temporarily? Anyone can buy the equipment, and no licenses or permits are required to use it. Political, social, and legal issues develop in parallel with this, as with all high impact technologies. Europe, China, Russia, India, and Japan all have independent satellite systems that provide GPS navigation, although not all available worldwide.

Position Navigation

Your GPS position is indicated on the display screen in latitude and longitude, specified to the nearest one-thousandth of a minute, such as 47° 38.532' N, 122° 24.795' W. Recall that 1' of latitude is about 6,000 ft, so a precision of 0.01' corresponds to about 60 ft. The remarkable thing is that the numbers you see in that decimal place are usually correct. This small hand held gadget communicating with satellites 10,000 miles away can tell you where you are on the 200 million square miles of the earth's surface to within a couple boat lengths! Generally they are accurate to within about 10 meters, or about 30 ft or so. The last decimal place, 0.001' of latitude, corresponds to 6 ft, so this number will bounce around as the unit is not accurate to that level.

If the unit suspects that the data may not be good, it will provide various warning signals or icons on the screen, with codes that tell of the problem such as missing satellites, weak signals, etc. In modern units, most interactions with the satellites are all done automatically. Most will tell you some parameter that is a measure of the accuracy of the fix with the present satellite configuration, expressed in feet. This is a statistical number, meaning if you wrote down the position it gives many times, or made a continuous plot of your position, it would have some spread of values and this accuracy number is a measure of the width of that spread. Any one reading could be off more than that, but that is the average error. Other than that, this is truly a "black box." You turn it on, and it tells you where you are.

Without echart software, using GPS, position navigation reduces to plotting your known latitude and longitude on the chart—to find out where you really are! This is not always a trivial task in a small boat at sea, especially going to weather and especially if you wish to retain anywhere near the actual accuracy you know. In fact in most cases, you cannot plot the accuracy you know, no matter how or where you do it, because of the limitations of the chart scales. On a 1:25,000 chart (the largest scale typically available), a pencil dot 1/16th of an inch across spans 130 ft on the chart. If you can get that dot on that chart in the right place, you know you are in the middle of it. Plot the position wrong by one dot width, and you have thrown away twice your accuracy. On a 1:40,000 chart, that dot is 208 ft across.

An efficient approach underway in a small boat is to have latitude and longitude lines already drawn on the chart at convenient intervals and then to locate your position relative to them, either by simply estimating the place or using a special tool. Some lines are, of course, printed on the chart to begin with, but they are too far apart to be convenient. On a 1:40,000 chart, the parallel lines of latitude are typically printed only every 5', which spaces them about 9 inches apart. If you draw lines at every 1' of latitude and longitude, it is much easier to estimate where your position lies by interpolation without other tools.

The procedure can be improved by constructing a special plotting tool from cardboard or plastic. See Figure 11.3-1. It must be customized to specific latitudes and chart scales, and it requires that the chart be prepared with latitude and longitude lines. I have used this plotting technique extensively in sailboat racing whenever quick plotting was essential and echarts were not an option. It is faster than conventional methods, regardless of the tools or space available.

Keep in mind, however, that no matter how you plot it, or even how you obtained the position fix in the first place, recording that position on a paper chart and labeling it with the corresponding time remains the key to good navigation. The more often you do it, the more you will learn from it and the better off you will be when you need it. (This is obviously using a paper chart. If you use echart navigation, the paper chart position can be recorded much less frequently.)

COG and SOG

A GPS receiver includes a computer and a clock. The clock displays the precise UTC accurate to the second at any time. The entire position analysis is based on very accurate timing, so this clock is updated continually from the satellites.

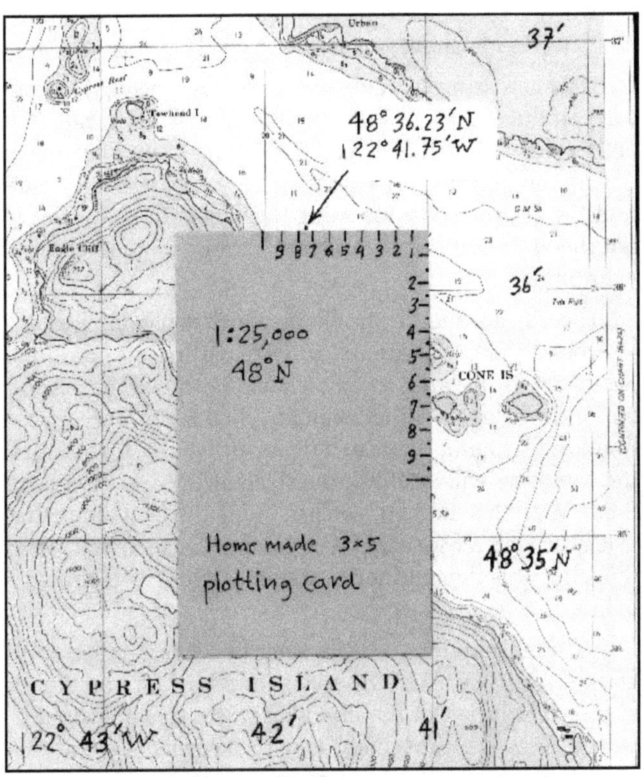

Figure 11.3-1 *Fast position plotting with a hand-made card.*

With a computer memory and a clock, the unit not only knows where you are, it knows where you were. From this it can calculate how you got from there to here. In other words, it can figure your true course and speed at any time. It is important to understand that the speed and course it tells you are your true speed and true course, called speed over the ground (SOG) and course over the ground (COG)—both treated already as acronyms these days, with both pronounced to rhyme with fog. This is not the same speed that a knotmeter would read, and not the course that your compass reads. SOG and COG are measures of your true motion across the chart (the "ground" part of the name) that takes into account your boat speed through the water, the speed of the current, and any leeway you might have when the wind is blowing. In most cases, these are the primary numbers you need to know to navigate.

The phrases course or speed "over ground" and course or speed "made good" are often used interchangeably, but they are technically quite different concepts in terms of official definitions. Our navigation can benefit from the distinctions. See starpath.com/glossary.

If you were moving at 6 kts according to the knotmeter through a tidal stream moving at 2 kts, the GPS would show a SOG of 8 kts, assuming the current was flowing in the same direction you were headed. In this case, your COG would be the same as your compass course. If, on the other hand, you were sailing 6 kts due north) across a current flowing toward the northeast at 2 kts, the GPS would show a SOG of 7.5 and a COG of 011. It has told you very plainly you are not going the direction you are headed, which is what the compass reads.

On a long passage or in dangerous waters, it is the COG and (to a lesser extent) the SOG, that you really care about, not so much about your actual position at any one time. This is the information that warns you immediately that you may be getting into trouble, or that you are at least not doing what you think you are. It is, nevertheless, the high accuracy of the position data that allows the instrument to determine the course and speed accurately and quickly.

Since the COG and SOG are so crucial to navigation, it is important that they be displayed in the most useful manner. The high accuracy of the instrument can work against us some times. When sailing in gusty winds or bigger seas, your actual course and speed change every few minutes or even every few seconds as you adjust or respond to the seas or gusts, whether surfing or pounding. But since the instrument is so accurate, it measures each of these intermittent changes. Each time you look at the screen you see a new course, which means you are back to not knowing which way you are going. To correct this, go back to the initialization procedure and select an averaging time for the COG and SOG that will wipe out the fluctuations.

This is a powerful practical feature of the instruments: you can display your instantaneous speed and course, or display the average value of these over the past few minutes or seconds, as you choose. This is an important feature to check when selecting models. Not all console units have this option, and few handhelds do.

The measured SOG and COG can be used (with care) to calibrate the knotmeter and compass. You must be certain, however, that your measured motion is not being influenced by current or leeway. The COG can also be useful for steering in areas of magnetic disturbance or in the high latitudes of the Arctic, where magnetic compasses are not reliable.

Another derived speed available in most GPS units is the velocity made good (VMG) toward the active waypoint. This is an important performance indicator for sailboat or predicted log racing, and also valuable in general navigation situations, but, for the most part, these are secondary data to the more immediate and basic value of SOG. VMG tells you how fast you are moving in a particular direction, whereas SOG is how fast you are moving in the direction of COG. Related discussion is in Section 11.30, which reviews several aspects of ocean navigation.

Waypoints and Routes

Navigation with GPS is facilitated by setting up specific locations called *waypoints* and sequences of these called *routes*. A planned trip would begin at home or at the dock, by selecting from the chart various points (usually turning points) along the intended route and then entering the latitude and longitude of these points into the GPS unit as you would a computer. Most models will accept several hundred such points, which can be numbered and given names. The sequence itself can then be named and stored as a specific route. Waypoints can also be copied from a previously stored route and built into a new one. Or you could define, say, waypoint 22 as 2.4 miles NE of waypoint 57. The format is very versatile in many units. It is also possible at any time when you are underway, to store your present position as a numbered waypoint. With this option, you could travel a route you have not programmed and store key points along the way to use for a programmed return trip.

Once a route is entered, you can run through the route on the keypad of the instrument (still sitting at home), asking for the course and distance between each waypoint to sum up the trip or for other planning. And this is exactly what you would do underway as you proceed from point to point. From your starting position, you call up the route of interest and the first waypoint on it. Then from your present position, the unit tells you the course and distance to that waypoint. As you proceed in that direction, it will figure your speed and tell how long it will take to get there at that average speed. If you wander off the direct line route to the waypoint, it will tell you that, as we discuss later; but regardless of where you are, it continually tells you the course and distance to the assigned waypoint. When you arrive at the waypoint, select the next one, and carry on; or use the automatic mode which will automatically switch to the next waypoint when you pass within a certain distance to the first one.

Currents, Cross-track Error, and Plotters

There are two basic ways to navigate with GPS using waypoints. The first is just to activate the desired destination waypoint, read the course to it, and head off in that direction. As you proceed, set up the display screen to show your COG and then watch how this compares to the desired course to the waypoint. If you are in current, or your compass is wrong, or you are simply not steering the course you intended to, then soon the COG will show that you are not making good the desired course, so you must alter course until these two agree.

For example, suppose the computed course to the waypoint is 050 and steering that course for a few minutes you notice the COG is 070, although the compass still reads 050 and you have held this fairly well. In other words, you are getting set to the south, most likely by a southerly current. In this case, you will have to point north of the desired course, into the current, in order to track straight to the waypoint.

As a first guess, since you are getting set 20° south, you could just steer 20° north of 050, toward 030, and then watch how that develops. If you are then tracking to the mark, you are done—assuming you remain sailing or motoring at the same rate. If you speed up or slow down, the numbers will change, but in any event the unit will tell you immediately what course to steer to achieve your desired course. Or, if you cared to, you could just stop all together, and then the COG and SOG would be a direct measure of the current speed and direction—providing there is no significant wind pushing you across the water.

When crossing currents in this manner, using just one waypoint and the COG, it is important that you monitor both courses (desired course and COG) simultaneously during the process, because if you are getting set by current the desired course is going to change. In short, this is not the optimum way to navigate because you are chasing your target.

The way around this problem, which is most important in crossing strong currents or when setting off on a long passage with hazards to either side, is to use the second option mentioned earlier, namely choose not only a destination waypoint, but also a departure point, from which the computer will establish the straight line track between them. With this method, you can guide the boat along that track through all sorts of hazards, in strong current, or in thick fog. It is the mariner's version of flying by the instruments.

Using this option, you can steer by what is called cross track error (XTE). This display shows how far you are off to the right or left of the intended track. In some circumstances this is a convenient way to navigate. Typical displays that you might select underway might read:

TO SMITH ROCK		ROUTE 10 LEG 3
050° M, 2.48 NM	or	47°38.41'N, 124°35.03'W
XTE 0.03 NM RIGHT		COG 057 M, SOG 3.9.

The first shows that you have called your immediate destination Smith Rock and that it is located 2.48 nmi away in magnetic (compass) direction 050, and at the moment you are 0.03 nmi to the right of the track you planned to travel. As often is the case, it pays to recall that 1 mile is about 6,000 ft, so this means you are 180 ft (0.03 × 6,000) off course to the right. It remains impressive: you can draw a precise line mathematically between two points that are, say, 10 miles apart, and at any position along that route know immediately whenever you wander more than 60 ft off that line!

The alternative display shows that Smith Rock is the destination of the 3rd leg of what you have numbered the 10th route of your travels. Your present position is shown, along with the fact that at the moment you are making good a course of 057 at a speed of 3.9 kts. If you want to get back on track, you will have to point more to the left.

In this case, if you happened to be steering 050, and then used the previous reasoning, you would alter course to steer about 7° high to correct for the set. What would likely happen, however, is when you steadied out headed toward 043, you would indeed start making good the course you wanted of 050, but you would not be back on the track you wanted. You just straightened out your course made good to be parallel to your desired track. You will have to over correct for a while to get back on to the actual track and then fall back to 043.

Remember, these are all average courses. You cannot, usually, steer a specific course of, say, 043 precisely; in all circumstances, your compass course swings around as you proceed. But whenever you are willfully choosing to put the boat back onto a specific course, you do have one in mind, and in this case it would be just under 045 on the compass or halfway between 040 and 045, or some such guide to what the compass should read when it is right. And in fact, you can make good fairly precise courses, especially when you have such a powerful tool as GPS to help. Just do what ever you are doing, and watch the average course on the GPS; if it is not quite right, do a little more or little less of it.

As an alternative to using digital values of cross-track error, some GPS models offer a graphic plot display to show this information. Stand-alone plotters are another option for this, or screens of other electronics such as depth sounders, electronic charts, or radars can be used to plot GPS data when the proper interfacing is available. The same screens used for numerical display become blank charts or plotting sheets of the region around your present position. The extent of the plot can span hundreds of miles or just a few tenths of a mile. You can show an entire route, traced between many waypoints, or zoom in on the display to show just 200 yards or so either side of your position. Usually, the present position is marked with a dot with an emanating arrow that clearly points in the direction of your present COG. As you proceed along the route, the computer leaves a trail of dots to show the route you followed. At any time, you can tell at a glance where you are relative to the track line and which way you are making good at the moment.

This type of track plotting can be a very convenient option for inland and ocean. Depending on the format of this feature, which varies among the brands, actual tracks of a trip can be saved, rather than just a series of waypoints along it. A saved track can then be reversed to use as a guide (actual path) for a return trip, or later scanned at home and transferred to a chart for a precise record of your cruise or race. Despite the potential conveniences of this feature, however, it remains prudent and still of utmost importance to record your position on a real chart with the corresponding time as frequently as possible. If you put all your eggs in one little plastic box, you might get caught up the creek with your batteries down.

All GPS units have some form of plotter to use as mentioned, but if you use an electronic charting system (ECS), you can follow your position right along a real chart. This is an obvious way to navigate these days. Most GPS come with some form of vector charts, but there is more flexibility and more realistic charts using a computer or tablet app. Combined with a Bluetooth GPS, you have a simple, very portable system for use in about any size vessel. You can even navigate on the larger format phones.

Another modern trick is to save your GPS track from the GPS as a GPS exchange file (.gpx). Then you can email that to a friend to display on Google Earth or their own echart program.

Note on Antennas

Many users have found that portable GPS units appear to work fine when located below-decks at the nav station, without any further external antenna. Nevertheless, an external antenna is highly recommended. When restricted to below-decks reception, the unit may not be using the best satellite combination, which in turn could influence the accuracy of your COG and SOG. Also, what seems to work well in one location, may not work as well in others, where there is, say, some part of the horizon blocked by terrain.

When locating the antenna, start out with a temporary location to test its practicality and then later make it permanent. On sailboats, it might be best to start out at as low as practical (on the stern rail, for example) to minimize quick motion of the antenna which, again, could influence COG and SOG.

Solar panels on deck over the nav station area could block the GPS signals, and we discovered this nuance: the external antennas for Iridium Go satcom units are for the Iridium connections only. Each unit has its own GPS unit for tracking, but the GPS antenna is the one on the box itself, not improved with the external antenna. Thus it could have poor GPS data from below decks, even though the satcom connections are good.

Electronic Compasses

In the modern nav station, electronic compasses are standard equipment. We have them to run the autopilot, and we have them for a heading sensor input to the radar so we can run it in a stabilized display mode. Another virtue is with networked nav stations and vessels in general; it means that with one of these we can view our heading from anywhere on the boat via numerous wifi transmitters to mobile apps.

Unlike conventional compasses, which find magnetic north from gimbaled needles pushed that way by magnetic forces (as wind vanes line up with the wind), electronic compasses find the field direction using gimbaled circuitry that figures that direction without actually pointing anything toward it. The underlying principles are the same ones that make electric motors work, although highly refined here with extensive micro-processing of the signals. The circuit design that senses the field is called a fluxgate, which is why these units are often called fluxgate compasses.

This technology has widespread applications on all vessels because it can be used for inputting digitized compass headings into other electronics for computing currents or for dead reckoning. If a computer knows the compass heading and the knotmeter speed, and also knows the course and speed over ground from GPS, then it can calculate the current, which is what causes these two sets of data to be different.

Some (few) mariners have become so enthralled with these devices that they forgo a standard magnetic steering compass, but that is a serious mistake. Sparing the sea stories to back this up, I would never head off on any voyage that might require any level of navigation without a conventional magnetic compass, regardless of the kind or size of the vessel, and especially regardless of what other electronic wonders I might have along. Fundamental prudent seamanship requires that all electronics in a marine environment be regarded as luxuries (regardless of their costs), to be used when convenient but not depended upon.

Handheld GPS units and many smartphones include a heading sensor, as also some include barometers, heel angle sensors, and electronic tide tables. But be sure to check the compass function for sensitivity to being level. Some work reasonably well, others are completely useless, because if you tilt them by 2°, the bearing changes 15°.

In one sense, we owe the long life of celestial navigation to electronic compasses. Once you have more than one compass on the boat, chances are that at some point they are not going to agree with each other. When that happens, we need to check them with celestial navigation by taking a simple bearing to a celestial body and then computing its true azimuth. See Section 11.21 for details. The COG from GPS might give you a rough idea of the compass error in favorable conditions (including no current or leeway), but there is no replacement for the cel nav sight.

The amazing navigation functions available in phones and tablets are increasing daily, but their dependability is not. Just the contrary; these devices are evolving toward consumer-grade products that are cheap and replaceable, but not intended for long-term use. Their attraction as a dependable tool for navigation at sea is simply not there. The value of knowing cel nav for the prudent mariner will not diminish for a long time.

11.4 Mercator Charts

Outside of the Polar Regions, nautical charts are made on a map projection called Mercator. This is just one of various ways to represent the spherical earth on a flat sheet of paper. At very high latitudes including the pole, for example, navigation is often done on what is called a polar azimuthal equidistant projection, which is similar to a radar plotting sheet centered at the pole. That type of projection is easy to interpret for position plotting but difficult to use for routine chart navigation—there is no direction that is uniquely north and it is difficult to measure bearings or courses from one point to another.

The Mercator projection is specifically designed to achieve these desired features of a navigational chart. Namely we want a chart with a unique north direction, toward the top of the chart, valid across the whole chart, and we want to be able to easily measure the bearing between points that will take us from one to the other.

Figure 11.4-1 shows schematically how this is accomplished without going into the math of the process. In a Mercator projection both the latitude and the longitude are distorted to achieve the desired behavior. The results of the math are included in what are called the meridonal parts for each latitude, which can be used to create an accurate Mercator chart. Approximate Mercator charts over limited regions can be made using the nomogram from a universal plotting sheet. In Section 11.23, we cover how to carry out computations using Mercator sailings.

Referring to Figure 11.4-1, in Part A we see the globe with two round lakes of the same size, one at a high latitude and one near the equator. In Part B, we peel open the cover of the earth and lay it flat on a chart, which shows all the surface of the earth but not usable for navigation. Next in Part C we distort the longitude by pulling apart the meridians until we achieve the first goal of having north be a unique direction toward the of the chart. This calls for more longitude distortion at higher latitudes and hardly any near the equator. The result is shown in Part D, where we see that our round lake at high latitude has been distorted into an ellipse. If we want to measure useful bearings from one point to another, we must have landmasses with the proper shapes. Thus the next step is to distort the latitude until the shapes of the land masses are correct. Again, this calls for more distortion at higher latitudes.

In Part E we have a proper Mercator projection. That is north is straight up everywhere, and we can measure the direction between any two points.

But we have paid a price for this. Although the shapes of land masses (and lakes) are now correct, their relative sizes are not correct. We have made high latitude lands appear much bigger than they are. Greenland, for example, looks bigger than Australia on a Mercator chart, whereas in fact it is notably smaller.

A consequence of this type of distortion is that the inches per degree of latitude increases with latitude. It is still true that 1° of Lat equals 60 nmi, but the length of this 1° is longer at higher latitudes. We can still use the latitude scale as a miles scale, but we must do the conversion at the latitude of interest.

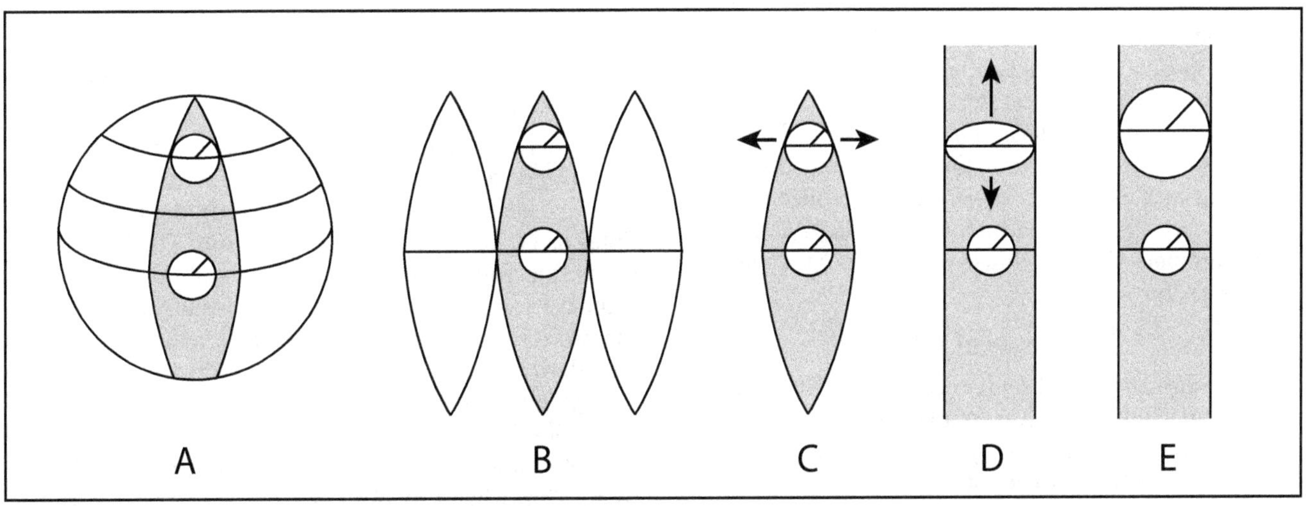

Figure 11.4-1 *Schematic evolution of a Mercator projection with north straight up and proper bearings.*

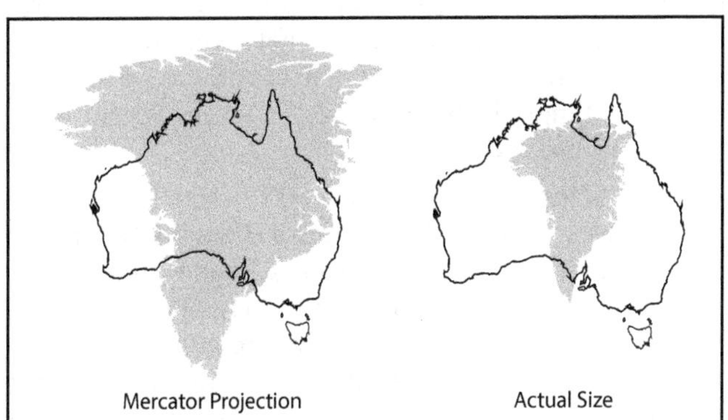

Figure 11.4 -2. *On a Mercator chart, Greenland looks much bigger than Australia, but it is actually notably smaller.*

11.5 Timekeeping in Navigation

There are a dozen or so timekeeping systems used in navigation and weather, and we cannot avoid using several of them from the nav station. In the end, the main time we care about is UTC, universal coordinated time.

Universal Coordinated Time

UTC is the world standard time system used by all nations to coordinate weather and navigation information. It corresponds to the time used in Greenwich, England for half of the year, formerly called Greenwich Mean Time. The town of Greenwich actually switches to daylight saving time in the summer, but all scientists and navigators continue with UTC. The official UTC system (like GMT) does not employ any form of daylight saving time.

Since all weather maps and GPS information uses UTC, it would seem we would want to keep our watches and ship's clocks on UTC for convenience, but it turns out this is not very convenient in practice. For daily activity—at home or underway—it is much better to have our clocks reading close to what we are used to, which is often referred to as local time.

"Local time," however, is a nebulous term, which when used should always be followed up with the definition of what we mean. There are two basic times it could mean. Local time could be the local *standard time* (that is well defined) or it could be the local *zone time* (also well defined). To confuse matters more, local time is also sometimes used in phrases such as Pacific Time, which is intended to be Pacific Standard Time in the winter and Pacific Daylight Time in the summer—the one phrase covering both, depending on the season.

Sources of UTC

These days the easiest source of accurate UTC is through a GPS connection. Whenever your GPS is indeed in contact with the satellites giving you a position, the time it displays will be accurate (in between satellite connections, it is just a good clock). On land, our cell phones and computers are usually connected to a network that itself gets this time from the GPS satellites; so phone and computer are also generally good—so long as they are connected to a network. As with the GPS receivers, when not connected they are just clocks, which we would have to monitor as we do other sources of time, which we cover later. To check your computer time, use www.time.gov.

The traditional way of getting UTC, which is still available and used widely, is to tune into a HF radio station that is broadcasting the time. This can be done with the same SSB transceiver used for communications, or from a shortwave receiver, which is the absolute minimum long distance radio we should have onboard. You can also get time tics from a sat phone using the telephone numbers, which also lists frequencies of the WWV and WWVH time broadcasts. These stations provide a tic at each second, and then they announce the time at each minute. The 29th and 59th tick are skipped, which gives you a way to prepare for the announcement on the 59th, and then to check your watch setting on the 30th. If you have not heard these broadcasts before and practiced setting or checking your watch, call one of the numbers to practice—not toll free, but well worth the few cents it takes to call.

WWV (Ft. Collins, CO)	303-499-7111
WWVH (Kauai, HI)	808-335-4363

There are a dozen or so other broadcast stations worldwide that provide UTC time. They are listed in NGA *Pub. 117, Radio Aids to Navigation,* which includes a detailed discussion of these services. See www.starpath.com/celnavbook.

Nuances of the UTC definition along with how to learn UTC to the tenth of a second are mentioned in the Glossary, but *Pub. 117* and the Time and Frequency Division at NIST are the primary sources: www.nist.gov/pml/div688 .

Zone Time

Zone time (ZT) is the system used by merchant ships and navies when crossing an ocean—or we all use when sitting at the USCG office taking a license exam. The time zone used in the zone time system is determined entirely by the longitude of your vessel at the time you record it. ZT will differ from UTC by a whole number of hours called the zone description (ZD).

In this time system, the world is divided into 24 1-hour time zones, each 15° of longitude wide, centered at the standard meridians, which are the longitudes that are multiples of 15, i.e., 0, 15, 30, 45... 165, 180. The borders between time zones thus take place at 7° 30' either side of the standard meridians. The only exceptions to this pattern are the two zones on either side of the International Date Line (standard meridian 180°, ZD = ±12). These two zones are only 30 minutes wide (each spanning only 7° 30' of longitude). See Figure 11.5-1. The labels of the times zones (ZD) are determined by the nearest standard meridian divided by 15. Thus when 120 W is the nearest standard meridian, the ZD would be 120/15 = +8.

If you are keeping ZT, then you find UTC from:

$$UTC = ZT + ZD,$$

where, again, the ZD is determined by your longitude. This formula essentially defines the sign (±) of the ZD. If your location is slow on UTC, i.e., any west longitude, then the ZD of that location is +. Eastern longitudes have negative ZDs.

To find the ZD of any arbitrary longitude:

(1) Round the longitude to the nearest whole degree.

(2) Divide by 15.

(3) Then round the result off to the nearest whole hour.

For example, at Lon 036° 48', we would get 37/15 = 2.46, so ZD = 2. At 37° 40', we get 38/15 = 2.53, so ZD = 3.

Zone time zones are also assigned a letter to facilitate radio communications, as shown in Figure 11.5-1. ZD of +8, for example is letter U, "Uniform." In this system UTC is letter z, which has led to the common zulu abbreviation for UTC or GMT. Thus the valid time of a weather map can be listed as 1200z. This is a convenient notation, so long as we know what we mean and write clearly.

We leave it to those interested in history to discover why there is no J zone. There was a reason. And if you want to ask trick questions on your navigation tests, remember ZD +12 and ZD -12 are just 30m wide, not the normal 1h. Using watch time, however, this fact and the Date Line itself will not affect us underway at all.

Zone time is used worldwide; it never adjusts for daylight saving time. Your ZD is determined by your longitude regardless of the season. Zone time is not used in civilian matters; it is designed for ocean navigation. A vessel using zone time will change the ship's clocks each time they cross into a new time zone. This serves a good purpose for those working at sea protected by labor laws and it keeps their daily schedules in tune with the sun, but this system adds a totally unnecessary layer of complexity to navigation. Vessels that are not forced to use it, should avoid it. Small-craft navigators crossing oceans are far better off using watch time, as discussed later. This recommendation cannot be over stressed!

00h vs. 24h

It is often crucial to understand the conventions used to mark the beginning and end of a day, especially in weather work. The first moment of any day is 00h 00m 00s, and the last moment of the day is called 24h 00m 00s. In practice, we should not have occasion to use the time 24h at all, and instead this time should be written as 00h with the date it is starting. If you see a map or position report listed as 00h on a given date, then you can assume that the date associated with it will be the same as the date an hour later at 01h. Likewise, we might want to avoid phrases such as "midnight on Jan 4th," and just say 00h Jan 4. This may seem trivial, but it is always valuable to keep in mind if you are doing something when you are tired... i.e., interpreting the valid time and date of a 48h forecast issued at 00z when you have not had any z's yourself for 24h.

Standard Time (EST, PST, etc)

Standard time is the time system used for civilian matters and for near coastal and inland navigation. Some coastal weather forecasts specify the local standard time in addition to the UTC of the report. Standard time is essentially the zone time of the location modified by politics and geography, and then susceptible to changes for daylight saving time.

Standard time zones do not follow longitude lines rigorously as do the zone-time zones, but they will often be approximately along those lines, diverting to follow state and country boundaries, or maybe a river flow. We still speak of the zone descriptions of standard zones in the same way as zone times, namely Eastern Standard Time (EST) has ZD = +5. Eastern Daylight Time would be ZD = +4, and so on. In other words, we would have UTC = EDT + 4h.

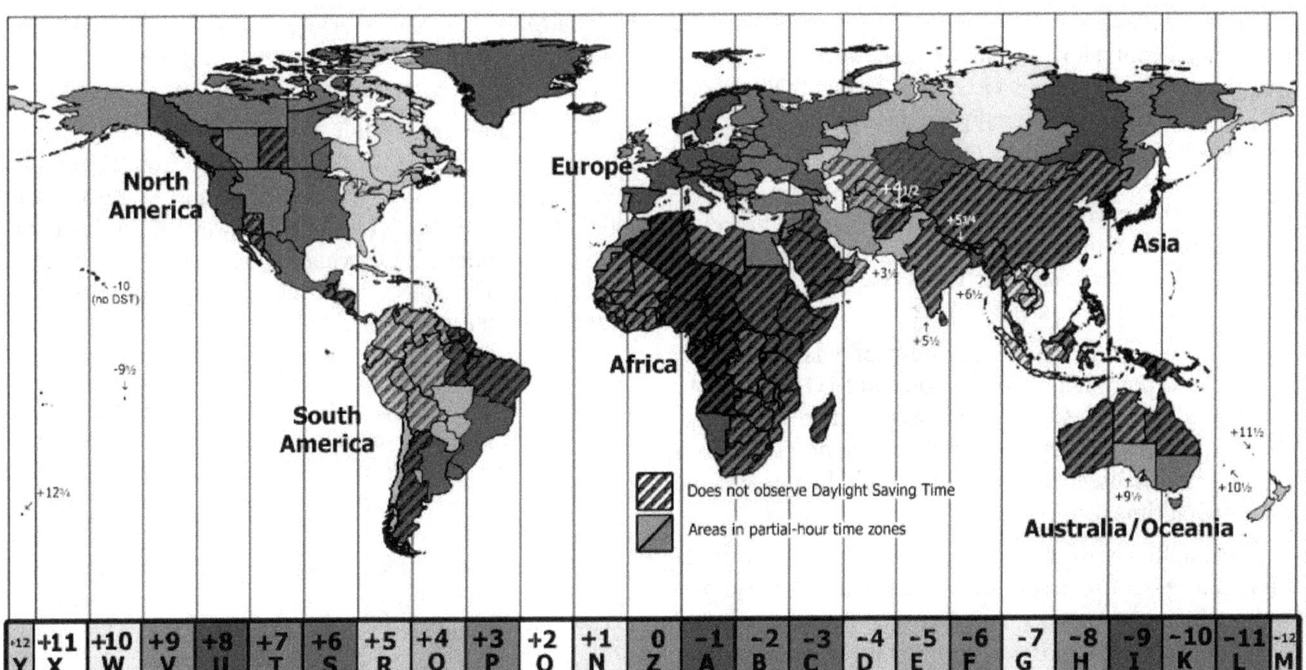

Figure 11.5-1 Zone-time *zones defined by the gray meridians compared to various* standard time *zones outlined on the land masses. The zone descriptions and their alphabetic label are shown at the bottom. These are navigator's definitions of the ZD. Beware that computers and phones might label the time zones with the signs reversed. The label "z" (zulu) for ZD = 0 gives rise to the common notation of 1800z to mean 1800 UTC.*

A complexity arises because standard times are often described outside of marine navigation circles as, for example, EDT being 4h behind UTC or slow on UTC. This leads to writing EDT = UTC – 4h. This is the same equation (with sides swapped), but in this line of thinking the time zone is described or labeled as -4h. Thus we often see computer and smart phone apps using reversed signs for the time zones. That is, when you want to select, for example, Pacific Standard Time for your phone, you will likely have to choose a number that says -8, whereas the navigator would describe this zone as having ZD = +8.

Watch Time

Watch time (WT) is the practical solution to timekeeping in navigation and weather. It is simply the time on your watch. Thus to navigate by WT, I just need to know the zone description *of my watch.* If I happen to have my watch set on Pacific Daylight Time, that would correspond to ZD = +7. Thus the ZD of my watch is +7 and that is all I need to know, no matter what longitude I am at as I cross the Pacific. In fact, I can go back and forth across the Date Line and never have to worry what date or time it is.

No matter where I am in the world, I find UTC by:

UTC = WT + ZD.

This is by far the best way to navigate, and we should always do so unless we are compelled to use ZT by labor laws or unions or some government regulation. It is easy to see that if you work day and night on ocean crossing vessels, you would want some semblance of order to your daylight and meal times, which would justify changing the ship's clocks each time you cross a time zone.

On a private vessel, however, this time changing adds tremendous confusion to your weather work and navigation. It is much better to just live with the fact that mid day might be 2 pm on your watch by the time you arrive—or set it ahead before you leave. In other words, you go an hour or two off local time as you proceed, but that is not distracting. To minimize timekeeping errors do not change your watch time when underway. Wait till you arrive. You are free to set the ZD of your watch that works best for you, but then do not change it till you arrive.

It is so important, one might guess there is more to say about it, but there is not. When you want UTC read your watch and add the ZD you have assigned to the watch. There will be a watch error to apply before doing sight reductions, as discussed later, but that would be the same no matter what timekeeping system you used.

You might say we have so many ways to get accurate time on a vessel these days why bother with all these precautions? The answer is we are teaching cel nav here as if that is all you have to go by, and good timekeeping practice is a key factor. With no other source of time but your watch, you do not want to risk losing the time, and changing the time zone—or in fact pushing any setting buttons at all—is the most probable time to lose it. More details are in the Chronometer Log and Watch Error section later.

Chronometer Time

For completeness, we include here also the very worst type of timekeeping, the one called *chronometer time* (CT). It is UTC kept on a 12-hour watch face, without specifying AM or PM! Absolutely no one in the world would consider using such a time system—that is, almost no one. This is the time system used on USCG celestial navigation exams. It is the way the USCG helps support navigation schools, and we are grateful to them.

When a sight time on an exam is listed as 04h 16m 32s CT, the first thing the candidate must do is use other peripheral information in the question to determine if this is 04h or 16h UTC. It is certainly doable; all problems have a ZT and a DR position, so we can DR to the location of the sight, figure the ZD and from that the UTC of that DR position, and this must be consistent with what we are doing. Evening star sights should be just after sunset, for example. It does require an overall awareness of what is going on, but this is rather more *gestalt* than called for on a navigation exam, especially since no one uses that system.

Local Mean Time

Local mean time (LMT) is the system used in the *Nautical Almanac* to tabulate meridian passage and the rising and setting times of the sun and moon, as well as twilight times. The actual watch times you will observe these events depends on your longitude, and LMT provides a way to tabulate the base values independent of longitude so that they can be used worldwide. LMT is intended to be referenced to the nearest standard meridian, assuming you are keeping the proper zone time at the moment. However, this gets ugly fast, and we can avoid all of that by using watch time.

In the watch time system, LMT is considered simply the UTC of the event as it would be observed from Greenwich meridian (Lon=0). Our job then is to correct these tabulated values with our longitude. The way we do this is the same for all phenomena whose times are tabulated. First figure the UTC of the event observed from your present location. For example:

UTC (sunset) = LMT (sunset) ± Lon

Your longitude must be converted from an angle to a time, using the Arc to Time table in the Nautical Almanac. Use the + sign for Lon W and the - sign for Lon E. Recall that the GP of the sun is moving from E to W, which helps us remember this. That is, if we are west of Greenwich, the sun goes by Greenwich before getting to us, but if we are east of Greenwich, the sun goes by us on the way to Greenwich so our UTC of the event is earlier than the UTC of the event at Greenwich.

Once we have the UTC of the event, we can convert that back to WT:

WT = UTC - ZD,

where again we are referring to the ZD we have the watch set to. We do not care what longitude we happen to be on.

International Date Line

What happens when we sail across the Date Line? When we are using the watch time method, the answer is Nothing at all—except if our longitude had been increasing, it will now be decreasing, and vice versa, but since all of our timekeeping does not depend on our longitude, we will find UTC from our WT just as we did before crossing. Read your watch and add the ZD to it to get UTC. You are, as always, also reading the WT date, and when you add the ZD to it if the number is bigger than 24 you will need to up the day by one for the UTC. But that is true no matter where you are when you add the ZD to the WT. Nothing special at the Date line.

Chronometer Log and Watch Error

Every watch gains or loses time as time goes by. This is referred to as watch error (WE). It could be a few seconds per month for a typical quartz watch or it could be milliseconds per month for some super accurate time pieces. Any practical time piece we have will lose accuracy with time so we will need to know what this error is and correct for it.

There are now watches (and phones of course) with GPS connection that correct themselves frequently, but they are expensive; we might as well look at the GPS for such times. If you have a watch with a GPS in it, then you won't have to navigate till the watch fails; just push the Position button, instead of the Time button.

The watch error of traditional watch will always get bigger with time—that is a requirement for chronometer. A *chronometer* is just a clock with a constant rate, meaning the number of seconds it gains or loses per some time period. The watch I navigated with for years had a rate of +3 sec/10 days. If I set it on the first of the month, on the 20th it would be 6 sec fast.

The first task of good timekeeping is to prove your time piece has a constant rate, and in doing so discover what that rate is. Again, we are talking here about traditional watches that you wear on your wrist, and we recommend that you do wear such a watch at sea and navigate by it. If you should get stuck in some emergency without other navigation aids, you can sail fairly easily to any port in the world by accurate time alone, but without a watch, you will struggle to DR for 100 miles accurately. I leave the details of the procedures to the book *Emergency Navigation.*

A chronometer log is just a list of what your watch reads and the corresponding correct time, and the difference between them. Checking once or twice a day, you should learn something in a week or two, but several months is better. You do not need to check every day, but the more often you do, the better statistics you get. Every entry is an estimate, because you have to round or estimate the tenths of a second. The more you do it, the better you become at that estimate. Figure 11.5-2 shows two chronometer rate plots—such a plot of WE versus time is a good way to see how good your data are and figure the best rate.

The procedure for a voyage is then to rate your watch before leaving and then just check and record the error frequently in an ongoing chronometer log so you can confirm that the rate has not changed. Once you get to your destination, you can set the watch again and start over.

We have to recognize that is part of traditional navigation technique, and the likelihood we will need it is small, but even in the satellite age the value of navigating by the watch you wear and knowing its rate remains prudent. Many of us have some time ago given up watches to our cell phones, which have become more amazing every year— but they have not become more dependable, they have actually become more disposable.

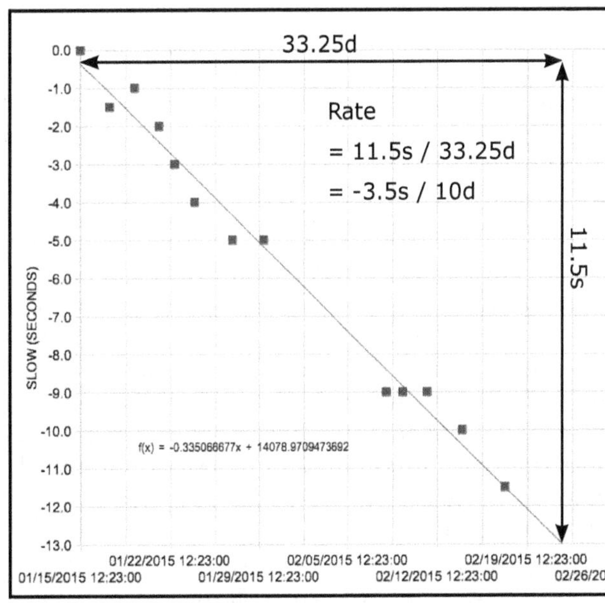

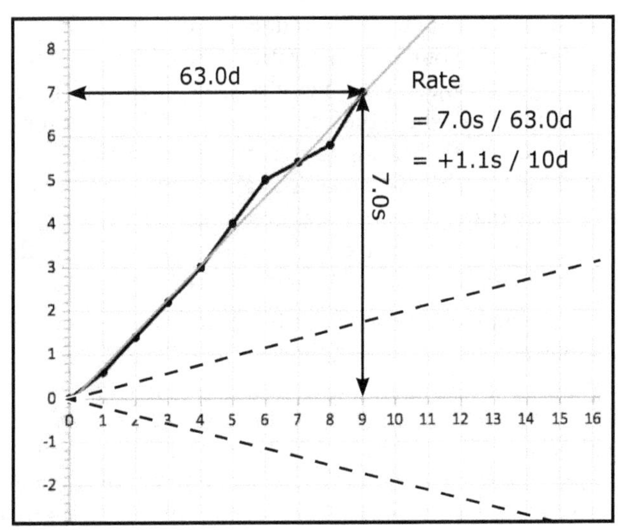

Figure 11.5-2 *Chronometer log plots. Top is an inexpensive quartz watch, which is slow, showing a rate -3.5s/10d. Bottom is a $600 watch with a guaranteed rate of <10s/year (dashed lines), but actual rate was +1.1s/10d, which shows we need to check these things. Bottom data compliments of Shawn Cook.*

11.6 Dip Short

Sometime after Chapter 3 the next and critical step is to practice the sextant sights. On land, without a clear view to a good sea horizon, this sometimes presents a problem. The best-known solution is the so-called artificial horizon (Section 11.19), which is nothing more than a pan of liquid—in the old days, they used mercury. But this best-known solution is not the best-working solution—at least as far as learning to use the sextant is concerned. With water nearby (lake, sound, river), the best way to practice sextant sights is to use the opposite shoreline under the object for a horizon. Use the land-water line for a sky-water line, and take your sights in the usual way.

On larger bodies of water, you can often do sights this way without any special corrections at all, just as if you were in the middle of the ocean. The conditions necessary for this are explained later, but even if you must make a special correction, it is a simple one, and one that does not distract from the learning process. The method of using an artificial horizon, on the other hand, requires sextant sight and sight reduction procedures that are rather different from the standard ones, so it is not the best way to learn to use a sextant.

To use a shoreline for a horizon you need to know how high your eye is above the water surface (HE) and you need to know the distance from you to the point on the opposite shoreline directly below the body sighted (D). It is most convenient to express HE in feet and D in nautical miles. If you are standing at the water's edge, HE is just your height. If you are up on a dock, HE is your height plus the dock height, and so on. This number can be found accurately, and for best results you should determine it to within an accuracy of 1 foot.

The distance to the shoreline (D) can be read from a chart once you have the bearing to the object sighted, which you get from the sight reduction, or .draw a line on the chart from your known position toward the direction of the sighted object, then measure the distance from you to the shoreline, where the line hits the land. You can measure the magnetic bearing to the star or sun with a hand-held compass when you take its sight, but you don't even have to do that. Again, the sight reduction process you do to follow up on the sight gives the true bearing (Zn) of the body at the sight time, and this bearing is all you need.

Once you have HE and D in hand, you can then decide whether special corrections are needed. Take the square root of HE in feet and compare it to D in nautical miles. If D is greater than square root of HE, then no special corrections are needed (Table 11.6-1). Proceed with your sight reduction just as if you were looking at an ocean horizon. For example an HE of 9 ft has a square root of 3. At this height, if you are using a shoreline that is 3 miles or more away from you (as would be the case, for example, looking across Puget Sound), then you are fine; no special corrections needed. This test tells us that we are not actually looking at the shoreline, but rather at the curvature of the earth between us and the shoreline, which is what we want for a good horizon.

If from an HE of 9 ft, the shoreline is less than 3 miles away, we are too close and must make the correction. The correction is called *dip short of the horizon*. And as the name implies, the only part of the standard sight reduction procedure that must be altered when using a shoreline instead of an ocean horizon is the dip correction—everything else remains standard. Instead of looking up the standard dip correction in the *Nautical Almanac*, we must calculate the dip correction (dip short) ourselves from a special formula. The dip short correction to use is figured from:

$$\text{dip short} = 0.416' \times D + 0.566' \times (HE/D),$$

where HE is in feet and D is in nautical miles. The dip correction will then be given in minutes of arc. For example, if HE is 8.5 ft and D is 1.35 miles, then figure the dip as: dip = 0.416 × 1.35 + 0.566 × (8.5/1.35) = 0.562 + 3.56 = 4.1', and use this value instead of the 2.8' that you would find in the *Nautical Almanac* for an HE of 8.5 ft. Remember that the dip correction is always negative, so it might be better to say, use - 4.1' instead of - 2.8'. Then do all the rest of the sight reduction in the normal way.

When HE is big and D is small you can end up with fairly large dip corrections, 30' or more, compared to the few minutes of normal Dip, but don't worry about this. Go ahead and use it; you will find that your sights work out well. But you must be precise about the numbers used to calculate the dip. As you practice a few, you will see that in some cases, if you just change the HE or the D by a small amount, it can have a large effect on the dip correction. Nevertheless, if you do this carefully, you can make corrections to your sights the size of a county that will put you right back onto a small inland lake.

You might want to stuff the dip short formula down into your bag of tricks for use in real navigation, not just

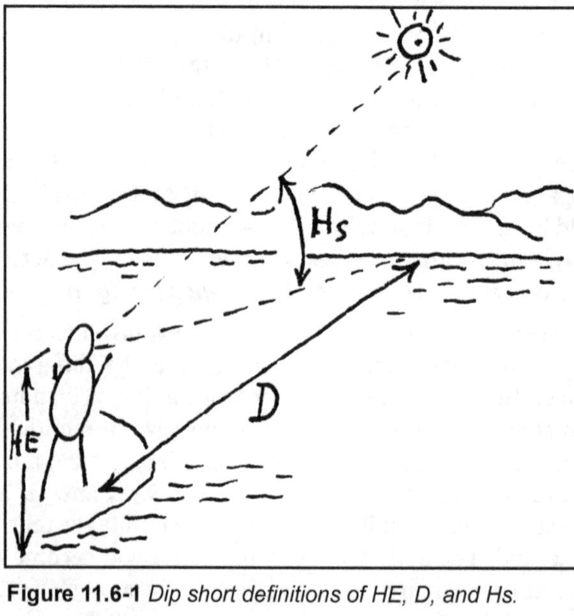

Figure 11.6-1 *Dip short definitions of HE, D, and Hs.*

practice. It was developed for coastwise navigation to allow for sun sights when you are very close to shore and the sun is over land. If a mile or so accuracy would help you out in coastwise navigation, you can always take a sun line. With this in mind, there is a Dip Short Table in Bowditch's *American Practical Navigator*, but the formula given previously is much better; the Bowditch table increments are large, so you must usually interpolate.

Remember too, that the dip short procedure is still an approximation. It is a good one, but it will never be as good as a proper horizon. So don't look for pin point accuracy when the corrections it calls for are very large. Individual sights may still be off a few miles when using it, especially if the horizon is not even a shoreline, but a houseboat dock or the waterlines of boats moored on the other side. Think of dip short in Samuel Johnson's words: "Sir, a woman's preaching is like a dog's walking on his hind legs. It is not done well; but you are surprised to find it done at all."

If you have the chance to plan your practice when sun or star bearings are in favorable directions (over the most distant shoreline) where the corrections are small or nil according to the previous guidelines, then you will get good results. In any event, this a good trick to know.

For comparison, the formula for open ocean dip used in the *Nautical Almanac* is

dip = 0.97' × Sqrt [HE(ft)],

which can be used for comparison or stashed away in a calculator if ever needed. We do not need this equation for routine work as it is solved in the dip correction table.

Dip Short Practice Exercise

Use the dip short formula to figure the proper dip correction for the following cases, then compare the answer to what the Almanac says the correction would be at sea from the same height of eye.

(1) Your eye height above the water level is 8.5 ft and the distance to the shoreline is 1.35 miles. What is the proper dip correction to use? (Worked in the text.)

(2) Your eye height above the water level is 6 ft and the distance to the shoreline is 0.42 miles. What is the proper dip correction to use?

(3) Your eye height is 25 ft and the distance to the shoreline is 1.4 miles. What is the proper dip correction to use?

(4) You checked the last sights, (3), above, and found that the distance is really 1.9 miles. How much does this change the dip correction?

(5) Your eye height is 12 ft and the distance to the shoreline is 0.9 miles. What is the proper dip correction to use?

(6) You checked the last sights (problem 5) and found that the height is closer to 15 ft than to 12 ft. With the distance still at 0.9 miles, how much does the dip correction change when you put in the right height?

(7) Your eye height is 28 ft and the distance to the shoreline is 0.9 miles for a set of sun sights and 0.65 miles for a set of moon sights. What is the proper dip correction to use for each set of sights?

Table 11.6-1 Dip Short vs Dip*

D nmi	*HE = 9 ft Dip = 2.9' Dip short*	*HE = 25 ft Dip = 4.9' Dip short*	*HE = 49 ft Dip = 6.8' Dip short*
0.25	20.5	56.7	111.0
0.50	10.4	28.5	55.7
0.75	7.1	19.2	37.3
1.00	5.5	14.6	28.2
1.25	4.6	11.8	22.7
1.50	4.0	10.1	19.1
1.75	3.6	8.8	16.6
2.00	3.4	7.9	14.7
2.25	3.2	7.2	13.3
2.50	3.1	6.7	12.1
2.75	3.0	6.3	11.2
3.00	2.9	6.0	10.5
3.25	2.9	5.7	9.9
3.50	2.9	5.5	9.4
3.75	2.9	5.3	9.0
4.00	2.9	5.2	8.6
4.25		5.1	8.3
4.50		5.0	8.0
4.75		5.0	7.8
5.00		4.9	7.6
5.25		4.9	7.5
5.50		4.9	7.3
5.75		4.9	7.2
6.00		4.9	7.1
6.25			7.0
6.50			7.0
6.75			6.9
7.00			6.9
7.25			6.8
7.50			6.8
7.75			6.8
8.00			6.8

** This table shows how the dip short approaches the distant horizon dip, and that the square root of HE is a good estimate of when we should check it.*

At farther distances the dip short computation goes back up, so we should not use it whenever we are far enough away to use the normal dip correction.

11.7 Solar Index Correction

This is an old method, used routinely by those explorers who did most sights on land with an artificial horizon (Lewis and Clark, David Thompson, for example. See www.northwestjournal.ca/dtnav.html.) The method was described by Maskelyne in his *Tables Requisite* as early as 1766.

It can be quite accurate, and offers a quick consistency check by measuring the sun's semidiameter at the time of the sight, which can be compared with the value listed in the *Nautical Almanac* or found online at www.starpath.com/usno. It is not entirely clear, however, if this solar IC method is superior for routine sights at sea using a true sea horizon. In these cases, it could be that the conventional methods we discuss elsewhere might be preferred. For lunar distance sights, on the other hand, this solar method is likely best, and landlocked using an artificial horizon this is the best method. It could also be the best method in all conditions, we are just not 100% sure of that—our perception of the horizon enters into the standard method, which could be a value?

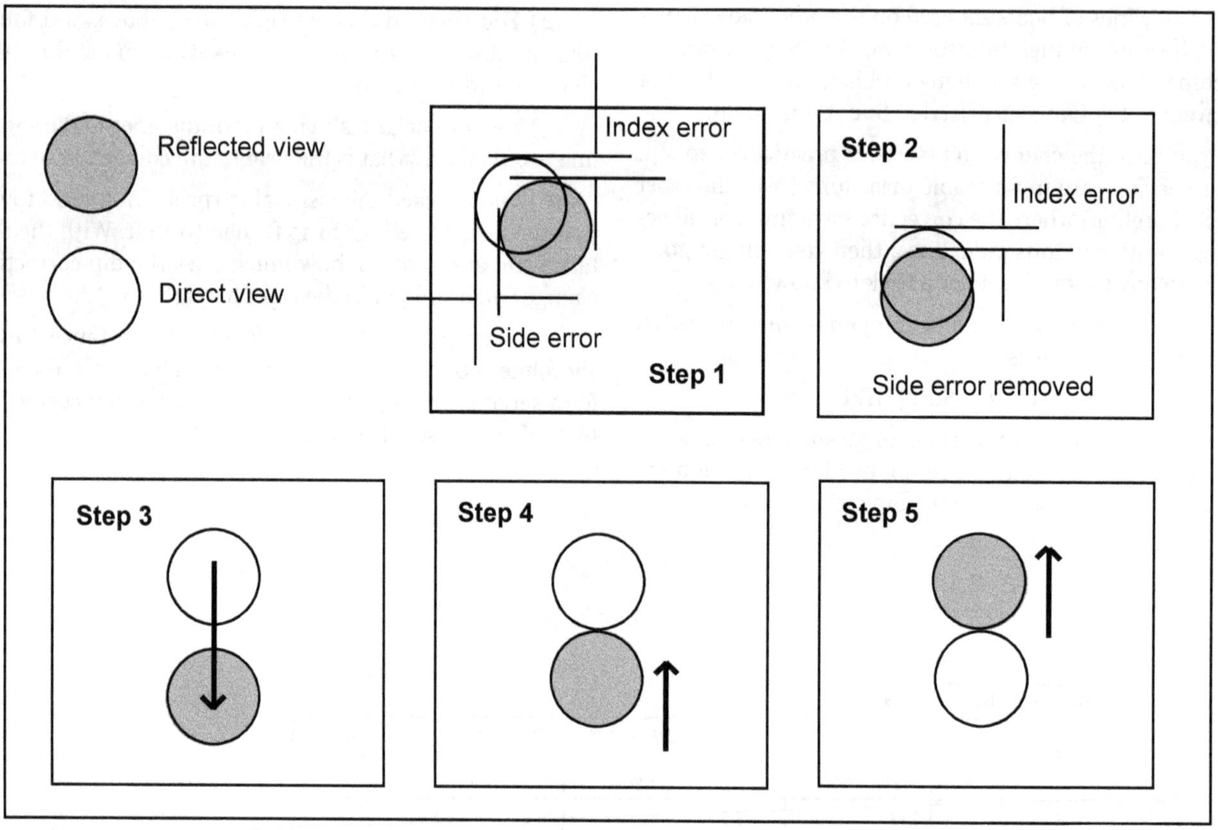

Figure 11.7-1 *Steps in the process of solar index correction. Dark disks are the reflected views.*

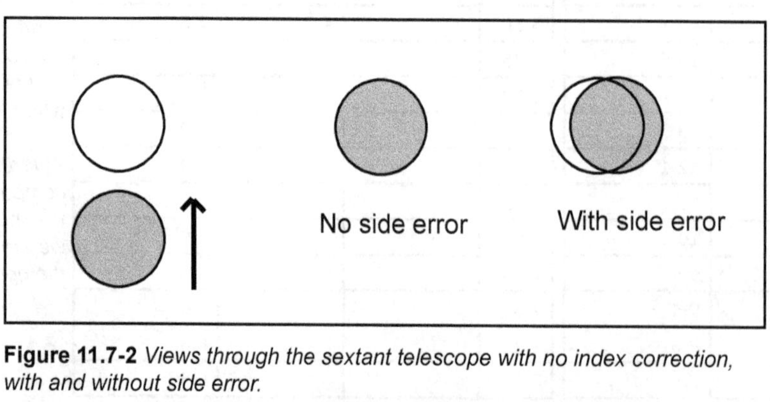

Figure 11.7-2 *Views through the sextant telescope with no index correction, with and without side error.*

CAUTION!

You will be looking straight toward the sun for this method and through a telescope to boot. So you must be very careful that all sun shades are in place and you do not somehow distort your view and look around the edge of the shades. *Do not under any circumstances look directly at the sun without it being completely covered by the shades.*

Procedure

Use the highest power scope you have for this. Monocular 6x35 or 7x30 are best if you have one. Adjust the shades if you have that option so the reflected and direct view of the sun appear as different colors.

(1) Set the sextant to 0° 0.0' and look toward the sun on a clear day. You will see something like shown in Figure 11.7-1, Step 1, in which we use the convention that shaded sun is the reflected view on the right side of the horizon mirror and the unshaded one is the direct view through the clear glass of the left side of the horizon glass.

(2) Adjust the side error to remove it by first adjusting the index mirror to be perpendicular to the frame of the arc and then adjusting the horizon mirror so it is parallel to the frame as well. Then you will see the picture shown in Figure 11.7-1, Step 2, which is almost all index error with no side error.

We use the rotation directions "toward" and "away," for convenience, but they must be defined carefully. The terms come from viewing the drum as you read it. Toward means turning the drum clockwise, with the numbers decreasing—the numbers on the top of the dial are moving *toward* you. Away means the opposite; counterclockwise, with numbers increasing, as the they move *away* from you.

During the actual sights you can benefit from this concept to keep track of which step you are on, but the logic of toward and away are lost as the drum is then sideways. During the sights, clockwise and counterclockwise can be confusing, so this convention helps us keep this crucial part of the process in order.

First we measure the "Toward value of the IC."

(3) Turn the micrometer away from you until all of the reflected image is well below the direct image.

(4) Now turn micrometer toward you slowly and uniformly so that the reflected image rises until the top edge of it just touches the bottom edge of the direct image. And then read the dial. It should read something like 32' on the scale—depending on your IC. Record this ON value. Accurate to the tenth. In this running example we will call this 34.0' ON. There is a form showing this example and several others in Figure 11.7-3.

(5) Now continue to turn, slowly and uniformly, in the toward direction until the bottom edge of the reflected image aligns with the top edge of the direct image. If you overshoot, we need to start all over again! The idea is to be turning only in one direction when we stop. This time the dial will read about 28' but this will be an OFF the scale measurement, so we have to subtract whatever it reads from 60. In this example, let's assume micrometer read 29.2', which would be 60.0'-29.2' = 30.8' OFF the scale. Record this OFF value.

(6) Now take the difference between the ON value and the OFF value and divide that by 2 to find your IC. Just subtract the smaller from the larger. The label of your result will be the same as the label of the larger value. In this example: 34.0 - 30.8 = 3.2' and 3.2'/2 = 1.6' and since 34 was ON, the answer is ON, i.e., our IC is 1.6' ON the scale.

(7) Now check your result by comparing to the actual semidiameter (SD) of the sun at the time of the sight. Our example was measured on 02/28/01 using an Astra 3b deluxe model sextant with traditional mirror. From the *Nautical Almanac*, we get that SD = 16.2'. The SD of the sun equals the ON value plus the OFF value divided by 4. In this example, 34.0+30.8 = 64.8 and 64.8/4 = 16.2 which is right.

More Notes

A quick and dirty method to measure the IC this way, or maybe to double-check the result to see that it all makes sense, is just to align the reflected and direct images on top of each other and read the dial. That reading will be your IC, it is just that the above procedure is a more accurate way to get the value. In this case we would see what is shown here, depending on whether or not we had side error. In our example, the dial would read 1.6' ON the scale when either of the two right-side alignments were set.

Now you can repeat the full process turning always in the Away direction to get the "Away value of the IC." Careful data will often show a slight difference for the Toward and Away values, even for a metal sextant. For plastic sextants, on the other hand, the toward and away values will almost always be rather large, some few minutes or so.

Forms like those of Figure 11.7-3 are included in the Forms Appendix that you can reproduce and use for practice.

The homemade Bader solar filters described in the book *How to Use Plastic Sextants: With Applications to Metal Sextants and a Review of Sextant Piloting* are ideal for this method. When using one of these filters this process is very easy and fast.

For Best Results

Because an important part of this method is that it includes a measurement of the sun's SD, choose a sun height above 20° or so to reduce uncertainty from refraction when comparing your measured SD with the actual SD. At low heights the refraction is changing fast with angle. At 5°, for example, this would cause an error of about 0.8', and worse lower. At 10° this error is down to 0.3' and it is essentially gone at 30° and higher. An outstretched hand span held vertical (tip of little finger to tip of thumb) is roughly 30° on many hands.

Date 2/28/01 SD 16.2’

[Toward] or Away

	ON	OFF	Diff	Check SD
1.	34.0	60.0	34.0	34.0
		− 29.2	− 30.8	+ 30.8
		= 30.8	= 3.2 ÷ 2	= 64.8 ÷ 4
			= 1.6 on	= 16.2

	ON	OFF	Diff	Check SD
2.	33.8	60.0	33.8	33.8
		− 29.8	− 30.2	+ 30.2
		= 30.2	= 3.6 ÷ 2	= 64.0 ÷ 4
			= 1.8 on	= 16.0

	ON	OFF	Diff	Check SD
3.	33.8	60.0	33.8	33.8
		− 29.2	− 30.4	+ 30.4
		= 30.8	= 3.4 ÷ 2	= 64.2 ÷ 4
			= 1.7	= 16.05

	ON	OFF	Diff	Check SD
4.	34.0	60.0	34.0	34.0
		− 29.6	− 30.4	+ 30.4
		= 30.4	= 3.6 ÷ 2	= 64.4 ÷ 4
			= 1.8	= 16.1

	ON	OFF	Diff	Check SD
5.		60.0		
		−	−	+
		=	= ÷ 2	= ÷ 4
			=	=

	ON	OFF	Diff	Check SD
6.		60.0		
		−	−	+
		=	= ÷ 2	= ÷ 4
			=	=

average = (1.6+1.8+1.7+1.8) / 4 = 1.7’ On when turning in the Toward direction.

Date 2/28/01 SD 16.2’

Toward or [Away]

	ON	OFF	Diff	CheckSD
1.	33.6	60.0	33.6	33.6
		− 28.8	− 31.2	+ 31.2
		= 31.2	= 2.4 ÷ 2	= 64.8 ÷ 4
			= 1.2 on	= 16.2

	ON	OFF	Diff	Check SD
2.	33.4	60.0	33.4	33.4
		− 29.0	− 31.0	+ 31.0
		= 31.0	= 2.4 ÷ 2	= 64.4 ÷ 4
			= 1.2	= 16.1

	ON	OFF	Diff	Check SD
3.	33.4	60.0	33.4	33.4
		− 29.0	− 31.0	+ 31.0
		= 31.0	= 2.4 ÷ 2	= 64.4 ÷ 4
			= 1.2	= 16.1

	ON	OFF	Diff	Check SD
4.	33.6	60.0	33.6	33.6
		− 29.2	− 30.8	+ 30.8
		= 30.8	= 2.8 ÷ 2	= 64.4 ÷ 4
			= 1.4	= 16.1

	ON	OFF	Diff	Check SD
5.	33.6	60.0	33.6	33.6
		− 29.2	− 30.8	+ 30.8
		= 30.8	= 2.8 ÷ 2	= 64.4 ÷ 4
			= 1.4	= 6.1

	ON	OFF	Diff	Check SD
6.		60.0		
		−	−	+
			= ÷ 2	= ÷ 4
			=	=

average = (1.2+1.2+1.2+1.4+1.4)/5 = 1.3’ On when turning in the Away direction.

Figure 11.7-3 *These data are from friend and navigator Lanny Petitjean using an Astra IIIb sextant with a traditional mirror. He has since used the results to achieve numerous sights from land with accuracies all below 0.4 miles and lunar distance sights leading to UTC accuracies below 30 seconds. Thanks Lanny. A form like this developed by Lanny is included in the Forms Appendix.*

11.8 Optimizing Plastic and Metal Sextant Sights

Plastic sextants are often disparaged for lack of inherent accuracy and vulnerability to the effects of the sun. But although it is true that they are not as accurate as metal sextants and they are indeed more sensitive to the sun than metal sextants are—thermal expansion coefficients of plastic are about 10 to 30 times higher than for metals—plastic sextants can with special care still be used quite successfully for practical navigation at sea and do provide a less-expensive alternative for new navigators to get their feet wet with sights of their own. Indeed, plastic sextants are in practice easier to use than metal sextants for the actual sight taking because they are so light weight, but this ease of handling is rather outweighed by the extra care required in procedures and analysis. The task at hand here is to explain the issues and then propose a way to compensate for these limitations by presenting a systematic method for taking sights with plastic sextants.

In my opinion the question of thermal effects of the sun have never been a real issue, since we have no reason to leave them for extended periods in the sun, just as we would not leave a $2000 metal sextant in the sun. Whether or not they might thermally change during a particular sight session in the bright sun is not clear, we have one set of sights from our studies that might be explained by that, but it is not at all conclusive.

There has been a published study that showed a large temperature dependence of the index correction of plastic sextants, but it is not at all clear that the study is pertinent to practical navigation—nor that the authors actually did measure what they set out to ("Temperature Dependence of Index Error," R. Egler, Navigation, Journal of the Institute of Navigation, 42, No.3, Fall 1995). That experiment should be repeated in more realistic circumstances before its conclusions can be extended to real navigation underway.

Figure 11.8-1 *Close up of the notched arc and worm gear on a metal sextant. Plastic sextants have the same basic mechanism, although the worm gear is hidden by a plastic cover.*

To understand the limitations and issues at hand we need to look briefly at how sextants work. Most sextants have a series of notches cut precisely 1° apart into the outside edge of the arc of the instrument (Figure 11.8-1). The notches are labeled in degrees along the side of the arc. A worm gear at the base of the index arm presses into these notches as it moves along the arc. Large changes in sextant angle are made by squeezing two levers that disengage the worm gear and allow the index arm to slide along the arc. Releasing the levers, engages the worm gear once again, but sometimes a slight twist of the micrometer drum is needed to seat the gear properly. The degrees part of the new sextant angle is read from a reference mark on the index arm against the degrees scale printed or engraved into the side of the arc.

Angle settings in between whole degrees are made by rotating the micrometer drum. This rotation changes the angle continuously from one degree to the next. The drum settings can typically be read to a precision of 0.1' of arc making use of a Vernier scale printed along the edge of the drum. Hence if a sextant were set to an angle of 32° 21.8', we would read the 32° from the scale on the arc, the 21' from the micrometer drum, and the 0.8' from the Vernier scale (Figure 11.8-2).

An ideal sextant has a very positive action of the micrometer drum, meaning no slack in the gears. Turn it to the right by 1' and immediately the angle increases by 1'. Stop and turn it to the left and it immediately starts to go down. A good metal sextant in good condition will behave properly in this regard. Plastic sextants, on the other hand, tend to have a bit of slack in this mechanism, consequently we get slightly different results when turning to the right to achieve alignment as opposed to turning to the left to achieve the same alignment. This is a well known issue with plastic sextants and it is mentioned in the manuals for the Davis Mark 15 and Mark 25 plastic sextants (it does not apply to the more basic Mark 3 model that does not have a micrometer drum). This crucial point is not mentioned at all in the Egler article cited earlier.

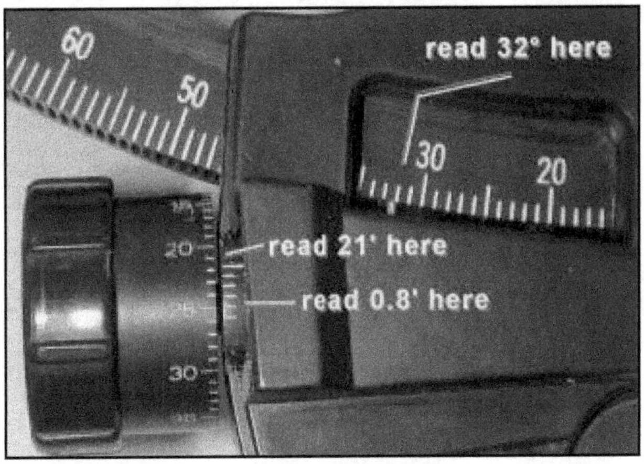

Figure 11.8-2 *Micrometer drum and Vernier scale on a Davis Mark 15 Plastic sextant. Metal sextants are read the same way.*

But there is more to this story. We cannot investigate slack in the gears without some means of observing the effects of our rotation of the drum. In other words, we have to decide what is or is not in alignment once we rotate the drum. An obvious time to study this effect is during the IC measurement, which is typically done with the sextant set to 0° 0.0' while viewing a distant sea horizon.

The sea horizon is the most convenient and most commonly used method, but for precision work it has the limitation of not often presenting a perfectly sharp line between sky color and sea color. Look very carefully at the best horizon and you often see—or at least appear to see—a very narrow line of some other color right at the horizon, or some other slight disruption of a perfect line. Consequently, even when we have a perfect sextant with no gear slack at all, we can still get the appearance of a slight gear slack because the imprecision of the reference line leads to some variance from sight to sight in what the observer might call perfectly aligned. The amount of this variance will depend on the nature of the horizon, the skill of the observer, the power of the telescope, and with the sextant model. A 6- or 7-power scope is better for IC checks than the 4-power scopes that are standard on most sextants, and this effect is naturally larger when viewed in the 2-power scopes on plastic sextants.

Testing for Gear Slack

First remove the side error of the sextant by adjusting the horizon mirror until you can rock (roll) the sextant set at 0°0' and not detect any splitting of the horizon (Figure 11.8-2).

This may also require some collateral adjustment of the index mirror. With plastic sextants we have found that it is often useful to give each mirror housing (not the mirror itself) a bit of a flick with the finger to help the seating of the mirrors before and after the adjustments. If the flick changes things, you have to keep working on it. (Don't flick it any harder than you would flick your own nose!)

Then with the sextant set to 0° 0.0', view the horizon and turn the drum "toward" you (clockwise, arc angle decreasing–see Section 11.7) to clearly separate the two horizons viewed directly and by reflection. Then slowly turn the drum "away" from you (counterclockwise, arc angle increasing) until the horizons just first appear as a smooth straight line, which is what we call in alignment. Be sure to sneak up on this very slowly so you do not overshoot the alignment. We want the reading just as they first become aligned.

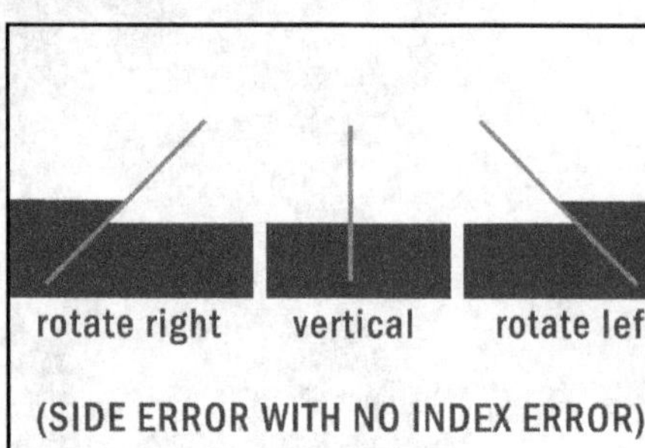

Figure 11.8-3 *Three views through the sextant telescope with side error but no index error as you rock it to the right and left.*

Confirm that you are aligned by panning (yawing) the sextant right and left a bit to verify that there is no detectable motion along the horizon (Figure 11.8-4). This is a more accurate method than just looking straight at it and concluding it is aligned. If you are just very slightly unaligned, you will notice a slight bump moving right and left at the intersection of the two views, direct and reflected. Once confirmed, record the IC reading to the nearest 0.1' and label this IC measurement with an "A" to note that you were turning the drum in that direction and a "touch" to note that this was the setting for the first touch of the two horizon views in alignment. If you have overshot the alignment, start all over again.

Now to continue, first double-check your notes to confirm which way you are turning and think through the motion, then very slowly and carefully continue turning in the away direction until you can first detect that you are no longer aligned. Again, this is best done by doing a slight rotation then panning the horizon, then another and another pan, until you can detect some motion along the horizon which indicates that you are no longer aligned. Then read and record the new IC and label it with "A" and "leave," meaning this was the value when you left the alignment.

Repeat this five or six times in the away direction and then do the same in the toward direction. This type of measurement will show what we are up against. You have effectively measured the angular width of "perfect alignment." With a metal sextant and a sharp horizon, the touch and leave values will typically differ by only a few tenths, which reflects our limits on locating the horizon precisely. Put another way, if we just randomly set the sextant to alignment on a series of sights, we could fairly expect to get at least this level of spread in the values we measured, since anywhere between "touch" and "leave" gives the same appearance of alignment.

More to the point at hand, however, is that with a metal sextant, the spread in the touch and leave values will show

Figure 11.8-4 *View through the sextant telescope with the index mirror almost exactly parallel to the horizon mirror. Look for this small bump moving along the horizon to detect that you are very close but not quite perfect yet on the alignment for an IC check.*

little if any difference when measured in the toward or away direction. With a typical plastic sextant, this is not the case. Not only will you detect larger spreads in the touch and leave values, you will also most often notice a significant difference in the IC values measured in the toward and away directions, which is a measure of the slack in the gears—or, if not that, at least some measure of the general behavior of the device (the actual worm gear in the plastic sextants is metal, but it seats into notches in plastic).

These IC differences in plastic sextants can also vary from day to day and from the beginning to the end of a given sight session—even if the temperature of the device has not changed at all during the session. Sometimes the toward and away differences might be zero and other times on the same device (without having adjusted the mirrors) be as large as 4' or 5'. We must stress here, however, that we are describing operational behavior, and not necessarily a limit on the ultimate accuracy obtainable with the sextants. The exercise is intended to show how users might verify for themselves why special care must be taken when doing celestial sights with plastic sextants. Next we show procedures that will to a large extent compensate for these limitations.

Set and Wait Method

This method can optimize metal and plastic sextant sights. For plastic sextants, measure the IC values as explained earlier. The sextant should be in thermal equilibrium with the ambient temperature.

For objects that are setting (i.e., bearing to the west of south) get object and horizon in view, then turn the drum in the away direction till the object is well below the horizon. Then slowly and smoothly turn the drum in the toward direction until the body is about one-eighth of a sun diameter above the horizon (about 4' or so) when using the sun or moon, so that the lower limb is just very clearly above the horizon. The goal is to get to this point by only turning in the toward direction and then stopping with no backlash on the drum. Then do not touch the drum any longer but just wait for the sun to set onto the horizon as you *continually rock the sextant* back and forth to ensure a perpendicular measurement. When the lower limb touches the horizon, note the time, and read the dial. Note the reading and that it was a toward sight.

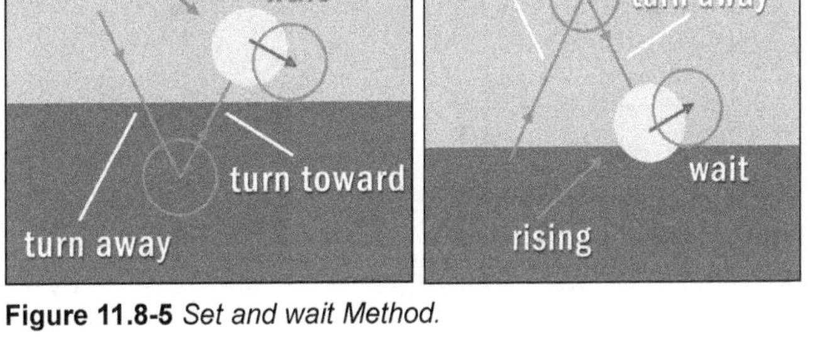

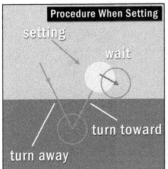

Figure 11.8-5 *Set and wait Method.*

When the body is rising, do the reverse. Turn toward till the body is above the horizon, then carefully and slowly use the away rotation to get the lower limb about 4' or so below the horizon and then wait for it to rise up to perfect alignment.

It will help to remember that turning what we are calling toward you (micrometer rotates clockwise) makes the reflected image rise in your view; turning away makes it descend in the sextant view. You may want to use other words in your mind to describe these two opposite rotations.

Then do at least four or five sights of each body. Use the appropriate toward or away IC for correcting the data.

And finally for the best results analyze your data using the fit-slope method of Section 11.24 to choose the best sight of the lot for your fix. There is no need to sight reduce all of them if you are doing it by hand, just the best representative of the set that you find this way. The slope analysis will essentially pile all the statistics of the set into that one sight.

Remember, too, that when you compute the Hc values for the theoretical slope of the line over the time range of your sights (explained in Section 11.24) you must use the proper DR position for each computation if they are different. When moving at any significant speed, this means updating the DR used at each computation. Sailing south at 8 kts, for example, any two sights of the same body taken more or less to the south that are 30 minutes apart in time would be some 4' different in sextant height. We must account for this in the slope analysis.

I would propose this set and wait method as standard operating procedure for taking sights with plastic sextants, but just add that this is a good way to do sights in general with any sextant if conditions are a bit rough. It is longer, but much easier, and creates much less internal stress. If you miss it, just start all over again. Trying to cut corners and guess what time it really was aligned is not reliable.

I would also propose—as a broad generalization—that using these procedures one should be able to obtain accuracies of about 5 or 6 miles as a general rule with plastic sextants. Maybe better in some cases, maybe a bit worse in others. Naturally, one needs to follow good procedures to obtain good fixes, which means well selected bodies (three near 120° apart) with careful correction for the motion of the vessel during the sight session. With metal sextants using good procedures in good conditions, on the other hand, we should strive for 1 or 2 miles routinely.

See also the notes on the advantages of sight reduction by computation in Section 11.28.

11.9 Longitude from LAN

The peak height of the sun at noon offers quick and accurate latitude. We cover the method in Chapter 3. When the sun is at its peak height, we know it is located precisely on our meridian, hence the obvious question: if you know when the sun is on your meridian, why can't we just look up the GHA of the sun and thereby know what our precise longitude is as well?

The answer is, yes, that is exactly right. The principle of finding longitude this way is most basic and would indeed be the mainstay of emergency navigation, as outlined in Chapter 10 (Section 10.1). One could, when dead in the water, time the sunrise and sunset, find the midpoint, look up the GHA of the sun at that UTC and that is your longitude—or at least very close to it.

The issue here is more one of ultimate accuracy and practicality rather than principle. The principle is easy, your longitude is equal to the GHA of the sun when it crosses your meridian. The problem is determining when the sun crosses your meridian—especially when you are changing latitudes during the measurement. We can say that although finding accurate latitude from LAN is easy, finding accurate longitude this way is not easy. The very thing that makes the latitude easy is the flat top of the LAN curve of Hs versus WT. If we miss taking a sight at the exact peak, we will not suffer much in latitude accuracy because the curve is flat at the top. But this very flatness makes selecting the peak time very difficult. From a practical point of view, to find longitude from the sun alone, one is better off doing a conventional running fix between two sun lines, as we cover in detail in Chapter 6.

Figure 11.9-1 shows a hypothetical plot of LAN data (we show examples of real data in Chapter 3). The task in Lon from LAN is selecting the exact center of this curve. Just taking the time of the highest value would not give a reliable midpoint in most cases. One approach is to plot on tracing paper, then fold it in half and crease it. Another is to take several horizontal samples across the data such as midpoint from A to B, then from C to D, etc and then average the midpoints. Some such technique is required to find the center from this type of data.

More or less regardless of how this is done, on the average (seasons, latitudes, length of sight series, etc) one will be lucky to find the center of such a curve to any better accuracy than about plus or minus 1 minute. Sometimes better, when the sun is high and you have good data, but more often worse. It is not that the answer will be wrong by that amount, but your uncertainty will be that large, which is almost equivalent in crucial navigation. One minute of time is the same as 15' of longitude; so as a broad rule of thumb, one might say that this method could give you longitude to within about 15'. This is far worse than one can obtain with a conventional running fix over some few hours.

But the problem is rather worse than that. Two matters of principle make the previous simple approach not quite right. One depends on the date, the other on your motion north-south. We won't analyze these in detail, the results vary with about everything, but we will add one numerical example at the end.

The date issue is related to changes in the declination of the sun between morning and afternoon sights used as the two reference points. Near the equinoxes, the declination changes about 1' per hour. So a 6-hour run up and over the peak would result in a declination change of 6'. This could yield an error in the longitude of as much as 3 or 4', depending on latitude.

The more important issue is the vessel's travel to the north or south during the extent of the sights used to find LAN. The situation is illustrated in Figure 11.9-2. Here we assume the vessel moves from Lat A, the location of the first sight, to Lat B, the location of the last sight. Note that when underway the path of the sun (Hs vs. WT) is not symmetric. So figuring the mid point between A and B will yield a time error in LAN by one-half of the difference between A' and B. In the following example this is about two-and-a-half minutes, or an error in longitude of about 40'.

When not moving, only the declination issue must be resolved, and certainly when moving one could make all the corrections needed to get good data from these "double-altitude" sights for longitude. But the corrections needed are long and tedious. One is better off just doing a running fix, which is easy and standard.

We stress this, since so many modern texts simply state the simplest form of this procedure without warning of errors and uncertainties, which might give the navigator the impression that it might yield standard accuracy, which it does not. It is best to reserve this procedure to emergency situations where other tools and procedures might not be available.

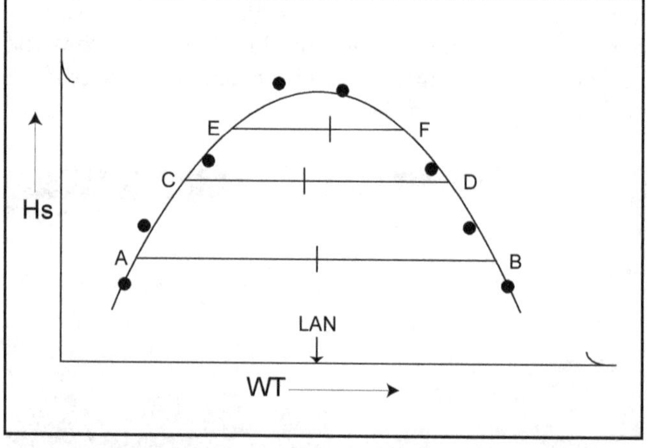

Figure 11.9-1 *Finding the midpoint of an LAN curve for longitude. An example of a real LAN data curve is shown in Figure 3.2-5.*

Double Altitude Example

April 2, 2002. Lat A = 50 N, Lon = 0, speed = 10 kt, course = 180. The first sight is 3 hours before LAN (12:03:36) and the second sight about 3 hours after LAN. At 09:03:36 we get Ho = 31° 13.7', then in principle if we measured Ho again at 15:03:36 we should get again 31° 13.7' and halfway between these two we would get 12:03:36 and sure enough the GHA of the sun at that time is 0°.

But that will not be what you get. You will not get that even if you do not move, because of the 6' declination change during the 6 hours that transpired (you will get 31° 18.5'), but it will be worse when traveling 60 nmi to the south between the two sights. The conventional instructions on these sights is to measure the height at the first sight (09:03:36 to get 31° 13.7') and then wait till the afternoon and just set your sextant to that height and wait till the sun touches the horizon. If you do this, you will find that the sun falls to this exact height again in the PM at 15:08:17. Then if you figure the midpoint between these two times, you get LAN = 12:05:57, which is indeed wrong from the correct 12:03:36 by an amount of 2m and 21s. This yields a longitude error of about 40', i.e., we were traveling due south on Lon = 0°, which is the locations we used to compute the heights.

This example was chosen more or less at random. We could find much worse cases, and some where the error would be smaller. In summary, this is not a recommended way to find longitude for routine navigation. In other words, could I do DR for 6 hours and be off by 40' of longitude? The answer is not likely, which means a running fix would yield a more accurate longitude.

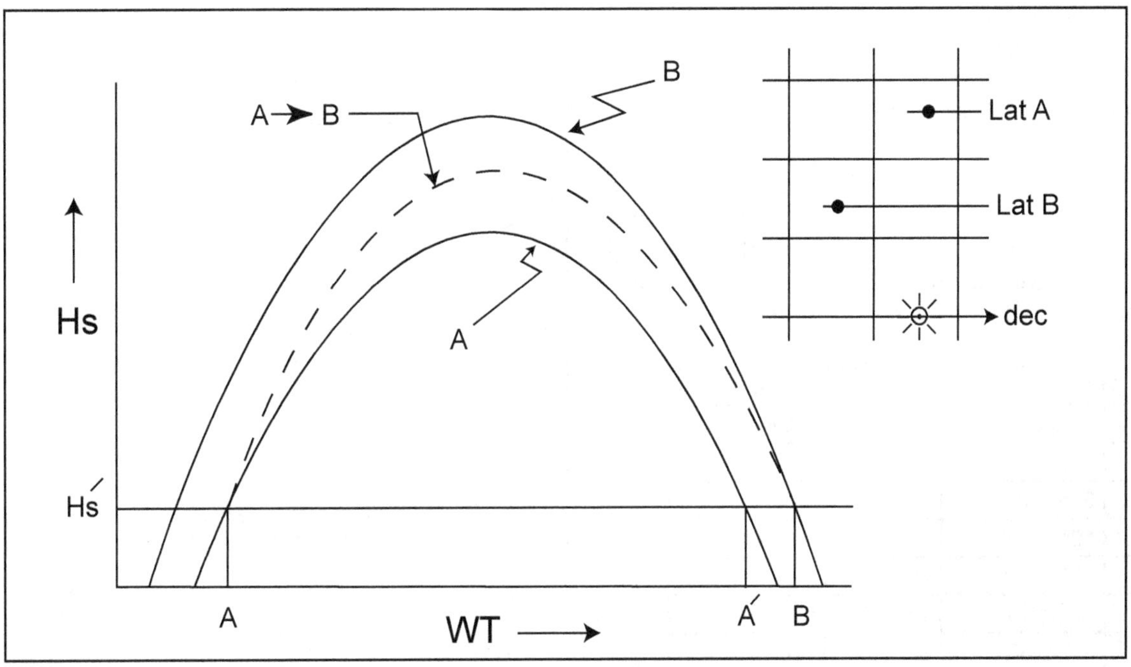

Figure 11.9-2 *Path of the sun at Lat A and Lat B and how it appears if measured while traveling from A to B. The time difference A' to B is twice the error in true longitude without corrections.*

11.10 Ocean Plotting Sheets

In the text, we describe and use universal plotting sheets available in pads of 50 sheets printed both sides, about 13 inches tall and 14 inches wide. Besides their use in cel nav, they are also valuable for weather route planning underway when new winds or currents are anticipated. They can also be used for radar maneuvering plots, or indeed any standard maneuvering board solutions.

On USCG cel nav tests, candidates are provided with an NGA Ocean Plotting Sheet. These are large sheets, 3 ft × 4 ft, that are preset to specific latitudes; so the longitude scale is printed right on them. At first glance, these might be considered superior for cel nav plotting, and indeed for the USCG exams they are. But underway in a small boat at sea they are not practical at all. First they are too big for a typical chart table, and second they are expensive, costing about the same as a nautical chart, some of which you would cross in a day or two.

Also they are no longer available in lithographic printing, so we have only the print on demand editions, and some companies that print these use a paper that is not very friendly to erasing pencil lines. Not all paper options have this problem, but it is something that would need clarification. The sheets available are listed in Table 11.10-1. Except for No. 920 that spans the equator, the labels N or S are not given, as these sheets are symmetric on either side of the equator.

Other, more useful options include free downloads of pdf files of universal plotting sheets with various designs, usually intended to be printed on standard letter or tabloid size paper. We have a list of these at www.starpath.com/celnavbook. The pdfs would not be valuable underway without a printer, but they could be printed in advance. They are also useful for practice on land.

Table 11.10-1 NGA Ocean Plotting Sheets (POD)

No.	Range	Mid Lat	Scale = 1 to:
920	4°S to 4°N	0°	1,095,679
921	3° to 11°	7°	1,087,566
922	10° to 18°	14°	1,063,344
923	17° to 24°	20° 30'	1,026,715
924	23° to 30°	26° 30'	981,220
925	29° to 36°	32° 30'	924,1984
926	35° to 41°	38°	864,517
927	40° to 46°	43°	802,596
928	45° to 50°	47° 30'	741,597
929	49° to 54°	51° 30'	683,493
930	53° to 57°	55°	629,889
931	56° to 60°	58°	582,040
932	59° to 63°	61°	532,576
933	62° to 65°	63° 30'	490,222
934	64° to 71°	67° 30'	841,029
935	70° to 75°	72° 30	660,992
936	74° to 78°	76°	531,840

Another option for plotting cel nav LOPs is to use any standard echart plotter, or more generally an electronic charting system (ECS) using a computer interface. In this approach you plot the assumed position precisely as a waypoint and do the remainder of the standard plotting with either the range and bearing tool, or use the route tool. We have an example of this type of plotting in the Answer to Exercise 9.7.

Those who want to be more self-reliant still, can make their own plotting sheets on any blank paper or chart using the guidelines that can be discerned from the way we draw the meridians in on the universal sheets. Figure 11.10-1 is a reminder of the method.

Keep in mind that any of these universal chart sections begin to lose accuracy for distances of much more than 100 nmi from the center once you are above about 40° Lat.

As a historical note, the first universal plotting sheets were invented by Capt. Fritz Uttmark in 1918. We have a sample of his original sheet in Figure 10.6-6.

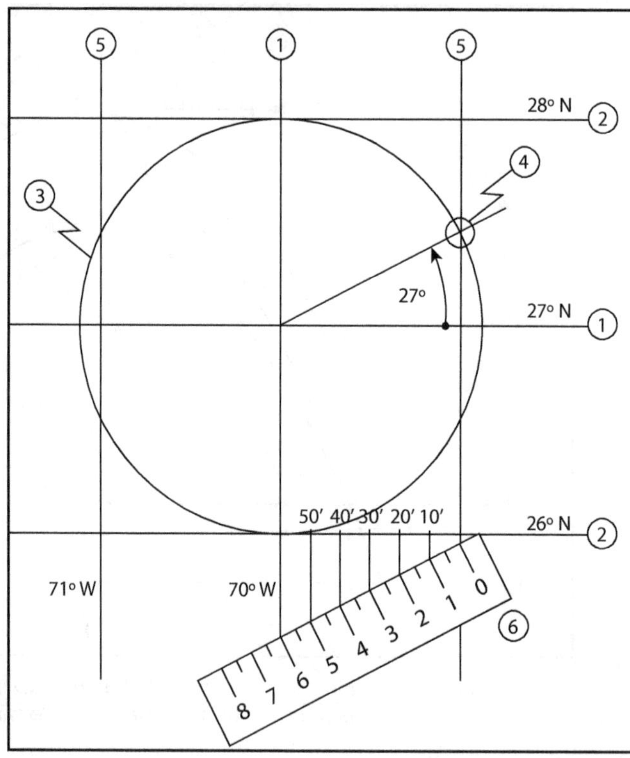

Figure 11.10-1 *Make a universal plotting sheet. (1) Draw mid-Lat and mid-Lon and label them. (2) Choose Lat spacing and draw in two parallels. (3) Draw a circle between the two Lat lines, centered on mid-Lat. (4) With a protractor draw an angle above the mid-Lat equal to the mid-Lat , and mark where that line crosses the circle. (5) Draw in a meridian parallel to mid-Lon through that point. (6) Use any ruler or scale marked in tenths to subdivide the Lat and Lon intervals. Alternatively, use graph paper (crosshatch) and draw the parallels 60 divisions apart, then the meridian spacing will be 60xCos(mid-Lat).In the above example, 60 divisions = 60' of Lat and 60xCos(27) = 53.5 divisions = 60' of Lon.*

11.11 Ocean Dead Reckoning

The ultimate goal of sound ocean navigation is learning how to do accurate dead reckoning for your vessel. That means knowing how to navigate by compass and log alone, enhanced by knowledge of your boat's performance and estimates of currents, so in the event you get stuck with nothing more to go by, you are prepared to carry on. With good cel nav skills, you will be less anxious about your electronics working right, and with good DR practice, you will be less anxious about clear skies and the possible loss of the tools you need for that.

The only way to learn how well you can do DR is to practice it. For this we need a log (or knotmeter and watch), a compass, and a logbook. We can check our DR with the GPS just as well as with cel nav, even easier, but in the spirit of the cel nav course we are assuming navigation without electronics. The reality is, however, that many of us do not get out into the ocean very often for this type of practice with cel nav, so tests on coastal or inland waters using GPS can be very productive.

The idea is to simply make a voyage and keep a careful logbook, and then periodically compare your DR position to your true position, make a note of the differences, then start over again. The more practice you get in various conditions, the more you learn.

Your compass should be calibrated if that has not been done already—which is easy to do with the sun underway at sea (Section 11.21). This is an extremely valuable skill and very easy to do. By compass calibration I mean checking the deviation, or confirming that it has no deviation. A typical binnacle mounted compass on a non-steel vessel should have no deviation if adjusted properly, but it has to be checked. For now we just assume that the compass is correct.

Next, we need some form of log. A log in this sense is just an odometer that counts miles traveled through the water. One option that immediately comes to mind is just using Speed × Time to figure Distance run. That is, if I am traveling at 6.0 kts for 3 hours then I have traveled 18 nmi. All well and good in principle. And indeed if that is all we have, then that is what we would use. The problem is that it is very unlikely that any small-craft vessel, especially a sailing vessel, will travel for 3 hours at precisely the same speed. And not only will your speed vary, but also your course will vary. In short, if you use speed and time, then you have another task of figuring out what the right average speed should be for a given leg of the trip. Not impossible, but just more work.

Whenever possible, it is best to use a log that accumulates the miles traveled. Most knotmeters also measure your total miles traveled as well as your actual speed—there is a spinning paddle wheel with magnets in it, and each revolution past an electric coil makes a pulse. The rate of the pulses is converted into a speed; the total number of pulses is converted into a distance run. Generally, it is the same calibration constant that adjusts both functions.

As a rule, the accumulated log miles is a more accurate means of gauging distance run than using average Speed × Time. On ocean racing yachts that have competition between watches for highest average speed, the way they compute the average speed is subtract log readings from beginning and end of watch periods and divide by the duration of the watch. (In principle they should compete on speed made good toward the desired waypoint, because it does not really matter how fast you go if not in the right direction.)

The log can be an electronic type as discussed, or it could be the traditional taffrail log such as the classic Walker log, which dates to the times of the civil war. The taffrail logs, however, are not very convenient for shorter runs on inland waters. Electronic logs, like the compass, must also be calibrated. This is more a topic of inland and coastal navigation. It involves timing several circuits along a known distance. It is fundamental to all navigation that the log and compass (and depth sounder) be properly calibrated.

Assuming log and compass are in order, we then look to the logbook. This is a simple step, but equally important. Using a log for DR, we actually only need two numbers: the log reading and the course at each course change. As a rule, we generally keep much more info in the logbook, but the fundamental practice of DR you only need to know what courses you steered and at what log reading you turned to that course. In Chapter 4 we have several exercises that show typical log book entries along with plotting exercises.

The simple rule on when to make a logbook entry is anytime anything changes. For doing DR, we only need to know when the course changes, but for other aspects of weather watching or performance analysis, you will want to make more frequent entries. If nothing changes at all, then it is still a good idea to make a logbook entry every couple of hours during a passage.

Figure 11.11-1 shows a DR track plotted from the logbook segment in Figure 11.11-2. The track is adjusted at each cel nav fix, and to learn about the past DR accuracy we need to also record the range and bearing from DR to fix at each fix. A sample of these data are in Figure 11.11-2. This line tells us how much our DR went wrong since the last fix.

Assuming our compass and log are well calibrated (meaning in practice compass right on all headings within 2° or better and log right to 2% or better at all speeds), the reasons the DR could go wrong beyond these instrument uncertainties would typically be a combination of these factors: (1) ocean current, (2) leeway, (3) helm bias, and (4) blunder in the logbook entry.

(1) Ocean currents average about 0.5 kts worldwide, but in special cases like the Gulf Stream they can be well over 4 kts, although such strong current patterns are well

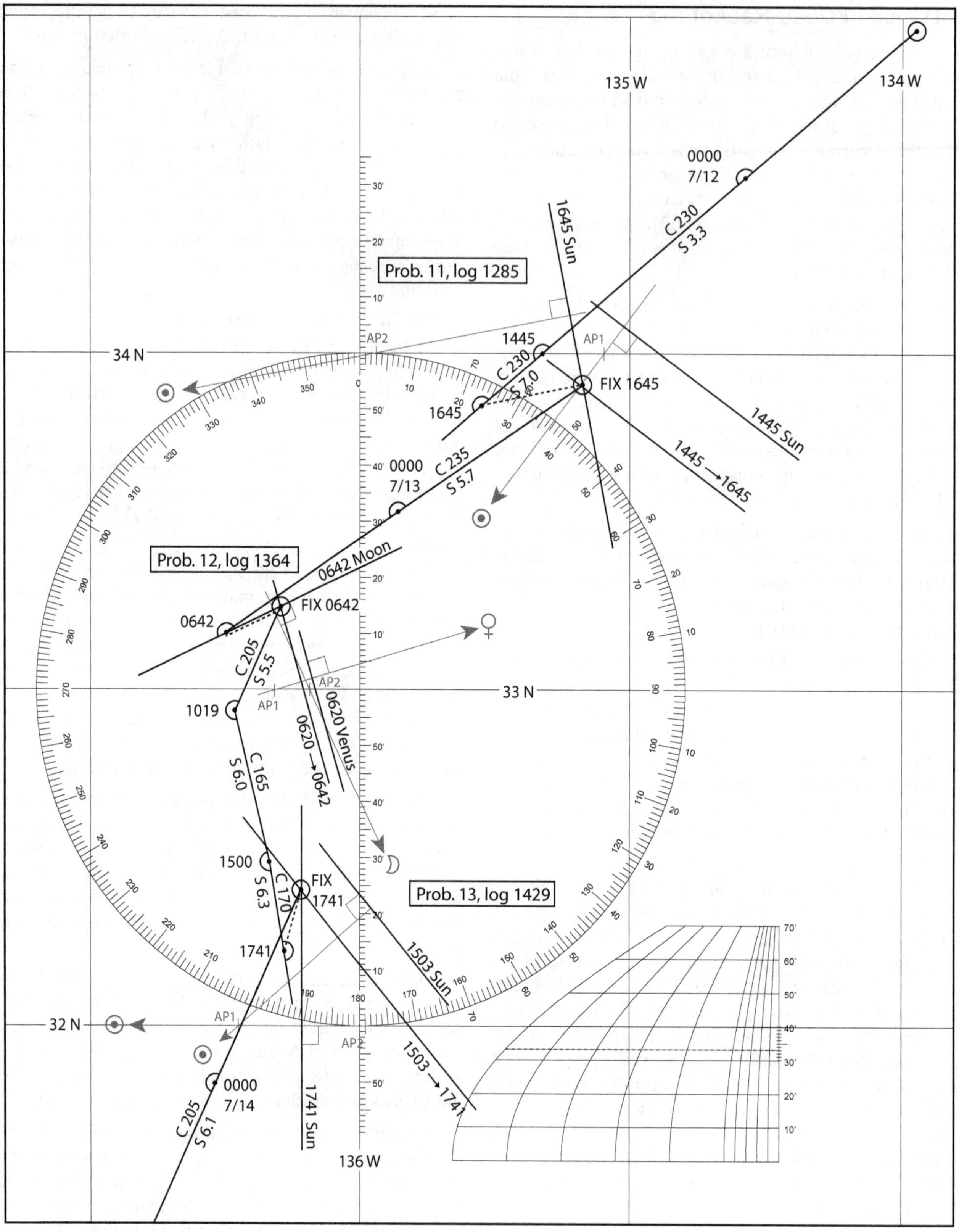

Figure 11.11-1 *Section of a plotting sheet from* Hawaii by Sextant. *The first point on the sheet (top right) is just a Lat-Lon reference mark used to start this sheet based on a position from the last sheet. The Dr track is based on the logbook segment of Figure 11.11-2. After each position fix, the range and bearing DR to Fix (dashed line) is then recorded. Seen here is a running fix from the sun at log 1285; a moon-Venus fix at log 1364; and another running fix from the sun at 1429, which is all the cel nav done over these two days. The percentage errors are larger than we would expect based on our guidelines, so this offset was likely due to real current. The only way to make this type of conclusion, however, is to accumulate this DR-Fix data over many fixes.*

monitored and reported. The worst enemy of good DR are mesoscale current eddies that float around the ocean in unpredictable locations. They can have currents of 1 or 2 kts spanning areas of up to several hundred miles. Atlas predictions of climatic currents and numerical ocean model predictions for recent currents are available, but they do not account well for the specific eddies we might encounter. See www.starpath.com/currents. We can detect ocean current ourselves underway by comparing course and speed made good with our logbook records of course and speed. With GPS we can do so in real time, but using cel nav it takes a day or so to piece this together.

(2) Leeway sets us downwind when sailing to weather in strong wind. Although typically in the 3° to 6° range, it can be as much as 15° or so, but not likely more as we tend to fall off at some point, which dramatically lessens the leeway. Leeway, unlike current, changes only our direction made good, not our speed. Leeway is also an important factor in very light air. In short, whenever our vessel is not operating in the conditions it was designed for, we will slip downwind.

(3) Helm bias is an insidious factor known to be a challenge to good DR since the 18th century. It means simply you are not making good the course you think you are steering and subsequently record in the logbook. In big waves we tend to fall off briefly at each wave to keep from pounding and sailing downwind we might come up more often on the wind to keep our speed in light air, or again fall off in stronger wind to surf down waves. Or we might simply steer a course that is easier to keep the sails full or we might steer a course that makes the boat go faster because it is more fun. In short, for one reason or another, we are not making good the course we think we are steering and consequently record in the logbook. Without GPS, the only way to learn something of this is for the navigator to sit quietly for some time and watch the helm.

Logbook Segment from *Hawaii by Sextant*

#	*July*	*Prob*	*WT*	*Log*	*C*	*S*	*Computed*		*Plotted*	*Range*	*Bearing*
41	11	P10 FIX	1110	1181	230	3.3	35.024 , 133.554		34.58 , 133.55	3	166
42	12		0000	1222	230	3.3					
43	12		1445	1271	230	7.0					
44	12	P11 DR	1645	1285					33.51 , 135.32		
45	12	P11 FIX	1645	1285	235	5.7	33.554 , 135.101		33.54 , 135.11	19	078
46	13		0000	1326	235	5.7					
47	13	P12 DR	0642	1364					33.10 , 136.30		
48	13	P12 FIX	0642	1364	205	5.5	33.150 , 136.175		33.15 , 136.18	11	065
49	13		1019	1384	165	6.0					
50	13		1500	1412	170	6.3					
51	13	P13 DR	1741	1429					32.13 , 136.17		
52	13	P13 FIX	1741	1429	205	6.1	32.254 , 136.129		32.24 , 136.13	11	016

DR Error Analysis*

Prob	*WT*	*dT*	*dT(h)*	*Log*	*dLog*		*Error*	*%*		*Drift*	*Set*	
P10	7/11 1110	05:05	05.08	1181	20		3	15 %		0.6	166	E-SE
P11	7/12 1645	29:35	29.58	1285	104		19	18 %		0.6	078	E-NE
P12	7/13 0642	13:57	13.95	1364	79		11	14 %		0.8	065	E-NE
P13	7/13 1741	11:01	11.02	1429	65		11	17 %		1.0	016	N
P14	7/14 1418	20:35	20.58	1554	125		4	3 %		0.2	150	S-SE

Figure 11.11-2 *Segments of the Logbook (Top) and DR Error Analysis (bottom) from the book* Hawaii by Sextant (HBS). *The watch was set to ZD +7. Column 1 top just numbers the entries on this sheet; no nav significance. Problem numbers are from HBS. Positions are given in hybrid units often used in mobile apps, namely: 43.268 = 43° 26.8', and 128.095 = 128° 09.5'. Courses and bearings are True. Range and Bearing is DR to Fix. We add another reminder that logbooks should be kept to the nearest tenth of a mile. We had that data underway, but it was not included in the abbreviated logbook used in HBS.*

*In the Error Analysis, dT is time difference between fixes in hh:mm; dT(h) is same time interval in decimal hours. dLog is log difference, or distance run between fixes. Error is the range from DR to Fix. The % listed is (Error/dLog)*100. The Drift is Error/dT(h), which is the speed of the error current. The Set is bearing from DR to Fix, which is the direction of the error current.*

With GPS tracking this is easy to see as you have your actual course painted out on the computer screen, but without electronics we must simply be aware of this and watch for it. It can also take the form of writing in the logbook the course you were supposed to steer rather than the one that was actually steered most of the watch—that is, not making an honest effort to recall the best average course.

(4) Logbook blunder is just that. You record the time as 1534 when you meant 1543 or a course as 306 when you meant 316. This source of error cannot be ruled out and it can take some detective work to track this down if an obvious error somewhere is apparent. It is something to look for if after good results for an extended time, your DR is suddenly off a lot—though this could also be caused by sailing into a strong current eddy.

All of this analysis assumes that you have a handle on the uncertainty of your celestial fix. We must come to conclusions more slowly when the fix is weak, such as a running fix in which one of the sight sessions had only one or two LOPs.

Evaluating DR Accuracy

Once we have this DR offset data we need a way to evaluate it. Is the error we see large or small? Are we doing a good job at DR or not? The expected uncertainty in a DR position depends on how far you have sailed since the last fix *and* it depends on how long this took. We are talking here about DR uncertainty, not DR error. Your DR position could be spot on, even though it does indeed have a larger uncertainty. Likewise, when looking at our measured DR errors we want to know if these are within expected uncertainties.

The conclusion we have come to over the years is that in a typical small craft at sea, we should expect our DR position to become uncertain by about 7% of the distance run or by the distance set in a current of about 0.7 kts in an unknown direction. We are generally safe to just use the larger of the two and not combine them. Short distances over a long time are generally dominated by the "error current" concept, whereas long distances over a short time are dominated by the percentage of distance covered. Typical voyage legs might have these two evaluations about the same.

After running 4h at 30 kts, you would DR for 120 nmi and be best to assume that this position is uncertain by about 8.4 nmi (0.07 × 120). The current factor would be just 0.7 × 4 = 2.8 nmi. But sailing at 3 kts for 40h (still covering 120 nmi) the uncertainty is no longer 8.4 nmi, but closer to 0.7 × 40 = 28 nmi. Again, this is not the error to expect, it is just the uncertainty you should keep in mind when evaluating the next fix, or when making any crucial route decisions before the next fix. We would hope that our next fix would show us that our DR was much closer than these uncertainties, and this would mean that none of the four sources of DR error listed earlier has dominated our navigation.

If you consistently do better than these guidelines, then you are doing fine. If you cannot achieve that on average, then a systematic analysis of the errors themselves might help you discover the source of the error. In other words, if you are on a long more or less constant course over several days, and your DR error direction is almost always straight ahead but 6% ahead of where you thought your were, then chances are your log is reading too low. From then on you can just bump your runs up by 6% and be back on track.

Compass errors will also show up nicely after holding a steady course downwind for some days. Sailing upwind in strong wind, on the other hand, you are almost certainly going to find DR errors to leeward. The log will be about right, but the course made good will be some 10° to 20° downwind of expected. Helm bias, wind-driven current, and leeway are all small on their own, but they add up in the same downwind direction.

To make a quick estimate of the effect of sailing the wrong course, recall the Small Angle Rule that 6° = 10%. It scales down forever and up to 18° = 30%. This means a right triangle of 6° has sides in ratio of 1 to 10. A 3° triangle has sides 1 to 20. For 12° triangle the sides are about 1 to 5, and so on. It is a very useful shortcut for navigators to remember; it has numerous applications.

Put into our context, if you sail 100 miles and your compass is wrong by 6° you will be off your intended track by 10 nmi, which is 10% of the distance run. The goal of 7% DR means you must make good a course within about 4° of what is recorded in the logbook, assuming everything else has no error at all.

The saving grace, meaning why this is not quite as hard as it seems, is we are assuming we have taken systematic errors into account on some level, meaning we correct for current and leeway as best we can when needed. In this case, our remaining errors are random, and could be just as well to the left as to the right, and so on.

11.12 Practice with Time Prediction

The base times of sunrise, sunset, twilights, and LAN are given in the *Nautical Almanac*; the procedures for figuring the Watch Time (WT) and UTC of these events based on your DR position is described in Section 3.2 for LAN and further in Section 5.2. The process is exactly the same, we just start with different times from the *Almanac*. Please review that section for the instructions. Then here are several practice problems to be sure this procedure is mastered. Figure 11.12-1 shows how the twilight times appear in the *Almanac*.

(1) ZD = +8, DR position 40° 00' N 126° 32' W,

27 March 1981.

1a. Determine WT of LAN

1b. Determine WT of Morning Civil Twilight

1c. Determine WT of Sunrise

(2) ZD = +4 , DR Position 20° 00' S, 030° 15' W,

26 October 1978.

2a. Determine WT of Sunset

2b. Determine WT of LAN

(3) ZD = +9, DR Position 52° 00'N, 133° 20' W,

25 July 1978. Determine:

3a. WT of Morning Nautical Twilight

3b. WT of Morning Civil Twilight

3c. WT of Sunrise

(4) ZD +5, DR Position 30° 00'N, 075° 20'W,

26 March 1981

4a. At what WT will we begin our morning star sights?

4b. At what WT will we end our evening star sights?

Trick for Choosing Time to Start Sights

The normal method is to look up *Almanac* times and then correct for longitude. An alternative to computing absolute times is to just look up the time relative to sunset. If sunset is listed as 1832 and civil twilight is listed as 1855, then you know without any further computations or corrections that you can start taking sights 1855-1832 = 23 minutes after the sun sets. If you are on deck, note the time of sunset and you have that many minutes to get ready.

Unfortunately, this does not help you when it comes to predicting the sights, and that is always the best way to do it. For that you need to know the UTC, which will indeed require the usual solution.

11.13 Practice Choosing the AP

Instructions for choosing the assumed longitude (a-Lon) are in Step 4 of the work form instructions in Section 5.3. The goal in East or West longitudes is to choose an assumed longitude that is within 30' of the DR longitude, but still has the minutes part selected properly so that they go away in the next step of the process when we figure the LHA. Namely, in western longitudes, the a-Lon minutes must equal the GHA minutes, and in eastern longitudes, the a-Lon minutes must equal 60' - GHA minutes.

As for the degrees part of a-Lon, in 75% of the cases you will run across, the correct degrees part of a-Lon will equal the degrees part of your DR-Lon, but about 25% of the time you will need to raise or lower the degrees part of a-Lon by 1° to get the result within 30' of the DR-Lon.

Here is a 75% type case: GHA = 302° 45.8', DR-Lon = 124° 22.5'W. Choose a-Lon = 124° 45.8'W and from this you note that the difference between DR-Lon and a-Lon is 124° 45.8' - 124° 22.5' = 23.3', which is less than 30'. This, then, is not only OK, it is the best we can do. There are never two choices that meet the minutes requirement and the less than 30' from DR-Lon requirement. Note too that when you make this comparison, you do not need to worry

1981 MARCH 26, 27, 28 (THURS., FRI., SAT.)

UT	SUN G.H.A.	SUN Dec.	MOON G.H.A.	MOON v	MOON Dec.	MOON d	MOON H.P.	Lat.	Twilight Naut.	Twilight Civil	Sunrise	2
d h	° ′	° ′	° ′	′	° ′	′	′	°	h m	h m	h m	h
								N 72	02 30	04 12	05 23	02
26 00	178 32.4	N 2 05.0	300 24.7	13.2	S16 25.0	6.4	54.2	N 70	02 58	04 24	05 27	01
01	193 32.6	06.0	314 56.9	13.3	16 31.4	6.4	54.2	68	03 19	04 34	05 31	01
02	208 32.8	07.0	329 29.2	13.2	16 37.8	6.3	54.2	66	03 35	04 42	05 34	00
03	223 33.0	· · 08.0	344 01.4	13.1	16 44.1	6.2	54.3	64	03 48	04 48	05 37	00
04	238 33.1	08.9	358 33.5	13.1	16 50.3	6.2	54.3	62	03 58	04 54	05 39	00
05	253 33.3	09.9	13 05.6	13.1	16 56.5	6.1	54.3	60	04 07	04 59	05 41	00
06	268 33.5	N 2 10.9	27 37.7	13.0	S17 02.6	6.0	54.3	N 58	04 15	05 03	05 43	24
07	283 33.7	11.9	42 09.7	13.0	17 08.6	5.9	54.3	56	04 22	05 07	05 44	24
T 08	298 33.9	12.9	56 41.7	13.0	17 14.5	5.9	54.3	54	04 27	05 10	05 46	24
H 09	313 34.1	· · 13.8	71 13.7	12.8	17 20.4	5.7	54.3	52	04 32	05 13	05 47	24
U 10	328 34.3	14.8	85 45.5	12.9	17 26.1	5.7	54.3	50	04 37	05 16	05 48	24
R 11	343 34.5	15.8	100 17.4	12.8	17 31.8	5.7	54.3	45	04 46	05 21	05 50	24
S 12	358 34.7	N 2 16.8	114 49.2	12.8	S17 37.5	5.5	54.4	N 40	04 53	05 25	05 52	23
D 13	13 34.9	17.8	129 21.0	12.7	17 43.0	5.5	54.4	35	04 59	05 29	05 54	23
A 14	28 35.0	18.7	143 52.7	12.7	17 48.5	5.4	54.4	30	05 04	05 32	05 56	23

Figure 11.12-1 *Section of the* Nautical Almanac *daily pages showing twilight and sunrise times. A similar section shows the sunset sequence. Refer back to Figure 5.2-1 for the perspective on the horizon.*

about negatives. If you happen to write them in the other order, 124° 22.5' - 124° 45.8' , don't worry about the -23.3. We do not care what side it is on, just how far apart they are.

Now here is a 25% case: GHA = 302° 45.8', DR-Lon = 124° 02.5'W. The same GHA, but from a different DR-Lon. In this case, we start out the same, a-Lon = 124° 45.8'W, so we get our minutes right, but now when we make the test we get: a-Lon - DR-Lon = 124° 45.8'W - 124° 02.5'W = 43.5'. This is more than 30', which tells us there is another choice that is better, and it means changing the degrees of a-Lon by 1. You might see from just looking that the best choice is 123° 45.8'W, but you can check it: a-Lon - DR-Lon = 123° 45.8'W - 124° 02.5'W = 123° 45.8'W - 123° 62.5'W = -16.7', which is less than 30', so this is the right one.

If a sequence of steps might appeal in getting started with this, here is one proposed set of guidelines. After you do a few by any means it becomes almost automatic to choose the a-Lon and then correct the degrees as needed.

We are given DR-lon° and DR-Lon' as well as GHA° and GHA', such that if DR-Lon = 122° 45.6', then DR-Lon° = 122, and DR-Lon' = 45.6.

Western Longitudes

Step 1. Choose a-Lon° = DR-Lon° and choose a-Lon' = GHA'

Step 2. Now look at the difference between DR-Lon and a-Lon. Call this Delta

Step 3. If Delta is less than or equal to 30' you are done. The AP = a-Lon° a-Lon' = DR-Lon° GHA'

Step 4. If Delta is greater than 30', then we need to change a-Lon° by 1°, either up or down according to Step 5.

Step 5. When Delta is greater than 30', if GHA' is greater than 30, then decrease a-Lon° by 1°, but if GHA' is less than 30, increase a-Lon° by 1°.

Eastern Longitudes

Step 1. Choose a-Lon° = DR-Lon° and choose a-Lon' = 60' - GHA'

Step 2. Now look at the difference between DR-Lon and a-Lon. Call this Delta

Step 3. If Delta is less than or equal to 30' you are done. The AP = a-Lon° a-Lon' = DR-Lon° GHA'

Step 4. If Delta is greater than 30', then we need to change a-Lon° by 1°, either up or down according to Step 5.

Step 5. When Delta is greater than 30', if GHA' is greater than 30, then increase a-Lon° by 1°, but if GHA' is less than 30, decrease a-Lon° by 1°.

Again, after a few practice ones, you will not need these sort of formal guidelines.

Practice Choosing the Assumed Position

In each of the following cases, find a-Lat and a-Lon.

(1)	DR GHA Sun	= 13° 48' N, 122° 16' W = 145° 40.5'
(2)	DR GHA Sun	= 13° 12' N, 152° 16' W = 245° 20.8'
(3)	DR GHA Sun	= 19° 18' S, 75° 05' W = 321° 55.3'
(4)	DR GHA Sun	= 48° 23' N, 132° 56' W = 43° 12.4'
(5)	DR GHA Sun	= 5° 28' S, 150° 43' W = 300° 04.9'
(6)	DR GHA Sun	= 22° 20' N, 153° 35' W = 12° 13.6'
(7)	DR GHA Sun	= 46° 45' N, 56° 20' W = 345° 56.1'
(8)	DR GHA Sun	= 33° 51' S, 122° 16' W = 145° 12.5'
(9)	DR GHA Sun	= 13° 48' N, 122° 16' E = 145° 40.5'
(10)	DR GHA Sun	= 13° 12' N, 152° 16' E = 245° 20.8'
(11)	DR GHA Sun	= 19° 18' S, 75° 55' E = 321° 55.3'
(12)	DR GHA Sun	= 48° 23' N, 132° 56' E = 43° 12.4'
(13)	DR GHA Sun	= 5° 28' S, 150° 03' E = 300° 04.9'
(14)	DR GHA Sun	= 22° 20' N, 153° 35' E = 12° 13.6'
(15)	DR GHA Sun	= 46° 45' N, 56° 20' E = 345° 56.1'
(16)	DR GHA Sun	= 33° 51' S, 122° 06' E = 145° 12.5'

11.14 Practice with Pub. 249 Vol. 2, 3

Follow the instructions in Step (5) of Section 5.3 to confirm and complete these further examples of using Pub. 249, Vol 2 or 3. Solutions to last 3 are in the Answers. The Z to Zn rules (bottom of the page) are the same for all sights.

4			5						6	
LHA	10°		tab Hc	25°	21′	d + -	-59	Z 170	Zn =	190
Dec deg	19°	N S **S**	d. corr.	Pub. 249	-23.3′	Dec min	23.3′		a - Lat =	
a-Lat	45°	N S **N**	Hc	24°	57.7′				a - Lon =	

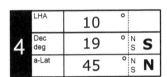

(1) Notes: Use table T-20; Contrary name; 25° 21′ - 23.3′ = 24° 81′ - 23.3′ = 24° 57.7′; N Lat for Z to Zn; exact values are 24° 58.1′, 190.4.

4			5						6	
LHA	330°		tab Hc	50°	46′	d + -	+49	Z 130	Zn =	130
Dec deg	15°	N S **N**	d. corr.	Pub. 249	+37.2′	Dec min	45.2′		a - Lat =	
a-Lat	45°	N S **N**	Hc	51°	23.2′				a - Lon =	

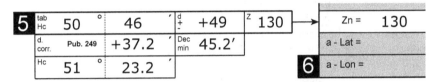

(2) Notes: Use table T-18; Same name; 50° 46′ + 37.2′ = 50° 83.2′ = 51° 23.2′; N Lat for Z to Zn; exact values are 51° 23.1′, 129.6.

4			5						6	
LHA	74°		tab Hc	13°	24′	d + -	+43	Z 099	Zn =	279
Dec deg	3°	N S **S**	d. corr.	Pub. 249	+11.0′	Dec min	15.6′		a - Lat =	
a-Lat	45°	N S **S**	Hc	13°	35.0′				a - Lon =	

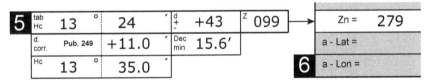

(3) Notes: Use table T-20; Same name; S Lat for Z to Zn; exact values are 13° 34.8′, 279.1.

4			5						6	
LHA	3°		tab Hc	°	′	d + -		Z	Zn =	
Dec deg	22°	N S **N**	d. corr.	Pub. 249	′	Dec min	5.6′		a - Lat =	
a-Lat	45°	N S **N**	Hc	°	′				a - Lon =	

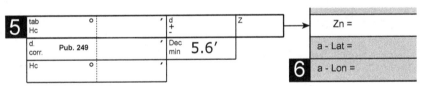

(4) Find Hc and Zn. See Answers.

4			5						6	
LHA	29°		tab Hc	°	′	d + -		Z	Zn =	
Dec deg	6°	N S **N**	d. corr.	Pub. 249	′	Dec min	29.6′		a - Lat =	
a-Lat	45°	N S **S**	Hc	°	′				a - Lon =	

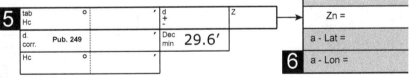

(5) Find Hc and Zn. See Answers.

4			5						6	
LHA	313°		tab Hc	°	′	d + -		Z	Zn =	
Dec deg	8°	N S **N**	d. corr.	Pub. 249	′	Dec min	48.9′		a - Lat =	
a-Lat	45°	N S **N**	Hc	°	′				a - Lon =	

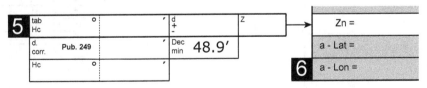

(6) Find Hc and Zn. See Answers.

North Latitudes		South Latitudes	
LHA greater than 180°	Zn = Z	LHA greater than 180°	Zn = 180° - Z
LHA less than 180°	Zn = 360° - Z	LHA less than 180°	Zn = 180° + Z

11.15 AM to PM Running Fixes

The standard way to navigate by the sun is to do a running fix between two sun lines. The two lines can be two morning lines, two afternoon lines, a morning line and an LAN line, an LAN line and an afternoon line, or you can straddle LAN with a morning line and an afternoon line—which is the subject at hand.

This last method has several advantages. First, it gives us a near midday fix—which is a convenient way to keep records—and yet does not require an LAN sight, which can be inconvenient since it requires taking sights at a specific time. Second, this type of running fix is typically the fastest, meaning you must wait the minimum time between sun lines. This, in turn, reduces the DR uncertainty between sights which improves the accuracy of the fix. And finally, it is especially easy to figure how long this minimum time between sun sights must be in order to get an adequate LOP intersection angle (often called the cut angle). Recall that we want this cut angle to be at least 30° or so, to ensure that the accuracy of the fix is not overly sensitive to the precision of the sight, sight reduction, and plotting.

To figure the sight times for this AM-to-PM running fix, we need to know what the approximate height of the sun at LAN will be. To figure this approximate observed height (Ho) we need to figure our approximate DR-Lat (which we here just call Lat) and then look up the sun's declination (dec). Then note if Lat and Dec are of Same or Contrary names. The noon height of the sun can then be figured from:

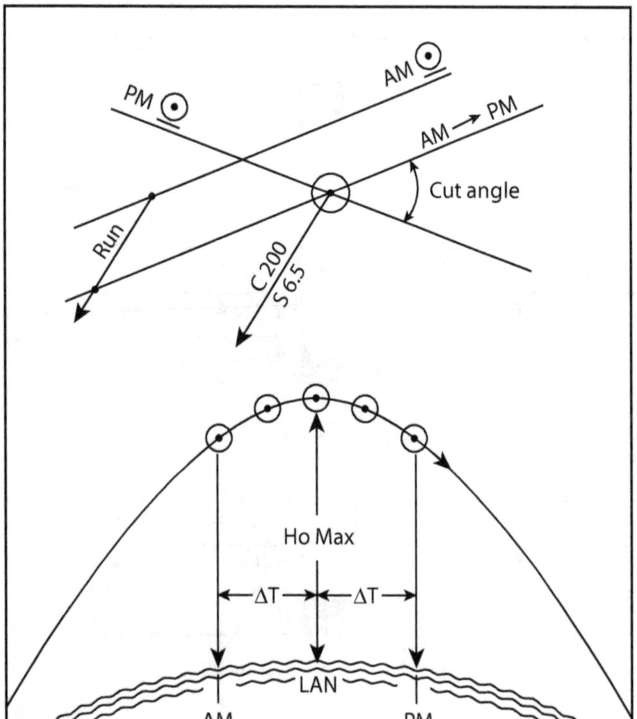

Figure 11.15-1 *Schematic of sun positions as it crosses your meridian and the corresponding LOPs plotted above. Their intersection is called the cut angle.*

For Contrary Names: Ho = 90° - (sum of Lat and dec)

For Same Names: Ho = 90° - (difference between Lat and dec).

If you are so close to the equator that you "don't know your name" (don't know if you're north or south of it), then your latitude must be near 0° and the two formulas for Ho are the same—that is, it doesn't matter.

Here are a few examples so you can check that you are figuring the expected Ho properly. For each Lat and Dec given, use the formulas above to figure and check the given Ho.

Lat	dec	Ho
40° S	S 10° —>	60°
5° S	S 20° —>	75°
0° ?	S 10° —>	80°

Lat	dec	Ho
50° N	S 10° —>	30°
30° N	N 5° —>	65°
35° N	N 14° —>	69°

Once you figure the expected Ho, Table 11.15-1 tells what cut angles to expect from taking sights at different times. Here it is assumed that the sights are taken at roughly equal times before and after LAN. But approximate values alone are good enough. For example, from my DR-Lon I figure the WT of LAN is 13:20. Then from the sun's Dec and my DR-Lat, I figure that Ho will be about 65°. Looking

Approximate Angular "Cuts" Between LOP's Before and After Local Apparent Noon

Ho at LAN	Minutes befoie and after LAN ΔT→											
	4	8	12	16	20	24	28	32	36	40	44	48
30°											19°	21°
40								18°	20°	22°	25	27
50						17°	20°	23	26	29	31	34
60					20°	23	27	31	35	38	42	45
65				19°	23	28	32	37	41	45	49	53
70			17°	23	29	34	39	45	50	55	59	64
75		15°	23	30	37	44	51	57	63	69	74	79
80	11°	22	33	43	53	62	70	78	85	89	83	78
81	13	25	36	48	58	67	76	83	90	83	77	72
82	14	28	41	53	63	73	82	90	83	77	71	66
83	16	31	44	59	70	81	90	82	75	69	64	59
84	18	36	52	66	79	89	82	74	67	61	56	51
85	22	42	60	76	89	80	71	64	58	52	48	43
86	27	51	72	88	79	68	60	53	47	42	38	35
87	35	65	88	75	63	54	46	41	36	32	29	
88	52	87	69	54	44	37	31	27				
89	87	55	36	28								

Example: Altitude of sun about 75° at LAN; sights 12 minutes before and after LAN will result in LOP'S with "cut" of 23°.

Table 11.15-1 *Cut angles for sun line LOPs from an old book on navigation (original source has been lost).*

at the table, if I take the first sight 32 minutes before LAN (at roughly 13:20 - 00:32 = 12:48) and the second sight at 32 minutes after LAN (13:20 + 00:32 = 13:52), then the two sun lines will intersect at an angle of about 37° when I advance the first to the second.

If time permits, work a few of the exercises that follow and then store this table somewhere. After some actual practice at sun lines and running fixes at sea, I think you will find that this is a pretty handy table.

Practice with Cut Angles (See Answers)

(1) Sun's Dec is S 21°, my Lat is 20° N, and I take sun lines 44 minutes before and after LAN. What will be the cut angle in the running fix?

(2) Sun's Dec is N 18°, my Lat is 30° N, and I take sun lines 28 minutes before and after LAN. What will be the cut angle in the running fix?

(3) Sun's Dec is S 15°, my Lat is 35° N. What is the shortest time I can wait either side of LAN for a running fix with cut angle of 30° or larger?

(4) Sun's Dec is N 15°, my Lat is 48° N. What is the shortest time I can wait either side of LAN for a running fix with cut angle of 30° or larger?

(5) Sun's Dec is S 12°, my Lat is 20° S. What is the shortest time I can wait either side of LAN for a running fix with cut angle of 30° or larger?

11.16 An Ocean-Going Nav Station

Every practicing navigator has an ideal nav station in mind—the place of work, its location, its layout, its tools. The ideal usually comes about the hard way, by ruling out, piece by piece, systems, locations, and things that don't work well. Somehow things that don't work make a bigger impression than things that do. As it is with learning any aspect of sailing, the best way to find your own ideal is to sail and navigate on different boats. At least with navigation, it won't take too long to find out what works well for you.

Here I will share some of my ideals and try to point out ones that I think most navigators would agree on as opposed to ones that are just my preference. For example, I prefer to sit facing forward, because it is easier for me to think through course changes, tacking angles, wind shifts, and so on when I am facing the way I am going. But this is just a preference. Chart table work in rough seas is not much different in any direction, if the seat is well designed, and I suspect that if I did it always one way, regardless of what way it was, I would also learn to think more easily in that orientation.

First the seat. A comfortable seat is important because you sit a lot when navigating. Or, rather, you should sit if you can. It's hard to think standing up, as the old saying goes. Especially if your back aches, and even the strongest backs ache leaning over a chart table for an hour or so. Luckily it's a rare stand-up chart table that won't accommodate some form of seat. With some ingenuity you can design one that can be removed when not in use to free up the space they were intended to provide in the first place.

One kind of chart table seat I found very comfortable was cut on an arc so that (when facing forward) you are always sitting straight up-and-down regardless of the boat's heel. The seat is easy to make from 3/4-inch plywood front and back plates cut with an arc, and then the seat itself made from 1 × 2 slats screwed into the plywood.

The other end of the problem is the feet. For rough going you need some way to get wedged into the chart seat. One nice solution is a small foot stool built into the sole under the table, or a ledge on the bulkhead in front of the table. These can be custom-made to your leg length so that when in use your legs are pinned against the bottom of the chart table, holding you in place with hands free. It's best to arrange the design so that you can sit comfortably without using this brace since you only need it in rough conditions.

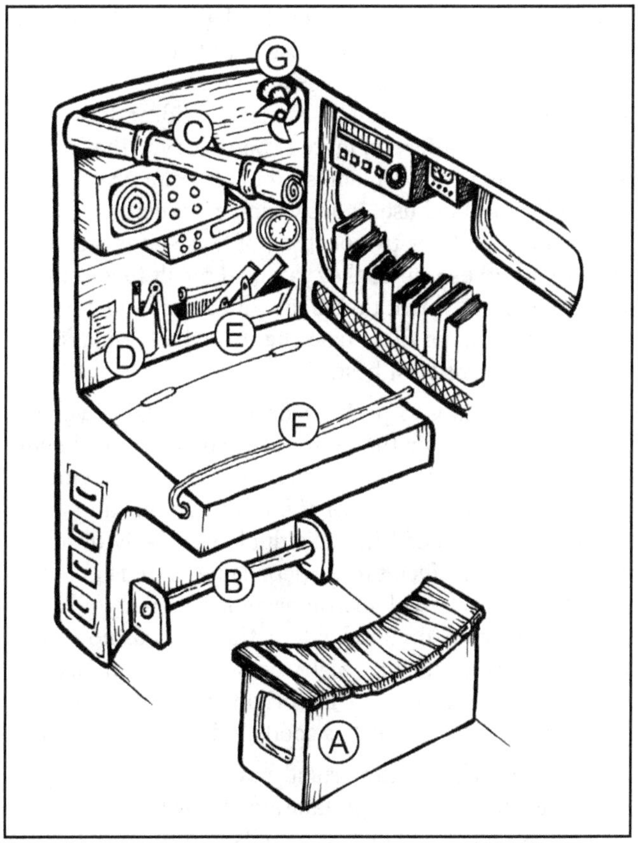

Figure 11.16-1 *An ocean-going nav station. A. Curved seat helps you stay vertical when heeled. B. Footrest so knees can be wedged up under the table to hold you in place in the waves. C. Spray Curtain to keep light in at night, and water out always. Some boats use two; one clear for daylight, one opaque for night. D. Pencil holder, also holds dividers and flashlight. E. Holder for parallel rulers and plotters. F. Bungee to hold chart table lid down. It also holds charts and books in place when underway. G. Fan for navigator's comfort!*

The location of the nav station doesn't really matter much. They usually get placed next to the companionway, which is good since you can yell back and forth to the cockpit from there. But this is also a very wet place. So it pays to have a spray curtain built that hangs between you and the companionway. This serves two purposes. First, it keeps your gear dry—or more precisely, limits the water on your charts to that which runs off of your own rain gear. Second, it blocks out the light so that your work at night does not interfere with the helmsman.

This last point is an important one. You almost always have to work at night, but it is equally important that no light at all get out to the cockpit. As you know, even the faintest light makes steering at night very difficult. Going fast in big waves on a dark night, the helmsman has very little for orientation and it can be dangerous to interfere with that. Often even stock steering compass lights are too bright in these cases. In short, it pays to think this through so you don't end up duct taping yourself into a cocoon.

As for the nav table lights themselves, I have never seen a specialized nav table light that found its way onto the ideal list. I refer here to the special ones of various designs intended to emit focused light or dim light or red light and so on. The famous, standard goose neck light, for example, is near useless since, goose neck or not, you can't see the whole chart with them. Lift the chart table lid, and you can't see anything. A different, more expensive type that comes close to solving the problem is mounted on a pivot and is detachable for hand use. It has variable intensity and a red light option. Perhaps two or three of these—one stored in a bag for hand use, since they can be difficult to get in and out of the pivot—might do the job, but it is not just a matter of buying one of these fancy lights and screwing it into wherever it seems to fit best.

For longer jobs, I prefer a fixed white light over the table and then cover the entire area someway. For short jobs, a hand held crew light does the job well provided it has a permanent home near the table so you can always find it when you need it. Individuals will likely differ on this, but I find it difficult to see pencil lines in red light. Also the coloring on charts looks different in red light and takes some getting used to. Red light, by the way, has no special significance to protecting night vision. The main factor is intensity, and red lights are not bright, hence their value. A low level white light is just as good, and to me preferable.

Seat and light are important, but not the most important. The single most important aid to navigation without doubt is a pencil holder (for pencils and dividers) and a holder for your parallel rulers that is within arm's reach in front of you, *outside of the chart table*. With these holders, you can always find your tools when you need them and you always have a place to put them between uses. Otherwise, they will get lost or broken. Without these holders, sometime in life you will want to draw a line, can't find a pencil, won't draw the line, and later regret it.

For many years I preferred thin-lead mechanical pencils, with the lead advance button down near the point, but this is obviously just a personal preference. In later years, I tend to prefer standard pencils with standard sharpener—on larger vessels you might consider an electric pencil sharpener. Any pencil and a way to keep it sharp will do. A No. 2 lead is traditionally considered optimum, with a No. 1 lead claimed to be so soft that it smears, and No. 3 too hard to see or erase. If your situation leads to damp charts, then No.1 is called for. Or at least have one at hand. Harder leads do not work well on damp charts.

The space inside the chart table, under the lid, is essentially useless space to navigation. This may seem surprising, but check under the lids of a few chart tables when you visit other boats to get the point—and you may get just that, the point of the dividers. The chart table is simply too convenient a place to store what ever has to be put down in a hurry. My standard advice is this: make an absolute rule that nothing gets put in the chart table. Then when it fills to overflowing, just forget about it.

My favorite pencil holder is a short tube attached to a shelf or bulkhead. The tube from an empty toilet paper roll is ideal—duct taped over the bottom, with tissue stuffed inside to protect the bottom from divider points, then taped to the wall. This elegant design has made it across oceans more than once. It holds pencils, pencil-type erasers, and dividers. As soon as engine keys, sunglasses, and various other things start appearing in it, remind people what the chart table is for. A tall square plastic fruit juice bottle is convenient for this type of pencil holder, and this is the type I have used for years, always having a few on hand and taking one onto each new boat. In a magazine story once about the Volvo Round the World race, they showed the nav station of one boat that had more than $75,000 worth of electronic nav gear, and right in the middle of this stuff was taped to the bulkhead this exact type of (Odwalla) juice bottle used for a pencil holder. Needless to say, this vessel won my heart immediately.

If you carry a backup steering compass, the chart table top is a good place to store it; so it can be used for navigation reference at the table. When mounting it keep in mind what might be stored under it in drawers. Check it occasionally with the steering compass, and if they disagree start pulling drawers open to see if the compass needle moves. If it does, you found the villain.

Some handheld bearing compasses can be mounted on or near the chart table and used for reference, but a dedicated, adjustable compass is the best bet. These days digital fluxgate compasses are common and they provide the ideal nav station readout. Often they input into the GPS, or other electronics and you can use that for the course readout. I prefer to mount the handheld bearing compass just inside the companionway so that it can be reached from the cockpit without going below. Again, it will be used more often if it is easy to get to.

Besides the compass, it is very convenient to have electronic readouts below deck at the nav station for all navigation instruments. This makes logbook entries easier for everyone and makes the tactics easier for the navigator. But this is clearly a luxury, especially the wind instruments. Electronic log readouts are usually located at the nav station anyway, since there is little call for their values on deck.

If you want to figure current set and drift from the GPS values of speed and course over ground, it is best, almost necessary, to have a compass and knotmeter readout below deck. Without this application, however, it is not so important to have a knotmeter readout at the nav station.

Unless it is intended for decoration, the barometer should be mounted in the nav station in clear view of someone standing next to the chart table—this is where most crew stand when filling in the logbook. To be of any value at all you must be able to see straight into the barometer and be able to tap it—assuming it is an aneroid device; this is not needed for modern electronic barometers. Generally, one is looking for small changes in pressure and you simply can't gauge these from an angle, leaning over some obstruction. It should also have a crew light mounted next to it for nighttime reading. Again, if it is not convenient to get readings from it, logbook entries of pressure will be of little value. A well-positioned barometer can be valuable even for inland day sailing or racing.

A sextant case rack is vital for offshore work and can be very valuable for inland and coastal sailing as well. Distance off by vertical sextant angle is an important practical technique in navigation that doesn't get used much, in part because most boats don't have a sextant handy. The technique is easy to learn and apply. Even if a sextant is on board, it is often buried. The solution is a convenient rack for the box, or better still some arrangement that mounts the box itself to the bulkhead. I have often found that the bulkhead between nav station and quarter berth is a good place to mount such a rack. The sextant is then in the quarter berth but high enough to not take up useful space and easy to reach standing next to the nav station.

With the box mounted, you take the sextant out and don't have to worry about storing the box. A sextant sight to measure the angular height of a hill is then just as convenient as taking a bearing to it. A bearing and a sextant height give you a fix. If this hill is the only thing in sight, you have just done a nice piece of navigation.

For extended sailing, it pays to have headphone adaptors on all radios. This way the navigator can listen to weather reports without disturbing the off watch. It's also very helpful to have a built-in tape recorder, or a rack for your personal tape recorder near the radios. You can then tape weather broadcasts. If reception is poor you need the tape to replay several times to get the message. Other times you may be busy or needed on deck. You can have the tape set up, the radio tuned, and then just turn things on when your wrist alarm goes off and go back to what ever duty calls. Or you can ask someone to turn on the tape and radio at a particular time and let you sleep.

One thing I have seen on several big boats that I always wanted to try but haven't yet, although I know it will be good, is a small, battery-operated nav station fan. Its purpose is simply to help cool off the navigator in hot weather. And before you start hollering wimp, wimp, wimp, let me give a scenario. It's 90° on deck in the tropics with plenty of wind and over 100° below decks with no wind. The head has been semi-clogged for more than a week, eight sailors have been living in a 9 × 25 × 6-foot space for 2 weeks with no laundry service, a forgotten can of frozen orange juice somehow got misplaced in a quarter berth locker and exploded 1 week ago, the boat is pitching and rolling in the trades, the other seven crew are on deck having a great time in the fresh air—but the navigator is below decks with head spinning in the wooze, working out sun sights that must be done in an hour for the afternoon position report. Now wouldn't you grant this poor soul a small fan?

11.17 Offshore Navigation Checklist

This list was prepared for participants in a Vic-Maui ocean yacht race, but it will serve for any offshore trip. Special pubs and charts refer to both departure and arrival.

Celestial

—Metal sextant (with light or dim penlight on lanyard)

—Davis Mark 3 plastic backup sextant

—Digital quartz watch (shows seconds, 24h, stopwatch, countdown timer, alarm, and waterproof, indiglo type lighting)

—Back-up watch (plus check rate of a crewmember's watch)

—Calculator or mobile app for sight reduction.

—Back-up calculator (same type, from crewmember)

—Waterproof container for calculators

—Spare batteries for calculator

—Sight reduction tables (229, 249, or rely on NAO tables in the Almanac, but if so take Starpath work form)

—Pub. 249 Vol. 1 Selected Stars for star-sight prep

— *Nautical Almanac*

—Universal plotting sheets (1 pad of 50)

—2102-D Star finder

—Small notebook for sight notes on deck

—List of potential star planet sights, dawn and dusk, start, mid, and end race locations.

—List of sun moon fix opportunities underway

Basic Tools and Supplies

—Parallel rulers (or parallel plotter, or triangles)

—Dividers + extra divider points

—Pencils (0.5 mm mechanical #1 or #2 lead)
— Big eraser + Pencil-type eraser
—Pencils with colored lead
—Highlight markers (three colors)
—Sharpie pens to label things, several colors
—Vis-a-vis overhead projector marker for radar screen
—Pen-type flashlight (Maglite or Pelican)
—8 AA batteries for pen light
—Ruler (at least 12", 15" or 18" is better)
—Large protractor
—Large rubber bands (to organize things in nav table)
—Notebook for all nav notes (different from logbook)
—Graph paper if notebook not cross-hatched
—Extra fuses for all nav instruments (read manuals carefully)
—Waterproof bags for nav supplies, books, and charts
—Roll of Blue Painter's Tape for notes and labels
—Bearing compass
—Digital voltmeter (if not part of instruments or electrical system)

Nav Station

—Pencil holder outside of chart table (very important)
—Plotter holder outside of chart table
—Foot brace to pin yourself in going to weather
—Curtain to keep light in and water out of nav area
—Rig for pen light backup to nav table light
—12V or D-cell operated small fan
—Bungee cord to wrap around table to hold down charts
—Alarm clock (or phone) that will wake you up
—Head phones for radios

Charts and Publications

—Paper charts (departure and approach)
—Coast Pilot
—Sailing Directions (if appropriate)
—Light List
—Local Notices to Mariners (past month)
—Tide Tables
—Current Tables
—Navigation Rules (printed copy)
—Racing Rules (plus set of appeals)
—Chart No. 1 (chart symbols)
—International Code of Signals book, Pub. 102
—Radio Navigation Aids, Pub. 117
—Cruising Guide to Hawaii
—Race Instructions
—Instruction manuals for all instruments
—Chart catalog marked with onboard charts
—List of VHF channel usages
—List of SSB frequencies and usages
—Emergency Navigation Card

Weather Prep

—MSC charts or equivalent.
—Barometer calibration table or graph
—Blank weather charts for plotting weather
—List of voice and fax broadcasts (times, freqs, contents, map times) spare fax paper and stylus, if used.
—Has fax machine been maintained lately? (as needed)
—Fax machine and SSB manuals
—Backup copies of your weather software (as needed)
—Telephone numbers and emails of software and services support.
—Unlock key for your satellite phone! (as needed)

11.18 Checking a Sextant with the Stars

In early 1982, a Chinese sextant appeared at several local outlets in the Seattle area, imported for the first time to the US by a local importer. It was a standard-sized metal sextant, with a modern full-view mirror and lighted arc, priced at $395. The novelty of its origin and low price brought several inquiries to me about the quality of the instrument. I tested it, but before these results were published, advertising and interest in the sextant seemed to evaporate.

In early 1984 it reappeared at a still lower price, even more novel for a sextant with its features. Consequently I dusted off these earlier tests and used them as a classroom example of how to test any sextant for accuracy. As you might have guessed, this sextant was a forerunner of the Astra IIIb (then called a Luna), which is now—after notable improvements—the most popular sextant worldwide. I have since visited the factory in Shanghai and am very familiar with this instrument. We have tested it extensively and used it on several ocean crossings. It remains an excellent bargain in sextants—but that is not the topic at hand; it is just the story of how this section on sextant checks came about.

The index error of a sextant is easy to check. It is the zero offset caused by slight misalignment of the mirrors. Checking it is equivalent to reading a scales with no weight applied, to see if you need to add or subtract a bit from the reading when you weigh something.

Index error is important, but not what we mean when we speak of the accuracy of a sextant. For this, we assume that we know the index correction precisely. The question now is, if I measure the height of a star to be 35° 28.5', after making the necessary index correction, is this result indeed the right height of the star?

The simplest way to check a questionable sextant is to measure a sun or star height several times in quick succession, alternating each sight with measurements (also by you) with another sextant of unquestioned accuracy and well known index error. Then plot the series of sights (sextant height versus watch time) on graph paper to see if they fall on the same line. With a good horizon and well-known position, this relative accuracy can be further checked by sight reduction to see if the resulting lines of position go through your known position. This is the quickest way to get a fairly useful answer, but you do need an unquestioned sextant and well-known position with a good horizon available. This can be done inland using a shoreline and the dip short correction (Section 11.6), or better still using an artificial horizon (Section 11.19).

Furthermore, you need to repeat this at various sextant heights to check the accuracy at several angles along the arc, and this complicates the matter since the mathematical and physical approximations of celestial navigation then begin to enter the problem. On land or sea, however, another method is more reliable. It takes time to do properly, but you don't need to do it often—most navigators never do it at all. A new model of a traditional metal sextant would rarely have any significant arc error of the type we are discussing, but a used sextant (after having been dropped) or a plastic sextant of any kind are better candidates for checking. High quality sextants from the past used to include a statement of the small arc corrections at various points along the arc, but this practice has long since disappeared. Now at best we get a statement (from any manufacturer) that the instrument is "free of errors," and then we check what overall accuracy specs are given.

The procedure is to measure the angular distances between selected star pairs (Figure 11.18-1) and then compare these measured separations to the true distances between them which can be calculated. The procedure is straight forward, but the measurements and sight reductions are not standard. Sight reduction by computation is best for this and we make use of a special refraction correction, given below. A good reference for the method is John Letcher's book *Self-contained Celestial Navigation using HO 208,* which is an outstanding book, despite his choice of Sight Reduction Tables. He shows, for example, how to do sextant accuracy checks without a calculator at all. John Letcher, by the way, is the fellow who invented wind-vane steering, which almost all cruising sailors rely upon daily.

Procedure

(1) Measure the index correction (IC) of the sextant very carefully, preferably by viewing direct and reflected views of a single star instead of the conventional way of using the horizon.

(2) Choose two known stars that are separated by the approximate angle you want to test. To check the center of the arc, for example, look for stars roughly 45° apart. The stars can be as high as you like, but neither should be lower than about 20°. Hold the sextant in line with the pair, meaning diagonal to the horizon, unless the two happen to be in the same direction. Then treat the lower star (kept in direct view) as a single-point horizon and bring the other star (reflected view) down to coincide with it. Record the sextant reading, called the sextant distance (Ds).

Then move the micrometer a degree or two to make the next sight independent of the first, and start over for a second or third measurement. Average the results and note the spread in values. Your test will be no better than this spread in the measurements, since these distances are essentially constant, even though the star heights are changing. Variation in these numbers probably represents operator errors, because even if the sextant is wrong at this angle, it is probably wrong by the same amount. To confirm that, check the gear slack using methods of Section 11.8.

(3) If you have a good horizon, also measure the conventional sextant heights of the two stars above the horizon. These need not be precise, and can be calculated if you don't have a horizon when doing this on land. Just carry out a routine sight reduction for each star for the time and place of the sights and get the calculated altitude H1 = Hc1 and H2 = Hc2.

(4) Apply the index correction to the average sextant distance to get the Apparent Distance (Da).

Da = Ds + IC

Then calculate the diagonal refraction (Rd) from:

Rd = 1.90' × (A - cos D)/sin D,

where

A = 0.5 (sin H1/sin H2) + 0.5 sin H2/sin H1.

Add Rd to Da to get the Observed Distance (Do):

Do = Da + Rd.

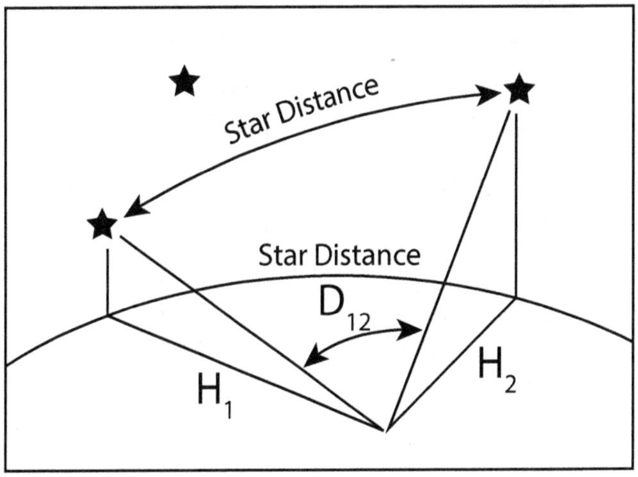

Figure 11.18-1 *Star distances measured to check sextant accuracy.*

(5) Now figure the True Distance (Dt) between the two stars using their sidereal hour angles (SHA) and declinations (dec) found in the *Nautical Almanac.* Do a regular sight reduction (by computation or Pub. 229) with these substitutions:

For Dec	use	Dec1
For LHA	use	(SHA1 - SHA2)
For Lat	use	Dec2.

Enter all values accurate to the tenth of a minute. You will get some calculated altitude (Hc) and azimuth (Zn). Forget the Zn, and figure the True Distance between stars as:

Dt = 89° 60.0' - Hc.

(6) And we are done. Sextant error (at the arc angle equal to the Sextant Distance used) is the difference between the True Distance and the Observed Distance.

Error = Dt - Do.

This method was used to test and compare four sextants. The results are shown in Figure 11.18-2. To practice with these you need the following star data from February 6th, 1984:

	Sextant A	Sextant B	Sextant C	Sextant D
		1932 51° 6.8'		
PST & Sext. Dist.	1934 51° 5.6'	1939 51° 8.4'	1936 51° 2.8'	1936 51°2.8'
	1941 51° 5.6'	1949 51° 7.4'	1943 51° 2.9'	1943 51°2.9'
Capella to Procyon	? 51° 5.6'	1953 51° 6.9'	1951 51° 3.2'	1951 51°3.2'
Avg. and Variation	51° 5.6' ±0.0'	51° 7.4' ±1.0'	51°3.0' ±0.2'	51°3.0' ±0.2'
Index Error	+0.6'	-0.5'	+4.5'	+4.5'
Apparent Distance	51° 6.2'	51° 6.9'	51° 7.5'	51°7.5'
Diagonal Refraction	+1.4'	+1.4'	+1.4'	+1.4'
Observed Distance	51° 7.6'	51° 8.3'	51° 8.9'	51°8.9'
True Distance	51° 7.6'	51° 7.6'	51° 7.6'	51°7.6'
Error	0.0'	0.7'	1.3'	1.3'
		1958 27° 5.0'		
PST & Sext. Dist.	1957 27° 4.8'	2007 27° 5.5'	2000 27° 1.3'	2002 27° 3.2'
Betelgeuse to Sirius	2005 27° 4.8'	2011 27° 5.3'	2081 27° 1.6'	2010 27° 3.5'
Avg. and Variation	27° 4.8' ±0.0'	27° 5.3' ±0.3'	27° 1.5' ±0.2'	27° 3.4' ±0.2'
Index Error	+0.6'	-0.5'	+4.5'	+0.6'
Apparent Distance	27° 5.4'	27° 4.8'	27° 6.0'	27°2.8'
Diagonal Refraction	+1.5'	+1.5'	+1.5'	+1.5'
Observed Distance	27° 6.9'	27° 6.3'	27° 7.5'	27°4.3'
True Distance	27° 6.2'	27° 6.2'	27° 6.2'	27°6.2'
Error	0.7'	0.1'	1.3'	1.9'
PST & Sext. Dist.	2024 65° 48.4'	2023 65° 48.1'	2025 65°48.1'	
Sirius to Capella	2028 65° 46.4'	2031 65° 48.3'	2033 65°48.3'	
Avg. and Variation	65° 47.4' ±1.0'	65° 48.2' ±1.0'	65°44.8' ±0.3'	
Index Error	+0.6'	-0.5'	+4.5'	
Apparent Distance	65° 48.0'	65° 47.7'	65°49.0'	
Diagonal Refraction	+2.2'	+2.2'	+2.2'	
Observed Distance	65° 50.2'	65° 49.9'	65°51.2'	
True Distance	65° 49.7'	65° 49.7'	65°49.7'	
Error	0.5'	0.2'	1.5'	

Note: To calculate the star heights needed for the Rd correction, use these values of GHA Aries for the time of the sights and then use any almanac for the minutes correction. GHA Aries (19h PST 2/6/84 = 03h UTC 2/7) = 181° 56.5' and at 20h PST = 04h UTC use 196° 59.0' The sights were taken from 47° 39' N, 122° 22' W.

Figure 11.18-2 *Data used in checking three sextants by stellar distances. PST is Pacific Standard Time.*

Star	Dec	SHA
Procyon	N 5° 16.0'	45° 22.9'
Capella	N45° 59.1'	281° 7.4'
Betelgeuse	N 7° 24.3'	271° 25.4'
Sirius	S16° 41.7'	258° 53.2'

As an example of figuring the True Distance between Procyon and Capella, do a sight reduction using: Dec= N 5° 16.0', Lat = N 45° 59.1', and LHA = 245° 22.9' - 281° 7.4' (+ 360°) = 324° 15.5'. The answer should be Hc = 38° 52.4' and Zn = 131.7°. Then Dt = 89° 60.0' - 38° 52.4' = 51° 7.6', as shown in Figure 11.18-2.

In the Procyon-Capella measurements, the Procyon height varied from 31° 24' to 31° 47' and the Capella heights varied from 81° 47' to 85° 15' during the full span of the sights of this pair. These height variations cause the A value in the refraction correction to vary from 1.213 to 1.166, which in turn causes Rd to vary from 1.4' to 1.3', and I used 1.4' for this. Generally, you need only figure this once for each star pair since it does not change much with small changes in star heights.

Conclusions

The sextants were chosen at random from new models. Only one of each was tested, so this does not test the consistent quality of many samples of any one model. The Chinese sextant (A) did measure the proper angles—in fact it did a very good job, although the exact reproducibility shown in the first sights must be considered accidental. Keep in mind, however, that regardless of the actual magnitude of the errors found, this error for each model has an inherent uncertainty in it of about 0.5' due to the method itself and the limited number of sights taken. These star tests also do not test the sun shades, which might introduce an error of up to 1' or so into sun sights with the same sextants, especially for plastic sextants with limited quality in the shades.

Furthermore, the error in the index correction itself enters the final answer. For example, sextant (C) was too high by about 1.3' on each star pair (arc location). This might reflect my error in measuring the IC, not an error in the sextant itself. Also, the first set of sights using (B) are not consistent with later ones with the same sextant. They were the first ones done, however, so I suspect this just reflects my getting tuned up to the sight taking. The index error on the plastic sextant (D) changed during the sights. The last star pair was not measured with (D) since measuring the index error carefully takes time and I was getting too cold by then to be careful.

Again, it is not likely that a navigator would often have to resort to this type of testing, but it is a good procedure to know about. It also provides a good backyard exercise for sextant practice—especially if you are looking forward to doing lunars for UTC later on.

11.19 Artificial Horizons

How do I practice celestial when I am landlocked, far from the ocean? This is a question we often get. Our usual first answer is, do you have any lakes near by, and then how big are they? If you have access to a lake or any other body of water, even just a quarter of a mile across, then your best method of practice is to use the dip short techniques we cover in Section 11.6. Those methods are accurate when done right, and do indeed provide realistic practice with sextant sights. We would recommend dip short over the use of artificial horizons if you have the option—and if, indeed, your goal is practice, as opposed to specifically studying artificial horizons.

With no water nearby for practice, or if planning something like desert or arctic travel where you want a backup to the GPS, or if you just want to do celestial the way Lewis and Clark did it, not to mention countless other land-based explorers throughout history, then you are left with some form of artificial horizon for the job.

What is an Artificial Horizon?

An artificial horizon is just the name of some device that will reflect the sun or stars so that sextant sights can be taken without reference to a real sea or distant flat land horizon. In the desert or some conditions in the Arctic, the actual visible land horizon might sometimes do the job, but not often. The reflecting surfaces used historically in artificial horizons include a small tray of Mercury (not so wise a choice for health reasons as we have learned over the years), or a pan of water, oil, molasses, or simply a mirror.

The only commercial one we know of these days is from Davis Instruments, the makers of plastic sextants and other boating gear. It consists of a small plastic tray with a glass tent over it as shown in Figure 11.19-1. The tray is for the reflecting liquid (a dark oil or molasses might work better than water but for the sun alone, it does not matter much what liquid is used.) The tent of glass is to keep the wind off the water. Even the *slightest* breeze puts tiny capillary

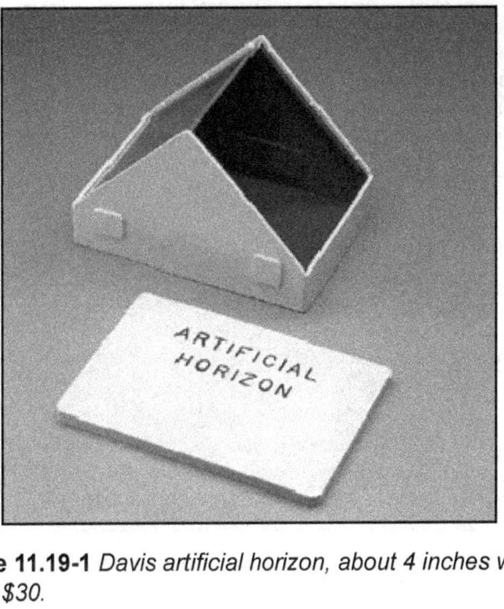

Figure 11.19-1 *Davis artificial horizon, about 4 inches wide, about $30.*

ripples on the surface that make sextant sights impossible. The Davis unit is designed to fold up into a small package when not in use and includes shades for use with the sun.

The glass covers on the Davis units (which is the same basic design used since before 1800) are in the form of a tent (two sides at 45°) for two reasons—I would guess. One is so any reflections from the glass itself are minimized and two, so that the light rays on to and off of the reflecting surface penetrate the glass at a near perpendicular angle. This is because the glass used is not high quality plate glass (which is much more expensive) and consequently the two surfaces of the glass pane may not be strictly parallel. A piece of glass with two sides not parallel is by definition a prism, and prisms bend light rays. If the light rays are bent at all, the measurement will be distorted. (If you have ever seen through glass in an authentically old house, you will see that things viewed through them are wavy and distorted to some extent.) The Davis units should work fine and are convenient for travel, but it is just as easy to build one yourself and you could end up with a better product for the job.

How to Make an Artificial Horizon

The simplest home solution using liquid, is just a pie pan filled with oil for calm nights, or covered with a quality piece of plate glass if there is a breeze. This should work well for the sun and bright planets, but will not be very useful for weaker bodies. It will certainly perform as good as any commercial device and perhaps better because the pie pan is bigger than the plastic tray.

It is best to arrange the device on a (very stable) post or table at about chest high so that you can comfortably look down onto it and be able to move around it to view different directions in the sky. You need to be able to look toward the surface of it from a small angle as well as from larger ones.

A liquid guarantees a flat surface but is some trouble to work with and it does not offer good reflection for stars. For stars we have found the best solution is to use a mirror. You will likely sacrifice some accuracy, but the sights will be much easier and this is about the only practical way to do stars, since the reflections from a liquid surface are weak. Use the same device to elevate the platform and then use a high quality machinist's level and shim the mirror to be level in all directions. For the last stages of shimming, we used business cards to make discrete controlled elevations. The mirror should be about a foot square or round and must be a quality plate glass mirror. We sacrifice some accuracy with the mirror because we cannot get it as level as a liquid surface.

For liquids, the containers and working areas should be all kept clean as any dust or dirt on the surface will interfere with the reflections, and sheltered from the wind to the extent possible. My favorite liquid is molasses; it will thicken after a few weeks, but a few drops of water and few seconds in the microwave and you are good as new. There are obvious (nutritional) advantages to this over dirty motor oil, which some navigators use. An example of molasses at work is in Figure 11.19-2

How to Take the Sights

First do the index correction using the sun or the stars themselves—we rule out the conventional method of using the horizon, but you may have distant hills or buildings that could be used. If using the sun, use the method described in Section 11.7 on Solar IC (this is the way Lewis and Clark did it). If using the stars at night, just set the sextant to 0° 0' and look to the star through the telescope. You will see two dots of light. The horizontal offset is the side error—not crucial if small—and the vertical offset is the index correction. Rotate the micrometer drum till the two dots line up vertically (or coincide if there is no side error) and then read the IC from the micrometer. As always, do it several times and average the results. Try it with bright stars and with fainter ones.

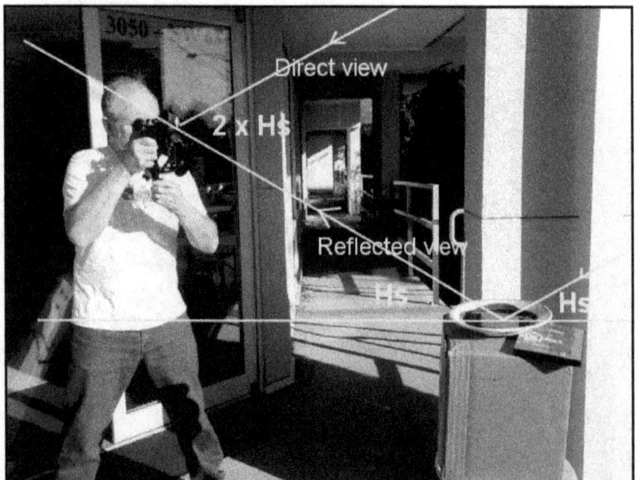

Figure 11.19-2 *Using a plate of molasses as an artificial horizon.*

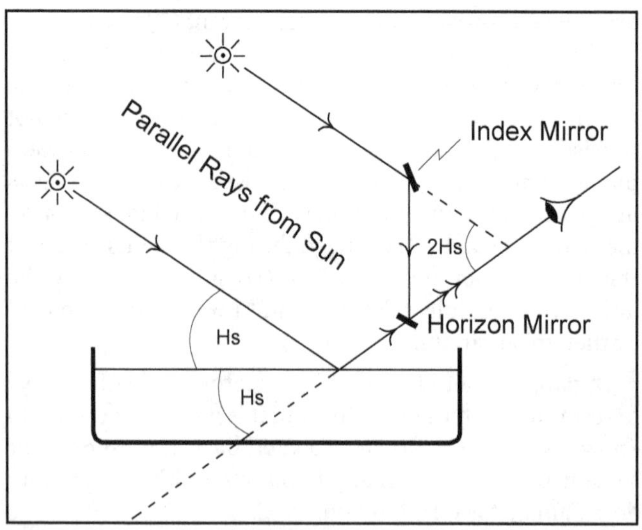

Figure 11.19-3 *Geometry for artificial Horizon, looking down toward the reflective surface.*

A fundamental issue with using a reflected image as a reference is that the angle you will end up measuring is twice the actual angular Hs of the body above the horizon (Figure 11.19-3). The geometry of a normal sight is shown in Figure 11.19-4. This fact has two effects on the process. One is once we measure the sextant height of the body we must divide the results by 2. If we measure Hs' = 36° 28.4' then we first convert this to Hs = 18° 14.2' and call this the measured height. The second practical consequence of this is we can only measure bodies that are about 55° to 60° high in the sky since most sextants only read to about 110°—some to as high as 150°, if this application was in mind at the time. In the old days, special artificial horizon sextants built on a fixed tripod oriented to the liquid surface usually had these higher arc ranges.

The first step in taking the sights is to precompute the altitude of the body you wish to shoot. Even for the sun this could save time, but for stars and planets it is essentially mandatory. Set the sextant to twice the precomputed value, and then orient yourself so that you can see the image you wish to shoot on the surface of the liquid through the direct (open glass) side of the horizon mirror. Since you are on firm land, it might be possible to jury-rig some arrangement for you to lean your arm on for the sights. Explorers often laid or sat on the ground and used their elbows onto knees or ground for support.

When looking to the image on the surface you should see the reflected image in the mirrored side of the sextant as well (if your DR and time used was close in the precompute). Then for stars or planets, just rotate the drum till the two images coincide, or are precisely beside each other (if you have a side error in effect). Then read the time and record the Hs.

For sun sights, you can do the same thing, that is overlap the images, and this is actually the easiest way to be sure you have what you want, although this is not the most precise way to do the sights. At least do it this way once or twice to get underway on the process. When touching limb to limb (the more precise alternative), it is easy to get confused as which limb is which. The sight reduction procedure in the following section explains this further. You will need some sun shades for the job, both on horizon and index mirrors or just use one over the roof, or just one over the front of the telescope. Generally you can get by with the shades on the sextant alone, as if you were doing sights from a glaring sea horizon.

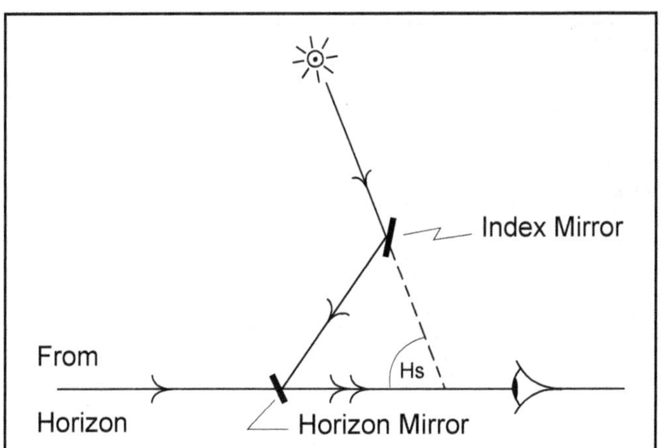

Figure 11.19-4 *Geometry of a normal sextant sight, looking toward the horizon.*

For doing limb-to-limb, use the lower limb of one image to just touch the upper limb of the other. Then after index correction, half the result will be the Ha of the upper or lower limb of the true sun according to the limb used as reference on the image reflected from the liquid surface.

It can be tricky to keep track of which limb is which, especially if you rotate one past the other. You have plenty of time, however, so these methods are learned with practice.

In any view or time of day, the two suns will be either coming together with time if you just watch them both in view, called *closing suns,* or they will be separating with time called *opening suns.* If you keep the suns from crossing over each other, this behavior will reverse from morning (closing suns) to afternoon (opening suns) as the sun changes from rising to setting. In the morning use the upper limb of the surface reflected sun as your reference. In the afternoon, the lower limb is used.

When the timed sight is recorded, note upper or lower limb as if it were done with a sea horizon, but use the definitions given earlier. If we do it wrong it will be apparent in the sight reduction.

For the most accurate sights when you must use a glass roof, you might want to try taking sights again with roof or cover glass turned over so you are looking at the other side of the glass, and then if the values are different, average them. To see if there is any effect from this you will need to take multiple sights and study the results. Just turn it over, do not turn and rotate. This is a rather long process for star-sight fixes or sun-moon fixes, because you need multiple sights from each side which you can plot; so you can choose an effective simultaneous time for each body (Section 11.24). This step would certainly not be required for practice sights or routine fixes, although since you will want to take multiple sights in any event, you might think ahead to turn over the glass on alternating sights of a sequence. If it is dead calm at the artificial horizon, you can leave off the roof and this is not an issue.

How to Reduce the Sights

For star or planet sights, first apply the index correction to the Hs you measured. Next divide the result by two and call this Ha, the apparent altitude (with artificial horizon sights there is no dip correction). Sight reduction of stars are otherwise done in the normal manner to obtain an LOP. That is, look up the altitude correction of the body and subtract it to get Ho and fill out the rest of the form in the normal manner to get Hc and Zn.

For sun sights taken by overlapping the images (as opposed to touching limbs), just do the same as a star, listed previously, being sure to use the Stars and Planets column to find the altitude correction. Do not use the sun corrections for anything when doing overlapped images. For this case there is no upper or lower limb corrections.

When using limb-to-limb, be sure you have identified the limb properly and then sight reduce using the proper upper or lower limb column of the sun's almanac altitude corrections. When doing this method, we always like to refer to the overlapped suns method to be sure we got the right limb. If you did it wrong, the answer will be off by some 32'.

If done carefully, artificial horizon sights can be just as accurate as or more so than those using a real sea horizon in typical conditions from a moving vessel. The only reason we don't promote the process more if you have a lake or other water around is that the overall process is sufficiently different from normal sights that it does not offer that much real practice in typical seagoing navigation. The process is, however, definitely a way to prove to yourself that celestial navigation really does work—but you could just take our word for that till you find a real horizon.

11.20 Star and Planet Brightness

The brightness of a star is often a valuable aid to its identification. Brightness is specified by the body's *magnitude*. Star magnitudes are given in the star list at the back of the Nautical Almanac, not on the daily pages; star magnitudes change very little, if at all, throughout the year. The magnitude of the selected navigational stars are also reproduced in the Index to Selected Stars at the back of the Almanac (for years on page xxxiii). The latter is often reproduced on a yellow card bookmark. Planet magnitudes are listed at the head of the planet columns on each daily page, because their brightness changes slowly throughout the year. The same magnitude scale applies to stars and planets. Samples are shown in Figure 11.20-1.

There is not a simple correspondence between the numerical magnitude of a star and the visual brightness that we perceive. Each magnitude difference of 1.0 implies a brightness difference of 2.5. The magnitude scale is logarithmic, which means we need special tables, such as Table 11.20-1, to figure the actual brightness difference between two stars, or between a star and planet. And to complicate things even further, the scale is inverted; the lower the magnitude, the brighter the star. (The system dates to Ptolemy in about 150 AD, who decided that the brightest stars we see are 100 times brighter than the faintest we can see, and then choose to divide the range into 5 magnitudes, so we end up with each being a factor of the fifth root of 100 (2.511) brighter than the next.)

Table 11.20-1. Brightness vs. Magnitude

Magnitude Difference	*Brightness Difference*
0.0	1.0
0.2	1.2
0.4	1.4
0.6	1.7
0.8	2.1
1.0	2.5
1.2	3.0
1.4	3.6
1.6	4.4
1.8	5.2
2.0	6.3
2.2	7.6
2.4	9.1
2.6	11
2.8	13
3.0	16
3.2	19
3.4	23
3.6	28
3.8	33
4.0	40
4.5	63
5.0	100
5.5	158
6.0	251
6.5	398

The faintest stars we might navigate by would have a magnitude of about 3.0 although it would be rare to use such a faint star. A typical bright star has magnitude 1.0, which we could say is "two magnitudes brighter" than a faint magnitude-3 star. But the actual brightness difference between the two would not be a factor of 2.0; the bright one would appear just over 6 times brighter than the faint one.

The magnitude scale can also go negative for very bright objects. Venus, for example, at magnitude -4.0 would be 5.5 magnitudes brighter than a star with magnitude 1.5. Only two stars, the southern stars Sirius (-1.5) and Canopus (-0.7), are bright enough to have negative magnitudes. Venus and Jupiter are always negative, meaning always very bright, but Mars and Saturn are only rarely negative.

The sign of the magnitude difference is not important; the object with the lower magnitude is always the brighter object. Remember -1 is less than +1; and -3 is less than -2,

1982 DECEMBER 21, 22, 23 (TUES., WED., THURS.)

G.M.T.	ARIES	VENUS −3.4		MARS +1.3		JUPITER −1.3		SATURN +0.9		STARS		
	G.H.A.	G.H.A.	Dec.	G.H.A.	Dec.	G.H.A.	Dec.	G.H.A.	Dec.	Name	S.H.A.	Dec.
	° ′	° ′	° ′	° ′	° ′	° ′	° ′	° ′	° ′		° ′	° ′
21 00	89 14.2	168 01.1	S23 59.0	138 05.7	S19 21.8	212 18.4	S19 07.6	238 31.9	S 9 58.4	Acamar	315 35.7	S40 22.6
01	104 16.7	183 00.1	58.9	153 06.1	21.3	227 20.3	07.8	253 34.2	58.5	Achernar	335 43.7	S57 19.8
02	119 19.1	197 59.2	58.7	168 06.6	20.7	242 22.2	07.9	268 36.4	58.6	Acrux	173 35.6	S62 59.9
03	134 21.6	212 58.2	·· 58.5	183 07.1	·· 20.2	257 24.2	·· 08.0	283 38.7	·· 58.6	Adhara	255 30.5	S28 56.8
04	149 24.1	227 57.2	58.4	198 07.5	19.7	272 26.1	08.1	298 40.9	58.7	Aldebaran	291 15.8	N16 28.5
05	164 26.5	242 56.3	58.2	213 08.0	19.2	287 28.0	08.2	313 43.2	58.8			

INDEX TO SELECTED STARS, 1982

Name	No.	Mag.	S.H.A.	Dec.
			°	°
Acamar	7	3·1	316	S. 40
Achernar	5	0·6	336	S. 57
Acrux	30	1·1	174	S. 63
Adhara	19	1·6	256	S. 29
Aldebaran	10	1·1	291	N. 16

No.	Name	Mag.	S.H.A.	Dec.
			°	°
1	*Alpheratz*	2·2	358	N. 29
2	*Ankaa*	2·4	354	S. 42
3	*Schedar*	2·5	350	N. 56
4	*Diphda*	2·2	349	S. 18
5	*Achernar*	0·6	336	S. 57

Figure 11.20-1 *Planet magnitudes, i.e., -3.4 for Venus, are on the daily pages; Magnitudes of the navigational stars, i.e., 0.6 for Achernar, are on the Index to Selected Stars (page xxxiii) shown here. For other stars, see the list of stars in the back of the Almanac.*

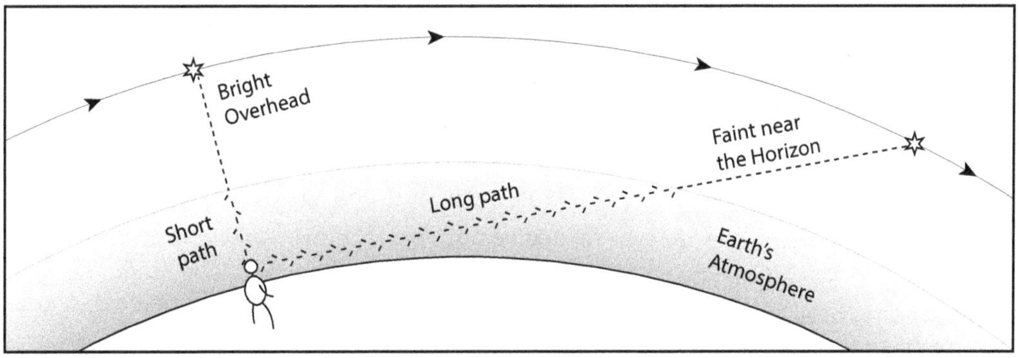

11.20-2 *How star brightness changes with the height of the star. All stars fade as they descend toward the horizon because more of their light is lost to scattering. Polaris, for example, can rarely be seen at latitudes lower than about 10 to maybe 5° N.*

and so forth. Objects with the same magnitude are equally bright—in Table 11.20.-1) this is indicated by showing that a zero magnitude difference means an object is 1.0 times brighter than another object with the same magnitude.

For all practical star identification it is not necessary to be very technical about brightness and magnitudes. It is sufficient to classify stars in three rough categories: ***Magnitude-1 stars***, being the 20 or so brightest ones—pick a favorite and use it as your standard. ***Magnitude-2 stars*** are stars about as bright as the Big Dipper stars. There are only about 70 of these, each two to three times fainter than magnitude-one stars. And finally the ***Magnitude-3 stars*** like Pherkad, which is the lesser of the two Guards on the cup edge of the Little Dipper. Kochab, nearest the Pole is a magnitude-2 star; Pherkad below it is a perfect 3.0 magnitude-3 star. The two trailing stars of Cassiopeia, Ruchbah (2.65) and Segin (3.35), are both magnitude-3 stars. There are only about 200 of these in all of the sky. The vast majority of celestial navigation is done with magnitude-1 stars, and magnitude-3 stars are hardly ever used.

Tip on star ID

It is rare to see stars 10° or lower (a hand width) on the horizon, because there we view them through the thickest layer of the earth's atmosphere, where much of their light intensity is lost to scattering. Even the brightest stars fade as they descend toward the horizon, as shown in Fig. 11.20-2. Consequently, if you see an isolated star low on the horizon, you can bet it is a bright one, even if it appears faint. Since bright stars are well known stars, this observation alone often identifies the star for you.

Or, an isolated low "star" could be Venus or Jupiter. But this confusion is unlikely since navigators tend to keep pretty close track of where these guys are, and even low on the horizon they remain notably bright. On a clear night, a low, bright Venus can startle a weary helmsman who sees it for the first time.

For more sophisticated star ID, it helps to know that several stars are distinctly reddish. These are in a class of stars called the Red Giants, and knowing these can be a valuable aid to their identification. See The Star Finder Book for more details on star and planet ID.

Practice with magnitudes

(1) Arcturus has magnitude 0.2 and Dubhe has magnitude 2.0. The magnitude difference is 2.0 - 0.2 = 1.8, and from Table 11.20-1, Arcturus is 5.2 times brighter than Dubhe.

(2) Sirius has magnitude -1.6 and Antares has magnitude 1.2 The magnitude difference is 1.2 - (-1.6) = 1.2 + 1.6 = 2.8, and from Table 11.20-1, Sirius is 13 times brighter than Antares.

(3) Jupiter, on some date, has magnitude -2.1 and Canopus has magnitude -0.9. The magnitude difference is -2.1 - (-0.9) = -2.1 + 0.9 = -1.2, and from Table 11.20-1, Jupiter is 3 times brighter than Canopus.

(4) Venus can be routinely as bright as magnitude -4.3 and the North Star, Polaris, has magnitude +2.1. The magnitude difference is 2.1 - (-4.3) = 6.4. From Table 11.20-1 we can estimate that Venus is roughly 400 times brighter than Polaris. Venus can be as bright as -4.8.

11.21 Compass Checks at Sea

One of the virtues of knowing celestial navigation is the ability that it gives you to check your compass at sea without landmarks for reference. There are tricks for compass checks with no information at all, but the best procedure requires that you have a reasonable DR position, have correct UTC, and know the local magnetic variation. For a review of compass use and conversions see *Inland and Coastal Navigation* (Starpath Publications, 2014)

Procedure

(1) Do the necessary sights or chart work to establish your position, and from an ocean chart (paper or electronic) determine the local magnetic variation (Var).

(2) Choose and identify a celestial body that lies near dead ahead on your intended course. Head directly toward it and note the compass course (C) and the UTC at this time.

(3) Then do a normal sight reduction of the object using the UTC and DR position at the time the compass heading (C) was recorded. Disregard the calculated altitude (Hc)

obtained but record the azimuth of the body (Zn). This azimuth was the object's true bearing (ZnT) at the time (ZnT = Zn). Figure the magnetic bearing of the object from: ZnM = ZnT - Var(East) or ZnM = ZnT + Var(West).

(4) Compass error (deviation) on heading C is then the difference between C and ZnM. The compass should have read ZnM when headed toward the object. Remember, however, that this only checks the compass on heading C. A compass might have no error on heading C, but still significant error on headings just about 30° or so to either side of C. When in doubt check the compass on several headings across the quadrant of your desired course.

Short-Cut Compass Checks

A convenient variation of this method for binnacle compasses with shadow pins is as follows: Record the heading of the boat while on course and note the compass direction of the sun's shadow on the compass card (Figure 11.21-1). Then the sun's compass bearing is the shadow bearing plus 180°. Then compare sun's compass bearing with its magnetic bearing found from a sight reduction as mentioned earlier. This way you can check the compass on the desired heading during the day without altering course. Note that although the sun's bearing is at another angle, this method checks the compass error only for the present heading of the boat. If called for, this is an easy way to swing ship to check the compass on all headings.

Important Practice Exercise

If you do this once at home, you will be prepared for doing it at sea. Or do it at home, then check the steering compass on your boat or a friend's boat. You can often do the boat check without leaving the dock.

(1) On land, look for a shadow of a vertical pole on a flat surface, then with a hand bearing compass or with your cellphone compass measure the compass bearing of the sun (C = opposite the shadow direction) and note the time. Cellphone compasses have to be calibrated with various rotation routines explained with the app.

(2) Then figure UTC and then get the true bearing to the sun by shortcut method at www.starpath.com/usno. That gives you Zn, the true bearing of the sun at the time.

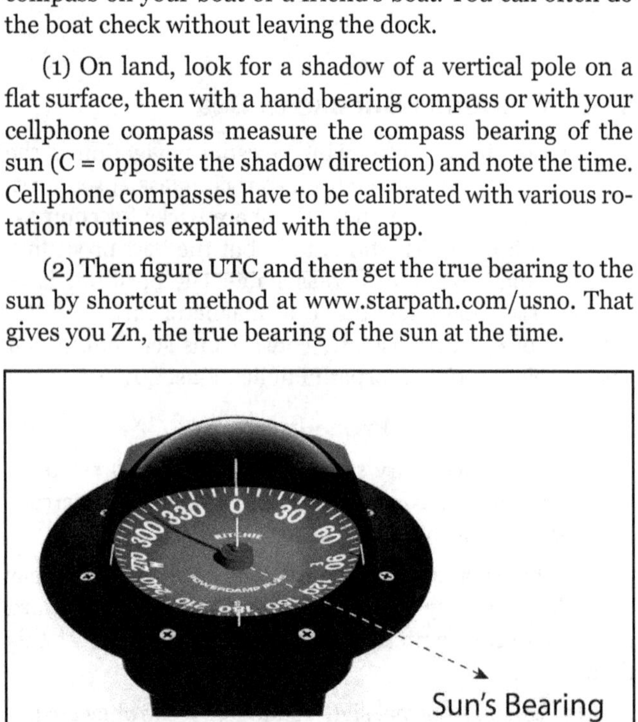

Figure 11.21-1 *Finding the compass bearing to the sun from the shadow direction.*

(3) Look up your Lat-Lon on Google Earth if needed; and also look up your variation if needed (www.ngdc.noaa.gov/geomag-web).

(4) Find sun magnetic bearing M = Zn ± variation. (Review compass correction rules as needed)

(5) Find compass error = M - C.

Remember this finds the error only on heading C. When extending this to use underway, you have to do the sight reduction for Zn from a DR position and look up the variation on the chart.

11.22 Great Circle Sailing

The shortest distance between any two points on earth–assuming the earth is spherical–is called the great circle (GC) route between them. The GC route is the intersection of a plane through the center of the earth and the surface, so it cuts the earth in half. Unlike a rhumb-line (RL) route which is a straight line on a Mercator chart, a GC route plotted on a Mercator chart is always a curved route, bowing out toward the poleward side (Figure 11.22-1). It is not often we need to know the route of shortest distance between two distant points, because usually wind or other matters dominate the routing. But sometimes we do care to know the initial heading of the route.

Furthermore, the difference in distance between GC and RL routes between two points is only significant when both departure and arrival are at high latitudes *and* the distance is about 2,000 miles or more. But there are times we still care to know at least the initial heading of the GC route so we can evaluate our present progress. Note that we refer to *initial* heading on a GC route. On a RL route, the true heading is constant all along the route, but in great circle sailing the route heading is continually changing, always starting out poleward of the RL.

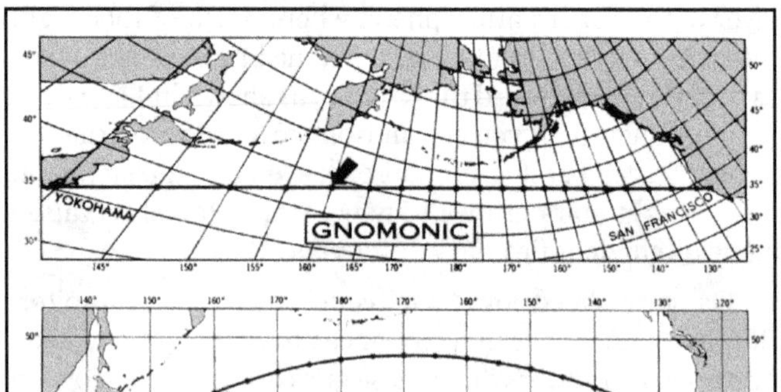

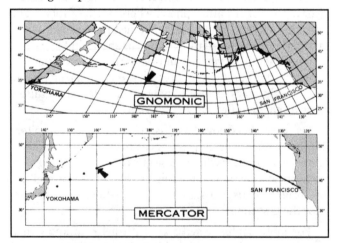

Figure 11.22-1 *Comparison of a great circle chart (top, called here gnomonic) compared to the same route transferred point by point to a Mercator chart. This is the main purpose of a Great Circle Chart, also called Tracking Chart. Bearings and distances cannot be read directly from gnomonic charts. Image from* Bowditch.

For example, on the route from Cape Flattery, WA (48° 24'N, 124° 45'W) to Maui, HI (21° 10'N, 156° 25'W) the difference in RL versus GC distance is only 14 miles, but the difference in initial heading is 11° (GC = 234T, RL = 223T). Thus, if you are in wind conditions that do not let you sail the RL route as you might want to (which might not be best choice anyway), we then have to look at what course we can make good. If we are making good a course about 10° to 15° higher (poleward) of the RL, we are not actually losing ground at all. In fact, we are getting closer to Maui on every mile than we would be sailing the same mile on the RL route. On the other hand, if we are forced south of the RL, we are losing miles compared to both the GC route and the RL route. On this particular sailing route, on the other hand, that might still be the way we would choose to go, but that is not the topic at hand.

From a tactical point of view, even if we wanted to get south fast, we might still prefer going on the GC route for a day or so, since every mile sailed due south is not getting us much closer to HI—again, however, not the topic at hand, but just to point out that in ocean sailing, it is not often the geometric route that dominates our choice of course. The guy on the GC route looking very good the first few days, better get south pretty soon or he risks sailing into the pacific High and not be able to get out of it, etc.

In any event, it can pay to calculate and keep in mind the difference between GC and RL headings, even if we do not care much about the few miles we might save on the GC route.

The best practical solution to figuring the GC route is just type the Lat-Lon of your departure and destination into an electronic charting system (ECS) or a computer or calculator program and push the button for GC route. You get all you need instantly. See starpath.com/calc for an online solution. The basic results are the distance between the two points and the initial heading of the route. Just be careful when using ECS that you are set to get GC data and not RL between two points. Usually that is the case, but some systems offer an option.

You can also get the answer from a GPS unit, which in one sense will be more accurate. They know what chart datum you have selected, and so they tell you the ellipsoidal distance, which takes into account the shape of the earth. GC sailing by definition is spherical earth, just like cel nav is. I believe all ECS programs use spherical earth solutions, so you might see slight differences between a GPS solution and an ECS solution—a mile or two out of a couple thousand.

In GC sailing the heading changes continuously along the route with the initial heading poleward of the RL. If you plot out the GC route on a Mercator chart, once you get beyond the halfway point on that initial route track, the GC heading will be on the other side of the RL, but if you recompute the GC route from a new position, it will again start poleward, but maybe an indistinguishable amount.

Thus, to layout a GC route we need waypoints along the route to navigate the changing heading. This is usually accomplished in navigation programs by telling them a Lon interval, and then the program tells you the Lat at each of these Lon intervals along the route—in other words, a set of waypoints. The solution is to break the CG route into a series of RL routes.

Another parameter often provided by computed solutions is the vertex of the route, which is the Lat-Lon of the highest Lat along the route. Since the GC route only differs notably from the RL route for high Lat at departure and destination, we often learn that the vertex hits the ice, so we can't use this route anyway!

If you do not have an ECS program, or a GPS, or a navigation program in a computer or mobile app—essentially a big mistake when it comes to shaping a course!—you have several other ways to determine a GC route.

Great Circle Charts

One way is to draw the line from point to point on a gnomonic chart—GC routes are straight lines on this projection—and then transfer the route by fixed distance or longitude intervals onto a Mercator chart (Figure 11.22-1). Read the Lat-Lon on the GC chart and plot it on the Mercator chart. Then on the Mercator chart you can read the course and bearing along each RL segment.

You cannot read course headings or bearings from a generic GC (gnomonic) chart. They are primarily meant for this transfer operation, although some older editions from the US government did include special diagrams and instructions to assist with distance and bearing estimates from specific locations. Also, note that the initial GC heading you get from the basic transfer method may not be very accurate, because it is sensitive to precise location readings and it depends on the length of the first interval you choose.

Again, it is not very often that this will be the best route to sail, but at least when plotted out it shows the track of where you would had sailed the shortest route. Chances are in most ocean crossings, you could sail 10% or 20% farther than the shortest route and still be quite a bit faster than following the "shortest route." GC charts are available in print on demand at most official chart outlets. They are, like all charts today, only print on demand. The GC charts readily available are NGA No. 5274 North Atlantic and No. 5270 North Pacific. These are the ones that are available in the USCG exam room. These particular charts, however, do not include instructions or diagrams for reading distances and bearings, so they can only be used for transferring a GC route to a Mercator chart, which frankly is not something needed for any exam question they give.

Sight Reduction for Great Circle

Without computer solution or GC plotting sheets we are down to two options: use Sight Reduction Tables Pub. 229 or NAO tables, or calculate the results with the basic formula using a trig calculator.

The Pub. 229 solution is standard for the most part. Recall that the zenith distance (z = 90° - Hc) is the distance between AP and GP, so we can get this from Pub. 229 by replacing the AP with the departure position, and replacing the GP with the destination position. Then when we get Hc, we can find z (in this case the GC distance) and convert this to distance using 1° = 60 nmi.

Likewise, the Zn we get from Pub. 229 is the bearing from AP to GP relative to the elevated pole, which we can convert to Zn in the usual manner, and this is indeed the initial GC heading we want. We cannot use Pub. 249 for this process, because it only has declinations up to 29°.

Thus the principle of using Pub. 229 is all pretty clear; it is just the actual numerical solution that gets a bit muddy. The problem is we are accustomed to using an AP chosen specifically to make the table look up easy. Now for accurate results we must do the computation from the actual position, not an AP, so there are a lot of small corrections to make.

One way to make the corrections numerically is to interpolate all the values we get from the tables, but that is a long process, susceptible to error. A simpler approach is just carry on as with a normal sight reduction, from an AP, then find the necessary correction graphically.

As an example, we return to the WA to HI route: depart 48° 24'N, 124° 45'W to 21° 10'N, 156° 25'W. Here the a-Lat is 48N, the Dec = N21° 10', and the a-Lon = 124° 25', giving us an LHA of 32°. We find from Pub. 229 that Hc = 52° 53.6' and Z = 125.0, leading to Zn = initial GC heading = 235 (correct is 234.1, but we got this close without any interpolations at all).

The GC distance is then (90° - 52° 53.6') × 60 nmi/1° = 2226.4 nmi. This, however, is from the AP to the destination, not the proper departure. Figure 11.22-2 shows a way to figure the correction by plotting. We find it is +3.0 nmi for a total distance of 2229.4, which is the correct value.

The NAO Sight Reduction Tables included in every *Nautical Almanac* can also do this job very nicely, and the precision will always be adequate. The NAO tables for the last example given Hc = 52° 54' with Zn = 235.7. The correction of Figure 11.22-2 is still required.

Direct Trig Calculation

The Pub. 229 solution using plot corrections rather than interpolations is fairly quick. You might want to interpolate Z for dec minutes, but again, except for inside the USCG license exam room, we would rarely care about the tenths.

The final GC solution option is a direct trig calculator solution by simply solving the sight reduction formula, rather than looking up the answers in the tables. The formulas are given in Section 10.6. In our example, a-Lat = 48.400°, dec = 21.167°, and LHA = 31.667° (note we use GHA - a-Lon directly here, no need for an AP), leading to Hc = 52.662 with z = 37.158 and GC distance = 2229.5 and Z = 125.4, or Zn = GC initial heading of 234.1. These computed solutions are by definition the exact solutions.

Summary

Besides keeping in mind at all times the direction of the shortest route, even if we can't sail it, the call for GC computations comes up in yacht racing every day, as we need to compute who is ahead at each daily report and you get that from the difference in the GC distance to the mark between you and your competitors. For this application, a computed solution is mandatory.

For completion, the GC charts readily available are NGA No. 5274 North Atlantic and No. 5270 North Pacific. They are available from print-on-demand chart outlets; these are the ones that are available in the USCG exam room. These particular charts, however, do not include instructions or diagrams for reading distances and bearings, so they can only be used for transferring a GC route to a Mercator chart.

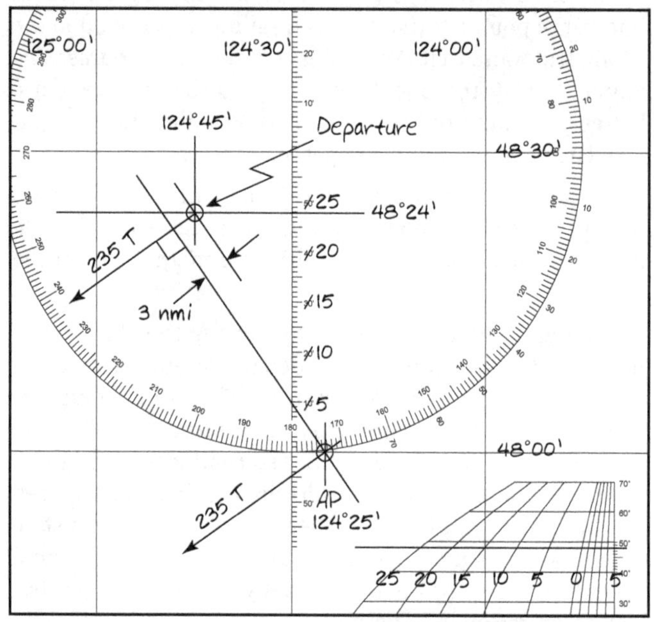

Figure 11.22-2 *Correction to Pub. 229 or NAO Table solutions to GC distance by plotting.*

Procedure:

(1) First look at the scale needed to include both AP and departure, and make a universal plotting sheet as large as possible to include both. Here we use 30' per standard parallel. Note that this changes the Lon scale as well.

(2) Plot both AP and departure points.

(3) Draw a line in the initial GC heading from both positions.

(4) Draw a line from the AP to intersect the heading line from the departure point at a right angle.

(5) Read the correction, which is the distance between that line and the AP, which is 3.0 nmi in this example. The correction can be plus or minus, and could be up to 20 nmi or so.

11.23 Rhumb-line Sailing

The *sailings* in marine navigation refers to the various ways to figure a course and distance between two points on the globe, historically called "shaping a course." The related task is figuring a new Lat, Lon after sailing on a given course for a given distance. We might have thought that the course and distance from A to B would have a unique answer in navigation discussions, but it does not. The answers to these questions (although often very similar) depend on the type of sailing used. There are several solutions, each with pros and cons.

There are two general types of sailings: great-circle (GC) sailing, which yields the shortest distance between two points, and rhumb-line (RL) sailing, which yields a straight line on a Mercator chart (Section 11.4), the common map projection used on nautical charts. We cover GC sailing in Section 11.22. Commercial ships at higher latitudes often strive for GC routes, but it is not common in small-craft navigation, not to mention that sailing vessels must take the route the wind allows. As a rough guide, the difference between GC and RL solutions is only significant if *both* departure and arrival are at latitudes higher than about 45°, and the total distance is more than about 2,000 miles. Nevertheless, it can be valuable for a small-craft navigator to know how GC heading and distance compares to the RL solution when it comes to route selection, especially when you cannot steer the RL course for some reason.

Rhumb Line by Plotting

In one sense, the fundamental solution to RL sailings is just plot the two positions on a nautical chart and draw a straight line between them. After doing this, the course is easy to read relative to any meridian it crosses. The main virtue of a RL route is that the true heading remains constant along the full voyage—although we still have to correct for variation to get the magnetic heading, which will likely change over a long voyage.

For shorter routes, the RL distance between the two points is also easy to measure with dividers using the latitude scale of the chart. For longer distances, this is not so easy, because the chart scale (miles per inch) increases with the latitude on a Mercator chart. For moderate distances (whole route fits on a 1:80,000 chart) this can be accomplished by breaking the full route up into shorter latitude intervals and using corresponding scale for each latitude range.

For long route lengths, however, and especially those that cross from one chart to another, the plotted solution is not very convenient, and it grows less accurate in practice the longer the route. Because of this, a direct mathematical computation is often the best solution. With programmed calculators, mobile apps, or computer software available, the direct computation is the obvious solution. Fast and accurate.

Rhumb Line by Computation

There are two ways to solve RL sailings mathematically. You can use a shortcut method that is easy to solve with a trig calculator called *mid-latitude sailing* or you can compute a more generalized solution called *Mercator sailing*. This latter method is often done in conjunction with special tables found in *Bowditch* called Meridonal Parts, but it can be computed from scratch if needed. A software program or mobile app would almost certainly use the Mercator solution, because mid-latitude sailing is limited to route legs shorter than about 300 miles, especially for latitudes above 60° or so. Starpath.com/calc offers an online computation that can be used to compare the relative accuracies of these two methods.

Besides the mathematical approximations used, the two methods also differ in the shape of the earth they are based upon. Mid-latitude sailing assumes a spherical earth, whereas Mercator sailing incorporates the eccentricity of the earth, presumed flattened (to some very small extent) into the shape of a doorknob. With the computations matching the same earth shape used in the nautical chart datum, we get closer agreement with plotted values—if we had a way to plot to very high precision.

Alert to Reader!

Before proceeding, please note that computing RL sailing must be considered an advanced or specialized part of navigation training. This is true for two reasons. First, most calls for this underway or in planning can be done by plotting right on the chart, and second, if we are to use this formalism in the practical world, we should have a calculator or mobile app programmed for instant solutions. We include this here because USCG tests require this knowledge (without *programmed* devices) and we do work on the premise that we should be prepared to do *anything* we need on our own—assuming here that "on our own" includes using a trig calculator! We would also like to present our procedures for this, which differ in some important details from standard treatments.

Mid-latitude DR

Both RL sailing solutions used the same definitions as shown in Figure 11.23-1, because both are going to be straight lines on a Mercator chart. Furthermore, the latitude interval for a given run along a course will be the same for each solution. It is just how they compute the longitude interval over this run that changes.

First, we look at doing DR by mid-latitude sailing. That is, leaving from a Lat 1, Lon 1 and sailing for a distance D along course C, what is then your new Lat 2, Lon 2?

The definitions are illustrated in Figure 11.23-1. The first step in any sailing computation is to draw a small sketch that orients you for the solution. The importance of this step cannot be overstressed. In most cases we are computing intervals, and you must use your sketch to decide if the Lat and Lon are getting bigger or smaller based on the course direction.

Definitions:

D = distance run

C = true course

α = course angle

ℓ = Lat interval in nmi

dLat = Lat interval in degrees and minutes

p = *departure* = Lon interval in nmi

dLon = Lon interval in degrees and minutes

From trig we can compute the two sides of the right triangle:

$\ell = D \times \cos C$

$p = D \times \sin C$.

Since the latitude scale is the miles scale, we get directly

$dLat = \ell = D \times \cos C$.

Now we define the mid-latitude:

$Lm = (Lat\ 1 + Lat\ 2)/2$

Then we make the assumption that the meridians of longitude are getting closer as we leave the equator in proportion to the cos of the latitude, and choose the midpoint between the first and second positions to use for this.

$dLon = p/\cos Lm$

Then having computed the two angular intervals we can find the new values.

$Lat\ 2 = Lat\ 1 + dLat$

$Lon\ 2 = Lon\ 1 + dLon$

Note: Crossing the equator dLat = Lat 1+Lat 2. Crossing Greenwich, dLon = Lon 1+Lon 2, and crossing the Date Line, dLon = 360 - (Lon 1+Lon 2). This question should not be asked for distances much larger than 500 nmi outside of the tropics as the method becomes less accurate.

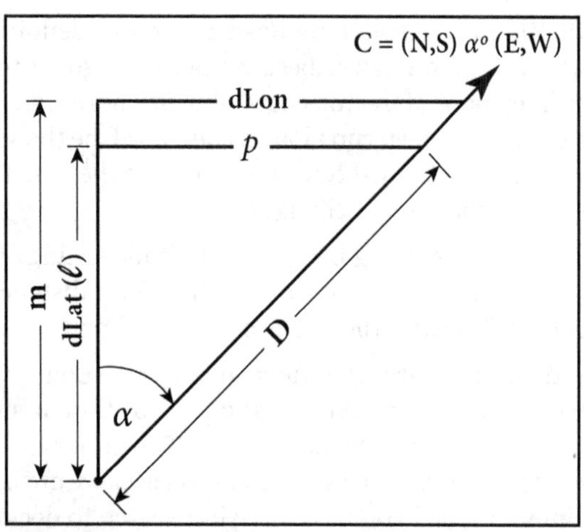

Figure 11.23-1 *Rhumb line sailing terms.*

Mid-Latitude Route

Now we look at the same solution applied to route planning. That is, given starting point (Lat 1, Lon 1) and destination (Lat 2, Lon 2) ,what is the distance between them and the course between them?

The procedure is to find ℓ and p, and then find C from

$C = (N,S)\ \alpha^o\ (E,W)$,

where

$\alpha = \arctan(p/\ell)$.

$p = dLon \times \cos Lm$

$\ell = dLat$

Then we can find D from Pythagorean Theorem:

$D^2 = \ell^2 + p^2$

$D = sqrt(\ell^2 + p^2)$.

Mid-Latitude Examples

Here are two questions from a USCG licence exam.

DR by mid-latitude

Example 1: A vessel steams 720 miles on course 058°T from LAT 30°06.0'S, LONG 31°42.0'E. What are the latitude and longitude of the point of arrival by mid-latitude sailing?

Solution: Make a rough sketch (Figure 11.23-3) for orientation and to ID dLat, dLon, course, distance run, and departure.

Lat 2 = Lat 1 + dLat.

$dLat = D \times \cos C = 720 \times \cos(58) = 381.5' = 6^o\ 21.5'$.

So Lat 2 = $30^o\ 06' - 6^o\ 21.5' = 23^o\ 44.5'$ S.

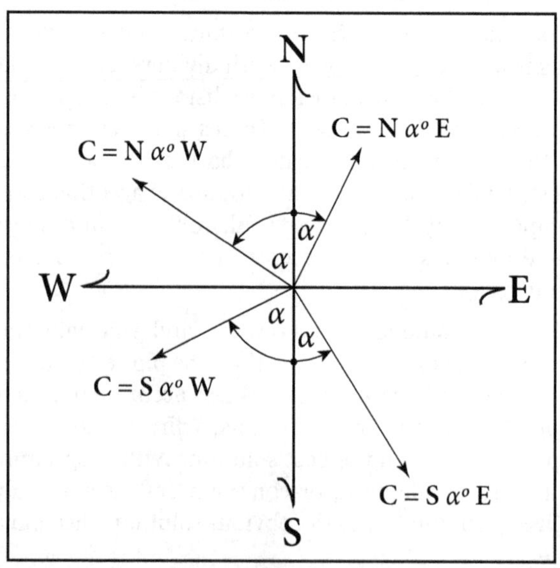

Figure 11.23-2 *How the angle α (called course angle) is used to determine the course direction.*

Lon 2 = Lon 1 - dLon

dLon = dep / cos (Lm)

p = D × sin C = 720 × sin (58) = 610.6'.

Lm = (23 44.5 + 30 06)/2 = (53 50.5)/2 = 26° 30' + 25.3' = 26 55.3' = 26.92°.

dLon = 610.6 / cos (26.92) = 684.8' = 11° 24.8'

Lon 2 = Lon 1 + dLon = 31°42.0' + 11° 24.8' = 42° 66.8' = 43° 6.8'E

Route by mid-latitude

Example 2: You depart LAT 28° 55.0'N, LONG 89° 10.0'W, enroute to LAT 24° 25.0'N, LONG 83° 00.0'W. Determine the true course and distance by mid-latitude sailing?

Solution: First make a rough sketch for orientation (Figure 11.23-4), roughly to scale, but precise scale is not crucial. From this we see that the course is given by C = S α E. Then find ℓ and p, and from these find C and D.

Lat 1 = 28° 55.0'N	Lon 1 = 89° 10.0'W
Lat 2 = 24° 25.0'N	Lon 2 = 83° 00.0'W
dLat = 4° 30.0' = 270.0'	dLon = 6° 10.0' = 370.0'

ℓ = dLat = 270.0'

Lm = (28° 55' + 24° 25')/2 = 52° 80' / 2 = 26° 40' = 26.67°

p = dLon × cos(Lm) = 370 × cos(26.67) = 370 × 0.89363 = 330.6 nmi

α = arctan(p/ℓ) = arctan(330.6/270.0) = 50.8°

Referring to Figure 11.23-4,

C = S α° E, or 180 - 50.8 = 129.2°

D = sqrt (270.0^2 + 330.6^2) = 426.8 nmi.

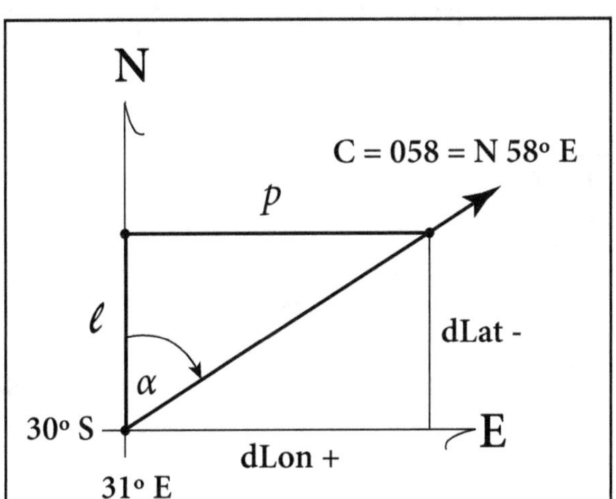

Figure 11.23-3 *Example 1 sketch to determine if dLat and dLon are plus or minus.*

Mercator Sailing

The Mercator sailing solution is a more accurate representation of a RL on a Mercator chart than mid-latitude sailing, especially for longer distances at higher latitudes. This is achieved by using directly the data that define the Mercator chart, namely the Meridonal Parts. The meridonal part (M) for a given latitude is the distance along a meridian from that latitude to the equator on a Mercator chart, expressed in minutes of longitude at the equator. This is just the data needed to construct an accurate Mercator chart to match a specific chart datum, usually WGS-84.

In mid-latitude sailing we just assumed there is 1 nmi per 1' of lat, which is no longer true on a non-spherical earth, and we approximated the distance between them (the departure) with the cos (Lat). Thus, we no longer use ℓ and p to find the course angle, but now use the difference between the meridonal parts (m) and dLon directly. A key to remembering the new equations is the fact that m has units of longitude minutes.

We still need to make the sketch to figure the course angle (α) and the directions for Lat and Lon increments.

Mercator Route

For a Mercator route between two positions, use:

α = arctan (dLon/m),

where m = M1 ± M2. This difference in meridonal parts is - when both positions are on the same side of the equator, but + when the route crosses the equator.

C = (N,S) α (E,W),

D = dLat/cos C,

The M values for Lat 1 and Lat 2 can be looked up in Table 6 of *Bowditch* (Figure 11.23-5, available online and always in the USCG test room), which lists them for every 1' of Lat, or compute directly from:

M(Lat) = 7915.704468 × log [tan (45° + Lat/2)] - 23.0133633 × sin (Lat) -0.051353 × sin ^{3} (Lat) - 0.000206 × sin^5 (Lat).

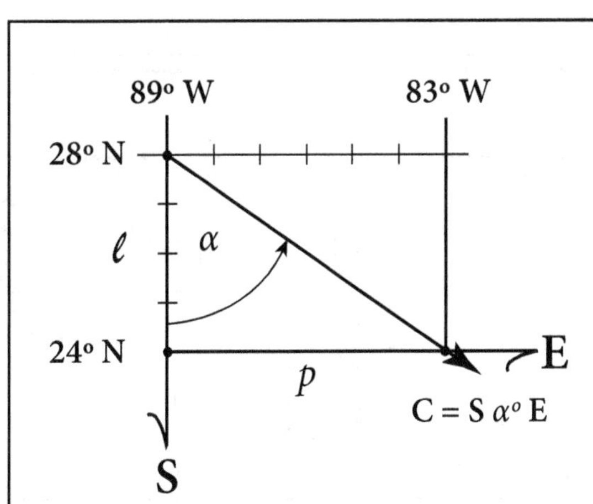

Figure 11.23-4 *Example 2 sketch of the example question to determine C from the course angle α.*

This equation is added for completeness or for your own programming. We would not be expected to memorize this.

Mercator DR

DR by Mercator sailing uses the same equations from a different approach. Here we are given C and D, Lat 1, Lon 1, and we need to compute dLat and dLon to find the second position. Thus:

dLat = D × cos C;

Lat 2 = Lat 1 ± dLat.

Look up M1 and M2 to find m = M1 ± M2.

Look at your sketch to figure α from C, then

dLon = m × tan α.

Lon 2 = Lon 1 ± dLon.

Mercator Sailing Examples

Here are sample questions from a USCG license exam.

Route by Mercator

Example 3: A vessel at LAT 21° 18.5'N, LON 157° 52.2'W, heads for a destination at LAT 8° 53.0'N, LON 79° 31.0'W. Determine the true course and distance by Mercator sailing.

Solution: Using Table 6 from *Bowditch*, Interpolate M1: 21° 18' = 1300.1 and 21° 19' = 1301.2, so 21° 18.5' = 1300.65. M2 (8° 53.0') = 531.6', so m = M1 - M2 = 769.0'

dLon = 157° 52.2'W - 79° 31.0'W = 78° 21.2' = 4701.2'

α = arctan (dLon/m)= arctan (4701.2'/769.0') = 80.710°, then check sketch (Figure 11.23-6) to see C = 180 - α = 099.291 =099.3.

dLat = 21° 18.5' N - 8° 53.0'N = 12° 25.5' = 745.5'

D = 745.5'/cos 99.291 = 4617.5 nmi.

We must use three decimals on the C to get D right to the mile.

Here is another example, with nuances.

Example 4: A vessel at LAT 10° 22.0'S, LON 7° 18.0'E heads for a destination at LAT 6° 52.0'N, LON 57° 23.0'W. Determine the true course and distance by Mercator sailing.

Solution: From Table 6, M1 = 621.3; M2 = 410.2, but recalling these are distances from the parallel of latitude to the equator, when we cross the equator the difference we want between the two latitudes is now a sum, so m = M1 + M2 = 1031.5'.

Since we are crossing the Greenwich meridian, the longitude difference (dLon) is numerically the sum of the two, not the difference as it is when they are both on the same side.

dLon = 7° 18.0'E + 57° 23.0'W = 64° 41' = 3881'.

α = arctan (dLon/m)= arctan (3881'/1031.5') = 75.116°, then check sketch (Figure 11.23-7) to see C = 360 - 75.116 = 284.884 = 284.9.

dLat = 10° 22.0'S + 6° 52.0'N = 16° 74.0' = 1034.0'

D = dLat/cos C = 1034.0/cos 284.884 = 4025.5 nmi.

Again, since we are crossing the equator, the difference in Lat is the sum, rather than the difference when they are both on the same side.

DR by Mercator

Example 5: You depart LAT 22° 35.0'N, LON 157° 30.0'W and steam 4505.0 miles on course 135°T. What are the latitude and longitude of your arrival by Mercator sailing?

Solution: Make a sketch for orientation (Figure 11.23-8).

dLat = D × cos C = 4505 × cos 135 = -3185.5' = -53° 5.5'

Lat 2 = Lat 1 ± dLat = 22° 35.0'N - 53° 5.5', which means you are at 22° 35.0'N and you are going to a latitude that is 53° 5.5' to the south of you. Thus the answer is a south Lat = 53° 5.5' - 22° 35.0' = 52° 65.5' - 22° 35.0' = 30° 30.5' S = Lat 2.

TABLE 6

Meridional Parts

Lat.	40°	41°	42°	43°	44°	45°	46°
'							
0	2607. 9	2686. 5	2766. 3	2847. 4	2929. 8	3013. 6	3099. 0
1	09. 2	87. 8	67. 6	48. 7	31. 2	15. 1	3100. 4
2	10. 5	89. 1	69. 0	50. 1	32. 6	16. 5	01. 8
3	11. 8	90. 4	70. 3	51. 5	34. 0	17. 9	03. 3
4	13. 1	91. 8	71. 7	52. 8	35. 4	19. 3	04. 7
5	2614. 4	2693. 1	2773. 0	2854. 2	2936. 7	3020. 7	3106. 2
6	15. 7	94. 4	74. 3	55. 6	38. 1	22. 1	07. 6
7	17. 0	95. 7	75. 7	56. 9	39. 5	23. 5	09. 0
8	18. 3	97. 1	77. 0	58. 3	40. 9	24. 9	10. 5
9	19. 6	98. 4	78. 4	59. 7	42. 3	26. 4	11. 9
10	2620. 9	2699. 7	2779. 7	2861. 0	2943. 7	3027. 8	3113. 3
11	22. 2	2701. 0	81. 1	62. 4	45. 1	29. 2	14. 8

Figure 11.23-5 *Sample of* Bowditch *Table 6, Meridonal Parts. At Lat 42° 6', N or S, M = 2774.3. Interpolate as needed for decimal minutes of Lat.*

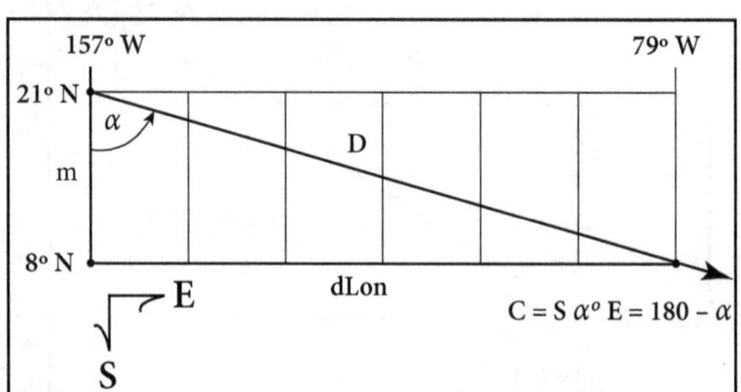

Figure 11.23-6 *Example 3 sketch to determine C from the relative bearing α.*

Now in Table 6 look up M1 (22° 35.0') and M2 (30° 30.5') to find m = M1 ± M2 = 1382.7 ± 1912.0 (interpolated).

Look at your sketch to figure out if we are crossing the equator in these 4000 miles to the SE. One way to estimate this is to realize we are in the tropics so the Lat-Lon grid is about square, so it is easy to make the sketch close to scale at 10° = 600 nmi, and from this we see we are definitely going to end up in S Lat, so we add the meridonal parts.

m = 1912.0 + 1382.7 = 3294.7'. Now check your sketch again (Figure 11.23-7) to see that C = 135 is the same as S 45 E, so α = 45°.

dLon = m × tan α = 3294.7' × tan 45 = 3294.7' = 54° 54.7'.

Lon 2 = Lon 1 ± dLon = 157° 30.0'W - 54° 54.7' = 102° 35.3'W.

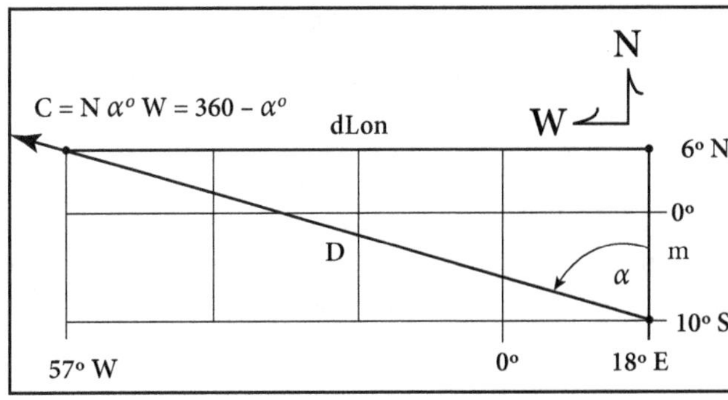

Figure 11.23-7. *Example 4 sketch to determine C from the relative bearing α.*

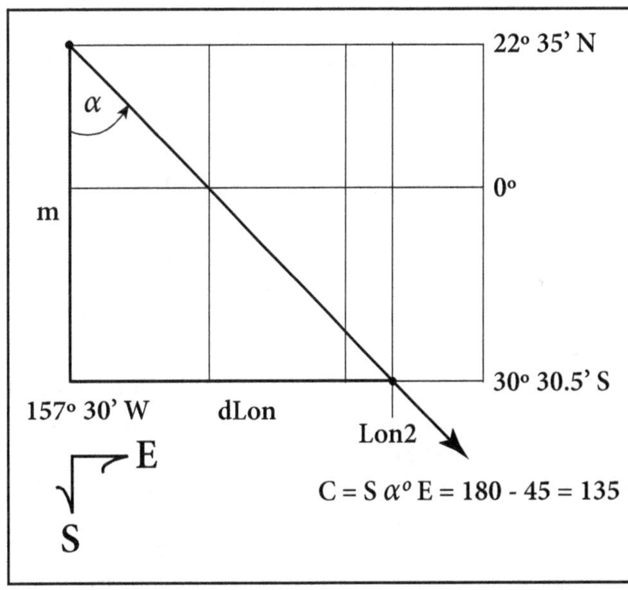

Figure 11.23-8 *Example 5 sketch for orientation. For this sketch we needed to find dLat to get Lat 2 before we could mock up a rough scale.*

Plain Sailing and Parallel Sailing

With the *Bowditch* Table 6 at hand, Mercator sailing is just as fast, if not faster, than the less accurate mid-latitude sailing, but not quite as fast as *Plain Sailing,* which is just mid-latitude sailing using either Lat 1 or Lat 2 in place of Lm. This works fine for short runs less than 60 miles or so.

When headed due east or west, so that your latitude does not change, the solution is called *Parallel Sailing*, and all tasks reduce to finding

dLon = departure / cos Lat.

Your course is always 090 or 270 in parallel sailing.

Summary

If you have read all the way to here, then I do not really need to say this, but if you are doing ocean sailing you need a convenient *computed solution* for your sailings. We do, indeed, have frequent use for them; after every fix we need to consider the best route to either an active waypoint or to the destination. And the planning of any voyage starts out with laying out the routes and figuring distances and estimated travel times.

11.24 Optimizing Celestial Fixes

The beauty of celestial navigation is its transparency, meaning when we get a position fix using standard good procedures we can be completely confident that it is right; if we make an error on the way to this fix, it is usually obvious even before we get the fix completed. With celestial navigation, we not only find our position independent of the external world, but we also have a way to evaluate its accuracy. This is not the case, for example, with GPS. We have to believe the GPS output based on our faith in the system, a procedure rather more appropriate to religion than to navigation.

Take Multiple Sights

Part of standard good procedure is taking multiple sights of each body used in the fix. If we take just one or two sights, we run the risk of starting out with less than the best possible data. These are human measurements, and we can all make errors, even in the best of conditions—an imperceptible little bump-twist of the dial just as we release it, or some chance coincidence of the vessel's heel angle and our sextant rocking angle can lead to an imprecise sight—or we can just blunder: we read the dial (of sextant or watch) as 23 and then record 32. Each of these is possible, but it is very unlikely that they would happen twice in the same series of sights.

The motivation of taking multiple sights is to average out these individual errors. Even if there were no blunders or mistakes, conventional celestial navigation is right on the edge of the ultimate capability of both man and sextant. About the best accuracy we can hope for is about ± 0.5 miles in final position, and this level of accuracy depends mostly on how we correct the process for vessel motion during the sights. Not to mention that we are striving for this level of accuracy using a handheld instrument that measures angles only to within about ±0.2 miles and astronomical data that is only accurate to within about ±0.1 miles. In short, to get the optimum accuracy in the final product, we must do every thing as carefully as possible and beat down the inherent uncertainties with statistics.

A key question then is simply how accurate are the sights themselves? Any navigator taking multiple sights of the same body will naturally observe some spread in the data. The sights will not be precise, but will scatter about the proper value. The extent of the scatter is some fraction of an arc minute—maybe optimistically about ±0.2' in ideal conditions with a good instrument in experienced hands, but more likely it will be about twice that (±0.4') in good conditions. In poor conditions, it may be more like ±1' or even ±2'. The question at hand here is, how do you know what that scatter is, and how do we average it out. We should note here, that even beginners, after good instruction, can do a series of sights well within ±1' in good conditions. The use of a sextant is not a magic art, and all who care to learn it can do so with only modest practice and good instruction.

The other very important point to note here is that the actual extent of the scatter is not crucial to the final accuracy of the fix, assuming it is truly random, and assuming we know how to evaluate it properly. In other words, we can get just as good a fix out of sights that scatter by an arc minute or more among individual sights as we can from a set of sights that are consistent to within a few tenths of a minute of each other.

Start with the Right Stars

The first step toward a good fix is a good selection of the bodies we use (stars or star-planet combination). We want to choose three bodies that are as near 120° apart in bearing as possible. This is the most important criteria, because it minimizes any constant (systematic) error that is common to each of the sights, such as an index error or personal bias on what proper alignment is.

The intersection of three LOPs from perfect sights will intersect in a single point, but if there is a constant error in each sight, we end up with a triangle of intersecting LOPs, often called a cocked hat. With no random error and just this constant error in each sight, each line of a 120° fix will be offset from the proper fix by the amount equal to that error, but the center of the triangle remains an accurate fix. On the other hand, if the sights are not 120° apart, this is no longer true, and indeed the proper fix could be outside of the cocked hat (Figure 11.24-1). So step one is a proper bearing distribution whenever possible.

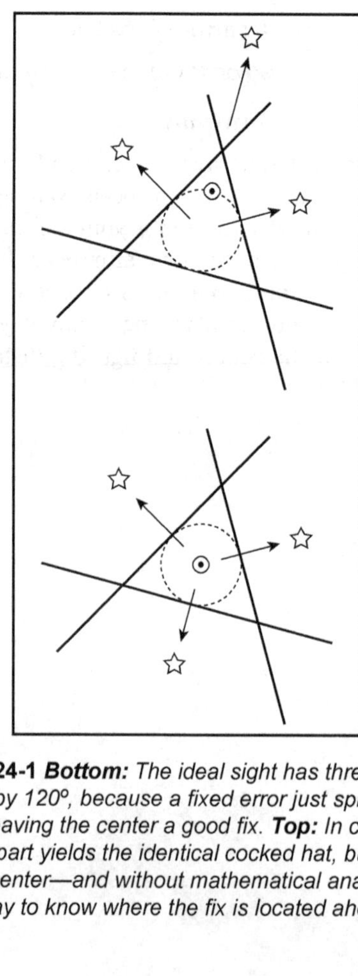

Figure 11.24-1 ***Bottom:*** *The ideal sight has three stars differing in bearing by 120°, because a fixed error just spreads the cocked hat apart leaving the center a good fix.* ***Top:*** *In contrast, three stars 60° apart yields the identical cocked hat, but the fix is no longer in the center—and without mathematical analysis, we would have no way to know where the fix is located ahead of time.*

Next we would choose the brightest bodies to fill the triad, if we have a choice without sacrificing bearings, simply because they are easier to see when the horizon is still sharp. Next if we have the choice, again without sacrificing bearing quality, we would choose stars at about the same height. This would tend to minimize differences in refraction among them, and refraction is usually the main uncertainty in many sights. This is why we always choose sights above about 15° whenever possible. Likewise, for routine work we would avoid sights above some 75° when possible. Very high sights are more difficult to take accurately because when getting close to overhead we do not know which way to look when we rock the sextant.

Very high sights also cannot be reduced in the normal manner, because the approximation of the circle of position as a short line segment is no longer valid (Section 10.6). For these sights we need to plot the actual circle of position on the chart as a circle of radius equal to the zenith distance, centered at the GP.

For the more general case of a set of three sights, at separations that are not exactly 120° apart, with a constant error among them, along with potentially different random uncertainties on each body (i.e., horizon better in one direction than another or one star notably fainter or lower than the others), we have a mathematical solution for the most likely position in Section 11.32—although most navigators would tend to choose some centroid location within the cocked hat, and just increase the assigned fix uncertainty to account for all of the intersections.

Check Assumed Positions when Plotting

Before we start to evaluate a full set of sights for optimum accuracy, we should pause at the end of the sight reduction to check that our basic assumptions are in order for the sights at hand. How we do this depends on how we are doing the sight reduction. If we are using a computer or nav app for sight reduction and position fixing, this step can be skipped completely, because the location of the assumed position (AP) does not matter when computing a fix. With calculator solutions, we generally use our DR at the fix time as the basis of the computations, and even if the DR is way off, the programs will work around this either by solving for intersecting circles of position, or iterating lines of position (LOPs) automatically, as explained in the manual approach below. In any event the choice of AP is not a concern for computed solutions, but we must consider this when doing manual solutions using plotting.

When doing sight reduction by hand using tables and manual plotting, we must check that none of the lines leading to our plotted fix are too long. This can happen with manual sight reduction as we must choose an AP based on the minutes part of the GHA and our DR Lat and Lon. We can always choose the AP to be within 30' of the DR, but even then with various configurations of body bearings and APs, we can end up with large a-values. If the DR position was wrong by a lot, meaning the distance between the DR position and the fix found using the APs chosen properly for each sight, then the a-values can get even much larger. In this case the distance between the fix and the azimuth line measured along the LOP can get large as well. The lines that can get too long are illustrated in Figure 11.24-2.

We might consider that any crucial line in our plotted fix that is over (or approaching) 60 nmi should be considered too long for best results, meaning they may violate our basic assumptions in the plotting. Underlying the manual plotting solution is the assumption that the LOP itself is a valid straight-line approximation to a segment of a circle of equal altitude (see Section 10.6), and we assume that the azimuth line is a segment of a great circle, even though we are plotting it as a straight rhumb line. These approximations can break down when the lines get too long. The consequences of this also depends on the direction they are oriented, but a generic filter on the lengths should catch all cases.

The solution to long lines on the plot, is to plot the fix in the normal way, then read that Lat and Lon and call that the new DR for these sights. Then do the sight reduction again using this DR, which will call for new APs, and then the lines will all be shorter, and the fix you get will be more accurate.

In most cases of routine cel nav—see *Hawaii by Sextant* for examples—we can proceed as normal, and will not find any excessively long lines, but if we do, we can fix it. On the other hand, if we suspect ahead of time that our DR could be wrong by over 40 miles or so, then we might do a quick 2-LOP fix to check the lines and find a new best DR to use before any further analysis.

The instructions to Pub 229 include a Table of Offsets for curving the LOPs to help with this correction. That table shows corrections of several miles for lines L1 or L2 of just 45 miles. Errors due to long a-values are more subtle and depend on the azimuths; they occur when a straight line approximation to the azimuth line diverges from the curved great circle track between AP and GP.

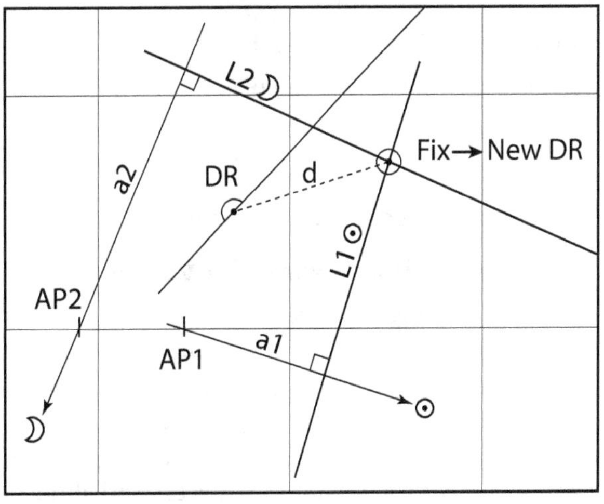

Figure 11.24-2 *Crucial lengths defined. If any of these are approaching 60 nmi long, we should use the fix for a new DR and redo the sight reduction.*

In summary, any of the crucial lines in a fix plot approaching 60 nmi long should call for getting a new DR from the fix and redoing the sight reduction. Errors of several miles can occur without this precaution. Such errors are larger for high sights, above 70° or so, and line lengths can get enhanced when DR Lat is about halfway between two parallels. See starpath.com/celnavbook for more.

Evaluating a Sight Sequence

Before we can plot the LOPs, however, we need some way to evaluate each set of sights of an individual body. In other words, we are taking say five sights of one star, and we want to somehow average these into just one sight to take advantage of the statistic nature of measurements.

The problem is not a trivial one, because the sextant height itself is changing with time; so we naturally expect each one to be different from the last one. Looking to the east, the sight angle will be getting bigger with time as the body rises, and looking west they will get smaller as the body sets. Measuring a sextant altitude for a fix is not like measuring your pulse rate, which you can just do many times in a row and then perform a simple average to get an accurate value. We must evaluate a sequence of sights and use their relative values to determine if individual ones might be in doubt. Furthermore, we are moving while we take the sights, so even if the stars did not rise and set, their heights in our sextant would change because we are changing positions.

A set of sample data taken on land is shown below. This shows clearly that you can practice this important method even at a lake shore, but when underway we have to account for our motion in the process.

DR 47° 38' N, 122° 20'W (Gasworks Park on Lake Union in Seattle, where we once did student practice sights), ZD=+8h, WE = 7s fast, HE = 7 ft. IC = 3.5' off the scale. Sights of the sun's lower limb. Note that we must use dip short for the ultimate evaluation of these sights, but that is not the issue at hand.

WT	Hs
14h 43m 11s	27° 42.3'
14h 45m 46s	27° 29.0'
14h 47m 53s	27° 12.0'
14h 49m 23s	27° 02.5'

This data is plotted in Figure 11.24-3

Averaging Advanced a-Values

One way to average these sights for the best LOP if you have a computer solution, is the following:

Do the sight reductions of each one from the DR position to get an a-value and Zn for each. (When underway, these sights would have to be advanced to the time of the DR used—a numerical way to do that is covered at the end of this section.)

For example, using the DR position above and HE=0 (which does not matter for this analysis) we get the following values:

14h 43m 11s a = 17.8' T 221

14h 45m 46s a = 21.6' T 221

14h 47m 53s a = 18.8' T 222

14h 49m 23s a = 19.4' T 222

At this point, since we have removed the time dependence of the sight altitude, we can simply average the four a-values to get: a = 19.4' T 222.

This would seem a reasonably good way to combine the four independent sights into one best value that averages out the random errors of individual sights–but there are nuances.

Looking at the list of LOPs and also at the plot of the Hs values, it appears that the second sight (14:45:46) is too high. It might seem reasonable to drop this one out of the list and average the rest. This would give: a = 18.7' T 222, which is a big effect (19.4 to 18.7 is a shift of 0.7 miles in this average LOP). We could take the attitude that our careful detection of one sight that was out of line has improved our accuracy by more than half a mile.

In other words, computing all the a-values, noting if any are well outside the other values, throwing them out, and averaging the rest could be considered one way of "sight averaging." All of this presumes we are computing our sight reductions; this approach would be essentially impossible in any reasonable time if each had to be reduced and advanced by hand.

Furthermore, we will show that this simplified averaging of computed solutions is not guaranteed to yield the correct result. It could well be that shifting the 19.4 to the 18.7 was a mistake. The motivation for throwing out the second sight was that it was well off the line *that the other three fit onto*. We assumed that nature was kind in this regard, i.e., three in a row must be right. Clearly, we need some method to evaluate which sights are far enough off to be discarded, i.e., to conclude that they may be blunders or isolated errors. For example, if a sight is 5 miles off, it is almost certainly wrong, and if we keep it, we will be pulling the average off the proper value. So how do we proceed?

Fit-Slope Method

The trick is simple. We fine tune the line we are fitting to. In the last example, we simply took the best line that fit the most data points and drew it. It could have been any line, meaning in this case a line with any slope to it. But the trick is that we know the slope. This does not have to be a free ranging option in selecting the best line. We can calculate the proper slope and then just slide that line up and down the page for the best fit to the data. Once we have that line in place, we have firmer ground to stand on as we pitch out some of our sights.

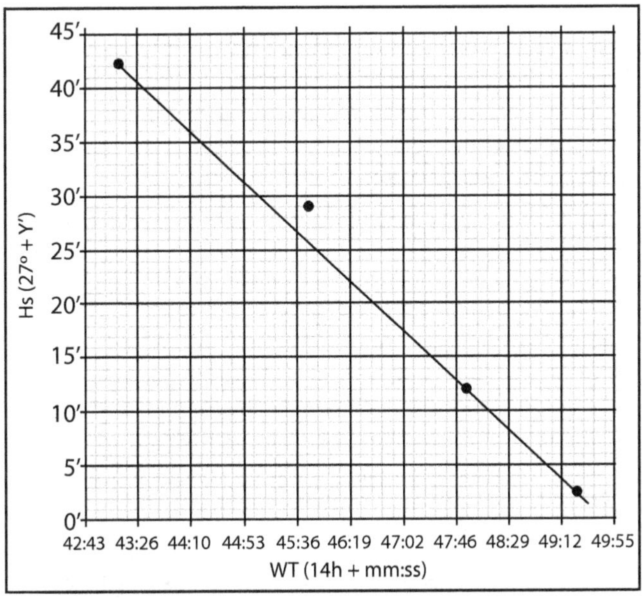

Figure 11.24-3 *Sextant height plotted versus time. It appears that the second sight is inconsistent with the other three.*

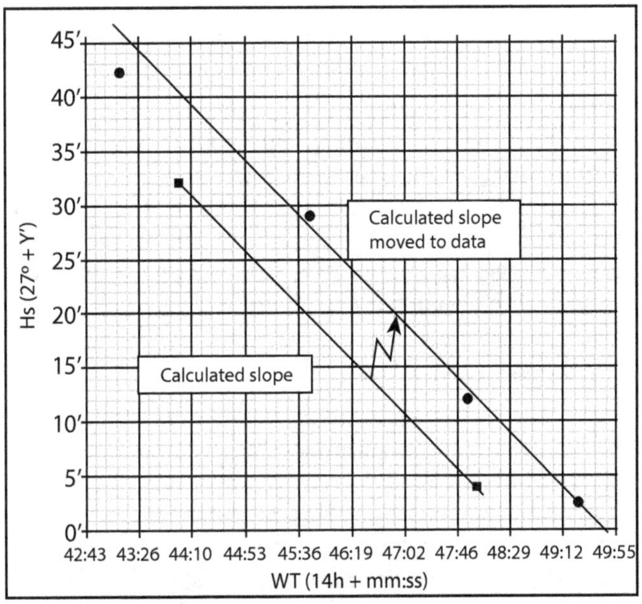

Figure 11.24-4 *Same data as Figure 11.24-3 with the calculated slope plotted. Forcing the fit line to the proper slope we see that it was not the second sight that was wrong, but the first one.*

To calculate the slope, we do a sight reduction at some time near the beginning of the sight session to get Hc and Zn (we do not need the latter) and then do the same thing at some time near the end of the sight session. In the previous example, we chose to do the computation at 14h 44m 00s to get Hc = 26° 3.3', and then again at 14h 48m 00s to get Hc = 25° 35.7'. This tells us that the sun at this time and place was setting at a rate of 63.3-35.7 = 27.6' per 4 minutes of time.

We can now draw in that line on the same plot with the data and then use parallel rules or plotter to move it up to fit the data (Figure 11.24-4). Just slide this line up and down to get the best fit position. There is no rotating it now for the best fit. We know that all good sights will be rising or falling at this rate. To draw the line, just choose any convenient place on the 1444 line to mark the first Hc then at 1448 mark another Hc that is 28' lower. Note that actual values of Hc used here do not matter so long as they are plotted on the right times and are 28' apart.

If we are computing Hc, it is trivial to do these two sight reductions; it takes just a minute or two. But if we are using tables, we must do one more trick to make it work. We can't just choose two arbitrary times, since we won't be able to get a whole-degrees value of LHA for use in the tables. So we simply do it once properly from a time early in the sights or just before it (in this case 1444), and then get Hc from that, and then look up the Hc for the same declination and latitude but for an LHA which is 1° higher. This will give the Hc for 4 minutes later (1448). You can then use these two values to figure the slope. If the d-value in the sight reduction tables is the same at both LHAs, then you do not even need to figure the d-correction, since that will not change the slope. Using Pub. 249 for the above calculations, you get Hc at 1444 (Lat = 48° N, Dec = S 6°, LHA = 38°) = 26° 32' and at 1448 (Lat = 48° N, Dec = S 6°, LHA = 39°) = 26° 04', which gives the same 28' per 4 minutes slope that we got by computer.

Figure 11.24-4 shows this result applied to the sight data at hand. Note the interesting result that poor old Sight No.2 that we were so ready to throw out was probably quite OK. The problem sight was No. 1, which looks off by more than 4' or so! That is one we can effectively throw out by simply ignoring it. What we want now as a best estimate of the full set is any point on the best fit line, and generally we do that by just choosing a sight that is on the line. Thus we end up with just one sight, but this process has effectively averaged the others to let us know this one is a good representation of the lot.

It's too late to say "in short," but at least in summary, this is a good trick to know for evaluating sextant sights. It is especially valuable on those days when the electronics have failed completely and the sky has been overcast for some days and you are anxious for at least a good LOP, and all you get is three hurried sights in broken cloud cover and choppy seas, and you have to make the best of these. Once the data are analyzed in this manner, we then just select one sight from the good data line and sight reduce it. In this example, we could use the last sight, right on the line, or we could use sight No 2 and take 1' off the value (it was not way out of line at all!), or sight No. 3 and add 1' or use the purely fictitious sight at 47:02 with an Hs of 27° 19.0'. We did not actually measure a height at this last time, but if we had, that is most likely what we would have gotten. Any one of these sights is a proper average of the full set of four, but it took the full set of four, and some reasoning, to pick it out.

Remember when you are underway, the two sight reductions for the slope will be from different DR positions to account for the slope you expect to see when moving. In contrast to just averaging the a-values (when all sights must be advanced to a single time), in the fit-slope method you do not advance the sights because the predicted slope from the two DRs is what you would expect to see when moving between these two positions. Later when you have found the best line from a sequence at a specific time, and then also another best line from another body at a specific time, these two (or more) lines will need to be advanced to a common time for the final fix.

Automatic Advancement of LOPs

We know that typical running fixes from the sun must be advanced as they are typically taken over a period of several hours, but it is equally important for the best star fix to advance *all* LOPs, even those from the same session. If you find two best lines that are 20 minutes apart when moving at 6 kts, you have a 2-mile uncertainty on the sights if this is not accounted for.

The typical plotting scale we use on universal plotting sheets, however, makes it difficult to precisely make corrections that are just a mile or two long. Thus we can use a trick to compute the shift in the a-value that will account for the advancement to a common time. It is a trick we have used since the early 1980s, but it is definitely in the finesse category. That is, with careful plotting, you can always do the advancement in the standard way using parallel rulers or roller plotter. The formula and its derivation are shown in Figure 11.24-5.

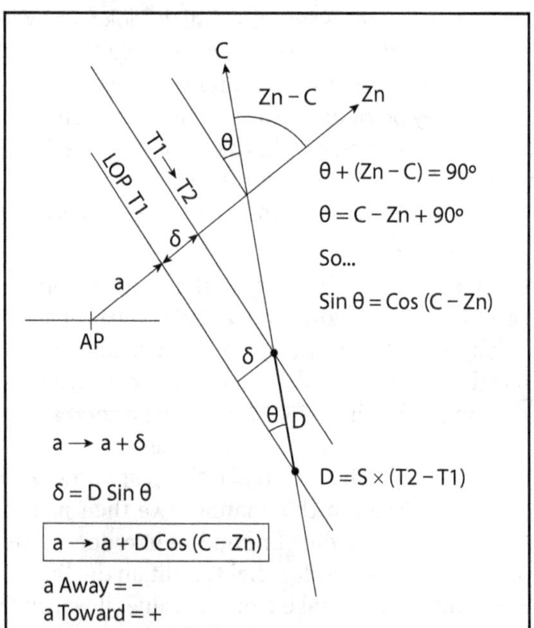

Figure 11.24-5. *To advance or retard an LOP that has an a-value and azimuth Zn for a distance D run in true direction C, add algebraically to the a-value a correction given by D × Cos (Zn - C). D is figured from the speed made good between sights, times the time difference between the two sights. This correction can be positive or negative. Initial and corrected a-values Toward Zn are positive; those Away from Zn are negative. Then plot from the same assumed position and Zn, but use the corrected a-value in place of the original. Thus a = 5T, with correction +2, the new a is 7T. A correction of -8 would give a new a = 3A. An initial a=5A with a correction of +6, yields a new a = 1T.*

This trick can be used for standard sun line running fixes or for a star series if you do not plan to use the fit-slope method. It is especially valuable if you are computing your solutions but your program does not do the running fixes automatically, which is the case with many of the packaged cel nav programs.

In this case, you just make a list of the times, a-values and Zns, compute the distance run from the base time you are using as the DR for the computations, and then correct each one, see if any really stands out as likely wrong, and then average the rest. As noted earlier, you might miss the outliers this way, compared to a full fit-slope analysis, but most of the time this will be fine. For this procedure it is usually best to choose the DR to be at the time of the last fix, then the individual run distances are quicker to calculate.

We have even seen cases, where a plot of Hs versus WT for the raw data seemed to imply one sight was wrong, but when advancing all to the same time, we learned that it was in fact another that was off—similar to what we saw with the fit-slope example.

You can also use this method to advance the three best sights from a fit-slope solution to a common time.

A good way to see these special analyses techniques in action is our new book *Hawaii by Sextant* (Starpath Publications, 2015). It includes some 250 sights making up 27 fixes, many of which use these methods. It uses real data from a 1982 voyage that used nothing but cel nav for an ocean passage. Samples of fixes from that book using the methods of this section are in Figure 11.28-1.

11.25 Star and Planet ID

A navigator does not need to know any stars by heart, nor even how to point out in the sky the very stars being used for a routine celestial fix. We have covered how to select the best stars ahead of time and then precompute their heights and bearings, and in doing so we could just call them Star-A, Star-B, etc. We do not care what constellation they are in, how they move, or how long they might be visible. All the paperwork and procedures have been worked out over the years to take care of that for us. We can even take sights of stars we do not know at all and did not predict, and then do a bit of paperwork after the fact to figure out which star we used and carry on routinely.

On the other hand, there is certainly much satisfaction in learning something of the stars for our own enlightenment, not to mention that others on the boat are going to assume we know something about the stars and might ask us questions about them. So if you wish to be prepared for that eventuality, a little diversion on star gazing will be useful.

Furthermore, take away our standard tools and we are left with our knowledge alone. And for emergency navigation without instruments or tables, the more you know about the stars, the better off you will be.

Identifying Stars and Planets

To identify a particular star or planet from its approximate height and bearing, the traditional maritime tool since the early 1940s has been the 2102-D Star Finder (Figure 11.25-1). This is a set of plastic plates about 10 inches in diameter that will identify the body seen at a specific height in a specific direction at a specific time from your latitude. You

Figure 11.25-1 *2102-D Star Finder and book on how to use it.*

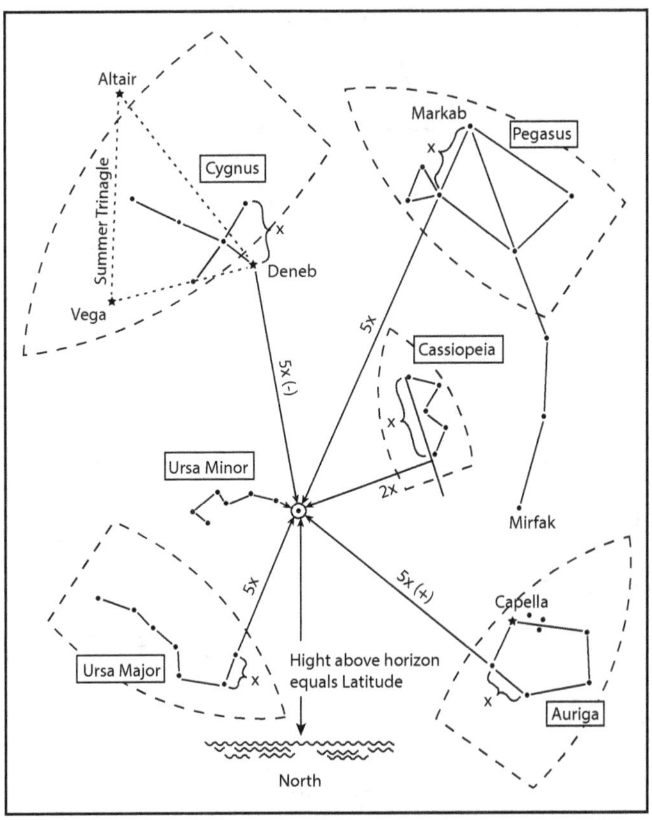

only need the *Nautical Almanac* to compute the local hour angle of Aries at the sight time.

This device is a powerful navigation aid that can be used for much more than just star ID, including selecting the best star-planet sight options, predicting rise and set times, choosing optimum sun-moon sight times, and more. Because of its value to navigators, we have a short book devoted to how to use it: *The Star Finder Book: A Complete Guide to the Many Uses of the 2102-D Star Finder* (Starpath Publications, 2008). Please refer to that book for the details.

These days there are numerous mobile apps that will also identify celestial bodies, often by just pointing the phone at the unknown body. The phone has a compass in it so it knows which way you are looking; it has an inclinometer in it so it knows the height above the horizon; it has a clock in it so it knows what time it is; and it has a GPS in it so it knows where you are. Needless to say, all of the sensors have to be calibrated, but when that is done, these work remarkably well. These astro apps were one of the first hot apps for the phones. They are more sophisticated than the 2102-D—until they get wet, get dropped, or run out of power, which is when we start looking for that bag of essentially indestructible plastic disks.

Thus during routine sights, if we get caught having to take a sight of an unknown body, the only thing extra we have to do is take an approximate bearing to the body. Then with the precise time and Hs of the sight, along with its approximate Zn (measured with a compass and corrected for variation), we can easily figure out what the body was. The bearing taken does not have to be precise. I recall once just pointing to a star and asking the helmsman which way I was pointing, and that was good enough.

Learning the Stars

There is a certain satisfaction in getting to know the stars. They are dependable, probably the most dependable of all the things about us. In foreign lands where everything else is different, the stars are still the same. In unfamiliar places, it can be pleasantly reassuring to spot a few familiar stars. Besides the ethereal comfort of a familiar overhead, stars provide the more mundane service of orientation in time as well as space, not to mention the overwhelming physical objects they are to think about themselves. Anyone who spends much time outdoors, in boats or boots, can benefit from knowing something of the stars.

To travel very far into unknown places requires some means of keeping track or bearing. A compass is the obvious tool for the job, and compasses are indeed very reliable

Figure 11.25-2 *Pointing stars of the northern sky. Each set points to Polaris at the end of the handle of the Little Dipper (Ursa Minor); in each case, the distance to Polaris is approximately five times the pointer spacing. In the Big Dipper (Ursa Major), the pointers are the leading stars. In this group, the cup leads and the handle trails. Auriga is a prominent pentagon, led by the bright star Capella and a small group of faint stars called the Kids. Its pointers are the trailing two stars of the pentagon. The Great Square of Pegasus is led by a small triangle of stars, with the handle of a "Giant Dipper" trailing behind. Deneb, at the head of the Northern Cross (Cygnus), together with Vega and Altair make up a prominent right triangle (the Summer Triangle) which is led across the sky by the brilliant Vega at the right angle. Note that in each of these groups, the pointers are either the leading or trailing stars. Polaris is always located at an angular height above the horizon equal to your latitude. Adapted from the book* Emergency Navigation *(McGraw-Hill 2008).*

devices, ranking not far behind the wheel in their utility-to-simple ratio. Nevertheless, they are still fallible devices that can be lost or broken. They can also give misleading readings whenever iron metal is nearby. If a compass reading is in doubt, there are various ways to check it, on land or sea, but without practice at these checks, the check itself can be in doubt. Stars take away the doubt. If a compass does not agree with the stars, the compass is wrong. With no compass at all available, stars can provide the bearings you need to carry on.

One might think that the sun would be a better choice of stellar reference for bearings out of doors. It is certainly the most conspicuous star during most of the time we might need this help. In some circumstances, with special preparation for the job, the sun can tell directions throughout the day. But as a rule the sun is not reliable for this purpose—without a watch, it is outright difficult to use. Well-known rules about the sun are of little value when specific directions are needed. "The sun rises in the east" for example, is a broad guideline at best. Along the Canadian-American border during early summer, the sun rises about 40° north of east, and in the early winter about 40° south of east. Even at the equator during these periods, this rule is wrong by roughly 24°—recall that if your bearing is wrong by just 6° you will go off 1 mile for every 10 you travel. In Alaska, this sunrise rule is useless most of the time. In contrast, the trick of pointing the hour hand of your watch toward the sun and calling 12 o' clock south works pretty well in northern Alaska (hence the name Eskimo Watch Method), but it is nearly useless most of the time at lower latitudes. The basic principles of star steering, on the other hand, work anywhere on earth, any time of the night.

The North Star, Polaris, is the most popular star for direction finding. It bears within 2° of due north at any sighting; so if it happens to be visible and can be identified, you can figure the bearing of any direction relative to it without training or knowledge. But Polaris is not bright and cannot be counted on when needed—it is also not visible below about 5° N. Limited to it alone the resource is not that great. Stellar bearings, however, can be found from any star or group of stars, so the resource is indeed a great one. The process of steering by the stars consists of several individual tricks for specific stars and times of night together with an overlying philosophy of orientation. Which aspect of the process dominates at any one time depends on how much and what part of the sky you can see. For now we will take a brief look at the philosophy and then a more specific look at a few tricks for northern stars.

One productive approach to learning the stars is to learn to find directions from the stars. This way you get involved with a few at a time while you can still use streets and other landmarks to test yourself. Then move to the next group.

To read directions from the stars requires a bit of memory and work and reckoning to begin with, but with practice, the process becomes much more intuitive and natural. The principle is easy; it is no different than learning geography—with a twist, if you will, from the rotating earth. Viewing a map of North America, for example, you could easily point to north on the map, or any other direction, if you choose to. Even if the map were spinning and tumbling through the air as you watched it, you could still point north on the map whenever you got a glimpse of it, regardless of the orientation of the map at that moment. We can do this because we have memorized the shape and orientation of the continent. More to the point, even if just one province or state could be seen outlined on the rotating map for a moment, you would know north on the map as a whole for the same reason.

In stellar geography, the constellations are the states and provinces, and groups of constellations are the continents. By knowing the shapes and orientation of the con-

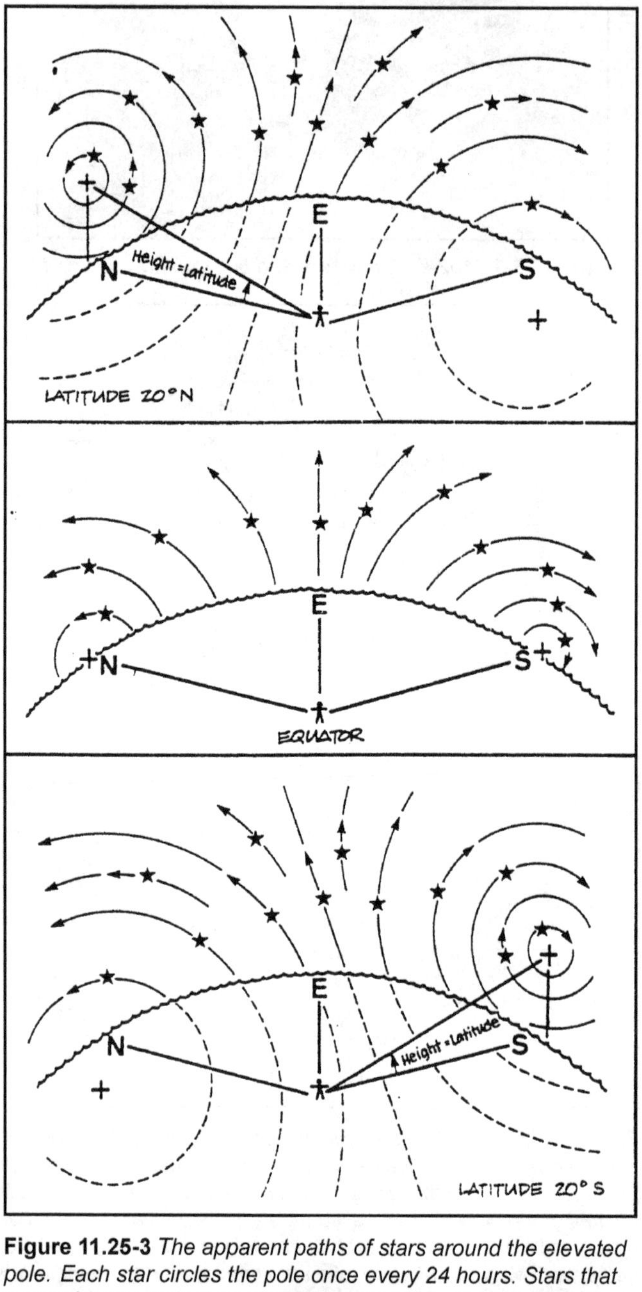

Figure 11.25-3 *The apparent paths of stars around the elevated pole. Each star circles the pole once every 24 hours. Stars that never rise or set as they circle are called circumpolar stars; they remain in view all night long, every night of the year.*

stellations, or any grouping of stars, north can be read from them just as it would be from a map. The slow rotation of the stars across the sky presents different perspectives of the group throughout the night, but their relative orientation to the North Pole of the sky does not change. The main problem is that constellations aren't as prominent as state boundaries and we need tricks to help with learning and recognizing them. An advantage we do have with the stars, however, is our freedom to define the constellations however we choose for this purpose. Just form a group in your mind from whatever guys are prominent in the neighborhood and give them a name. An example is the *Summer Triangle* also called the *Navigator's Triangle* made up of Altair, Vega, and Deneb, the three brightest stars of neighboring constellations—see top left part of Figure 11.25-2.

To help remember the orientation and relative locations of the stars, we can imagine figures in the sky, just as stargazers have done since the beginning of time. The stars all move along predictable paths; so once a particular group is chosen, it pays to memorize which stars or parts of the group are leading and which are trailing as they proceed across the sky. One way is to think of the group as a vessel, and memorize which parts are the bow and which parts are the stern. Then each group becomes a boat sailing counterclockwise around Polaris, located at the hub on the northern sky. Due north on the horizon is directly below this point. With a sky full of boats all sailing in a circle around the North Pole it is easy to keep track of the north. Even if you only see one boat you know north is on her port beam. By knowing how far the pole is off the beam of that boat relative to star spacing within the group north can be found more precisely from that group alone.

This description of the philosophy applies best when looking toward the northern sky. A similar model works looking south toward the southern stars sailing the opposite direction around the South Pole of the sky (Figure 11.25-3). Looking east or west, the philosophy can be thought of another way. We know that stars rise from the eastern horizon and set on the western horizon. Consequently, if we know which side of the horizon is west, we can tell which direction stars are headed for. To steer by the stars, use the same approach in reverse: learn which way the stars are moving (by knowing the bows and sterns of various groups), and from this figure out where west is.

With this picture in mind and a broad view of the horizon you can end up steering by the "shape of the sky" as a whole rather than relying on individual stars or groups of stars. Some form of this method was probably used by early seafaring cultures that traveled long distances without compasses. Arabian, Scandinavian, and Polynesian methods are the best documented and the only ones that are to some extent still practiced today. I have found only indirect references to this type of philosophy in the literature, but it is easy to imagine how early navigators made up pictures of the sky for this purpose. People or animals chasing each other across the sky would do as well as boats, and they might be easier to build stories around so that the pictures could be passed on without written records.

Even with this guiding philosophy, however, more specific tricks for individual star groups are often helpful in finding precise directions. Polynesian navigators had many such tricks but in most cases these worked only in the latitudes of their islands, and most were incorporated into routes from one island to another rather than being general ways to find directions. For general use we need more general tricks. Again, we are free to make these up to suit our needs. Figure 11.25-2 illustrates one approach that covers most of the northern sky. These are just one set of tricks; the same stars can be regrouped and used in different ways to find directions.

The methods shown in Figure 11.25-2 use *pointing stars* to locate the position of Polaris, since it is this position that is needed to locate north and not the star itself. North can be found with any of these pointing stars nearly as well as it can be with Polaris itself, and at least one set of these pointers is likely to be visible when Polaris is obscured by haze, clouds, or hills. Figure 11.25-2 illustrates the use of pointers to find due north on the horizon.

The pointers in Figure 11.25-2 are each chosen to have a distance to Polaris of five times the pointer spacing. To remember the factor: you point with your finger, each hand has five fingers. The (±) labels indicate distances slightly larger or smaller than exactly five.

Mintaka

The leading star of Orion's belt (the three close stars, evenly-spaced, at the center of the figure) is the special one for star steering (Figure 11.25-4). The name of this special star is Mintaka, and, setting aside small differences, it is special because it is neither a southern star nor a northern star, as it straddles the celestial equator (halfway between

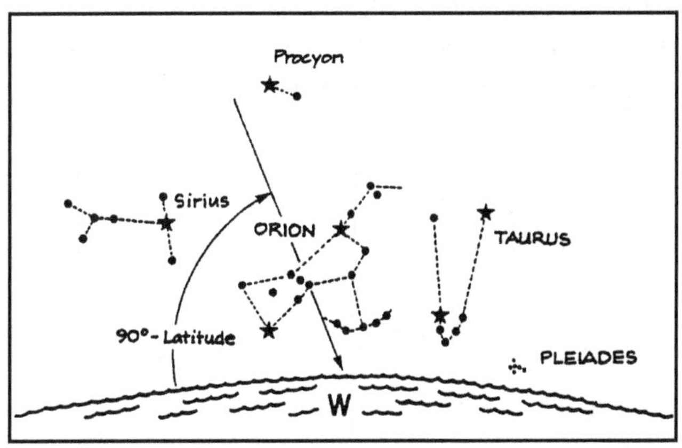

Figure 11.25-4 *Orion on the horizon. From any point on earth, at any time of night, Orion's belt always rises due east and sets due west. The Seven Sisters, Pleiades, lead the chase of nearby stars. Taurus the Bull follows, fighting off Orion whose faithful hunting dogs, Sirius and Procyon. trail close behind. Betelgeuse, at the base of Orion's raised arm, and Aldebaran, at the eye of the Bull, are brilliant red giant stars. Mintaka is the leading star of the belt, closest to the horizon.*

the South Pole and the North Pole), circling the earth daily directly above the earth's equator. And just as the sun does on the equinoxes—when it happens to be directly over the equator—Mintaka always rises due east and sets due west, from wherever and whenever it is sighted. Unlike the sun, however, which spends only a few days each year over the equator, Mintaka lives there permanently. Any time you happen to see Orion's Belt on the horizon (in Canada or Australia), it is just as good as a big letter "E" marking due east when rising, or a big letter "W" marking due west when setting.

Even more important, however, we need not see Mintaka just as it crosses the horizon in order to use it for accurate bearings. By knowing the angle that stars rise and set, we can project the star forward (when setting) or backward (when rising) to locate where it actually will or did cross the horizon. The proper angle to use is 90° minus your latitude, as illustrated in Figure 11.25-4. In Hawaii or Rio de Janerio, at latitudes of about 20° (north or south does not matter here), eastern stars rise steeply at 70°; whereas at high latitudes such as Anchorage or Tierra del Fuego at latitudes of about 60°, eastern or western stars rise and set gently at only 30°. To do this pointing to the horizon, the rising or setting angle must be estimated by eye, but the angle need not be precise to get a good indication of east or west (see Figure 11.25-4). Near the equator, Mintaka bearings are especially easy, and they are useful at any time. Near the equator, stars rise straight up from the horizon (90° - 0°), so viewed from anywhere near the equator, Mintaka not only rises due east but it remains due east throughout the night until it passes over head, after which it remains due west until it sets.

Other tricks can be developed from special stars at certain latitudes. Some work in only special cases, such as high in the sky or low on the horizon, but the practice of creating and testing them is both functional and instructive. For more information on navigation in general without conventional instruments, please see *Emergency Navigation.*

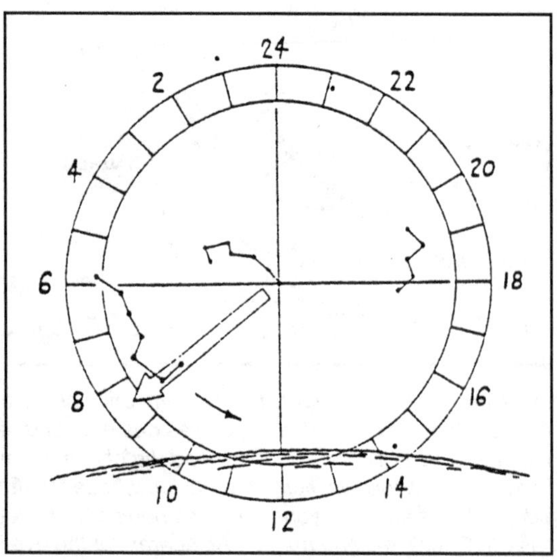

Figure 11.25-5 *Big Dipper star clock as it would appear reading 0830 hours*

For an informative and enjoyable treatment of the stars and constellations with excellent star maps see *North Star to Southern Cross* by Will Kyselka and Ray Lanterman. Another pleasant introduction to the stars is by H.A. Rey, called *The Stars: A New Way to See Them.*

Telling Time by the Stars

Any of the pointing stars can also be used to tell the time, although the need to do so is not likely to be as crucial as reading bearings from the stars might be. Most people who care about time wear a watch or carry a cell phone, and even without a watch we can usually get by without time more easily than without bearings. In any event, it can be done and it is a resource that is potentially more than a novelty. Learning to tell time from the stars requires learning the rate at which stars circle the pole and which paths they follow across the sky, for example, and this extra understanding of star motions will ultimately help in reading bearings from the sky.

As is the case with tricks for finding bearings, there is no exclusive way to tell time from the stars; so we are free to make up whatever method works. To make up generalized star clocks that work on any arbitrary day of the year, however, does require some background in celestial navigation which we now have. It is much easier to make up specific clocks on the spot, using a correct watch to calibrate it for the present date, and then use it on following nights by applying a simple daily correction. This does not require special reference books and calculations.

To tell time from the Big Dipper, as one example of a generalized star clock, imagine its pointers as the end of clock hands whose pivot point is Polaris and imagine a 24-hour clock face printed backward on the sky around Polaris as shown in Figure 11.25-5. Midnight (0000 hours or 2400 hours) is straight up from Polaris; 0600 hours is to the west of Polaris and 1800 hours to the east. In 24 hours, the pointers sweep counterclockwise once around this clock face.

When the clock hand points straight up from the horizon, the clock reads midnight; when the hands point east with the pointers lying parallel to the horizon, the clock reads 1800, and so forth. To read the clock at any time of the night, estimate the hour and fraction of an hour from the relative orientation of the pointers on the imaginary clock face. That's all there would be to it if the sun kept pace with the stars. But the sun does not keep pace with the stars, and our daily timekeeping is based on the sun so we must make a correction for this.

All star clocks are fast; they gain 4 minutes every day, because we keep track of time relative to the location of the sun, and we are moving around the sun relative to the stars at a rate of about 1° per day (360°/365d). Thus, when we make our daily 24-hour rotation from noon to noon (relative to the sun), we are then 1° farther along our orbit; so we have passed any stars overhead by 1°. At our daily rotation rate of 360°/24 hours, this 1° is equivalent to 4 minutes.

If you look at the same star on successive nights at the same time, it will be 1° farther (more westward) along its path across the sky. Thus, if you want to see it at the same place on successive nights, you have to look 4 minutes earlier. This is basically how new stars appear on the eastern horizon at sunset as the seasons progress—although that is a bit more complicated because the time of sunrise is also changing. (We learn star positions relative to Aries, so check out the value of GHA Aries on successive days at the same time and you will see that it increases by about 1°.)

At a gain of 4 minutes per day, star clocks gain a whole day in 1 year; so all star clocks reset themselves on a particular date that depends on the particular star clock in use—and by star clock we mean any two stars with the same SHA so that the line between them rotates around the pole. The Big Dipper star clock resets itself on March 8th so all corrections must be reckoned from that date. (Official scientific star time used by astronomers resets on the Vernal Equinox, March 21st; the shift to March 8th comes about because scientific star time does not use the Big Dipper pointers for a reference line.)

To tell time from the Big Dipper, we need to know how many days have passed since March 8th. The time we read directly from the star clock is then fast by 4 minutes for each of these days. As an example, suppose the date was September 22nd and the stars looked as they do in Figure 11.25-5, with the star clock reading 0830. September 22nd is 198 days past March 8th, so the clock is fast by 198 × 4 minutes, which equals 792 minutes, or 13 hours and 12 minutes. The first 12 hours of the correction just switches the time from AM to PM, so the correct time of night is 2030 - 0112, which equals 1918, or 7:18 PM local time.

Figuring the correction is a bit involved, but this preparation need only be done once, after which the results can be rearranged to be more convenient. On September 22nd, for example, you could make an equivalent new rule for reading this star clock: change the star clock time from AM to PM (or vice versa, later in the night) and then subtract 1 hour and 12 minutes. Each subsequent night, you would subtract an extra 4 minutes, because the clock is still gaining time each night.

The time you figure from the corrected star clock will be the proper standard time for your time zone to within, at worst, about 30 minutes. It would be exact only if you happened to be located right in the middle of a time zone, each of which is about 1 hour wide according to star time. Star clocks also do not know about daylight saving time, so when daylight saving time is in effect, you must add 1 hour to the final result. Corrections for both longitude (the time zone correction) and for daylight saving time can be made simultaneously if you calibrate the star clock with a known time. In the last example, if the uncorrected star clock read 0830 at a time you knew was 8:10 AM Pacific Daylight Time, the rule becomes much simpler: subtract 20 minutes tonight, and then 4 minutes less each subsequent night.

The final accuracy of the time obviously depends on how accurately the star clock itself is read, which requires an estimate of the angle between the clock hand and the horizon—similar to reading a stylish watch with no numbers on the dial. Sticks held in one line with the Pointers and one with the horizon can help with this. The angle found this way can then be transferred to a sketch of the clock or to the compass rose of a chart. Reading the clock by eye alone, however, is usually adequate. Note that in normal circumstances most people have an adequate sense of time even without a watch, but under a great deal of stress this is not the case at all. During long storms at sea, it is possible to even lose track of how many days have passed. This is not likely to happen in a routine cruising, but one could imagine getting caught in coastal waters at night without a safe harbor nearby. If the wind and seas began to build on top of this, one could easily muster enough stress to lose track of time. Without a watch, you could monitor the duration of the adventure with the stars.

(Note: A star clock resets when the common SHA of the two stars making up the clock hand leads to GHA = 0° 0' at 00 UTC. For the Big Dipper clock, Dubhe and Merak have SHA = 194° 4.2' ±14.3', so recalling that GHA * = GHA Aries + SHA *, we need the nearest date when GHA Aries = 360° - 194° 4.2' = 165° 55.8' at 00 UTC. You can get a rough estimate from the Planet Diagram, or interpolate the Almanac to find that this is March 8.)

Stargazing for orientation in time and space clearly requires some hands-on practice. It is not like learning the combination to a lock, that once memorized can be opened at will. It is more like learning to play a kazoo. You start by learning to play a few notes well, and pretty soon you are playing a fine tune. And the enjoyment to be had from exercising this skill can be just as rewarding. It is one way to get in a little more in tune with a dependable part of the environment.

11.26 Emergency Procedures

The *Nautical Almanac,* which includes Sight Reduction Tables, is the fundamental reference for celestial navigation. If you have these, you have all you need once the sextant sights are in hand. What you might lose, however, are the tools needed to take the sights, a sextant and correct UTC.

You can read your latitude from the stars that pass directly overhead since your latitude equals the declination of your zenith stars (Section 10.1). With practice and the almanac's list of star declinations you can find latitude this way to within 1° or so without sextant or UTC. The almanac also includes star maps that will help identify unknown stars from their positions relative to known ones.

The uncorrected sextant altitude of Polaris at unknown UTC will equal your latitude to within about 1° at worst from any location in the Northern Hemisphere. The Polaris Tables of the *Nautical Almanac* explain in detail how to apply corrections to a timed sight of Polaris to remove this 1° uncertainty.

With everything but a sextant, you can time the sunset or sunrise for an LOP. Call Hs (upper limb) 0° 0' at sunset or sunrise and carry out a normal sight reduction—although care must be taken in applying the sign (±) corrections and picking the altitude intercept label (Away or Toward), because one or more of the altitudes will be negative.

Approximate longitude can be found by calling the time halfway between sunrise and sunset equal to LAN and then looking up the sun's GHA at that UTC. The method is most accurate when not moving. Or, from a known latitude, figure what your longitude must be to have the observed UTC of sunrise or sunset agree with the *Nautical Almanac* prediction for your date and latitude.

Remember that even if your watch has an unknown watch error, two star sights will give the right latitude. The longitude, however, will be off by 15' for each 1 minute of watch error.

Steering without a compass is easily accommodated with celestial navigation by carrying out sight reductions of the sun periodically throughout the day and likewise for a few key stars at night to obtain true bearings. The 2102-D Star Finder (Section 11.25) is very convenient for this application, because it must be set up only once to use throughout the day or night.

Emergency navigation as a whole is discussed in detail in the book *Emergency Navigation*. This book remains the main reference for improvised and makeshift navigation techniques on all waters—the second edition even explains how to get an emergency LOP from a cell phone photo of the sun or moon low on the horizon. If a star or planet happened to be in view as well, you could get an actual fix.

The Starpath *Emergency Navigation Card* is a single sheet (two sides) that summarizes several emergency techniques for position finding and steering. It includes an abbreviated long-term almanac for the sun as well as extremely short set of Sight Reduction Tables that we call the N(x) Table (Section 11.30).

A more practical, user friendly solution to long-term cel nav is the *Long Term Almanac* by Geoffrey Kolbe (Starpath Publications, 2008). This includes accurate almanac data for the sun and stars valid until 2050, along with a complete set of the NAO Sight Reduction Tables, as well as Dip and Altitude Corrections tables. This is a complete and practical one-book celestial navigation solution that will last for many decades.

Lunars

If you have lost accurate time but still have all of your other equipment and books, you can find the time with the 18th century technique of lunar distance. This method relies on the fact that the moon moves rapidly enough through the stars that by careful measurement of its location relative to a star or planet along its path compared to the computed location of the moon from the *Nautical Almanac*, we can deduce the time of our measurement. The technique is relatively straight forward but tedious if the solution is to be made by tables alone, which is the only practical application in that with a computer or mobile app running we likely have other options for navigation.

The primary reference for lunars is *The Stark Tables for Clearing the Lunar Distance and Finding Universal Time from Sextant Observation* (Starpath Publications, 2010). With careful sights, a practiced user can routinely find the correct time to within about ± 30s and sometimes better. See http://davidburchnavigation.blogspot.com/2014/06/finding-longitude-by-lunar-distance.html for related discussion and links.

Lunar Altitudes

Without the special publications and measurements of a traditional lunar measurement, we can also find UTC from the moon in special circumstances, namely whenever we have a moon bearing roughly east or west at twilight.

To do this take a series of careful sights of two stars and the moon, rotating through them several times. Then use the Automatic Running Fix method of Section 11.24 to find the best average values of the three sights at one specific time on the watch whose error you do not know. Then sight reduce and plot the lines. The stars will intersect at your correct latitude but the moon line (near vertical as it was near east or west) will defer by an amount that reflects the error in your watch.

Then you just iterate the process with guess of the watch error till all three lines coincide and that is then the correct watch error. The procedure is illustrated with additional tricks to expedite the iterations at http://davidburchnavigation.blogspot.com/2013/01/utc-by-lunar-altitudes.html. This is an important process to add to your bag of tricks. Testing it on your own will be a worthwhile and instructive exercise.

11.27 Pub. 249 Vol. 1, Selected Stars

This first volume of Pub. 249 is distinctly different from the Vols. 2 and 3 that we use in the text for sight reduction. Vol. 1 can be used for two purposes. One is to precompute star sights to prepare for the actual sight taking, and the other is to actually reduce the star sights once they are taken. In other words, we can use Pub. 249 to predict the sights, and then reduce them however we like best, or we can also reduce them with that publication.

We do not start the course with the Vol. 1 star method, because we have to learn the basic procedures represented in Vols. 2 and 3 sight reduction, because it is the basis for traditional cel nav for all sights. It is also essentially the same method you would use with Pub. 229, which is the next step up in table precision.

With that said, we can now look at the special technique of star sight reduction by Pub. 249, Vol 1, and indeed some navigators might choose to use this method. It is relatively fast, although sometimes slightly less accurate, and we would still have to bounce back to the standard methods for sun, moon, and planets. On the other hand, since this method is quicker, we might end up taking more star sights, which is a positive.

For this application, you need Pub. 249 Vol. 1 Selected Stars. It is the first volume of the sight reduction tables we have used for the sun, moon, and planets, although this is a different type of book from Vols. 2 and 3. The name and volume sequencing is misleading, at best. Vols. 2 and 3, for example, are permanent publications, whereas Vol. 1 must be purchased every 5 years.

Instructions by Example

Here we will work through an example that shows both the prediction step (precomputation) and also the subsequent sight reduction. We will use evening star sights on October 25, 1978 from a DR position of (45° 22' N, 140° 15' W) as an example. The other data needed are: IC = 3.6' Off, HE = 9 ft, WE = 5s slow, ZD = + 9h.

Step 1. Predict the UTC that you will start the sights by looking up the time of evening civil twilight in the *Nautical Almanac*. The tabulated time is the UTC of civil twilight at Greenwich; so to find the time of twilight at your position, add your west longitude of 140° 15' in time units. (For morning sights, use the time of Nautical Twilight).

From T-4 (Daily pages), evening civil Twilight = 17h 28m at Lat 45° N.

From T-7 (Arc to time), 140° 15' W = + 9h 21m,

so UTC of civil twilight at your position = 26h 49m = 02h 49m October 26.

Step 2. Find LHA Aries at twilight just as we did for Polaris sights in Section 7.8. In this example the time is 02h 49m UTC on October 26.

From T-3 GHA Aries at 02h = 64° 5.7'

From T-11 the 49m 00s corr = +12° 17.0'

or GHA Aries at 02h 49m = 76° 22.7'

Now subtract DR-Lon West = -140° 15.0'

+360°

LHA Aries = 296° 7.7' rounded ⊠ 296.0°

Step 3. Use Pub. 249 Vol. 1 to find your stars by rounding off your DR-Lat to the nearest whole degree (45° N) and go to that page in Pub. 249 Vol.1, and then to the row labeled with the LHA Aries (296°). You will then find the predicted heights and bearings of the seven stars best suited for sights at this time. See example in Figure 11.27-1, which also lists the actual sights taken of the predicted stars.

Step 4. The three best of the seven are marked with an *, meaning these are the ones closest to 120° apart in bearing. Stars in CAPS are the bright ones. Take several sights of the three best in rotation as soon as the stars are visible.

LAT 45°N

LHA ♈	Hc	Zn	Hc	Zn	Hc	Zn	Hc	Zn	Hc	Zn	Hc	Zn	Hc	Zn
	♦Mirfak		Alpheratz		♦ALTAIR		Rasalhague		♦ARCTURUS		Alkaid		Kochab	
285	15 54	033	28 56	077	52 15	160	52 44	216	26 33	271	39 03	305	50 20	338
286	16 17	034	29 38	077	52 29	161	52 19	218	25 51	272	38 28	305	50 04	338
287	16 41	034	30 19	078	52 42	163	51 52	219	25 08	273	37 54	306	49 48	338
288	17 05	035	31 01	079	52 54	164	51 25	221	24 26	273	37 19	306	49 32	338
289	17 29	035	31 42	079	53 05	166	50 57	222	23 44	274	36 45	306	49 16	338
290	17 53	036	32 24	080	53 15	168	50 28	223	23 01	275	36 11	307	48 59	338
291	18 18	036	33 06	080	53 23	169	49 59	225	22 19	275	35 37	307	48 43	338
292	18 44	037	33 48	081	53 30	171	49 29	226	21 37	276	35 03	308	48 27	338
293	19 09	037	34 30	082	53 36	173	48 58	227	20 55	277	34 30	308	48 11	337
294	19 35	038	35 12	082	53 41	174	48 26	228	20 13	277	33 57	308	47 54	337
295	20 01	038	35 54	083	53 45	176	47 54	230	19 31	278	33 23	309	47 38	337
296	20 28	039	36 36	084	53 47	178	47 22	231	18 49	279	32 50	309	47 22	337
297	20 54	039	37 18	084	53 48	179	46 49	232	18 07	279	32 18	310	47 06	337
298	21 21	040	38 00	085	53 48	181	46 15	233	17 25	280	31 45	310	46 49	337
299	21 49	040	38 43	086	53 46	183	45 41	234	16 43	281	31 13	311	46 33	337
	Mirfak		•Alpheratz		Enif		•ALTAIR		Rasalhague		Alphecca		•Kochab	
300	22 16	041	39 25	086	48 23	140	53 44	184	45 06	235	34 43	275	46 17	337
301	22 44	041	40 07	087	48 50	141	53 40	186	44 31	237	34 01	275	46 01	338
[illegible]	[illegible]	[illegible]	[illegible]	[illegible]	[illegible]	[illegible]	[illegible]	[illegible]	[illegible]5	238	33 19	276	45 44	338

<u>Predictions from 249 Vol.1</u> / <u>Actual sights taken</u>

	Star	Hc	Zn	WT	Hs	GMT
*	Mirfak	20° 28'	039° →	18h 04m 01s	22° 21.6'	03h 04m 06s
	Alpheratz	36° 36'	084°			
*	ALTAIR	53° 47'	178° →	17h 51m 10s	53° 32.0'	02h 51m 15s
	Raselhague	47° 22'	231°			
*	ARCTURUS	18° 49'	279° →	17h 48m 15s	19° 07.2'	02h 48m 20s
	Alkaid	32° 50'	309°			
	Kochab	47° 22'	337°			

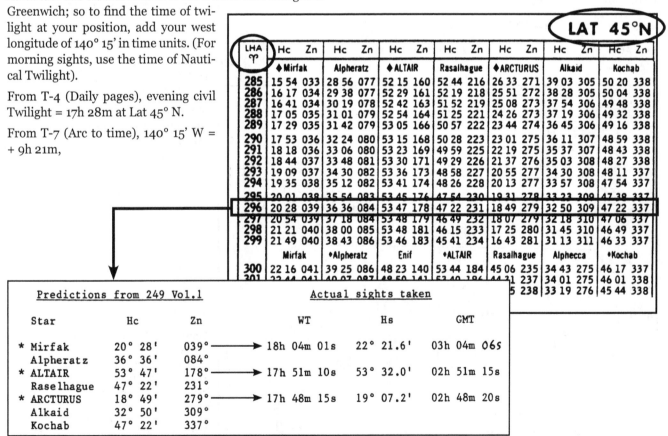

Figure 11.27-1 *Top right is a sample section of a page from* Pub. 249, Vol 1. Selected Stars, *showing the stars it proposes you use when your Lat = 45N and the time is such that the LHA of Aries = 296°. Stars in caps are the bright ones. The three marked with diamonds are the triad they propose for the best fix, taking into account relative bearings (i.e., closest to 120° apart), brightness, and altitude. The bottom left shows a list of these stars, and the bottom right shows the actual sights taken of the three proposed stars. See Steps 4 and 5 for how to sight reduce these sights. They are then plotted in Figure 11.27-2.*

Set your sextant to Hc and look in the true direction Zn. The stars will be in view near the horizon in the telescope. Adjust the sextant and record the watch time as usual for each one.

Step 5. At this point, you could do the sight reductions in the usual way using Pub. 229 or some other set of tables to get your LOPs. Note that you typically cannot use Pub. 249 Vols. 2 and 3 as we did for the earlier star sights, since Vols. 2 and 3 include only declinations less than 29°, whereas the seven predicted stars will have all declinations. But there is an easier way to get the LOPs using Vol. 1 itself.

Sight Reduction with Pub. 249, Vol. 1

The procedure is nearly the same as we used to make the predictions. The only difference is the time we use. For the sight reductions, we must find the LHA Aries for the precise times we did each sight rather than the one time of twilight we used for the predictions. The process is illustrated as follows:

STAR	Mirfak	Altair	Arcturus
UTC =	03 04 06	02 51 15	02 48 20
GHA Aries (h) =	79° 8.2'	64° 5.7'	64° 5.7'
GHA Aries (m, s)	+ 1° 1.7'	12° 50.9'	+ 12° 7.0'
GHA Aries =	80° 9.9'	76° 56.6'	76° 12.7'
a-Lon	-140° 9.9'	-139° 56.6'	-140° 12.7'
	+360.0°	+360.0°	+360.0°
LHA Aries =	300.0°	297.0°	296.0°

Then from Pub. 249, Vol. 1 at Lat 45° N and the appropriate LHA Aries find:

Hc =	22° 16'	53° 48'	18° 49'
Zn =	041°	179°	279°

Notice this is one step, no corrections.

Step 6. Convert Hs to Ho for each sight in the usual manner.

STAR	Mirfak	Altair	Arcturus
Hs =	22° 21.6'	53° 32.0'	19°07.2'
IC =	+3.6'	+3.6'	+3.6'
Dip =	-2.9'	-2.9'	-2.9'
Alt corr =	-2.3'	-0.7'	-2.8'
Ho =	22° 20.0'	53° 32.0'	19° 05.1'
Hc =	22° 16'	53° 48'	18° 49.0'*

We get the HC above from the sight reductions, just done.

And now we have the three LOPS we need:

	Mirfak	Altair	Arcturus
a =	4.0' T	16.0' A	16.1' T
Zn =	041.0°	179.0°	279.0°
a-Lat =	45.0° N	45.0° N	45.0° N
a-Lon =	40° 9.9'W	39° 56.6'W	140° 12.7'W

These lines are plotted in Figure 11.27-2. Figure 11.27-3 compares the Altair and Arcturus sight reductions this way with the same ones done with Vol. 3. The different procedures lead to different assumed positions, but still the same fix, as shown plotted in Figure 11.27-4.

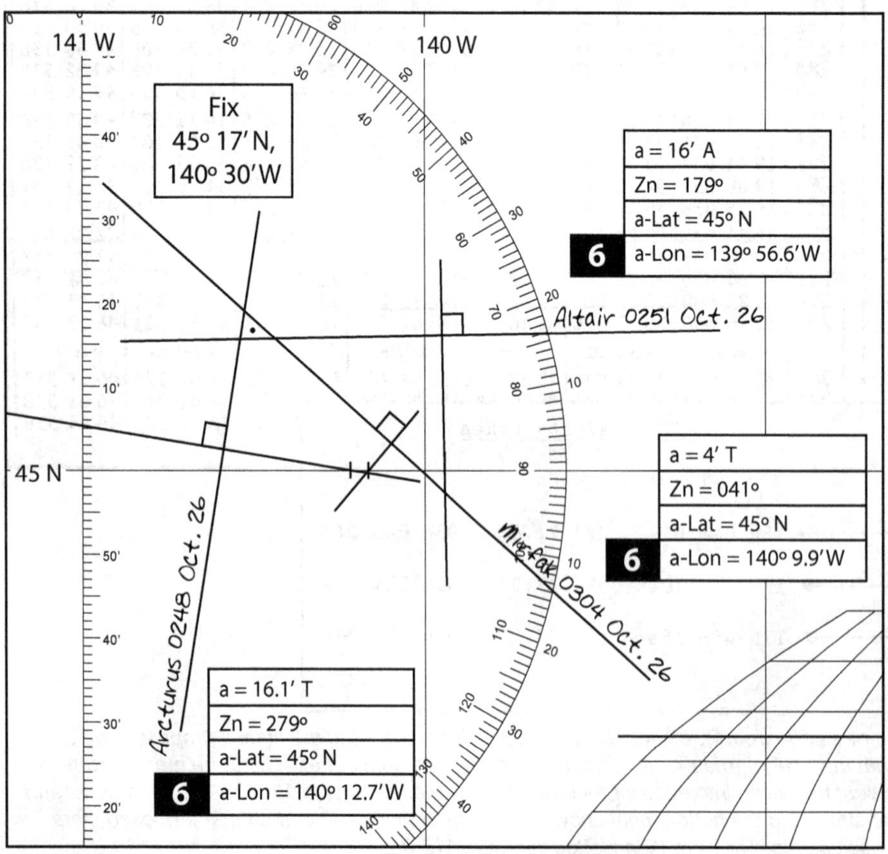

Figure 11.27-2 *Plot of the three star sights reduced with Pub. 249, Vol. 1. The data are presented at the end of Step 6. They have been transferred to Box 6 of our regular sight reduction form.*

The Arcturus and Altair sights are also plotted again in Figure 11.27-4 to illustrate using different a-values from different assumed positions but still ending up with the same fix. The Vol. 1 method leads to different assumed positions than the Vol. 3 method, but you still get the same fix.

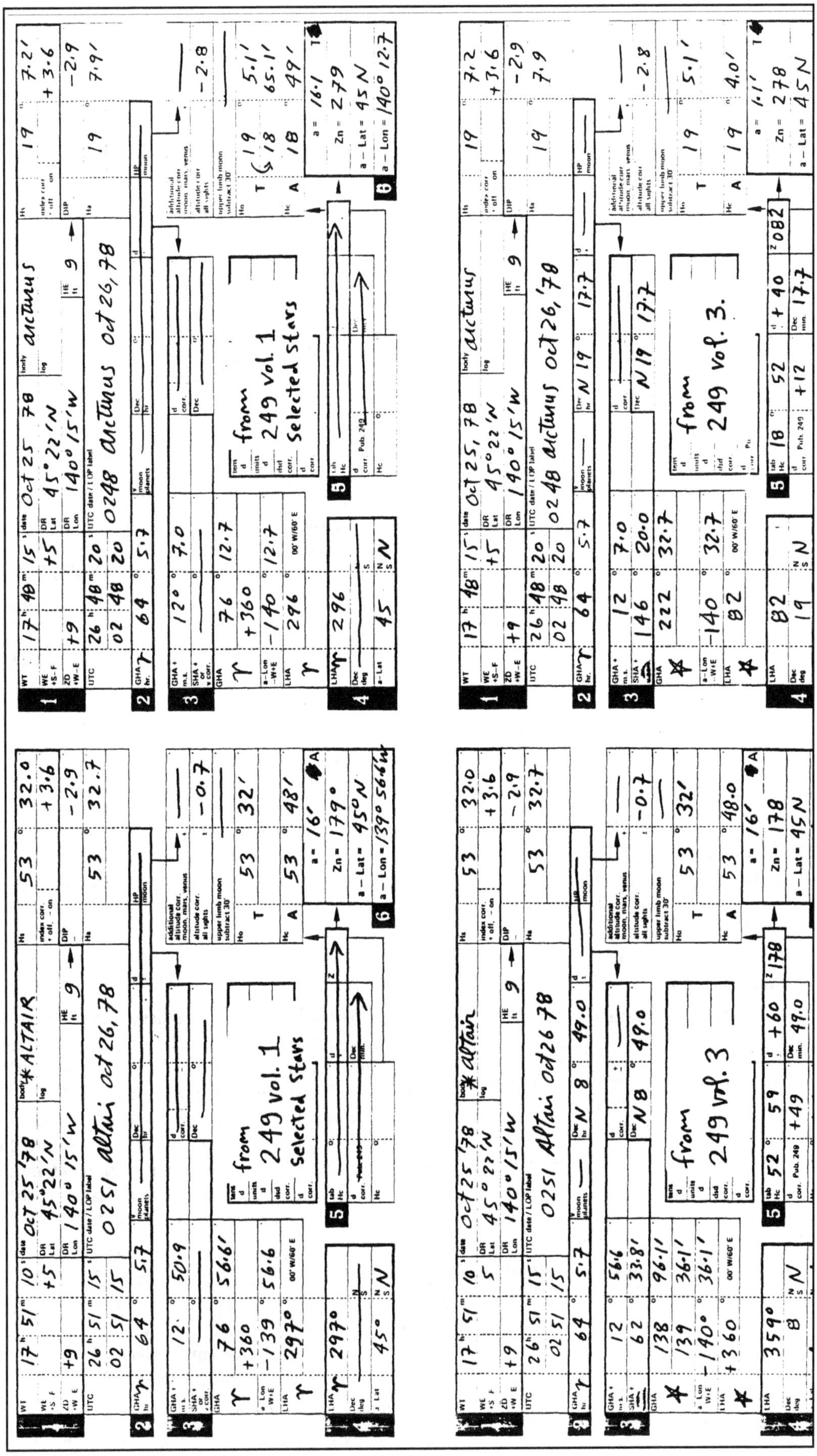

Figure 11.27-3 *Comparison of star sight reduction by Pub. 249 Vol. 1 (Selected Stars) and by Vol. 3. The Vol. 3 method can be applied to any star whose declination is between N29 and S29, but not others. That method is the standard method for sun, moon, and planets. The Vol. 1 method is for stars alone, but it only works on the stars they select as the best for the circumstances. The Vol. 1 method for stars uses the same tables for sight reduction that are used for precomputation.*

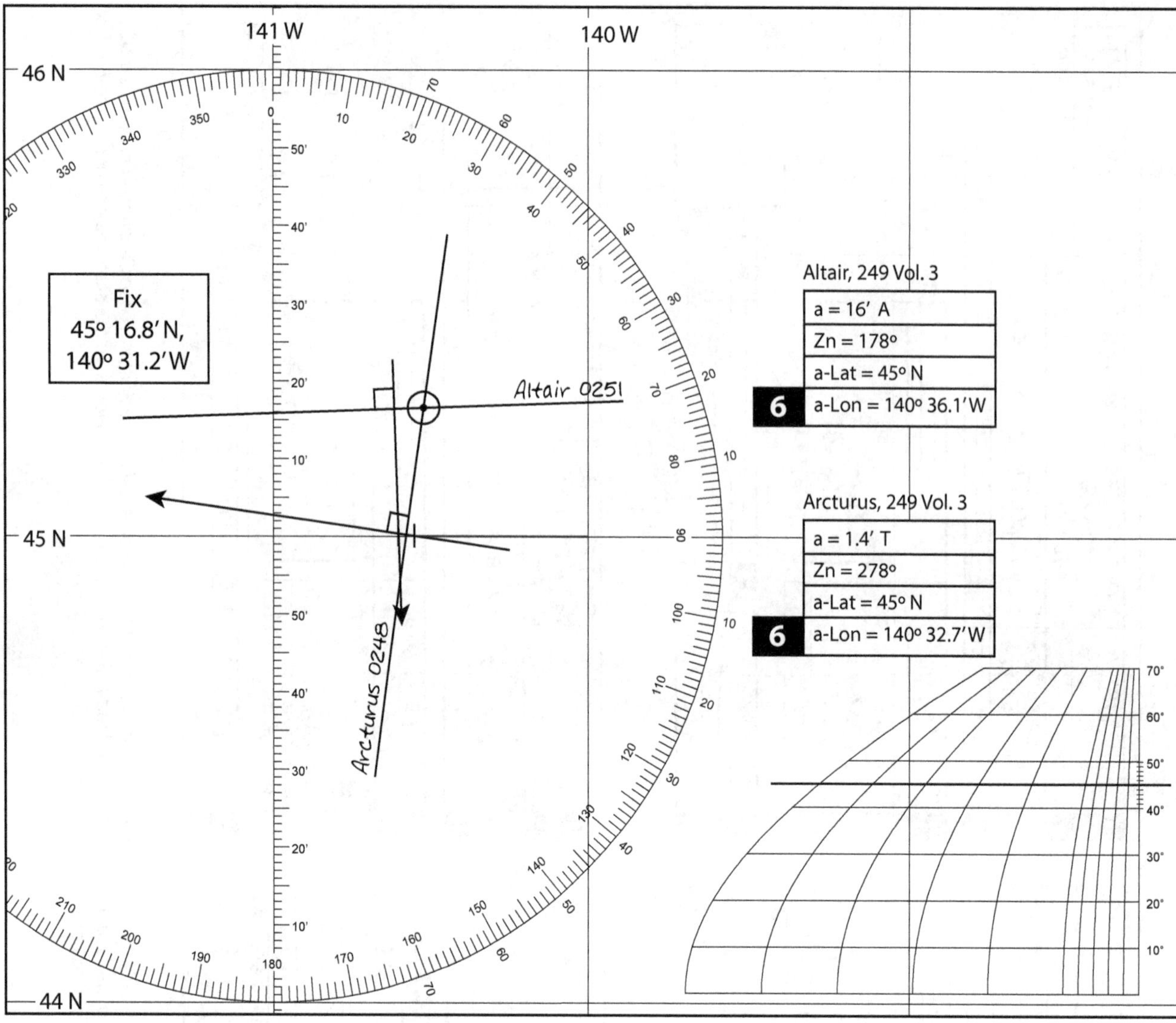

Figure 11.27-4 *Plot of the LOPs from Figure 11.27-3 showing that different sight reduction methods lead to the same fix, even when they have different assumed positions. We get different assumed longitudes in the two methods because one uses LHA of the star and the other uses LHA of Aries.*

Advantages

(1) Fast and easy—no hunting for the stars.

(2) Don't have to know the stars you're shooting.

(3) With a preset sextant and sextant telescope you can see the stars very early in twilight. This means you are sighting with a sharp horizon that gives more accurate sights and since you start as early as possible you have longer for your sights.

(4) You can get GHA Aries from the back of Pub. 249 Vol. 1, which makes this one volume a self-contained method of star sights. The altitude corrections and Arc to Time tables are also included, so you don't need an almanac to do star sights this way.

Disadvantages

(1) Basically, there are no disadvantages providing two or three of the seven stars it predicts are out when you need them—and they will be most of the time.

(2) Occasionally, you will predict a star at one LHA Aries but not get the sight until a later one. And sometimes at the later LHA Aries the star is not listed. We see this in our example if the Mirfak and Arcturus sights were taken in the other order. At LHA Aries = 300°, Arcturus is not listed. If missing by only 1°, choose a new assumed longitude, and you're back in business. If missing by more than 1°, you must do the sight reduction for that star with some other means, like your backup set of the NAO Tables.

(3) Vol. 1 of Pub. 249 is printed every 5 years. Near the limits of the printing period (called the Epoch of the edition), errors in the fix may be as large as 2 or 3 miles. There is, however, a table in the back of Vol. 1 for making this correction. Usually you can neglect this correction, but there is no need to. It is an easy one to make.

(4) There are alternative sources of star precompuation, namely the 2102-D Star Finder (Section 11.24), and

using that device has the advantage of combining stars with planets for the best choice of sights at a given time.

An historical note: Pub. 249 Vol. 1 was once an official US government publication, but this is no longer the case. In 2014, it was discontinued. It is now only available from commercial sources. This in itself is not a disadvantage. The publication no longer has the sanction of the USNO or NAO, but there is no reason to believe the commercial edition is not just as good, if not better than the historic government publication. The 2102-D Star Finder is in the same category: once a government publication, now only commercial, and it has survived in this format and served the needs of celestial navigators for many decades.

11.28 Computed Solutions

Computed solutions here means using a programmed calculator, computer program, or mobile app to assist with your cel nav. This assistance can include almanac data computations (replaces the *Nautical Almanac*), sight reduction (replaces Sight Reduction Tables), and even position fixing by direct computation or by graphic plots (replaces plotting). Needless to say, we want to have a minimum set of paper book references at hand, but they can be in a zip-lock bag somewhere.

There is good reason that many experienced celestial navigators use calculator or computer assisted cel nav whenever possible. They all know how to do it without electronic aids, but once they have mastered that, they switch over to computed solutions.

A main reason is the time you save. With programmed computation you can do in 10 minutes what it would take an hour to do by traditional table methods. It is reasonable to take pride in knowing the traditional methods of navigation that do not require computers, and it is even prudent for safety to have this knowledge, but in practice at sea, there are other chores to attend to besides navigation. With limited time available at the nav station, it is better to figure out where you are as quickly as possible, and use remaining time for gathering and thinking about weather patterns, planning your routes, and so on.

Besides being quicker, computed solutions are also easier. You don't have to unstow and stow large books, and you are less likely to make errors because you don't have to look numbers up in tables and the arithmetic is all done for you in the computer. Furthermore, when doing things like route planning (great circle and Mercator sailings are covered in Sections 11.22 and 11.23), a computer or mobile app becomes particularly valuable, because the proper ways to do this planning without calculators is involved, requiring special tables or charts. With a dedicated app, you push a few buttons and the answer appears.

The biggest advantage of computed navigation, however, is the end product. You will inevitably end up with more accurate navigation when using a calculator than when doing it by hand. There are several reasons for this. One is the more sights you take, the more accurate your navigation will be. With a calculator to quickly reduce the sights, you will do more fixes, and each fix you take can include enough sights for an accurate result. Accurate fixes require multiple sights of several bodies. In short, routine fixes can all become optimum fixes, something you cannot do without a calculator because it simply takes too long to reduce them.

Another advantage that leads to better navigation is the very method that calculators use to carry out the sight reduction process. When using the traditional table method of celestial navigation, each sight must be reduced from a separate assumed position. With a calculator, all sight reduction is effectively done from a single position, usually an appropriate DR position. This results in smaller intercepts that are much easier to interpret and evaluate, and also much easier to plot, if you care to carry out this extra step, although it is not actually required in most cases.

Celestial navigation by calculator, therefore, allows for a much more convenient interplay between DR and position fixing, which not only leads to more accurate fixes but also provides a convenient way to test the accuracy of the DR position itself (Section 11.11). *In the long run, it is your ability to do accurate dead reckoning that leads to the most confidence in navigation.* You could do excellent celestial navigation for an entire crossing, for example, but if it is overcast on the last few days, your landfall must be done by dead reckoning. A calculator or program that facilitates DR in the most convenient manner will be the one that serves you best in the long run.

Finally, assuming the computed almanac data are correct and the sights themselves are accurate, the final accuracy of a celestial fix ultimately hinges on how the motion of the boat is accounted for during the time the sights are taken. If it takes 30 minutes to take a round of star sights and you are traveling at 8 kts, then you have moved 4 miles during the time you are figuring out where you are. If you wish to know your position to a precision greater than 4 miles then you must correct the sights for this motion. This correction is a tedious process when done by hand plotting. A calculator can do it automatically.

The same problem arises during the day, since most daytime position fixing is done by running fixes of the sun—you take one set of sun sights; carry on for a few hours or so; take another round of sun sights; and then advance the first set to the second for a running fix. This involves careful analysis, DR, and plotting to do by hand, whereas a computer can do it automatically. Furthermore, to properly evaluate a series of sights, they must be compared after the time span between them and the boat's motion have been corrected for. In short, you must reduce every sight and advance it to a common time before a series of sights of the same object can be compared to decide if poor sights are included. This is tedious and time consuming to do by hand. If this process is not well organized in the computed solution, the apparent precision of the results can be misleading.

In a nutshell, celestial navigation by computation is faster, easier, and more accurate than using traditional methods with tables and plotting. The choice of handheld device versus computer has some nuances. If you have your computer rigged safely at the nav station and you use it routinely, a computer solution is likely most convenient, otherwise you might prefer a mobile app or calculator. Calculators are more easily protected from the environment at sea and they take up less space on the chart table if you are computing and plotting. They also offer more options for working other places on the boat.

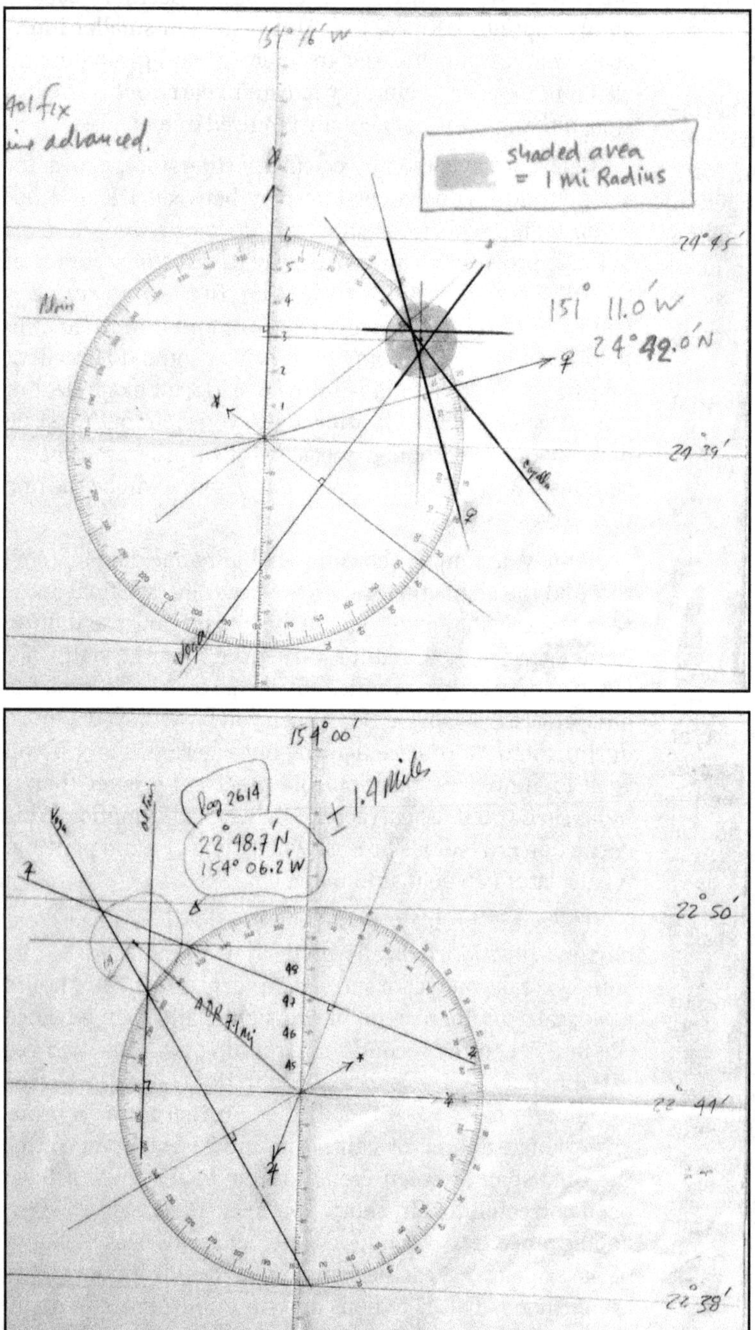

There are numerous mobile apps for cel nav for iOS and for Android devices found in the app stores of each device, and likewise a search online finds several comprehensive computer program packages as free downloads. Most are still PC-based, but more Mac versions are likely to appear. There are also numerous commercial products available. For practice on land, you have the excellent USNO computations we link to at www.starpath.com/usno. Sight reduction and ocean sailings can also be computed at www.starpath.com/calc and links given there.

When comparing your course work solutions with computed solutions, remember that to get a one-to-one comparison on the a-values and Zns, we need to use the assumed position (AP) for the sight rather than the DR position. Most computed solutions default to using the DR, because they have no need to invoke an AP.

Indeed, one way we have found to be an instructive way to do practical navigation is to combine the methods. Namely, compute all the sights from a selected DR position, each automatically corrected to that DR position for boat motion, and then plot the fix manually on a universal plotting sheet centered at the chosen DR. This calls for a custom scale on the plotting sheet, but since the a-values will be small with this method, the scale can be expanded, often from 60' per parallel to 6'. A sample of this type of plot is shown in Figure 11.28-1. Optimizing the fixes is discussed in Section 11.24, which includes a trick for numerical advancement of LOPs over short distances.

For extensive practice with sight reductions using real sextant sights from an ocean passage that are presented with both traditional paper solutions as well as computed solutions see the book *Hawaii by Sextant* (Starpath Publications, 2014).

If you do intend to rely on computed solutions—after, of course, learning the traditional methods covered in this book—then you only need a few plotting sheets and a *Nautical Almanac* as a back up. It includes the NAO Sight Reduction Tables, so that will do all of it. The use of these tables is covered in Section 11.29. Alternatively, if you want to back up just sun and star sights, you can use Geoffrey Kolbe's *Long Term Almanac* (Starpath Publications, 2008). It is a one-thin-book cel nav solution that lasts until 2050.

Figure 11.28-1 *Sample fixes made by combining computed solutions with traditional plotting on a universal plotting sheet centered at the DR with enhanced scale of 6' per parallel. Sights taken underway on 40 ft vessel at about 7 kts. Top is a very good fix; bottom is more typical. Each LOP represents the best average of four or five sights using methods of Section 11.24. From* Hawaii by Sextant.

11.29 NAO Sight Reduction Tables

Starting in 1989, there was a significant change in the available tables for celestial navigation. As we have learned so far, the tables required are an almanac and a set of Sight Reduction Tables. In the past, Sight Reduction Tables were usually chosen from Pub. 249 (most popular with yachtsmen) and Pub. 229, which is required on USCG license exams. The latter have more precision, but this extra precision would rarely affect the final accuracy of a celestial fix in routine circumstances. Pub. 229 is much heavier, more expensive, and slightly more difficult to use. Our course materials use Pub. 249, up to this point, although our work forms include instructions and form slots for use of Pub. 229.

As of 1989, the Nautical Almanac Office (NAO) began to include a set of Sight Reduction Tables at the back of the *Nautical Almanac*. Now when you buy an almanac, you get a set of Sight Reduction Tables with it, even if you don't intend to use these tables. As always, the almanac data must be replaced each new year with a new almanac, but the Sight Reduction Tables they include each year will be the same. Like all standard Sight Reduction Tables, these are not dated and can be used for sights from any year.

The new tables (which, as we originally predicted, have come to be called the "NAO Tables") are very short, but they will reduce any sight, and provide the same Hc precision as the Pub. 249 tables (0.5', rounded to nearest 1') and the same azimuth precision (0.05°, rounded to nearest 0.1°) as the Pub. 229 tables. The price we pay, however, for a free set of concise tables is the amount of work necessary to get the numbers out of them.

All Sight Reduction Tables start with Lat, LHA, and Dec and end up with Hc and Zn. With Pub. 249, the answer is obtained in two steps. With Pub. 229, it takes three steps, sometimes four, and with the new NAO tables it always takes four steps with some adding and subtracting between the steps.

At first glance, the new tables are awkward to use and not an attractive alternative to Pub. 249. There are several reasons, however, to not rule them out too quickly. First, they will always be there. As of 1989, everyone has them, like it or not. Second, celestial itself is a backup navigation method to most sailors these days. Most rely on GPS, only using celestial to test it or to replace it if it fails. Sailors who rely on celestial daily, on the other hand, usually do not use tables at all, but instead do all the paperwork with a calculator. In short, traditional navigation using tables is becoming less and less common. Since we are not using tables often, it is not so bad that the tables take a bit longer to use.

In short, if we take the time to learn these new tables and are comfortable with the knowledge that we can use them if we need to, we can save space, money, and complexity in the long run by not having to bother with various sources of tables. With this in mind, we have developed a work form that makes the use of these tables considerably easier than just following the instructions given in the almanac. With the use of our work form, the NAO tables do not take much longer than Pub. 249 does for this step of the work. Naturally, the first few times go slowly, but after a few examples it becomes automatic and easy. The form guides you through the steps.

We have included here a few of the earlier examples, redone using the new tables. Try a few if you care to see how it goes.

A Bit of History

The NAO tables were the invention of Admiral Thomas Davies and Dr. Paul Janiczek, then Head of the Astronomical Applications Department of the US Naval Observatory They were originally published as the *Concise Tables for Sight Reduction* by Cornell Maritime Press. This type of tables is referred to as "concise," or "compact" tables, as opposed to the full form tables such as Pub. 229 and 249, which are referred to as "inspection tables," since they require fewer steps.

Forerunners of these short tables were the Ageton Tables (Pub. 211) and the Dreisenstock Tables (Pub. 208). The Ageton Tables were included in Bowditch, Vol. 2 (editions prior to 1985) but not included in later editions, perhaps because they are now in the *Nautical Almanac*. Both Ageton and Dreisenstock are long out of print. US Power Squadron courses on celestial switched to the new NAO tables shortly after they were published, with the help of USPS National Education Director Dr. Allan Bayless, who had published his own version of the tables called *Compact Sight Reduction Tables*.

Admiral Davies was aware of the Starpath work form (Form 106) for the NAO tables and suggested at the time that it be included in the *Nautical Almanac*, which was agreed upon by the US NAO. The almanac, however, is a joint publication with the British NAO, and at the time they did not want to include any forms in the almanac, so this was dropped. In 2006, there was a change of heart in the UK, and a single-column work form does now appear in the almanac for these tables. It is better than none, but it remains valuable to keep a Starpath form for these tables in the almanac, since it takes you step by step through the process with no further instructions required.

Using the NAO Tables

This procedure is the same as presented in the Almanac, except for a change in notation explained below. In the work form, row numbers are marked with white letters in black boxes. For Hs below 1° or above 87°, see special instructions at the end.

The angle notation used in the form is as follows:

X = 35° 48'	— an angle
X° = 35°	— degrees part of X
X' = 48'	— minutes part of X
$\overline{X}$ = 36°	— x rounded to nearest whole degree.

Work Form for NAO Sight Reduction Tables included in the *Nautical Almanac*

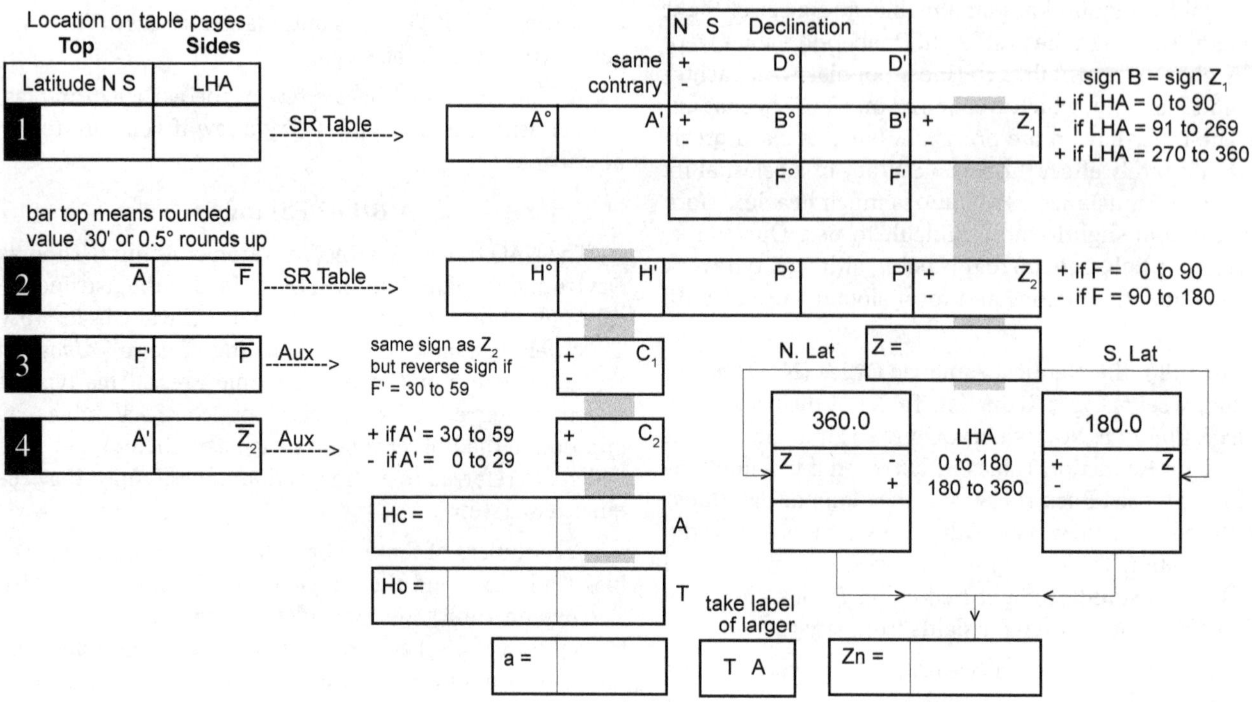

Short Instructions

1 In row 1, record assumed Lat, LHA, and Dec (D). Mark the signs of D, B, and Z1.

2 In row 1, with Lat and LHA, enter Sight Reduction Table (SR Table) and record A, B, and Z1.

3 Add D and B to get F, and record it in row 1.

4 Copy A' to row 4 and mark the sign of C2.

5 Round off A to nearest whole degree and record it as A-bar in row 2.

6 Mark the signs of Z2 and C1 in rows 2 and 3.

7 Round off F to nearest whole degree and record it as F-bar in row 2.

8 With A-bar and F-bar, enter SR Table and record H, P, and Z2 in row 2.

9 Round off P and Z2 to nearest whole degrees and record them as as P-bar and Z2-bar in rows 3 and 4.

10 With F' and P-bar, enter Auxiliary Table (Aux) and record C1 in row 3.

11 With A' and Z2-bar, enter Aux table and record C2 in row 4.

12 Add C1 and C2 to H to get Hc.

13 Add Z1 and Z2 to get Z. Copy Z to space below it, rounding to nearest degree. Drop minus sign if present.

14 Convert Z to Zn by chosing appropriate Z sign next to LHA.

15 Record Ho below Hc; take their difference and record it as "a" with the proper label.

Figure 11.29-1 *Form for NAO sight reduction, plus short set of instructions. The text has more detail. With little practice the form will guide you through the process without need for separate instructions. It is valuable to print this form with short instructions and keep a copy in the almanac. The Forms Appendix include a 2-up version without the instructions.*

Step 1. In the top lines of row 1, record assumed Latitude, LHA, and Declination (degrees in D°; minutes in D'). Circle the sign (+ or -) of D according to Same or Contrary name—or mark out the sign that does not apply.

Step 2. From the rules beside the Z1 box, determine the sign of B and Z1 (depends on LHA) and circle these signs in row 1 of the work form. B and Z1 have the same sign.

Step 3. With LAT and LHA, enter the main Sight Reduction Table (SR Table on the form) and record A, B, and Z1 in the spaces provided in row 1, separating degrees and minutes parts. Lat is found at the top of the Sight Reduction Tables; LHA on either side. Note the reminder of this arrangement at the top left of the form. This applies to all table entries.

Step 4. Copy A' to row 4 and circle the sign of C2 according to the size of A'.

Step 5. Round off A to the nearest whole degree and record it as A-bar in row 2.

Step 6. Add D and B algebraically to get F, and record F-bar and F' in the spaces provided in row 1.

Step 7. From the size of F and the notes provided, determine the signs of Z2 and C1 and circle them in rows 2 and 3.

Step 8. Round off F to the nearest whole degree and record it as F-bar in row 2.

Step 9. With A-bar and F-bar, enter Sight Reduction Table and record H, P, and Z2 into the spaces provided in row 2.

Step 10. Round off P and Z2 to nearest whole degrees and record them as as P-bar and Z2-bar in rows 3 and 4.

Step 11. With F' and P-bar, enter the Auxiliary Table (Aux) and record C1 in row 3. The Aux table is at the end of the Sight Reduction Table.

Step 12. With A' and Z2-bar, enter the Auxiliary Table and record C2 in row 4.

Step 13. Apply the corrections C1 and C2 (with their appropriate signs) to H to get Hc and record it in the space provided.

Step 14. Combine Z1 and Z2 (with their appropriate signs) to get Z and record it in the space provided. The result can be negative or positive (depending on the signs of Z1 and Z2), but this resulting sign is to be ignored—Z is to be treated as a positive number when later converting it to Zn.

Step 15. Record Ho in the space provided below Hc, then take their difference and record it as "a" in the space provided. Mark the proper label of the a-value using the rule if Hc is greater than Ho, then the label is "A," otherwise it is "T."

Step 16. Convert Z to Zn using the traditional rules located below the box for Z, and record the result in the space provided.

Step 17. Plot the LOP using the a-value, its label, and Zn

Low-altitude Sights (Hs below 1° or so)

For Hs values below 1° or so (sights that are usually only taken in desperation when other sights are not available), Ho, Hc, or both can be negative. In these cases, the Hs to Ho conversion must be done carefully, as signs can change as corrections are applied. Also, the procedure must be modified as follows: in Step 6 if F is negative (can only happen for very low sights), treat it as positive until the final Hc is determined in Step 13. And in Step 9, change Z2 to 180° - Z2 (remembering that the original Z2 has a sign). In Step 13, if F was negative, change Hc to negative.

High-altitude Sights (Hs above 87° or so)

For very high sights, the standard plotting procedure of intersecting two straight LOPs does not provide a reliable fix, because these lines are no longer good approximations to the circles of position measured with the sextant. For high sights, it is best to plot the GP and then swing an arc from this point, using a radius equal to the zenith distance (90° - Ho). This arc is then a section of your circle of position.

It is difficult to estimate the errors caused by neglecting this procedure because they depend on the heights of all sights used for the fix. In any event, when a fix is made from data including a high sight, it is best to check this effect. Also, our preliminary study shows that the NAO type of Sight Reduction Table does not provide consistently accurate Zn values for very high sights. We have not analyzed this effect in detail. We have found no Zn problems for heights below 87°.

Several examples follow on the next pages. A form with instructions that can be reproduced is in Figure 11.29-1. Further work forms are in the Appendix.

For more practice, take any sight from the book (i.e., a-Lat, dec, and LHA) and then solve for Hc and Zn with the NAO tables—and for even more precise comparison, check your results with the computed sight reduction online at www.starpath.com/calc.

The NAO tables are an excellent back up method, especially if you are relying on computed cel nav solutions routinely. With little practice, you will see the process goes very quickly, at which time it evolves from a complex solution to an elegant solution.

Work Form for NAO Sight Reduction Tables included in the *Nautical Almanac*

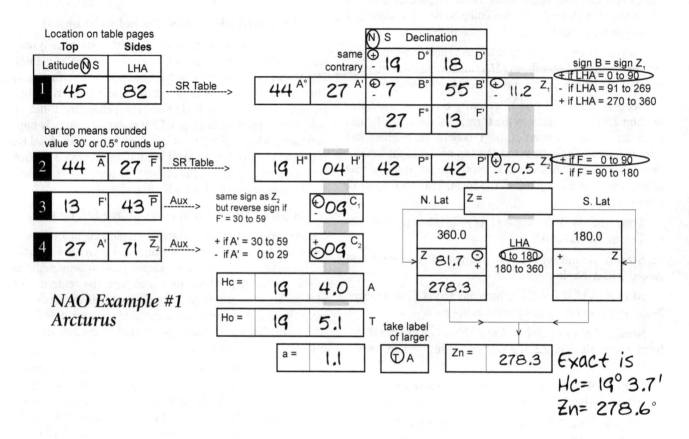

NAO Example #1 — *Arcturus*

Location on table pages: Top / Sides

bar top means rounded value 30' or 0.5° rounds up

	Latitude (N) S (Top)	LHA (Sides)		
1	45	82	SR Table --->	
2	44 $\bar{A}$	27 $\bar{F}$	SR Table --->	
3	13 F'	43 $\bar{P}$	Aux --->	same sign as Z_2 but reverse sign if F' = 30 to 59: (+) 09 C_1
4	27 A'	71 $\bar{Z}_2$	Aux --->	+ if A' = 30 to 59, - if A' = 0 to 29: (-) 09 C_2

Declination (N) S — same (+) / contrary -: D° 19, D' 18

A°	A'	B°	B'	Z_1
44	27	(+) 7	55	(+) 11.2
		F° 27	F' 13	

sign B = sign Z_1: (+ if LHA = 0 to 90) - if LHA = 91 to 269, + if LHA = 270 to 360

H°	H'	P°	P'	Z_2
19	04	42	42	(+) 70.5

(+ if F = 0 to 90) - if F = 90 to 180

Z = ; N. Lat: 360.0; Z 81.7 (-) +; 278.3. LHA (0 to 180) 180 to 360. S. Lat: 180.0; + Z -

Hc =	19	4.0	A
Ho =	19	5.1	T
a =		1.1	take label of larger: (T) A

Zn = 278.3

Exact is Hc= 19° 3.7' Zn= 278.6°

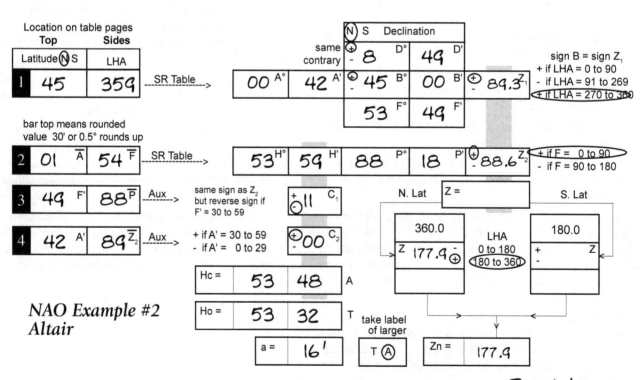

NAO Example #2 — *Altair*

Location on table pages: Top / Sides

bar top means rounded value 30' or 0.5° rounds up

	Latitude (N) S (Top)	LHA (Sides)		
1	45	359	SR Table --->	
2	01 $\bar{A}$	54 $\bar{F}$	SR Table --->	
3	49 F'	88 $\bar{P}$	Aux --->	same sign as Z_2 but reverse sign if F' = 30 to 59: (-) 11 C_1
4	42 A'	89 $\bar{Z}_2$	Aux --->	+ if A' = 30 to 59, - if A' = 0 to 29: (+) 00 C_2

Declination (N) S — same (+) / contrary -: D° 8, D' 49

A°	A'	B°	B'	Z_1
00	42	(+) 45	00	(+) 89.3
		F° 53	F' 49	

sign B = sign Z_1: + if LHA = 0 to 90, - if LHA = 91 to 269, (+ if LHA = 270 to 360)

H°	H'	P°	P'	Z_2
53	59	88	18	(+) 88.6

(+ if F = 0 to 90) - if F = 90 to 180

Z = ; N. Lat: 360.0; Z 177.9 - (+). LHA 0 to 180 (180 to 360). S. Lat: 180.0; + Z -

Hc =	53	48	A
Ho =	53	32	T
a =		16'	take label of larger: T (A)

Zn = 177.9

Exact is Hc= 53° 48.4' Zn= 178.3°

Compare to sample sights in Section 11.27 using Pub. 249

Work Form for NAO Sight Reduction Tables included in the *Nautical Almanac*

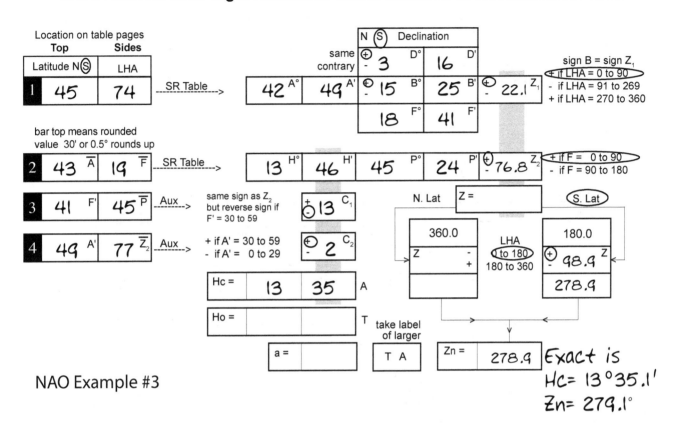

NAO Example #3

Location on table pages

	Top: Latitude N (S)	Sides: LHA		
1	45	74	SR Table -->	
2	43 $\bar{A}$	19 $\bar{F}$	SR Table -->	
3	41 F'	45 $\bar{P}$	Aux -->	
4	49 A'	77 $\bar{Z}_2$	Aux -->	

bar top means rounded value 30' or 0.5° rounds up

		N (S) Declination			
	same (+) / contrary -	3 D°	16 D'		
42 A°	49 A'	(+) - 15 B°	25 B'	(+) - 22.1 Z_1	
		18 F°	41 F'		
13 H°	46 H'	45 P°	24 P'	(+) - 76.8 Z_2	

sign B = sign Z_1
(+ if LHA = 0 to 90)
- if LHA = 91 to 269
+ if LHA = 270 to 360

(+ if F = 0 to 90)
- if F = 90 to 180

same sign as Z_2 but reverse sign if F' = 30 to 59: + (-) 13 C_1

+ if A' = 30 to 59
- if A' = 0 to 29: (+) - 2 C_2

Hc =	13	35
Ho =		
a =		

A / T — take label of larger: T A

N. Lat | Z = | (S. Lat)

360.0	LHA	180.0
Z - / +	(0 to 180) / 180 to 360	(+) - 98.9 Z
		278.9

Zn = 278.9

Exact is
Hc= 13°35.1'
Zn= 279.1°

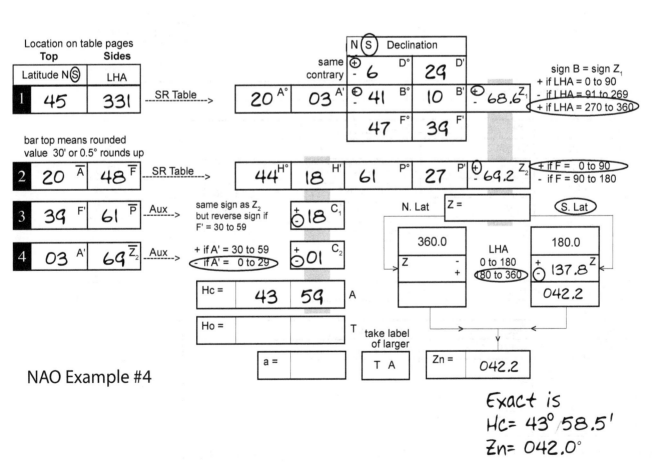

NAO Example #4

Location on table pages

	Top: Latitude N (S)	Sides: LHA		
1	45	331	SR Table -->	
2	20 $\bar{A}$	48 $\bar{F}$	SR Table -->	
3	39 F'	61 $\bar{P}$	Aux -->	
4	03 A'	69 $\bar{Z}_2$	Aux -->	

bar top means rounded value 30' or 0.5° rounds up

		N (S) Declination			
	same (+) / contrary -	6 D°	29 D'		
20 A°	03 A'	(+) - 41 B°	10 B'	(+) - 68.6 Z_1	
		47 F°	39 F'		
44 H°	18 H'	61 P°	27 P'	(+) - 69.2 Z_2	

sign B = sign Z_1
+ if LHA = 0 to 90
- if LHA = 91 to 269
(+ if LHA = 270 to 360)

(+ if F = 0 to 90)
- if F = 90 to 180

same sign as Z_2 but reverse sign if F' = 30 to 59: + (-) 18 C_1

+ if A' = 30 to 59
(- if A' = 0 to 29): + (-) 01 C_2

Hc =	43	59
Ho =		
a =		

A / T — take label of larger: T A

N. Lat | Z = | (S. Lat)

360.0	LHA	180.0
Z - / +	0 to 180 / (180 to 360)	+ (-) 137.8 Z
		042.2

Zn = 042.2

Exact is
Hc= 43° 58.5'
Zn= 042.0°

11.30 N(x) Table

This optional section is way outside of routine cel nav. It is for those who might like the novelty of doing a sight reduction with the world's shortest Sight Reduction Table, which we have called the N(x) table. The examples here use that table (T-27) and the Emergency Sun Almanac (T-28), from the Tables Selections. In Figure 11.30-1 the emergency almanac is used to find GHA and Dec of the sun; in Figure 11.30-2 the N(x) table is used for sight reduction. The results are then compared to Sun #6 & Sun #7 worked by Pub. 249 in the Answers section and by USNO computations in Table 11.30-1.

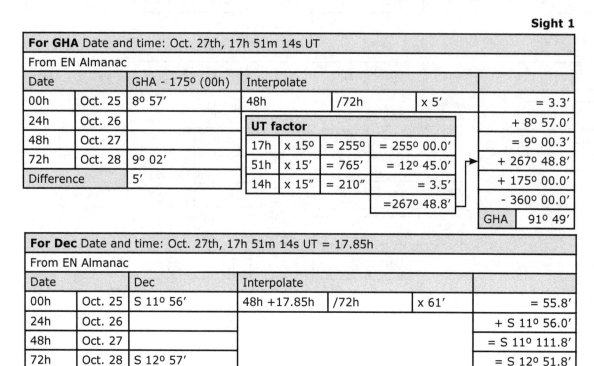

Sight 1

For GHA Date and time: Oct. 27th, 17h 51m 14s UT							
From EN Almanac							
Date		GHA - 175° (00h)	Interpolate				
00h	Oct. 25	8° 57′	48h	/72h	x 5′		= 3.3′
24h	Oct. 26		**UT factor**				+ 8° 57.0′
48h	Oct. 27		17h	x 15°	= 255°	= 255° 00.0′	= 9° 00.3′
72h	Oct. 28	9° 02′	51h	x 15′	= 765′	= 12° 45.0′	+ 267° 48.8′
Difference		5′	14h	x 15″	= 210″	= 3.5′	+ 175° 00.0′
						=267° 48.8′	- 360° 00.0′
							GHA 91° 49′

For Dec Date and time: Oct. 27th, 17h 51m 14s UT = 17.85h						
From EN Almanac						
Date		Dec	Interpolate			
00h	Oct. 25	S 11° 56′	48h +17.85h	/72h	x 61′	= 55.8′
24h	Oct. 26					+ S 11° 56.0′
48h	Oct. 27					= S 11° 111.8′
72h	Oct. 28	S 12° 57′				= S 12° 51.8′
Difference		61′				Dec S 12° 52′

Sight 2

For GHA Date and time: Oct. 27th, 21h 06m 49s							
From EN Almanac							
Date		GHA - 175° (00h)	Interpolate				
00h	Oct. 25	8° 57′	48h	/72h	x 5′		= 3.3′
24h	Oct. 26		**UT factor**				+ 8° 57.0′
48h	Oct. 27		21h	x 15°	= 315°	= 315° 00.0′	= 9° 00.3′
72h	Oct. 28	9° 02′	06h	x 15′	= 90′	= 1° 30.0′	+ 316° 42.3′
Difference		5′	49h	x 15″	= 735″	= 12.3′	+ 175° 00.0′
						=316° 42.3′	- 360° 00.0′
							GHA 140° 43′

For Dec Date and time: Oct. 27th, 21h 06m 49s = 21.1h						
From EN Almanac						
Date		Dec	Interpolate			
00h	Oct. 25	S 11° 56′	48h +21.1h	/72h	x 61′	= 58.5′
24h	Oct. 26					+ S 11° 56.0′
48h	Oct. 27					= S 12° 54.5′
72h	Oct. 28	S 12° 57′				
Difference		61′				Dec S 12° 54.5′

Figure 11.30-1 *Use of the Emergency Sun Almanac from the Emergency Navigation Card. See T-28 in Table Selections.*

Sight Reduction of Sight 1 using N(x) Tables				
Time	DR Lat	DR Lon	GHA	Dec
17:51:14	45° 27′ N	131° 34′ W	91° 49′	S 12° 52′
	a-Lat = **45°**	a-Lon = 131° 49′		= **S 12.9°**
		- GHA (91° 49′)		
		t = 40° E		

N(v) = N(90-12.9) + N(40)

N(v) = N(77.1) + N(40)

N(v) = 25.6* + 442

N(v) = 467.6

So **v = 38.8***

N(w) = N(12.9) - N(90-38.8)

N(w) = N(12.9) - N(51.2)

N(w) = 1500 - 249.2

N(w) = 1250.8

So **w = 16.65**

u = 90 - w - lat

u = 90 - 16.65 - 45

So **u = 28.35**

N(Hc) = N(90-38.8) + N(28.35)

N(Hc) = N(51.2) + N(28.35)

N(Hc) = 249.2 + 744.8

N(Hc) = 994.0

So **Hc = 21.73° = 21° 44′**

N(Z) = N(38.8) - N(90-21.73)

N(Z) = N(38.8) - N(68.27)

N(Z) = 467.6 - 74.1

N(Z) = 393.5

So **Z = 042.5**

Since Dec and Lat are contrary name:

Z = 180 - Z

Z = 180 - 42.5 = 137.5

Since LHA>180 and Lat is North Zn = Z

Therefore, **Zn = 137.5**

Figure 11.30-2 *Use of the N(x) Sight Reduction Tables. The sights are plotted in Figure 11.30-3. The instructions are located with the N(x) Table in Table Selections T-27.*

Optional Practice with N(x) Table Sight Reduction

(A) t = 49 W, Dec = N 13, Lat = 32 N

(B) t = 49 W, Dec = N 50, Lat = 20 N

(C) t = 30 W, Dec = S 20, Lat = 12 N

(D) t = 62 E, Dec = N 10.4, Lat = 11 S

*Note on interpolation: Several of these steps involve interpolation.
For example, N(v) = 467.6, so what is v? Using the N(x) table:

N(38) = 485
N(39) = 463
Difference = 22

467.6 - 463 = 4.6

4.6/22 = 0.2 Correction

Therefore, v = 39 - 0.2 = 38.8

Another example: What is N(28.35)?

N(28) = 756
N(29) = 724
Difference = 32

0.35 × 32 = 11.2 correction

Therefore, N(28.35) = 756 - 11.2 = 744.8

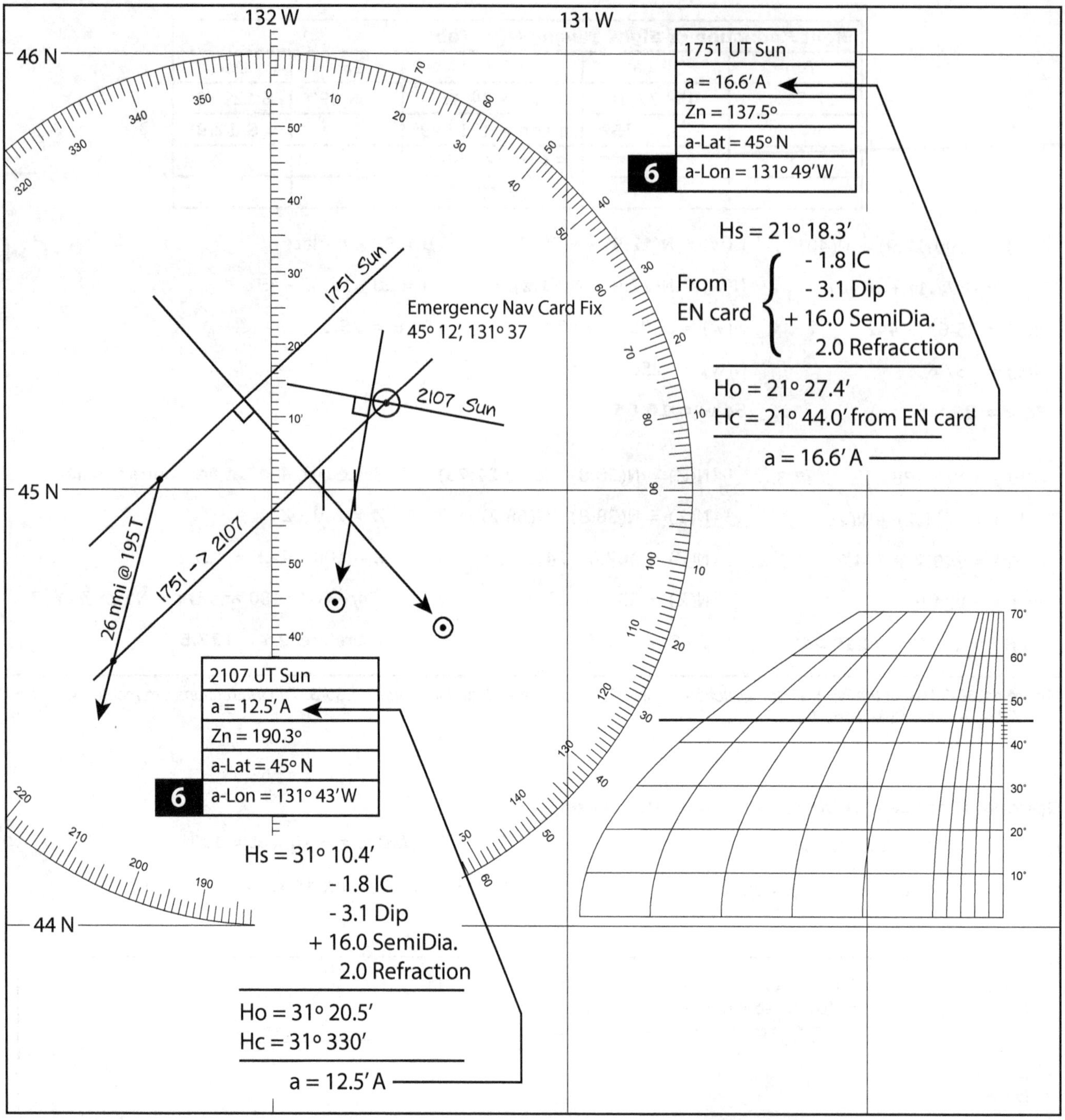

Figure 11.30-3 *Sample plot of Sights 1 & 2 from 11.30-1. Reduction of Sight 2 is not shown but the process is the same as for Sight 1.*

Table 11.30-1. Summary of EN Card accuracies.

Sight 1	*GHA*	*Dec*	*Hc*	*Zn*
EN Card	91° 49′	12° 52′	21° 44′	137.5°
USNO	91° 49.9′	12° 50.3′	21° 47.2′	137.6°
NA + Pub. 249	91° 49.9′	12° 50.3′	21° 46.7′	137°
Sight 2	*GHA*	*Dec*	*Hc*	*Zn*
EN Card	140° 43′	12° 54.5′	31° 33′	190.3°
USNO	140° 43.8′	12° 53.0′	31° 32.6′	190.3°
NA + Pub. 249	140° 43.9′	12° 53.0′	31° 33.0′	190°

11.31 Nuts and Bolts of Ocean Navigation

There is a lot we learn from a first ocean passage that we wish we had known before we left. We will look at a few of these from the navigator's perspective, and focus on those that might not be on the standard list of forethoughts. Some are personal preferences, with obvious options, others are nuances. We raise the issues so that you can think on your own solutions. The many declarative sentences are for the sake of brevity, not authority. Experienced sailors will have valid differences.

Navigation means knowing where you are on a chart and then choosing the best route to where you want to go. It is always the latter task that is the biggest challenge, meaning it requires the most knowledge and skill. This is especially true in the GPS age, but it was just as true when we had only celestial navigation to go by.

So we will talk about navigation and not even worry about where we are! We get that from the GPS, and if all the backups fail, we get out the sextant. We look instead at the broader picture of successful navigation of a sailboat in the typical environment we have at sea on an ocean passage. There are some differences racing and cruising, but the basics are the same if you choose to get there in the most efficient manner, which includes of course just getting there at all if many things go wrong at once.

Accurate Time

Dealing with that last thought first, it is important to know the correct time (UTC) at sea, because we can navigate to any port in the world with accurate time alone—we don't even need a sextant—so it pays to wear an old-fashioned watch and navigate by the time on that watch. Then maintain a chronometer log of the watch error from which we can confirm the rate of the watch, meaning how many seconds it gains or loses per day or week, and from that we can figure the right time by applying the ever-increasing watch error on any date in the future.

And most important, do not change time zones while underway. Choose the zone you want for ship's time before you leave and stick with it till you arrive. Changing times underway, or changing anything on it, is just asking for trouble, even if everything is working properly. We have notes on timekeeping in Section 11.5.

Notebooks and Logbooks

The more we rely on echarts and GPS, the higher the temptation to under-do good old fashioned written records. It is fundamental to good seamanship to keep a written record of your navigation. Use log readings if you have them, or speed and time, and course steered. Also while all is working properly, record COG and SOG and GPS position, as well as wind info needed for sailing. More entries will be discussed later. Believe it or not, it also pays to record what tack or jibe you are on, although in most cases we should be able to figure that out—it depends on the wind and how well our records are kept.

There is a simple rule: make a logbook entry whenever anything changes. If nothing changes, make an entry every couple of hours. The on-watch crew should generally make the entries, but you may find in the logbook only the navigator's handwriting for the first half of the passage... till the value of this sinks in.

Also maintain at least one other notebook for navigation notes. In this, you record everything related to navigation that you compute or think about. Do not use scratch paper for any computation. A book with numbered cross-hatched pages is ideal, such as National Brand Computation Notebook, No. 43-648, because you can then plot various graphs right in the notebook.

You might even want a separate one for notes on weather and a place to record forecasts and related routing notes. This one should include a time table of weather reports and forecasts. We have data from many sources, and they are valid at different times and then only available at certain times after that, and we need these times in UTC and in watch time, and we need a note of where we get each one, which may include radio or fax channel information. This is a very important schedule, which takes some time to prepare, and is easier done before departure. In any event, you will have it made by the time you arrive, but may have missed a couple reports in the process. The times of GRIB file updates as well as latest weather map broadcasts and voice reports can be sorted out at home.

Chart Table and Plotting Tools

The value of pencil and tools holders outside of the chart table cannot be over emphasized. If you can't find a pencil you can't draw a line that could be crucial. Unless it is built in, we also need to devise a way to protect the laptop used for navigation. It has to be fixed so it cannot slide around or bounce off the table and include some quick way to cover it to protect it from water when you are not there. The most vulnerable parts might be the connectors to it: power cable, USB and serial connectors. I have seen a person fall across the cabin in rough conditions and reach out to brace the fall and hit just the right place to break off the only serial connector of an otherwise bulletproof laptop.

A laptop stand that is raised a couple of inches from the chart table is handy, so you can lay out plotting sheets or charts underneath it. We have notes on the nav station in Section 11.16.

Share Navigation and Radio Information

Teach the SSB radio and sat phone usage to all of the crew. SSB transceivers can be complex, so posting a cheat sheet on how to use it is valuable. Even modern VHF radios might call for a note or two.

In the ideal world, you would have at least one person on each watch who is in tune with the navigation. That would mean knowing how to use the echart program and be aware of latest goals, weather tactics, and possible hazards. They can also encourage logbook participation. On larger racing boats the crew can get departmentalized, and important navigation information is not shared enough to be as safe and effective as it might be.

One way to help with this is to post a small-scale chart showing the full ocean route that is readily in view to all crew—sections of tracking charts no. 5270 or 5274 would do the job. Then plot and date your position once a day. The crew will get more interested in the navigation and indeed know where you are along the course. Discussing at any common meal times the latest weather forecasts and tactics can help as well. On a tight watch system this might not happen very often, so the navigator's helpers can fill in.

Also in this same vein, use some modern version of a route box in sight of the helm and deck crew. This could be just several strips of blue tape on which you write in big letters with a Sharpie the present course to steer. Or you could make something more elegant. The main idea, however, is to have a list of these courses, not just a white board where you post only the active course. We want to see the old course crossed out, and the new course written below it. This keeps all in tune with what is going on with the course over time.

Having the active course in view gives the helmsman a quick reference on what to come back to when thrown off course for any reason. Memory could hurt us if we had been on 220 for 2 days, but now the course is 200. Also we could get confused if the course was 200 then 210 but now it is back to 200.

Sail Waypoints

If we are not sailing to specific waypoints, we are not navigating; we are just out sailing. Even on an ocean passage we need waypoints. There is essentially no efficient ocean crossing that has just one waypoint at the destination. Needless to say we want one there, and we should always keep an eye on the VMG to that one, but there will be intermediate ones we set and change as we proceed, and the immediate navigation is to maximize VMG to that active waypoint.

Sailing around the corner of the Pacific High, for example, you might use some guideline to mark the corner such as two full isobars off the central high pressure. This choice depends on how far you are from that point. If you have a 3- or 4-day forecast of the winds that might let you cut it a bit closer, then you can try that. But the main job is to set one and optimize speed to it until you have good reason to move it. The forecast might change and call for heading more south toward the trades for a while, or let you sail a bit closer to the rhumb line.

Once around the corner, you might set another waypoint based on the forecast of the trade winds closer to your destination. In other words, with the present forecast of the trades out to 800 nmi you might choose the point that sets you up for your best wind angles if you were at that point and the trades did indeed stay as forecasted in speed and direction (Figure 11.31-1). Then you again watch that and adjust as needed. Both the speed and the direction of the trades could cause the waypoint to shift.

When sailing waypoints in this manner, sometimes the course is crucial—that is, if we do not make that waypoint we could lose a lot of efficiency; so we have to fight to make it. In this case the navigator's job is to stress this point and also keep a more careful watch on what is actually being steered and recorded in the logbook. With all the electronics working, we have an exact trail on the echart of what we are making good; so if we are not making it, we need to study the situation to find out why and try to correct it. Not to sound too crass, but you may have one watch that just wants to go fast, so they are reaching a little extra all the time–not looking ahead to the consequences. Again, we are back to getting the crew involved with the navigation.

On the other hand, there can be circumstances when you have a lot more freedom and you can simply say go as fast as you can (with present sails set), always looking ahead to see if a crucial waypoint might be developing.

Selecting waypoints and approach cone from forecasted winds. Adapted from *Modern Marine Weather*.

Stay on the Right Jibe

This may sound obvious, but in a long ocean race it might slip by us, especially in wonderful sailing conditions. Thus, the task of a continual monitoring of the VMG to the next waypoint is crucial. It is also crucial to monitor this progress on both jibes. It could be the time to jibe is affected by the sea state, because in the same wind, one jibe is much better than the other because of the direction of the waves. This could take some testing; the interaction of wind and waves can be unique.

Depending on the boat and crew and sailing conditions, the decision could also be affected by how you want to spend the night. It could also be a time to decide, depending on where you are relative to the waypoint you want, if it might be valuable to set a head sail over night. If your route calls for fairly close reaching at the moment, it could be that the extra progress to weather could balance out a slower speed and reduced risk of sail trouble for the overnight run.

One way to make a quick estimate of the consequences of steering the wrong course is what we call the Small Angle Rule. Namely, a 6° right triangle has sides in proportion of 1:10. Thus if I sail the wrong course by 6° for 100 nmi, I will be 10 nmi off my intended track. The rule can be scaled up to 18° and down to 1°. It can also be used to estimate current set and other applications.

Every Mile Counts

Sometimes, it is hard to keep this in mind when we are in the middle of the ocean with 1,000 miles to go, but it is a constantly crucial matter. Just imagine what that one mile looks like if your competitor is one mile ahead at the finish line. This gives us the burden to compute once a day who is ahead and by how much in a precise manner, which is not a trivial process. Sometimes, it is difficult because it depends on what we think is going to happen ahead with the wind, but it must always start from the best geometric computation, which means you must use accurate great circle computations—in fact, we should probably not even use great circle, which assumes a round earth, but rather use ellipsoidal distance, which takes into account the best datum for the ocean we are in. You can test these things, i.e., great circle versus ellipsoidal, by computing long distances with your GPS, since most of these do in fact read the datum you have selected, and use it, compared to standard round earth great circle, which you compute at www.starpath.com/calc. On the other hand, most echart programs use only great circle, unless they specifically ask you for the datum. Spread sheets can be set up to do this, or there are good old-fashioned great circle plotting tricks using universal plotting sheets if the computers fail.

Evaluating the Forecasts

We set the waypoints based on the forecasts; so it is important to remember that there will always be a forecast, and they are not marked good or bad. (Eventually we will get more probability forecasting into marine weather, but for now this evaluation is up to us.)

One obvious way to evaluate the forecasts is to see if the present surface analysis agrees with our own observations. To do this, we need calibrated wind instruments (to compute true wind speed and direction) and a good barometer. Then we plot our position on the weather map, read off wind speed and direction and pressure, and compare to what we have recorded for these at the valid map time. If they agree, we have more confidence in the forecast. To the extent they do not, we have less confidence.

There are also well-known properties of the winds aloft at 500 mb that tell us if the surface forecast might be strong or weak. These depend on the flow pattern and speed of the winds, as well as the shape and location of the surface patterns below them. Guidelines for these procedures are in *ModernMarine Weather* (Starpath Publications).

If we have surface forecast conditions that are very enticing for making a bold move, but our evaluation of the forecast is weak, then we should be cautious. You might then do just half of what you want to do, or do it for just half as long, then wait till you get another map (6 hours) to see how things are panning out.

Another simple and important guideline is to not rely on just the ubiquitous GRIB formated GFS model output. The minimum to do is download the actual weather maps produced by the Ocean Prediction Center, and use them as an important criteria in evaluating the GRIB data. Once the GRIB maps are confirmed, then you can have more confidence in using their extremely convenient format. The first map in a GRIB forecast sequence will usually coincide with the latest synoptic time of the OPC surface analysis. As noted earlier, making a weather services time table is crucial to putting this together.

When you are setting off on an ocean voyage, be sure that your echart program options has magnetic variation set to automatic. This may be something you never ever looked at, so it could be on manual, which means it will not change till you change it. I know of two real cases where this caused serious issues to the navigation, and one other that was caught just before that. Put another way, we need to be comparing the COG and heading all day every day. It is how we spot current.

A unique new Kindle ebook by Will Oxley called *Modern Racing Navigation* discusses the latest technology available to the navigator. We have looked earlier at a few of the old-fashioned ideas; Oxley's book is the place to learn about the powerful new resources, including specific recommendations for software, hardware, and apps. He focuses on the popular Expedition software as the base for navigation, performance, and weather analysis.

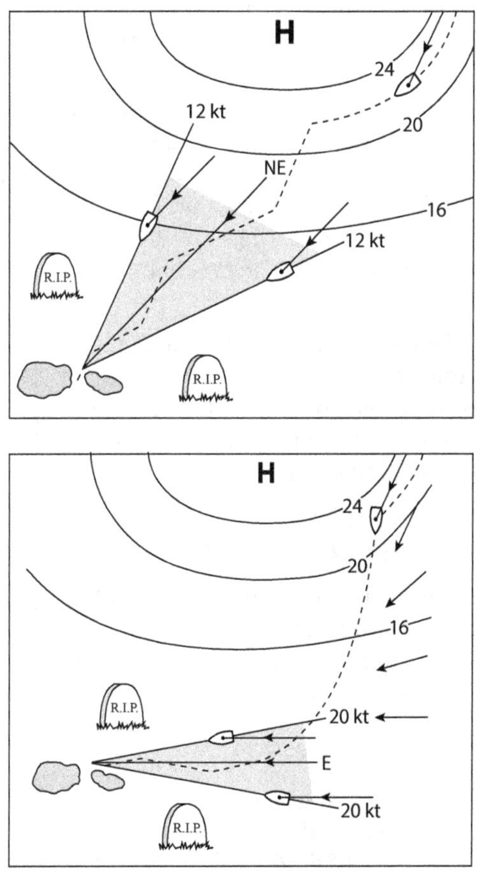

Figure 11.31-1 *Setting waypoints and approach cone based on sailing performance and anticipated wind conditions ahead.*

11.32 Most Likely Position from 3 LOPs

In Section 11.24 we mentioned that practicing navigators tend to choose the best position within a triad of intersecting LOPs (cocked hat) as a centroid value of their choice, based on their experience and the actual sights at hand. In most cases this is an adequate solution, but in rare cases we might need to choose the very best location based on all that we know about the three LOPs. These can be celestial sights, or they could be three compass bearing lines, or more to the point they could be two typical compass bearings and a natural range line (a very accurate LOP) or equivalently one very good celestial sight and two that were not as good due to poor horizon or fewer sights in the sequence.

In short, if we are to apply more sophisticated analysis, we need to have enough extra data to justify it, which can be expressed as the individual uncertainties in each sight, called their variances.

It can be shown that if these variances are all the same (no one sight better than another), and there is no systematic error that applies to all of them, then the most likely position is located at what is called the symmedian point of the triangle, which is discussed at length at online math resources. It is frankly fairly tedious to graphically plot this point, but worth noting that it is *not* any of the common centroids we might have considered. This does not distract from the practical solution we usually use underway, because we are fine-tuning the analysis here, and assuming knowledge we do not always have.

Once you are convinced that the variances are not the same, then the symmedian point is no longer correct. For example, if one line (of a terrestrial fix) is a range, then that should bias the fix toward that line, and the other two compass bearings are effectively just showing where you are on that line.

In a recent research paper [Note 1], we have developed a solution to the most likely position that is relatively easy to evaluate by hand, and very easy to solve with a calculator or programmed function. The result for the most likely position P can be written as:

$P = q_1Q_1 + q_2Q_2 + q_3Q_3$,

where $q_i = s_i^2\ \sigma_i^2 \ /\ \Sigma\ (s_j^2\ \sigma_j^2)$.

In this formalism the most likely point is determined from the sides of the triangle (s_i) and the variance of each line (σ_i) without reference to the intersection angles.

Note 1. *"Most Likely Position from n LOPs with Random and Systematic Variances" by Richard Rice and David Burch, to be published. This paper presents the derivation of the full probability distribution and includes an app that displays the distribution graphically for user-selected inputs, with and without a systematic error that applies to all sights.*

Consider a sample triangle of sides 10, 9, and 13 that have corresponding variances of 1, 2, and 3. The units are arbitrary, chosen for convenience of measurement on the nautical chart or plotting sheet in use. Once the LOPs have been plotted, it is the task of the navigator to assign the corresponding variances.

For a graphic solution, it is easiest to use rectilinear coordinates (x.y), as shown in Figure 11.32-1. The orientation of the coordinates is chosen to align with one of the LOPs, and the location of the third point is measured from the chart in the same units, (5.7, 6.9) in this case. In this example:

$\Sigma\ (s_j^2\ \sigma_j^2) = 100 \times 1 + 81 \times 4 + 169 \times 9 = 1945$, and

$q_1 = 100/1945 = 0.051$,

$q_2 = 324/1945 = 0.167$,

$q_3 = 1521/1945 = 0.782$.

Then with $Q_1 = (0, 0)$, $Q_2 = (13, 0)$, and $Q_3 = (5.7, 6.9)$, we get:

$P = 0.051 \times (0,0) + 0.167 \times (13,0) + 0.782 \times (5.7,6.9)$

$= (0, 0) + (2.2, 0) + (4.5, 5.4)$

$= (6.7, 5.4)$.

The history of this most basic of navigation questions is reviewed in the paper [1], along with other examples and extended discussion. This is the first solution we have seen that offers a fast practical way to answer this question if it should be needed underway.

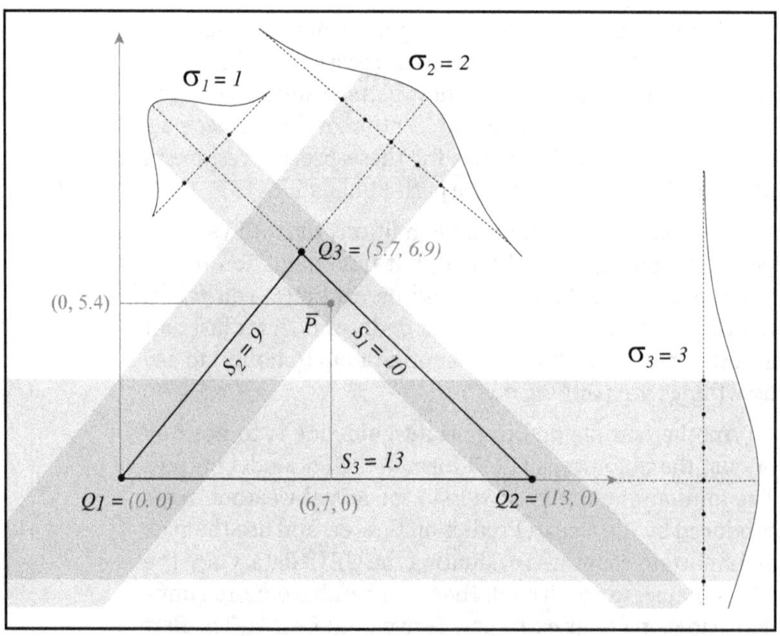

Figure 11.32-1 *Most likely point P (6.7, 5.4) determined from three LOPs, without systematic error. The variance of each LOP is shown schematically to match the units chosen to measure the sides of the triangle from the chart. If the units were miles, a centroid choice would be wrong by 3 miles.*

Appendix 1

Glossary

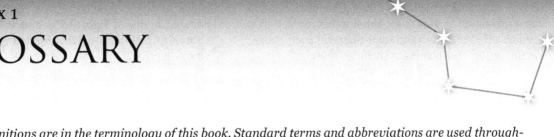

These definitions are in the terminology of this book. Standard terms and abbreviations are used throughout, although the interpretations of some are simplified or expanded for clarity. This glossary includes content details expanded in some cases beyond the presentation in the text. A list of ***Abbreviations*** *alone is at the end of the Glossary.*

a-value — Same as altitude intercept. Called the "a-value," it is the difference, found in the last step of a sight reduction, between the calculated height (Hc) and the observed height (Ho) of a celestial body. It is used for plotting the LOP. It is labeled A (away) if Hc is greater than Ho, or T (toward) if Hc is less than Ho. In physical terms, "a" tells if we are closer or farther from the GP than the assumed position is. An a-value of 20' T, for example, means your true position is 20' (20 nmi) closer to the GP than the assumed position is.

Accuracy — The difference between your true position and the fix position found from a round of celestial sights. Generally this is better thought of as the uncertainty in your fix, which, with good procedures and a good sextant, should be less than 3 or 4 miles routinely. This can be improved to about 0.5 miles, but this requires special care, especially when moving. Anything more than about 10 miles indicates some problem with procedures or equipment. A rough way to judge your accuracy is the size of the triangle of crossed lines of position, assuming that each side of the triangle represents the average of several sights of the same body. The most accurate fix comes from sights of three bodies, bearing about 120° apart. See Sextant Sights and Fix.

Accuracy in dead reckoning is the difference between your fix position and your DR position at the time of the fix. With calibrated instruments and careful dead reckoning this should be no worse than about 15% of the distance run since the last fix, although this depends very much on the conditions present. See Dead Reckoning.

Additional Altitude Correction — Used only in the sight reduction of the moon, Mars, or Venus (the three closest celestial bodies), this correction accounts for the parallax of their light rays—that is, since each of these bodies is so close to the earth, the light ray we see it with is not strictly parallel to the light ray from it that passes through its geographical position (GP). The theory of celestial navigation assumes that the distance along the earth's surface between the observer and the GP is equal to the zenith distance (z) of the body, but this is only true if these two light rays are parallel. So for these three close bodies this extra correction is required. See Parallax.

Another, completely different, type of Additional Altitude Correction is also discussed and tabulated in the Table A4 of the *Nautical Almanac*. These are additional corrections for non-standard refraction in unusual atmospheric conditions. In principle, these corrections apply to all sights, but from a practical point of view they can be neglected. The corrections are very small for all sights except those near the horizon (which should be avoided anyway if possible). There is no space for this type of additional correction on the Starpath work forms. It is recommended that this atmospheric correction just be ignored, but bear in mind that any sights within about 5° of the horizon will be uncertain by plus or minus 5' or so. See Refraction.

Advanced LOP — A line of position that has been shifted on the chart or plotting sheet to correct for the boat's motion since the time of the sight. Section 11.24 includes a method of numerically advancing an LOP by adjusting the a-value. See Running Fix.

Air Almanac — A questionable alternative to the *Nautical Almanac* that some very few marine navigators prefer. It is not as convenient to use, nor as complete, nor as easy to obtain. As of 2008, only available on CD. It is not recommended.

Altitude — Same as Height. A general name for the angular height of a celestial body above the horizon that is determined from a sextant measurement or sight reduction. Angular height is often called "altitude" in other textbooks. When a body is right on the horizon, its height is 0°; when a body is overhead, its height is 90°. The term is used more precisely depending on the number of corrections that have been made to the sextant measurement. See Sextant Height, Apparent Height, Observed Height, and Calculated Height.

Altitude Correction — When doing a sight reduction, this is the final correction to the sextant height needed to get the observed height. This term actually describes several different corrections (although we don't need to know this detail to use it): for the sun this correction is primarily the refraction and semi-diameter corrections; for the moon and planets it includes these and also a parallax correction; and for stars the altitude correction includes only refraction. See Refraction, Semi-diameter, Parallax, and Additional Altitude Correction.

Altitude Intercept (a-value) —The difference, found in the last step of a sight reduction, between the calculated height (Hc) and the observed height (Ho) of a celestial body. It is used for plotting the LOP. It is labeled A (away) if Hc is greater than Ho, or T (toward) if Hc is less than Ho. In physical terms, the a-value tells if we are closer or farther from the GP than the assumed position is. An a-value of 20' T, for example, means your true position is 20' closer to the GP than the assumed position is.

Amplitude — A convenient term (although little used in routine navigation) that describes the bearing of any celestial body on the horizon (when rising or setting). It is the number of degrees away from due east or west that a body rises or sets. It is labeled North or South according to its location relative to east or west. If a body has an amplitude of 30° N, it rises 30° north of east (at 060 T) and sets 30° north of west (at 300 T). The name (N or S) of the amplitude is always the same as that of the declination. With a calculator, amplitude can be found from: Sin(Amp) = Sin(dec) / Cos(Lat), but this is technically Hc =0, which is not precisely what we observe because of refraction. USCG exams cover this topic as a way to do compass checks, but we do not cover amplitude in this course.

Apparent Height (Ha) — Every sight reduction starts with the sextant height (Hs) and ends up with the observed height (Ho). But to do this we must first figure this intermediate value, called the apparent height, which has only the index and dip corrections removed: Ha = Hs + IC - Dip. This height should be agreed upon by all observers who took sights at the same time, even though they used different sextants (different ICs) and stood at different elevations (different dips). It is only "apparent," however, because it is not correct.

Aries (♈) — Also called the *First Point of Aries*, this is the celestial equivalent to the Greenwich meridian. Longitude lines on a star globe (called sidereal hour angles, SHA) are all relative to Aries, just as earth longitudes are all relative to Greenwich. As the earth turns, the Aries meridian circles the earth once every 24 hours. In star sight reductions, to find the star's GHA from the *Nautical Almanac*, add the permanent SHA of the star to the GHA of Aries at the time of the sight. The meridian of Aries passes approximately through Polaris and Caph, the leading star of Cassiopeia; extended backwards from Polaris, it passes through Phecda, inside the cup of the Big Dipper.

Assumed Latitude (a-Lat)— The latitude of the assumed position chosen during a sight reduction to facilitate the use of Sight Reduction Tables. It is always chosen to be your DR-Lat rounded off to the nearest whole degree. If DR-Lat = 35° 20' N, a-Lat = 35° N. If DR-Lat = 35° 46' S, a-Lat = 36° S. If the minutes part of DR-Lat is exactly 30', a-Lat can be rounded up or down. See Assumed Position.

Assumed Longitude (a-Lon) — The longitude of the assumed position chosen during a sight reduction to facilitate the use of Sight Reduction Tables. The proper choice depends on your DR-Lon and the minutes part of the sighted body's GHA at the time of the sight. In west longitudes, it is the one longitude that lies within 30' of your DR-Lon that has the same minutes part as that of the GHA. In east longitudes, it is the one longitude that lies within 30' of DR-Lon that has a minutes part equal to 60' minus the minutes part of GHA. With a-Lon chosen properly, the local hour angle (LHA) of the sighted body will be a whole number of degrees. See Assumed Position.

Assumed Position (AP) — The position (a-Lat, a-Lon) chosen by the navigator during the sight reduction process to facilitate the use of Sight Reduction Tables. This is a purely fictitious position (no boat or celestial body is located there) that must be chosen as a reference point for the calculations since Sight Reduction Tables give solutions for only whole degrees of Lat and LHA. Each sextant sight will have a unique assumed position, and the LOP of that sight must be plotted from that position. It is recorded in Box 6 of the work form. Sight reductions by programmed calculators do not require or use an assumed position.

Azimuth (Zn) — The true bearing (between 0° and 360°) of a celestial body from the assumed position at the time of the sight. In a sight reduction (work form, Boxes 5 and 6), it is obtained from applying the azimuth rules to the azimuth angle (Z). These rules are given on the work forms and on each page of the Sight Reduction Tables. Azimuth is also used outside of celestial navigation as a general term for any true bearing.

Azimuth Angle (Z) — The relative bearing (between 0° and 180°) of a celestial body viewed from the assumed position at the time of the sight. It is found in the Sight Reduction Tables (work form, Box 5); it is measured relative to due north in north latitudes and relative to due south in south latitudes. The abbreviation is capital Z, as opposed to the azimuth, which is abbreviated Zn. Rules for converting Z to Zn are different in the NH and SH because we use the North Pole for reference in both hemispheres. See elevated pole and Navigational Triangle.

Azimuth Line — In plotting the LOP, it is the line drawn through the assumed position in the direction of Zn. The azimuth line points to the GP. See Plotting LOPs.

Bearing — The direction on earth of some point relative to the true North (True bearings) or magnetic north (Magnetic bearings). If the bearing to Mount St. Helens is 135 T, you find this direction by facing north and then rotating 135° to the right. Due east has a true bearing of 090°. A phrase like "due east" always implies true bearings unless specified otherwise. If the bearing to Deception Pass is 050 M, you would face magnetic north and turn 50° to the right. If your steering compass has no deviation, it should read 050 when Deception Pass is on the bow. The difference between true and magnetic bearings at any one place is called the magnetic variation at that place. It is given on all nautical charts. See Deviation and Variation.

Bowditch — Nickname for the navigational encyclopedia called the *American Practical Navigator*, originally by Nathaniel Bowditch. The first edition was in 1802, the latest was a special bicentennial edition in 2002. It includes most tables needed for navigation as well as an extensive authoritative glossary. It is NGA Pub. No. 9. All navigation questions are answered there, but it is not easy reading in many places. Notably good (in earlier editions) and quite easy reading, however, are its sections on sextant care and use, star identification, and chapters on weather and oceanography. A complete electronic copy of the latest as well as earlier ones are available online. See Section 11.1.

Calculated Height (Hc) — Found from Sight Reduction Tables or mathematical computation, it is the height of the celestial body that would have been observed from the assumed position at the time of the sight, assuming no refraction and no HE. At the end of a sight reduction, Hc is compared to Ho (observed height) to figure the altitude intercept (a-value) which in turn is used to plot the line of position. It is also called calculated altitude. The mathematical determination of Hc is found from solving the navigational triangle.

Calculators — Meaning, here, handheld calculators or apps in mobile devices specially programmed for celestial navigation calculations. They can do sight reductions and calculate celestial positions (declinations and Greenwich hour angles) normally found in an almanac. Another, perhaps even more valuable, function is their ability to do dead reckoning. See Section 11.28.

Celestial Body — Stars, sun, moon, and planets.

Celestial Navigation — The process of finding your position from timed sextant sights of celestial bodies. Related work under this same general title includes calculating bearings to celestial bodies for compass checks, figuring great-circle routes and distances between ports, and star identification. Outside of the US, this is often called *astro navigation*. An astronomer might call it *positional astronomy*.

Chronometer — Any watch that gains or loses time at a constant rate. These days, essentially any quartz watch is a chronometer with constant rate of less than about 15 seconds per month. See Watch Rate, Watch Time, and Watch Error.

Chronometer Log — That part of your logbook devoted to recording the daily checks of your watch error. It is best to plot the daily watch errors versus the date to see that the watch rate is constant, meaning that these daily points make a straight line. The slope of this line is your watch rate. See Logbook, Watch Time, Watch Error, and Watch Rate.

Circle of Equal Altitude — Any circle of points on the earth's surface that is equal distance from the geographical position (GP) of a celestial body at a precise moment of time. All observers located anywhere on this circle would measure the same sextant height of the body at that moment. The center of the circle is the GP of the body, the radius of the circle is the zenith distance (z). The Ho they would observe is Ho = 90° - z. When taking the sights, the observers would all be looking toward the body in the center of the circle, which means some would be looking north, others, south or west, etc.. If the body were 60° high, the zenith distance would be 30°, which means the distance to the GP would be 30° × (60 miles/1°), or 1,800 miles. The LOPs used in celestial navigation are short segments of the circumference of this circle, which we approximate as straight lines.

Circle of Position — A line of position that is curved into a circle. These are obtained only rarely in celestial navigation from high-altitude sights, or much more frequently in coastal navigation from distance off measurements. See Line of Position and High-Altitude Sights.

Circumpolar Stars — The disk of stars, centered at the pole, which never rise or set and consequently are visible all night, every night of the year. In Seattle, the end of the handle of the Big Dipper (Alkaid) and the bright star Capella in Auriga, opposite it across the pole, represent the approximate extent of the circumpolar stars for this latitude. In Hawaii, the Big Dipper swings below the horizon, but the Little Dipper remains circumpolar.

Civil Twilight — That time of evening, listed in the *Nautical Almanac*, when we first see the brightest stars, typically about 20 to 40 minutes after sunset depending on latitude and time of year. In the morning, this time is interpreted as when the brightest stars fade into the daylight sky, about 20 to 40 minutes before sunrise. Evening star sights are taken between civil and nautical twilight; morning sights between nautical and civil twilight. See Nautical Twilight.

Compass Rose — The 360° protractor in the center of a plotting sheet, or located throughout nautical charts. The name is somewhat misleading, since even the scales referenced to true north are called "compass" roses. On nautical charts, there are both true and magnetic scales, but on plotting sheets there are only true scales. See Protractor.

Contrary Name – The term used to describe a declination that has the opposite name (North or South) from your latitude. A star with Dec N 19° has Contrary Name if you are at 30° S, but Same Name is you are at 30° N.

Course – The direction you want to travel, usually read from a nautical chart by drawing a line from here to there (a rhumb-line course) and then reading this direction from the compass rose. It can be specified True, Magnetic, or Compass. With no deviation, Magnetic and Compass are the same. See Heading, Bearing, and Course Over Ground

Course Over Ground (COG) – Your true course made good relative to the fixed earth measured with a GPS. It is the actual direction you are traveling at the moment regardless of the course steered and temporary variations in heading around this course. Factors that cause COG to differ from the course being steered include: current, leeway, helm bias, and compass errors. See also Speed Over Ground.

Daily Pages – The main body of the *Nautical Almanac* that includes daily data for the celestial bodies.

d-Correction (d-corr) – When doing a sight reduction, it is a correction to the declination that accounts for its change during the minutes part of the sight time. The same term is used for another correction done during the sight reduction to correct the tabulated value of the calculated height (Hc) for the minutes part of the declination. See Sight Reduction, Sight Reduction Tables, and d-Value.

d-Value – Numbers given in celestial navigation tables that are used for interpolation. The d-value for declination (work form, Box 2), given in the *Nautical Almanac*, is the number of minutes the declination changes each hour. We must determine its sign (±) by inspection. This varies with the sun from 0 (near solstices) to 1' per hour (near equinoxes). For the stars this d is effectively 0, as they do not change. For the moon it can be rather large, up to 13' per hour or so, and it changes rather quickly with time. Declination of Venus can change up to 1.3' per hour; the other planets have very low d-values, less than 0.3' or so. The d-value for the calculated height (work form, Box 5), given in Sight Reduction Tables, is the number of minutes that this height (Hc) changes if declination increases by 1°; its sign is given. This use and definition of "d-value" is totally different from the one above.

Davies Tables – Nickname for the *Concise Tables for Sight Reduction* by Admr. Thomas D. Davies. These were originally published by Cornell Maritime Press. They have evolved into the tables now called NAO Tables, which are included in each *Nautical Almanac* since 1989. See NAO Tables.

Dead Reckoning (DR) – Keeping track of your position from your log (odometer) reading and compass course recorded in a logbook and then adjusting this position by your knowledge of leeway and current. In this course, we consider the process of DR to be using everything you know about your position, short of an actual fix or other piloting information. See DR Position.

Declination (Dec) – This is a fundamental concept in celestial navigation. It is the latitude of the geographical position of any celestial body. Stars have very nearly constant declinations; they can have any value between N 90° and S 90°. The sun's declination varies slowly throughout the year from N 23.4° to S 23.4°. The declinations of the moon and planets vary in a more complex manner between about N 30° to S 30°. The N, S label is conventionally placed before the declination to distinguish it from geographic latitude, which is written with the label after the value, i.e., a star with declination N 19° passes once a day over all points on earth that have latitude 19° N. See Geographical Position.

Declination Increment – This is an official name of the minutes part of the declination. We do not use this term in our course, but it is used in the Pub. 229 Sight Reduction Tables. In our course, we call this "the minutes part of the declination."

Deviation – A compass error caused by magnetic materials on the boat. If your compass reads too high on a particular heading, the deviation is called "west," if too low, it is called "east." If you have deviation on any one heading, you will have different errors on other headings.

Dip – A correction to the sextant height to account for the height of eye (HE) at the sight time. In math terms, it is the angle between the geometric horizon (true horizontal) and the visible horizon which is tilted because of the observer's height above the water. The effect of the dip is to make every sextant height too large by a small amount (equal to 0.97' times the square root of HE in feet). Dip corrections are tabulated in the *Nautical Almanac*. The dip correction expressed in miles (1' = 1 mile) is approximately equal to the distance from the observer to the last visible point on the horizon.

Dividers – A plotting tool used in navigation to transfer distances from one place to another on a chart or plotting sheet, such as distance between buoys to a miles scale.

DR Latitude – The latitude of your DR position. See DR Position.

DR Longitude – The longitude of your DR position. See DR Position.

DR Plot – A plot on the plotting sheet of your DR track records (from the logbook), showing how far and in what direction you traveled since your last fix. Once a new fix is obtained, this plot is abandoned and a new one started from the latest fix. This plot is the most important part of ocean navigation. It must be done carefully if you are to test the accuracy of your DR. See Accuracy, Dead Reckoning, and Plotting.

DR Position – In this course we treat this as your best evaluation of your position taking into account everything you know about your progress since the last fix. Besides log and compass records, you also have leeway, estimated currents, and helm bias as typical corrections to make. See Section 11.11.

DR Track – Same as DR plot.

Drift – The speed of a current, expressed in knots or nautical miles per day. Pilot charts plot ocean currents. There are also world maps showing currents in *Bowditch*, along with a discussion of the currents. See set.

Easy LAN Rule – A reminder that once you have declination and zenith distance, your LAN latitude is the sum or difference of these two. There are standard rules to decide when to do which, or this rule says simply add them, and if that does not make sense, subtract them. Comparison with your DR Lat will usually answer this.

Ecliptic – The annual path of the sun through the stars. The 12 zodiac constellations are located along the ecliptic. The sun moves along this path at 1° per day relative to the stars (from 360° divided by 365 days). The First Point of Aries is astronomically defined as the intersection of the ecliptic and the celestial equator (the line across the sky that separates northern stars from southern stars). The term ecliptic is not directly used in the practice of navigation. The zodiac constellation observed on the horizon just before the rising sun and just following the setting sun tells the position of the sun along the ecliptic, and has served for thousands of years as a stellar calendar. Because the orbits of the moon and planets lie in the same plane with the earth's orbit, these bodies are also always seen along the ecliptic. Whenever the moon and planets can be seen together, they will form a line (giant arc) across the sky. At twilight, this line also includes the point on the horizon that the sun crosses. See Aries.

Elevated Pole – A navigator's term referring to the north pole of the sky in the Northern Hemisphere and the south pole of the sky in the Southern Hemisphere. This concept allows for precise shorthand descriptions, such as the azimuth angle is measured "relative to the elevated pole," instead of saying, "relative to N in the NH and relative to S in the SH" .

Ellipsoidal Distance – Shortest distance on the earth between two points taking into account the geodedic datum used to describe the shape of the earth. It will vary slightly from the great circle distance.

EPIRB – Emergency Position-Indicating Radio Beacon, a small portable radio that emits distress signals when activated. Monitored by satellites and aircraft, they are an important emergency aid. The system is improving rapidly; every vessel should carry one.

Equation of Time (EqT) – The time difference between the actual UTC of local apparent noon at Greenwich and 12:00:00. It varies throughout the year in a smooth but irregular way from about +14 minutes to about -16 minutes. EqT is listed twice daily in the *Nautical Almanac*. This variation is caused by the tilt of the earth's rotation axis and the varying orbital speed of the earth along its slightly elliptical path around the sun.

Equinoxes – The 2 days of the year when the sun crosses the equator as its declination changes from south to north (March 21) and then back to south again (September 23). On the equinoxes, the sun rises due east at 6 am and sets due west at 6 pm solar time everywhere on earth. Hence the name, equinox, which means "equal nights," or day and night of equal length.

Fix – A position, latitude and longitude, found by the navigator from the intersection of two or more LOPs, or given to the navigator from GPS or radar.

Full-View Mirror – Although this may be a trade name for one specific model, it generally refers to that type of sextant horizon mirror with a special horizon glass that replaces the traditional split mirror with an optically coated glass that both reflects and transmits light over the full range of view. It makes easy sights easier, but hard sights harder, since its principle of operation loses light intensity at the horizon glass. Nevertheless, they are attractive to first time sextant users because most sights fall into the easy category. Problems occur for faint stars, or when checking the index correction, or inverting the sextant when there is little contrast between sky and water color. Full-view mirrors are also difficult to use for sextant piloting. See Index Correction, Inverting the Sextant, and Horizon Glass, Sextant Piloting.

Geographical Position (GP) – The point on earth directly below a celestial body; or put another way, a star can appear directly overhead only if you are standing at its GP. The latitude of the GP of a celestial body is called its declination; the longitude of the GP is called its Greenwich hour angle (GHA). As the earth rotates, the GPs of all celestial bodies move westward at about 15° of longitude each hour along the surface of the earth, locked in tracks of fixed latitudes equal to their declinations. (The moon is the only body whose declination track slips north or south a noticeable amount during a single day's pass around the earth). The main function of the *Nautical Almanac* is to tell us the precise location of the GPs of all celestial bodies, at all times, throughout the year.

Global Positioning System (GPS) – The name of the satellite navigation system that began public operation in the mid-1980s. It offers continuous, high-accuracy navigation. See Section 11.3.

Great Circle (GC) – The intersection of a plane and a sphere (the earth) on the surface of the sphere is a circle. If the plane passes through the center of the sphere the circle is a great circle. The shortest distance between two points on the surface of the earth (assumed a sphere) is the segment of the great circle passing between the two points. For any angular segment of a great circle on the earth 1° = 60 nmi. See also Ellipsoidal Distance.

Great-Circle Route – The shortest route between two points on earth. It is rarely possible to follow such a route in a sailboat, but there is also rarely any advantage to trying. The difference in distance between a rhumb-line route and a great-circle route is insignificant unless both the departure and destination are at high latitudes (above 45° or so) and the trip itself is more than 2,000 miles long. Most voyages are planned with simple rhumb-line routes through prevailing wind patterns. See Course, Rhumb line.

Greenwich Hour Angle (GHA) – The longitude of the geographical position (GP) of a celestial body, given in the *Nautical Almanac* as a positive angle between 0° and 360°. It is the Almanac's way of telling how far a GP is west of Greenwich. If GHA = 30°, the longitude of this GP is 30° West. If GHA = 270°, the longitude of the GP is 90° East. The GHAs of celestial bodies move westward at about 15° of longitude each hour.

Greenwich Mean Time (GMT) – The historic name of what is now called universal time. See Universal Time.

Greenwich Meridian – The meridian line passing through Greenwich (London) England, which is defined as longitude equals 0°. See Meridian.

H.O. – A now out-dated abbreviation for Hydrographic Office that used to precede the title numbers of various navigation tables published by the government, but it is no longer used. See Publication No.

H.O. 208 – Sight Reduction Tables, called the Dreisenstock method, similar to H.O. 211 that survive only because of an excellent book by John Letcher on how to use them.

H.O. 211 – An out-dated set of Sight Reduction Tables, called the Ageton method, which was once reproduced in *Bowditch*, Vol. 2. as an emergency or backup means of sight reduction. These have now been replaced in most similar applications by the NAO Tables.

H.O. 214 – The older Sight Reduction Tables that were replaced with Pub. No. 229.

Heading – The direction a boat is pointed. In a seaway, the heading generally swings back and forth across your desired course. "Course heading" is a redundant, and possibly confusing, phrase for "course." The question "What is your course?" means, "which way do you want to go?" "What is your heading?" means, "which way are you going right now?" See Course and Bearing.

Height – A general name for the angular height of a celestial body above the horizon that is determined from a sextant measurement or sight reduction. Angular height is often called "altitude" in other textbooks. When a body is right on the horizon, its height is 0°; when a body is overhead, its height is 90°. The term is used more precisely depending on the number of corrections that have been made to the sextant measurement. See Sextant Height, Apparent Height, Observed Height, and Calculated Height.

Height of Eye (HE) – The vertical distance from an observer's eye to the water level. It is used for the dip correction to the sextant height in a sight reduction and to estimate the visible range of land and lights. It is best expressed in feet.

High-Altitude Sights – Sextant sights of celestial bodies that are more than about 80° high. These sights are special for two reasons. First, they are difficult to take because it is difficult to tell which way to point the sextant as you rock it; and second, once taken, they must be reduced by special methods.

A standard sight reduction will not yield an accurate line of position for high-altitude sights. It is important to remember this whenever you sail under the sun. At heights of 75° to 85° or so, you can still do a standard sight reduction, but you must interpolate for the azimuth angle as explained in the Work-form Instructions, and then you should also adjust the slopes of the lines as explained in the instructions to the Sight Reduction Tables.

Above 85°, it will be necessary to plot the geographical position on the plotting sheet and then plot a circle of position around it with a radius equal to the zenith distance of the sight. The book Emergency Navigation explains these sights with examples. See Rocking the Sextant, Sextant Sights, Sight Reduction, Circle of Position, and Zenith Distance.

Horizon Glass – Part of a sextant, it is the half-mirrored glass in line with the telescope. On "full-view" sextants this glass is not split into a mirror-half and a glass-half, but is transparent throughout. See Full-view Sextants.

Horizon mirror – The more common name for Horizon Glass.

Horizontal Parallax (HP) – The maximum value of the parallax angle of a celestial body, corresponding to its observation on the horizon. It is only used for moon-sight reductions (work forms, Box 2) and is tabulated in the *Nautical Almanac*. Geometrically, HP is the angle between two lines, one from the center of the moon to the center of the earth, the other from the center of the moon to the edge of the earth. This angle is about 56', but it changes slightly from day to day as the distance to the moon changes along its elliptical path around the earth. See Parallax.

Increments and Corrections — The corrections tables at the back of the *Nautical Almanac* that are used to find the incremental increase to the Greenwich hour angle (GHA) for the minutes and seconds part of the sight time and for finding the d-correction to the declination and the v-correction to GHA. See d-correction, Greenwich Hour Angle, and v-value.

Index Arm — Part of a sextant, it is the arm that rotates about the center of the arc. The index mirror is at the top of this arm, and the micrometer is at the bottom.

Index Correction (IC) — The sextant error caused by a misalignment of the two mirrors when the index arm is set to 0° and the micrometer is set to 0.0'. The correction is measured by aligning the direct and reflected views of the horizon or a star and then reading the micrometer. If the reading is a small number, the IC is "on the scale" and the correction is to be subtracted. If the reading is a large number such as 58.2' the correction is 60' minus 58.2', or 1.8' "off the scale" and the correction is to be added. The rule is, "If it's on, take it off; if it's off, put it on." It is important to measure IC carefully at some point, and then check it at each sight. The primary disadvantage of plastic sextants are unavoidable variations of the index correction, which means it must be checked frequently during any sight session.

Index Error — See Index Correction.

Index Mirror — A part of the sextant, it is the mirror on the end of the index arm at the center of the arc.

Inverting the Sextant — The standard way to do star or planet sights that have not been precomputed. Set the sextant to 0° 0', turn it upside down in the left hand, then looking up toward the star, keep the star in direct view as you use the right hand to adjust the sextant to bring the horizon up to the star. Once star and horizon are both in view, turn the sextant back over and complete the sight in the normal manner. See Precomputation and Sextant Sights.

Jupiter — One of the five planets visible to the naked eye (Jupiter, Venus, Mercury, Saturn, and Mars). Jupiter and Venus are the two main planets for navigation since they are always brighter than the brightest stars and therefore their sights can be taken immediately after sunset or just before sunrise when the stars are not visible. Unlike Venus, however, Jupiter moves rather slowly through the stars. Check the planet diagram in the *Nautical Almanac* to get a feeling for how it moves in any particular year. See Planet Diagram

Knot — The unit of speed used in navigation and meteorology. One knot equals one nautical mile per hour. "Knots per hour" is not correct terminology these days, but the point should not be pushed too hard, because that is how it was originally used in 19th century logbooks.

Knotmeter — A boat's speedometer.

Latitude (Lat) — Latitude and longitude are an imaginary grid used to locate positions on the earth's surface. Latitude is the side of the grid that tells how far a place is north or south of the equator. It is the angular distance of a point from the equator, measured north or south along a meridian line. To picture the angle, imagine the earth cut in half along any meridian line. Since a meridian line is a great circle, the latitude of a place can be literally considered the number of miles it is from the equator. Latitude 30° N, for example, means all points on earth that are 30° × (60 miles/1°), or 1,800 miles north of the equator. See Meridian, Great Circle, and Nautical Mile.

Latitude by Polaris — The procedure for finding your latitude from the sextant height of Polaris. This unique star sight is especially convenient since no precomputation is required; just set your sextant to your DR-Lat, look north, and Polaris will be in view with the horizon. The simple sight reduction required is explained with examples in the *Nautical Almanac*—interestingly, this is the only place in the *Nautical Almanac* that explains a way to navigate with the data provided in the book. Once you have found your latitude this way it is plotted on the chart as a line of position and used with other sights to find a fix. See Polaris, Precomputation, and Polaris Corrections.

Line of Position (LOP) — Any line that marks the location of a boat, such as a bearing to a lighthouse in coastal waters or a sun line from a celestial sight at sea. With one known LOP, the boat is known to be located somewhere on that line, but the precise place on the line is not known. Generally, a position fix is found from the intersection of two or more LOPs. In celestial navigation, each sextant sight yields one LOP, so it takes at least two sights of different bodies to get a fix. See Plotting LOPs, Sun Lines, and Circle of Equal Altitude.

Local Apparent Noon (LAN) — The time of meridian passage of the sun. Often used as a name for the series of midday sights of the sun taken to find latitude.

Local Hour Angle (LHA) — Used in a sight reduction, it is the number of longitude degrees that the geographical position of a body is west of the assumed longitude (a-Lon). It is figured from the Greenwich hour angle (GHA) as: LHA = GHA - a-Lon(West) or LHA = GHA + a-Lon(East). The GHA is listed in the *Nautical Almanac*. Although the rules for figuring it are different in east and west longitudes, the meaning of the result is the same. When using Sight Reduction Tables, a-Lon is always chosen such that LHA will be a whole number of degrees with no minutes part. At meridian passage, LHA equals 0°. See Greenwich Hour Angle and Assumed Longitude.

Local Mean Time (LMT) — The UTC of any event observed from the Greenwich meridian. All times (sunrise, twilights, meridian passage, etc) listed in the *Nau-*

tical Almanac are given in terms of LMT - that is, they tell you what time this will happen in UTC for observers at Greenwich. To figure the actual UTC you should observe for these events from a western DR-Lon, convert your DR-Lon to time using the Arc to Time table in the *Nautical Almanac* and then add this time interval to the listed LMT of the event. In east longitudes, subtract this interval from the tabulated LMT. Once you have figured the UTC of the event this way, you can figure watch time, by reversing whatever you normally do to your watch time to figure UTC from it.

Log – A boat's odometer, it counts miles traveled through the water by summing knotmeter signals. Logs, however, cannot detect motion of the water itself, so they tell nothing about currents present. Taffrail or Walker (a brand name) logs are mechanical ones whose signals come from a propeller pulled at the end of a drag line about 50 ft astern. The prop turns the drag line that turns a geared clock dial that is mounted on the stern rail, which counts the miles.

Logbook – The boat's written record of course changes and other data pertinent to the voyage. Logbook entries should be made whenever the course changes by a consistent 5° or more, or at least once every 4 hours, even if nothing changes.

Longitude (Lon) – Latitude and longitude are an imaginary grid used to locate positions on the earth's surface. Longitude is the side of the grid that tells how far a place is east or west of the Greenwich meridian. The longitude of a place is the angular distance "around" the earth from Greenwich to the place, when the earth is viewed from the top, looking down at the North Pole. Lines of constant longitude are called meridians, and since they converge at the poles the number of miles between them decreases with increasing latitude.

At the equator, and to a good approximation throughout the tropics, 1° of longitude is 60 nmi (the same as 1° of latitude), but at higher latitudes this distance must be read from a chart or plotting sheet. Although there is rarely any need to do so, the length of a longitude degree at some arbitrary latitude can be found with a calculator from: 1° of Lon = 60 nmi × Cos(Lat). At 48° North, there are 40 miles to a degree of longitude. Traveling west from Greenwich, longitude is labeled west and increases until you reach 180°, and then it decreases and is labeled east. The meridian that lies 300° west of Greenwich, for example, is called 60° East.

Lower Limb (LL) – The bottom edge of the sun or moon. The top edge of the sun or moon is called the upper limb. Most sights of the sun are taken relative to the lower limb. Only when the lower limb is obscured would one typically use the upper limb for the sun. For moon sights, we must use whatever limb is full at the time.

Lower Transit – The time a celestial body crosses a longitude equal to your longitude plus 180°—in a sense, the exact opposite of meridian passage. This time and concept have little practical application in celestial navigation, other than the application to circumpolar stars discussed under meridian passage. Upper transit, on the other hand, is just another name for meridian passage.

Lunar Distance – The procedure of finding longitude and UTC by measuring the angular distance between the moon and another celestial body. Sights taken for lunar distance are called *lunars*. With care and practice, one can find UTC in this manner to within about 30s of time, sometimes better, more often not quite that good. The sights are difficult, even on land, and must be accurate, along with accurate index correction. There are several procedures for solving the special sight reduction. The *Nautical Almanac* stopped printing the required tables in 1905, but navigation historian Bruce Stark published a modern set with instructions called *Stark Tables for Clearing the Lunar Distance and Finding Universal Time by Sextant Observation* (Starpath Publications, 2010). There are excellent lunar distance resources online for those who wish to practice this.

Magnitude – A logarithmic scale for the brightness of celestial bodies. The smaller the magnitude number, the brighter the object, so negative magnitudes mean very bright objects. There are 20 magnitude-one stars (the brightest stars), about 70 magnitude-two stars (two to three times fainter than the first group, about as bright as an average Big Dipper star), about 200 magnitude-three stars (about six times fainter than the first group, similar to stars in the Little Dipper), and about 500 magnitude-four stars (about 16 times fainter than the bright guys). On a reasonably clear night in Seattle one can see magnitude-four stars. In navigation we use almost exclusively first and second magnitude stars. The planets are typically brighter than the stars by as much as 1 to 4 magnitudes. The magnitudes of planets are listed on the *Nautical Almanac* daily pages, but to find star magnitudes you must look in the back of the *Nautical Almanac*, in the special star lists.

Mars – One of the five planets visible to the naked eye (Jupiter, Venus, Mercury, Saturn, and Mars). Usually Mars is not particularly bright, so is not special for navigation, but it does go through periods every few years of being very bright, as in mid 2003. Mars usually appears reddish when viewed through binoculars. All planets appear as tiny disks when viewed through binoculars, as opposed to stars which are always points of light.

Mercury – One of the five planets visible to the naked eye (Jupiter, Venus, Mercury, Saturn, and Mars). Mercury is not used for navigation. It is usually too close to the sun; so it is rarely more than a few degrees above the horizon at sunset or sunrise, and we try to avoid low sights when possible due to refraction uncertainties. The Almanac will often discuss Mercury in the Planet Diagram discussion section, but usually just a warning of when it might be confused with Venus, etc.

Meridian — Any line at constant longitude. Special ones are the Greenwich meridian (the reference line), the International Date Line (where west turns to east), and your local meridian which marks the high point in the arc of all celestial bodies as they pass. The corresponding name for a constant latitude line is a "parallel" of latitude.

Meridian Angle (t) — An equivalent, but less convenient way to measure the local hour angle (LHA), which is used in a few navigation publications, but not this one. It is the number of longitude degrees between the assumed position and the geographical position, measured either East or West of the assumed longitude (a-Lon). It is defined as: t = GHA - a-Lon. If t is negative (-) the body is east of the observer (t-East); if positive (+), the body is west of the observer (t-West).

Meridian Passage (mer pass) — The moment any celestial body crosses over your longitude line (meridian), bearing precisely due north or south. A body approaching your meridian from the east will have a large LHA (local hour angle) that reaches 360° and starts over at 0° just as it crosses the meridian at its peak height in the sky. Meridian passage of the sun is called local apparent noon. Meridian passage of other bodies do not have a special name, although looking north, meridian passage of circumpolar stars crossing your meridian over the top Polaris headed west are described as upper transit (at their peak height in the sky), whereas those crossing the meridian below Polaris headed east (at their lowest point in the sky) are described as crossing your meridian at lower transit. Once you have found your latitude this way (from any body, although sun is by far most common) it is plotted on the chart as a line of position and used with other sights to find a fix.

Micrometer Drum — That part of a modern sextant used to measure the minutes part of the sextant angle. The micrometer scale can usually be read to a precision of 1' and the tenths of minutes are read from the Vernier scale. The degrees part of the angle is read from a scale on the arc of the sextant.

Mid-Latitude — A type of rhumb-line sailing that uses the mid-latitude (Lm) defined as the average of the departure and arrival latitudes. It also refers to the center latitude on a universal plotting sheet. As one word, midlatitudes refers to the region on earth between the tropics and the polar regions.

Minutes Boxes — Starpath course jargon for the Increments and Corrections Tables in the *Nautical Almanac*. See Increments and Corrections.

Name — The label (north or south) of latitudes and declinations. See Same Name and Contrary Name.

NAO Tables — Originally a nickname, now in essence the official name, for the Nautical Almanac Office's Concise Sight Reduction Tables, which are included in each edition of the *Nautical Almanac*. These 20 pages can reduce any sight, but the process is a bit longer than using inspection tables such as Pub. 249 or 229, which are typically several volumes each of large books.

Nautical Almanac — The annual government publication that tabulates the locations of all celestial bodies each second of the year. It also includes correction tables for sextant sights and related data. Commercial reproductions of the government edition are also available. The official government editions (a joint US and UK publication) has an orange hard cover with black spine; a popular commercial edition has an all blue paper cover.

Nautical Charts — Maps of the waterways, from lakes to entire oceans, designed specifically for marine navigation. Charts of American waters are published by NOS, a division of NOAA; charts of foreign waters are from NGA. See www.starpath.com/getcharts

Nautical Mile (nmi) — A unit of distance equal to a latitude change of 1' at constant longitude. Cape Flattery is at latitude 48° N, San Francisco is at 38° N. It is 10° south, so it must be 600 nmi south. A nautical mile is very nearly 6,000 ft long, which makes it about 15% longer than a statute mile. The official definition (required because the earth is not strictly round) is 1 nmi = 1852 meters, exactly. To figure the precise length of a nmi in other units, start with 1852 meters, then 1 meter equals 100 centimeters, and then use the official definition of an inch as 2.54 centimeters, exactly. In navigation, miles means nautical miles.

Nautical Twilight — That time of day, listed in the *Nautical Almanac*, when the horizon fades into or out of darkness. In the morning it marks the end of night when star sights begin; in the evening, it marks the beginning of night when star sights end. See Civil Twilight and Local Mean Time.

Navigational Stars — The 57 stars listed on the daily pages of the Nautical Almanac, also listed in the Index of Selected Stars on page xxxiii of the Almanac.

Navigational Triangle — The sight reduction process we use in cel nav is based on this triangle drawn on the earth's surface. You do not, however, need to know anything at all about this triangle to do celestial navigation and do it well. See Section 10.6.

Observed Height (Ho) — The final, fully corrected sextant height. It is figured by applying the altitude corrections to the apparent height (Ha), or Ho = Ha + altitude corrections. The observed height is the true height of the body in that the distance to the geographical position (called the zenith distance of the body) can be found from it: zenith distance = 90° - Ho. See Apparent Height, Sextant Height, and Altitude Corrections.

Parallax — The difference in the apparent position of an object viewed from different locations. See Section 10.2. See also Horizontal Parallax.

Parallel — A line of constant latitude, special ones are the equator, which separates north from south latitudes, the tropics (at 23.4° North and South) that mark the limits of the sun's north and south excursions, and the polar circles (at 90° - 23.4° North and South) that mark the latitudes above which it is possible for the sun to stay above or below the horizon for more than 24 hours.

In this usage, a parallel of latitude is analogous to a meridian of longitude.

Parallel can, of course, also refer geometrically to two lines in a plane that never intersect, or two planes in space that never touch.

Parallel Plotter — A plotting tool that does the same job as parallel rulers by rolling without sliding, sometimes called a Weems plotter. They are convenient for work at home or on large chart tables, but must often be backed up with parallel rulers at sea, because they can't reach the edges of the chart and they often slip when used on folded charts. See Parallel Rulers.

Parallel Rulers — A plotting tool used to draw a line on a chart parallel to another line located elsewhere on the chart. One application is transferring a course direction from the compass rose to your present position; another is to lay off the azimuth line from the assumed position when plotting celestial lines of position. Parallel rulers come in various lengths, although 15 inches is about optimum in most small chart table applications.

Pilot Charts — Monthly charts of the oceans used for voyage planning. They include prevailing winds and currents, isobars of average pressures, magnetic variation, gale frequencies, shipping lanes, traditional sailing routes (although they tend to be more downwind than required by modern yachts), and limits of ice flow where applicable. British Pilot Charts are similar to the American ones. Some Pilot Charts can now be downloaded online. See www.starpath.com/navpubs.

Piloting — Keeping track of position relative to charted landmarks. Piloting techniques include magnetic bearings, natural ranges, various methods of finding distance off, depth sounding, and radio direction finding. Piloting should be distinguished from dead reckoning, which is navigation by instruments alone, without reference to charted landmarks. Celestial navigators with a sextant at hand can do very accurate piloting by measuring vertical and horizontal angles between landmarks. See Sextant Piloting and Shipping Lanes.

Planet Diagram — A diagram in the front of the *Nautical Almanac* that shows the locations of planets throughout the day relative to the location of the sun and how this evolves during the year. It takes some practice to learn to use this diagram, but worth it if you care for an overview of planet positions throughout the year. For any given day, on the other hand, you can simply do a sight reduction to get a planet's height and bearing.

Planets — In celestial navigation this means the visible planets Venus, Mars, Jupiter, and Saturn. Mercury is also visible to the naked eye at times, but always too low to be used for sights. Mercury data are not given in the *Nautical Almanac*. Only Venus and Jupiter have special significance to celestial navigation. Because of their extreme brightness their sights can be taken during the brightest part of twilight with a daylight horizon, which makes them accurate sights that are easy to do. Every 16 years or so, Mars becomes unusually bright (even brighter than Jupiter) and then enters the Venus-Jupiter category of special value.

Plotting — The third and final step to finding a fix from celestial sights, the first two being the sextant sight and the sight reduction. The sight reduction leaves you with the four numbers in work form, Box 6 (a-Lat, a-Lon, Zn, and a-value). These four numbers constitute the line of position (LOP) that this one sight has provided. This LOP is then plotted on a plotting sheet using dividers and parallel rulers or protractor. Your boat is located somewhere on this LOP.

The procedure is to plot a point at the assumed position (a-Lat, a-Lon). Then through this point draw the azimuth line in the direction of Zn. The LOP is perpendicular to this azimuth line, at a distance (in nautical miles) from the assumed position equal to the a-value. When the a-value is labeled "T," the LOP is on the side of the assumed position "Toward" the Zn direction; when a-value is labeled "A," it is on the other side of the assumed position, "Away" from the Zn direction. The perpendicular is best drawn using the cross lines printed on the protractor. See Assumed Position, Altitude Intercept (a-value), and Azimuth (Zn).

Plotting Sheet — A blank chart of the ocean used for plotting celestial lines of position and a DR track. Government issues come with the proper grid for various latitudes, and you draw in the longitudes. These plotting sheets for specific latitudes are, however, rather hard to come by, fairly expensive, and too large for typical small-craft chart tables. A better alternative is the universal plotting sheets which can be used for any latitude. See Universal Plotting Sheets.

Polaris — The North Star, a magnitude-two star located 48' off the true celestial pole of the northern sky (2019 declination N 89° 20'), at the tip of the handle of the Little Dipper. The sextant height of Polaris is equal to your latitude to within 1° with no further corrections. The *Nautical Almanac* explains how to remove this uncertainty to find latitude more precisely—which is the only actual cel nav procedure explained in that book. See Polaris Corrections and Latitude by Polaris.

Polaris Corrections (a0, a1, a2) — Corrections given at the back of the *Nautical Almanac* used to find latitude from Polaris, a technique that is similar to finding latitude from the sun at local apparent noon. The largest correction (a0) accounts for the position of Polaris on its circle about the pole, and the other two account for the shape of the earth and slight motions of the polar axis and Polaris. See Polaris and Latitude by Polaris.

Precomputation — The process of predicting the heights and bearings of celestial sights before the sight session, and then choosing the best objects to use. This is the standard way to do star sights and also recommended for sights of Venus and Jupiter, even though they are bright and easy to find. With precomputed sights, you set the sextant to the predicted height, look in the predicted direction, and the star will appear in view near the horizon. To complete the sight, bring it in line with the horizon and record watch time and sextant height. Star precomputation can be done with Pub. No. 249, Vol. 1, or with the 2102-D Star Finder that has the advantage of showing the best star-planet combination to use. Precomputation can also be done by standard sight reduction when you already know what sights you want. This is best done with a calculator, however, if you have many sights to precompute. See Pub. No. 249, Vol.1, Star Finder, Calculators, and Sextant Sights.

Protractor — A plotting tool used to lay off angles or mark azimuths when plotting lines of position.

The compass rose on any chart or plotting sheet is just a permanent protractor that you use with parallel rulers. See Compass Rose and Plotting.

Pub. 229 — Sight Reduction Tables for all celestial bodies, presented in volumes of 15° of Lat each. Official editions are large, hardbound, maroon volumes, with answers given to the nearest 0.1', although this extra precision requires an extra step in the d-correction to the calculated height (Hc). The layout is slightly different from Pub. 249, but the basic use of the tables are the same except for the d-correction step at the end. These do not go out of date. If you find some in a used bookstore or swap meet for a good price, they will do the job just fine.

Pub. 249, Vol. 1 — A special volume of the Pub. 249 Sight Reduction Tables (with a red spine tape) that is used for precomputing star sights and then for sight reduction of these sights. Unlike Vols. 2 and 3, however, this volume must be purchased every 5 years, because the star positions change slightly over the years.

Pub. 249, Vols. 2 and 3 — Sight Reduction Tables (white (v2) and blue (v3)) for sun, moon, and planets, and any star with declination less than 30°, north or south. The answers are given to the nearest whole minute, which implies a precision of 0.5'. This precision limit, however, will rarely place a limitation on the practical accuracy of a typical celestial fix. A sharp pencil and correction for boat motion are more important. Vol. 2 covers north or south latitudes of 0° to 40°; Vol. 3 covers 39° to 89°.

These do not go out of date. If you find some in a used bookstore or swap meet for a good price, they will do the job just fine.

Refraction — In cel nav, this describes the bending of light rays as they enter the earth's atmosphere. The effect takes place because the light ray is traveling from the vacuum of space into the atmosphere, which slows down the light wave. An analogy is shown online at http://davidburchnavigation.blogspot.com/2012/05/refraction-in-sink.html. The effect makes all sextant angles too large, although the correction is very small except for low sights. Sights near the horizon have a maximum refraction of about 35', but at heights of only 10° the refraction has dropped to 5'; at 5° it increases to 10'. At a sextant height of 40° the correction is only 1'. All sights must be corrected for refraction, which is included in the *Nautical Almanac* under the general name altitude correction. Recall that very roughly a 1' sextant angle error translates into a 1 nmi error in a fix, so small corrections do matter. For heights above 6°, the refraction correction is nearly equal to 60' divided by the sextant height in degrees. The Almanac refraction values can be reproduced with the Bennett formula: R = cot[Ha + 7.31/(Ha + 4.4)] for T= 10° C and P = 1010 mb. Correct for temperature and pressure by multiplying by (P/1010) (283/(273+T). See Altitude Corrections.

Rhumb Line (RL) — The straight line between two points on a standard nautical chart (Mercator projection). The true course direction remains constant along a rhumb-line route, although the magnetic course direction changes as the variation does. See Great Circle Route.

Right Ascension (RA) — An alternative to sidereal hour angle (SHA) for labeling star longitudes on a star globe. It is used by astronomers and some star maps but rarely by navigators. It uses time units instead of angle units and runs backward relative to SHA. A star with SHA 300° would have an RA equal to (360° - 300°) × (1 hour/15°) = 4h 00m 00s. The 2102-D uses RA, but this is all sorted out in *The Star Finder Book*. If you have a star map marked in RA, you can convert it to SHA as: SHA = (24h - RA) × 15°.

Rocking the Sextant — A motion of the sextant that must be done when taking a sight to ensure that the proper vertical height of the object is measured. "Rocking" means rotating the sextant, without moving the head, about an imaginary line from your eye to the image of the object on the horizon. For actual sights, you need to rock very little, about 20° or so, to either side, but it is good to practice rocking even farther to begin with as this teaches you how to keep the object in view on a moving boat. As you rock the sextant you must willfully keep it pointed toward the object, since the tendency is to rotate as you rock (yawl as you roll). As you rock, the image will appear to move along an arc. You want the object to just touch the horizon at the lowest point of the arc. Achieve this by adjusting the micrometer as you rock the sextant. See Sextant and Sextant Sight.

Running Fix (rfix) – The procedure of finding a fix from two sights taken at different times when the boat is moving. At the time of the second sight, you will have moved off of the first line of position (LOP); so it must be corrected before it can be crossed with the second LOP to get a fix. The only exception is a first sight taken of an object precisely on the beam, then no course changes till the second sight. In this case the first LOP is your course line and your fix is simply where the second LOP crosses the first.

The procedure for arbitrary sights and course changes between sights is to plot a special, between-sights DR track of the distance run and all course changes made between the two sights, starting at any point on the first LOP. Generally it is best to plot this track from a far end of the LOP, away from your main DR plot. Then use parallel rulers to advance the first LOP to the end of this between-sights DR track. The running fix is the intersection of the second LOP with the advanced first LOP. See Advanced LOP.

Same Name – Means that the label (north or south) of a sighted body's declination is the same as your DR-Lat. A star with declination S 56° has "Same Name" if you are at any south latitude when you did the sight, otherwise it is called "Contrary Name." See Name and Contrary Name.

Saturn – One of the five planets visible to the naked eye (Jupiter, Venus, Mercury, Saturn, and Mars). Saturn is rarely as bright as the brightest stars; so its main role in navigation is to confuse us by appearing as a star where no star should be. There, of course, will be exceptions, and we will be very happy to have Saturn right where it is for a nice combination of star-planet sights. It is an outer planet like Jupiter and moves slowly across the stars, as opposed to Venus and Mercury, which move much more quickly.

Semidiameter (SD) – One half of the angular width of the sun or moon. This width is accidentally about the same for the sun and moon at about 16' on the average. The moon is much smaller than the sun, but it is also much closer; its semi-diameter is coincidentally about the same as the sun's. The SD of sun and moon both vary with time since their distances from us change with orbital position. Normally, half the diameter of a circle is called its radius, but because of refraction, the apparent shape of the sun or moon, especially when low in the sky, is not a circle but an ellipse. Half of an ellipse is called its semi-diameter. Perhaps that is a source of this terminology, since the term was first used as a correction, but the value tabulated is not related to that. It is a geometric factor determined by the distance to the sun. Because of refraction, however, if you wish to measure the SD, it should be done when the sun is above 30° high. See Refraction and Solar Method of IC.

Set – The true direction toward which a current flows. Pilot charts plot ocean currents. There are also world maps showing currents in *Bowditch*, along with a discussion of the currents. Best data come from modern ocean model predictions. See Drift.

The word "set" is often used to refer to the difference between a vessel's heading and its actual course over ground. If I am steering 200 and making good a course of 215, then I am getting set 15° to the right. This latter common usage is more parlance than official terminology.

Sextant – A device used to measure the angular heights of celestial bodies above the horizon. It can also be used for coastal piloting to find distance off from the angular heights of landmarks with charted elevations. The inherent precision of top-line metal models (costing $600 to $3,000) is about 0.2' or so, but this does not mean any single sight will be this accurate. Even highly experienced navigators will get variations of up to 1.0' in a series of nominally identical sights. Consequently, to approach a fix accuracy equivalent to the quality of a good sextant, several sights must be taken and then averaged. Plastic sextants have a lower inherent precision, 1' to 2', with even higher variations within a series of sights. Nevertheless, celestial fixes to within 3 or 4 miles accuracy can still be achieved with a plastic sextant by averaging many sights and checking the index correction frequently (See Section 11.18 on use of plastic sextants).

The sextant was invented by Sir Issac Newton in the mid 1700's. Early models used a Vernier scale, which was replaced with more convenient micrometer drums some time in the 1930's. Important features to look for are large mirrors, a wide, unobstructed field of view, with lighted arc and micrometer. An optimum all-purpose telescope is about a 4 × 40. The most popular sextant worldwide is the Astra IIIb, which marks a peak in performance per dollar. These are made in China. Top quality metal sextants are made also by Freiberger (German) and Tamaya (Japan). See Sextant Sights, Accuracy, Vernier, Index Correction, and Side Error.

Sextant arc – The bottom circumference of the sextant frame. The degrees scale is usually attached or engraved into the arc of the sextant. Sextant accuracy is not dependent on the arc scale itself, but rather on the precise spacing of the notches on the bottom of the arc that engage the worm gear.

Sextant Height (Hs) — The actual sextant reading at the time of a sextant sight, without any corrections applied. The degrees part is read from the sextant arc; the minutes part from the micrometer drum. Modern sextants give these angles in degrees, minutes, and tenths of a minute; older sextants are marked in degrees, minutes, and seconds. The Hs angle itself is the one between the two lines of sight, eye-to-horizon and eye-to-star. See Sextant Sight, High-Altitude Sights, and Rocking the Sextant.

Sextant Sight — The process of measuring the sextant height of a celestial body and recording the watch time of the measurement to the second. Once the object and horizon are both in view (achieved in sun sights by just hunting around the arc, or in star sights by precomputation or by inverting the sextant), the sight is completed by adjusting the micrometer until the object just skims the horizon while rocking the sextant.

Log readings should be recorded before and after each sight session, to identify the sight or to use later in a running fix.

Whenever possible, sextant sights should be of objects higher than 15° and lower than 75°. Lower sights are less accurate due to refraction uncertainties, and higher sights require special sight reduction techniques. Within these limits, sun sights can be taken any time of day, but star sights are typically limited to the period between civil and nautical twilight when it is dark enough to see the stars, yet not too dark to see the horizon. Checking the index correction is an important part of any sight session. Sun sights require no preparation, but star or planet sights should be precomputed before the sight session. See Index Correction, High-Altitude Sights, Precomputation, Rocking the Sextant, and Inverting the Sextant.

Sextant Piloting — The process of using a sextant to measure vertical angles (i.e., height of a hill or bridge clearance) or horizontal angles (i.e., width of an islet or bay entrance, or distance between two landmarks) to find a distance off or position on a chart. Sextant piloting is the most accurate means of piloting, so much so that it is often called surveying. Examples are given in the book *How to Use Plastic Sextant: With Applications to Metal Sextants and a Review of Sextant Piloting*.

Shipping Lanes — The great-circle routes between major ports that are followed by marine traffic at sea. They are shown on pilot charts. Crossing them, keep special watch for traffic; in an emergency, they are the best bet for finding help. See Pilot Charts.

Shooting a Star — Parlance for taking a sextant sight of a star.

Side Error — A sextant misalignment that affects the view through the telescope but not the measured height. Side error is present when the two mirrors (horizon and index) are not perpendicular to the arc of the sextant. On a traditional sextant with half-silvered horizon glass, this error causes the image to jump from one side of the glass to the other as you scan the object with the sextant set to 0° 0'. It will also cause a smooth horizon to split apart as you rock the sextant, which is a good way to detect even a small side error independent of index error.

On full-view sextants, side error shows up as a light blue smear to one side of a distant object with a light yellow smear to the other side when the sextant is set to 0°. Instruction manuals (or *Bowditch*) tells how to remove this error with the adjustment screws at the mirrors. See Index Correction, *Bowditch*, and Full-View Sextants.

Sidereal Hour Angle (SHA) — The name of a star's longitude on a star globe, it is how far the star is west of the Aries meridian. The location of a star on the star globe or in the sky is given by its declination and SHA just as points on earth are located with latitude and longitude. The SHAs and declinations of individual stars remain essentially constant throughout the years. See Aries and Declination.

Sight — See Sextant Sight.

Sight Reduction — The book and paperwork of celestial navigation. It is the intermediate step to finding a fix from celestial sights; the first step is the sight itself, the last step is plotting the lines of position. Using Starpath work forms, sight reduction begins in work form, Box 1 with the sextant height (Hs) and watch time (WT) of a particular sight. Using the *Nautical Almanac* and Sight Reduction Tables, it ends with the four numbers in work form, Box 6 (a-Lat, a-Lon, Zn, and a-value) that are used to plot the line of position. Once the procedures and work forms are familiar, the process takes about 15 minutes using tables. The same process can be completed with a programmed calculator in about 1 minute. In either case, the key to good sight reduction is to double-check yourself at each stage. Blunders will usually stand out, but not until near the end of the process. See Work Forms, Calculators, *Nautical Almanac*, and Sight Reduction Tables.

Sight Reduction Tables — Required books for celestial navigation that last indefinitely as they are just tables of mathematical solutions to the navigational triangle. There are several styles available, the most popular amongst sailors are Pub. 249 Vols. 2 and 3 (used in this course). The set called Pub. 229 is used on USCG exams and by the Navy. For backup or a viable alternative for your primary tables, the NAO Tables are the best bet. Regardless of the table style, however, all do the same job: you tell the tables three numbers (LHA, Dec, and a-Lat) and the tables tell you two numbers (Hc and Zn). Programmed calculators will do what these tables do, but you still need some set of tables on board to backup the calculator. See Pub. 249, Pub. 229, NAO Tables, Navigational Triangle, and Calculators.

Solar Method of IC — Using the alignment of upper and lower limbs of the sun to measure the index correction, which measures the SD of the sun as a check. See Section 11.7.

Solstices — The 2 days of the year when the "sun stands still" over one of the two tropics as it turns from an increasing to a decreasing declination. In northern latitudes, these are the longest day of the year (June 21 with the sun at declination N 23.4°) and the shortest day of the year (December 21 with the sun at declination S 23.4°). These 2 days mark the maximum excursion of the sunrise and sunset off of due east and west. The exact date when the declination is maximum can change slightly from year to year. See Amplitude and Equinoxes.

Speed Over Ground (SOG) — A GPS computed value of your speed relative to the fixed earth taking into account all factors that affect your motion. See also Course Over Ground.

Standard Time — The time system that uses time zone boundaries marked by government and geographical considerations, such as Pacific Standard Time and Eastern Standard Time. Each time zone is roughly 15° of longitude wide, but large discrepancies can be found. Places that switch from standard time to daylight saving time, change the zone description of their time zone by 1 hour during the summer half of the year. The standard time zone that applies to a particular place (and whether they switch to daylight saving time) can be looked up in the back of the *Nautical Almanac*, but there is no practical navigational need to know this—other than helping a thirsty navigator guess whether the Pioneer Inn in Lahaina, or equivalent stations around the world, might still be open when you arrive. See Universal Time, Watch Time, Zone Time, and Zone Description.

Star Finder — Meaning the 2102-D Star Finder or the equivalent British version called NP 323, it is a plastic device that can predict angular heights and bearings of all celestial bodies to within a few degrees, at any time, from any place on earth. Its primary use is for identifying unknown stars in partly cloudy skies, although it has many other valuable applications such as precomputation for star sights, planning running fixes, and calling the best time of day for sun-moon fixes. The device is explained in detail in *The Star Finder Book*. See Precomputation and Star Finder book.

Summer Triangle — A prominent right triangle of three bright stars, each from a different constellation, that often appears over head in the northern summer as the first visible stars. Deneb, at the head of the Northern Cross (Cygnus), together with Vega and Altair make up a prominent right triangle, which is led across the sky by the brilliant Vega at the right angle. See extended discussion in *Emergency Navigation* by David Burch

Sun line — A line of position obtained from a sextant sight of the sun. "Take a sun line," means do a sun sight, reduce it, and plot it. Similar use for star line, moon line, etc. Sometimes written as "sunline." See Sextant Sight.

Sunrise — The moment the top edge (upper limb) of the sun first appears on the visible horizon. This time depends on your latitude and the date and is listed every 3 days in the *Nautical Almanac*. See Local Mean Time, and Civil and Nautical Twilights.

Sunset — The moment the top edge (upper limb) of the sun disappears below the visible horizon. This time depends on your latitude and the date and is listed every 3 days in the *Nautical Almanac*. See Local Mean Time, and Civil and Nautical Twilights.

The Star Finder Book — A recommended supplement to this book. It covers all aspects and usage of the 2102-D Star Finder as well as many tips on star and planet motions and identification.

Time Zone — Most generally speaking, this means a geographical region within which the same time is used. The time system in use, however, can be either a "zone time," more common for navigation, or a "standard time," which is more common for daily use outside of navigation — although there are no hard and fast rules for practical navigation. In the end, we need to know UTC, and it does not matter at all what time system we work with so long as we can in an error-free manner always know UTC. See Zone Time, Standard Time, and UT.

Transit — In astronomy and celestial navigation, it means the same as meridian passage. See Meridian Passage, Upper Transit, and Lower Transit. In England, the word "transit" is used in coastal navigation as we use "range." Transit is also the name of the present satellite navigation system.

Tropics — Has two meanings: tropics, the specific latitudes of 23.4° S (the Tropic of Capricorn) and 23.4° N (the Tropic of Cancer) or tropics, the region on earth between these two latitudes. The tropics span the latitude range of the sun's geographical position. At each latitude within the tropics the sun will appear directly overhead twice a year. Outside of the tropics the sun will never reach a height of 90°. The tropics are the latitudes of the sun's declination on the solstices. The Equator is the latitude of the sun's declination on the equinoxes. See Declination, Solstices, and Equinoxes.

Twilight — In general use, that time period between daylight and darkness. It is used more precisely in celestial navigation since star sights must be taken during this period. Twilight times in navigation refer to specific times of day, not to time periods. See Civil Twilight and Nautical Twilight.

Universal Plotting Sheets — Blank charts of the ocean with latitude lines spaced 3 inches apart and no longitude lines shown. The longitude lines must be drawn in by the navigator using a universal scale provided on each sheet. This way the proper grid can be set up to match any latitude. Near the equator, 1° grids are nearly square; at higher latitudes they are rectangular. They come in pads of 50 sheets, printed both sides, which cost about $10. The implied scale is 3 inches equals 60 miles, but any scale can be used by re-labeling the latitude lines and adjusting the longitude diagram accordingly. For accurate celestial fixes, it is usually necessary to expand the scale to 3 inches equals 6 miles.

Your DR track can also be plotted on these same sheets, making it your primary chart for the open ocean part of the voyage. They are also useful for weather plotting and tactics.

Universal Time (UT, UTC, UT1) — The international time system used in navigation that used to be called Greenwich Mean Time (GMT). You will see this abbreviated in various references as UT, UTC, and UT1. The *Nautical Almanac* prints "UT" on the daily pages where it used to print GMT. Technically, GMT = UT1, which is tied to the rotation rate of the earth, whereas UTC is an absolute clock time independent of the earth. These two differ by at most 0.9s, as the rotation rate of earth changes slightly with time. The two are synchronized about once a year with the adjustment of a *leap second* to UT1. Although interesting in their own right, these details have little significance to practical celestial navigation in a small boat at sea. See links to time references at www.starpath.com/celnavbook.

Update the DR Plot — Jargon that means transfer your course changes from the logbook to the plotting sheet, so that you can determine your present DR position. The chart and plotting work of dead reckoning. In practice, this process can take more time than the actual sights and sight reductions. It can be done more efficiently and accurately using a programmed calculator that does dead reckoning. See Dead Reckoning, DR Plot, DR Position, Logbook, Plotting Sheets, and Calculators.

Upper Limb (UL) — The top edge of the sun or moon, used for sun sights when the lower limb is obscured by clouds. For moon sights, we use what ever limb is full at the time. See Lower Limb and Semi-diameter.

Upper Transit — Same as meridian passage. The moment any celestial body crosses your meridian, bearing precisely due north or south. See Meridian Passage.

USNO — United States Naval Observatory (usno.navy.mil). See especially their Astronomical Applications department that has many wonderful resources for celestial navigators. See www.starpaath.com/usno.

v-correction — The correction given in the *Nautical Almanac* that accounts for the changing rate of the GHA motion of the moon and planets. See v-value.

v-value — A number given in the *Nautical Almanac* that is used to correct the Greenwich hour angles (GHAs) of the moon and planets. This correction is not needed for the sun and stars because they circle the earth at precisely constant rates according to UTC. The stars do this because they are stationary and the earth rotates at a constant rate (15° 02.5' of longitude per hour). The sun also does so (at a slightly different constant rate, 15° of longitude per hour, exactly) despite its annual motion through the stars as we circle it, because UTC is defined in such a way as to make this happen. But because of the orbital motions of the moon and planets, their GHAs do not circle the earth at constant rates, but rather vary slightly throughout the month for the moon and throughout the year for the planets.

The *Nautical Almanac* accounts for this variation by assigning each a constant average value (15° 00.0' per hour for the planets and 14° 19.0' per hour for the moon), and then lists the excess of this rate at a particular time as the v-value. For example, if the moon's v-value is listed as 14.0' at a UTC of 22h 00m, it means that at this time of day, the moon's geographical position is moving west at a rate of 14° 19.0' + 14.0', or 14° 33.0' of longitude per hour. If you wanted the moon's GHA at 22h 49m 10s, you would look up the GHA at 22h on the daily pages and then find the 49m 10s increment on the 49-minute page of the Increments and Corrections Table. This answer should be (49m 10s) × (14° 19.0') / (60m) = (49.167/60) × (14.317) = 11.732° = 11° 43.9', which must be added to the 22h value. Then find in the same table the v-correction that corresponds to a v-value of 14.0'. This should be (49.5m/60m) × (14.0') = 11.6'. Add this v-correction and you have found the proper GHA. Note that the corrections table uses the half-minute value (49.5 instead of 49) for all times.

The v-value and subsequent v-corrections are positive in all cases except occasionally for Venus, in which case it is clearly marked in the *Nautical Almanac*.

Variation — The difference in bearing between true north and magnetic north. It is different for different parts of the world and changes very slowly over the years. It is clearly marked on all nautical charts and pilot charts.

Velocity Made Good (VMG) — The speed you are making good in a particular direction. Two common choices are VMG to a waypoint and VMG relative to the true wind direction.

Venus — One of the five planets visible to the naked eye (Jupiter, Venus, Mercury, Saturn, and Mars). Jupiter and Venus are the two primary planets for navigation, because they are always brighter than the brightest stars, and therefore their sights can be taken immediately after sunset or just before sunrise when the stars are not visible. Venus is seen in the morning or evening, never more than about 45° from the sun. It changes from morning star to evening star about once a year. Check the Planet Diagram in the *Nautical Almanac* to learn how it moves in any particular year.

Vernier — The type of scale used on sextants to interpolate tenths of minutes on the micrometer drum. The Vernier scale lies adjacent to the micrometer scale, with 9 units on the micrometer scale divided into 10 units on the Vernier scale. With this clever arrangement, you read the proper fractional part of the minutes from the Vernier scale by noting which unit of the Vernier scale most closely aligns with any unit of the micrometer scale. Technically speaking, "Vernier scale" may be redundant, since "Vernier" does mean a type of scale, but this is obviously not an important point.

Watch Error (WE) — The difference between watch time and the standard time the watch is set to. The technical meaning is the same as the common meaning: how much any watch is fast or slow. If your watch is set to Pacific Daylight Time (PDT), and it reads 14h 12m 20s, when you hear the proper time announced from some source to be 14h 12m exactly, then your watch error is 20 seconds fast. Since every watch has some rate of gaining or losing time, watch error increases as a voyage progresses. The size of the watch error is not important as long as your know what it is. Watch error can be checked underway with the WWV time broadcasts. A GPS in contact with satellites is also a dependable source of accurate time.

Watch Rate — The number of seconds a watch, or any timepiece, gains or loses per day or week. The rate of a typical quartz watch might be a gain of 3 seconds every 10 days. The size of the rate is not so important, but it must be constant if the watch is to be useful for navigation. A watch with constant rate is called a chronometer. Most quartz watches can be adjusted to minimize the rate, but the cost when done by a jeweler is comparable to the watch cost. See Watch Error and Chronometer Log.

Watch Time (WT) — The actual time indicated on the chronometer or wrist watch used for navigation, without any corrections, recorded to an accuracy of 1 second at the precise time of the sight. Watch time can be kept on any time zone that is convenient, but should not be changed during a voyage. There is no particular virtue to keeping watch time set to UTC, because you must correct even this watch time for watch error. You might as well pick a more useful time to carry around on your arm and add this correction as well when you correct for watch error. Also, you need some ship's time that everyone on the boat goes by for watch changes and meals. It is best if this matches your watch time; UTC is very awkward for this purpose.

Waypoint — A Lat-Lon position chosen to mark a point along a route. Under sail, the waypoints are typically determined by forecasted wind patterns.

Work Forms — Blank forms used to guide you through the steps of a sight reduction. After some practice, you can do without forms, but they help when learning or underway when its hard to think, very sick, or very tired, or both. See Sight Reduction.

Zenith — The point in the sky directly overhead. If a star appears at an observer's zenith, at that instant the observer is at the geographical position of that star. See zenith distance.

Zenith Distance (z) — The angular distance between the point directly overhead (the zenith) and the celestial body sighted. It is the complement of the observed height (Ho) figured from: $z = 90° - Ho$. Zenith distance is a key concept in celestial navigation since it can be shown to be numerically equivalent to the distance between the observer and the geographical position (GP) of the sighted body. If a star is 70° above the horizon, its zenith distance is 20°, and at that moment you are located precisely 20° × (60 miles/1°), or 1,200 miles from the GP. The *Nautical Almanac* tells precisely where the GP is located at all times; so this observation alone has established a giant circle of position. The rest of celestial navigation covered in a sight reduction is just a trick to get a segment of this circle onto a plotting sheet, so we can call it a line of position. See Geographical Position, Observed Height, Sight Reduction, Circle of Position, and Nautical Mile.

Zenith Passage — The moment when a star passes directly overhead, at a peak height of 90°. Any star that does this must have a declination equal to your latitude, or vice versa, if you spot a star overhead, your latitude equals the star's declination. Look it up (or recall it from memory), and you know your latitude. This is an emergency method of finding latitude without sextant or tables, although it takes practice to determine whether the star was indeed at your zenith at meridian passage. If the star passes 2° north of your zenith (zenith distance of 2°), your latitude is 2° south of the star's declination, and so forth. See Zenith Stars and Meridian Passage.

Zenith Star — Any star that crosses your zenith (passes directly overhead), also used to describe stars that cross your destination as in "Sirius is a zenith star for Tahiti," since you will know you are at the right latitude when you see these guys overhead. See Zenith Passage.

Zone Description (ZD) — When referred to a watch, it is the number of whole hours between the watch time (WT) and universal time (UTC). If your watch reads 13:04:20 as you hear UTC (also called universal coordinated time, UT or GMT) announced on the WWV broadcast as 21:04:00, then the ZD of your watch is +8 hours. You know this because you now know that you get UTC from your WT by adding 8 hours. As long as you don't change your watch time, this correction to the hours part will remain constant, even though the error in the seconds part of your watch time will increase as time goes by. In the previous example, the watch error was 20 seconds fast. As long as you don't change your watch time, UTC is your watch time, corrected for the watch error, plus 8 hours, no matter what time of day you look at it, and no matter where on earth you are when you do look.

When referred to a place on earth (as in the zone time or standard time systems), the zone description describes the local time zone of the place, telling how many hours it differs from UTC. But in practical navigation there is little use for this conventional definition of the term. To navigate, the only time you need to know is UTC, and to get UTC you need to know only the time zone of your watch, not the time zone you happen to be in. Just forget that you are sailing across several time zones as you cross an ocean; it has no bearing on the important part of navigation. Midday will gradually slip an hour or two off of 12:00, but this is no problem at all compared to the timekeeping problems you expose yourself to once you start changing your watch time. Once you get to your destination, set your watch to their time and go on from there. See Time Zone.

Zone Time (ZT) — A time system used in commercial and government navigation that changes time zones at specific longitudes, regardless of what is going on at that place. The central time meridian of each zone is a whole multiple of 15°, called the zone description of that zone. The boundaries of each zone are 7° 30' of longitude to either side of the central meridian. According to the Zone Time system, every point on earth between 127° 30' W and 112° 30' W keeps time that is 8 hours behind UTC (ZD = +8h, since 8 × 15 = 120°). There is no daylight saving time in this system, and it is assumed that all ship's clocks change by 1 hour when a time zone boundary is crossed. Zone time is like standard time with straight boundaries along specific meridians and no daylight changes. See also Standard Time, Watch Time, and Time Zone.

Abbreviations

a	a-Value
A	Away
a-Lat	Assumed Latitude
a-Lon	Assumed Longitude
ao, a1, a2	Polaris Corrections
alt cor	Altitude Correction
Amp	Amplitude
AP	Assumed Position
C	Course
COG	Course Over Ground
d	d-Value
d-corr	d correction to Hc
Dec	Declination
DR	Dead Reckoning
DR-Lat	DR Latitude
DR-Lon	DR Longitude
EqT	Equation of Time
G	Greenwich Meridian
GHA	Greenwich Hour Angle
GMT	Greenwich Mean Time
GP	Geographical Position
GPS	Global Positioning System
H	Altitude or angular height
Ha	Apparent Height
Hc	Calculated Height
HE	Height of Eye
Ho	Observed Height
HP	Horizontal Parallax
Hs	Sextant Height
IC	Index Correction
LAN	Local Apparent Noon
Lat	Latitude

LHA	Local Hour Angle
LL	Lower Limb
Lm	Mid-Latitude
LMT	Local Mean Time
Lon	Longitude
LOP	Line of Position
NA	Nautical Almanac
NAO	Nautical Almanac Office
NIST	*National Institute of Standards and Technology*
nmi	*Nautical Mile*
Mer Pass	Meridian Passage
RA	Right Ascension
SD	Semidiameter
SHA	Sidereal Hour Angle
SOG	Speed over ground
t	Meridian Angle
T	Toward
T-3	Table 3 in the Table Selections
UL	Upper Limb
USNO	United States Naval Observatory
UT	Universal time
UTC	Universal Coordinated Time (=UT)
v	v-value
VOS	Voluntary Observing Ship
WAAS	Wide Area Augmentation System
WE	Watch Error
WT	Watch Time
Z	Azimuth Angle
z	Zenith Distance
ZD	Zone Description
Zn	Azimuth
ZT	Zone Time
ZD	Zone Description

Appendix 2

ANSWERS

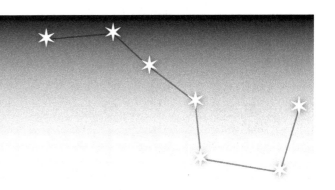

Examples with Full Work Form Solutions*					
Sight	*Body*	*Date*	*DR*	*Exercise*	*Solution*
Sun #1	LL	25 Oct 78	44 50 N, 139 15 W	68	68
Sun #2	LL	26 Jul 78	44 40 N, 123 00 W	71	223
Sun #3	LL	24 Jul 78	44 50 N, 123 36 W	71	223
Sun #4	LL	25 Jul 78	45 26 N, 134 30 W	72	224
Sun #5	LL	25 Jul 78	45 26 N, 134 30 W	72	224
Sun#6	LL	27 Oct 78	45 53 N, 131 24 W	79	226
Sun #7	LL	27 Oct 78	45 53 N, 131 24 W	79	226
Sun #8	LL	26 Jul 78	45 21 N, 122 39 W	104	237
Sun #9	LL	11 Jul 86	25 13 N, 147 15 W	274	274
Star #1	Altair	24 Jul 78	45 30 N, 126 27 W	85	85
Star #2	Arcturus	24 Jul 78	45 30 N, 120 58 W	85	230
Star #3	Altair	24 Jul 78	44 36 N, 122 14 W	86	230
Star #4	Antares	24 Jul 78	44 36 N, 122 14 W	86	231
Star #5	Arcturus	25 Jul 78	44 40 N, 126 27 W	87	232
Star #6	Regulus	27 Mar 81	45 21 N, 130 03 W	87	233
Star #7	Hamal	26 Oct 78	45 05 N, 160 25 E	98	234
Star #8	Sirius	25 Jul 78	45 30 S, 033 40 W	98	235
Star #9	Arcturus	26 Oct 78	45 05 N, 160 25 E	105	239
Star #10	Rigil Kent.	2 Sep 86	31 09 S, 157 48 E	276	276
Planet #1	Venus	27 Oct 78	44 50 S, 015 10 E	96	96
Planet #2	Jupiter	26 Oct 78	45 05 N, 160 25 E	97	234
Planet #3	Venus	25 Jul 78	45 30 S, 033 40 W	97	235
Planet #4	Venus	2 Sep 86	31 09 S, 157 48 E	277	277
Moon #1	UL	25 Oct 78	44 50 N, 40 20 W	103	236
Moon #2	UL	26 Jul 78	44 58 N, 122 24 W	104	238
Moon #3	UL	26 Oct 78	45 05 N, 160 25 E	105	239
Moon #4	LL	27 Mar 81	45 16 N, 140 20 W	106	240
Moon #5	LL	11 Jul 86	25 13 N, 147 15 W	276	276

* *Over the years we have learned that having this indexed list of fully worked examples is helpful for cross referencing. Please note the list is here and use it as called for. The last example of each body is in the Instructions to using Work Form 104 in the Appendix. On the right are the page numbers.*

1.6 Exercise on Adding and Subtracting Angles

(a)	153° 58.4’	(g)	330° 0.0’
(b)	54° 17.1’	(h)	64° 43.5’
(c)	164° 25.2’	(i)	11.6’
(d)	1° 42.7’	(j)	38° 9.4’
(e)	308° 5.4’	(k)	53° 58.6’
(f)	315° 36.9’	(l)	93° 18.7’

1.7 Exercise on Adding and Subtracting Times

(a)	23h 22m 43s	May 2
(b)	19h 38m 20s	May 22
(c)	11h 46m 03s	May 1
(d)	04h 06m 38s	May 3
(e)	22h 22m 14s	May 4
(f)	11h 23m 48s	May 9
(g)	11h 06m 11s	Apr 30
(h)	13h 11m 45s	May 19
(i)	23h 45m 58s	May 2
(j)	01h 41m 04s	May 9
(k)	21h 34m 46s	May 28
(L)	05h 00m 04s	May 11

2.4 Exercise on Sextant Reading

(1) 46° 7.2’	(2) 49° 57.6’
(3) 14° 37.0’	(4) 81° 22.3’
(5) 32° 58.9’	(6) 56° 2.8’
(7) 0.4’ ON	(8) 1.5’ OFF
(9) 2.3’ OFF	

3.3 Exercise Looking up Sun’s Dec

(a) S 12° 2.7’

(b) N 3° 13.4’

(c) N 19° 53.0’

(d) S 12° 54.5’

3.4 Exercise on LAN Sights for Latitude

(1) 55° 19.0’ N	(2) 9° 55.4’ S
(3) 36° 13.6’ N	(4) 37° 45.5’ N
(5) 21° 39.1’ N	(6) 27° 1.2’ S
(7) 27° 40.0’ S	(8) 44° 02.5’ N
(9) 16° 47.5’ S	(10) 34° 32.5’ N

4.3 Exercise on Universal Plotting Sheets

(1)	A:	45° 00’ N, 122° 00’ W,
	B:	45° 37’ N, 122° 50’ W,
	C:	44° 40’ N, 123° 26’ W,
	D:	44° 14’ N, 121° 36’ W

(3a) 37’	(3b) 57’
(4a) 50’	(4b) 1° 50’
(5a) 51.5 n mi,	(5b) 83.0 n mi
(6a) 136°	(6b) 316°
(6c) 340°	(6d) 204°

4.5 Exercise on Plotting LOPs

A (1 & 2) 35° 34.9’ N, 144° 32.3’ W

B (3 & 4) 34° 16.8’ N, 146° 16.0’ W

C (5 & 6) 35° 21.2’ N, 145° 35.3’ W

D (7 & 8) 34° 25.9’ N, 146° 13.8’ W

E (9 & 10) 35° 24.7’ N, 146° 48.5’ W

4.6 DR Plotting. Final positions

(1) 24° 23.0’N, 43° 26.3’ W

(2) 24° 50.1’N, 44° 06.4’ W

(3) 26° 16.2’N, 45° 33.9’ W

(4) 24° 34.6’N, 44° 45.5’ W

(5) 23° 38.0’N, 44° 22.9’ W

Note: These answers are accurate to 0.1’ from computer calculations. If you plot carefully you should agree with the correct answer to within 1’ or 2’ (about 1 or 2 miles).

5.4 Sun #2

1

	h	m	s				
WT	14	49	10	date	26 July 1978	body	☉ LL SUN
WE +S -F			-13	DR Lat	44° 40′ N	log	882.0
ZD +W -E	+7			DR Lon	123° 00′ W	HE ft	16 →
UTC	21	48	57	UTC date / LOP label	2148 ☉ 26 July		

	°	′
Hs	58	24.8
index corr. + off - on		0.0′
DIP -		-3.9′
Ha	58	20.9

2

GHA hr.	133°	23.3′	v moon planets	–	Dec hr	N 19°	22.3′	d + -	-0.5	HP moon	–

3

	°	′			
GHA + m.s.	+ 12	14.3	d corr.	+ -	-0.4
SHA + or v corr.	–	–	stars or moon, planets Dec	N 19°	Dec min 21.9
GHA	145	37.6			
a-Lon -W+E	- 122	37.6			
LHA	23	00′ W / 60′ E			

tens d		d upper
units d		d lower
dsd corr.	+	dsd ←
d. corr.	Pub. 229	

additional altitude corr. moon, mars, venus	–
altitude corr. all sights	+15.4′
upper limb moon subtract 30′	–
Ho	58° 36.3′
Hc	58° 3.9′

T A

4

LHA	23°	
Dec deg	19°	N S: N
a-Lat	45°	N S: N

5

	°	′			
tab Hc	57	45	d + -	+ 51	Z 136°
d. corr.	Pub. 249	+ 18.9	Dec min	21.9′	
Hc	57	63.9			

6

a =	32.4′ T
Zn =	224°
a - Lat =	45° N
a - Lon =	122° 37.6′ W

5.5 Sun #3

1

	h	m	s				
WT	19	05	32	date	24 July 1978	body	☉ LL SUN
WE +S -F			+8	DR Lat	44° 50′ N	log	0605
ZD +W -E	+7			DR Lon	122° 36′ W	HE ft	16 →
UTC	26	05	40	UTC date / LOP label	0205 ☉ 25 July		
	02	05	40				

	°	′
Hs	15	20.5
index corr. + off - on		- 1.8′
DIP -		-3.9′
Ha	15	14.8

2

GHA hr.	208°	23.4′	v moon planets	–	Dec hr	N 19°	45.7′	d + -	-0.5	HP moon	–

3

	°	′			
GHA + m.s.	+ 1	25.0	d corr.	+ -	+0.0
SHA + or v corr.	–	–	stars or moon, planets Dec	N 19°	Dec min 45.7
GHA	209	48.4			
a-Lon -W+E	- 122	48.4			
LHA	87	00′ W / 60′ E			

tens d		d upper
units d		d lower
dsd corr.	+	dsd ←
d. corr.	Pub. 229	

additional altitude corr. moon, mars, venus	–
altitude corr. all sights	+12.5′
upper limb moon subtract 30′	–
Ho	15° 27.3′
Hc	15° 54.0′

T A

4

LHA	87°	
Dec deg	19°	N S: N
a-Lat	45°	N S: N

5

	°	′			
tab Hc	15	23	d + -	+ 41	Z 78°
d. corr.	Pub. 249	+ 31.0	Dec min	45.7′	
Hc	15	54.0			

6

a =	26.7′ A
Zn =	282°
a - Lat =	45° N
a - Lon =	122° 48.4′ W

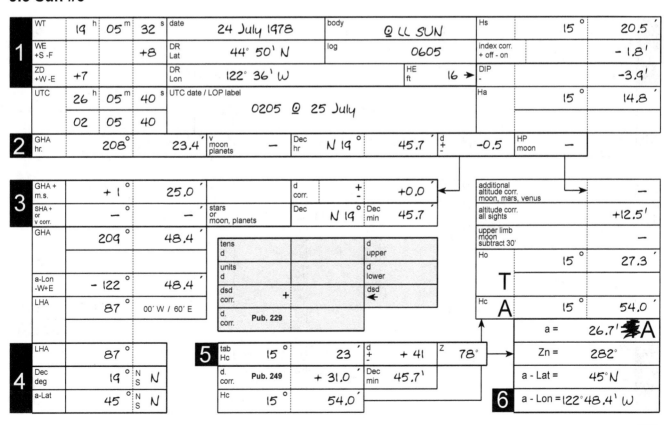

5.6 Sun #4

1

	h	m	s						°	'
WT	11	05	23	date	25 July 1978	body	LL SUN	Hs	54	05.0
WE +S -F		-1	10	DR Lat	45° 26' N	log	6605.5	index corr. + off - on		-2.0'
ZD +W -E	+8			DR Lon	134° 30' W	HE ft	9 →	DIP -		-2.9'
UTC	19	04	13	UTC date / LOP label	1904 LL SUN 25 July 1978			Ha	54	00.1

2

GHA hr.	103°	23.3'	v moon planets	—	Dec hr	N 19°	36.6'	d + -	-0.5	HP moon —

3

	°	'				
GHA + m.s.	+1	3.3		d corr.	+ -	-0.0'
SHA + or v corr.	—	—	stars or moon, planets	Dec	N 19°	Dec min 36.6'
GHA	104	26.6				
a-Lon -W+E	- 134	26.6				
LHA	- 30	00' W / 60' E				
	+360					

tens d		d upper
units d		d lower
dsd corr. +		dsd ←
d. corr. Pub. 229		

	°	'
additional altitude corr. moon, mars, venus		—
altitude corr. all sights		+15.3'
upper limb moon subtract 30'		—
Ho	54	15.4
T		
Hc A	54	30.6

4

	°	N/S
LHA	330	
Dec deg	19	N
a-Lat	45	N

5

	°	'			
tab Hc	54	01	d + -	+ 48	Z 126
d. corr. Pub. 249		+ 29.6	Dec min	36.6'	
Hc	54	30.6			

6

a =	15.2' A
Zn =	126°
a - Lat =	45° N
a - Lon =	134°26.6' W

5.7 Sun #5

1

	h	m	s						°	'
WT	15	05	44	date	25 July 1978	body	LL SUN	Hs	54	05.0
WE +S -F		-1	10	DR Lat	45° 26' N	log	6605.5	index corr. + off - on		-2.0'
ZD +W -E	+8			DR Lon	134° 30' W	HE ft	9 →	DIP -		-2.9'
UTC	23	04	34	UTC date / LOP label	2304 ⊙ 25 July			Ha	54	00.1

2

GHA hr.	163°	23.3'	v moon planets	—	Dec hr	N 19°	34.4'	d + -	-0.5	HP moon —

3

	°	'				
GHA + m.s.	+ 1	8.5		d corr.	+ -	-0.0'
SHA + or v corr.	—	—	stars or moon, planets	Dec	N 19°	Dec min 34.4'
GHA	164	31.8				
a-Lon -W+E	- 134	31.8				
LHA	30	00' W / 60' E				

tens d		d upper
units d		d lower
dsd corr. +		dsd ←
d. corr. Pub. 229		

	°	'
additional altitude corr. moon, mars, venus		
altitude corr. all sights		+15.3'
upper limb moon subtract 30'		—
Ho	54	15.4
T		
Hc A	54	28.4

4

	°	N/S
LHA	30	
Dec deg	19	N
a-Lat	45	N

5

	°	'			
tab Hc	54	01	d + -	+ 48	Z 126°
d. corr. Pub. 249		+ 27.4	Dec min	34.4'	
Hc	54	28.4			

6

a =	13.0' A
Zn =	234°
a - Lat =	45° N
a - Lon =	134°31.8' W

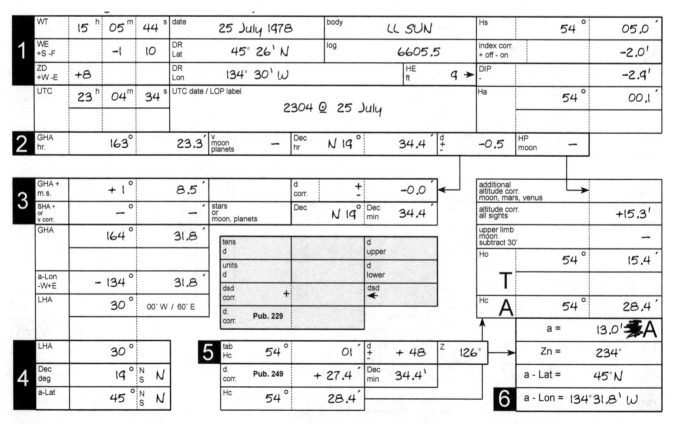

5.8 Sight Reducing LAN Data

Sight Reduction of LAN Data (uses Table T-26)						
#	LHA	Dec Deg	a-Lat	Hc	a-value	Lat
1	0°	N 19°	56° N	53° 34.4’	41.0’ T 180°	55° 19.0’ N
2	0°	S 12°	10° S	87° 05.5’	4.6’ A 180°	09° 55.4’ S
3	360°	S 11°	36° N	42° 00.2’	13.6’ A 180°	36° 13.6’ N
4	0°	N 2°	38° N	54° 41.4’	14.5’ T 180°	37° 45.5’ N
5	360°	N 2°	23° N	69° 59.7’	1° 20.9’ T 180°	21° 39.1’ N
6	360°	S 12°	27° S	75° 15.4’	1.2’ A 000°	27° 01.2’ S
7	0°	N 19°	29° S	41° 10.0’	1° 20.0’ T 000°	27° 40.0’ S
8	0°	N 19°	44° N	65° 35.6’	2.5’ A 180°	44° 02.5’ N
9	0°	N 3°	17° S	69° 46.6’	12.5’ T 000°	16° 47.5’ S
10	360°	S 12°	34° N	43° 57.3’	32.5’ A 180°	34° 32.5’ N

6.4 Answers

(1) 31° 15’ N, 143° 35’ W (Plot in Figure 6.4-1)

(2) 29° 12.1’ N, 144° 51.9’ W

(3) 30° 10’ N, 146° 37’ W

(4) 31° 18.4’ N, 145° 24.0’ W

6.5 AM Sun #6

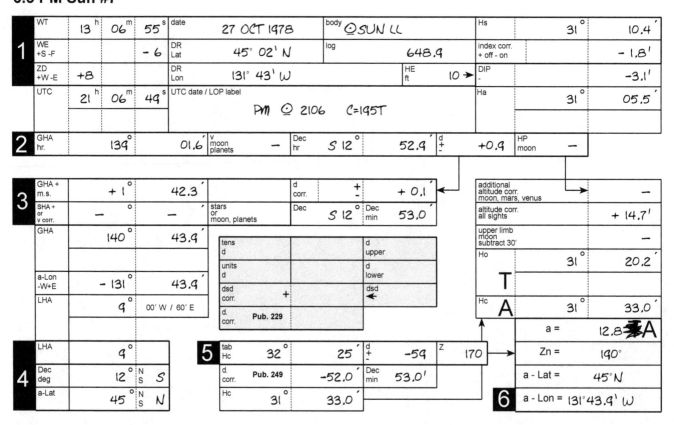

1	WT	9h 51m 20s	date	27 OCT 1978	body	☉ SUN LL	Hs	21° 18.3′
	WE +S -F	-6	DR Lat	45° 27′ N	log	622.8	index corr. + off - on	-1.8′
	ZD +W -E	+8	DR Lon	131° 34′ W	HE ft	10 →	DIP -	-3.1′
	UTC	17h 51m 14s	UTC date / LOP label	AM ☉ 1751 C=195T			Ha	21° 13.4′
2	GHA hr.	79° 01.4′	v moon planets	—	Dec hr	S 12° 49.5′	d + -	+0.9
	HP moon	—						
3	GHA + m.s.	12° 48.5′	d corr. + -	+0.8′	additional altitude corr. moon, mars, venus	—		
	SHA + or v corr.	—° —′	stars or moon, planets		Dec	S 12° Dec min 50.3′	altitude corr. all sights	+ 13.8′
	GHA	91° 49.9′	tens d		d upper		upper limb moon subtract 30′	—
		+ 360	units d		d lower		Ho	21° 27.2′
	a-Lon -W+E	- 131° 49.9′	dsd corr.	+	dsd	←	T	
	LHA	320° 00′ W / 60′ E	d. corr.	Pub. 229			Hc A	21° 46.7′
							a =	19.5′ A
4	LHA	320°	5 tab Hc	22° 31′	d + -	- 53	Z	137
	Dec deg	12° N/S S	d. corr.	Pub. 249 - 44.3′	Dec min	50.3′		
	a-Lat	45° N/S N	Hc	21° 46.7′				
6	Zn =	137°	a - Lat =	45° N	a - Lon =	131°49.9′ W		

6.5 PM Sun #7

1	WT	13h 06m 55s	date	27 OCT 1978	body	☉ SUN LL	Hs	31° 10.4′
	WE +S -F	-6	DR Lat	45° 02′ N	log	648.9	index corr. + off - on	-1.8′
	ZD +W -E	+8	DR Lon	131° 43′ W	HE ft	10 →	DIP -	-3.1′
	UTC	21h 06m 49s	UTC date / LOP label	PM ☉ 2106 C=195T			Ha	31° 05.5′
2	GHA hr.	139° 01.6′	v moon planets	—	Dec hr	S 12° 52.9′	d + -	+0.9
	HP moon	—						
3	GHA + m.s.	+ 1° 42.3′	d corr. + -	+ 0.1′	additional altitude corr. moon, mars, venus	—		
	SHA + or v corr.	—° —′	stars or moon, planets		Dec	S 12° Dec min 53.0′	altitude corr. all sights	+ 14.7′
	GHA	140° 43.9′	tens d		d upper		upper limb moon subtract 30′	—
			units d		d lower		Ho	31° 20.2′
	a-Lon -W+E	- 131° 43.9′	dsd corr.	+	dsd	←	T	
	LHA	9° 00′ W / 60′ E	d. corr.	Pub. 229			Hc A	31° 33.0′
							a =	12.8 A
4	LHA	9°	5 tab Hc	32° 25′	d + -	-59	Z	170
	Dec deg	12° N/S S	d. corr.	Pub. 249 -52.0′	Dec min	53.0′		
	a-Lat	45° N/S N	Hc	31° 33.0′				
6	Zn =	190°	a - Lat =	45° N	a - Lon =	131°43.9′ W		

Plot of Sun Lines #6 and #7, Advanced for a Running Fix from Exercise 6.5

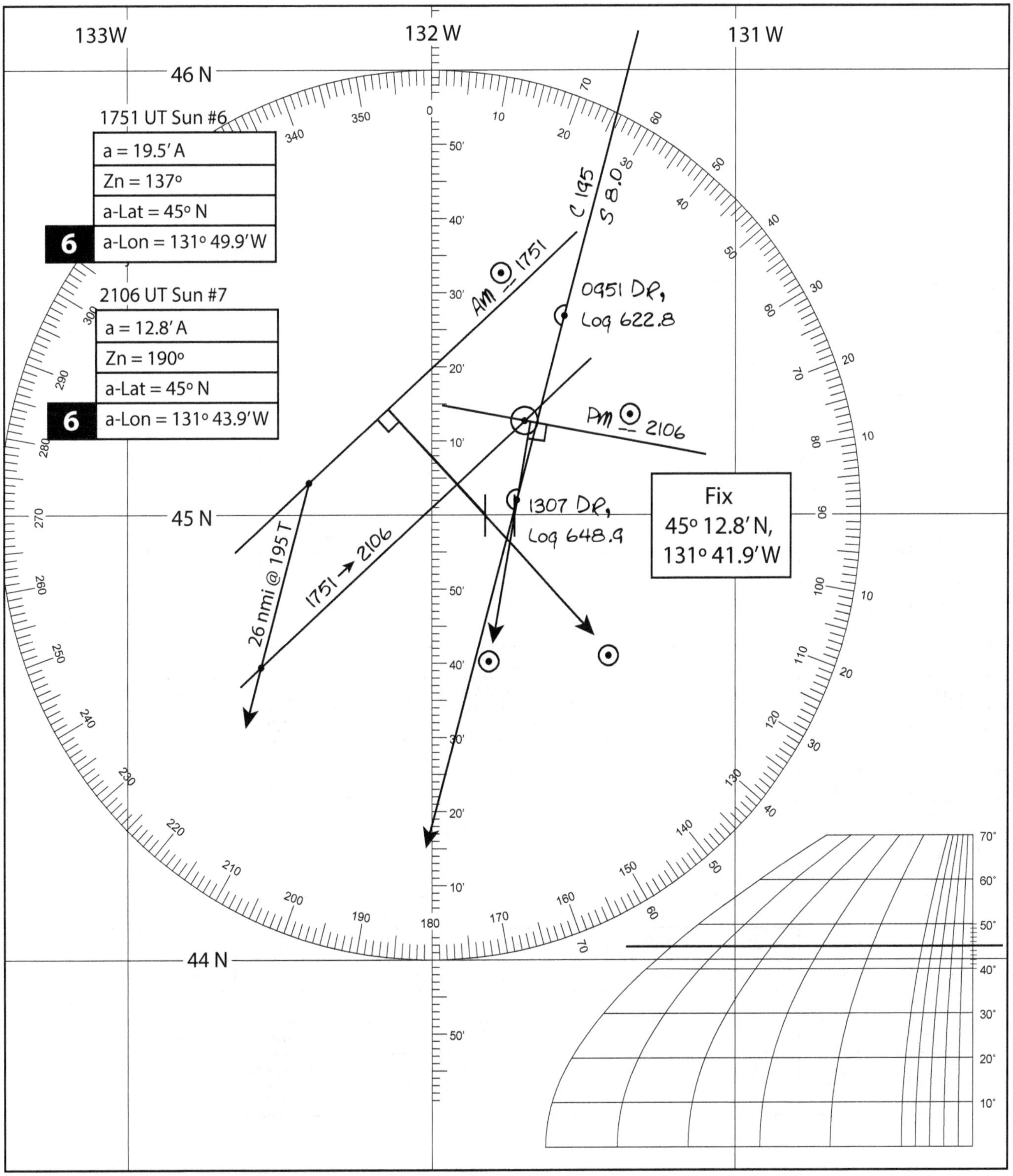

6.6 Running Fix Final Answers (See Intermediate Answers for Details)

(Example) 26° 38.7’ S, 62° 58.9’ E

(1) 21° 28.1’ N, 125° 26.3’ W

(2) 27° 54.5’ N, 005° 23.2’ W

(3) 26° 43.3’ N, 135° 13.6’ E

(4) 20° 54.6’ S, 032° 57.4’ W

(5) 29° 08.7’ S, 034° 57.8’ E

Intermediate Answers for Exercise 6.6

					For Plot			
	Run		DR			For Sight Reduction		
WT	Time	Distance	Lat	Lon	a-Lon	a-Lat	LHA	dec
Example 1016	01 16	19.0	28° 11.7’ S	62° 36.9’ E	62° 11.1’ E	28° S	335°	N14°
Example 1230	02 14	33.5	27° 38.7’ S	62° 43.5’ E	62° 42.1’ E	28° S	9°	N 14°
Example 1620	03 50	57.5	26° 42.1’ S	62° 54.8’ E	63° 9.7’ E	27° S	67°	N 14°
(1) 1015	01 15	16.3	21° 50.8’ N	124° 26.9’ W	124° 47.1’ W	22° N	328°	N 14°
(1) 1156	01 41	21.9	21° 43.3’ N	124° 49.1’ W	125° 4.1’ W	22° N	353°	N 14°
(1) 1425	02 29	32.3	21° 32.3’ N	125° 21.7 W	125° 18.1’ W	22° N	30°	N 14°
(2) 1015	01 35	14.3	28° 17.0’ N	6° 4.1’ W	6° 0.4’ W	28° N	328°	S 23°
(2) 1200	01 45	15.8	28° 9.2’ N	5° 48.6’ W	6° 17.4’ W	28° N	354°	S 23°
(2) 1420	02 20	21.0	27° 58.7’ N	5° 28.0’ W	5° 8.4’ W	28° N	30°	S 23°
(3) 1013	02 13	24.4	27° 50.1’ N	135° 32.5’ E	135° 20.3’ E	28° N	332°	N 21°
(3) 1255	02 42	29.7	27° 20.8’ N	135° 26.7’ E	135° 47.2’ E	27° N	13°	N 21°
(3) 1646	03 51	42.4	26° 39.1’ N	135° 18.4’ E	135° 6.9’ E	27° N	40°	N 21°
(4) 1018	02 03	20.5	20° 21.5’ S	32° 27.0’ W	32° 12.0’ W	20° S	331°	N 21°
(4) 1255	02 37	26.2	20° 41.6’ S	32° 45.0’ W	32° 30.8’ W	21° S	10°	N 21°
(4) 1404	01 09	11.5	20° 50.4’ S	32° 52.9’ W	32° 42.2’ W	21° S	27°	N 21°
(5) 1000	01 45	21.0	29° 37.8’ S	36° 4.0’ E	35° 53.2’ E	30° S	335°	N 3°
(5) 1235	02 35	31.0	29° 24.7’ S	35° 31.7” E	35° 8.9’ E	29° S	13°	N 3°
(5) 1455	02 20	28.0	29° 12.9’ S	35° 2.6’ E	35° 3.5’ E	29° S	48°	N 3°

More Intermediate Answers for Exercise 6.6

These can be used to check your work, but note that you may not get the precise values of Hc and Zn shown here because these have been calculated, not solved from tables. These are correct however, and differences show the limitations of the tables and the procedures used. In particular, note that the Zn values will differ by a degree or so in some cases. When using 249 or 229, this comes about primarily because the Z value is typically not corrected for the minutes part of the declination.

Usually, you can account for most of this by taking the Z from the next highest declination whenever the minutes part of the declination is greater than 30'. Remember, however, that you must always take Hc in the normal manner and then correct for it as done earlier. In other words, whenever the minutes part of the declination is greater than 30 and you notice that the Z value for the next declination is different, then take it to the forms, but do everything else the same.

	WT	a-Lat	LHA	Dec	Hc	Zn
Example	1016	28° S	335°	N 14° 45.4'	40° 51.8'	032.7
	1230	28° S	9°	N 14° 43.9'	46° 23. 3'	347.1
	1620	27° S	67°	N 14° 40.8'	12° 48.6'	294.1
(1)	1015	22° N	328°	N 14° 54.51'	58° 53.6'	097.6
(1)	1156	22° N	353°	N 14° 53.2'	80° 16.4'	135.8
(1)	1425	22° N	30°	N 14° 51.3'	60° 42.7'	261.1
(2)	1015	28° N	328°	S 23° 26.5'	30° 00.9'	145.8
(2)	1200	28° N	354°	S 23° 26.4'	39° 13. 7'	172.8
(2)	1420	28° N	30°	S 23° 26.4'	30° 59.1'	212.2
(3)	1013	28° N	332°	N 21° 54.0'	63° 57. 3'	097.2
(3)	1255	27° N	13°	N 21° 53.1'	77° 07.0'	249.4
(3)	1646	27° N	40°	N 21° 52.4'	53° 22.5'	270.9
(4)	1018	20° S	331°	N 21° 58.6'	39° 21.5'	035.6
(4)	1255	21° S	10°	N 21° 57.7'	45° 56.6'	346.6
(4)	1404	21° S	27°	N 21° 57.3'	39° 36.4'	326.9
(5)	1000	30° S	335°	N 3° 41.2'	48° 41.2'	039.7
(5)	1235	29° S	13°	N 3° 43.7'	54° 58.3'	337.0
(5)	1455	29° S	48°	N 3° 46.0'	33° 30.8'	297.2

These values can also be used for practice with the NAO Sight Reduction Tables. You have the three values needed (a-Lat, dec, and LHA) and the answers (Hc and Zn) you should get. It does not matter where they come from–sun, moon, stars, or planets. The sight reduction option at starpath.com/calc can also be used for such tests.

7.3 Arcturus Sight Exercise, Star #2

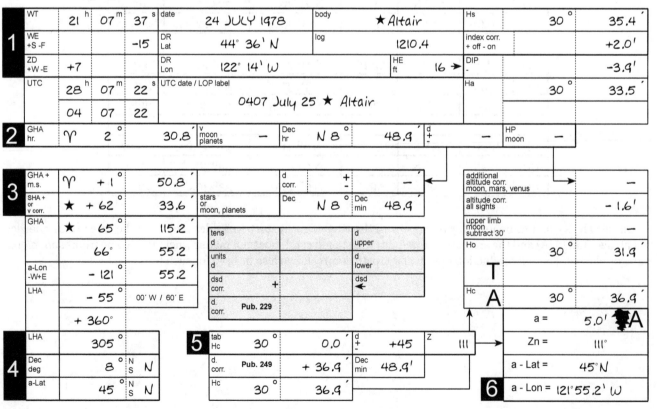

1

WT	20h 48m 55s	date	24 JULY 1978	body	★ Arcturus	Hs	57° 57.4′
WE +S -F	+8	DR Lat	45° 30′ N	log	6605.5	index corr. + off - on	-1.8′
ZD +W -E	+7	DR Lon	120° 58′ W	HE ft	16 →	DIP -	-3.9′
UTC	27h 48m 63s 03 49 03	UTC date / LOP label	0349 July 25 ★ Arcturus			Ha	57° 51.7′

2

GHA hr.	v moon planets	Dec hr	d + -	HP moon
♈ 347° 28.3′	—	N 19° 17.9′	—	—

3

GHA + m.s.	♈ + 12° 17.8′	d corr. + -	—	additional altitude corr. moon, mars, venus	—
SHA + or v corr.	★ + 146° 19.8′	stars or moon, planets — Dec	N 19° / Dec min 17.9′	altitude corr. all sights	- 0.6′
GHA	★ 505° 65.9′ 506° 05.9′	tens d / d upper		upper limb moon subtract 30′	—
a-Lon -W+E	- 121° 05.9′	units d / d lower		Ho	57° 51.1′
		dsd corr. + / dsd ←		T	56° 111.1′
LHA	385° (00′ W / 60′ E) - 360°	d. corr. Pub. 229		Hc A	56° 58.9′
				a =	52.2′ T

4

LHA	25°
Dec deg	19° N
a-Lat	45° N

5

tab Hc	56° 44′	d + -	+50	Z	133 → Zn = 227°
d. corr. Pub. 249	+ 14.9′	Dec min	17.9′		
Hc	56° 58.9′				

6

a =	52.2′ T
Zn =	227°
a - Lat =	45° N
a - Lon =	121° 05.9′ W

7.4 Altair Sight, Star #3

1

WT	21h 07m 37s	date	24 JULY 1978	body	★ Altair	Hs	30° 35.4′
WE +S -F	-15	DR Lat	44° 36′ N	log	1210.4	index corr. + off - on	+2.0′
ZD +W -E	+7	DR Lon	122° 14′ W	HE ft	16 →	DIP -	-3.9′
UTC	28h 07m 22s 04 07 22	UTC date / LOP label	0407 July 25 ★ Altair			Ha	30° 33.5′

2

GHA hr.	v moon planets	Dec hr	d + -	HP moon
♈ 2° 30.8′	—	N 8° 48.9′	—	—

3

GHA + m.s.	♈ + 1° 50.8′	d corr. + -	—	additional altitude corr. moon, mars, venus	—
SHA + or v corr.	★ + 62° 33.6′	stars or moon, planets — Dec	N 8° / Dec min 48.9′	altitude corr. all sights	- 1.6′
GHA	★ 65° 115.2′ 66° 55.2	tens d / d upper		upper limb moon subtract 30′	—
a-Lon -W+E	- 121° 55.2′	units d / d lower		Ho	30° 31.9′
		dsd corr. + / dsd ←		T	
LHA	- 55° (00′ W / 60′ E) + 360°	d. corr. Pub. 229		Hc A	30° 36.9′
				a =	5.0′ A

4

LHA	305°
Dec deg	8° N
a-Lat	45° N

5

tab Hc	30° 0.0′	d + -	+45	Z	111 → Zn = 111°
d. corr. Pub. 249	+ 36.9′	Dec min	48.9′		
Hc	30° 36.9′				

6

a =	5.0′ A
Zn =	111°
a - Lat =	45° N
a - Lon =	121° 55.2′ W

Plot of Exercise 7.4, note that all scales have been increased by a factor of 2

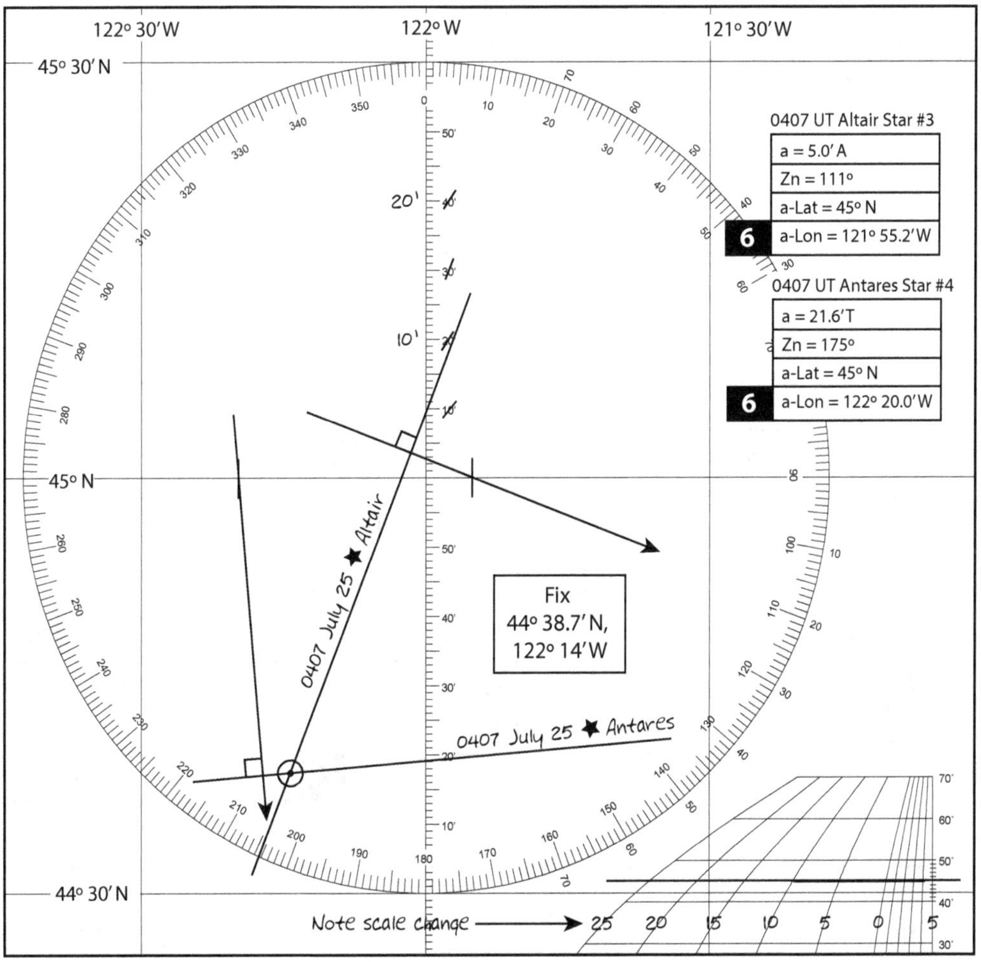

7.5 Antares Sight, Star #4

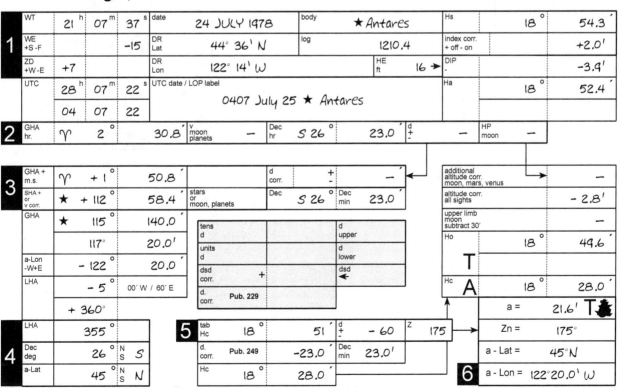

1

WT	21 h	07 m	37 s	date	24 JULY 1978	body	★ Antares	Hs 18° 54.3′
WE +S -F			-15	DR Lat	44° 36′ N	log	1210.4	index corr. + off - on +2.0′
ZD +W-E	+7			DR Lon	122° 14′ W	HE ft	16 →	DIP - -3.9′
UTC	28 h	07 m	22 s	UTC date / LOP label	0407 July 25 ★ Antares			Ha 18° 52.4′
	04	07	22					

2

GHA hr.	♈ 2° 30.8′	v moon planets	—	Dec hr	S 26° 23.0′	d +- —	HP moon —

3

GHA + m.s.	♈ +1°	50.8′		d corr.	+- —
SHA + or v corr.	★ +112°	58.4′	stars or moon, planets	Dec S 26°	Dec min 23.0′
GHA	★ 115°	140.0′			
	117°	20.0′			
a-Lon -W+E	-122°	20.0′			
LHA	-5°	00′ W / 60′ E			
	+360°				

tens d		d upper	
units d		d lower	
dsd corr.	+	dsd ←	
d. corr. Pub. 229			

additional altitude corr. moon, mars, venus		—
altitude corr. all sights		- 2.8′
upper limb moon subtract 30′		—
Ho	18°	49.6′
T		
Hc A	18°	28.0′

4

LHA	355°	
Dec deg	26°	N S: S
a-Lat	45°	N S: N

5

tab Hc	18°	51′	d +- - 60	Z 175
d. corr. Pub. 249		-23.0′	Dec min 23.0′	
Hc	18°	28.0′		

6

a =	21.6′ T
Zn =	175°
a - Lat =	45° N
a - Lon =	122° 20.0′ W

7.6 Arcturus Sight , Star #5

1

	h	m	s				
WT	21	49	25	date	25 JULY 1978	body	★ Arcturus
WE +S -F		-1	08	DR Lat	45° 30' N	log	369.8
ZD +W -E	+7			DR Lon	126° 27' W	HE ft	12 →
UTC	28	48	17	UTC date / LOP label	0448 July 26 ★ Arcturus		
	04	48	17				

	°	'
Hs	50	50.9
index corr. + off - on		0.0'
DIP -		-3.4'
Ha	50	47.5

2

GHA hr.	♈ 3°	29.9'	v moon planets	—	
Dec hr	N 19°	17.9'	d + -	—	
HP moon	—				

3

	°	'
GHA + m.s.	♈ + 12	6.2
SHA + or v corr.	★ + 146	19.8
GHA	★ 161	55.9
a-Lon -W+E	- 126	55.9
LHA	35	00' W / 60' E

d corr.	+ -	—	
Dec (stars or moon, planets)	N 19°	Dec min	17.9'

tens d		d upper
units d		d lower
dsd corr.	+	dsd ←
d. corr. Pub. 229		

additional altitude corr. moon, mars, venus	—
altitude corr. all sights	- 0.8'
upper limb moon subtract 30'	—
Ho	50° 46.7'
T	
Hc A	50° 77.9'

4

LHA	35°	
Dec deg	19°	N
a-Lat	45°	N

5

tab Hc	51°	04'	d + -	+46
d. corr. Pub. 249		+ 13.9'	Dec min	17.9'
Hc	51°	17.9'		
Z	120			

6

a =	31.2' A
Zn =	240°
a - Lat =	45° N
a - Lon =	126° 55.9' W

Plot of Polaris, Star #1, and Star #5

The plot also shows how a Latitude by Polaris would be plotted as an LOP.

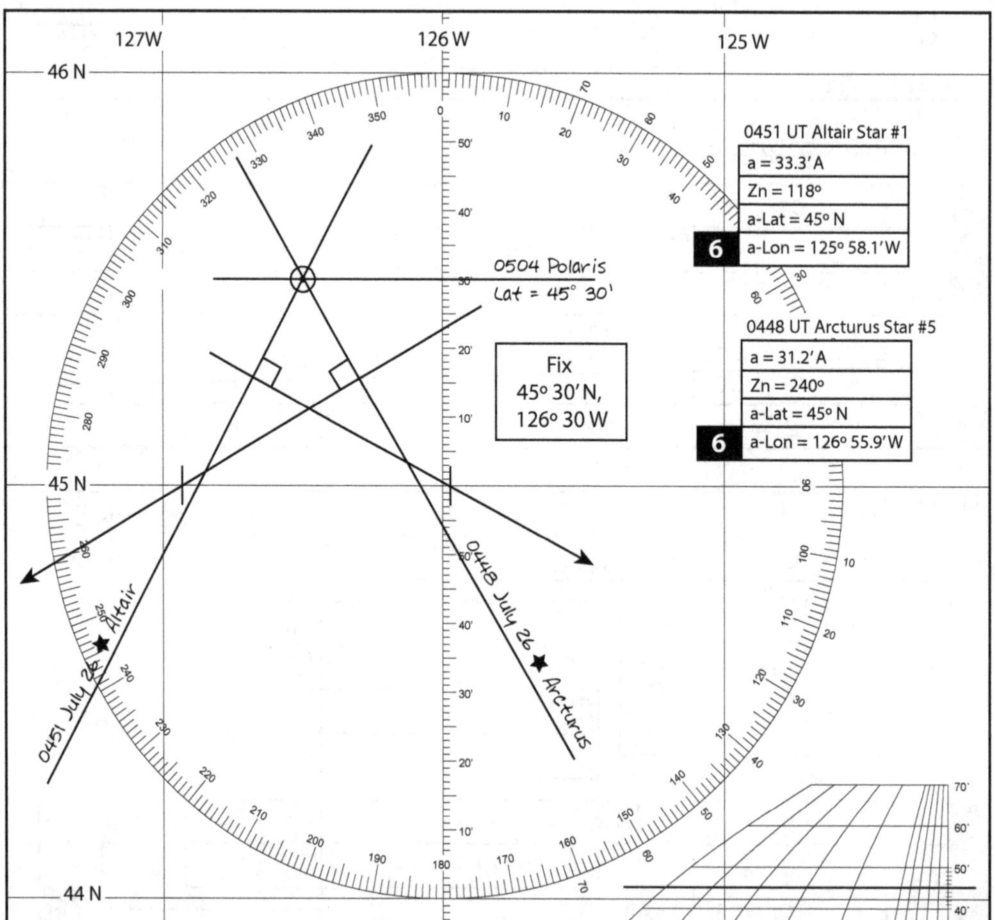

7.7 Regulus Sight, Star #6

1

WT	19 h	48 m	58 s	date	27 Mar 1981	body	★ Regulus	Hs	42° 58.5′
WE +S -F			+7	DR Lat	45° 21′ N	log	505.5	index corr. + off - on	+1.2′
ZD +W -E	+8			DR Lon	130° 03′ W	HE ft	9 →	DIP -	- 2.9′
UTC	27 h	49 m	05 s	UTC date / LOP label	★ Regulus 0349 Mar 28, 1981			Ha	42° 56.8′
	=03	49	05						

2

GHA hr.	♈ 230° 26.8′	v moon planets	—	Dec hr	N 12° 3.5′	d + -	HP moon —

3

GHA + m.s.	♈ + 12°	18.3′	d corr.	+ -	- 0.0′
SHA + or v corr.	★ 208°	09.4′ stars or moon, planets	Dec	N 12°	Dec min 03.5′
GHA	★ 450°	54.5′			
a-Lon -W+E	- 129°	54.5′			
LHA	321°	00′ W / 60′ E			

tens d		d upper
units d		d lower
dsd corr.	+	dsd ←
d. corr.	Pub. 229	

additional altitude corr. moon, mars, venus	—
altitude corr. all sights	-1.0′
upper limb moon subtract 30′	—
Ho	42° 55.8′
T	
Hc A	42° 74.5′

4

LHA	321°	
Dec deg	12°	N S N
a-Lat	45°	N S N

5

tab Hc	43°	12′	d + - + 47	Z 122
d. corr. Pub. 249		+ 2.5′	Dec min 03.5′	
Hc	43°	14.5′		

6

a =	18.7′ [redacted] A
Zn =	122°
a - Lat =	45° N
a - Lon =	129° 54.5′ W

7.9 Latitude by Polaris Exercises

(1) See text example example.

(2)

GHA Aries 3h = 346° 29.2’
49m 20s = 012° 22.0’

GHA Aries = 358° 51.2’
-DR-Lon(W) = -60° 13.0’

LHA Aries = 298° 38.2’

Ho = 24° 55.0’
constant = -1°
(298° 38.2’) ao = +1° 2.8’ (with interpolation for LHA Aries)
(25° 0’) a1 = + 0.4’
(July) a2 = + 0.6’

Latitude = 24° 58.8’

(3) Lat = 42° 49.6’

(4) Lat = 45° 28.4’

(5) All north, because you cannot see the North Star in southern latitudes!

8.3 and 8.5 Jupiter-Hamal Fix, Planet #2

1

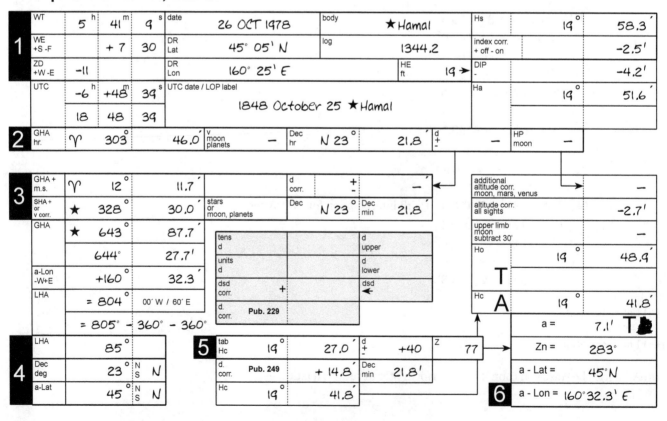

WT	5 h	56 m	58 s	date	26 OCT 1978	body	Jupiter ♃	Hs 62° 51.9′
WE +S -F		+ 7	30	DR Lat	45° 05′ N	log	1344.2	index corr. + off - on: -2.5′
ZD +W -E	-11			DR Lon	160° 25′ E	HE ft	19 →	DIP -: -4.2′
UTC	-6 h	+63 m	88 s	UTC date / LOP label	1904 October 25 ♃			Ha 62° 45.2′
	19	04	28					

2

GHA hr. 188° 45.9′	v moon planets +2.2	Dec hr N 18° 44.7′	d + - -0.1	HP moon —

3

GHA + m.s.	+1°	7.0′	d corr. + - -0.0′
SHA + or v corr.	°	+ 0.2′	stars or moon, planets — Dec N 18°, Dec min 44.7′
GHA	189°	53.1′	
a-Lon -W+E	+160°	06.9′	
LHA	= 349°	00′ W / 60′ E	
	= 350		

tens d		d upper
units d		d lower
dsd corr.	+	dsd ←
d. corr. Pub. 229		

additional altitude corr. moon, mars, venus	—
altitude corr. all sights	-0.5′
upper limb moon subtract 30′	—
Ho	62° 44.7′
T	
Hc A	62° 27.7′

4

LHA	350°	
Dec deg	18°	N/S: N
a-Lat	45°	N/S: N

5

tab Hc	61°	44′	d + - +58	Z	160
d. corr. Pub. 249		+ 43.7′	Dec min 44.7′		
Hc	61°	87.7′			

6

a =	17′ T
Zn =	160°
a - Lat =	45°N
a - Lon =	160°06.9′ E

The plot of these sights is in Chapter 8.

8.5 Jupiter-Hamal Fix, Star #7

1

WT	5 h	41 m	9 s	date	26 OCT 1978	body	★Hamal	Hs 19° 58.3′
WE +S -F		+ 7	30	DR Lat	45° 05′ N	log	1344.2	index corr. + off - on: -2.5′
ZD +W -E	-11			DR Lon	160° 25′ E	HE ft	19 →	DIP -: -4.2′
UTC	-6 h	+48 m	39 s	UTC date / LOP label	1848 October 25 ★Hamal			Ha 19° 51.6′
	18	48	39					

2

GHA hr. ♈ 303° 46.0′	v moon planets —	Dec hr N 23° 21.8′	d + - —	HP moon —

3

GHA + m.s.	♈ 12°	11.7′	d corr. + - —′
SHA + or v corr.	★ 328°	30.0′	stars or moon, planets — Dec N 23°, Dec min 21.8′
GHA	★ 643°	87.7′	
	644°	27.7′	
a-Lon -W+E	+160°	32.3′	
LHA	= 804°	00′ W / 60′ E	
	= 805° - 360° - 360°		

tens d		d upper
units d		d lower
dsd corr.	+	dsd ←
d. corr. Pub. 229		

additional altitude corr. moon, mars, venus	—
altitude corr. all sights	-2.7′
upper limb moon subtract 30′	—
Ho	19° 48.9′
T	
Hc A	19° 41.8′

4

LHA	85°	
Dec deg	23°	N/S: N
a-Lat	45°	N/S: N

5

tab Hc	19°	27.0′	d + - +40	Z	77
d. corr. Pub. 249		+ 14.8′	Dec min 21.8′		
Hc	19°	41.8′			

6

a =	7.1′ T
Zn =	283°
a - Lat =	45°N
a - Lon =	160°32.3′ E

8.6 Venus-Sirius Fix, Star #8

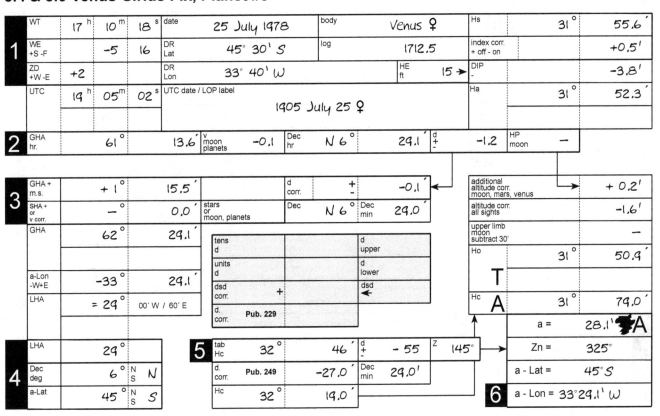

1

WT	16 h 54 m 37 s	date	25 July 1978	body	★Sirius	Hs	11° 5.2′
WE +S -F	-5 16	DR Lat	45° 30′ S	log	1712.5	index corr. + off - on	+0.5′
ZD +W -E	+2	DR Lon	33° 40′ W	HE ft	15 →	DIP -	-3.8′
UTC	18 h 49 m 21 s	UTC date / LOP label	1849 July 25 ★Sirius			Ha	11° 1.9′

2

GHA hr.	♈ 213°	05.3′	v moon planets	—	Dec hr	S 16° 41.2′	d +-	—	HP moon —

3

GHA + m.s.	♈ + 12°	22.3′	d corr. +-	
SHA + or v corr.	★ 258°	57.3′	stars or moon, planets — Dec	S 16° ; Dec min 41.2′
GHA	★ 483°	84.9′		
	484	24.9′		
a-Lon -W+E	-33°	24.9′		
LHA	= 451°	00′ W / 60′ E		
	-360°			

tens d		d upper
units d		d lower
dsd corr.	+	dsd ←
d. corr. Pub. 229		

additional altitude corr. moon, mars, venus	—
altitude corr. all sights	-4.8′
upper limb moon subtract 30′	
Ho	10° 57.1′
T	
Hc A	10° 62.0′
a =	4.9′ A
Zn =	258°
a - Lat =	45° S
6 a - Lon =	33°24.9′ W

4

LHA	91°	
Dec deg	16°	N/S S
a-Lat	45°	N/S S

5

tab Hc	10°	33′	d +- + 42	Z 078°
d. corr. Pub. 249		+ 29.0′	Dec min 41.2′	
Hc	10°	62.0′		

The plot of these sights are on the following page.

8.4 & 8.6 Venus-Sirius Fix, Planet #3

1

WT	17 h 10 m 18 s	date	25 July 1978	body	Venus ♀	Hs	31° 55.6′
WE +S -F	-5 16	DR Lat	45° 30′ S	log	1712.5	index corr. + off - on	+0.5′
ZD +W -E	+2	DR Lon	33° 40′ W	HE ft	15 →	DIP -	-3.8′
UTC	19 h 05 m 02 s	UTC date / LOP label	1905 July 25 ♀			Ha	31° 52.3′

2

GHA hr.	61°	13.6′	v moon planets	-0.1	Dec hr	N 6° 29.1′	d +-	-1.2	HP moon —

3

GHA + m.s.	+ 1°	15.5′	d corr. +-	-0.1′
SHA + or v corr.	—°	0.0′	stars or moon, planets — Dec	N 6° ; Dec min 29.0′
GHA	62°	29.1′		
a-Lon -W+E	-33°	29.1′		
LHA	= 29°	00′ W / 60′ E		

tens d		d upper
units d		d lower
dsd corr.	+	dsd ←
d. corr. Pub. 229		

additional altitude corr. moon, mars, venus	+ 0.2′
altitude corr. all sights	-1.6′
upper limb moon subtract 30′	—
Ho	31° 50.9′
T	
Hc A	31° 79.0′
a =	28.1′ A
Zn =	325°
a - Lat =	45° S
6 a - Lon =	33°29.1′ W

4

LHA	29°	
Dec deg	6°	N/S N
a-Lat	45°	N/S S

5

tab Hc	32°	46′	d +- - 55	Z 145°
d. corr. Pub. 249		-27.0′	Dec min 29.0′	
Hc	32°	19.0′		

8.6 Venus-Sirius Fix, Plotted

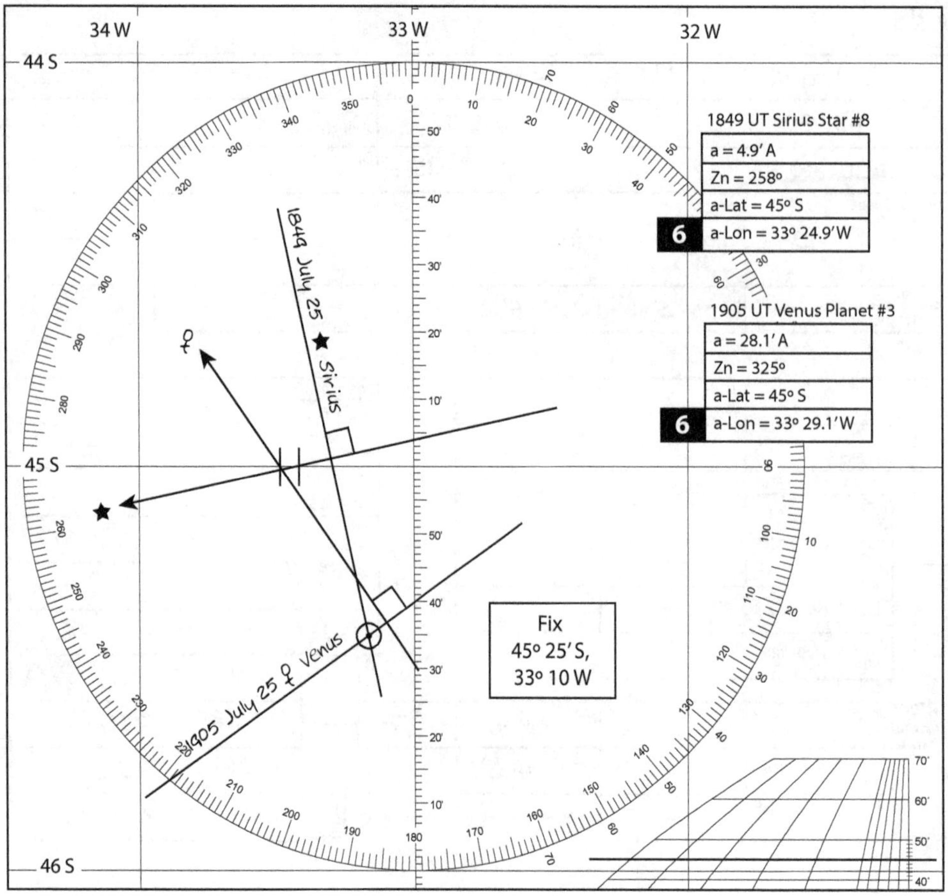

9.3 Converting Moon's Hs to Ho

(A) Ho = 58° 59.2'.

(B) Ho = 25° 7.8'

9.4 Moon #1

1

	h	m	s				
WT	04	51	13	date: Oct 25, 1978	body: UL Moon	Hs	42° 38.1′
WE +S -F			-3	DR Lat: 44° 50′ N	log	index corr. + off - on	0.0
ZD +W -E	+2			DR Lon: 40° 20′ W	HE ft: 10 →	DIP -	
UTC	06	51	10	UTCdate / LOP label: 0651 Oct 25 UL Moon		Ha	42° 35.0′

2

GHA hr.		v moon planets	Dec hr		d +/-	HP moon
347°	3.4′	13.7	N 13°	5.6′	-6.6	54.4

3

	°	′			
GHA + m.s.	+ 12	12.5		d corr. +/-	-5.7′
SHA + or v corr.	+	11.8	stars or moon, planets	Dec N 12°	Dec min 59.9′
GHA	359	27.7			
a-Lon -W+E	40	27.7′ W			
LHA	319	00′ W / 60′ E			

tens d		d upper
units d		d lower
dsd corr.	+	dsd ←
d. corr.	Pub. 229	

additional altitude corr. moon, mars, venus	+ 2.1′
altitude corr. all sights	+52.0′
upper limb moon subtract 30′	-30.0′
Ho	42° 59.1′
T	
Hc A	42° 45.9′

4

LHA	319°	
Dec deg	12°	N
a-Lat	45°	N

5

	°	′			
tab Hc	42	00.0	d +/-	+46	Z 119*
d. corr. Pub. 249		45.9	Dec min	59.9	
Hc	42	45.9			

6

a =	13.2 T
Zn =	119
a - Lat =	45° N
a - Lon =	40° 27.7′ W

** In this case since we are so close to 13° on the declination, we should get Z from Dec 13. In principle, however, when doing this we should always use the proper dec degrees (12 in this case) for finding Hc, but in this case that will not matter.*

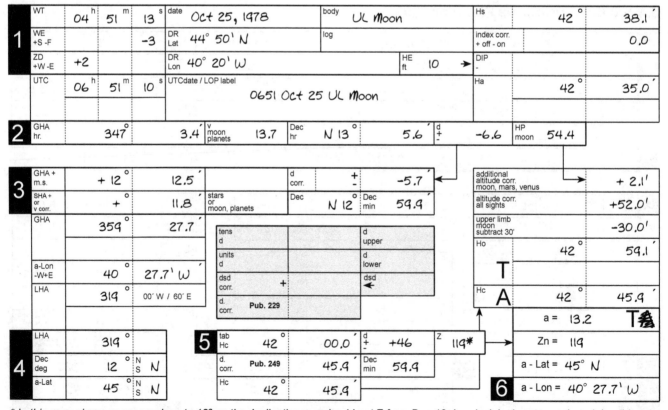

9.5 Moon-Sun Running Fix, Moon #2

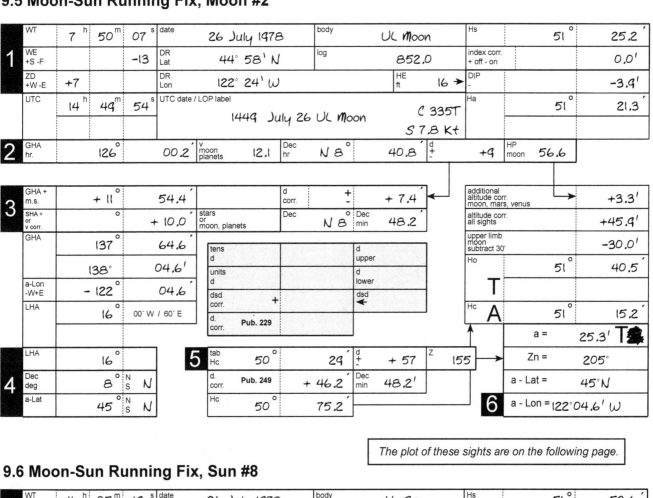

1

WT	7 h	50 m	07 s	date: 26 July 1978	body: UL Moon	Hs: 51° 25.2′
WE +S -F			-13	DR Lat: 44° 58′ N	log: 852.0	index corr. + off - on: 0.0′
ZD +W -E	+7			DR Lon: 122° 24′ W	HE ft: 16 →	DIP -: -3.9′
UTC	14 h	49 m	54 s	UTC date / LOP label: 1449 July 26 UL Moon	C 335T S 7.8 Kt	Ha: 51° 21.3′

2

GHA hr.	126°	00.2′	v moon planets: 12.1	Dec hr: N 8° 40.8′	d + -: +9	HP moon: 56.6

3

GHA + m.s.	+ 11°	54.4′	d corr. + -: + 7.4′
SHA + or v corr.	°	+ 10.0′	stars or moon, planets — Dec: N 8° Dec min: 48.2′
GHA	137°	64.6′	
	138°	04.6′	
a-Lon -W+E	- 122°	04.6′	
LHA	16°	00′ W / 60′ E	

tens d		d upper
units d		d lower
dsd corr.	+	dsd ←
d. corr.	Pub. 229	

additional altitude corr. moon, mars, venus	+3.3′
altitude corr. all sights	+45.9′
upper limb moon subtract 30′	-30.0′
Ho	51° 40.5′
Hc	51° 15.2′

4

LHA	16°	
Dec deg	8°	N S: N
a-Lat	45°	N S: N

5

tab Hc	50°	29′	d + -: + 57	Z: 155
d. corr. Pub. 249		+ 46.2′	Dec min: 48.2′	
Hc	50°	75.2′		

6

a =	25.3′ T[redacted]
Zn =	205°
a - Lat =	45° N
a - Lon =	122° 04.6′ W

The plot of these sights are on the following page.

9.6 Moon-Sun Running Fix, Sun #8

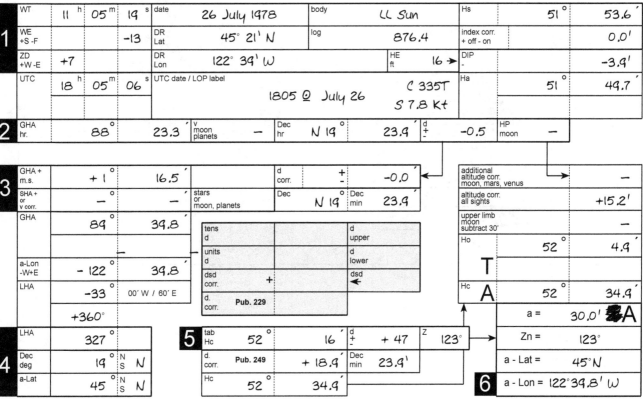

1

WT	11 h	05 m	19 s	date: 26 July 1978	body: LL Sun	Hs: 51° 53.6′
WE +S -F			-13	DR Lat: 45° 21′ N	log: 876.4	index corr. + off - on: 0.0′
ZD +W -E	+7			DR Lon: 122° 39′ W	HE ft: 16 →	DIP -: -3.9′
UTC	18 h	05 m	06 s	UTC date / LOP label: 1805 ☉ July 26	C 335T S 7.8 Kt	Ha: 51° 49.7′

2

GHA hr.	88°	23.3′	v moon planets: —	Dec hr: N 19° 23.9′	d + -: -0.5	HP moon: —

3

GHA + m.s.	+ 1°	16.5′	d corr. + -: -0.0′
SHA + or v corr.	—	—	stars or moon, planets — Dec: N 19° Dec min: 23.9′
GHA	89°	39.8′	
	—		
a-Lon -W+E	- 122°	39.8′	
LHA	-33°	00′ W / 60′ E	
	+360°		

tens d		d upper
units d		d lower
dsd corr.	+	dsd ←
d. corr.	Pub. 229	

additional altitude corr. moon, mars, venus	—
altitude corr. all sights	+15.2′
upper limb moon subtract 30′	—
Ho	52° 4.9′
Hc	52° 34.9′

4

LHA	327°	
Dec deg	19°	N S: N
a-Lat	45°	N S: N

5

tab Hc	52°	16′	d + -: + 47	Z: 123°
d. corr. Pub. 249		+ 18.9′	Dec min: 23.9′	
Hc	52°	34.9′		

6

a =	30.0′ [redacted]A
Zn =	123°
a - Lat =	45° N
a - Lon =	122° 39.8′ W

Plot of Moon-Sun Running Fix, Moon #2, Sun #8

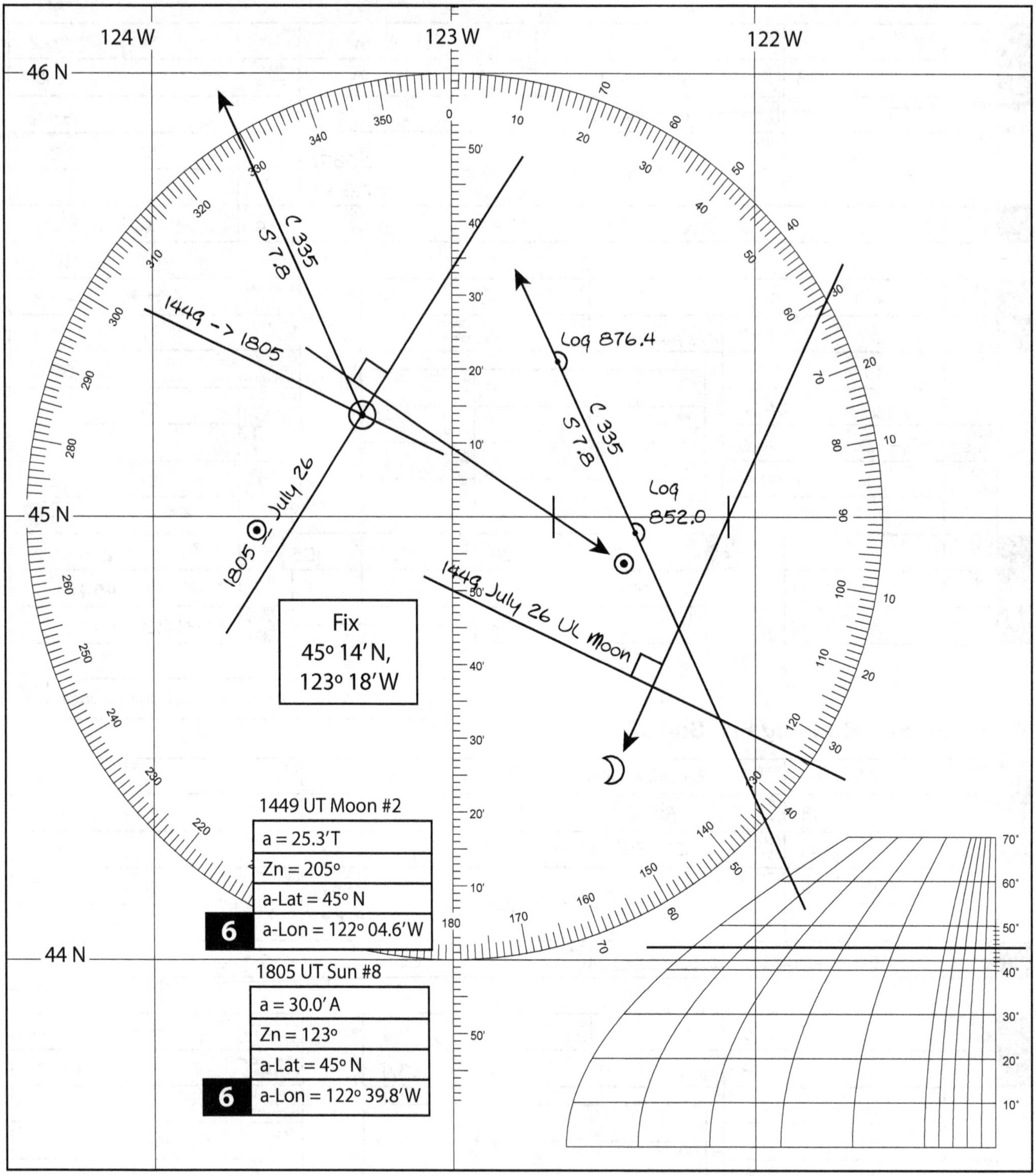

9.7 Moon-Arcturus Fix, Moon #3

1

	h	m	s						
WT	5	59	32	date	26 Oct 1978	body	UL Moon	Hs	51° 42.9′
WE +S -F		+7	30	DR Lat	45° 05′ N	log	3951.8	index corr. + off - on	-2.5′
ZD +W -E	-11			DR Lon	160° 25′ E	HE ft	19 →	DIP -	-4.2′
UTC	-6	+66	62	UTC date / LOP label	UL Moon 1907 Oct 25 1978			Ha	51° 36.2′
	19	07	02						

2

GHA hr.		v moon planets	Dec hr		d + -	HP moon
176°	09.7′	+13.9	N 11°	35.0′	-7.4	54.5

3

	°	′			
GHA + m.s.	1	40.7	d corr. + -	-0.9	
SHA + or v corr.	—	+ 1.7	stars or moon, planets	Dec N 11°	Dec min 34.1
GHA	177	52.1			
a-Lon -W+E	+ 160	7.9			
LHA	337	00′ W / 60′ E			
	338°				

tens d		d upper	
units d		d lower	
dsd corr.	+	dsd ←	
d. corr.	Pub. 229		

additional altitude corr. moon, mars, venus	+2.6′
altitude corr. all sights	+45.7′
upper limb moon subtract 30′	-30.0′
Ho (T)	51° 54.5′
Hc (A)	51° 38.1′

4

LHA	338°	
Dec deg	11°	N
a-Lat	45°	N

5

	°	′			
tab Hc	51	07	d + -	+ 55	Z 144°
d. corr.	Pub. 249	+ 31.1	Dec min	34.1′	
Hc	51	38.1			

6

a =	16.4 T[redacted]
Zn =	144°
a - Lat =	45° N
a - Lon =	160° 07.9′ E

North Latitudes
LHA greater than 180° .... Zn = Z
LHA less than 180° .... Zn = 360° - Z

South Latitudes
LHA greater than 180° .... Zn = 180° - Z
LHA less than 180° .... Zn = 180° + Z

The plot of these sights are on the following page.

9.8 Moon-Arcturus Fix, Star #9

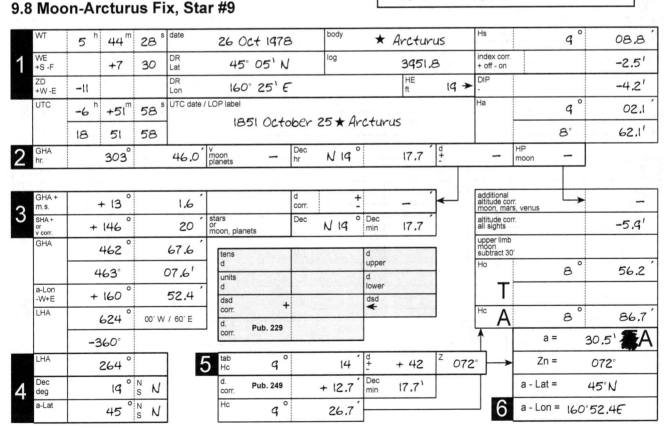

1

	h	m	s						
WT	5	44	28	date	26 Oct 1978	body	★ Arcturus	Hs	9° 08.8′
WE +S -F		+7	30	DR Lat	45° 05′ N	log	3951.8	index corr. + off - on	-2.5′
ZD +W -E	-11			DR Lon	160° 25′ E	HE ft	19 →	DIP -	-4.2′
UTC	-6	+51	58	UTC date / LOP label	1851 October 25 ★ Arcturus			Ha	9° 02.1′
	18	51	58						8° 62.1′

2

GHA hr.		v moon planets	Dec hr		d + -	HP moon
303°	46.0′	—	N 19°	17.7′	—	—

3

	°	′			
GHA + m.s.	+ 13	1.6	d corr. + -	—	
SHA + or v corr.	+ 146	20	stars or moon, planets	Dec N 19°	Dec min 17.7
GHA	462	67.6			
	463°	07.6′			
a-Lon -W+E	+ 160	52.4			
LHA	624	00′ W / 60′ E			
	-360°				

tens d		d upper	
units d		d lower	
dsd corr.	+	dsd ←	
d. corr.	Pub. 229		

additional altitude corr. moon, mars, venus	—
altitude corr. all sights	-5.9′
upper limb moon subtract 30′	
Ho (T)	8° 56.2′
Hc (A)	8° 86.7′

4

LHA	264°	
Dec deg	19°	N
a-Lat	45°	N

5

	°	′			
tab Hc	9	14	d + -	+ 42	Z 072°
d. corr.	Pub. 249	+ 12.7	Dec min	17.7′	
Hc	9	26.7			

6

a =	30.5′ [redacted]A
Zn =	072°
a - Lat =	45° N
a - Lon =	160° 52.4E

Plot of Moon-Arcturus Fix, Moon #3, Star #9.

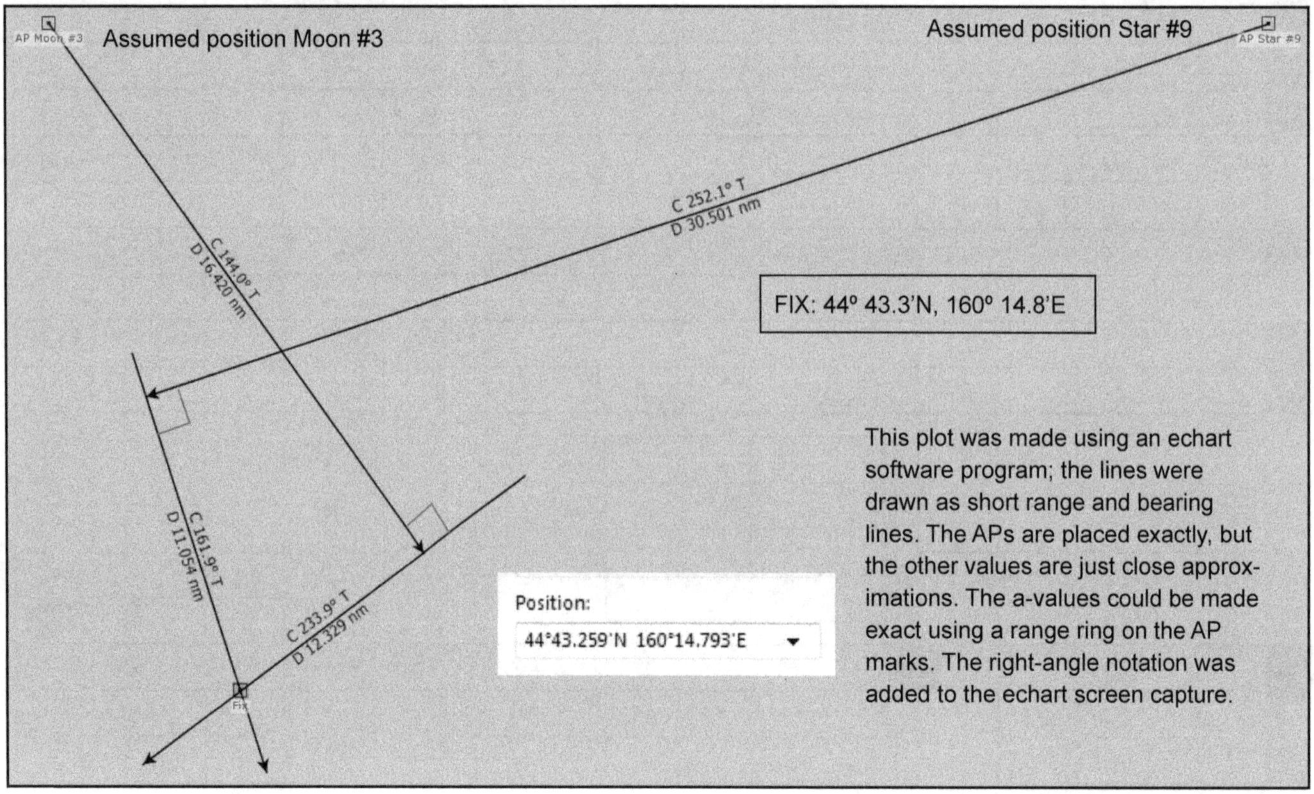

9.9 Moon #4

1

WT	05 h	49 m	26 s	date	27 Mar 1981	body	LL Moon	Hs	24°	49.7′
WE +S -F			+03	DR Lat	45° 16′ N	log	0102.7	index corr. + off - on		- 0.1′
ZD +W -E	+9			DR Lon	140° 20′ W	HE ft	10 →	DIP -		-3.1′
UTC	14 h	49 m	29 s	UTC date / LOP label	1449 Mar 27 LL Moon			Ha	24°	46.5′

2

GHA hr.	132°	20.5′	v moon planets	+11.6	Dec hr	S 19°	35.4′	d + -	+3.4	HP moon 54.8

3

GHA + m.s.	+ 11°	48.4′		d corr.	+ -	+2.8′
SHA + or v corr.	°	+9.6′	stars or moon, planets	Dec	S 19°	Dec min 38.2′
GHA	143°	78.5′				
	=144°	18.5′				
a-Lon -W+E	- 140°	18.5′				
LHA	004°	00′ W / 60′ E				

tens d		d upper
units d		d lower
dsd corr.	+	dsd ←
d. corr. Pub. 229		

additional altitude corr. moon, mars, venus		+1.6′
altitude corr. all sights		+ 60.9′
upper limb moon subtract 30′		–
Ho	25°	49.0′
T		
Hc A	25°	15.8′

4

LHA	004°	
Dec deg	19°	N S S
a-Lat	45°	N S N

5

tab Hc	25°	54.0′	d + -	-60	Z 176°
d. corr. Pub. 249		-38.2′	Dec min	38.2′	
Hc	25°	15.8′			

6

a =	33.2′ T
Zn =	184°
a - Lat =	45° N
a - Lon =	140° 18.5′ W

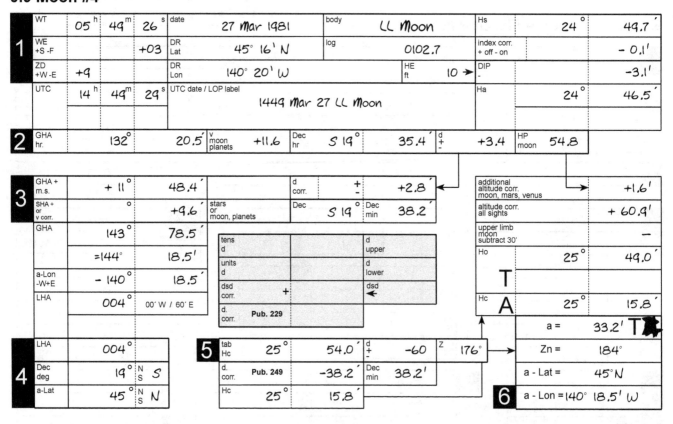

11.6 Dip Short

(1) HE = 8.5 ft. Dist = 1.35 miles. SQRT 8.5 = 2.9, so we need dip short. Dip = 0.416 x 1.35 + 0.566 x (8.5/1.35) = 0.516 + 3.563 = -4.1'

(2) HE 6 ft. Dist = 0.42 miles. SQRT 6 = 2.4, so we need dip short. Dip = 0.416 x 0.42 + 0.566 x (6/0.42) = 0.174 + 8.085 = -8.3'

(3) HE = 25 ft. Dist = 1.4 miles. Clearly need dip. Dip = 0.416 x 1.4 + 0.566 x (25/1.4) = 0.582 + 10.107 = -10.7'

(4) HE = 25 ft. Dist = 1.9 miles. Dip = 0.416 x 1.9 + 0.566 x (25/1.9) = 0.790 + 7.447 = -8.2'. The correction is smaller by 2.5'; i.e., big effect.

(5) HE = 12 ft. Dist = 0.9 miles. Dip = 0.416 x 0.9 + 0.566 x (12/0.9) = 0.374+ 7.547 = -7.9'

(6) HE = 15 ft. Dist = 0.9 miles. Dip = 0.416 x 0.9 + 0.566 x (15/0.9) = 0.374 + 9.433 = -9.8'. The correction is larger by 1.9', again, shows to use this we must measure everything carefully.

(7-Sun) HE = 28 ft. Dist = 0.9 miles. Dip = 0.416 x 0.9 + 0.566 x (28/0.9) = 0.374 + 17.609 = -18.0' Sun Correction

(7-Moon) HE = 28 ft. Dist = 0.65 miles. Dip = 0.416 x 0.65 + 0.566 x (28/0.65) = 0.270 + 24.381 = -24.7' Moon Correction

11.12 Time Predictions

(1a). UTC (at Greenwich)= 12h 00m 00s + (Equation of Time) 05m 23s = 12h 05m 23s, Longitude 126° 32'W = (Arc to Time) 08h 26m 08s + 12h 05m 23s = 20h 31m 31s, Minus ZD (+8) = 12h 31m 31s LAN

(1b). Tabular UTC (at Greenwich) 05h 25m, Longitude 126° 32'W = (Arc to Time) 08h 26m 08s + 05h 25m 00s = 13h 51m 08s, Minus ZD (+8) = 05h 51m 08s

(1c). Tabular UTC (at Greenwich) 05h 52m, Longitude 126° 32'W = (Arc to Time) 08h 26m 08s + 05h 52m 00s = 14h 18m 08s, Minus ZD (+8) = 06h 18m 08s

(2a). Tabular UTC (at Greenwich) 18h 06m, Longitude 030° 15' W = (Arc to Time) 02h 01m 00s + 18h 06m 00s = 20h 07m 00s, Minus ZD (+4) = 16h 07m 00s

(2b). UTC (at Greenwich) = 12h 00m 00s - (Equation of Time) 15m 58s = 11h 44m 02s, Longitude 030° 15' W = (Arc to Time) 02h 01m 00s + 11h 44m 02s = 13h 45m 02s, Minus ZD (+4) = 09h 45m 02s

(3a). WT of Morning Nautical Twilight 02h 20m 20s
(3b). WT of Morning Civil Twilight = 03h 20m 20s
(3c). WT of Sunrise = 04h 04m 20s

(4a). Nautical Twilight = 05h 05m 20s
(4b). Nautical Twilight = 19h 09m 20s

11.13 Choosing the Assumed Position

a-Lat, a-Lon	*a-Lat, a-Lon*
(1) 14° N, 122° 40.5' W	(9) 14° N, 122° 19.5' E
(2) 13° N, 152° 20.8' W	(10) 13° N, 152° 39.2' E
(3) 19° S, 74° 55.3' W	(11) 19° S, 76° 04.7' E
(4) 48° N, 133° 12.4' W	(12) 48° N, 132° 47.6' E
(5) 05° S, 151° 4.9' W	(13) 05° S, 149° 55.1' E
(6) 22° N, 153° 13.6' W	(14) 22° N, 153° 46.4' E
(7) 47° N, 55° 56.1' W	(15) 47° N, 56° 03.9' E
(8) 34° S, 122° 12.5' W	(16) 34° S, 121° 47.5' E

11.14 Practice Using Pub. 249

4			5					6	
LHA	3°		tab Hc	66°	52'	d ± +60	Z 173 →	Zn =	187
Dec deg	22°	N	d. corr. Pub. 249		+5.6'	Dec min 5.6'		a - Lat =	
a-Lat	45°	N	Hc	66°	57.6'			a - Lon =	

(4) Notes: Use table T-17; Same name; N Lat for Z to Zn; exact values are 66° 57.7', 187.1.

4			5					6	
LHA	29°		tab Hc	32°	46'	d ± -55	Z 145 →	Zn =	325
Dec deg	6°	N	d. corr. Pub. 249		-27.6'	Dec min 29.6'		a - Lat =	
a-Lat	45°	S	Hc	32°	18.4'			a - Lon =	

(5) Notes: Use table T-18; Contrary name; S Lat for Z to Zn; exact is 32° 18.7', 325.3.

4			5					6	
LHA	313°		tab Hc	35°	10'	d ± +46	Z 118 →	Zn =	118
Dec deg	8°	N	d. corr. Pub. 249		+37.9'	Dec min 48.9'		a - Lat =	
a-Lat	45°	N	Hc	35°	47.9'			a - Lon =	

(6) Notes: Use table T-15; Same name; N Lat for Z to Zn; exact values are 35° 47.8', 117.0. Round to Dec 9° in Pub. 249 to find that Z = 117 is better.

11.15 Cut angles from special table

#	*Ho-max*	*Cut angle*	*Time interval*
1	49°	~30°	44 min
2	78°	~67°	28 min
3	40°	30°	>48 min
4	57°	30°	~42 min
5	82°	30°	~10 min

This type of cut angle question can also be solved by doing a simple sight reduction at the time of the proposed first and second sights, although when doing it by hand this takes a long time. The process can be made much shorter by just looking at the Z column of the SR tables to see how long it takes for Z to increase by 30 or so degrees. Then recall that each 15° of LHA is the same as 1 hr, which means each 1° of LHA is 4 minutes. Alternatively, when using a calculator or computer it is a simple matter to just do a few sight reductions at various times to see how long you have to wait. This takes just a minute or two.

11.30 Sight Reduction by N(x) Table

Answers derived from calculator are shown at the end as [Hc, Zn], to illustrate that the method really works!

(A) t = 49 W, Dec = N 13, Lat = 32 N

N(v) = N(90 - 13) + N(49) = 26 + 281 = 307, so v = 47.4. N(w)=N(13)-N(90 - 47.4)=1492 - 391 = 1101, so w = 47.4 and (same name) u = 90 - 19.4 + 32 = 102.6 which is > 90, so u = 180 - 102.6 = 77.4

N(Hc) = N(90 - 44.7) + N(77.4) = 391 + 24 = 415, so Hc = 41.4°. N(Z) = N(47.4) - N(90 - 41.4) = 307 - 287 = 20, so Z = 78.7, but u > 90, so Z = 180 - 78.7 = 101.3° and Zn = 258.7. [41.40, 258.6]

(B) t = 49 W, Dec = N 50, Lat = 20 N

N(v) = N(90 - 50) + N(49) = 442 + 281 = 723, so v = 29.0. N(w) = N(50) - N(90 - 29.0) = 267 - 134 = 133, so w = 61.1 and (same name) u = 90 - 61.1 + 20 = 48.9 N(Hc) = N(90 - 29.0) + N(48.9) = 134 + 283 = 417, so Hc = 41.3°. N(Z) = N(29.0) - N(90 - 41.3) = 724 - 286 = 438, so Z = 40.2° and Zn = 319.8. [41.17, 319.8]

(C) t = 30 W, Dec = S 20, Lat = 12 N

N(v) = N(90 - 20) + N(30) = 62 + 693 = 755, so v = 28.0. N(w) = N(20) - N(90 - 28.0) = 1073 - 124 = 949, so w = 22.8 and (contrary name) u = 90 - 22.8 - 12 = 55.2 N(Hc) = N(90 - 28.0) + N(55.2) = 124 + 197 = 321, so Hc = 46.5°. N(Z) = N(28.0) - N(90 - 46.5) = 756 - 374 = 382, so Z = 43.1, but since contrary name Z = 180 - 43.1 = 136.9° and Zn = 223.1. [46.46, 223.0]

(D) t =62 E, Dec N 10.4, Lat 11 S

N(v) = N(90 - 10.4) + N(62) = 16.6 + 124 = 140.6, so v = 60.3. N(w) = N(10.4) - N(90 - 60.3) = 1713 - 702.3 = 1010.7, so w = 21.4 and (contrary name) u = 90 - 21.4 - 11 = 57.6 N(Hc) = N(90 - 60.3) + N(57.6) = 702.3 + 169.4 = 871.7, so Hc = 24.7°. N(Z) = N(60.3) - N(90 -24.7) = 140.6 - 95.6 = 45.0, so Z = 73.0, but since contrary name Z = 180 - 73.0 = 107.0° and Zn = 73.0. [24.76, 73.0]

Appendix 3

TABLE SELECTIONS

CONTENTS

The notation "T-1," "T-2," etc, is for easy cross reference within this book or classroom only. This notation is not used elsewhere in navigation, and it does not appear in the *Nautical Almanac.* These Table Selections are available as a free pdf download from www.starpath.com/celnavbook, if it might be more convenient to have them separate from the book.

T-1

1978 JULY 24, 25, 26 (MON., TUES., WED.)

Day	UT d h	ARIES G.H.A. ° ′	VENUS −3.7 G.H.A. ° ′	VENUS Dec. ° ′	MARS +1.7 G.H.A. ° ′	MARS Dec. ° ′	JUPITER −1.4 G.H.A. ° ′	JUPITER Dec. ° ′	SATURN +0.9 G.H.A. ° ′	SATURN Dec. ° ′
	24 00	301 21.8	136 16.3	N 7 21.2	127 29.6	N 3 22.1	188 46.6	N21 59.1	149 02.2	N12 55.3
	01	316 24.2	151 16.2	20.0	142 30.7	21.4	203 48.5	59.0	164 04.4	55.2
	02	331 26.7	166 16.1	18.8	157 31.8	20.8	218 50.3	58.9	179 06.5	55.1
	03	346 29.2	181 16.0	·· 17.6	172 32.9	·· 20.2	233 52.2	·· 58.8	194 08.7	·· 55.0
	04	1 31.6	196 16.0	16.4	187 34.0	19.5	248 54.1	58.8	209 10.9	54.9
	05	16 34.1	211 15.9	15.2	202 35.1	18.9	263 55.9	58.7	224 13.1	54.8
	06	31 36.6	226 15.8	N 7 14.0	217 36.1	N 3 18.3	278 57.8	N21 58.6	239 15.3	N12 54.7
	07	46 39.0	241 15.8	12.7	232 37.2	17.7	293 59.7	58.5	254 17.5	54.6
	08	61 41.5	256 15.7	11.5	247 38.3	17.0	309 01.5	58.4	269 19.7	54.5
MONDAY	09	76 44.0	271 15.6	·· 10.3	262 39.4	·· 16.4	324 03.4	·· 58.3	284 21.8	·· 54.4
	10	91 46.4	286 15.5	09.1	277 40.5	15.8	339 05.3	58.3	299 24.0	54.3
	11	106 48.9	301 15.5	07.9	292 41.6	15.1	354 07.1	58.2	314 26.2	54.2
	12	121 51.3	316 15.4	N 7 06.7	307 42.7	N 3 14.5	9 09.0	N21 58.1	329 28.4	N12 54.1
	13	136 53.8	331 15.3	05.5	322 43.7	13.9	24 10.9	58.0	344 30.6	54.0
	14	151 56.3	346 15.3	04.3	337 44.8	13.3	39 12.8	57.9	359 32.8	53.9
	15	166 58.7	1 15.2	·· 03.1	352 45.9	·· 12.6	54 14.6	·· 57.9	14 34.9	·· 53.8
	16	182 01.2	16 15.1	01.9	7 47.0	12.0	69 16.5	57.8	29 37.1	53.6
	17	197 03.7	31 15.1	7 00.7	22 48.1	11.4	84 18.4	57.7	44 39.3	53.5
	18	212 06.1	46 15.0	N 6 59.4	37 49.2	N 3 10.7	99 20.2	N21 57.6	59 41.5	N12 53.4
	19	227 08.6	61 15.0	58.2	52 50.3	10.1	114 22.1	57.5	74 43.7	53.3
	20	242 11.1	76 14.9	57.0	67 51.3	09.5	129 24.0	57.5	89 45.9	53.2
	21	257 13.5	91 14.8	·· 55.8	82 52.4	·· 08.9	144 25.8	·· 57.4	104 48.0	·· 53.1
	22	272 16.0	106 14.8	54.6	97 53.5	08.2	159 27.7	57.3	119 50.2	53.0
	23	287 18.5	121 14.7	53.4	112 54.6	07.6	174 29.6	57.2	134 52.4	52.9
	25 00	302 20.9	136 14.6	N 6 52.2	127 55.7	N 3 07.0	189 31.5	N21 57.1	149 54.6	N12 52.8
	01	317 23.4	151 14.6	51.0	142 56.8	06.3	204 33.3	57.0	164 56.8	52.7
	02	332 25.8	166 14.5	49.7	157 57.8	05.7	219 35.2	57.0	179 59.0	52.6
	03	347 28.3	181 14.5	·· 48.5	172 58.9	·· 05.1	234 37.1	·· 56.9	195 01.1	·· 52.5
	04	2 30.8	196 14.4	47.3	188 00.0	04.4	249 38.9	56.8	210 03.3	52.4
	05	17 33.2	211 14.3	46.1	203 01.1	03.8	264 40.8	56.7	225 05.5	52.3
	06	32 35.7	226 14.3	N 6 44.9	218 02.2	N 3 03.2	279 42.7	N21 56.6	240 07.7	N12 52.2
	07	47 38.2	241 14.2	43.7	233 03.3	02.6	294 44.5	56.6	255 09.9	52.1
	08	62 40.6	256 14.2	42.5	248 04.3	01.9	309 46.4	56.5	270 12.1	52.0
	09	77 43.1	271 14.1	·· 41.2	263 05.4	·· 01.3	324 48.3	·· 56.4	285 14.2	·· 51.9
	10	92 45.6	286 14.0	40.0	278 06.5	00.7	339 50.2	56.3	300 16.4	51.8
TUESDAY	11	107 48.0	301 14.0	38.8	293 07.6	3 00.0	354 52.0	56.2	315 18.6	51.7
	12	122 50.5	316 13.9	N 6 37.6	308 08.7	N 2 59.4	9 53.9	N21 56.1	330 20.8	N12 51.6
	13	137 52.9	331 13.9	36.4	323 09.8	58.8	24 55.8	56.1	345 23.0	51.5
	14	152 55.4	346 13.8	35.2	338 10.8	58.1	39 57.6	56.0	0 25.2	51.4
	15	167 57.9	1 13.8	·· 34.0	353 11.9	·· 57.5	54 59.5	·· 55.9	15 27.3	·· 51.3
	16	183 00.3	16 13.7	32.7	8 13.0	56.9	70 01.4	55.8	30 29.5	51.2
	17	198 02.8	31 13.7	31.5	23 14.1	56.3	85 03.3	55.7	45 31.7	51.1
	18	213 05.3	46 13.6	N 6 30.3	38 15.2	N 2 55.6	100 05.1	N21 55.6	60 33.9	N12 51.0
	19	228 07.7	61 13.6	29.1	53 16.3	55.0	115 07.0	55.6	75 36.1	50.9
	20	243 10.2	76 13.5	27.9	68 17.3	54.4	130 08.9	55.5	90 38.3	50.8
	21	258 12.7	91 13.5	·· 26.7	83 18.4	·· 53.7	145 10.7	·· 55.4	105 40.4	·· 50.7
	22	273 15.1	106 13.4	25.4	98 19.5	53.1	160 12.6	55.3	120 42.6	50.6
	23	288 17.6	121 13.4	24.2	113 20.6	52.5	175 14.5	55.2	135 44.8	50.4
	26 00	303 20.1	136 13.3	N 6 23.0	128 21.7	N 2 51.8	190 16.4	N21 55.2	150 47.0	N12 50.3
	01	318 22.5	151 13.3	21.8	143 22.7	51.2	205 18.2	55.1	165 49.2	50.2
	02	333 25.0	166 13.2	20.6	158 23.8	50.6	220 20.1	55.0	180 51.3	50.1
	03	348 27.4	181 13.2	·· 19.3	173 24.9	·· 49.9	235 22.0	·· 54.9	195 53.5	·· 50.0
	04	3 29.9	196 13.1	18.1	188 26.0	49.3	250 23.8	54.8	210 55.7	49.9
	05	18 32.4	211 13.1	16.9	203 27.1	48.7	265 25.7	54.7	225 57.9	49.8
	06	33 34.8	226 13.0	N 6 15.7	218 28.2	N 2 48.0	280 27.6	N21 54.7	241 00.1	N12 49.7
	07	48 37.3	241 13.0	14.5	233 29.2	47.4	295 29.5	54.6	256 02.3	49.6
	08	63 39.8	256 12.9	13.2	248 30.3	46.8	310 31.3	54.5	271 04.4	49.5
	09	78 42.2	271 12.9	·· 12.0	263 31.4	·· 46.2	325 33.2	·· 54.4	286 06.6	·· 49.4
	10	93 44.7	286 12.8	10.8	278 32.5	45.5	340 35.1	54.3	301 08.8	49.3
	11	108 47.2	301 12.8	09.6	293 33.6	44.9	355 36.9	54.2	316 11.0	49.2
WEDNESDAY	12	123 49.6	316 12.7	N 6 08.4	308 34.6	N 2 44.3	10 38.8	N21 54.2	331 13.2	N12 49.1
	13	138 52.1	331 12.7	07.1	323 35.7	43.6	25 40.7	54.1	346 15.3	49.0
	14	153 54.6	346 12.7	05.9	338 36.8	43.0	40 42.6	54.0	1 17.5	48.9
	15	168 57.0	1 12.6	·· 04.7	353 37.9	·· 42.4	55 44.4	·· 53.9	16 19.7	·· 48.8
	16	183 59.5	16 12.6	03.5	8 39.0	41.7	70 46.3	53.8	31 21.9	48.7
	17	199 01.9	31 12.5	02.3	23 40.0	41.1	85 48.2	53.7	46 24.1	48.6
	18	214 04.4	46 12.5	N 6 01.0	38 41.1	N 2 40.5	100 50.0	N21 53.7	61 26.3	N12 48.5
	19	229 06.9	61 12.5	5 59.8	53 42.2	39.8	115 51.9	53.6	76 28.4	48.4
	20	244 09.3	76 12.4	58.6	68 43.3	39.2	130 53.8	53.5	91 30.6	48.3
	21	259 11.8	91 12.4	·· 57.4	83 44.4	·· 38.6	145 55.7	·· 53.4	106 32.8	·· 48.2
	22	274 14.3	106 12.3	56.1	98 45.4	37.9	160 57.5	53.3	121 35.0	48.1
	23	289 16.7	121 12.3	54.9	113 46.5	37.3	175 59.4	53.2	136 37.2	48.0
	Mer. Pass.	h m 3 50.0	v −0.1	d 1.2	v 1.1	d 0.6	v 1.9	d 0.1	v 2.2	d 0.1

STARS

Name	S.H.A. ° ′	Dec. ° ′
Acamar	315 38.5	S40 23.2
Achernar	335 46.4	S57 20.5
Acrux	173 39.0	S62 59.1
Adhara	255 33.6	S28 56.6
Aldebaran	291 19.9	N16 27.9
Alioth	166 44.1	N56 04.9
Alkaid	153 19.7	N49 25.6
Al Na'ir	28 16.4	S47 03.7
Alnilam	276 13.4	S 1 13.0
Alphard	218 22.3	S 8 34.0
Alphecca	126 33.2	N26 47.5
Alpheratz	358 10.6	N28 58.3
Altair	62 33.6	N 8 48.9
Ankaa	353 41.5	S42 25.1
Antares	112 58.4	S26 23.0
Arcturus	146 19.8	N19 17.9
Atria	108 23.5	S68 59.5
Avior	234 29.4	S59 26.5
Bellatrix	279 00.6	N 6 19.8
Betelgeuse	271 30.1	N 7 24.1
Canopus	264 08.3	S52 41.0
Capella	281 13.8	N45 58.4
Deneb	49 48.9	N45 12.3
Denebola	183 00.7	N14 41.6
Diphda	349 22.2	S18 06.1
Dubhe	194 24.5	N61 52.2
Elnath	278 46.2	N28 35.2
Eltanin	90 57.9	N51 29.8
Enif	34 12.7	N 9 46.7
Fomalhaut	15 52.8	S29 43.9
Gacrux	172 30.5	S56 59.8
Gienah	176 19.6	S17 25.4
Hadar	149 25.3	S60 16.4
Hamal	328 30.5	N23 21.6
Kaus Aust.	84 18.4	S34 23.6
Kochab	137 18.9	N74 15.0
Markab	14 04.3	N15 05.4
Menkar	314 42.7	N 4 00.3
Menkent	148 38.7	S36 16.0
Miaplacidus	221 46.0	S69 37.9
Mirfak	309 18.3	N49 46.9
Nunki	76 30.6	S26 19.3
Peacock	54 00.1	S56 48.1
Pollux	244 00.3	N28 04.7
Procyon	245 27.6	N 5 16.8
Rasalhague	96 30.7	N12 34.8
Regulus	208 11.8	N12 04.4
Rigel	281 37.7	S 8 13.6
Rigil Kent.	140 27.6	S60 44.9
Sabik	102 42.5	S15 41.8
Schedar	350 10.3	N56 25.0
Shaula	96 57.4	S37 05.3
Sirius	258 57.3	S16 41.2
Spica	158 59.1	S11 02.9
Suhail	223 12.2	S43 20.9
Vega	80 56.4	N38 46.1
Zuben'ubi	137 34.5	S15 57.1

	S.H.A. ° ′	Mer. Pass. h m
Venus	193 53.7	14 55
Mars	185 34.8	15 27
Jupiter	247 10.5	11 20
Saturn	207 33.7	13 58

1978 JULY 24, 25, 26 (MON., TUES., WED.)

UT d	UT h	SUN G.H.A. ° ′	SUN Dec. ° ′	MOON G.H.A. ° ′	MOON v ′	MOON Dec. ° ′	MOON d ′	MOON H.P. ′
24	00	178 23.7	N19 59.3	306 42.0	10.0	S 1 55.1	11.1	59.0
	01	193 23.7	58.8	321 11.0	10.2	1 44.0	11.0	59.0
	02	208 23.7	58.3	335 40.2	10.2	1 33.0	10.9	59.0
	03	223 23.7	·· 57.8	350 09.4	10.2	1 22.1	11.0	58.9
	04	238 23.7	57.2	4 38.6	10.3	1 11.1	11.0	58.9
	05	253 23.7	56.7	19 07.9	10.3	1 00.1	11.0	58.8
	06	268 23.7	N19 56.2	33 37.2	10.4	S 0 49.1	10.9	58.8
	07	283 23.6	55.7	48 06.6	10.4	0 38.2	11.0	58.8
	08	298 23.6	55.2	62 36.0	10.5	0 27.2	10.9	58.7
M	09	313 23.6	·· 54.6	77 05.5	10.6	0 16.3	10.9	58.7
O	10	328 23.6	54.1	91 35.1	10.5	S 0 05.4	10.9	58.6
N	11	343 23.6	53.6	106 04.6	10.7	N 0 05.5	10.9	58.6
D	12	358 23.6	N19 53.1	120 34.3	10.6	N 0 16.4	10.8	58.6
A	13	13 23.6	52.5	135 03.9	10.8	0 27.2	10.9	58.5
Y	14	28 23.6	52.0	149 33.7	10.7	0 38.1	10.8	58.5
	15	43 23.5	·· 51.5	164 03.4	10.8	0 48.9	10.8	58.4
	16	58 23.5	51.0	178 33.2	10.9	0 59.7	10.8	58.4
	17	73 23.5	50.4	193 03.1	10.9	1 10.5	10.8	58.4
	18	88 23.5	N19 49.9	207 33.0	10.9	N 1 21.3	10.7	58.3
	19	103 23.5	49.4	222 02.9	11.0	1 32.0	10.7	58.3
	20	118 23.5	48.9	236 32.9	11.0	1 42.7	10.7	58.2
	21	133 23.5	·· 48.3	251 02.9	11.0	1 53.4	10.7	58.2
	22	148 23.5	47.8	265 32.9	11.1	2 04.1	10.6	58.2
	23	163 23.5	47.3	280 03.0	11.2	2 14.7	10.6	58.1
25	00	178 23.4	N19 46.7	294 33.2	11.1	N 2 25.3	10.6	58.1
	01	193 23.4	46.2	309 03.3	11.3	2 35.9	10.6	58.0
	02	208 23.4	45.7	323 33.6	11.2	2 46.5	10.5	58.0
	03	223 23.4	·· 45.1	338 03.8	11.3	2 57.0	10.5	58.0
	04	238 23.4	44.6	352 34.1	11.3	3 07.5	10.5	57.9
	05	253 23.4	44.1	7 04.4	11.3	3 18.0	10.4	57.9
	06	268 23.4	N19 43.5	21 34.7	11.4	N 3 28.4	10.4	57.8
	07	283 23.4	43.0	36 05.1	11.4	3 38.8	10.3	57.8
	08	298 23.4	42.5	50 35.5	11.5	3 49.1	10.4	57.8
T	09	313 23.4	·· 41.9	65 06.0	11.5	3 59.5	10.3	57.7
U	10	328 23.4	41.4	79 36.5	11.5	4 09.8	10.2	57.7
E	11	343 23.4	40.9	94 07.0	11.5	4 20.0	10.3	57.7
S	12	358 23.3	N19 40.3	108 37.5	11.6	N 4 30.3	10.1	57.6
D	13	13 23.3	39.8	123 08.1	11.6	4 40.4	10.2	57.6
A	14	28 23.3	39.3	137 38.7	11.6	4 50.6	10.1	57.5
Y	15	43 23.3	·· 38.7	152 09.3	11.7	5 00.7	10.1	57.5
	16	58 23.3	38.2	166 40.0	11.7	5 10.8	10.0	57.5
	17	73 23.3	37.6	181 10.7	11.7	5 20.8	10.0	57.4
	18	88 23.3	N19 37.1	195 41.4	11.7	N 5 30.8	9.9	57.4
	19	103 23.3	36.6	210 12.1	11.8	5 40.7	9.9	57.3
	20	118 23.3	36.0	224 42.9	11.8	5 50.6	9.9	57.3
	21	133 23.3	·· 35.5	239 13.7	11.8	6 00.5	9.8	57.3
	22	148 23.3	34.9	253 44.5	11.8	6 10.3	9.8	57.2
	23	163 23.3	34.4	268 15.3	11.9	6 20.1	9.7	57.2
26	00	178 23.3	N19 33.8	282 46.2	11.8	N 6 29.8	9.7	57.2
	01	193 23.3	33.3	297 17.0	11.9	6 39.5	9.6	57.1
	02	208 23.3	32.7	311 47.9	12.0	6 49.1	9.6	57.1
	03	223 23.3	·· 32.2	326 18.9	11.9	6 58.7	9.5	57.0
	04	238 23.3	31.7	340 49.8	12.0	7 08.2	9.5	57.0
	05	253 23.3	31.1	355 20.8	11.9	7 17.7	9.4	57.0
	06	268 23.3	N19 30.6	9 51.7	12.0	N 7 27.1	9.4	56.9
W	07	283 23.3	30.0	24 22.7	12.1	7 36.5	9.4	56.9
E	08	298 23.3	29.5	38 53.8	12.0	7 45.9	9.3	56.9
D	09	313 23.3	·· 28.9	53 24.8	12.0	7 55.2	9.2	56.8
N	10	328 23.3	28.4	67 55.8	12.1	8 04.4	9.2	56.8
E	11	343 23.3	27.8	82 26.9	12.1	8 13.6	9.1	56.7
S	12	358 23.3	N19 27.3	96 58.0	12.1	N 8 22.7	9.1	56.7
D	13	13 23.3	26.7	111 29.1	12.1	8 31.8	9.0	56.7
A	14	28 23.3	26.2	126 00.2	12.1	8 40.8	9.0	56.6
Y	15	43 23.3	·· 25.6	140 31.3	12.2	8 49.8	8.9	56.6
	16	58 23.3	25.1	155 02.5	12.1	8 58.7	8.9	56.6
	17	73 23.3	24.5	169 33.6	12.2	9 07.6	8.8	56.5
	18	88 23.3	N19 23.9	184 04.8	12.2	N 9 16.4	8.8	56.5
	19	103 23.3	23.4	198 36.0	12.2	9 25.2	8.7	56.5
	20	118 23.3	22.8	213 07.2	12.2	9 33.9	8.6	56.4
	21	133 23.3	·· 22.3	227 38.4	12.2	9 42.5	8.6	56.4
	22	148 23.3	21.7	242 09.6	12.2	9 51.1	8.5	56.4
	23	163 23.3	21.2	256 40.8	12.3	9 59.6	8.5	56.3
		S.D. 15.8	d 0.5	S.D. 16.0		15.7		15.5

Lat. °	Twilight Naut. h m	Twilight Civil h m	Sunrise h m	Moonrise 24 h m	Moonrise 25 h m	Moonrise 26 h m	Moonrise 27 h m
N 72	▭	▭	▭	21 54	21 49	21 44	21 39
N 70	▭	▭	▭	21 57	21 57	21 59	22 02
68	////	////	01 32	21 59	22 04	22 11	22 20
66	////	////	02 16	22 01	22 10	22 21	22 34
64	////	00 38	02 44	22 02	22 15	22 29	22 46
62	////	01 43	03 06	22 03	22 19	22 37	22 56
60	////	02 16	03 23	22 05	22 23	22 43	23 05
N 58	00 35	02 40	03 38	22 06	22 27	22 49	23 13
56	01 34	02 59	03 50	22 07	22 30	22 53	23 20
54	02 04	03 14	04 01	22 07	22 32	22 58	23 26
52	02 27	03 27	04 11	22 08	22 35	23 02	23 31
50	02 44	03 39	04 19	22 09	22 37	23 06	23 36
45	03 18	04 02	04 37	22 11	22 42	23 14	23 47
N 40	03 42	04 20	04 51	22 12	22 46	23 20	23 56
35	04 01	04 35	05 04	22 13	22 50	23 26	24 04
30	04 16	04 48	05 14	22 14	22 53	23 31	24 11
20	04 41	05 09	05 33	22 16	22 58	23 40	24 23
N 10	05 00	05 26	05 48	22 17	23 03	23 48	24 33
0	05 15	05 41	06 03	22 19	23 08	23 56	24 43
S 10	05 29	05 55	06 17	22 21	23 12	24 03	00 03
20	05 42	06 09	06 33	22 22	23 17	24 11	00 11
30	05 55	06 25	06 50	22 24	23 23	24 20	00 20
35	06 02	06 33	07 00	22 25	23 26	24 26	00 26
40	06 09	06 42	07 12	22 27	23 30	24 32	00 32
45	06 17	06 53	07 25	22 28	23 35	24 39	00 39
S 50	06 26	07 05	07 41	22 30	23 40	24 47	00 47
52	06 29	07 11	07 49	22 31	23 42	24 51	00 51
54	06 33	07 17	07 58	22 32	23 45	24 56	00 56
56	06 38	07 24	08 07	22 33	23 48	25 00	01 00
58	06 43	07 32	08 18	22 34	23 51	25 06	01 06
S 60	06 48	07 40	08 31	22 35	23 55	25 12	01 12

Lat. °	Sunset h m	Twilight Civil h m	Twilight Naut. h m	Moonset 24 h m	Moonset 25 h m	Moonset 26 h m	Moonset 27 h m
N 72	▭	▭	▭	09 50	11 38	13 24	15 08
N 70	▭	▭	▭	09 50	11 32	13 11	14 46
68	22 35	////	////	09 51	11 27	13 00	14 29
66	21 54	////	////	09 51	11 23	12 51	14 16
64	21 26	23 23	////	09 51	11 19	12 44	14 04
62	21 05	22 26	////	09 51	11 16	12 37	13 55
60	20 48	21 54	////	09 51	11 13	12 32	13 47
N 58	20 34	21 31	23 27	09 52	11 11	12 27	13 40
56	20 21	21 13	22 35	09 52	11 09	12 23	13 33
54	20 11	20 57	22 06	09 52	11 07	12 19	13 28
52	20 01	20 44	21 44	09 52	11 05	12 15	13 23
50	19 53	20 33	21 27	09 52	11 04	12 12	13 18
45	19 35	20 10	20 54	09 52	11 00	12 06	13 08
N 40	19 21	19 52	20 30	09 52	10 57	12 00	13 00
35	19 09	19 37	20 11	09 52	10 55	11 55	12 53
30	18 58	19 24	19 56	09 52	10 53	11 51	12 47
20	18 40	19 04	19 32	09 53	10 49	11 43	12 36
N 10	18 24	18 47	19 13	09 53	10 46	11 37	12 27
0	18 10	18 32	18 57	09 53	10 42	11 31	12 18
S 10	17 56	18 18	18 44	09 53	10 39	11 25	12 10
20	17 40	18 04	18 31	09 53	10 36	11 18	12 00
30	17 23	17 49	18 18	09 53	10 32	11 11	11 50
35	17 13	17 40	18 11	09 53	10 30	11 07	11 44
40	17 02	17 31	18 04	09 53	10 28	11 02	11 37
45	16 48	17 20	17 56	09 53	10 25	10 56	11 29
S 50	16 32	17 08	17 48	09 53	10 21	10 50	11 19
52	16 24	17 02	17 44	09 53	10 20	10 46	11 15
54	16 16	16 56	17 40	09 53	10 18	10 43	11 10
56	16 06	16 49	17 36	09 53	10 16	10 39	11 04
58	15 55	16 42	17 31	09 53	10 14	10 35	10 58
S 60	15 43	16 33	17 26	09 53	10 12	10 31	10 52

Day	SUN Eqn. of Time 00ʰ m s	SUN Eqn. of Time 12ʰ m s	SUN Mer. Pass. h m	MOON Mer. Pass. Upper h m	MOON Mer. Pass. Lower h m	MOON Age d	MOON Phase
24	06 25	06 26	12 06	03 41	16 06	19	
25	06 26	06 27	12 06	04 31	16 55	20	◑
26	06 27	06 27	12 06	05 19	17 43	21	

1978 OCTOBER 25, 26, 27 (WED., THURS., FRI.)

	UT	ARIES	VENUS −3.8		MARS +1.7		JUPITER −1.7		SATURN +1.1		STARS		
	d h	G.H.A. ° ′	G.H.A. ° ′	Dec. ° ′	G.H.A. ° ′	Dec. ° ′	G.H.A. ° ′	Dec. ° ′	G.H.A. ° ′	Dec. ° ′	Name	S.H.A. ° ′	Dec. ° ′
	25 00	33 01.7	165 27.4	S24 38.1	161 15.0	S19 13.3	263 03.8	N18 45.7	230 09.7	N 8 59.2	Acamar	315 37.8	S40 23.3
	01	48 04.1	180 30.6	37.8	176 15.6	13.8	278 06.0	45.6	245 11.9	59.1	Achernar	335 45.7	S57 20.7
	02	63 06.6	195 33.7	37.5	191 16.3	14.2	293 08.2	45.6	260 14.1	59.0	Acrux	173 39.2	S62 58.7
	03	78 09.1	210 36.9	·· 37.1	206 16.9	·· 14.7	308 10.5	·· 45.5	275 16.4	·· 59.0	Adhara	255 33.0	S28 56.4
	04	93 11.5	225 40.0	36.8	221 17.6	15.1	323 12.7	45.5	290 18.6	58.9	Aldebaran	291 19.2	N16 28.0
	05	108 14.0	240 43.2	36.5	236 18.2	15.6	338 14.9	45.4	305 20.9	58.8			
	06	123 16.4	255 46.3	S24 36.2	251 18.8	S19 16.1	353 17.1	N18 45.4	320 23.1	N 8 58.7	Alioth	166 44.3	N56 04.5
	07	138 18.9	270 49.5	35.9	266 19.5	16.5	8 19.3	45.3	335 25.3	58.6	Alkaid	153 20.1	N49 25.2
W	08	153 21.4	285 52.7	35.6	281 20.1	17.0	23 21.5	45.2	350 27.6	58.5	Al Na'ir	28 16.4	S47 03.9
E	09	168 23.8	300 55.9	·· 35.2	296 20.8	·· 17.4	38 23.8	·· 45.2	5 29.8	·· 58.5	Alnilam	276 12.8	S 1 12.9
D	10	183 26.3	315 59.0	34.9	311 21.4	17.9	53 26.0	45.1	20 32.0	58.4	Alphard	218 21.9	S 8 33.9
N	11	198 28.8	331 02.2	34.6	326 22.1	18.4	68 28.2	45.1	35 34.3	58.3			
E	12	213 31.2	346 05.4	S24 34.2	341 22.7	S19 18.8	83 30.4	N18 45.0	50 36.5	N 8 58.2	Alphecca	126 33.6	N26 47.4
S	13	228 33.7	1 08.6	33.9	356 23.4	19.3	98 32.6	45.0	65 38.8	58.1	Alpheratz	358 10.3	N28 58.6
D	14	243 36.2	16 11.8	33.6	11 24.0	19.7	113 34.8	44.9	80 41.0	58.0	Altair	62 33.8	N 8 49.0
A	15	258 38.6	31 15.0	·· 33.2	26 24.7	·· 20.2	128 37.1	·· 44.9	95 43.2	·· 58.0	Ankaa	353 41.2	S42 25.3
Y	16	273 41.1	46 18.2	32.9	41 25.3	20.6	143 39.3	44.8	110 45.5	57.9	Antares	112 58.8	S26 23.0
	17	288 43.6	61 21.4	32.5	56 26.0	21.1	158 41.5	44.8	125 47.7	57.8			
	18	303 46.0	76 24.6	S24 32.2	71 26.6	S19 21.5	173 43.7	N18 44.7	140 50.0	N 8 57.7	Arcturus	146 20.0	N19 17.7
	19	318 48.5	91 27.8	31.8	86 27.3	22.0	188 45.9	44.7	155 52.2	57.6	Atria	108 24.5	S68 59.4
	20	333 50.9	106 31.0	31.5	101 27.9	22.5	203 48.2	44.6	170 54.4	57.5	Avior	234 28.7	S59 26.2
	21	348 53.4	121 34.3	·· 31.1	116 28.5	·· 22.9	218 50.4	·· 44.5	185 56.7	·· 57.5	Bellatrix	278 59.9	N 6 19.8
	22	3 55.9	136 37.5	30.8	131 29.2	23.4	233 52.6	44.5	200 58.9	57.4	Betelgeuse	271 29.5	N 7 24.2
	23	18 58.3	151 40.7	30.4	146 29.8	23.8	248 54.8	44.4	216 01.2	57.3			
	26 00	34 00.8	166 43.9	S24 30.1	161 30.5	S19 24.3	263 57.0	N18 44.4	231 03.4	N 8 57.2	Canopus	264 07.5	S52 40.9
	01	49 03.3	181 47.2	29.7	176 31.1	24.7	278 59.3	44.3	246 05.6	57.1	Capella	281 12.9	N45 58.4
	02	64 05.7	196 50.4	29.3	191 31.8	25.2	294 01.5	44.3	261 07.9	57.0	Deneb	49 49.3	N45 12.7
	03	79 08.2	211 53.7	·· 29.0	206 32.4	·· 25.6	309 03.7	·· 44.2	276 10.1	·· 57.0	Denebola	183 00.7	N14 41.5
	04	94 10.7	226 56.9	28.6	221 33.0	26.1	324 05.9	44.2	291 12.4	56.9	Diphda	349 21.9	S18 06.1
	05	109 13.1	242 00.2	28.2	236 33.7	26.5	339 08.2	44.1	306 14.6	56.8			
	06	124 15.6	257 03.4	S24 27.9	251 34.3	S19 27.0	354 10.4	N18 44.1	321 16.8	N 8 56.7	Dubhe	194 24.3	N61 51.8
	07	139 18.1	272 06.7	27.5	266 35.0	27.4	9 12.6	44.0	336 19.1	56.6	Elnath	278 45.5	N28 35.3
T	08	154 20.5	287 09.9	27.1	281 35.6	27.9	24 14.8	44.0	351 21.3	56.5	Eltanin	90 58.6	N51 29.9
H	09	169 23.0	302 13.2	·· 26.7	296 36.3	·· 28.3	39 17.1	·· 43.9	6 23.6	·· 56.5	Enif	34 12.7	N 9 46.9
U	10	184 25.4	317 16.5	26.3	311 36.9	28.8	54 19.3	43.9	21 25.8	56.4	Fomalhaut	15 52.7	S29 44.1
R	11	199 27.9	332 19.7	26.0	326 37.5	29.2	69 21.5	43.8	36 28.0	56.3			
S	12	214 30.4	347 23.0	S24 25.6	341 38.2	S19 29.7	84 23.7	N18 43.8	51 30.3	N 8 56.2	Gacrux	172 30.6	S56 59.5
D	13	229 32.8	2 26.3	25.2	356 38.8	30.1	99 26.0	43.7	66 32.5	56.1	Gienah	176 19.6	S17 25.3
A	14	244 35.3	17 29.6	24.8	11 39.5	30.6	114 28.2	43.6	81 34.8	56.1	Hadar	149 25.7	S60 16.1
Y	15	259 37.8	32 32.9	·· 24.4	26 40.1	·· 31.0	129 30.4	·· 43.6	96 37.0	·· 56.0	Hamal	328 30.0	N23 21.8
	16	274 40.2	47 36.2	24.0	41 40.7	31.5	144 32.6	43.5	111 39.3	55.9	Kaus Aust.	84 18.8	S34 23.7
	17	289 42.7	62 39.5	23.6	56 41.4	31.9	159 34.9	43.5	126 41.5	55.8			
	18	304 45.2	77 42.8	S24 23.2	71 42.0	S19 32.4	174 37.1	N18 43.4	141 43.7	N 8 55.7	Kochab	137 20.3	N74 14.7
	19	319 47.6	92 46.1	22.8	86 42.7	32.8	189 39.3	43.4	156 46.0	55.6	Markab	14 04.2	N15 05.7
	20	334 50.1	107 49.4	22.4	101 43.3	33.3	204 41.5	43.3	171 48.2	55.6	Menkar	314 42.2	N 4 00.4
	21	349 52.5	122 52.7	·· 22.0	116 43.9	·· 33.7	219 43.8	·· 43.3	186 50.5	·· 55.5	Menkent	148 38.9	S36 15.8
	22	4 55.0	137 56.0	21.6	131 44.6	34.2	234 46.0	43.2	201 52.7	55.4	Miaplacidus	221 45.3	S69 37.5
	23	19 57.5	152 59.3	21.2	146 45.2	34.6	249 48.2	43.2	216 54.9	55.3			
	27 00	34 59.9	168 02.6	S24 20.8	161 45.8	S19 35.1	264 50.5	N18 43.1	231 57.2	N 8 55.2	Mirfak	309 17.4	N49 47.1
	01	50 02.4	183 05.9	20.3	176 46.5	35.5	279 52.7	43.1	246 59.4	55.2	Nunki	76 30.9	S26 19.3
	02	65 04.9	198 09.3	19.9	191 47.1	36.0	294 54.9	43.0	262 01.7	55.1	Peacock	54 00.5	S56 48.4
	03	80 07.3	213 12.6	·· 19.5	206 47.7	·· 36.4	309 57.1	·· 43.0	277 03.9	·· 55.0	Pollux	243 59.7	N28 04.5
	04	95 09.8	228 15.9	19.1	221 48.4	36.9	324 59.4	42.9	292 06.2	54.9	Procyon	245 27.1	N 5 16.8
	05	110 12.3	243 19.3	18.6	236 49.0	37.3	340 01.6	42.9	307 08.4	54.8			
	06	125 14.7	258 22.6	S24 18.2	251 49.7	S19 37.8	355 03.8	N18 42.8	322 10.6	N 8 54.8	Rasalhague	96 31.0	N12 34.8
	07	140 17.2	273 26.0	17.8	266 50.3	38.2	10 06.1	42.8	337 12.9	54.7	Regulus	208 11.6	N12 04.3
	08	155 19.7	288 29.3	17.4	281 50.9	38.6	25 08.3	42.7	352 15.1	54.6	Rigel	281 37.0	S 8 13.5
F	09	170 22.1	303 32.7	·· 16.9	296 51.6	·· 39.1	40 10.5	·· 42.7	7 17.4	·· 54.5	Rigil Kent.	140 28.2	S60 44.7
R	10	185 24.6	318 36.0	16.5	311 52.2	39.5	55 12.8	42.6	22 19.6	54.4	Sabik	102 42.9	S15 41.8
I	11	200 27.0	333 39.4	16.0	326 52.8	40.0	70 15.0	42.6	37 21.9	54.3			
D	12	215 29.5	348 42.7	S24 15.6	341 53.5	S19 40.4	85 17.2	N18 42.5	52 24.1	N 8 54.3	Schedar	350 09.9	N56 25.4
A	13	230 32.0	3 46.1	15.2	356 54.1	40.9	100 19.4	42.5	67 26.4	54.2	Shaula	96 57.8	S37 05.3
Y	14	245 34.4	18 49.5	14.7	11 54.7	41.3	115 21.7	42.4	82 28.6	54.1	Sirius	258 56.7	S16 41.2
	15	260 36.9	33 52.8	·· 14.3	26 55.4	·· 41.7	130 23.9	·· 42.4	97 30.8	·· 54.0	Spica	158 59.2	S11 02.9
	16	275 39.4	48 56.2	13.8	41 56.0	42.2	145 26.1	42.3	112 33.1	53.9	Suhail	223 11.8	S43 20.6
	17	290 41.8	63 59.6	13.3	56 56.6	42.6	160 28.4	42.3	127 35.3	53.9			
	18	305 44.3	79 03.0	S24 12.9	71 57.3	S19 43.1	175 30.6	N18 42.2	142 37.6	N 8 53.8	Vega	80 56.9	N38 46.2
	19	320 46.8	94 06.4	12.4	86 57.9	43.5	190 32.8	42.2	157 39.8	53.7	Zuben'ubi	137 34.8	S15 57.1
	20	335 49.2	109 09.8	12.0	101 58.5	44.0	205 35.1	42.1	172 42.1	53.6		S.H.A. ° ′	Mer. Pass. h m
	21	350 51.7	124 13.2	·· 11.5	116 59.1	·· 44.4	220 37.3	·· 42.1	187 44.3	·· 53.5			
	22	5 54.2	139 16.5	11.0	131 59.8	44.8	235 39.5	42.0	202 46.6	53.5	Venus	132 43.1	12 50
	23	20 56.6	154 19.9	10.6	147 00.4	45.3	250 41.8	42.0	217 48.8	53.4	Mars	127 29.7	13 13
											Jupiter	229 56.2	6 23
	Mer. Pass.	h m 21 40.4	v 3.3	d 0.4	v 0.6	d 0.5	v 2.2	d 0.1	v 2.2	d 0.1	Saturn	197 02.6	8 34

1978 OCTOBER 25, 26, 27 (WED., THURS., FRI.)

UT (d h)	SUN G.H.A.	SUN Dec.	MOON G.H.A.	v	MOON Dec.	d	H.P.
25 00 (Wednesday)	183 57.1	S11 53.9	259 47.5	13.6	N13 44.1	6.3	54.3
01	198 57.2	54.8	274 20.1	13.6	13 37.8	6.3	54.3
02	213 57.2	55.7	288 52.7	13.6	13 31.5	6.4	54.3
03	228 57.3	·· 56.5	303 25.3	13.7	13 25.1	6.4	54.3
04	243 57.4	57.4	317 58.0	13.7	13 18.7	6.5	54.3
05	258 57.5	58.2	332 30.7	13.7	13 12.2	6.6	54.4
06	273 57.5	S11 59.1	347 03.4	13.7	N13 05.6	6.6	54.4
07	288 57.6	12 00.0	1 36.1	13.7	12 59.0	6.7	54.4
08	303 57.7	00.8	16 08.8	13.8	12 52.3	6.8	54.4
09	318 57.8	·· 01.7	30 41.6	13.7	12 45.5	6.8	54.4
10	333 57.8	02.6	45 14.3	13.8	12 38.7	6.8	54.4
11	348 57.9	03.4	59 47.1	13.8	12 31.9	6.9	54.4
12	3 58.0	S12 04.3	74 19.9	13.8	N12 25.0	7.0	54.4
13	18 58.1	05.2	88 52.7	13.8	12 18.0	7.0	54.4
14	33 58.1	06.0	103 25.5	13.8	12 11.0	7.1	54.4
15	48 58.2	·· 06.9	117 58.3	13.9	12 03.9	7.2	54.5
16	63 58.3	07.7	132 31.2	13.8	11 56.7	7.2	54.5
17	78 58.3	08.6	147 04.0	13.9	11 49.5	7.2	54.5
18	93 58.4	S12 09.5	161 36.9	13.8	N11 42.3	7.3	54.5
19	108 58.5	10.3	176 09.7	13.9	11 35.0	7.4	54.5
20	123 58.6	11.2	190 42.6	13.9	11 27.6	7.4	54.5
21	138 58.6	·· 12.0	205 15.5	13.9	11 20.2	7.4	54.5
22	153 58.7	12.9	219 48.4	13.9	11 12.8	7.6	54.5
23	168 58.8	13.8	234 21.3	14.0	11 05.2	7.5	54.5
26 00 (Thursday)	183 58.8	S12 14.6	248 54.3	13.9	N10 57.7	7.6	54.6
01	198 58.9	15.5	263 27.2	13.9	10 50.1	7.7	54.6
02	213 59.0	16.3	278 00.1	14.0	10 42.4	7.7	54.6
03	228 59.0	·· 17.2	292 33.1	13.9	10 34.7	7.8	54.6
04	243 59.1	18.0	307 06.0	14.0	10 26.9	7.8	54.6
05	258 59.2	18.9	321 39.0	14.0	10 19.1	7.9	54.6
06	273 59.2	S12 19.8	336 12.0	13.9	N10 11.2	7.9	54.7
07	288 59.3	20.6	350 44.9	14.0	10 03.3	8.0	54.7
08	303 59.4	21.5	5 17.9	14.0	9 55.3	8.0	54.7
09	318 59.4	·· 22.3	19 50.9	14.0	9 47.3	8.1	54.7
10	333 59.5	23.2	34 23.9	14.0	9 39.2	8.1	54.7
11	348 59.6	24.0	48 56.9	14.0	9 31.1	8.2	54.7
12	3 59.6	S12 24.9	63 29.9	14.0	N 9 22.9	8.2	54.7
13	18 59.7	25.7	78 02.9	14.0	9 14.7	8.2	54.8
14	33 59.8	26.6	92 35.9	14.0	9 06.5	8.3	54.8
15	48 59.8	·· 27.5	107 08.9	14.0	8 58.2	8.4	54.8
16	63 59.9	28.3	121 41.9	14.0	8 49.8	8.4	54.8
17	79 00.0	29.2	136 14.9	14.0	8 41.4	8.4	54.8
18	94 00.0	S12 30.0	150 47.9	14.0	N 8 33.0	8.5	54.9
19	109 00.1	30.9	165 20.9	14.0	8 24.5	8.5	54.9
20	124 00.1	31.7	179 53.9	14.0	8 16.0	8.6	54.9
21	139 00.2	·· 32.6	194 26.9	14.0	8 07.4	8.6	54.9
22	154 00.3	33.4	208 59.9	14.0	7 58.8	8.6	54.9
23	169 00.3	34.3	223 32.9	14.0	7 50.2	8.7	54.9
27 00 (Friday)	184 00.4	S12 35.1	238 05.9	14.0	N 7 41.5	8.7	55.0
01	199 00.4	36.0	252 38.9	14.0	7 32.8	8.8	55.0
02	214 00.5	36.8	267 11.9	14.0	7 24.0	8.8	55.0
03	229 00.6	·· 37.7	281 44.9	14.0	7 15.2	8.8	55.0
04	244 00.6	38.5	296 17.9	13.9	7 06.4	8.9	55.0
05	259 00.7	39.4	310 50.8	14.0	6 57.5	9.0	55.1
06	274 00.7	S12 40.2	325 23.8	14.0	N 6 48.5	8.9	55.1
07	289 00.8	41.1	339 56.8	13.9	6 39.6	9.0	55.1
08	304 00.9	41.9	354 29.7	14.0	6 30.6	9.0	55.1
09	319 00.9	·· 42.8	9 02.7	13.9	6 21.6	9.1	55.2
10	334 01.0	43.6	23 35.6	13.9	6 12.5	9.1	55.2
11	349 01.0	44.5	38 08.5	13.9	6 03.4	9.2	55.2
12	4 01.1	S12 45.3	52 41.4	14.0	N 5 54.2	9.1	55.2
13	19 01.2	46.2	67 14.4	13.9	5 45.1	9.2	55.2
14	34 01.2	47.0	81 47.3	13.8	5 35.9	9.3	55.3
15	49 01.3	·· 47.8	96 20.1	13.9	5 26.6	9.3	55.3
16	64 01.3	48.7	110 53.0	13.9	5 17.3	9.3	55.3
17	79 01.4	49.5	125 25.9	13.8	5 08.0	9.3	55.3
18	94 01.4	S12 50.4	139 58.7	13.9	N 4 58.7	9.4	55.4
19	109 01.5	51.2	154 31.6	13.8	4 49.3	9.4	55.4
20	124 01.5	52.1	169 04.4	13.8	4 39.9	9.4	55.4
21	139 01.6	·· 52.9	183 37.2	13.8	4 30.5	9.5	55.4
22	154 01.6	53.8	198 10.0	13.8	4 21.0	9.5	55.5
23	169 01.7	54.6	212 42.8	13.7	4 11.5	9.5	55.5
	S.D. 16.1	d 0.9	S.D. 14.8		14.9		15.0

Lat.	Twilight Naut.	Twilight Civil	Sunrise	Moonrise 25	Moonrise 26	Moonrise 27	Moonrise 28
°	h m	h m	h m	h m	h m	h m	h m
N 72	05 40	07 00	08 19	22 55	24 33	00 33	02 11
N 70	05 39	06 51	08 00	23 14	24 44	00 44	02 16
68	05 38	06 43	07 45	23 29	24 54	00 54	02 20
66	05 37	06 37	07 32	23 41	25 01	01 01	02 23
64	05 35	06 31	07 22	23 51	25 08	01 08	02 26
62	05 34	06 26	07 13	24 00	00 00	01 13	02 29
60	05 33	06 22	07 06	24 07	00 07	01 18	02 31
N 58	05 32	06 18	06 59	24 14	00 14	01 22	02 33
56	05 31	06 15	06 53	24 19	00 19	01 26	02 35
54	05 30	06 11	06 48	24 24	00 24	01 29	02 36
52	05 29	06 08	06 43	24 29	00 29	01 32	02 38
50	05 28	06 06	06 39	24 33	00 33	01 35	02 39
45	05 25	05 59	06 30	24 42	00 42	01 41	02 42
N 40	05 22	05 54	06 22	24 49	00 49	01 46	02 44
35	05 20	05 49	06 15	00 02	00 56	01 50	02 46
30	05 17	05 45	06 09	00 09	01 01	01 54	02 48
20	05 10	05 36	05 59	00 22	01 11	02 01	02 51
N 10	05 03	05 28	05 49	00 32	01 19	02 07	02 54
0	04 55	05 19	05 41	00 43	01 27	02 12	02 57
S 10	04 45	05 10	05 32	00 53	01 35	02 17	02 59
20	04 33	04 59	05 22	01 03	01 44	02 23	03 02
30	04 17	04 46	05 11	01 16	01 53	02 30	03 05
35	04 07	04 38	05 05	01 23	01 59	02 33	03 07
40	03 54	04 29	04 57	01 31	02 05	02 38	03 09
45	03 39	04 17	04 49	01 40	02 12	02 42	03 11
S 50	03 19	04 03	04 38	01 52	02 21	02 48	03 14
52	03 10	03 56	04 33	01 57	02 25	02 51	03 16
54	02 58	03 49	04 28	02 03	02 30	02 54	03 17
56	02 45	03 40	04 22	02 09	02 34	02 57	03 19
58	02 30	03 30	04 15	02 16	02 40	03 01	03 20
S 60	02 11	03 19	04 08	02 24	02 46	03 05	03 22

Lat.	Sunset	Twilight Civil	Twilight Naut.	Moonset 25	Moonset 26	Moonset 27	Moonset 28
°	h m	h m	h m	h m	h m	h m	h m
N 72	15 07	16 26	17 46	15 51	15 46	15 41	15 37
N 70	15 27	16 35	17 47	15 31	15 33	15 34	15 35
68	15 42	16 43	17 49	15 15	15 22	15 28	15 33
66	15 54	16 50	17 50	15 02	15 14	15 23	15 32
64	16 05	16 56	17 51	14 51	15 06	15 19	15 31
62	16 14	17 01	17 52	14 42	15 00	15 15	15 30
60	16 21	17 05	17 54	14 34	14 54	15 12	15 29
N 58	16 28	17 09	17 55	14 27	14 49	15 09	15 28
56	16 34	17 13	17 56	14 21	14 45	15 06	15 27
54	16 39	17 16	17 57	14 15	14 41	15 04	15 27
52	16 44	17 19	17 58	14 10	14 37	15 02	15 26
50	16 48	17 22	17 59	14 05	14 34	15 00	15 26
45	16 58	17 28	18 02	13 56	14 26	14 56	15 25
N 40	17 06	17 33	18 05	13 47	14 20	14 52	15 24
35	17 13	17 38	18 08	13 40	14 15	14 49	15 23
30	17 19	17 43	18 11	13 34	14 11	14 46	15 22
20	17 29	17 52	18 18	13 23	14 03	14 42	15 21
N 10	17 39	18 00	18 25	13 13	13 56	14 37	15 20
0	17 47	18 09	18 33	13 04	13 49	14 33	15 18
S 10	17 56	18 18	18 43	12 55	13 42	14 29	15 17
20	18 06	18 29	18 56	12 45	13 35	14 25	15 16
30	18 17	18 42	19 12	12 34	13 27	14 20	15 15
35	18 24	18 50	19 22	12 28	13 22	14 17	15 14
40	18 31	19 00	19 35	12 20	13 17	14 14	15 13
45	18 40	19 12	19 50	12 12	13 10	14 10	15 12
S 50	18 51	19 26	20 10	12 01	13 03	14 06	15 10
52	18 56	19 33	20 20	11 56	12 59	14 03	15 10
54	19 01	19 41	20 32	11 51	12 55	14 01	15 09
56	19 07	19 50	20 45	11 45	12 51	13 59	15 08
58	19 14	20 00	21 01	11 38	12 46	13 56	15 08
S 60	19 22	20 11	21 21	11 31	12 41	13 53	15 07

Day	SUN Eqn. of Time 00ʰ	SUN Eqn. of Time 12ʰ	SUN Mer. Pass.	MOON Mer. Pass. Upper	MOON Mer. Pass. Lower	Age	Phase
	m s	m s	h m	h m	h m	d	
25	15 48	15 52	11 44	06 53	19 16	23	
26	15 55	15 58	11 44	07 38	20 00	24	
27	16 01	16 04	11 44	08 23	20 45	25	

UT	ARIES	VENUS −3.5		MARS +1.3		JUPITER −2.0		SATURN +0.6		STARS		
	G.H.A.	G.H.A.	Dec.	G.H.A.	Dec.	G.H.A.	Dec.	G.H.A.	Dec.	Name	S.H.A.	Dec.
d h	° ′	° ′	° ′	° ′	° ′	° ′	° ′	° ′	° ′		° ′	° ′
26 00	183 21.1	180 52.7	S 0 27.6	176 44.3	N 2 04.9	357 39.3	S 0 43.8	356 18.5	S 0 09.3	Acamar	315 37.3	S40 23.1
01	198 23.6	195 52.3	26.3	191 45.0	05.7	12 42.0	43.7	11 21.1	09.3	Achernar	335 45.6	S57 20.2
02	213 26.0	210 51.9	25.1	206 45.7	06.5	27 44.8	43.5	26 23.8	09.2	Acrux	173 36.1	S62 59.7
03	228 28.5	225 51.5	·· 23.8	221 46.4	·· 07.3	42 47.6	·· 43.4	41 26.4	·· 09.1	Adhara	255 31.8	S28 57.1
04	243 30.9	240 51.1	22.6	236 47.1	08.0	57 50.3	43.3	56 29.1	09.0	Aldebaran	291 17.8	N16 28.2
05	258 33.4	255 50.8	21.3	251 47.8	08.8	72 53.1	43.2	71 31.7	09.0			
06	273 35.9	270 50.4	S 0 20.1	266 48.5	N 2 09.6	87 55.8	S 0 43.0	86 34.3	S 0 08.9	Alioth	166 41.7	N56 03.7
07	288 38.3	285 50.0	18.8	281 49.2	10.4	102 58.6	42.9	101 37.0	08.8	Alkaid	153 17.8	N49 24.4
T 08	303 40.8	300 49.6	17.6	296 49.9	11.2	118 01.4	42.8	116 39.6	08.7	Al Na'ir	28 14.9	S47 03.1
H 09	318 43.3	315 49.3	·· 16.3	311 50.6	·· 12.0	133 04.1	·· 42.6	131 42.3	·· 08.6	Alnilam	276 11.4	S 1 13.0
U 10	333 45.7	330 48.9	15.1	326 51.3	12.7	148 06.9	42.5	146 44.9	08.6	Alphard	218 20.0	S 8 34.8
R 11	348 48.2	345 48.5	13.8	341 52.0	13.5	163 09.6	42.4	161 47.5	08.5			
S 12	3 50.7	0 48.1	S 0 12.5	356 52.7	N 2 14.3	178 12.4	S 0 42.3	176 50.2	S 0 08.4	Alphecca	126 31.6	N26 46.5
D 13	18 53.1	15 47.7	11.3	11 53.4	15.1	193 15.2	42.1	191 52.8	08.3	Alpheratz	358 09.3	N28 59.0
A 14	33 55.6	30 47.4	10.0	26 54.1	15.9	208 17.9	42.0	206 55.5	08.2	Altair	62 32.3	N 8 48.9
Y 15	48 58.0	45 47.0	·· 08.8	41 54.8	·· 16.7	223 20.7	·· 41.9	221 58.1	·· 08.2	Ankaa	353 40.3	S42 24.7
16	64 00.5	60 46.6	07.5	56 55.5	17.4	238 23.4	41.7	237 00.8	08.1	Antares	112 56.3	S26 23.4
17	79 03.0	75 46.2	06.3	71 56.2	18.2	253 26.2	41.6	252 03.4	08.0			
18	94 05.4	90 45.9	S 0 05.0	86 56.8	N 2 19.0	268 29.0	S 0 41.5	267 06.1	S 0 07.9	Arcturus	146 17.9	N19 16.7
19	109 07.9	105 45.5	03.8	101 57.5	19.8	283 31.7	41.4	282 08.7	07.9	Atria	108 20.0	S68 59.4
20	124 10.4	120 45.1	02.5	116 58.2	20.6	298 34.5	41.2	297 11.3	07.8	Avior	234 27.8	S59 27.2
21	139 12.8	135 44.7	S 0 01.2	131 58.9	·· 21.4	313 37.2	·· 41.1	312 14.0	·· 07.7	Bellatrix	278 58.5	N 6 19.8
22	154 15.3	150 44.4	0 00.0	146 59.6	22.1	328 40.0	41.0	327 16.6	07.6	Betelgeuse	271 28.0	N 7 24.1
23	169 17.8	165 44.0	N 0 01.3	162 00.3	22.9	343 42.8	40.8	342 19.3	07.5			
27 00	184 20.2	180 43.6	N 0 02.5	177 01.0	N 2 23.7	358 45.5	S 0 40.7	357 21.9	S 0 07.5	Canopus	264 07.1	S52 41.5
01	199 22.7	195 43.2	03.8	192 01.7	24.5	13 48.3	40.6	12 24.6	07.4	Capella	281 10.9	N45 58.8
02	214 25.2	210 42.8	05.0	207 02.4	25.3	28 51.0	40.5	27 27.2	07.3	Deneb	49 48.5	N45 12.5
03	229 27.6	225 42.5	·· 06.3	222 03.1	·· 26.1	43 53.8	·· 40.3	42 29.8	·· 07.2	Denebola	182 58.4	N14 40.6
04	244 30.1	240 42.1	07.5	237 03.8	26.8	58 56.6	40.2	57 32.5	07.1	Diphda	349 20.9	S18 05.6
05	259 32.5	255 41.7	08.8	252 04.5	27.6	73 59.3	40.1	72 35.1	07.1			
06	274 35.0	270 41.3	N 0 10.1	267 05.2	N 2 28.4	89 02.1	S 0 39.9	87 37.8	S 0 07.0	Dubhe	194 21.1	N61 51.3
07	289 37.5	285 41.0	11.3	282 05.9	29.2	104 04.9	39.8	102 40.4	06.9	Elnath	278 43.8	N28 35.5
08	304 39.9	300 40.6	12.6	297 06.6	30.0	119 07.6	39.7	117 43.1	06.8	Eltanin	90 57.5	N51 29.2
F 09	319 42.4	315 40.2	·· 13.8	312 07.3	·· 30.7	134 10.4	·· 39.6	132 45.7	·· 06.8	Enif	34 11.5	N 9 47.1
R 10	334 44.9	330 39.8	15.1	327 08.0	31.5	149 13.1	39.4	147 48.3	06.7	Fomalhaut	15 51.4	S29 43.4
I 11	349 47.3	345 39.4	16.3	342 08.7	32.3	164 15.9	39.3	162 51.0	06.6			
D 12	4 49.8	0 39.1	N 0 17.6	357 09.4	N 2 33.1	179 18.7	S 0 39.2	177 53.6	S 0 06.5	Gacrux	172 27.8	S57 00.5
A 13	19 52.3	15 38.7	18.9	12 10.1	33.9	194 21.4	39.0	192 56.3	06.4	Gienah	176 17.3	S17 26.3
Y 14	34 54.7	30 38.3	20.1	27 10.8	34.7	209 24.2	38.9	207 58.9	06.4	Hadar	149 22.3	S60 16.8
15	49 57.2	45 37.9	·· 21.4	42 11.5	·· 35.4	224 26.9	·· 38.8	223 01.6	·· 06.3	Hamal	328 28.8	N23 22.3
16	64 59.7	60 37.6	22.6	57 12.2	36.2	239 29.7	38.7	238 04.2	06.2	Kaus Aust.	84 16.4	S34 23.5
17	80 02.1	75 37.2	23.9	72 12.9	37.0	254 32.5	38.5	253 06.8	06.1			
18	95 04.6	90 36.8	N 0 25.1	87 13.6	N 2 37.8	269 35.2	S 0 38.4	268 09.5	S 0 06.0	Kochab	137 18.1	N74 13.8
19	110 07.0	105 36.4	26.4	102 14.3	38.6	284 38.0	38.3	283 12.1	06.0	Markab	14 03.1	N15 06.0
20	125 09.5	120 36.1	27.6	117 15.0	39.3	299 40.7	38.2	298 14.8	05.9	Menkar	314 41.0	N 4 00.8
21	140 12.0	135 35.7	·· 28.9	132 15.7	·· 40.1	314 43.5	·· 38.0	313 17.4	·· 05.8	Menkent	148 36.3	S36 16.6
22	155 14.4	150 35.3	30.2	147 16.4	40.9	329 46.3	37.9	328 20.1	05.7	Miaplacidus	221 44.3	S69 38.6
23	170 16.9	165 34.9	31.4	162 17.1	41.7	344 49.0	37.8	343 22.7	05.7			
28 00	185 19.4	180 34.5	N 0 32.7	177 17.8	N 2 42.5	359 51.8	S 0 37.6	358 25.3	S 0 05.6	Mirfak	309 16.0	N49 47.7
01	200 21.8	195 34.2	33.9	192 18.5	43.2	14 54.5	37.5	13 28.0	05.5	Nunki	76 28.8	S26 19.2
02	215 24.3	210 33.8	35.2	207 19.1	44.0	29 57.3	37.4	28 30.6	05.4	Peacock	53 58.1	S56 47.6
03	230 26.8	225 33.4	·· 36.4	222 19.8	·· 44.8	45 00.1	·· 37.3	43 33.3	·· 05.3	Pollux	243 57.6	N28 04.3
04	245 29.2	240 33.0	37.7	237 20.5	45.6	60 02.8	37.1	58 35.9	05.3	Procyon	245 25.3	N 5 16.3
05	260 31.7	255 32.7	38.9	252 21.2	46.4	75 05.6	37.0	73 38.6	05.2			
06	275 34.2	270 32.3	N 0 40.2	267 21.9	N 2 47.1	90 08.3	S 0 36.9	88 41.2	S 0 05.1	Rasalhague	96 29.2	N12 34.3
07	290 36.6	285 31.9	41.5	282 22.6	47.9	105 11.1	36.7	103 43.8	05.0	Regulus	208 09.4	N12 03.5
S 08	305 39.1	300 31.5	42.7	297 23.3	48.7	120 13.9	36.6	118 46.5	04.9	Rigel	281 35.8	S 8 13.6
A 09	320 41.5	315 31.2	·· 44.0	312 24.0	·· 49.5	135 16.6	·· 36.5	133 49.1	·· 04.9	Rigil Kent.	140 24.8	S60 45.2
T 10	335 44.0	330 30.8	45.2	327 24.7	50.3	150 19.4	36.4	148 51.8	04.8	Sabik	102 40.6	S15 42.1
U 11	350 46.5	345 30.4	46.5	342 25.4	51.0	165 22.1	36.2	163 54.4	04.7			
R 12	5 48.9	0 30.0	N 0 47.7	357 26.1	N 2 51.8	180 24.9	S 0 36.1	178 57.1	S 0 04.6	Schedar	350 09.2	N56 25.9
D 13	20 51.4	15 29.7	49.0	12 26.8	52.6	195 27.7	36.0	193 59.7	04.6	Shaula	96 55.2	S37 05.3
A 14	35 53.9	30 29.3	50.3	27 27.5	53.4	210 30.4	35.8	209 02.3	04.5	Sirius	258 55.4	S16 41.7
Y 15	50 56.3	45 28.9	·· 51.5	42 28.2	·· 54.2	225 33.2	·· 35.7	224 05.0	·· 04.4	Spica	158 56.9	S11 03.8
16	65 58.8	60 28.5	52.8	57 28.9	54.9	240 35.9	35.6	239 07.6	04.3	Suhail	223 10.3	S43 21.6
17	81 01.3	75 28.1	54.0	72 29.6	55.7	255 38.7	35.5	254 10.3	04.2			
18	96 03.7	90 27.8	N 0 55.3	87 30.3	N 2 56.5	270 41.5	S 0 35.3	269 12.9	S 0 04.2	Vega	80 55.6	N38 45.7
19	111 06.2	105 27.4	56.5	102 31.0	57.3	285 44.2	35.2	284 15.6	04.1	Zuben'ubi	137 32.4	S15 57.8
20	126 08.6	120 27.0	57.8	117 31.7	58.1	300 47.0	35.1	299 18.2	04.0		S.H.A.	Mer. Pass.
21	141 11.1	135 26.6	0 59.0	132 32.4	·· 58.8	315 49.7	·· 35.0	314 20.8	·· 03.9		° ′	h m
22	156 13.6	150 26.3	1 00.3	147 33.1	2 59.6	330 52.5	34.8	329 23.5	03.9	Venus	356 23.4	11 57
23	171 16.0	165 25.9	01.6	162 33.8	3 00.4	345 55.3	34.7	344 26.1	03.8	Mars	352 40.8	12 11
	h m									Jupiter	174 25.3	0 05
Mer. Pass.	11 40.7	v −0.4	d 1.3	v 0.7	d 0.8	v 2.8	d 0.1	v 2.6	d 0.1	Saturn	173 01.7	0 11

1981 MARCH 26, 27, 28 (THURS., FRI., SAT.)

Day	UT (d h)	SUN G.H.A. ° ′	SUN Dec. ° ′	MOON G.H.A. ° ′	v ′	MOON Dec. ° ′	d ′	H.P. ′
	26 00	178 32.4	N 2 05.0	300 24.7	13.2	S16 25.0	6.4	54.2
	01	193 32.6	06.0	314 56.9	13.3	16 31.4	6.4	54.2
	02	208 32.8	07.0	329 29.2	13.2	16 37.8	6.3	54.2
	03	223 33.0	·· 08.0	344 01.4	13.1	16 44.1	6.2	54.3
	04	238 33.1	08.9	358 33.5	13.1	16 50.3	6.2	54.3
	05	253 33.3	09.9	13 05.6	13.1	16 56.5	6.1	54.3
	06	268 33.5	N 2 10.9	27 37.7	13.0	S17 02.6	6.0	54.3
	07	283 33.7	11.9	42 09.7	13.0	17 08.6	5.9	54.3
T	08	298 33.9	12.9	56 41.7	13.0	17 14.5	5.9	54.3
H	09	313 34.1	·· 13.8	71 13.7	12.8	17 20.4	5.7	54.3
U	10	328 34.3	14.8	85 45.5	12.9	17 26.1	5.7	54.3
R	11	343 34.5	15.8	100 17.4	12.8	17 31.8	5.7	54.3
S	12	358 34.7	N 2 16.8	114 49.2	12.8	S17 37.5	5.5	54.4
D	13	13 34.9	17.8	129 21.0	12.7	17 43.0	5.5	54.4
A	14	28 35.0	18.7	143 52.7	12.7	17 48.5	5.4	54.4
Y	15	43 35.2	·· 19.7	158 24.4	12.6	17 53.9	5.3	54.4
	16	58 35.4	20.7	172 56.0	12.6	17 59.2	5.3	54.4
	17	73 35.6	21.7	187 27.6	12.5	18 04.5	5.1	54.4
	18	88 35.8	N 2 22.7	201 59.1	12.5	S18 09.6	5.1	54.4
	19	103 36.0	23.6	216 30.6	12.5	18 14.7	5.0	54.5
	20	118 36.2	24.6	231 02.1	12.4	18 19.7	5.0	54.5
	21	133 36.4	·· 25.6	245 33.5	12.3	18 24.7	4.8	54.5
	22	148 36.6	26.6	260 04.8	12.4	18 29.5	4.8	54.5
	23	163 36.8	27.6	274 36.2	12.2	18 34.3	4.6	54.5
	27 00	178 37.0	N 2 28.5	289 07.4	12.3	S18 38.9	4.6	54.5
	01	193 37.1	29.5	303 38.7	12.2	18 43.5	4.5	54.5
	02	208 37.3	30.5	318 09.9	12.1	18 48.0	4.5	54.6
	03	223 37.5	·· 31.5	332 41.0	12.1	18 52.5	4.3	54.6
	04	238 37.7	32.5	347 12.1	12.0	18 56.8	4.2	54.6
	05	253 37.9	33.4	1 43.1	12.0	19 01.0	4.2	54.6
	06	268 38.1	N 2 34.4	16 14.1	12.0	S19 05.2	4.1	54.6
	07	283 38.3	35.4	30 45.1	11.9	19 09.3	4.0	54.7
	08	298 38.5	36.4	45 16.0	11.9	19 13.3	3.9	54.7
F	09	313 38.7	·· 37.4	59 46.9	11.8	19 17.2	3.8	54.7
R	10	328 38.9	38.3	74 17.7	11.8	19 21.0	3.7	54.7
I	11	343 39.0	39.3	88 48.5	11.7	19 24.7	3.7	54.7
D	12	358 39.2	N 2 40.3	103 19.2	11.7	S19 28.4	3.5	54.7
A	13	13 39.4	41.3	117 49.9	11.6	19 31.9	3.5	54.8
Y	14	28 39.6	42.2	132 20.5	11.6	19 35.4	3.4	54.8
	15	43 39.8	·· 43.2	146 51.1	11.6	19 38.8	3.3	54.8
	16	58 40.0	44.2	161 21.7	11.5	19 42.1	3.1	54.8
	17	73 40.2	45.2	175 52.2	11.5	19 45.2	3.1	54.8
	18	88 40.4	N 2 46.2	190 22.7	11.4	S19 48.3	3.0	54.9
	19	103 40.6	47.1	204 53.1	11.4	19 51.3	2.9	54.9
	20	118 40.8	48.1	219 23.5	11.3	19 54.2	2.9	54.9
	21	133 40.9	·· 49.1	233 53.8	11.3	19 57.1	2.7	54.9
	22	148 41.1	50.1	248 24.1	11.3	19 59.8	2.6	55.0
	23	163 41.3	51.0	262 54.4	11.2	20 02.4	2.5	55.0
	28 00	178 41.5	N 2 52.0	277 24.6	11.1	S20 04.9	2.5	55.0
	01	193 41.7	53.0	291 54.7	11.2	20 07.4	2.3	55.0
	02	208 41.9	54.0	306 24.9	11.0	20 09.7	2.3	55.0
	03	223 42.1	·· 55.0	320 54.9	11.1	20 12.0	2.1	55.1
	04	238 42.3	55.9	335 25.0	11.0	20 14.1	2.1	55.1
	05	253 42.5	56.9	349 55.0	10.9	20 16.2	1.9	55.1
	06	268 42.7	N 2 57.9	4 24.9	10.9	S20 18.1	1.9	55.1
	07	283 42.8	58.9	18 54.8	10.9	20 20.0	1.7	55.2
S	08	298 43.0	2 59.8	33 24.7	10.8	20 21.7	1.7	55.2
A	09	313 43.2	3 00.8	47 54.5	10.8	20 23.4	1.5	55.2
T	10	328 43.4	01.8	62 24.3	10.8	20 24.9	1.5	55.2
U	11	343 43.6	02.8	76 54.1	10.7	20 26.4	1.3	55.3
R	12	358 43.8	N 3 03.7	91 23.8	10.6	S20 27.7	1.3	55.3
D	13	13 44.0	04.7	105 53.4	10.7	20 29.0	1.1	55.3
A	14	28 44.2	05.7	120 23.1	10.6	20 30.1	1.1	55.3
Y	15	43 44.4	·· 06.7	134 52.7	10.5	20 31.2	0.9	55.4
	16	58 44.5	07.6	149 22.2	10.5	20 32.1	0.9	55.4
	17	73 44.7	08.6	163 51.7	10.5	20 33.0	0.7	55.4
	18	88 44.9	N 3 09.6	178 21.2	10.4	S20 33.7	0.6	55.5
	19	103 45.1	10.6	192 50.6	10.4	20 34.3	0.6	55.5
	20	118 45.3	11.5	207 20.0	10.4	20 34.9	0.4	55.5
	21	133 45.5	·· 12.5	221 49.4	10.3	20 35.3	0.3	55.5
	22	148 45.7	13.5	236 18.7	10.3	20 35.6	0.2	55.6
	23	163 45.9	14.5	250 48.0	10.2	20 35.8	0.2	55.6
		S.D. 16.1	*d* 1.0	S.D. 14.8		14.9		15.1

Lat. °	Twilight Naut. h m	Twilight Civil h m	Sunrise h m	Moonrise 26 h m	Moonrise 27 h m	Moonrise 28 h m	Moonrise 29 h m
N 72	02 30	04 12	05 23	02 36	■	■	■
N 70	02 58	04 24	05 27	01 43	03 35	■	■
68	03 19	04 34	05 31	01 11	02 41	04 05	05 06
66	03 35	04 42	05 34	00 48	02 09	03 22	04 20
64	03 48	04 48	05 37	00 30	01 45	02 53	03 50
62	03 58	04 54	05 39	00 15	01 26	02 32	03 27
60	04 07	04 59	05 41	00 02	01 11	02 14	03 09
N 58	04 15	05 03	05 43	24 58	00 58	01 59	02 54
56	04 22	05 07	05 44	24 46	00 46	01 47	02 41
54	04 27	05 10	05 46	24 36	00 36	01 36	02 29
52	04 32	05 13	05 47	24 28	00 28	01 26	02 19
50	04 37	05 16	05 48	24 20	00 20	01 17	02 11
45	04 46	05 21	05 50	24 03	00 03	00 59	01 52
N 40	04 53	05 25	05 52	23 49	24 44	00 44	01 36
35	04 59	05 29	05 54	23 38	24 31	00 31	01 23
30	05 04	05 32	05 56	23 28	24 20	00 20	01 12
20	05 10	05 36	05 58	23 10	24 01	00 01	00 53
N 10	05 15	05 39	06 00	22 55	23 45	24 36	00 36
0	05 17	05 41	06 02	22 41	23 30	24 20	00 20
S 10	05 19	05 43	06 04	22 27	23 15	24 04	00 04
20	05 18	05 44	06 06	22 13	22 58	23 47	24 40
30	05 16	05 44	06 08	21 55	22 40	23 28	24 21
35	05 14	05 43	06 09	21 46	22 29	23 17	24 10
40	05 11	05 43	06 10	21 34	22 16	23 04	23 58
45	05 08	05 42	06 11	21 21	22 02	22 49	23 43
S 50	05 03	05 40	06 13	21 05	21 44	22 30	23 25
52	05 00	05 40	06 13	20 58	21 35	22 21	23 16
54	04 57	05 39	06 14	20 49	21 26	22 11	23 07
56	04 54	05 38	06 15	20 40	21 15	22 00	22 56
58	04 51	05 37	06 16	20 29	21 03	21 48	22 43
S 60	04 46	05 35	06 17	20 17	20 49	21 33	22 29

Lat. °	Sunset h m	Twilight Civil h m	Twilight Naut. h m	Moonset 26 h m	Moonset 27 h m	Moonset 28 h m	Moonset 29 h m
N 72	18 51	20 02	21 48	05 24	■	■	■
N 70	18 46	19 50	21 18	06 18	06 03	■	■
68	18 42	19 40	20 56	06 51	06 58	07 16	07 59
66	18 39	19 31	20 39	07 15	07 31	07 58	08 46
64	18 36	19 24	20 26	07 34	07 55	08 27	09 16
62	18 33	19 19	20 15	07 49	08 14	08 49	09 38
60	18 31	19 14	20 06	08 02	08 30	09 07	09 56
N 58	18 29	19 09	19 58	08 14	08 43	09 22	10 12
56	18 28	19 05	19 51	08 23	08 55	09 35	10 25
54	18 26	19 02	19 45	08 32	09 05	09 46	10 36
52	18 25	18 59	19 40	08 40	09 14	09 56	10 46
50	18 24	18 56	19 35	08 47	09 22	10 04	10 55
45	18 21	18 51	19 26	09 02	09 39	10 23	11 13
N 40	18 19	18 46	19 18	09 14	09 54	10 38	11 29
35	18 17	18 43	19 12	09 25	10 06	10 51	11 42
30	18 16	18 40	19 08	09 34	10 16	11 02	11 53
20	18 13	18 35	19 01	09 50	10 34	11 21	12 12
N 10	18 11	18 32	18 56	10 04	10 50	11 38	12 29
0	18 09	18 29	18 53	10 17	11 05	11 54	12 45
S 10	18 07	18 28	18 52	10 30	11 19	12 09	13 00
20	18 05	18 27	18 52	10 44	11 35	12 26	13 17
30	18 03	18 27	18 54	11 00	11 53	12 45	13 36
35	18 02	18 27	18 56	11 10	12 04	12 56	13 47
40	18 00	18 27	18 59	11 21	12 16	13 09	14 00
45	17 59	18 28	19 02	11 33	12 30	13 24	14 15
S 50	17 57	18 29	19 07	11 49	12 48	13 43	14 33
52	17 57	18 30	19 09	11 56	12 56	13 52	14 42
54	17 56	18 31	19 12	12 04	13 05	14 02	14 52
56	17 55	18 32	19 15	12 13	13 15	14 13	15 03
58	17 54	18 33	19 19	12 23	13 27	14 25	15 15
S 60	17 53	18 34	19 23	12 35	13 41	14 40	15 30

Day	SUN Eqn. of Time 00ʰ m s	SUN Eqn. of Time 12ʰ m s	SUN Mer. Pass. h m	MOON Mer. Pass. Upper h m	MOON Mer. Pass. Lower h m	Age d	Phase
26	05 51	05 42	12 06	04 06	16 29	20	
27	05 33	05 23	12 05	04 53	17 17	21	◑
28	05 14	05 05	12 05	05 42	18 07	22	

T-7

CONVERSION OF ARC TO TIME

0°–59°		60°–119°		120°–179°		180°–239°		240°–299°		300°–359°			0′·00	0′·25	0′·50	0′·75
°	h m	°	h m	°	h m	°	h m	°	h m	°	h m	′	m s	m s	m s	m s
0	0 00	60	4 00	120	8 00	180	12 00	240	16 00	300	20 00	0	0 00	0 01	0 02	0 03
1	0 04	61	4 04	121	8 04	181	12 04	241	16 04	301	20 04	1	0 04	0 05	0 06	0 07
2	0 08	62	4 08	122	8 08	182	12 08	242	16 08	302	20 08	2	0 08	0 09	0 10	0 11
3	0 12	63	4 12	123	8 12	183	12 12	243	16 12	303	20 12	3	0 12	0 13	0 14	0 15
4	0 16	64	4 16	124	8 16	184	12 16	244	16 16	304	20 16	4	0 16	0 17	0 18	0 19
5	0 20	65	4 20	125	8 20	185	12 20	245	16 20	305	20 20	5	0 20	0 21	0 22	0 23
6	0 24	66	4 24	126	8 24	186	12 24	246	16 24	306	20 24	6	0 24	0 25	0 26	0 27
7	0 28	67	4 28	127	8 28	187	12 28	247	16 28	307	20 28	7	0 28	0 29	0 30	0 31
8	0 32	68	4 32	128	8 32	188	12 32	248	16 32	308	20 32	8	0 32	0 33	0 34	0 35
9	0 36	69	4 36	129	8 36	189	12 36	249	16 36	309	20 36	9	0 36	0 37	0 38	0 39
10	0 40	70	4 40	130	8 40	190	12 40	250	16 40	310	20 40	10	0 40	0 41	0 42	0 43
11	0 44	71	4 44	131	8 44	191	12 44	251	16 44	311	20 44	11	0 44	0 45	0 46	0 47
12	0 48	72	4 48	132	8 48	192	12 48	252	16 48	312	20 48	12	0 48	0 49	0 50	0 51
13	0 52	73	4 52	133	8 52	193	12 52	253	16 52	313	20 52	13	0 52	0 53	0 54	0 55
14	0 56	74	4 56	134	8 56	194	12 56	254	16 56	314	20 56	14	0 56	0 57	0 58	0 59
15	1 00	75	5 00	135	9 00	195	13 00	255	17 00	315	21 00	15	1 00	1 01	1 02	1 03
16	1 04	76	5 04	136	9 04	196	13 04	256	17 04	316	21 04	16	1 04	1 05	1 06	1 07
17	1 08	77	5 08	137	9 08	197	13 08	257	17 08	317	21 08	17	1 08	1 09	1 10	1 11
18	1 12	78	5 12	138	9 12	198	13 12	258	17 12	318	21 12	18	1 12	1 13	1 14	1 15
19	1 16	79	5 16	139	9 16	199	13 16	259	17 16	319	21 16	19	1 16	1 17	1 18	1 19
20	1 20	80	5 20	140	9 20	200	13 20	260	17 20	320	21 20	20	1 20	1 21	1 22	1 23
21	1 24	81	5 24	141	9 24	201	13 24	261	17 24	321	21 24	21	1 24	1 25	1 26	1 27
22	1 28	82	5 28	142	9 28	202	13 28	262	17 28	322	21 28	22	1 28	1 29	1 30	1 31
23	1 32	83	5 32	143	9 32	203	13 32	263	17 32	323	21 32	23	1 32	1 33	1 34	1 35
24	1 36	84	5 36	144	9 36	204	13 36	264	17 36	324	21 36	24	1 36	1 37	1 38	1 39
25	1 40	85	5 40	145	9 40	205	13 40	265	17 40	325	21 40	25	1 40	1 41	1 42	1 43
26	1 44	86	5 44	146	9 44	206	13 44	266	17 44	326	21 44	26	1 44	1 45	1 46	1 47
27	1 48	87	5 48	147	9 48	207	13 48	267	17 48	327	21 48	27	1 48	1 49	1 50	1 51
28	1 52	88	5 52	148	9 52	208	13 52	268	17 52	328	21 52	28	1 52	1 53	1 54	1 55
29	1 56	89	5 56	149	9 56	209	13 56	269	17 56	329	21 56	29	1 56	1 57	1 58	1 59
30	2 00	90	6 00	150	10 00	210	14 00	270	18 00	330	22 00	30	2 00	2 01	2 02	2 03
31	2 04	91	6 04	151	10 04	211	14 04	271	18 04	331	22 04	31	2 04	2 05	2 06	2 07
32	2 08	92	6 08	152	10 08	212	14 08	272	18 08	332	22 08	32	2 08	2 09	2 10	2 11
33	2 12	93	6 12	153	10 12	213	14 12	273	18 12	333	22 12	33	2 12	2 13	2 14	2 15
34	2 16	94	6 16	154	10 16	214	14 16	274	18 16	334	22 16	34	2 16	2 17	2 18	2 19
35	2 20	95	6 20	155	10 20	215	14 20	275	18 20	335	22 20	35	2 20	2 21	2 22	2 23
36	2 24	96	6 24	156	10 24	216	14 24	276	18 24	336	22 24	36	2 24	2 25	2 26	2 27
37	2 28	97	6 28	157	10 28	217	14 28	277	18 28	337	22 28	37	2 28	2 29	2 30	2 31
38	2 32	98	6 32	158	10 32	218	14 32	278	18 32	338	22 32	38	2 32	2 33	2 34	2 35
39	2 36	99	6 36	159	10 36	219	14 36	279	18 36	339	22 36	39	2 36	2 37	2 38	2 39
40	2 40	100	6 40	160	10 40	220	14 40	280	18 40	340	22 40	40	2 40	2 41	2 42	2 43
41	2 44	101	6 44	161	10 44	221	14 44	281	18 44	341	22 44	41	2 44	2 45	2 46	2 47
42	2 48	102	6 48	162	10 48	222	14 48	282	18 48	342	22 48	42	2 48	2 49	2 50	2 51
43	2 52	103	6 52	163	10 52	223	14 52	283	18 52	343	22 52	43	2 52	2 53	2 54	2 55
44	2 56	104	6 56	164	10 56	224	14 56	284	18 56	344	22 56	44	2 56	2 57	2 58	2 59
45	3 00	105	7 00	165	11 00	225	15 00	285	19 00	345	23 00	45	3 00	3 01	3 02	3 03
46	3 04	106	7 04	166	11 04	226	15 04	286	19 04	346	23 04	46	3 04	3 05	3 06	3 07
47	3 08	107	7 08	167	11 08	227	15 08	287	19 08	347	23 08	47	3 08	3 09	3 10	3 11
48	3 12	108	7 12	168	11 12	228	15 12	288	19 12	348	23 12	48	3 12	3 13	3 14	3 15
49	3 16	109	7 16	169	11 16	229	15 16	289	19 16	349	23 16	49	3 16	3 17	3 18	3 19
50	3 20	110	7 20	170	11 20	230	15 20	290	19 20	350	23 20	50	3 20	3 21	3 22	3 23
51	3 24	111	7 24	171	11 24	231	15 24	291	19 24	351	23 24	51	3 24	3 25	3 26	3 27
52	3 28	112	7 28	172	11 28	232	15 28	292	19 28	352	23 28	52	3 28	3 29	3 30	3 31
53	3 32	113	7 32	173	11 32	233	15 32	293	19 32	353	23 32	53	3 32	3 33	3 34	3 35
54	3 36	114	7 36	174	11 36	234	15 36	294	19 36	354	23 36	54	3 36	3 37	3 38	3 39
55	3 40	115	7 40	175	11 40	235	15 40	295	19 40	355	23 40	55	3 40	3 41	3 42	3 43
56	3 44	116	7 44	176	11 44	236	15 44	296	19 44	356	23 44	56	3 44	3 45	3 46	3 47
57	3 48	117	7 48	177	11 48	237	15 48	297	19 48	357	23 48	57	3 48	3 49	3 50	3 51
58	3 52	118	7 52	178	11 52	238	15 52	298	19 52	358	23 52	58	3 52	3 53	3 54	3 55
59	3 56	119	7 56	179	11 56	239	15 56	299	19 56	359	23 56	59	3 56	3 57	3 58	3 59

The above table is for converting expressions in arc to their equivalent in time ; its main use in this Almanac is for the conversion of longitude for application to L.M.T. (*added* if *west*, *subtracted* if *east*) to give G.M.T. or vice versa, particularly in the case of sunrise, sunset, etc.

NOTE We have combined the planet data for two years 1978 and 1981 in this table. Normally this table has data for one year only. It is only the planet data that changes on this table from year to year.

T-8

A2 ALTITUDE CORRECTION TABLES 10°-90°—SUN, STARS, PLANETS

SUN OCT.—MAR. App. Alt.	Lower Limb	Upper Limb	SUN APR.—SEPT. App. Alt.	Lower Limb	Upper Limb	STARS AND PLANETS App. Alt.	Corr^n	DIP Ht. of Eye (m)	Corr^n	Ht. of Eye (ft.)
° ′	′	′	° ′	′	′	° ′	′	m	′	ft.
9 34	+10·8	−21·5	9 39	+10·6	−21·2	9 56	−5·3	2·4	−2·8	8·0
9 45	+10·9	−21·4	9 51	+10·7	−21·1	10 08	−5·2	2·6	−2·9	8·6
9 56	+11·0	−21·3	10 03	+10·8	−21·0	10 20	−5·1	2·8	−3·0	9·2
10 08	+11·1	−21·2	10 15	+10·9	−20·9	10 33	−5·0	3·0	−3·1	9·8
10 21	+11·2	−21·1	10 27	+11·0	−20·8	10 46	−4·9	3·2	−3·2	10·5
10 34	+11·3	−21·0	10 40	+11·1	−20·7	11 00	−4·8	3·4	−3·3	11·2
10 47	+11·4	−20·9	10 54	+11·2	−20·6	11 14	−4·7	3·6	−3·4	11·9
11 01	+11·5	−20·8	11 08	+11·3	−20·5	11 29	−4·6	3·8	−3·5	12·6
11 15	+11·6	−20·7	11 23	+11·4	−20·4	11 45	−4·5	4·0	−3·6	13·3
11 30	+11·7	−20·6	11 38	+11·5	−20·3	12 01	−4·4	4·3	−3·7	14·1
11 46	+11·8	−20·5	11 54	+11·6	−20·2	12 18	−4·3	4·5	−3·8	14·9
12 02	+11·9	−20·4	12 10	+11·7	−20·1	12 35	−4·2	4·7	−3·9	15·7
12 19	+12·0	−20·3	12 28	+11·8	−20·0	12 54	−4·1	5·0	−4·0	16·5
12 37	+12·1	−20·2	12 46	+11·9	−19·9	13 13	−4·0	5·2	−4·1	17·4
12 55	+12·2	−20·1	13 05	+12·0	−19·8	13 33	−3·9	5·5	−4·2	18·3
13 14	+12·3	−20·0	13 24	+12·1	−19·7	13 54	−3·8	5·8	−4·3	19·1
13 35	+12·4	−19·9	13 45	+12·2	−19·6	14 16	−3·7	6·1	−4·4	20·1
13 56	+12·5	−19·8	14 07	+12·3	−19·5	14 40	−3·6	6·3	−4·5	21·0
14 18	+12·6	−19·7	14 30	+12·4	−19·4	15 04	−3·5	6·6	−4·6	22·0
14 42	+12·7	−19·6	14 54	+12·5	−19·3	15 30	−3·4	6·9	−4·7	22·9
15 06	+12·8	−19·5	15 19	+12·6	−19·2	15 57	−3·3	7·2	−4·8	23·9
15 32	+12·9	−19·4	15 46	+12·7	−19·1	16 26	−3·2	7·5	−4·9	24·9
15 59	+13·0	−19·3	16 14	+12·8	−19·0	16 56	−3·1	7·9	−5·0	26·0
16 28	+13·1	−19·2	16 44	+12·9	−18·9	17 28	−3·0	8·2	−5·1	27·1
16 59	+13·2	−19·1	17 15	+13·0	−18·8	18 02	−2·9	8·5	−5·2	28·1
17 32	+13·3	−19·0	17 48	+13·1	−18·7	18 38	−2·8	8·8	−5·3	29·2
18 06	+13·4	−18·9	18 24	+13·2	−18·6	19 17	−2·7	9·2	−5·4	30·4
18 42	+13·5	−18·8	19 01	+13·3	−18·5	19 58	−2·6	9·5	−5·5	31·5
19 21	+13·6	−18·7	19 42	+13·4	−18·4	20 42	−2·5	9·9	−5·6	32·7
20 03	+13·7	−18·6	20 25	+13·5	−18·3	21 28	−2·4	10·3	−5·7	33·9
20 48	+13·8	−18·5	21 11	+13·6	−18·2	22 19	−2·3	10·6	−5·8	35·1
21 35	+13·9	−18·4	22 00	+13·7	−18·1	23 13	−2·2	11·0	−5·9	36·3
22 26	+14·0	−18·3	22 54	+13·8	−18·0	24 11	−2·1	11·4	−6·0	37·6
23 22	+14·1	−18·2	23 51	+13·9	−17·9	25 14	−2·0	11·8	−6·1	38·9
24 21	+14·2	−18·1	24 53	+14·0	−17·8	26 22	−1·9	12·2	−6·2	40·1
25 26	+14·3	−18·0	26 00	+14·1	−17·7	27 36	−1·8	12·6	−6·3	41·5
26 36	+14·4	−17·9	27 13	+14·2	−17·6	28 56	−1·7	13·0	−6·4	42·8
27 52	+14·5	−17·8	28 33	+14·3	−17·5	30 24	−1·6	13·4	−6·5	44·2
29 15	+14·6	−17·7	30 00	+14·4	−17·4	32 00	−1·5	13·8	−6·6	45·5
30 46	+14·7	−17·6	31 35	+14·5	−17·3	33 45	−1·4	14·2	−6·7	46·9
32 26	+14·8	−17·5	33 20	+14·6	−17·2	35 40	−1·3	14·7	−6·8	48·4
34 17	+14·9	−17·4	35 17	+14·7	−17·1	37 48	−1·2	15·1	−6·9	49·8
36 20	+15·0	−17·3	37 26	+14·8	−17·0	40 08	−1·1	15·5	−7·0	51·3
38 36	+15·1	−17·2	39 50	+14·9	−16·9	42 44	−1·0	16·0	−7·1	52·8
41 08	+15·2	−17·1	42 31	+15·0	−16·8	45 36	−0·9	16·5	−7·2	54·3
43 59	+15·3	−17·0	45 31	+15·1	−16·7	48 47	−0·8	16·9	−7·3	55·8
47 10	+15·4	−16·9	48 55	+15·2	−16·6	52 18	−0·7	17·4	−7·4	57·4
50 46	+15·5	−16·8	52 44	+15·3	−16·5	56 11	−0·6	17·9	−7·5	58·9
54 49	+15·6	−16·7	57 02	+15·4	−16·4	60 28	−0·5	18·4	−7·6	60·5
59 23	+15·7	−16·6	61 51	+15·5	−16·3	65 08	−0·4	18·8	−7·7	62·1
64 30	+15·8	−16·5	67 17	+15·6	−16·2	70 11	−0·3	19·3	−7·8	63·8
70 12	+15·9	−16·4	73 16	+15·7	−16·1	75 34	−0·2	19·8	−7·9	65·4
76 26	+16·0	−16·3	79 43	+15·8	−16·0	81 13	−0·1	20·4	−8·0	67·1
83 05	+16·1	−16·2	86 32	+15·9	−15·9	87 03	0·0	20·9	−8·1	68·8
90 00			90 00			90 00		21·4		70·5

STARS AND PLANETS — App. Alt. / Additional Corr^n

App. Alt.	Additional Corr^n
1981 VENUS	
Jan. 1-Sept. 27	
0° – 42°	+ 0′·1
Sept. 28-Nov. 13	
0° – 47°	+ 0′·2
Nov. 14-Dec. 10	
0° – 46°	+ 0′·3
Dec. 11-Dec. 26	
0° – 11°	+ 0′·4
11° – 41°	+ 0·5
Dec. 27-Dec. 31	
0° – 6°	+ 0′·5
6° – 20°	+ 0·6
20° – 31°	+ 0·7
MARS	
Jan. 1-Dec. 31	
0° – 60°	+ 0′·1
1978 VENUS	
July 21-Sept. 2	
0° – 47°	+ 0′·2
Sept. 3-Sept. 29	
0° – 46°	+ 0′·3
Sept. 30-Oct. 14	
0° – 11°	+ 0′·4
11° – 41°	+ 0·5
Oct. 15-Oct. 22	
0° – 6°	+ 0′·5
6° – 20°	+ 0·6
20° – 31°	+ 0·7
Oct. 23-Nov. 25	
0° – 4°	+ 0′·6
4° – 12°	+ 0·7
12° – 22°	+ 0·8

DIP

Ht. of Eye	Corr^n
m	′
1·0	− 1·8
1·5	− 2·2
2·0	− 2·5
2·5	− 2·8
3·0	− 3·0
See table ←	
m	′
20	− 7·9
22	− 8·3
24	− 8·6
26	− 9·0
28	− 9·3
30	− 9·6
32	− 10·0
34	− 10·3
36	− 10·6
38	− 10·8
40	− 11·1
42	− 11·4
44	− 11·7
46	− 11·9
48	− 12·2
ft.	′
2	− 1·4
4	− 1·9
6	− 2·4
8	− 2·7
10	− 3·1
See table ←	
ft.	′
70	− 8·1
75	− 8·4
80	− 8·7
85	− 8·9
90	− 9·2
95	− 9·5
100	− 9·7
105	− 9·9
110	− 10·2
115	− 10·4
120	− 10·6
125	− 10·8
130	− 11·1
135	− 11·3
140	− 11·5
145	− 11·7
150	− 11·9
155	− 12·1

App. Alt. = Apparent altitude = Sextant altitude corrected for index error and dip.
For daylight observations of Venus, see page 260.

T-9

4^m INCREMENTS AND CORRECTIONS 5^m

4^m	SUN PLANETS	ARIES	MOON	v or d	Corr^n	v or d	Corr^n	v or d	Corr^n
s	° ′	° ′	° ′	′	′	′	′	′	′
00	1 00·0	1 00·2	0 57·3	0·0	0·0	6·0	0·5	12·0	0·9
01	1 00·3	1 00·4	0 57·5	0·1	0·0	6·1	0·5	12·1	0·9
02	1 00·5	1 00·7	0 57·7	0·2	0·0	6·2	0·5	12·2	0·9
03	1 00·8	1 00·9	0 58·0	0·3	0·0	6·3	0·5	12·3	0·9
04	1 01·0	1 01·2	0 58·2	0·4	0·0	6·4	0·5	12·4	0·9
05	1 01·3	1 01·4	0 58·5	0·5	0·0	6·5	0·5	12·5	0·9
06	1 01·5	1 01·7	0 58·7	0·6	0·0	6·6	0·5	12·6	0·9
07	1 01·8	1 01·9	0 58·9	0·7	0·1	6·7	0·5	12·7	1·0
08	1 02·0	1 02·2	0 59·2	0·8	0·1	6·8	0·5	12·8	1·0
09	1 02·3	1 02·4	0 59·4	0·9	0·1	6·9	0·5	12·9	1·0
10	1 02·5	1 02·7	0 59·7	1·0	0·1	7·0	0·5	13·0	1·0
11	1 02·8	1 02·9	0 59·9	1·1	0·1	7·1	0·5	13·1	1·0
12	1 03·0	1 03·2	1 00·1	1·2	0·1	7·2	0·5	13·2	1·0
13	1 03·3	1 03·4	1 00·4	1·3	0·1	7·3	0·5	13·3	1·0
14	1 03·5	1 03·7	1 00·6	1·4	0·1	7·4	0·6	13·4	1·0
15	1 03·8	1 03·9	1 00·8	1·5	0·1	7·5	0·6	13·5	1·0
16	1 04·0	1 04·2	1 01·1	1·6	0·1	7·6	0·6	13·6	1·0
17	1 04·3	1 04·4	1 01·3	1·7	0·1	7·7	0·6	13·7	1·0
18	1 04·5	1 04·7	1 01·6	1·8	0·1	7·8	0·6	13·8	1·0
19	1 04·8	1 04·9	1 01·8	1·9	0·1	7·9	0·6	13·9	1·0
20	1 05·0	1 05·2	1 02·0	2·0	0·2	8·0	0·6	14·0	1·1
21	1 05·3	1 05·4	1 02·3	2·1	0·2	8·1	0·6	14·1	1·1
22	1 05·5	1 05·7	1 02·5	2·2	0·2	8·2	0·6	14·2	1·1
23	1 05·8	1 05·9	1 02·8	2·3	0·2	8·3	0·6	14·3	1·1
24	1 06·0	1 06·2	1 03·0	2·4	0·2	8·4	0·6	14·4	1·1
25	1 06·3	1 06·4	1 03·2	2·5	0·2	8·5	0·6	14·5	1·1
26	1 06·5	1 06·7	1 03·5	2·6	0·2	8·6	0·6	14·6	1·1
27	1 06·8	1 06·9	1 03·7	2·7	0·2	8·7	0·7	14·7	1·1
28	1 07·0	1 07·2	1 03·9	2·8	0·2	8·8	0·7	14·8	1·1
29	1 07·3	1 07·4	1 04·2	2·9	0·2	8·9	0·7	14·9	1·1
30	1 07·5	1 07·7	1 04·4	3·0	0·2	9·0	0·7	15·0	1·1
31	1 07·8	1 07·9	1 04·7	3·1	0·2	9·1	0·7	15·1	1·1
32	1 08·0	1 08·2	1 04·9	3·2	0·2	9·2	0·7	15·2	1·1
33	1 08·3	1 08·4	1 05·1	3·3	0·2	9·3	0·7	15·3	1·1
34	1 08·5	1 08·7	1 05·4	3·4	0·3	9·4	0·7	15·4	1·2
35	1 08·8	1 08·9	1 05·6	3·5	0·3	9·5	0·7	15·5	1·2
36	1 09·0	1 09·2	1 05·9	3·6	0·3	9·6	0·7	15·6	1·2
37	1 09·3	1 09·4	1 06·1	3·7	0·3	9·7	0·7	15·7	1·2
38	1 09·5	1 09·7	1 06·3	3·8	0·3	9·8	0·7	15·8	1·2
39	1 09·8	1 09·9	1 06·6	3·9	0·3	9·9	0·7	15·9	1·2
40	1 10·0	1 10·2	1 06·8	4·0	0·3	10·0	0·8	16·0	1·2
41	1 10·3	1 10·4	1 07·0	4·1	0·3	10·1	0·8	16·1	1·2
42	1 10·5	1 10·7	1 07·3	4·2	0·3	10·2	0·8	16·2	1·2
43	1 10·8	1 10·9	1 07·5	4·3	0·3	10·3	0·8	16·3	1·2
44	1 11·0	1 11·2	1 07·8	4·4	0·3	10·4	0·8	16·4	1·2
45	1 11·3	1 11·4	1 08·0	4·5	0·3	10·5	0·8	16·5	1·2
46	1 11·5	1 11·7	1 08·2	4·6	0·3	10·6	0·8	16·6	1·2
47	1 11·8	1 11·9	1 08·5	4·7	0·4	10·7	0·8	16·7	1·3
48	1 12·0	1 12·2	1 08·7	4·8	0·4	10·8	0·8	16·8	1·3
49	1 12·3	1 12·4	1 09·0	4·9	0·4	10·9	0·8	16·9	1·3
50	1 12·5	1 12·7	1 09·2	5·0	0·4	11·0	0·8	17·0	1·3
51	1 12·8	1 12·9	1 09·4	5·1	0·4	11·1	0·8	17·1	1·3
52	1 13·0	1 13·2	1 09·7	5·2	0·4	11·2	0·8	17·2	1·3
53	1 13·3	1 13·5	1 09·9	5·3	0·4	11·3	0·8	17·3	1·3
54	1 13·5	1 13·7	1 10·2	5·4	0·4	11·4	0·9	17·4	1·3
55	1 13·8	1 14·0	1 10·4	5·5	0·4	11·5	0·9	17·5	1·3
56	1 14·0	1 14·2	1 10·6	5·6	0·4	11·6	0·9	17·6	1·3
57	1 14·3	1 14·5	1 10·9	5·7	0·4	11·7	0·9	17·7	1·3
58	1 14·5	1 14·7	1 11·1	5·8	0·4	11·8	0·9	17·8	1·3
59	1 14·8	1 15·0	1 11·3	5·9	0·4	11·9	0·9	17·9	1·3
60	1 15·0	1 15·2	1 11·6	6·0	0·5	12·0	0·9	18·0	1·4

5^m	SUN PLANETS	ARIES	MOON	v or d	Corr^n	v or d	Corr^n	v or d	Corr^n
s	° ′	° ′	° ′	′	′	′	′	′	′
00	1 15·0	1 15·2	1 11·6	0·0	0·0	6·0	0·6	12·0	1·1
01	1 15·3	1 15·5	1 11·8	0·1	0·0	6·1	0·6	12·1	1·1
02	1 15·5	1 15·7	1 12·1	0·2	0·0	6·2	0·6	12·2	1·1
03	1 15·8	1 16·0	1 12·3	0·3	0·0	6·3	0·6	12·3	1·1
04	1 16·0	1 16·2	1 12·5	0·4	0·0	6·4	0·6	12·4	1·1
05	1 16·3	1 16·5	1 12·8	0·5	0·0	6·5	0·6	12·5	1·1
06	1 16·5	1 16·7	1 13·0	0·6	0·1	6·6	0·6	12·6	1·2
07	1 16·8	1 17·0	1 13·3	0·7	0·1	6·7	0·6	12·7	1·2
08	1 17·0	1 17·2	1 13·5	0·8	0·1	6·8	0·6	12·8	1·2
09	1 17·3	1 17·5	1 13·7	0·9	0·1	6·9	0·6	12·9	1·2
10	1 17·5	1 17·7	1 14·0	1·0	0·1	7·0	0·6	13·0	1·2
11	1 17·8	1 18·0	1 14·2	1·1	0·1	7·1	0·7	13·1	1·2
12	1 18·0	1 18·2	1 14·4	1·2	0·1	7·2	0·7	13·2	1·2
13	1 18·3	1 18·5	1 14·7	1·3	0·1	7·3	0·7	13·3	1·2
14	1 18·5	1 18·7	1 14·9	1·4	0·1	7·4	0·7	13·4	1·2
15	1 18·8	1 19·0	1 15·2	1·5	0·1	7·5	0·7	13·5	1·2
16	1 19·0	1 19·2	1 15·4	1·6	0·1	7·6	0·7	13·6	1·2
17	1 19·3	1 19·5	1 15·6	1·7	0·2	7·7	0·7	13·7	1·3
18	1 19·5	1 19·7	1 15·9	1·8	0·2	7·8	0·7	13·8	1·3
19	1 19·8	1 20·0	1 16·1	1·9	0·2	7·9	0·7	13·9	1·3
20	1 20·0	1 20·2	1 16·4	2·0	0·2	8·0	0·7	14·0	1·3
21	1 20·3	1 20·5	1 16·6	2·1	0·2	8·1	0·7	14·1	1·3
22	1 20·5	1 20·7	1 16·8	2·2	0·2	8·2	0·8	14·2	1·3
23	1 20·8	1 21·0	1 17·1	2·3	0·2	8·3	0·8	14·3	1·3
24	1 21·0	1 21·2	1 17·3	2·4	0·2	8·4	0·8	14·4	1·3
25	1 21·3	1 21·5	1 17·5	2·5	0·2	8·5	0·8	14·5	1·3
26	1 21·5	1 21·7	1 17·8	2·6	0·2	8·6	0·8	14·6	1·3
27	1 21·8	1 22·0	1 18·0	2·7	0·2	8·7	0·8	14·7	1·3
28	1 22·0	1 22·2	1 18·3	2·8	0·3	8·8	0·8	14·8	1·4
29	1 22·3	1 22·5	1 18·5	2·9	0·3	8·9	0·8	14·9	1·4
30	1 22·5	1 22·7	1 18·7	3·0	0·3	9·0	0·8	15·0	1·4
31	1 22·8	1 23·0	1 19·0	3·1	0·3	9·1	0·8	15·1	1·4
32	1 23·0	1 23·2	1 19·2	3·2	0·3	9·2	0·8	15·2	1·4
33	1 23·3	1 23·5	1 19·5	3·3	0·3	9·3	0·9	15·3	1·4
34	1 23·5	1 23·7	1 19·7	3·4	0·3	9·4	0·9	15·4	1·4
35	1 23·8	1 24·0	1 19·9	3·5	0·3	9·5	0·9	15·5	1·4
36	1 24·0	1 24·2	1 20·2	3·6	0·3	9·6	0·9	15·6	1·4
37	1 24·3	1 24·5	1 20·4	3·7	0·3	9·7	0·9	15·7	1·4
38	1 24·5	1 24·7	1 20·7	3·8	0·3	9·8	0·9	15·8	1·4
39	1 24·8	1 25·0	1 20·9	3·9	0·4	9·9	0·9	15·9	1·5
40	1 25·0	1 25·2	1 21·1	4·0	0·4	10·0	0·9	16·0	1·5
41	1 25·3	1 25·5	1 21·4	4·1	0·4	10·1	0·9	16·1	1·5
42	1 25·5	1 25·7	1 21·6	4·2	0·4	10·2	0·9	16·2	1·5
43	1 25·8	1 26·0	1 21·8	4·3	0·4	10·3	0·9	16·3	1·5
44	1 26·0	1 26·2	1 22·1	4·4	0·4	10·4	1·0	16·4	1·5
45	1 26·3	1 26·5	1 22·3	4·5	0·4	10·5	1·0	16·5	1·5
46	1 26·5	1 26·7	1 22·6	4·6	0·4	10·6	1·0	16·6	1·5
47	1 26·8	1 27·0	1 22·8	4·7	0·4	10·7	1·0	16·7	1·5
48	1 27·0	1 27·2	1 23·0	4·8	0·4	10·8	1·0	16·8	1·5
49	1 27·3	1 27·5	1 23·3	4·9	0·4	10·9	1·0	16·9	1·5
50	1 27·5	1 27·7	1 23·5	5·0	0·5	11·0	1·0	17·0	1·6
51	1 27·8	1 28·0	1 23·8	5·1	0·5	11·1	1·0	17·1	1·6
52	1 28·0	1 28·2	1 24·0	5·2	0·5	11·2	1·0	17·2	1·6
53	1 28·3	1 28·5	1 24·2	5·3	0·5	11·3	1·0	17·3	1·6
54	1 28·5	1 28·7	1 24·5	5·4	0·5	11·4	1·0	17·4	1·6
55	1 28·8	1 29·0	1 24·7	5·5	0·5	11·5	1·1	17·5	1·6
56	1 29·0	1 29·2	1 24·9	5·6	0·5	11·6	1·1	17·6	1·6
57	1 29·3	1 29·5	1 25·2	5·7	0·5	11·7	1·1	17·7	1·6
58	1 29·5	1 29·7	1 25·4	5·8	0·5	11·8	1·1	17·8	1·6
59	1 29·8	1 30·0	1 25·7	5·9	0·5	11·9	1·1	17·9	1·6
60	1 30·0	1 30·2	1 25·9	6·0	0·6	12·0	1·1	18·0	1·7

6^m INCREMENTS AND CORRECTIONS 7^m

6^m s	SUN PLANETS ° ′	ARIES ° ′	MOON ° ′	v or d ′	Corr^n ′	v or d ′	Corr^n ′	v or d ′	Corr^n ′
00	1 30·0	1 30·2	1 25·9	0·0	0·0	6·0	0·7	12·0	1·3
01	1 30·3	1 30·5	1 26·1	0·1	0·0	6·1	0·7	12·1	1·3
02	1 30·5	1 30·7	1 26·4	0·2	0·0	6·2	0·7	12·2	1·3
03	1 30·8	1 31·0	1 26·6	0·3	0·0	6·3	0·7	12·3	1·3
04	1 31·0	1 31·2	1 26·9	0·4	0·0	6·4	0·7	12·4	1·3
05	1 31·3	1 31·5	1 27·1	0·5	0·1	6·5	0·7	12·5	1·4
06	1 31·5	1 31·8	1 27·3	0·6	0·1	6·6	0·7	12·6	1·4
07	1 31·8	1 32·0	1 27·6	0·7	0·1	6·7	0·7	12·7	1·4
08	1 32·0	1 32·3	1 27·8	0·8	0·1	6·8	0·7	12·8	1·4
09	1 32·3	1 32·5	1 28·0	0·9	0·1	6·9	0·7	12·9	1·4
10	1 32·5	1 32·8	1 28·3	1·0	0·1	7·0	0·8	13·0	1·4
11	1 32·8	1 33·0	1 28·5	1·1	0·1	7·1	0·8	13·1	1·4
12	1 33·0	1 33·3	1 28·8	1·2	0·1	7·2	0·8	13·2	1·4
13	1 33·3	1 33·5	1 29·0	1·3	0·1	7·3	0·8	13·3	1·4
14	1 33·5	1 33·8	1 29·2	1·4	0·2	7·4	0·8	13·4	1·5
15	1 33·8	1 34·0	1 29·5	1·5	0·2	7·5	0·8	13·5	1·5
16	1 34·0	1 34·3	1 29·7	1·6	0·2	7·6	0·8	13·6	1·5
17	1 34·3	1 34·5	1 30·0	1·7	0·2	7·7	0·8	13·7	1·5
18	1 34·5	1 34·8	1 30·2	1·8	0·2	7·8	0·8	13·8	1·5
19	1 34·8	1 35·0	1 30·4	1·9	0·2	7·9	0·9	13·9	1·5
20	1 35·0	1 35·3	1 30·7	2·0	0·2	8·0	0·9	14·0	1·5
21	1 35·3	1 35·5	1 30·9	2·1	0·2	8·1	0·9	14·1	1·5
22	1 35·5	1 35·8	1 31·1	2·2	0·2	8·2	0·9	14·2	1·5
23	1 35·8	1 36·0	1 31·4	2·3	0·2	8·3	0·9	14·3	1·5
24	1 36·0	1 36·3	1 31·6	2·4	0·3	8·4	0·9	14·4	1·6
25	1 36·3	1 36·5	1 31·9	2·5	0·3	8·5	0·9	14·5	1·6
26	1 36·5	1 36·8	1 32·1	2·6	0·3	8·6	0·9	14·6	1·6
27	1 36·8	1 37·0	1 32·3	2·7	0·3	8·7	0·9	14·7	1·6
28	1 37·0	1 37·3	1 32·6	2·8	0·3	8·8	1·0	14·8	1·6
29	1 37·3	1 37·5	1 32·8	2·9	0·3	8·9	1·0	14·9	1·6
30	1 37·5	1 37·8	1 33·1	3·0	0·3	9·0	1·0	15·0	1·6
31	1 37·8	1 38·0	1 33·3	3·1	0·3	9·1	1·0	15·1	1·6
32	1 38·0	1 38·3	1 33·5	3·2	0·3	9·2	1·0	15·2	1·6
33	1 38·3	1 38·5	1 33·8	3·3	0·4	9·3	1·0	15·3	1·7
34	1 38·5	1 38·8	1 34·0	3·4	0·4	9·4	1·0	15·4	1·7
35	1 38·8	1 39·0	1 34·3	3·5	0·4	9·5	1·0	15·5	1·7
36	1 39·0	1 39·3	1 34·5	3·6	0·4	9·6	1·0	15·6	1·7
37	1 39·3	1 39·5	1 34·7	3·7	0·4	9·7	1·1	15·7	1·7
38	1 39·5	1 39·8	1 35·0	3·8	0·4	9·8	1·1	15·8	1·7
39	1 39·8	1 40·0	1 35·2	3·9	0·4	9·9	1·1	15·9	1·7
40	1 40·0	1 40·3	1 35·4	4·0	0·4	10·0	1·1	16·0	1·7
41	1 40·3	1 40·5	1 35·7	4·1	0·4	10·1	1·1	16·1	1·7
42	1 40·5	1 40·8	1 35·9	4·2	0·5	10·2	1·1	16·2	1·8
43	1 40·8	1 41·0	1 36·2	4·3	0·5	10·3	1·1	16·3	1·8
44	1 41·0	1 41·3	1 36·4	4·4	0·5	10·4	1·1	16·4	1·8
45	1 41·3	1 41·5	1 36·6	4·5	0·5	10·5	1·1	16·5	1·8
46	1 41·5	1 41·8	1 36·9	4·6	0·5	10·6	1·1	16·6	1·8
47	1 41·8	1 42·0	1 37·1	4·7	0·5	10·7	1·2	16·7	1·8
48	1 42·0	1 42·3	1 37·4	4·8	0·5	10·8	1·2	16·8	1·8
49	1 42·3	1 42·5	1 37·6	4·9	0·5	10·9	1·2	16·9	1·8
50	1 42·5	1 42·8	1 37·8	5·0	0·5	11·0	1·2	17·0	1·8
51	1 42·8	1 43·0	1 38·1	5·1	0·6	11·1	1·2	17·1	1·9
52	1 43·0	1 43·3	1 38·3	5·2	0·6	11·2	1·2	17·2	1·9
53	1 43·3	1 43·5	1 38·5	5·3	0·6	11·3	1·2	17·3	1·9
54	1 43·5	1 43·8	1 38·8	5·4	0·6	11·4	1·2	17·4	1·9
55	1 43·8	1 44·0	1 39·0	5·5	0·6	11·5	1·2	17·5	1·9
56	1 44·0	1 44·3	1 39·3	5·6	0·6	11·6	1·3	17·6	1·9
57	1 44·3	1 44·5	1 39·5	5·7	0·6	11·7	1·3	17·7	1·9
58	1 44·5	1 44·8	1 39·7	5·8	0·6	11·8	1·3	17·8	1·9
59	1 44·8	1 45·0	1 40·0	5·9	0·6	11·9	1·3	17·9	1·9
60	1 45·0	1 45·3	1 40·2	6·0	0·7	12·0	1·3	18·0	2·0

7^m s	SUN PLANETS ° ′	ARIES ° ′	MOON ° ′	v or d ′	Corr^n ′	v or d ′	Corr^n ′	v or d ′	Corr^n ′
00	1 45·0	1 45·3	1 40·2	0·0	0·0	6·0	0·8	12·0	1·5
01	1 45·3	1 45·5	1 40·5	0·1	0·0	6·1	0·8	12·1	1·5
02	1 45·5	1 45·8	1 40·7	0·2	0·0	6·2	0·8	12·2	1·5
03	1 45·8	1 46·0	1 40·9	0·3	0·0	6·3	0·8	12·3	1·5
04	1 46·0	1 46·3	1 41·2	0·4	0·1	6·4	0·8	12·4	1·6
05	1 46·3	1 46·5	1 41·4	0·5	0·1	6·5	0·8	12·5	1·6
06	1 46·5	1 46·8	1 41·6	0·6	0·1	6·6	0·8	12·6	1·6
07	1 46·8	1 47·0	1 41·9	0·7	0·1	6·7	0·8	12·7	1·6
08	1 47·0	1 47·3	1 42·1	0·8	0·1	6·8	0·9	12·8	1·6
09	1 47·3	1 47·5	1 42·4	0·9	0·1	6·9	0·9	12·9	1·6
10	1 47·5	1 47·8	1 42·6	1·0	0·1	7·0	0·9	13·0	1·6
11	1 47·8	1 48·0	1 42·8	1·1	0·1	7·1	0·9	13·1	1·6
12	1 48·0	1 48·3	1 43·1	1·2	0·2	7·2	0·9	13·2	1·7
13	1 48·3	1 48·5	1 43·3	1·3	0·2	7·3	0·9	13·3	1·7
14	1 48·5	1 48·8	1 43·6	1·4	0·2	7·4	0·9	13·4	1·7
15	1 48·8	1 49·0	1 43·8	1·5	0·2	7·5	0·9	13·5	1·7
16	1 49·0	1 49·3	1 44·0	1·6	0·2	7·6	1·0	13·6	1·7
17	1 49·3	1 49·5	1 44·3	1·7	0·2	7·7	1·0	13·7	1·7
18	1 49·5	1 49·8	1 44·5	1·8	0·2	7·8	1·0	13·8	1·7
19	1 49·8	1 50·1	1 44·8	1·9	0·2	7·9	1·0	13·9	1·7
20	1 50·0	1 50·3	1 45·0	2·0	0·3	8·0	1·0	14·0	1·8
21	1 50·3	1 50·6	1 45·2	2·1	0·3	8·1	1·0	14·1	1·8
22	1 50·5	1 50·8	1 45·5	2·2	0·3	8·2	1·0	14·2	1·8
23	1 50·8	1 51·1	1 45·7	2·3	0·3	8·3	1·0	14·3	1·8
24	1 51·0	1 51·3	1 45·9	2·4	0·3	8·4	1·1	14·4	1·8
25	1 51·3	1 51·6	1 46·2	2·5	0·3	8·5	1·1	14·5	1·8
26	1 51·5	1 51·8	1 46·4	2·6	0·3	8·6	1·1	14·6	1·8
27	1 51·8	1 52·1	1 46·7	2·7	0·3	8·7	1·1	14·7	1·8
28	1 52·0	1 52·3	1 46·9	2·8	0·4	8·8	1·1	14·8	1·9
29	1 52·3	1 52·6	1 47·1	2·9	0·4	8·9	1·1	14·9	1·9
30	1 52·5	1 52·8	1 47·4	3·0	0·4	9·0	1·1	15·0	1·9
31	1 52·8	1 53·1	1 47·6	3·1	0·4	9·1	1·1	15·1	1·9
32	1 53·0	1 53·3	1 47·9	3·2	0·4	9·2	1·2	15·2	1·9
33	1 53·3	1 53·6	1 48·1	3·3	0·4	9·3	1·2	15·3	1·9
34	1 53·5	1 53·8	1 48·3	3·4	0·4	9·4	1·2	15·4	1·9
35	1 53·8	1 54·1	1 48·6	3·5	0·4	9·5	1·2	15·5	1·9
36	1 54·0	1 54·3	1 48·8	3·6	0·5	9·6	1·2	15·6	2·0
37	1 54·3	1 54·6	1 49·0	3·7	0·5	9·7	1·2	15·7	2·0
38	1 54·5	1 54·8	1 49·3	3·8	0·5	9·8	1·2	15·8	2·0
39	1 54·8	1 55·1	1 49·5	3·9	0·5	9·9	1·2	15·9	2·0
40	1 55·0	1 55·3	1 49·8	4·0	0·5	10·0	1·3	16·0	2·0
41	1 55·3	1 55·6	1 50·0	4·1	0·5	10·1	1·3	16·1	2·0
42	1 55·5	1 55·8	1 50·2	4·2	0·5	10·2	1·3	16·2	2·0
43	1 55·8	1 56·1	1 50·5	4·3	0·5	10·3	1·3	16·3	2·0
44	1 56·0	1 56·3	1 50·7	4·4	0·6	10·4	1·3	16·4	2·1
45	1 56·3	1 56·6	1 51·0	4·5	0·6	10·5	1·3	16·5	2·1
46	1 56·5	1 56·8	1 51·2	4·6	0·6	10·6	1·3	16·6	2·1
47	1 56·8	1 57·1	1 51·4	4·7	0·6	10·7	1·3	16·7	2·1
48	1 57·0	1 57·3	1 51·7	4·8	0·6	10·8	1·4	16·8	2·1
49	1 57·3	1 57·6	1 51·9	4·9	0·6	10·9	1·4	16·9	2·1
50	1 57·5	1 57·8	1 52·1	5·0	0·6	11·0	1·4	17·0	2·1
51	1 57·8	1 58·1	1 52·4	5·1	0·6	11·1	1·4	17·1	2·1
52	1 58·0	1 58·3	1 52·6	5·2	0·7	11·2	1·4	17·2	2·2
53	1 58·3	1 58·6	1 52·9	5·3	0·7	11·3	1·4	17·3	2·2
54	1 58·5	1 58·8	1 53·1	5·4	0·7	11·4	1·4	17·4	2·2
55	1 58·8	1 59·1	1 53·3	5·5	0·7	11·5	1·4	17·5	2·2
56	1 59·0	1 59·3	1 53·6	5·6	0·7	11·6	1·5	17·6	2·2
57	1 59·3	1 59·6	1 53·8	5·7	0·7	11·7	1·5	17·7	2·2
58	1 59·5	1 59·8	1 54·1	5·8	0·7	11·8	1·5	17·8	2·2
59	1 59·8	2 00·1	1 54·3	5·9	0·7	11·9	1·5	17·9	2·2
60	2 00·0	2 00·3	1 54·5	6·0	0·8	12·0	1·5	18·0	2·3

48m INCREMENTS AND CORRECTIONS 49m

48m s	SUN PLANETS	ARIES	MOON	v or d	Corrn	v or d	Corrn	v or d	Corrn
s	° ′	° ′	° ′	′	′	′	′	′	′
00	12 00·0	12 02·0	11 27·2	0·0	0·0	6·0	4·9	12·0	9·7
01	12 00·3	12 02·2	11 27·4	0·1	0·1	6·1	4·9	12·1	9·8
02	12 00·5	12 02·5	11 27·7	0·2	0·2	6·2	5·0	12·2	9·9
03	12 00·8	12 02·7	11 27·9	0·3	0·2	6·3	5·1	12·3	9·9
04	12 01·0	12 03·0	11 28·2	0·4	0·3	6·4	5·2	12·4	10·0
05	12 01·3	12 03·2	11 28·4	0·5	0·4	6·5	5·3	12·5	10·1
06	12 01·5	12 03·5	11 28·6	0·6	0·5	6·6	5·3	12·6	10·2
07	12 01·8	12 03·7	11 28·9	0·7	0·6	6·7	5·4	12·7	10·3
08	12 02·0	12 04·0	11 29·1	0·8	0·6	6·8	5·5	12·8	10·3
09	12 02·3	12 04·2	11 29·3	0·9	0·7	6·9	5·6	12·9	10·4
10	12 02·5	12 04·5	11 29·6	1·0	0·8	7·0	5·7	13·0	10·5
11	12 02·8	12 04·7	11 29·8	1·1	0·9	7·1	5·7	13·1	10·6
12	12 03·0	12 05·0	11 30·1	1·2	1·0	7·2	5·8	13·2	10·7
13	12 03·3	12 05·2	11 30·3	1·3	1·1	7·3	5·9	13·3	10·8
14	12 03·5	12 05·5	11 30·5	1·4	1·1	7·4	6·0	13·4	10·8
15	12 03·8	12 05·7	11 30·8	1·5	1·2	7·5	6·1	13·5	10·9
16	12 04·0	12 06·0	11 31·0	1·6	1·3	7·6	6·1	13·6	11·0
17	12 04·3	12 06·2	11 31·3	1·7	1·4	7·7	6·2	13·7	11·1
18	12 04·5	12 06·5	11 31·5	1·8	1·5	7·8	6·3	13·8	11·2
19	12 04·8	12 06·7	11 31·7	1·9	1·5	7·9	6·4	13·9	11·2
20	12 05·0	12 07·0	11 32·0	2·0	1·6	8·0	6·5	14·0	11·3
21	12 05·3	12 07·2	11 32·2	2·1	1·7	8·1	6·5	14·1	11·4
22	12 05·5	12 07·5	11 32·4	2·2	1·8	8·2	6·6	14·2	11·5
23	12 05·8	12 07·7	11 32·7	2·3	1·9	8·3	6·7	14·3	11·6
24	12 06·0	12 08·0	11 32·9	2·4	1·9	8·4	6·8	14·4	11·6
25	12 06·3	12 08·2	11 33·2	2·5	2·0	8·5	6·9	14·5	11·7
26	12 06·5	12 08·5	11 33·4	2·6	2·1	8·6	7·0	14·6	11·8
27	12 06·8	12 08·7	11 33·6	2·7	2·2	8·7	7·0	14·7	11·9
28	12 07·0	12 09·0	11 33·9	2·8	2·3	8·8	7·1	14·8	12·0
29	12 07·3	12 09·2	11 34·1	2·9	2·3	8·9	7·2	14·9	12·0
30	12 07·5	12 09·5	11 34·4	3·0	2·4	9·0	7·3	15·0	12·1
31	12 07·8	12 09·7	11 34·6	3·1	2·5	9·1	7·4	15·1	12·2
32	12 08·0	12 10·0	11 34·8	3·2	2·6	9·2	7·4	15·2	12·3
33	12 08·3	12 10·2	11 35·1	3·3	2·7	9·3	7·5	15·3	12·4
34	12 08·5	12 10·5	11 35·3	3·4	2·7	9·4	7·6	15·4	12·4
35	12 08·8	12 10·7	11 35·6	3·5	2·8	9·5	7·7	15·5	12·5
36	12 09·0	12 11·0	11 35·8	3·6	2·9	9·6	7·8	15·6	12·6
37	12 09·3	12 11·2	11 36·0	3·7	3·0	9·7	7·8	15·7	12·7
38	12 09·5	12 11·5	11 36·3	3·8	3·1	9·8	7·9	15·8	12·8
39	12 09·8	12 11·7	11 36·5	3·9	3·2	9·9	8·0	15·9	12·9
40	12 10·0	12 12·0	11 36·7	4·0	3·2	10·0	8·1	16·0	12·9
41	12 10·3	12 12·2	11 37·0	4·1	3·3	10·1	8·2	16·1	13·0
42	12 10·5	12 12·5	11 37·2	4·2	3·4	10·2	8·2	16·2	13·1
43	12 10·8	12 12·8	11 37·5	4·3	3·5	10·3	8·3	16·3	13·2
44	12 11·0	12 13·0	11 37·7	4·4	3·6	10·4	8·4	16·4	13·3
45	12 11·3	12 13·3	11 37·9	4·5	3·6	10·5	8·5	16·5	13·3
46	12 11·5	12 13·5	11 38·2	4·6	3·7	10·6	8·6	16·6	13·4
47	12 11·8	12 13·8	11 38·4	4·7	3·8	10·7	8·6	16·7	13·5
48	12 12·0	12 14·0	11 38·7	4·8	3·9	10·8	8·7	16·8	13·6
49	12 12·3	12 14·3	11 38·9	4·9	4·0	10·9	8·8	16·9	13·7
50	12 12·5	12 14·5	11 39·1	5·0	4·0	11·0	8·9	17·0	13·7
51	12 12·8	12 14·8	11 39·4	5·1	4·1	11·1	9·0	17·1	13·8
52	12 13·0	12 15·0	11 39·6	5·2	4·2	11·2	9·1	17·2	13·9
53	12 13·3	12 15·3	11 39·8	5·3	4·3	11·3	9·1	17·3	14·0
54	12 13·5	12 15·5	11 40·1	5·4	4·4	11·4	9·2	17·4	14·1
55	12 13·8	12 15·8	11 40·3	5·5	4·4	11·5	9·3	17·5	14·1
56	12 14·0	12 16·0	11 40·6	5·6	4·5	11·6	9·4	17·6	14·2
57	12 14·3	12 16·3	11 40·8	5·7	4·6	11·7	9·5	17·7	14·3
58	12 14·5	12 16·5	11 41·0	5·8	4·7	11·8	9·5	17·8	14·4
59	12 14·8	12 16·8	11 41·3	5·9	4·8	11·9	9·6	17·9	14·5
60	12 15·0	12 17·0	11 41·5	6·0	4·9	12·0	9·7	18·0	14·6

49m s	SUN PLANETS	ARIES	MOON	v or d	Corrn	v or d	Corrn	v or d	Corrn
s	° ′	° ′	° ′	′	′	′	′	′	′
00	12 15·0	12 17·0	11 41·5	0·0	0·0	6·0	5·0	12·0	9·9
01	12 15·3	12 17·3	11 41·8	0·1	0·1	6·1	5·0	12·1	10·0
02	12 15·5	12 17·5	11 42·0	0·2	0·2	6·2	5·1	12·2	10·1
03	12 15·8	12 17·8	11 42·2	0·3	0·2	6·3	5·2	12·3	10·1
04	12 16·0	12 18·0	11 42·5	0·4	0·3	6·4	5·3	12·4	10·2
05	12 16·3	12 18·3	11 42·7	0·5	0·4	6·5	5·4	12·5	10·3
06	12 16·5	12 18·5	11 42·9	0·6	0·5	6·6	5·4	12·6	10·4
07	12 16·8	12 18·8	11 43·2	0·7	0·6	6·7	5·5	12·7	10·5
08	12 17·0	12 19·0	11 43·4	0·8	0·7	6·8	5·6	12·8	10·6
09	12 17·3	12 19·3	11 43·7	0·9	0·7	6·9	5·7	12·9	10·6
10	12 17·5	12 19·5	11 43·9	1·0	0·8	7·0	5·8	13·0	10·7
11	12 17·8	12 19·8	11 44·1	1·1	0·9	7·1	5·9	13·1	10·8
12	12 18·0	12 20·0	11 44·4	1·2	1·0	7·2	5·9	13·2	10·9
13	12 18·3	12 20·3	11 44·6	1·3	1·1	7·3	6·0	13·3	11·0
14	12 18·5	12 20·5	11 44·9	1·4	1·2	7·4	6·1	13·4	11·1
15	12 18·8	12 20·8	11 45·1	1·5	1·2	7·5	6·2	13·5	11·1
16	12 19·0	12 21·0	11 45·3	1·6	1·3	7·6	6·3	13·6	11·2
17	12 19·3	12 21·3	11 45·6	1·7	1·4	7·7	6·4	13·7	11·3
18	12 19·5	12 21·5	11 45·8	1·8	1·5	7·8	6·4	13·8	11·4
19	12 19·8	12 21·8	11 46·1	1·9	1·6	7·9	6·5	13·9	11·5
20	12 20·0	12 22·0	11 46·3	2·0	1·7	8·0	6·6	14·0	11·6
21	12 20·3	12 22·3	11 46·5	2·1	1·7	8·1	6·7	14·1	11·6
22	12 20·5	12 22·5	11 46·8	2·2	1·8	8·2	6·8	14·2	11·7
23	12 20·8	12 22·8	11 47·0	2·3	1·9	8·3	6·8	14·3	11·8
24	12 21·0	12 23·0	11 47·2	2·4	2·0	8·4	6·9	14·4	11·9
25	12 21·3	12 23·3	11 47·5	2·5	2·1	8·5	7·0	14·5	12·0
26	12 21·5	12 23·5	11 47·7	2·6	2·1	8·6	7·1	14·6	12·0
27	12 21·8	12 23·8	11 48·0	2·7	2·2	8·7	7·2	14·7	12·1
28	12 22·0	12 24·0	11 48·2	2·8	2·3	8·8	7·3	14·8	12·2
29	12 22·3	12 24·3	11 48·4	2·9	2·4	8·9	7·3	14·9	12·3
30	12 22·5	12 24·5	11 48·7	3·0	2·5	9·0	7·4	15·0	12·4
31	12 22·8	12 24·8	11 48·9	3·1	2·6	9·1	7·5	15·1	12·5
32	12 23·0	12 25·0	11 49·2	3·2	2·6	9·2	7·6	15·2	12·5
33	12 23·3	12 25·3	11 49·4	3·3	2·7	9·3	7·7	15·3	12·6
34	12 23·5	12 25·5	11 49·6	3·4	2·8	9·4	7·8	15·4	12·7
35	12 23·8	12 25·8	11 49·9	3·5	2·9	9·5	7·8	15·5	12·8
36	12 24·0	12 26·0	11 50·1	3·6	3·0	9·6	7·9	15·6	12·9
37	12 24·3	12 26·3	11 50·3	3·7	3·1	9·7	8·0	15·7	13·0
38	12 24·5	12 26·5	11 50·6	3·8	3·1	9·8	8·1	15·8	13·0
39	12 24·8	12 26·8	11 50·8	3·9	3·2	9·9	8·2	15·9	13·1
40	12 25·0	12 27·0	11 51·1	4·0	3·3	10·0	8·3	16·0	13·2
41	12 25·3	12 27·3	11 51·3	4·1	3·4	10·1	8·3	16·1	13·3
42	12 25·5	12 27·5	11 51·5	4·2	3·5	10·2	8·4	16·2	13·4
43	12 25·8	12 27·8	11 51·8	4·3	3·5	10·3	8·5	16·3	13·4
44	12 26·0	12 28·0	11 52·0	4·4	3·6	10·4	8·6	16·4	13·5
45	12 26·3	12 28·3	11 52·3	4·5	3·7	10·5	8·7	16·5	13·6
46	12 26·5	12 28·5	11 52·5	4·6	3·8	10·6	8·7	16·6	13·7
47	12 26·8	12 28·8	11 52·7	4·7	3·9	10·7	8·8	16·7	13·8
48	12 27·0	12 29·0	11 53·0	4·8	4·0	10·8	8·9	16·8	13·9
49	12 27·3	12 29·3	11 53·2	4·9	4·0	10·9	9·0	16·9	13·9
50	12 27·5	12 29·5	11 53·4	5·0	4·1	11·0	9·1	17·0	14·0
51	12 27·8	12 29·8	11 53·7	5·1	4·2	11·1	9·2	17·1	14·1
52	12 28·0	12 30·0	11 53·9	5·2	4·3	11·2	9·2	17·2	14·2
53	12 28·3	12 30·3	11 54·2	5·3	4·4	11·3	9·3	17·3	14·3
54	12 28·5	12 30·5	11 54·4	5·4	4·5	11·4	9·4	17·4	14·4
55	12 28·8	12 30·8	11 54·6	5·5	4·5	11·5	9·5	17·5	14·4
56	12 29·0	12 31·1	11 54·9	5·6	4·6	11·6	9·6	17·6	14·5
57	12 29·3	12 31·3	11 55·1	5·7	4·7	11·7	9·7	17·7	14·6
58	12 29·5	12 31·6	11 55·4	5·8	4·8	11·8	9·7	17·8	14·7
59	12 29·8	12 31·8	11 55·6	5·9	4·9	11·9	9·8	17·9	14·8
60	12 30·0	12 32·1	11 55·8	6·0	5·0	12·0	9·9	18·0	14·9

50ᵐ INCREMENTS AND CORRECTIONS 51ᵐ

50ᵐ	SUN PLANETS	ARIES	MOON	v or d	Corrⁿ	v or d	Corrⁿ	v or d	Corrⁿ
s	° ′	° ′	° ′	′	′	′	′	′	′
00	12 30·0	12 32·1	11 55·8	0·0	0·0	6·0	5·1	12·0	10·1
01	12 30·3	12 32·3	11 56·1	0·1	0·1	6·1	5·1	12·1	10·2
02	12 30·5	12 32·6	11 56·3	0·2	0·2	6·2	5·2	12·2	10·3
03	12 30·8	12 32·8	11 56·5	0·3	0·3	6·3	5·3	12·3	10·4
04	12 31·0	12 33·1	11 56·8	0·4	0·3	6·4	5·4	12·4	10·4
05	12 31·3	12 33·3	11 57·0	0·5	0·4	6·5	5·5	12·5	10·5
06	12 31·5	12 33·6	11 57·3	0·6	0·5	6·6	5·6	12·6	10·6
07	12 31·8	12 33·8	11 57·5	0·7	0·6	6·7	5·6	12·7	10·7
08	12 32·0	12 34·1	11 57·7	0·8	0·7	6·8	5·7	12·8	10·8
09	12 32·3	12 34·3	11 58·0	0·9	0·8	6·9	5·8	12·9	10·9
10	12 32·5	12 34·6	11 58·2	1·0	0·8	7·0	5·9	13·0	10·9
11	12 32·8	12 34·8	11 58·5	1·1	0·9	7·1	6·0	13·1	11·0
12	12 33·0	12 35·1	11 58·7	1·2	1·0	7·2	6·1	13·2	11·1
13	12 33·3	12 35·3	11 58·9	1·3	1·1	7·3	6·1	13·3	11·2
14	12 33·5	12 35·6	11 59·2	1·4	1·2	7·4	6·2	13·4	11·3
15	12 33·8	12 35·8	11 59·4	1·5	1·3	7·5	6·3	13·5	11·4
16	12 34·0	12 36·1	11 59·7	1·6	1·3	7·6	6·4	13·6	11·4
17	12 34·3	12 36·3	11 59·9	1·7	1·4	7·7	6·5	13·7	11·5
18	12 34·5	12 36·6	12 00·1	1·8	1·5	7·8	6·6	13·8	11·6
19	12 34·8	12 36·8	12 00·4	1·9	1·6	7·9	6·6	13·9	11·7
20	12 35·0	12 37·1	12 00·6	2·0	1·7	8·0	6·7	14·0	11·8
21	12 35·3	12 37·3	12 00·8	2·1	1·8	8·1	6·8	14·1	11·9
22	12 35·5	12 37·6	12 01·1	2·2	1·9	8·2	6·9	14·2	12·0
23	12 35·8	12 37·8	12 01·3	2·3	1·9	8·3	7·0	14·3	12·0
24	12 36·0	12 38·1	12 01·6	2·4	2·0	8·4	7·1	14·4	12·1
25	12 36·3	12 38·3	12 01·8	2·5	2·1	8·5	7·2	14·5	12·2
26	12 36·5	12 38·6	12 02·0	2·6	2·2	8·6	7·2	14·6	12·3
27	12 36·8	12 38·8	12 02·3	2·7	2·3	8·7	7·3	14·7	12·4
28	12 37·0	12 39·1	12 02·5	2·8	2·4	8·8	7·4	14·8	12·5
29	12 37·3	12 39·3	12 02·8	2·9	2·4	8·9	7·5	14·9	12·5
30	12 37·5	12 39·6	12 03·0	3·0	2·5	9·0	7·6	15·0	12·6
31	12 37·8	12 39·8	12 03·2	3·1	2·6	9·1	7·7	15·1	12·7
32	12 38·0	12 40·1	12 03·5	3·2	2·7	9·2	7·7	15·2	12·8
33	12 38·3	12 40·3	12 03·7	3·3	2·8	9·3	7·8	15·3	12·9
34	12 38·5	12 40·6	12 03·9	3·4	2·9	9·4	7·9	15·4	13·0
35	12 38·8	12 40·8	12 04·2	3·5	2·9	9·5	8·0	15·5	13·0
36	12 39·0	12 41·1	12 04·4	3·6	3·0	9·6	8·1	15·6	13·1
37	12 39·3	12 41·3	12 04·7	3·7	3·1	9·7	8·2	15·7	13·2
38	12 39·5	12 41·6	12 04·9	3·8	3·2	9·8	8·2	15·8	13·3
39	12 39·8	12 41·8	12 05·1	3·9	3·3	9·9	8·3	15·9	13·4
40	12 40·0	12 42·1	12 05·4	4·0	3·4	10·0	8·4	16·0	13·5
41	12 40·3	12 42·3	12 05·6	4·1	3·5	10·1	8·5	16·1	13·6
42	12 40·5	12 42·6	12 05·9	4·2	3·5	10·2	8·6	16·2	13·6
43	12 40·8	12 42·8	12 06·1	4·3	3·6	10·3	8·7	16·3	13·7
44	12 41·0	12 43·1	12 06·3	4·4	3·7	10·4	8·8	16·4	13·8
45	12 41·3	12 43·3	12 06·6	4·5	3·8	10·5	8·8	16·5	13·9
46	12 41·5	12 43·6	12 06·8	4·6	3·9	10·6	8·9	16·6	14·0
47	12 41·8	12 43·8	12 07·0	4·7	4·0	10·7	9·0	16·7	14·1
48	12 42·0	12 44·1	12 07·3	4·8	4·0	10·8	9·1	16·8	14·1
49	12 42·3	12 44·3	12 07·5	4·9	4·1	10·9	9·2	16·9	14·2
50	12 42·5	12 44·6	12 07·8	5·0	4·2	11·0	9·3	17·0	14·3
51	12 42·8	12 44·8	12 08·0	5·1	4·3	11·1	9·3	17·1	14·4
52	12 43·0	12 45·1	12 08·2	5·2	4·4	11·2	9·4	17·2	14·5
53	12 43·3	12 45·3	12 08·5	5·3	4·5	11·3	9·5	17·3	14·6
54	12 43·5	12 45·6	12 08·7	5·4	4·5	11·4	9·6	17·4	14·6
55	12 43·8	12 45·8	12 09·0	5·5	4·6	11·5	9·7	17·5	14·7
56	12 44·0	12 46·1	12 09·2	5·6	4·7	11·6	9·8	17·6	14·8
57	12 44·3	12 46·3	12 09·4	5·7	4·8	11·7	9·8	17·7	14·9
58	12 44·5	12 46·6	12 09·7	5·8	4·9	11·8	9·9	17·8	15·0
59	12 44·8	12 46·8	12 09·9	5·9	5·0	11·9	10·0	17·9	15·1
60	12 45·0	12 47·1	12 10·2	6·0	5·1	12·0	10·1	18·0	15·2

51ᵐ	SUN PLANETS	ARIES	MOON	v or d	Corrⁿ	v or d	Corrⁿ	v or d	Corrⁿ
s	° ′	° ′	° ′	′	′	′	′	′	′
00	12 45·0	12 47·1	12 10·2	0·0	0·0	6·0	5·2	12·0	10·3
01	12 45·3	12 47·3	12 10·4	0·1	0·1	6·1	5·2	12·1	10·4
02	12 45·5	12 47·6	12 10·6	0·2	0·2	6·2	5·3	12·2	10·5
03	12 45·8	12 47·8	12 10·9	0·3	0·3	6·3	5·4	12·3	10·6
04	12 46·0	12 48·1	12 11·1	0·4	0·3	6·4	5·5	12·4	10·6
05	12 46·3	12 48·3	12 11·3	0·5	0·4	6·5	5·6	12·5	10·7
06	12 46·5	12 48·6	12 11·6	0·6	0·5	6·6	5·7	12·6	10·8
07	12 46·8	12 48·8	12 11·8	0·7	0·6	6·7	5·8	12·7	10·9
08	12 47·0	12 49·1	12 12·1	0·8	0·7	6·8	5·8	12·8	11·0
09	12 47·3	12 49·4	12 12·3	0·9	0·8	6·9	5·9	12·9	11·1
10	12 47·5	12 49·6	12 12·5	1·0	0·9	7·0	6·0	13·0	11·2
11	12 47·8	12 49·9	12 12·8	1·1	0·9	7·1	6·1	13·1	11·2
12	12 48·0	12 50·1	12 13·0	1·2	1·0	7·2	6·2	13·2	11·3
13	12 48·3	12 50·4	12 13·3	1·3	1·1	7·3	6·3	13·3	11·4
14	12 48·5	12 50·6	12 13·5	1·4	1·2	7·4	6·4	13·4	11·5
15	12 48·8	12 50·9	12 13·7	1·5	1·3	7·5	6·4	13·5	11·6
16	12 49·0	12 51·1	12 14·0	1·6	1·4	7·6	6·5	13·6	11·7
17	12 49·3	12 51·4	12 14·2	1·7	1·5	7·7	6·6	13·7	11·8
18	12 49·5	12 51·6	12 14·4	1·8	1·5	7·8	6·7	13·8	11·8
19	12 49·8	12 51·9	12 14·7	1·9	1·6	7·9	6·8	13·9	11·9
20	12 50·0	12 52·1	12 14·9	2·0	1·7	8·0	6·9	14·0	12·0
21	12 50·3	12 52·4	12 15·2	2·1	1·8	8·1	7·0	14·1	12·1
22	12 50·5	12 52·6	12 15·4	2·2	1·9	8·2	7·0	14·2	12·2
23	12 50·8	12 52·9	12 15·6	2·3	2·0	8·3	7·1	14·3	12·3
24	12 51·0	12 53·1	12 15·9	2·4	2·1	8·4	7·2	14·4	12·4
25	12 51·3	12 53·4	12 16·1	2·5	2·1	8·5	7·3	14·5	12·4
26	12 51·5	12 53·6	12 16·4	2·6	2·2	8·6	7·4	14·6	12·5
27	12 51·8	12 53·9	12 16·6	2·7	2·3	8·7	7·5	14·7	12·6
28	12 52·0	12 54·1	12 16·8	2·8	2·4	8·8	7·6	14·8	12·7
29	12 52·3	12 54·4	12 17·1	2·9	2·5	8·9	7·6	14·9	12·8
30	12 52·5	12 54·6	12 17·3	3·0	2·6	9·0	7·7	15·0	12·9
31	12 52·8	12 54·9	12 17·5	3·1	2·7	9·1	7·8	15·1	13·0
32	12 53·0	12 55·1	12 17·8	3·2	2·7	9·2	7·9	15·2	13·0
33	12 53·3	12 55·4	12 18·0	3·3	2·8	9·3	8·0	15·3	13·1
34	12 53·5	12 55·6	12 18·3	3·4	2·9	9·4	8·1	15·4	13·2
35	12 53·8	12 55·9	12 18·5	3·5	3·0	9·5	8·2	15·5	13·3
36	12 54·0	12 56·1	12 18·7	3·6	3·1	9·6	8·2	15·6	13·4
37	12 54·3	12 56·4	12 19·0	3·7	3·2	9·7	8·3	15·7	13·5
38	12 54·5	12 56·6	12 19·2	3·8	3·3	9·8	8·4	15·8	13·6
39	12 54·8	12 56·9	12 19·5	3·9	3·3	9·9	8·5	15·9	13·6
40	12 55·0	12 57·1	12 19·7	4·0	3·4	10·0	8·6	16·0	13·7
41	12 55·3	12 57·4	12 19·9	4·1	3·5	10·1	8·7	16·1	13·8
42	12 55·5	12 57·6	12 20·2	4·2	3·6	10·2	8·8	16·2	13·9
43	12 55·8	12 57·9	12 20·4	4·3	3·7	10·3	8·8	16·3	14·0
44	12 56·0	12 58·1	12 20·6	4·4	3·8	10·4	8·9	16·4	14·1
45	12 56·3	12 58·4	12 20·9	4·5	3·9	10·5	9·0	16·5	14·2
46	12 56·5	12 58·6	12 21·1	4·6	3·9	10·6	9·1	16·6	14·2
47	12 56·8	12 58·9	12 21·4	4·7	4·0	10·7	9·2	16·7	14·3
48	12 57·0	12 59·1	12 21·6	4·8	4·1	10·8	9·3	16·8	14·4
49	12 57·3	12 59·4	12 21·8	4·9	4·2	10·9	9·4	16·9	14·5
50	12 57·5	12 59·6	12 22·1	5·0	4·3	11·0	9·4	17·0	14·6
51	12 57·8	12 59·9	12 22·3	5·1	4·4	11·1	9·5	17·1	14·7
52	12 58·0	13 00·1	12 22·6	5·2	4·5	11·2	9·6	17·2	14·8
53	12 58·3	13 00·4	12 22·8	5·3	4·5	11·3	9·7	17·3	14·8
54	12 58·5	13 00·6	12 23·0	5·4	4·6	11·4	9·8	17·4	14·9
55	12 58·8	13 00·9	12 23·3	5·5	4·7	11·5	9·9	17·5	15·0
56	12 59·0	13 01·1	12 23·5	5·6	4·8	11·6	10·0	17·6	15·1
57	12 59·3	13 01·4	12 23·8	5·7	4·9	11·7	10·0	17·7	15·2
58	12 59·5	13 01·6	12 24·0	5·8	5·0	11·8	10·1	17·8	15·3
59	12 59·8	13 01·9	12 24·2	5·9	5·1	11·9	10·2	17·9	15·4
60	13 00·0	13 02·1	12 24·5	6·0	5·2	12·0	10·3	18·0	15·5

T-13

ALTITUDE CORRECTION TABLES 35°-90°—MOON

App. Alt.	35°-39° Corrⁿ	40°-44° Corrⁿ	45°-49° Corrⁿ	50°-54° Corrⁿ	55°-59° Corrⁿ	60°-64° Corrⁿ	65°-69° Corrⁿ	70°-74° Corrⁿ	75°-79° Corrⁿ	80°-84° Corrⁿ	85°-89° Corrⁿ	App. Alt.
′	° ′	° ′	° ′	° ′	° ′	° ′	° ′	° ′	° ′	° ′	° ′	′
00	35 56·5	40 53·7	45 50·5	50 46·9	55 43·1	60 38·9	65 34·6	70 30·1	75 25·3	80 20·5	85 15·6	00
10	56·4	53·6	50·4	46·8	42·9	38·8	34·4	29·9	25·2	20·4	15·5	10
20	56·3	53·5	50·2	46·7	42·8	38·7	34·3	29·7	25·0	20·2	15·3	20
30	56·2	53·4	50·1	46·5	42·7	38·5	34·1	29·6	24·9	20·0	15·1	30
40	56·2	53·3	50·0	46·4	42·5	38·4	34·0	29·4	24·7	19·9	15·0	40
50	56·1	53·2	49·9	46·3	42·4	38·2	33·8	29·3	24·5	19·7	14·8	50
00	36 56·0	41 53·1	46 49·8	51 46·2	56 42·3	61 38·1	66 33·7	71 29·1	76 24·4	81 19·6	86 14·6	00
10	55·9	53·0	49·7	46·0	42·1	37·9	33·5	29·0	24·2	19·4	14·5	10
20	55·8	52·8	49·5	45·9	42·0	37·8	33·4	28·8	24·1	19·2	14·3	20
30	55·7	52·7	49·4	45·8	41·8	37·7	33·2	28·7	23·9	19·1	14·1	30
40	55·6	52·6	49·3	45·7	41·7	37·5	33·1	28·5	23·8	18·9	14·0	40
50	55·5	52·5	49·2	45·5	41·6	37·4	32·9	28·3	23·6	18·7	13·8	50
00	37 55·4	42 52·4	47 49·1	52 45·4	57 41·4	62 37·2	67 32·8	72 28·2	77 23·4	82 18·6	87 13·7	00
10	55·3	52·3	49·0	45·3	41·3	37·1	32·6	28·0	23·3	18·4	13·5	10
20	55·2	52·2	48·8	45·2	41·2	36·9	32·5	27·9	23·1	18·2	13·3	20
30	55·1	52·1	48·7	45·0	41·0	36·8	32·3	27·7	22·9	18·1	13·2	30
40	55·0	52·0	48·6	44·9	40·9	36·6	32·2	27·6	22·8	17·9	13·0	40
50	55·0	51·9	48·5	44·8	40·8	36·5	32·0	27·4	22·6	17·8	12·8	50
00	38 54·9	43 51·8	48 48·4	53 44·6	58 40·6	63 36·4	68 31·9	73 27·2	78 22·5	83 17·6	88 12·7	00
10	54·8	51·7	48·2	44·5	40·5	36·2	31·7	27·1	22·3	17·4	12·5	10
20	54·7	51·6	48·1	44·4	40·3	36·1	31·6	26·9	22·1	17·3	12·3	20
30	54·6	51·5	48·0	44·2	40·2	35·9	31·4	26·8	22·0	17·1	12·2	30
40	54·5	51·4	47·9	44·1	40·1	35·8	31·3	26·6	21·8	16·9	12·0	40
50	54·4	51·2	47·8	44·0	39·9	35·6	31·1	26·5	21·7	16·8	11·8	50
00	39 54·3	44 51·1	49 47·6	54 43·9	59 39·8	64 35·5	69 31·0	74 26·3	79 21·5	84 16·6	89 11·7	00
10	54·2	51·0	47·5	43·7	39·6	35·3	30·8	26·1	21·3	16·5	11·5	10
20	54·1	50·9	47·4	43·6	39·5	35·2	30·7	26·0	21·2	16·3	11·4	20
30	54·0	50·8	47·3	43·5	39·4	35·0	30·5	25·8	21·0	16·1	11·2	30
40	53·9	50·7	47·2	43·3	39·2	34·9	30·4	25·7	20·9	16·0	11·0	40
50	53·8	50·6	47·0	43·2	39·1	34·7	30·2	25·5	20·7	15·8	10·9	50

H.P.	L	U	L	U	L	U	L	U	L	U	L	U	L	U	L	U	L	U	L	U	L	U	H.P.
′	′	′	′	′	′	′	′	′	′	′	′	′	′	′	′	′	′	′	′	′	′	′	′
54·0	1·1	1·7	1·3	1·9	1·5	2·1	1·7	2·4	2·0	2·6	2·3	2·9	2·6	3·2	2·9	3·5	3·2	3·8	3·5	4·1	3·8	4·5	54·0
54·3	1·4	1·8	1·6	2·0	1·8	2·2	2·0	2·5	2·3	2·7	2·5	3·0	2·8	3·2	3·0	3·5	3·3	3·8	3·6	4·1	3·9	4·4	54·3
54·6	1·7	2·0	1·9	2·2	2·1	2·4	2·3	2·6	2·5	2·8	2·7	3·0	3·0	3·3	3·2	3·5	3·5	3·8	3·7	4·1	4·0	4·3	54·6
54·9	2·0	2·2	2·2	2·3	2·3	2·5	2·5	2·7	2·7	2·9	2·9	3·1	3·2	3·3	3·4	3·5	3·6	3·8	3·9	4·0	4·1	4·3	54·9
55·2	2·3	2·3	2·5	2·4	2·6	2·6	2·8	2·8	3·0	2·9	3·2	3·1	3·4	3·3	3·6	3·5	3·8	3·7	4·0	4·0	4·2	4·2	55·2
55·5	2·7	2·5	2·8	2·6	2·9	2·7	3·1	2·9	3·2	3·0	3·4	3·2	3·6	3·4	3·7	3·5	3·9	3·7	4·1	3·9	4·3	4·1	55·5
55·8	3·0	2·6	3·1	2·7	3·2	2·8	3·3	3·0	3·5	3·1	3·6	3·3	3·8	3·4	3·9	3·6	4·1	3·7	4·2	3·9	4·4	4·0	55·8
56·1	3·3	2·8	3·4	2·9	3·5	3·0	3·6	3·1	3·7	3·2	3·8	3·3	4·0	3·4	4·1	3·6	4·2	3·7	4·4	3·8	4·5	4·0	56·1
56·4	3·6	2·9	3·7	3·0	3·8	3·1	3·9	3·2	3·9	3·3	4·0	3·4	4·1	3·5	4·3	3·6	4·4	3·7	4·5	3·8	4·6	3·9	56·4
56·7	3·9	3·1	4·0	3·1	4·1	3·2	4·1	3·3	4·2	3·3	4·3	3·4	4·3	3·5	4·4	3·6	4·5	3·7	4·6	3·8	4·7	3·8	56·7
57·0	4·3	3·2	4·3	3·3	4·3	3·3	4·4	3·4	4·4	3·4	4·5	3·5	4·5	3·5	4·6	3·6	4·7	3·6	4·7	3·7	4·8	3·8	57·0
57·3	4·6	3·4	4·6	3·4	4·6	3·4	4·6	3·5	4·7	3·5	4·7	3·5	4·7	3·6	4·8	3·6	4·8	3·6	4·8	3·7	4·9	3·7	57·3
57·6	4·9	3·6	4·9	3·6	4·9	3·6	4·9	3·6	4·9	3·6	4·9	3·6	4·9	3·6	4·9	3·6	5·0	3·6	5·0	3·6	5·0	3·6	57·6
57·9	5·2	3·7	5·2	3·7	5·2	3·7	5·2	3·7	5·2	3·7	5·1	3·6	5·1	3·6	5·1	3·6	5·1	3·6	5·1	3·6	5·1	3·6	57·9
58·2	5·5	3·9	5·5	3·8	5·5	3·8	5·4	3·8	5·4	3·7	5·4	3·7	5·3	3·7	5·3	3·6	5·2	3·6	5·2	3·5	5·2	3·5	58·2
58·5	5·9	4·0	5·8	4·0	5·8	3·9	5·7	3·9	5·6	3·8	5·6	3·8	5·5	3·7	5·5	3·6	5·4	3·6	5·3	3·5	5·3	3·4	58·5
58·8	6·2	4·2	6·1	4·1	6·0	4·1	6·0	4·0	5·9	3·9	5·8	3·8	5·7	3·7	5·6	3·6	5·5	3·5	5·4	3·5	5·3	3·4	58·8
59·1	6·5	4·3	6·4	4·3	6·3	4·2	6·2	4·1	6·1	4·0	6·0	3·9	5·9	3·8	5·8	3·6	5·7	3·5	5·6	3·4	5·4	3·3	59·1
59·4	6·8	4·5	6·7	4·4	6·6	4·3	6·5	4·2	6·4	4·1	6·2	3·9	6·1	3·8	6·0	3·7	5·8	3·5	5·7	3·4	5·5	3·2	59·4
59·7	7·1	4·6	7·0	4·5	6·9	4·4	6·8	4·3	6·6	4·1	6·5	4·0	6·3	3·8	6·2	3·7	6·0	3·5	5·8	3·3	5·6	3·2	59·7
60·0	7·5	4·8	7·3	4·7	7·2	4·5	7·0	4·4	6·9	4·2	6·7	4·0	6·5	3·9	6·3	3·7	6·1	3·5	5·9	3·3	5·7	3·1	60·0
60·3	7·8	5·0	7·6	4·8	7·5	4·7	7·3	4·5	7·1	4·3	6·9	4·1	6·7	3·9	6·5	3·7	6·3	3·5	6·0	3·2	5·8	3·0	60·3
60·6	8·1	5·1	7·9	5·0	7·7	4·8	7·6	4·6	7·3	4·4	7·1	4·2	6·9	3·9	6·7	3·7	6·4	3·4	6·2	3·2	5·9	2·9	60·6
60·9	8·4	5·3	8·2	5·1	8·0	4·9	7·8	4·7	7·6	4·5	7·3	4·2	7·1	4·0	6·8	3·7	6·6	3·4	6·3	3·2	6·0	2·9	60·9
61·2	8·7	5·4	8·5	5·2	8·3	5·0	8·1	4·8	7·8	4·5	7·6	4·3	7·3	4·0	7·0	3·7	6·7	3·4	6·4	3·1	6·1	2·8	61·2
61·5	9·1	5·6	8·8	5·4	8·6	5·1	8·3	4·9	8·1	4·6	7·8	4·3	7·5	4·0	7·2	3·7	6·9	3·4	6·5	3·1	6·2	2·7	61·5

ALTITUDE CORRECTION TABLES 0°–35°—MOON

App. Alt.	0°–4° Corrⁿ	5°–9° Corrⁿ	10°–14° Corrⁿ	15°–19° Corrⁿ	20°–24° Corrⁿ	25°–29° Corrⁿ	30°–34° Corrⁿ	App. Alt.
′	° ′	° ′	° ′	° ′	° ′	° ′	° ′	′
00	0 33·8	5 58·2	10 62·1	15 62·8	20 62·2	25 60·8	30 58·9	00
10	35·9	58·5	62·2	62·8	62·1	60·8	58·8	10
20	37·8	58·7	62·2	62·8	62·1	60·7	58·8	20
30	39·6	58·9	62·3	62·8	62·1	60·7	58·7	30
40	41·2	59·1	62·3	62·8	62·0	60·6	58·6	40
50	42·6	59·3	62·4	62·7	62·0	60·6	58·5	50
00	1 44·0	6 59·5	11 62·4	16 62·7	21 62·0	26 60·5	31 58·5	00
10	45·2	59·7	62·4	62·7	61·9	60·4	58·4	10
20	46·3	59·9	62·5	62·7	61·9	60·4	58·3	20
30	47·3	60·0	62·5	62·7	61·9	60·3	58·2	30
40	48·3	60·2	62·5	62·7	61·8	60·3	58·2	40
50	49·2	60·3	62·6	62·7	61·8	60·2	58·1	50
00	2 50·0	7 60·5	12 62·6	17 62·7	22 61·7	27 60·1	32 58·0	00
10	50·8	60·6	62·6	62·6	61·7	60·1	57·9	10
20	51·4	60·7	62·6	62·6	61·6	60·0	57·8	20
30	52·1	60·9	62·7	62·6	61·6	59·9	57·8	30
40	52·7	61·0	62·7	62·6	61·5	59·9	57·7	40
50	53·3	61·1	62·7	62·6	61·5	59·8	57·6	50
00	3 53·8	8 61·2	13 62·7	18 62·5	23 61·5	28 59·7	33 57·5	00
10	54·3	61·3	62·7	62·5	61·4	59·7	57·4	10
20	54·8	61·4	62·7	62·5	61·4	59·6	57·4	20
30	55·2	61·5	62·8	62·5	61·3	59·6	57·3	30
40	55·6	61·6	62·8	62·4	61·3	59·5	57·2	40
50	56·0	61·6	62·8	62·4	61·2	59·4	57·1	50
00	4 56·4	9 61·7	14 62·8	19 62·4	24 61·2	29 59·3	34 57·0	00
10	56·7	61·8	62·8	62·3	61·1	59·3	56·9	10
20	57·1	61·9	62·8	62·3	61·1	59·2	56·9	20
30	57·4	61·9	62·8	62·3	61·0	59·1	56·8	30
40	57·7	62·0	62·8	62·2	60·9	59·1	56·7	40
50	57·9	62·1	62·8	62·2	60·9	59·0	56·6	50

H.P.	L	U	L	U	L	U	L	U	L	U	L	U	L	U	H.P.
′	′	′	′	′	′	′	′	′	′	′	′	′	′	′	′
54·0	0·3	0·9	0·3	0·9	0·4	1·0	0·5	1·1	0·6	1·2	0·7	1·3	0·9	1·5	54·0
54·3	0·7	1·1	0·7	1·2	0·7	1·2	0·8	1·3	0·9	1·4	1·1	1·5	1·2	1·7	54·3
54·6	1·1	1·4	1·1	1·4	1·1	1·4	1·2	1·5	1·3	1·6	1·4	1·7	1·5	1·8	54·6
54·9	1·4	1·6	1·5	1·6	1·5	1·6	1·6	1·7	1·6	1·8	1·8	1·9	1·9	2·0	54·9
55·2	1·8	1·8	1·8	1·8	1·9	1·9	1·9	1·9	2·0	2·0	2·1	2·1	2·2	2·2	55·2
55·5	2·2	2·0	2·2	2·0	2·3	2·1	2·3	2·1	2·4	2·2	2·4	2·3	2·5	2·4	55·5
55·8	2·6	2·2	2·6	2·2	2·6	2·3	2·7	2·3	2·7	2·4	2·8	2·4	2·9	2·5	55·8
56·1	3·0	2·4	3·0	2·5	3·0	2·5	3·0	2·5	3·1	2·6	3·1	2·6	3·2	2·7	56·1
56·4	3·4	2·7	3·4	2·7	3·4	2·7	3·4	2·7	3·4	2·8	3·5	2·8	3·5	2·9	56·4
56·7	3·7	2·9	3·7	2·9	3·8	2·9	3·8	2·9	3·8	3·0	3·8	3·0	3·9	3·0	56·7
57·0	4·1	3·1	4·1	3·1	4·1	3·1	4·1	3·1	4·2	3·1	4·2	3·2	4·2	3·2	57·0
57·3	4·5	3·3	4·5	3·3	4·5	3·3	4·5	3·3	4·5	3·3	4·5	3·4	4·6	3·4	57·3
57·6	4·9	3·5	4·9	3·5	4·9	3·5	4·9	3·5	4·9	3·5	4·9	3·5	4·9	3·6	57·6
57·9	5·3	3·8	5·3	3·8	5·2	3·8	5·2	3·7	5·2	3·7	5·2	3·7	5·2	3·7	57·9
58·2	5·6	4·0	5·6	4·0	5·6	4·0	5·6	4·0	5·6	3·9	5·6	3·9	5·6	3·9	58·2
58·5	6·0	4·2	6·0	4·2	6·0	4·2	6·0	4·2	6·0	4·1	5·9	4·1	5·9	4·1	58·5
58·8	6·4	4·4	6·4	4·4	6·4	4·4	6·3	4·4	6·3	4·3	6·3	4·3	6·2	4·2	58·8
59·1	6·8	4·6	6·8	4·6	6·7	4·6	6·7	4·6	6·7	4·5	6·6	4·5	6·6	4·4	59·1
59·4	7·2	4·8	7·1	4·8	7·1	4·8	7·1	4·8	7·0	4·7	7·0	4·7	6·9	4·6	59·4
59·7	7·5	5·1	7·5	5·0	7·5	5·0	7·5	5·0	7·4	4·9	7·3	4·8	7·2	4·7	59·7
60·0	7·9	5·3	7·9	5·3	7·9	5·2	7·8	5·2	7·8	5·1	7·7	5·0	7·6	4·9	60·0
60·3	8·3	5·5	8·3	5·5	8·2	5·4	8·2	5·4	8·1	5·3	8·0	5·2	7·9	5·1	60·3
60·6	8·7	5·7	8·7	5·7	8·6	5·7	8·6	5·6	8·5	5·5	8·4	5·4	8·2	5·3	60·6
60·9	9·1	5·9	9·0	5·9	9·0	5·9	8·9	5·8	8·8	5·7	8·7	5·6	8·6	5·4	60·9
61·2	9·5	6·2	9·4	6·1	9·4	6·1	9·3	6·0	9·2	5·9	9·1	5·8	8·9	5·6	61·2
61·5	9·8	6·4	9·8	6·3	9·7	6·3	9·7	6·2	9·5	6·1	9·4	5·9	9·2	5·8	61·5

DIP

Ht. of Eye	Corrⁿ	Ht. of Eye	Ht. of Eye	Corrⁿ	Ht. of Eye
m		ft.	m		ft.
2·4		8·0	9·5		31·5
	−2·8			−5·5	
2·6		8·6	9·9		32·7
	−2·9			−5·6	
2·8		9·2	10·3		33·9
	−3·0			−5·7	
3·0		9·8	10·6		35·1
	−3·1			−5·8	
3·2		10·5	11·0		36·3
	−3·2			−5·9	
3·4		11·2	11·4		37·6
	−3·3			−6·0	
3·6		11·9	11·8		38·9
	−3·4			−6·1	
3·8		12·6	12·2		40·1
	−3·5			−6·2	
4·0		13·3	12·6		41·5
	−3·6			−6·3	
4·3		14·1	13·0		42·8
	−3·7			−6·4	
4·5		14·9	13·4		44·2
	−3·8			−6·5	
4·7		15·7	13·8		45·5
	−3·9			−6·6	
5·0		16·5	14·2		46·9
	−4·0			−6·7	
5·2		17·4	14·7		48·4
	−4·1			−6·8	
5·5		18·3	15·1		49·8
	−4·2			−6·9	
5·8		19·1	15·5		51·3
	−4·3			−7·0	
6·1		20·1	16·0		52·8
	−4·4			−7·1	
6·3		21·0	16·5		54·3
	−4·5			−7·2	
6·6		22·0	16·9		55·8
	−4·6			−7·3	
6·9		22·9	17·4		57·4
	−4·7			−7·4	
7·2		23·9	17·9		58·9
	−4·8			−7·5	
7·5		24·9	18·4		60·5
	−4·9			−7·6	
7·9		26·0	18·8		62·1
	−5·0			−7·7	
8·2		27·1	19·3		63·8
	−5·1			−7·8	
8·5		28·1	19·8		65·4
	−5·2			−7·9	
8·8		29·2	20·4		67·1
	−5·3			−8·0	
9·2		30·4	20·9		68·8
	−5·4			−8·1	
9·5		31·5	21·4		70·5

MOON CORRECTION TABLE

The correction is in two parts; the first correction is taken from the upper part of the table with argument apparent altitude, and the second from the lower part, with argument H.P., in the same column as that from which the first correction was taken. Separate corrections are given in the lower part for lower (L) and upper (U) limbs. All corrections are to be **added** to apparent altitude, *but 30′ is to be subtracted from the altitude of the upper limb.*

For corrections for pressure and temperature see page A4.

For bubble sextant observations ignore dip, take the mean of upper and lower limb corrections and subtract 15′ from the altitude.

App. Alt. = Apparent altitude = Sextant altitude corrected for index error and dip.

T-15

LAT 45°

DECLINATION (0°-14°) SAME NAME AS LATITUDE

N. Lat. {LHA greater than 180°......Zn=Z; LHA less than 180°..........Zn=360−Z}

LHA	0° Hc	d	Z	1° Hc	d	Z	2° Hc	d	Z	3° Hc	d	Z	4° Hc	d	Z	LHA
	° ′	′	°	° ′	′	°	° ′	′	°	° ′	′	°	° ′	′	°	
0	45 00	+60	180	46 00	+60	180	47 00	+60	180	48 00	+60	180	49 00	+60	180	360
1	45 00	60	179	46 00	60	179	47 00	59	179	47 59	60	179	48 59	60	179	359
2	44 58	60	177	45 58	60	177	46 58	60	177	47 58	60	177	48 58	60	177	358
3	44 55	60	176	45 55	60	176	46 55	60	176	47 55	60	176	48 55	60	175	357
4	44 52	60	174	45 52	59	174	46 51	60	174	47 51	60	174	48 51	60	174	356
5	44 47	+60	173	45 47	+60	173	46 47	+59	173	47 46	+60	173	48 46	+60	172	355
6	44 41	60	172	45 41	60	171	46 41	59	171	47 40	60	171	48 40	59	171	354
7	44 35	59	170	45 34	60	170	46 34	59	170	47 33	60	170	48 33	59	169	353
8	44 27	59	169	45 26	60	169	46 26	59	168	47 25	59	168	48 24	60	168	352
9	44 18	59	167	45 17	59	167	46 16	60	167	47 16	59	167	48 15	59	166	351
10	44 08	+59	166	45 07	+59	166	46 06	+59	166	47 05	+59	165	48 04	+59	165	350
11	43 57	59	165	44 56	59	164	45 55	59	164	46 54	59	164	47 53	59	164	349
12	43 46	58	163	44 44	59	163	45 43	59	163	46 42	58	162	47 40	59	162	348
13	43 33	59	162	44 32	58	162	45 30	58	161	46 28	59	161	47 27	58	161	347
14	43 19	59	161	44 18	58	160	45 16	58	160	46 14	58	160	47 12	58	159	346
15	43 05	+58	159	44 03	+58	159	45 01	+58	159	45 59	+58	158	46 57	+57	158	345
16	42 49	58	158	43 47	58	158	44 45	58	157	45 43	57	157	46 40	58	156	344
17	42 33	57	157	43 30	58	156	44 28	57	156	45 25	58	155	46 23	57	155	343
18	42 16	57	155	43 13	57	155	44 10	57	155	45 07	57	154	46 04	57	154	342
19	41 58	57	154	42 55	56	154	43 51	57	153	44 48	57	153	45 45	57	152	341
20	41 39	+56	153	42 35	+57	152	43 32	+56	152	44 28	+57	151	45 25	+56	151	340
21	41 19	55	152	42 15	56	151	43 11	57	151	44 08	56	150	45 04	56	150	339
22	40 58	56	150	41 54	56	150	42 50	56	149	43 46	56	149	44 42	55	148	338
23	40 37	55	149	41 32	56	149	42 28	56	148	43 24	55	148	44 19	55	147	337
24	40 14	56	148	41 10	55	147	42 05	56	147	43 01	55	146	43 56	55	146	336
25	39 51	+56	147	40 47	+55	146	41 42	+55	146	42 37	+54	145	43 31	+55	145	335
26	39 28	55	145	40 23	54	145	41 17	55	144	42 12	54	144	43 06	55	143	334
27	39 03	55	144	39 58	54	144	40 52	54	143	41 46	54	143	42 40	54	142	333
28	38 38	54	143	39 32	54	143	40 26	54	142	41 20	54	141	42 14	54	141	332
29	38 12	54	142	39 06	54	141	40 00	53	141	40 53	54	140	41 47	53	140	331
30	37 46	+53	141	38 39	+54	140	39 33	+53	140	40 26	+53	139	41 19	+53	138	330
31	37 19	53	140	38 12	53	139	39 05	53	139	39 58	52	138	40 50	53	137	329
32	36 51	53	139	37 44	52	138	38 36	53	137	39 29	52	137	40 21	53	136	328
33	36 22	53	137	37 15	52	137	38 07	53	136	39 00	52	136	39 52	51	135	327
34	35 53	53	136	36 46	52	136	37 38	52	135	38 30	51	135	39 21	52	134	326
35	35 24	+52	135	36 16	+52	135	37 08	+51	134	37 59	+51	133	38 50	+52	133	325
36	34 54	51	134	35 45	52	134	36 37	51	133	37 28	51	132	38 19	51	132	324
37	34 23	51	133	35 14	51	133	36 05	51	132	36 56	51	131	37 47	50	131	323
38	33 52	51	132	34 43	51	132	35 34	50	131	36 24	51	130	37 15	50	130	322
39	33 20	51	131	34 11	50	131	35 01	51	130	35 52	50	129	36 42	49	129	321
40	32 48	+50	130	33 38	+50	130	34 28	+50	129	35 18	+50	128	36 08	+50	127	320
41	32 15	50	129	33 05	50	129	33 55	50	128	34 45	49	127	35 34	49	126	319
42	31 42	50	128	32 32	49	128	33 21	50	127	34 11	49	126	35 00	49	125	318
43	31 09	49	127	31 58	49	127	32 47	49	126	33 36	49	125	34 25	49	124	317
44	30 34	50	126	31 24	49	126	32 13	48	125	33 01	49	124	33 50	48	124	316
45	30 00	+49	125	30 49	+49	125	31 38	+48	124	32 26	+48	123	33 14	+48	123	315
46	29 25	49	124	30 14	48	124	31 02	48	123	31 50	48	122	32 38	48	122	314
47	28 50	48	123	29 38	48	123	30 26	48	122	31 14	48	121	32 02	47	121	313
48	28 14	48	123	29 02	48	122	29 50	48	121	30 38	47	120	31 25	47	120	312
49	27 38	48	122	28 26	48	121	29 14	47	120	30 01	47	120	30 48	47	119	311
50	27 02	+48	121	27 50	+47	120	28 37	+47	119	29 24	+47	119	30 11	+47	118	310
51	26 25	48	120	27 13	47	119	28 00	47	118	28 47	46	118	29 33	47	117	309
52	25 48	47	119	26 35	47	118	27 22	47	118	28 09	46	117	28 55	46	116	308
53	25 11	47	118	25 58	47	117	26 45	46	117	27 31	46	116	28 17	46	115	307
54	24 34	46	117	25 20	46	117	26 06	47	116	26 53	46	115	27 39	45	115	306
55	23 56	+46	116	24 42	+46	116	25 28	+46	115	26 14	+46	114	27 00	+45	114	305
56	23 18	46	116	24 04	46	115	24 50	45	114	25 35	46	113	26 21	45	113	304
57	22 39	46	115	23 25	46	114	24 11	45	113	24 56	45	113	25 41	46	112	303
58	22 00	46	114	22 46	46	113	23 32	45	112	24 17	45	112	25 02	45	111	302
59	21 22	45	113	22 07	45	112	22 52	45	112	23 37	45	111	24 22	45	110	301
60	20 42	+46	112	21 28	+45	112	22 13	+45	111	22 58	+44	110	23 42	+45	109	300
61	20 03	45	111	20 48	45	111	21 33	45	110	22 18	44	109	23 02	45	109	299
62	19 23	45	111	20 08	45	110	20 53	45	109	21 38	44	109	22 22	44	108	298
63	18 44	44	110	19 28	45	109	20 13	44	108	20 57	44	108	21 41	44	107	297
64	18 04	44	109	18 48	44	108	19 32	45	108	20 17	44	107	21 01	44	106	296
65	17 23	+45	108	18 08	+44	108	18 52	+44	107	19 36	+44	106	20 20	+44	105	295
66	16 43	44	108	17 27	44	107	18 11	44	106	18 55	44	105	19 39	43	105	294
67	16 02	44	107	16 46	44	106	17 30	44	105	18 14	44	105	18 58	43	104	293
68	15 22	44	106	16 06	43	105	16 49	44	105	17 33	44	104	18 17	43	103	292
69	14 41	44	105	15 25	43	105	16 08	44	104	16 52	43	103	17 35	43	102	291

LHA	5° Hc	d	Z	6° Hc	d	Z	7° Hc	d	Z	8° Hc	d	Z	9° Hc	d	Z	LHA
	° ′	′	°	° ′	′	°	° ′	′	°	° ′	′	°	° ′	′	°	
0	50 00	+60	180	51 00	+60	180	52 00	+60	180	53 00	+60	180	54 00	+60	180	360
1	49 59	60	179	50 59	60	178	51 59	60	178	52 59	60	178	53 59	60	178	359
2	49 58	60	177	50 58	60	177	51 58	60	177	52 58	60	177	53 58	60	177	358
3	49 55	60	175	50 55	60	175	51 55	60	175	52 55	59	175	53 54	60	175	357
4	49 51	60	174	50 51	60	174	51 51	59	174	52 50	60	173	53 50	60	173	356
5	49 46	+59	172	50 45	+60	172	51 45	+60	172	52 45	+60	172	53 45	+59	172	355
6	49 39	60	171	50 39	60	171	51 39	59	170	52 38	60	170	53 38	59	170	354
7	49 32	60	169	50 32	59	169	51 31	59	169	52 30	60	169	53 30	59	168	353
8	49 24	59	168	50 23	59	168	51 22	59	167	52 21	60	167	53 21	59	167	352
9	49 14	59	166	50 13	59	166	51 12	59	166	52 11	59	165	53 10	59	165	351
10	49 03	+59	165	50 02	+59	164	51 01	+59	164	52 00	+59	164	52 59	+58	164	350
11	48 52	58	163	49 50	59	163	50 49	59	163	51 48	58	162	52 46	59	162	349
12	48 39	58	162	49 37	59	161	50 36	58	161	51 34	58	161	52 32	59	160	348
13	48 25	58	160	49 23	58	160	50 21	58	160	51 19	58	159	52 17	58	159	347
14	48 10	58	159	49 08	58	158	50 06	58	158	51 04	58	158	52 02	57	157	346
15	47 54	+58	157	48 52	+58	157	49 50	+57	157	50 47	+58	156	51 45	+57	156	345
16	47 38	57	156	48 35	57	156	49 32	57	155	50 29	57	155	51 26	57	154	344
17	47 20	57	155	48 17	57	154	49 14	57	154	50 11	56	153	51 07	57	153	343
18	47 01	57	153	47 58	57	153	48 55	56	152	49 51	56	152	50 47	57	151	342
19	46 42	56	152	47 38	56	151	48 34	56	151	49 30	56	150	50 26	56	150	341
20	46 21	+56	150	47 17	+56	150	48 13	+56	149	49 09	+56	149	50 05	+55	148	340
21	46 00	55	149	46 55	56	149	47 51	56	148	48 47	55	147	49 42	55	147	339
22	45 37	56	148	46 33	55	147	47 28	55	147	48 23	55	146	49 18	55	145	338
23	45 14	55	146	46 09	55	146	47 04	55	145	47 59	55	145	48 54	54	144	337
24	44 51	54	145	45 45	55	145	46 40	54	144	47 34	54	143	48 28	54	143	336
25	44 26	+54	144	45 20	+55	143	46 15	+54	143	47 09	+53	142	48 02	+54	141	335
26	44 01	54	143	44 55	53	142	45 48	54	141	46 42	53	141	47 35	54	140	334
27	43 34	54	141	44 28	54	141	45 22	53	140	46 15	53	140	47 08	53	139	333
28	43 08	53	140	44 01	53	140	44 54	53	139	45 47	53	138	46 40	52	138	332
29	42 40	53	139	43 33	53	138	44 26	52	138	45 18	53	137	46 11	52	136	331
30	42 12	+52	138	43 04	+53	137	43 57	+52	136	44 49	+52	136	45 41	+51	135	330
31	41 43	52	137	42 35	52	136	43 27	52	135	44 19	52	135	45 11	51	134	329
32	41 14	51	135	42 05	52	135	42 57	51	134	43 48	52	133	44 40	50	133	328
33	40 43	52	134	41 35	51	134	42 26	51	133	43 17	51	132	44 08	51	132	327
34	40 13	51	133	41 04	51	133	41 55	51	132	42 46	50	131	43 36	50	130	326
35	39 42	+50	132	40 32	+51	131	41 23	+50	131	42 13	+50	130	43 03	+50	129	325
36	39 10	50	131	40 00	51	130	40 51	50	130	41 41	49	129	42 30	50	128	324
37	38 37	51	130	39 28	50	129	40 18	49	129	41 07	50	128	41 57	49	127	323
38	38 05	50	129	38 55	49	128	39 44	49	127	40 33	49	127	41 22	49	126	322
39	37 31	50	128	38 21	49	127	39 10	49	126	39 59	49	126	40 48	48	125	321
40	36 58	+49	127	37 47	+49	126	38 36	+48	125	39 24	+49	125	40 13	+48	124	320
41	36 23	49	126	37 12	49	125	38 01	48	124	38 49	48	124	39 37	48	123	319
42	35 49	48	125	36 37	49	124	37 26	48	123	38 14	47	123	39 01	48	122	318
43	35 14	48	124	36 02	48	123	36 50	48	122	37 38	47	122	38 25	47	121	317
44	34 38	48	123	35 26	48	122	36 14	47	121	37 01	47	121	37 48	47	120	316
45	34 02	+48	122	34 50	+47	121	35 37	+48	120	36 25	+46	120	37 11	+47	119	315
46	33 26	47	121	34 13	48	120	35 01	46	119	35 47	47	119	36 34	46	118	314
47	32 49	48	120	33 37	46	119	34 23	47	118	35 10	46	118	35 56	46	117	313
48	32 12	47	119	32 59	47	118	33 46	46	118	34 32	46	117	35 18	46	116	312
49	31 35	47	118	32 22	46	117	33 08	46	117	33 54	46	116	34 40	46	115	311
50	30 58	+46	117	31 44	+46	116	32 30	+46	116	33 16	+45	115	34 01	+46	114	310
51	30 20	46	116	31 06	46	116	31 52	45	115	32 37	46	114	33 23	45	113	309
52	29 41	46	115	30 27	46	115	31 13	45	114	31 58	45	113	32 43	45	112	308
53	29 03	46	115	29 49	45	114	30 34	45	113	31 19	45	112	32 04	45	111	307
54	28 24	46	114	29 10	45	113	29 55	45	112	30 40	45	111	31 25	44	111	306
55	27 45	+45	113	28 30	+45	112	29 15	+45	111	30 00	+45	111	30 45	+44	110	305
56	27 06	45	112	27 51	45	111	28 36	44	110	29 20	45	110	30 05	44	109	304
57	26 27	44	111	27 11	45	110	27 56	44	110	28 40	44	109	29 24	44	108	303
58	25 47	44	110	26 31	45	110	27 16	44	109	28 00	44	108	28 44	44	107	302
59	25 07	44	109	25 51	45	109	26 36	44	108	27 20	43	107	28 03	44	106	301
60	24 27	+44	109	25 11	+44	108	25 55	+44	107	26 39	+44	106	27 23	+43	106	300
61	23 47	44	108	24 31	44	107	25 15	43	106	25 58	44	106	26 42	43	105	299
62	23 06	44	107	23 50	44	106	24 34	43	106	25 17	44	105	26 01	43	104	298
63	22 25	44	106	23 09	44	106	23 53	43	105	24 36	43	104	25 19	43	103	297
64	21 45	43	105	22 28	44	105	23 12	43	104	23 55	43	103	24 38	43	102	296
65	21 04	+43	105	21 47	+43	104	22 30	+44	103	23 14	+42	102	23 56	+43	102	295
66	20 22	44	104	21 06	43	103	21 49	43	102	22 32	43	102	23 15	42	101	294
67	19 41	43	103	20 24	44	102	21 08	42	102	21 50	43	101	22 33	43	100	293
68	19 00	43	102	19 43	43	102	20 26	43	101	21 09	42	100	21 51	43	99	292
69	18 18	43	102	19 01	43	101	19 44	43	100	20 27	42	99	21 09	43	99	291

LHA	10° Hc	d	Z	11° Hc	d	Z	12° Hc	d	Z	13° Hc	d	Z	14° Hc	d	Z	LHA
	° ′	′	°	° ′	′	°	° ′	′	°	° ′	′	°	° ′	′	°	
0	55 00	+60	180	56 00	+60	180	57 00	+60	180	58 00	+60	180	59 00	+60	180	360
1	54 59	60	178	55 59	60	178	56 59	60	178	57 59	60	178	58 59	60	178	359
2	54 58	59	177	55 57	60	177	56 57	60	176	57 57	60	176	58 57	60	176	358
3	54 54	60	175	55 54	60	175	56 54	60	175	57 54	60	175	58 54	60	174	357
4	54 50	60	173	55 50	59	173	56 49	60	173	57 49	60	173	58 49	60	173	356
5	54 44	+60	172	55 44	+59	171	56 43	+60	171	57 43	+60	171	58 43	+59	171	355
6	54 37	60	170	55 37	59	170	56 36	60	169	57 36	59	169	58 35	59	169	354
7	54 29	59	168	55 28	60	168	56 28	59	168	57 27	59	167	58 26	59	167	353
8	54 20	59	166	55 19	59	166	56 18	59	166	57 17	59	166	58 16	59	165	352
9	54 09	59	165	55 08	59	164	56 07	59	164	57 06	58	164	58 04	59	163	351
10	53 57	+59	163	54 56	+59	163	55 55	+58	162	56 53	+59	162	57 52	+58	162	350
11	53 45	58	162	54 43	58	161	55 41	58	161	56 39	59	160	57 38	58	160	349
12	53 31	58	160	54 29	58	159	55 27	57	159	56 24	58	159	57 22	58	158	348
13	53 15	58	158	54 13	58	158	55 11	57	157	56 08	58	157	57 06	57	156	347
14	52 59	58	157	53 57	57	156	54 54	57	156	55 51	57	155	56 48	57	155	346
15	52 42	+57	155	53 39	+57	155	54 36	+57	154	55 33	+56	154	56 29	+57	153	345
16	52 23	57	154	53 20	57	153	54 17	56	153	55 13	57	152	56 10	56	151	344
17	52 04	56	152	53 00	57	152	53 57	56	151	54 53	56	150	55 49	55	150	343
18	51 44	56	151	52 40	56	150	53 36	55	149	54 31	56	149	55 27	55	148	342
19	51 22	56	149	52 18	56	149	53 14	55	148	54 09	55	147	55 04	55	147	341
20	51 00	+55	148	51 55	+55	147	52 50	+55	146	53 45	+55	146	54 40	+54	145	340
21	50 37	55	146	51 32	55	146	52 27	54	145	53 21	54	144	54 15	54	144	339
22	50 13	54	145	51 07	55	144	52 02	54	143	52 56	53	143	53 49	54	142	338
23	49 48	54	143	50 42	54	143	51 36	54	142	52 30	53	141	53 23	53	141	337
24	49 22	54	142	50 16	54	141	51 10	53	141	52 03	53	140	52 56	52	139	336
25	48 56	+53	141	49 49	+53	140	50 42	+53	139	51 35	+52	139	52 27	+53	138	335
26	48 29	53	139	49 22	52	139	50 14	52	138	51 06	52	137	51 58	52	136	334
27	48 01	52	138	48 53	52	137	49 45	52	137	50 37	52	136	51 29	51	135	333
28	47 32	52	137	48 24	52	136	49 16	51	135	50 07	51	135	50 58	51	134	332
29	47 03	51	136	47 54	52	135	48 46	51	134	49 37	50	133	50 27	51	132	331
30	46 32	+52	134	47 24	+51	134	48 15	+50	133	49 05	+51	132	49 56	+50	131	330
31	46 02	51	133	46 53	50	132	47 43	51	131	48 34	50	131	49 24	49	130	329
32	45 30	51	132	46 21	50	131	47 11	50	130	48 01	50	130	48 51	49	129	328
33	44 59	50	131	45 49	50	130	46 39	49	129	47 28	49	128	48 17	49	127	327
34	44 26	50	130	45 16	49	129	46 05	50	128	46 55	48	127	47 43	49	126	326
35	43 53	+50	128	44 43	+49	128	45 32	+48	127	46 20	+49	126	47 09	+48	125	325
36	43 20	49	127	44 09	48	127	44 57	49	126	45 46	48	125	46 34	47	124	324
37	42 46	48	126	43 34	49	125	44 23	48	125	45 11	47	124	45 58	48	123	323
38	42 11	49	125	43 00	48	124	43 48	47	124	44 35	48	123	45 23	46	122	322
39	41 36	48	124	42 24	48	123	43 12	47	122	43 59	47	122	44 46	47	121	321
40	41 01	+48	123	41 49	+47	122	42 36	+47	121	43 23	+47	121	44 10	+46	120	320
41	40 25	47	122	41 12	48	121	42 00	46	120	42 46	47	119	43 33	45	119	319
42	39 49	47	121	40 36	47	120	41 23	46	119	42 09	46	118	42 55	46	118	318
43	39 12	47	120	39 59	47	119	40 46	46	118	41 32	45	117	42 17	46	117	317
44	38 35	47	119	39 22	46	118	40 08	46	117	40 54	45	116	41 39	45	116	316
45	37 58	+46	118	38 44	+46	117	39 30	+46	116	40 16	+45	116	41 01	+44	115	315
46	37 20	46	117	38 06	46	116	38 52	45	115	39 37	45	115	40 22	44	114	314
47	36 42	46	116	37 28	45	115	38 13	45	114	38 58	45	114	39 43	44	113	313
48	36 04	46	115	36 50	45	114	37 35	44	114	38 19	45	113	39 04	44	112	312
49	35 26	45	114	36 11	45	113	36 56	44	113	37 40	44	112	38 24	44	111	311
50	34 47	+45	113	35 32	+44	113	36 16	+45	112	37 01	+43	111	37 44	+44	110	310
51	34 08	44	112	34 52	45	112	35 37	44	111	36 21	43	110	37 04	44	109	309
52	33 28	45	112	34 13	44	111	34 57	44	110	35 41	43	109	36 24	43	108	308
53	32 49	44	111	33 33	44	110	34 17	44	109	35 01	43	108	35 44	43	107	307
54	32 09	44	110	32 53	44	109	33 37	43	108	34 20	43	107	35 03	43	107	306
55	31 29	+44	109	32 13	+43	108	32 56	+44	107	33 40	+43	107	34 23	+42	106	305
56	30 49	43	108	31 32	44	107	32 16	43	107	32 59	43	106	33 42	42	105	304
57	30 08	44	107	30 52	43	107	31 35	43	106	32 18	42	105	33 00	43	104	303
58	29 28	43	106	30 11	43	106	30 54	43	105	31 37	42	104	32 19	42	103	302
59	28 47	43	106	29 30	43	105	30 13	43	104	30 56	42	103	31 38	42	102	301
60	28 06	+43	105	28 49	+43	104	29 32	+42	103	30 14	+42	102	30 56	+42	102	300
61	27 25	43	104	28 08	42	103	28 50	43	102	29 33	42	102	30 15	41	101	299
62	26 44	42	103	27 26	43	102	28 09	42	102	28 51	42	101	29 33	42	100	298
63	26 02	43	102	26 45	42	102	27 27	42	101	28 09	42	100	28 51	42	99	297
64	25 21	42	102	26 03	43	101	26 46	42	100	27 28	41	99	28 09	42	99	296
65	24 39	+43	101	25 22	+42	100	26 04	+42	99	26 46	+41	99	27 27	+42	98	295
66	23 57	43	100	24 40	42	99	25 22	42	99	26 04	41	98	26 45	41	97	294
67	23 16	42	99	23 58	42	99	24 40	42	98	25 22	41	97	26 03	41	96	293
68	22 34	42	99	23 16	42	98	23 58	41	97	24 39	42	96	25 21	41	96	292
69	21 52	42	98	22 34	42	97	23 16	41	96	23 57	42	96	24 39	41	95	291

S. Lat. {LHA greater than 180°......Zn=180−Z; LHA less than 180°..........Zn=180+Z}

DECLINATION (0°-14°) SAME NAME AS LATITUDE

32

LAT 45°

N. Lat. {LHA greater than 180°....... Zn=Z; LHA less than 180°............ Zn=360−Z}

DECLINATION (0°-14°) SAME NAME AS LATITUDE

LHA	0° Hc	d	Z	1° Hc	d	Z	2° Hc	d	Z	3° Hc	d	Z	4° Hc	d	Z	5° Hc	d	Z	6° Hc	d	Z	7° Hc	d	Z	8° Hc	d	Z	9° Hc	d	Z	10° Hc	d	Z	11° Hc	d	Z	12° Hc	d	Z	13° Hc	d	Z	14° Hc	d	Z	LHA
	° ′	′	°	° ′	′	°	° ′	′	°	° ′	′	°	° ′	′	°	° ′	′	°	° ′	′	°	° ′	′	°	° ′	′	°	° ′	′	°	° ′	′	°	° ′	′	°	° ′	′	°	° ′	′	°	° ′	′	°	
70	14 00	+43	104	14 43	+44	104	15 27	+43	103	16 10	+44	102	16 54	+43	102	17 37	+43	101	18 20	+42	100	19 02	+43	99	19 45	+42	99	20 27	+43	98	21 10	+42	97	21 52	+41	96	22 33	+42	96	23 15	+41	95	23 56	+41	94	290
71	13 19	43	104	14 02	44	103	14 46	43	102	15 29	43	102	16 12	43	101	16 55	43	100	17 38	43	99	18 21	42	99	19 03	42	98	19 45	42	97	20 27	42	96	21 09	42	96	21 51	42	95	22 33	41	94	23 14	41	93	289
72	12 37	44	103	13 21	43	102	14 04	43	102	14 47	43	101	15 30	43	100	16 13	43	99	16 56	43	99	17 39	42	98	18 21	42	97	19 03	42	96	19 45	42	96	20 27	42	95	21 09	41	94	21 50	42	93	22 32	41	93	288
73	11 56	43	102	12 39	43	102	13 22	44	101	14 06	42	100	14 48	43	99	15 31	43	99	16 14	42	98	16 56	43	97	17 39	42	96	18 21	42	96	19 03	42	95	19 45	41	94	20 26	42	93	21 08	41	93	21 49	41	92	287
74	11 14	44	102	11 58	43	101	12 41	43	100	13 24	43	99	14 07	42	99	14 49	43	98	15 32	42	97	16 14	43	96	16 57	42	96	17 39	42	95	18 21	42	94	19 03	41	93	19 44	42	93	20 26	41	92	21 07	41	91	286
75	10 33	+43	101	11 16	+43	100	11 59	+43	99	12 42	+43	99	13 25	+42	98	14 07	+43	97	14 50	+42	96	15 32	+42	96	16 14	+42	95	16 56	+42	94	17 38	+42	94	18 20	+42	93	19 02	+41	92	19 43	+41	91	20 24	+41	90	285
76	09 51	43	100	10 34	43	99	11 17	43	99	12 00	42	98	12 42	43	97	13 25	43	96	14 08	42	96	14 50	42	95	15 32	42	94	16 14	42	94	16 56	42	93	17 38	41	92	18 19	42	91	19 01	41	91	19 42	41	90	284
77	09 09	43	99	09 52	43	99	10 35	43	98	11 18	42	97	12 00	43	96	12 43	42	96	13 25	43	95	14 08	42	94	14 50	42	94	15 32	42	93	16 14	41	92	16 55	42	91	17 37	41	91	18 18	41	90	18 59	41	89	283
78	08 27	43	99	09 10	43	98	09 53	43	97	10 36	42	96	11 18	43	96	12 01	42	95	12 43	42	94	13 25	42	94	14 07	42	93	14 49	42	92	15 31	42	91	16 13	41	91	16 54	42	90	17 36	41	89	18 17	41	88	282
79	07 45	43	98	08 28	43	97	09 11	42	96	09 53	43	96	10 36	42	95	11 18	43	94	12 01	42	94	12 43	42	93	13 25	42	92	14 07	42	91	14 49	42	91	15 31	41	90	16 12	41	89	16 53	42	88	17 35	41	88	281
80	07 03	+43	97	07 46	+43	96	08 29	+42	96	09 11	+43	95	09 54	+42	94	10 36	+42	94	11 18	+43	93	12 01	+42	92	12 43	+42	91	13 25	+41	91	14 06	+42	90	14 48	+42	89	15 30	+41	88	16 11	+41	88	16 52	+41	87	280
81	06 21	43	96	07 04	42	96	07 46	43	95	08 29	42	94	09 11	43	94	09 54	42	93	10 36	42	92	11 18	42	91	12 00	42	91	12 42	42	90	13 24	42	89	14 06	41	88	14 47	42	88	15 29	41	87	16 10	41	86	279
82	05 39	43	96	06 22	42	95	07 04	43	94	07 47	42	94	08 29	42	93	09 11	43	92	09 54	42	91	10 36	42	91	11 18	42	90	12 00	42	89	12 42	41	89	13 23	42	88	14 05	41	87	14 46	42	86	15 28	41	86	278
83	04 57	42	95	05 39	43	94	06 22	42	94	07 04	43	93	07 47	42	92	08 29	42	91	09 11	42	91	09 53	42	90	10 35	42	89	11 17	42	89	11 59	42	88	12 41	41	87	13 22	42	86	14 04	41	86	14 45	42	85	277
84	04 14	43	94	04 57	42	94	05 39	43	93	06 22	42	92	07 04	42	91	07 46	43	91	08 29	42	90	09 11	42	89	09 53	42	89	10 35	42	88	11 17	42	87	11 59	41	86	12 40	42	86	13 22	41	85	14 03	41	84	276
85	03 32	+42	94	04 14	+43	93	04 57	+42	92	05 39	+43	91	06 22	+42	91	07 04	+42	90	07 46	+42	89	08 28	+43	89	09 11	+42	88	09 53	+41	87	10 34	+42	86	11 16	+42	86	11 58	+41	85	12 39	+42	84	13 21	+41	83	275
86	02 50	42	93	03 32	43	92	04 15	42	91	04 57	42	91	05 39	43	90	06 22	42	89	07 04	42	89	07 46	42	88	08 28	42	87	09 10	42	86	09 52	42	86	10 34	42	85	11 16	41	84	11 57	42	84	12 39	41	83	274
87	02 07	43	92	02 50	42	91	03 32	43	91	04 15	42	90	04 57	42	89	05 39	42	89	06 21	43	88	07 04	42	87	07 46	42	86	08 28	42	86	09 10	42	85	09 52	41	84	10 33	42	84	11 15	42	83	11 57	41	82	273
88	01 25	42	91	02 07	43	91	02 50	42	90	03 32	42	89	04 14	43	89	04 57	42	88	05 39	42	87	06 21	42	86	07 03	43	86	07 46	42	85	08 28	41	84	09 09	42	84	09 51	42	83	10 33	42	82	11 15	41	81	272
89	00 42	43	91	01 25	42	90	02 07	43	89	02 50	42	89	03 32	42	88	04 14	43	87	04 57	42	86	05 39	42	86	06 21	42	85	07 03	42	84	07 45	42	84	08 27	42	83	09 09	42	82	09 51	42	81	10 33	41	81	271
90	00 00	+42	90	00 42	+43	89	01 25	+42	89	02 07	+43	88	02 50	+42	87	03 32	+42	86	04 14	+43	86	04 57	+42	85	05 39	+42	84	06 21	+42	84	07 03	+42	83	07 45	+42	82	08 27	+42	82	09 09	+42	81	09 51	+42	80	270
91	−0 42	42	89	00 00	42	89	00 42	43	88	01 25	42	87	02 07	43	86	02 50	42	86	03 32	42	85	04 14	43	84	04 57	42	84	05 39	42	83	06 21	42	82	07 03	42	82	07 45	42	81	08 27	42	80	09 09	42	79	269
92	−1 25	43	89	−0 42	42	88	00 00	42	87	00 42	43	86	01 25	42	86	02 07	43	85	02 50	42	84	03 32	43	84	04 15	42	83	04 57	42	82	05 39	42	82	06 21	43	81	07 04	42	80	07 46	42	79	08 28	42	79	268
93	−2 07	42	88	−1 25	43	87	−0 42	42	86	00 00	43	86	00 43	42	85	01 25	43	84	02 08	42	84	02 50	42	83	03 32	43	82	04 15	42	82	04 57	43	81	05 40	42	80	06 22	42	79	07 04	42	79	07 46	42	78	267
94	−2 50	43	87	−2 07	42	86	−1 25	43	86	−0 42	42	85	00 00	43	84	00 43	42	84	01 25	43	83	02 08	42	82	02 50	43	82	03 33	42	81	04 15	43	80	04 58	42	79	05 40	42	79	06 22	43	78	07 05	42	77	266
95	−3 32	+43	86	−2 49	+42	86	−2 07	+43	85	−1 24	+42	84	−0 42	+43	84	00 01	+42	83	00 43	+43	82	01 26	+43	82	02 09	+42	81	02 51	+43	80	03 34	+42	79	04 16	+43	79	04 59	+42	78	05 41	+42	77	06 23	+43	77	265
96	−4 14	42	86	−3 32	43	85	−2 49	42	84	−2 07	43	84	−1 24	43	83	−0 41	42	82	00 01	43	82	00 44	43	81	01 27	42	80	02 09	43	79	02 52	43	79	03 35	42	78	04 17	43	77	05 00	42	77	05 42	43	76	264
97	−4 57	43	85	−4 14	43	84	−3 31	42	84	−2 49	43	83	−2 06	43	82	−1 23	42	82	−0 41	43	81	00 02	43	80	00 45	43	79	01 28	42	79	02 10	43	78	02 53	43	77	03 36	42	77	04 18	43	76	05 01	43	75	263
98	−5 39	43	84	−4 56	43	84	−4 13	42	83	−3 31	43	82	−2 48	43	82	−2 05	43	81	−1 22	42	80	−0 40	43	79	00 03	43	79	00 46	43	78	01 29	43	77	02 12	43	77	02 55	42	76	03 37	43	75	04 20	43	75	262
99	−6 21	43	84	−5 38	42	83	−4 56	43	82	−4 13	43	81	−3 30	43	81	−2 47	43	80	−2 04	43	79	−1 21	43	79	−0 38	43	78	00 05	42	77	00 47	44	77	01 31	42	76	02 13	43	75	02 56	43	75	03 39	43	74	261
100				−6 20	+42	82	−5 38	+43	81	−4 55	+43	81	−4 12	+43	80	−3 29	+43	79	−2 46	+43	79	−2 03	+43	78	−1 20	+43	77	−0 37	+43	77	00 06	+43	76	00 49	+44	75	01 33	+43	75	02 16	+43	74	02 59	+43	73	260
101							−6 20	43	81	−5 37	44	80	−4 53	43	79	−4 10	43	79	−3 27	43	78	−2 44	43	77	−2 01	43	77	−1 18	43	76	−0 35	44	75	00 09	43	74	00 52	43	74	01 35	43	73	02 18	43	72	259
102										−6 18	43	79	−5 35	43	79	−4 52	43	78	−4 09	43	77	−3 26	44	77	−2 42	43	76	−1 59	43	75	−1 16	44	74	−0 32	43	74	00 11	43	73	00 54	44	72	01 38	43	72	258
103													−6 17	44	78	−5 33	43	77	−4 50	43	77	−4 07	44	76	−3 23	43	75	−2 40	44	74	−1 56	43	74	−1 13	44	73	−0 29	43	72	00 14	43	72	00 57	44	71	257
104																−6 15	44	76	−5 31	43	76	−4 48	44	75	−4 04	43	74	−3 21	44	74	−2 37	44	73	−1 53	43	72	−1 10	44	72	−0 26	43	71	00 17	44	70	256
105																			−6 12	+43	75	−5 29	+44	74	−4 45	+44	74	−4 01	+43	73	−3 18	+44	72	−2 34	+44	72	−1 50	+44	71	−1 06	+44	70	−0 22	+43	70	255
106																						−6 10	44	74	−5 26	44	73	−4 42	44	72	−3 58	44	72	−3 14	44	71	−2 30	44	70	−1 46	44	70	−1 02	44	69	254
107																									−6 06	44	72	−5 22	44	72	−4 38	44	71	−3 54	44	70	−3 10	44	70	−2 26	44	69	−1 42	45	68	253
108																												−6 02	44	71	−5 18	44	70	−4 34	44	69	−3 50	45	69	−3 05	44	68	−2 21	45	67	252
109																															−5 58	44	69	−5 14	45	69	−4 29	45	68	−3 44	44	67	−3 00	45	67	251
110																																		−5 53	+45	68	−5 08	+44	67	−4 24	+45	67	−3 39	+45	66	250
111																																					−5 47	45	67	−5 02	45	66	−4 17	45	65	249
112																																								−5 41	45	65	−4 56	45	65	248
113																																											−5 34	45	64	247
114																																											−6 12	46	63	246

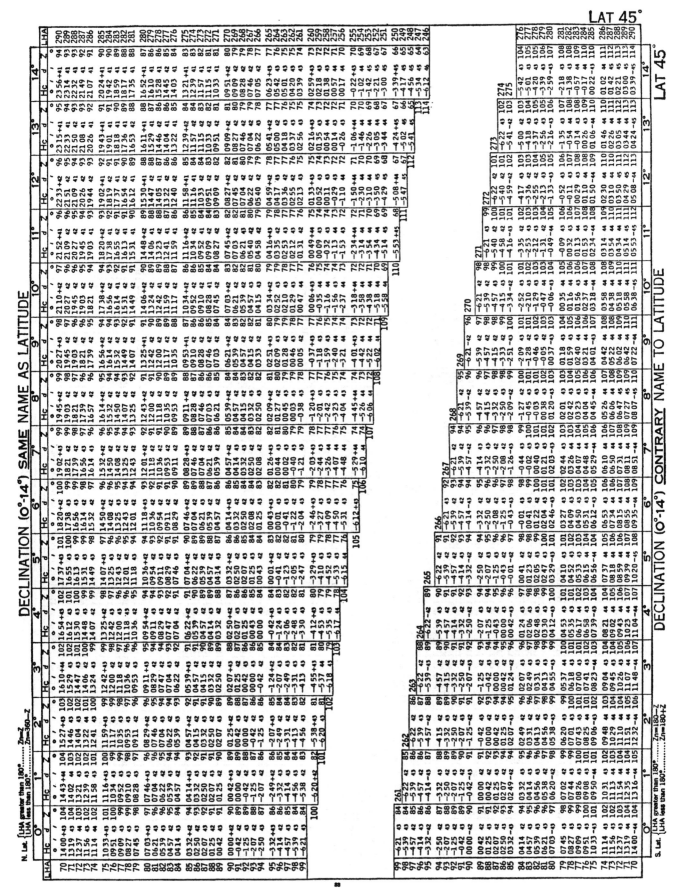

DECLINATION (0°-14°) CONTRARY NAME TO LATITUDE

LHA	0° Hc	d	Z	1° Hc	d	Z	2° Hc	d	Z	3° Hc	d	Z	4° Hc	d	Z	5° Hc	d	Z	6° Hc	d	Z	7° Hc	d	Z	8° Hc	d	Z	9° Hc	d	Z	10° Hc	d	Z	11° Hc	d	Z	12° Hc	d	Z	13° Hc	d	Z	14° Hc	d	Z	LHA
99	−6 21	43	84																																											261
98	−5 39	43	84	−6 22	42	85																																								262
97	−4 57	42	85	−5 39	43	86	−6 22	42	86																																					263
96	−4 14	43	86	−4 57	42	86	−5 39	43	87	−6 22	42	88																																		264
95	−3 32	−42	86	−4 14	−43	87	−4 57	−42	88	−5 39	−43	89	−6 22	−42	89																															265
94	−2 50	42	87	−3 32	43	88	−4 15	42	89	−4 57	42	89	−5 39	43	90	−6 22	42	91																												266
93	−2 07	43	88	−2 50	42	89	−3 32	43	89	−4 15	42	90	−4 57	42	91	−5 39	42	91	−6 21	43	92																									267
92	−1 25	42	89	−2 07	43	89	−2 50	42	90	−3 32	42	91	−4 14	43	91	−4 57	42	92	−5 39	42	93	−6 21	42	94																						268
91	−0 42	43	89	−1 25	42	90	−2 07	43	91	−2 50	42	91	−3 32	42	92	−4 14	43	93	−4 57	42	94	−5 39	42	94	−6 21	42	95																			269
90	00 00	−42	90	−0 42	−43	91	−1 25	−42	91	−2 07	−43	92	−2 50	−42	93	−3 32	−42	94	−4 14	−43	94	−4 57	−42	95	−5 39	−42	96	−6 21	−42	96																270
89	00 42	42	91	00 00	42	91	−0 42	43	92	−1 25	42	93	−2 07	43	94	−2 50	42	94	−3 32	42	95	−4 14	43	96	−4 57	42	96	−5 39	42	97	−6 21	42	98													271
88	01 25	43	91	00 42	42	92	00 00	42	93	−0 42	43	94	−1 25	42	94	−2 07	43	95	−2 50	42	96	−3 32	43	96	−4 15	42	97	−4 57	42	98	−5 39	42	98	−6 21	43	99										272
87	02 07	42	92	01 25	43	93	00 42	42	94	00 00	43	94	−0 43	42	95	−1 25	43	96	−2 08	42	96	−2 50	42	97	−3 32	43	98	−4 15	42	98	−4 57	43	99	−5 40	42	100	−6 22	42	101							273
86	02 50	43	93	02 07	42	94	01 25	43	94	00 42	42	95	00 00	43	96	−0 43	42	96	−1 25	43	97	−2 08	42	98	−2 50	43	98	−3 33	42	99	−4 15	43	100	−4 58	42	101	−5 40	42	101	−6 22	43	102				274
85	03 32	−43	94	02 49	−42	94	02 07	−43	95	01 24	−42	96	00 42	−43	96	−0 01	−42	97	−0 43	−43	98	−1 26	−43	98	−2 09	−42	99	−2 51	−43	100	−3 34	−42	101	−4 16	−43	101	−4 59	−42	102	−5 41	−42	103				275
84	04 14	42	94	03 32	43	95	02 49	42	96	02 07	43	96	01 24	43	97	00 41	42	98	−0 01	43	98	−0 44	43	99	−1 27	42	100	−2 09	43	101	−2 52	43	101	−3 35	42	102	−4 17	43	103	−5 00	42	103	−5 42	43	104	276
83	04 57	43	95	04 14	43	96	03 31	42	96	02 49	43	97	02 06	43	98	01 23	42	98	00 41	43	99	−0 02	43	100	−0 45	43	101	−1 28	42	101	−2 10	43	102	−2 53	43	103	−3 36	42	103	−4 18	43	104	−5 01	43	105	277
82	05 39	43	96	04 56	43	96	04 13	42	97	03 31	43	98	02 48	43	98	02 05	43	99	01 22	42	100	00 40	43	101	−0 03	43	101	−0 46	43	102	−1 29	43	103	−2 12	43	103	−2 55	42	104	−3 37	43	105	−4 20	43	105	278
81	06 21	43	96	05 38	42	97	04 56	43	98	04 13	43	99	03 30	43	99	02 47	43	100	02 04	43	101	01 21	43	101	00 38	43	102	−0 05	42	103	−0 47	44	103	−1 31	42	104	−2 13	43	105	−2 56	43	105	−3 39	43	106	279
80	07 03	−43	97	06 20	−42	98	05 38	−43	99	04 55	−43	99	04 12	−43	100	03 29	−43	101	02 46	−43	101	02 03	−43	102	01 20	−43	103	00 37	−43	103	−0 06	−43	104	−0 49	−44	105	−1 33	−43	105	−2 16	−43	106	−2 59	−43	107	280
79	07 45	43	98	07 02	42	99	06 20	43	99	05 37	44	100	04 53	43	101	04 10	43	101	03 27	43	102	02 44	43	103	02 01	43	103	01 18	43	104	00 35	44	105	−0 09	43	106	−0 52	43	106	−1 35	43	107	−2 18	43	108	281
78	08 27	43	99	07 44	43	99	07 01	43	100	06 18	43	101	05 35	43	101	04 52	43	102	04 09	43	103	03 26	44	103	02 42	43	104	01 59	43	105	01 16	44	106	00 32	43	106	−0 11	43	107	−0 54	44	108	−1 38	43	108	282
77	09 09	43	99	08 26	43	100	07 43	43	101	07 00	43	101	06 17	44	102	05 33	43	103	04 50	43	103	04 07	44	104	03 23	43	105	02 40	44	106	01 56	43	106	01 13	44	107	00 29	43	108	−0 14	43	108	−0 57	44	109	283
76	09 51	43	100	09 08	43	101	08 25	44	101	07 41	43	102	06 58	43	103	06 15	44	104	05 31	43	104	04 48	44	105	04 04	43	106	03 21	44	106	02 37	44	107	01 53	43	108	01 10	44	108	00 26	43	109	−0 17	44	110	284
75	10 33	−43	101	09 50	−44	101	09 06	−43	102	08 23	−44	103	07 39	−43	104	06 56	−44	104	06 12	−43	105	05 29	−44	106	04 45	−44	106	04 01	−43	107	03 18	−44	108	02 34	−44	108	01 50	−44	109	01 06	−44	110	00 22	−43	110	285
74	11 14	43	102	10 31	43	102	09 48	44	103	09 04	43	104	08 21	44	104	07 37	44	105	06 53	43	106	06 10	44	106	05 26	44	107	04 42	44	108	03 58	44	108	03 14	44	109	02 30	44	110	01 46	44	110	01 02	44	111	286
73	11 56	43	102	11 13	44	103	10 29	44	104	09 45	43	104	09 02	44	105	08 18	44	106	07 34	44	106	06 50	44	107	06 06	44	108	05 22	44	108	04 38	44	109	03 54	44	110	03 10	44	110	02 26	44	111	01 42	45	112	287
72	12 37	43	103	11 54	44	104	11 10	44	104	10 26	43	105	09 43	44	106	08 59	44	106	08 15	44	107	07 31	44	108	06 47	45	109	06 02	44	109	05 18	44	110	04 34	44	111	03 50	45	111	03 05	44	112	02 21	45	113	288
71	13 19	44	104	12 35	44	104	11 51	44	105	11 07	44	106	10 23	44	107	09 39	44	107	08 55	44	108	08 11	44	109	07 27	45	109	06 42	44	110	05 58	44	111	05 14	45	111	04 29	45	112	03 44	44	113	03 00	45	113	289
70	14 00	−44	104	13 16	−44	105	12 32	−44	106	11 48	−44	107	11 04	−44	107	10 20	−45	108	09 35	−44	109	08 51	−44	109	08 07	−45	110	07 22	−44	111	06 38	−45	111	05 53	−45	112	05 08	−44	113	04 24	−45	113	03 39	−45	114	290

S. Lat. {LHA greater than 180°....... Zn=180−Z; LHA less than 180°............ Zn=180+Z}

LAT 45°

T-17

LAT 45°

N. Lat. {LHA greater than 180°........ Zn=Z; LHA less than 180°........... Zn=360−Z}

DECLINATION (0°-14°) CONTRARY NAME TO LATITUDE

LHA	0° Hc	0° d	0° Z	1° Hc	1° d	1° Z	2° Hc	2° d	2° Z	3° Hc	3° d	3° Z	4° Hc	4° d	4° Z	5° Hc	5° d	5° Z	6° Hc	6° d	6° Z	7° Hc	7° d	7° Z	8° Hc	8° d	8° Z	9° Hc	9° d	9° Z	10° Hc	10° d	10° Z	11° Hc	11° d	11° Z	12° Hc	12° d	12° Z	13° Hc	13° d	13° Z	14° Hc	14° d	14° Z	LHA
	° ′	′	°	° ′	′	°	° ′	′	°	° ′	′	°	° ′	′	°	° ′	′	°	° ′	′	°	° ′	′	°	° ′	′	°	° ′	′	°	° ′	′	°	° ′	′	°	° ′	′	°	° ′	′	°	° ′	′	°	
69	14 41	44	105	13 57	44	106	13 13	44	107	12 29	45	107	11 44	44	108	11 00	44	109	10 16	45	109	09 31	45	110	08 46	44	111	08 02	45	111	07 17	45	112	06 32	45	113	05 47	45	113	05 02	45	114	04 17	45	115	291
68	15 22	44	106	14 38	45	107	13 53	44	107	13 09	44	108	12 25	45	109	11 40	44	109	10 56	45	110	10 11	45	111	09 26	45	111	08 41	45	112	07 56	45	113	07 11	45	114	06 26	45	114	05 41	45	115	04 56	45	115	292
67	16 02	44	107	15 18	44	107	14 34	45	108	13 49	44	109	13 05	45	110	12 20	45	110	11 35	45	111	10 50	45	112	10 05	45	112	09 20	45	113	08 35	45	114	07 50	45	114	07 05	46	115	06 19	45	116	05 34	45	116	293
66	16 43	44	108	15 59	45	108	15 14	45	109	14 29	44	110	13 45	45	110	13 00	45	111	12 15	45	112	11 30	45	112	10 45	46	113	09 59	45	114	09 14	45	114	08 29	46	115	07 43	45	116	06 58	46	116	06 12	46	117	294
65	17 23	−44	108	16 39	−45	109	15 54	−45	110	15 09	−45	110	14 24	−45	111	13 39	−45	112	12 54	−45	112	12 09	−45	113	11 24	−46	114	10 38	−45	114	09 53	−46	115	09 07	−46	116	08 21	−45	116	07 36	−46	117	06 50	−46	118	295
64	18 04	45	109	17 19	45	110	16 34	45	110	15 49	45	111	15 04	45	112	14 19	46	113	13 33	45	113	12 48	46	114	12 02	45	115	11 17	46	115	10 31	46	116	09 45	46	117	08 59	46	117	08 13	46	118	07 27	46	118	296
63	18 44	45	110	17 59	45	111	17 14	46	111	16 28	45	112	15 43	45	113	14 58	46	113	14 12	45	114	13 27	46	115	12 41	46	115	11 55	46	116	11 09	46	117	10 23	46	117	09 37	46	118	08 51	47	119	08 04	46	119	297
62	19 23	45	111	18 38	45	111	17 53	45	112	17 08	46	113	16 22	45	113	15 37	46	114	14 51	46	115	14 05	46	115	13 19	46	116	12 33	46	117	11 47	46	117	11 01	47	118	10 14	46	119	09 28	47	119	08 41	46	120	298
61	20 03	45	111	19 18	46	112	18 32	45	113	17 47	46	114	17 01	46	114	16 15	46	115	15 29	46	116	14 43	46	116	13 57	46	117	13 11	47	118	12 24	46	118	11 38	47	119	10 51	46	119	10 05	47	120	09 18	47	121	299
60	20 42	−45	112	19 57	−46	113	19 11	−45	114	18 26	−46	114	17 40	−46	115	16 54	−47	116	16 07	−46	116	15 21	−46	117	14 35	−47	118	13 48	−46	118	13 02	−47	119	12 15	−47	120	11 28	−47	120	10 41	−47	121	09 54	−47	122	300
59	21 22	46	113	20 36	46	114	19 50	46	114	19 04	46	115	18 18	46	116	17 32	47	116	16 45	46	117	15 59	47	118	15 12	47	118	14 25	46	119	13 39	47	120	12 52	47	120	12 05	48	121	11 17	47	122	10 30	47	122	301
58	22 00	45	114	21 15	46	115	20 29	47	115	19 42	46	116	18 56	46	117	18 10	47	117	17 23	47	118	16 36	47	119	15 49	47	119	15 02	47	120	14 15	47	121	13 28	47	121	12 41	48	122	11 53	47	122	11 06	48	123	302
57	22 39	46	115	21 53	46	115	21 07	47	116	20 20	46	117	19 34	47	117	18 47	47	118	18 00	47	119	17 13	47	119	16 26	47	120	15 39	47	121	14 52	48	121	14 04	47	122	13 17	48	123	12 29	48	123	11 41	47	124	303
56	23 18	47	116	22 31	46	116	21 45	47	117	20 58	47	118	20 11	47	118	19 24	47	119	18 37	47	120	17 50	47	120	17 03	48	121	16 15	47	122	15 28	48	122	14 40	48	123	13 52	48	123	13 04	47	124	12 17	49	125	304
55	23 56	−47	116	23 09	−46	117	22 23	−47	118	21 36	−47	118	20 49	−48	119	20 01	−47	120	19 14	−47	120	18 27	−48	121	17 39	−48	122	16 51	−47	122	16 04	−48	123	15 16	−48	124	14 28	−48	124	13 40	−49	125	12 51	−48	125	305
54	24 34	47	117	23 47	47	118	23 00	47	119	22 13	47	119	21 26	48	120	20 38	47	121	19 51	48	121	19 03	48	122	18 15	48	123	17 27	48	123	16 39	48	124	15 51	48	124	15 03	49	125	14 14	48	126	13 26	49	126	306
53	25 11	47	118	24 24	47	119	23 37	47	119	22 50	48	120	22 02	47	121	21 15	48	121	20 27	48	122	19 39	48	123	18 51	49	123	18 02	48	124	17 14	48	125	16 26	49	125	15 37	48	126	14 49	49	126	14 00	49	127	307
52	25 48	47	119	25 01	47	120	24 14	48	120	23 26	48	121	22 38	47	122	21 51	48	122	21 03	49	123	20 14	48	124	19 26	48	124	18 38	49	125	17 49	49	125	17 00	49	126	16 11	49	127	15 22	49	127	14 33	49	128	308
51	26 25	47	120	25 38	48	121	24 50	48	121	24 02	48	122	23 14	48	123	22 26	48	123	21 38	48	124	20 50	49	124	20 01	49	125	19 12	49	126	18 23	49	126	17 34	49	127	16 45	49	128	15 56	49	128	15 07	50	129	309
50	27 02	−48	121	26 14	−48	121	25 26	−48	122	24 38	−48	123	23 50	−48	123	23 02	−49	124	22 13	−49	125	21 24	−49	125	20 35	−49	126	19 46	−49	127	18 57	−49	127	18 08	−49	128	17 19	−50	128	16 29	−49	129	15 40	−50	130	310
49	27 38	48	122	26 50	48	122	26 02	48	123	25 14	49	124	24 25	48	124	23 37	49	125	22 48	49	126	21 59	49	126	21 10	50	127	20 20	49	127	19 31	50	128	18 41	49	129	17 52	50	129	17 02	50	130	16 12	50	130	311
48	28 14	48	123	27 26	48	123	26 38	49	124	25 49	49	125	25 00	49	125	24 11	49	126	23 22	49	126	22 33	50	127	21 43	49	128	20 54	50	128	20 04	50	129	19 14	49	129	18 25	50	130	17 35	51	131	16 44	50	131	312
47	28 50	49	123	28 01	48	124	27 13	49	125	26 24	49	125	25 35	49	126	24 46	50	127	23 56	49	127	23 07	50	128	22 17	50	129	21 27	50	129	20 37	50	130	19 47	50	130	18 57	50	131	18 07	51	131	17 16	50	132	313
46	29 25	49	124	28 36	49	125	27 47	49	126	26 58	49	126	26 09	50	127	25 19	49	128	24 30	50	128	23 40	50	129	22 50	50	129	22 00	50	130	21 10	51	131	20 19	50	131	19 29	51	132	18 38	51	132	17 47	50	133	314
45	30 00	−49	125	29 11	−49	126	28 22	−50	127	27 32	−49	127	26 43	−50	128	25 53	−50	129	25 03	−50	129	24 13	−51	130	23 22	−50	130	22 32	−50	131	21 42	−51	132	20 51	−51	132	20 00	−51	133	19 09	−51	133	18 18	−51	134	315
44	30 34	49	126	29 45	49	127	28 56	50	128	28 06	50	128	27 16	50	129	26 26	50	129	25 36	51	130	24 45	50	131	23 55	51	131	23 04	51	132	22 13	51	132	21 22	51	133	20 31	51	134	19 40	51	134	18 49	52	135	316
43	31 09	50	127	30 19	50	128	29 29	50	129	28 39	50	129	27 49	51	130	26 58	50	130	26 08	51	131	25 17	51	132	24 26	51	132	23 35	51	133	22 44	51	133	21 53	51	134	21 02	52	134	20 10	51	135	19 19	52	136	317
42	31 42	50	128	30 52	50	129	30 02	50	129	29 12	51	130	28 21	51	131	27 30	50	131	26 40	51	132	25 49	51	133	24 58	52	133	24 06	51	134	23 15	52	134	22 23	51	135	21 32	52	135	20 40	52	136	19 48	52	136	318
41	32 15	50	129	31 25	50	130	30 35	51	130	29 44	51	131	28 53	51	132	28 02	51	132	27 11	51	133	26 20	52	133	25 28	51	134	24 37	52	135	23 45	52	135	22 53	52	136	22 01	52	136	21 09	52	137	20 17	52	137	319
40	32 48	−51	130	31 57	−50	131	31 07	−51	131	30 16	−51	132	29 25	−52	133	28 33	−51	133	27 42	−52	134	26 50	−51	134	25 59	−52	135	25 07	−52	136	24 15	−52	136	23 23	−52	137	22 31	−53	137	21 38	−52	138	20 46	−53	138	320
39	33 20	51	131	32 29	51	132	31 38	51	132	30 47	51	133	29 56	52	134	29 04	52	134	28 12	52	135	27 20	52	135	26 28	52	136	25 36	52	136	24 44	52	137	23 52	53	138	22 59	52	138	22 07	53	139	21 14	53	139	321
38	33 52	51	132	33 01	52	133	32 09	51	133	31 18	52	134	30 26	52	135	29 34	52	135	28 42	52	136	27 50	52	136	26 58	53	137	26 05	52	137	25 13	53	138	24 20	53	138	23 27	53	139	22 34	53	140	21 41	53	140	322
37	34 23	51	133	33 32	52	134	32 40	52	134	31 48	52	135	30 56	52	136	30 04	53	136	29 11	52	137	28 19	53	137	27 26	52	138	26 34	53	138	25 41	53	139	24 48	53	139	23 55	53	140	23 02	54	140	22 08	53	141	323
36	34 54	52	134	34 02	52	135	33 10	52	135	32 18	53	136	31 25	52	137	30 33	53	137	29 40	52	138	28 48	53	138	27 55	53	139	27 02	53	139	26 09	54	140	25 15	53	140	24 22	54	141	23 28	53	141	22 35	54	142	324
35	35 24	−52	135	34 32	−53	136	33 39	−52	137	32 47	−53	137	31 54	−53	138	31 01	−52	138	30 09	−53	139	29 16	−54	139	28 22	−53	140	27 29	−53	140	26 36	−54	141	25 42	−54	141	24 48	−53	142	23 55	−54	142	23 01	−54	143	325
34	35 53	52	136	35 01	53	137	34 08	52	138	33 16	53	138	32 23	54	139	31 29	53	139	30 36	53	140	29 43	54	140	28 49	53	141	27 56	54	141	27 02	54	142	26 08	54	142	25 14	54	143	24 20	54	143	23 26	54	144	326
33	36 22	52	137	35 30	53	138	34 37	53	139	33 44	54	139	32 50	53	140	31 57	54	140	31 03	53	141	30 10	54	141	29 16	54	142	28 22	54	142	27 28	54	143	26 34	54	143	25 40	55	144	24 45	54	144	23 51	54	145	327
32	36 51	53	139	35 58	54	139	35 04	53	140	34 11	54	140	33 17	53	141	32 24	54	141	31 30	54	142	30 36	54	142	29 42	54	143	28 48	55	143	27 53	54	144	26 59	54	144	26 05	55	145	25 10	55	145	24 15	54	146	328
31	37 19	54	140	36 25	53	140	35 32	54	141	34 38	54	141	33 44	54	142	32 50	54	142	31 56	54	143	31 02	55	143	30 07	54	144	29 13	55	144	28 18	55	145	27 23	54	145	26 29	55	146	25 34	55	146	24 39	55	147	329
30	37 46	−54	141	36 52	−54	141	35 58	−54	142	35 04	−54	142	34 10	−54	143	33 16	−55	143	32 21	−54	144	31 27	−55	144	30 32	−55	145	29 37	−55	145	28 42	−55	146	27 47	−55	146	26 52	−55	147	25 57	−55	147	25 02	−55	148	330
29	38 12	54	142	37 18	54	143	36 24	54	143	35 30	55	144	34 35	55	144	33 40	54	145	32 46	55	145	31 51	55	146	30 56	55	146	30 01	55	146	29 06	55	147	28 11	56	147	27 15	55	148	26 20	56	148	25 24	55	149	331
28	38 38	54	143	37 44	55	144	36 49	55	144	35 54	54	145	35 00	55	145	34 05	55	146	33 10	55	146	32 15	56	147	31 19	55	147	30 24	55	148	29 29	56	148	28 33	55	148	27 38	56	149	26 42	56	149	25 46	56	150	332
27	39 03	54	144	38 09	55	145	37 14	55	145	36 19	55	146	35 24	56	146	34 28	55	147	33 33	55	147	32 38	56	148	31 42	55	148	30 47	56	149	29 51	56	149	28 55	56	149	27 59	56	150	27 03	56	150	26 07	56	151	333
26	39 28	55	145	38 33	56	146	37 37	55	146	36 42	55	147	35 47	56	147	34 51	55	148	33 56	56	148	33 00	56	149	32 04	56	149	31 08	56	150	30 12	56	150	29 16	56	150	28 20	56	151	27 24	56	151	26 28	57	152	334
25	39 51	−55	147	38 56	−55	147	38 01	−56	148	37 05	−56	148	36 09	−55	149	35 14	−56	149	34 18	−56	149	33 22	−56	150	32 26	−57	150	31 29	−56	151	30 33	−56	151	29 37	−56	152	28 41	−57	152	27 44	−56	152	26 48	−57	153	335
24	40 14	55	148	39 19	56	148	38 23	56	149	37 27	56	149	36 31	56	150	35 35	56	150	34 39	56	151	33 43	57	151	32 46	56	151	31 50	57	152	30 53	56	152	29 57	57	153	29 00	57	153	28 03	56	153	27 07	57	154	336
23	40 37	56	149	39 41	56	150	38 45	57	150	37 48	56	150	36 52	56	151	35 56	57	151	34 59	56	152	34 03	57	152	33 06	56	153	32 10	57	153	31 13	57	153	30 16	57	154	29 19	57	154	28 22	57	154	27 25	57	155	337
22	40 58	56	150	40 02	57	151	39 05	56	151	38 09	57	152	37 12	56	152	36 16	57	152	35 19	57	153	34 22	57	153	33 25	56	154	32 29	57	154	31 32	58	154	30 34	57	155	29 37	57	155	28 40	57	155	27 43	57	156	338
21	41 19	57	152	40 22	56	152	39 26	57	152	38 29	57	153	37 32	57	153	36 35	57	154	35 38	57	154	34 41	57	154	33 44	57	155	32 47	57	155	31 50	58	156	30 52	57	156	29 55	58	156	28 57	57	157	28 00	57	157	339
20	41 39	−57	153	40 42	−57	153	39 45	−57	154	38 48	−57	154	37 51	−57	154	36 54	−58	155	35 56	−57	155	34 59	−57	156	34 02	−58	156	33 04	−57	156	32 07	−58	157	31 09	−57	157	30 12	−58	157	29 14	−58	158	28 16	−57	158	340
19	41 58	58	154	41 00	57	154	40 03	57	155	39 06	57	155	38 09	58	156	37 11	57	156	36 14	58	156	35 16	57	157	34 19	58	157	33 21	58	157	32 23	57	158	31 26	58	158	30 28	58	158	29 30	58	159	28 32	58	159	341
18	42 16	58	155	41 18	57	156	40 21	58	156	39 23	57	157	38 26	58	157	37 28	58	157	36 30	57	158	35 33	58	158	34 35	58	158	33 37	58	159	32 39	58	159	31 41	58	159	30 43	58	159	29 45	58	160	28 47	58	160	342
17	42 33	58	157	41 35	57	157	40 38	58	157	39 40	58	158	38 42	58	158	37 44	58	158	36 46	58	159	35 48	58	159	34 50	58	159	33 52	58	160	32 54	58	160	31 56	58	160	30 58	59	161	29 59	58	161	29 01	58	161	343
16	42 49	58	158	41 51	57	158	40 54	58	159	39 56	59	159	38 57	58	159	37 59	58	160	37 01	58	160	36 03	58	160	35 05	59	161	34 06	58	161	33 08	58	161	32 10	59	161	31 11	58	162	30 13	59	162	29 14	58	162	344
15	43 05	−58	159	42 07	−58	160	41 09	−59	160	40 10	−58	160	39 12	−58	161	38 14	−59	161	37 15	−58	161	36 17	−59	161	35 18	−58	162	34 20	−59	162	33 21	−58	162	32 23	−59	163	31 24	−58	163	30 26	−59	163	29 27	−59	163	345
14	43 19	58	161	42 21	58	161	41 23	59	161	40 24	58	162	39 26	59	162	38 27	58	162	37 29	59	162	36 30	59	163	35 31	58	163	34 33	59	163	33 34	59	163	32 35	59	164	31 36	58	164	30 38	59	164	29 39	59	164	346
13	43 33	59	162	42 34	58	162	41 36	59	163	40 37	58	163	39 39	59	163	38 40	59	163	37 41	59	164	36 42	59	164	35 43	58	164	34 45	59	164	33 46	59	165	32 47	59	165	31 48	59	165	30 49	59	165	29 50	59	165	347
12	43 46	59	163	42 47	59	164	41 48	59	164	40 49	59	164	39 50	58	164	38 52	59	165	37 53	59	165	36 54	59	165	35 55	59	165	34 56	59	166	33 57	59	166	32 58	60	166	31 58	59	166	30 59	59	166	30 00	59	167	348
11	43 57	58	165	42 59	59	165	42 00	60	165	41 00	59	165	40 01	59	166	39 02	59	166	38 03	59	166	37 04	59	166	36 05	59	167	35 06	59	167	34 07	60	167	33 07	59	167	32 08	59	167	31 09	59	168	30 10	60	168	349
10	44 08	−59	166	43 09	−59	166	42 10	−59	167	41 11	−59	167	40 12	−60	167	39 12	−59	167	38 13	−59	167	37 14	−60	168	36 14	−59	168	35 15	−59	168	34 16	−59	168	33 17	−60	168	32 17	−59	168	31 18	−60	169	30 18	−59	169	350
9	44 18	59	167	43 19	60	168	42 19	59	168	41 20	59	168	40 21	60	168	39 21	59	168	38 22	59	169	37 23	60	169	36 23	59	169	35 24	60	169	34 24	59	169	33 25	60	169	32 25	59	170	31 26	60	170	30 26	59	170	351
8	44 27	60	169	43 27	59	169	42 28	60	169	41 28	59	169	40 29	60	170	39 29	59	170	38 30	60	170	37 30	59	170	36 31	60	170	35 31	59	170	34 32	60	170	33 32	59	171	32 33	60	171	31 33	60	171	30 33	59	171	352
7	44 35	60	170	43 35	60	170	42 35	59	171	41 36	60	171	40 36	59	171	39 37	60	171	38 37	60	171	37 37	59	171	36 38	60	171	35 38	60	172	34 38	59	172	33 39	60	172	32 39	60	172	31 39	59	172	30 40	60	172	353
6	44 41	59	172	43 42	60	172	42 42	60	172	41 42	60	172	40 42	59	172	39 43	60	172	38 43	60	172	37 43	59	173	36 44	60	173	35 44	60	173	34 44	60	173	33 44	59	173	32 45	60	173	31 45	60	173	30 45	60	173	354
5	44 47	−60	173	43 47	−60	173	42 47	−59	173	41 48	−60	173	40 48	−60	173	39 48	−60	174	38 48	−60	174	37 48	−59	174	36 49	−60	174	35 49	−60	174	34 49	−60	174	33 49	−60	174	32 49	−60	174	31 49	−59	174	30 50	−60	174	355
4	44 52	60	174	43 52	60	174	42 52	60	175	41 52	60	175	40 52	60	175	39 52	60	175	38 52	59	175	37 53	60	175	36 53	60	175	35 53	60	175	34 53	60	175	33 53	60	175	32 53	60	175	31 53	60	175	30 53	60	176	356
3	44 55	60	176	43 55	59	176	42 56	60	176	41 56	60	176	40 56	60	176	39 56	60	176	38 56	60	176	37 56	60	176	36 56	60	176	35 56	60	176	34 56	60	176	33 56	60	176	32 56	60	177	31 56	60	177	30 56	60	177	357
2	44 58	60	177	43 58	60	177	42 58	60	177	41 58	60	177	40 58	60	177	39 58	60	177	38 58	60	177	37 58	60	178	36 58	60	178	35 58	60	178	34 58	60	178	33 58	60	178	32 58	60	178	31 58	60	178	30 58	60	178	358
1	45 00	60	179	44 00	60	179	43 00	60	179	42 00	60	179	41 00	60	179	40 00	60	179	39 00	60	179	38 00	60	179	37 00	60	179	36 00	60	179	35 00	60	179	34 00	60	179	33 00	60	179	32 00	60	179	31 00	60	179	359
0	45 00	−60	180	44 00	−60	180	43 00	−60	180	42 00	−60	180	41 00	−60	180	40 00	−60	180	39 00	−60	180	38 00	−60	180	37 00	−60	180	36 00	−60	180	35 00	−60	180	34 00	−60	180	33 00	−60	180	32 00	−60	180	31 00	−60	180	360

S. Lat. {LHA greater than 180°........ Zn=180−Z; LHA less than 180°........... Zn=180+Z}

DECLINATION (0°-14°) CONTRARY NAME TO LATITUDE

LAT 45°

LAT 45°

N. Lat. {LHA greater than 180°.......Zn=Z; LHA less than 180°..........Zn=360−Z}

DECLINATION (15°-29°) SAME NAME AS LATITUDE

LHA	15° Hc	15° d	15° Z	16° Hc	16° d	16° Z	17° Hc	17° d	17° Z	18° Hc	18° d	18° Z	19° Hc	19° d	19° Z	20° Hc	20° d	20° Z	21° Hc	21° d	21° Z
	° ′	′	°	° ′	′	°	° ′	′	°	° ′	′	°	° ′	′	°	° ′	′	°	° ′	′	°
0	60 00	+60	180	61 00	+60	180	62 00	+60	180	63 00	+60	180	64 00	+60	180	65 00	+60	180	66 00	+60	180
1	59 59	60	178	60 59	60	178	61 59	60	178	62 59	60	178	63 59	60	178	64 59	60	178	65 59	60	178
2	59 57	60	176	60 57	60	176	61 57	60	176	62 57	60	176	63 57	60	176	64 57	60	176	65 57	60	175
3	59 54	59	174	60 53	60	174	61 53	60	174	62 53	60	174	63 53	60	174	64 53	59	173	65 52	60	173
4	59 49	59	172	60 48	60	172	61 48	60	172	62 48	59	172	63 47	60	171	64 47	60	171	65 47	59	171
5	59 42	+60	170	60 42	+59	170	61 41	+60	170	62 41	+59	170	63 40	+60	169	64 40	+59	169	65 39	+59	169
6	59 34	60	169	60 34	59	168	61 33	59	168	62 32	60	168	63 32	59	167	64 31	59	167	65 30	59	166
7	59 25	59	167	60 24	60	166	61 24	58	166	62 22	59	166	63 21	59	165	64 20	59	165	65 19	59	164
8	59 15	59	165	60 14	58	164	61 12	59	164	62 11	59	164	63 10	58	163	64 08	59	163	65 07	58	162
9	59 03	59	163	60 02	58	163	61 00	58	162	61 58	59	162	62 57	58	161	63 55	58	161	64 53	58	160
10	58 50	+58	161	59 48	+58	161	60 46	+58	160	61 44	+58	160	62 42	+58	159	63 40	+58	158	64 38	+57	158
11	58 36	57	159	59 33	58	159	60 31	58	158	61 29	57	158	62 26	58	157	63 24	57	156	64 21	57	156
12	58 20	57	158	59 17	58	157	60 15	57	156	61 12	57	156	62 09	57	155	63 06	57	154	64 03	56	154
13	58 03	57	156	59 00	57	155	59 57	57	155	60 54	57	154	61 51	56	153	62 47	56	153	63 43	56	152
14	57 45	57	154	58 42	56	153	59 38	57	153	60 35	56	152	61 31	56	151	62 27	55	151	63 22	56	150
15	57 26	+56	152	58 22	+56	152	59 18	+56	151	60 14	+56	150	61 10	+55	150	62 05	+55	149	63 00	+55	148
16	57 06	56	151	58 02	55	150	58 57	56	149	59 53	55	149	60 48	55	148	61 43	54	147	62 37	54	146
17	56 44	56	149	57 40	55	148	58 35	55	148	59 30	55	147	60 25	54	146	61 19	54	145	62 13	54	144
18	56 22	55	147	57 17	55	147	58 12	54	146	59 06	54	145	60 00	54	144	60 54	54	143	61 48	53	142
19	55 59	54	146	56 53	54	145	57 47	54	144	58 41	54	143	59 35	53	143	60 28	53	142	61 21	53	141
20	55 34	+54	144	56 28	+54	144	57 22	+54	143	58 16	+53	142	59 09	+52	141	60 01	+53	140	60 54	+52	139
21	55 09	54	143	56 03	53	142	56 56	53	141	57 49	53	140	58 42	52	139	59 34	51	138	60 25	52	137
22	54 43	53	141	55 36	53	140	56 29	52	140	57 21	52	139	58 13	52	138	59 05	51	137	59 56	51	136
23	54 16	53	140	55 09	52	139	56 01	52	138	56 53	52	137	57 45	51	136	58 36	50	135	59 26	50	134
24	53 48	52	138	54 40	52	138	55 32	52	137	56 24	51	136	57 15	50	135	58 05	50	134	58 55	50	133
25	53 20	+51	137	54 11	+52	136	55 03	+51	135	55 54	+50	134	56 44	+50	133	57 34	+50	132	58 24	+49	131
26	52 50	51	136	53 41	51	135	54 32	51	134	55 23	50	133	56 13	50	132	57 03	49	131	57 52	48	130
27	52 20	51	134	53 11	50	133	54 01	50	132	54 51	50	131	55 41	49	130	56 30	49	129	57 19	48	128
28	51 49	51	133	52 40	50	132	53 30	49	131	54 19	49	130	55 08	49	129	55 57	48	128	56 45	47	127
29	51 18	50	132	52 08	49	131	52 57	49	130	53 46	49	129	54 35	48	128	55 23	48	127	56 11	47	126
30	50 46	+49	130	51 35	+49	129	52 24	+49	128	53 13	+48	127	54 01	+48	126	54 49	+47	125	55 36	+46	124
31	50 13	49	129	51 02	49	128	51 51	48	127	52 39	48	126	53 27	47	125	54 14	47	124	55 01	46	123
32	49 40	48	128	50 28	49	127	51 17	48	126	52 05	47	125	52 52	47	124	53 39	46	123	54 25	45	122
33	49 06	48	127	49 54	48	126	50 42	48	125	51 30	46	124	52 16	47	123	53 03	46	122	53 49	45	121
34	48 32	48	125	49 20	47	124	50 07	47	124	50 54	46	123	51 40	46	122	52 26	46	121	53 12	45	119
35	47 57	+47	124	48 44	+47	123	49 31	+47	122	50 18	+46	121	51 04	+46	120	51 50	+45	119	52 35	+44	118
36	47 21	48	123	48 09	46	122	48 55	47	121	49 42	45	120	50 27	45	119	51 12	45	118	51 57	44	117
37	46 46	46	122	47 32	47	121	48 19	46	120	49 05	45	119	49 50	45	118	50 35	44	117	51 19	44	116
38	46 09	47	121	46 56	46	120	47 42	45	119	48 27	45	118	49 12	45	117	49 57	44	116	50 41	43	115
39	45 33	46	120	46 19	46	119	47 05	45	118	47 50	44	117	48 34	45	116	49 19	43	115	50 02	43	114
40	44 56	+46	119	45 42	+45	118	46 27	+45	117	47 12	+44	116	47 56	+44	115	48 40	+43	114	49 23	+43	113
41	44 18	46	118	45 04	45	117	45 49	44	116	46 33	44	115	47 17	44	114	48 01	43	113	48 44	42	112
42	43 41	45	117	44 26	45	116	45 11	44	115	45 55	44	114	46 39	43	113	47 22	42	112	48 04	42	111
43	43 03	44	116	43 47	45	115	44 32	44	114	45 16	43	113	45 59	43	112	46 42	43	111	47 25	41	110
44	42 24	45	115	43 09	44	114	43 53	44	113	44 37	43	112	45 20	42	111	46 02	43	110	46 45	41	109
45	41 45	+45	114	42 30	+44	113	43 14	+43	112	43 57	+43	111	44 40	+42	110	45 22	+42	109	46 04	+42	108
46	41 06	45	113	41 51	43	112	42 34	43	111	43 17	43	110	44 00	42	109	44 42	42	108	45 24	41	107
47	40 27	44	112	41 11	43	111	41 54	43	110	42 37	43	109	43 20	42	108	44 02	41	107	44 43	41	106
48	39 48	43	111	40 31	43	110	41 14	43	109	41 57	42	108	42 39	42	107	43 21	41	106	44 02	41	105
49	39 08	43	110	39 51	43	109	40 34	43	108	41 17	42	107	41 59	41	106	42 40	41	105	43 21	41	104
50	38 28	+43	109	39 11	+43	108	39 54	+42	107	40 36	+42	106	41 18	+41	105	41 59	+41	104	42 40	+40	103
51	37 48	43	108	38 31	42	107	39 13	42	106	39 55	42	106	40 37	41	105	41 18	41	104	41 59	40	103
52	37 07	43	107	37 50	42	106	38 32	42	106	39 14	42	105	39 56	41	104	40 37	40	103	41 17	40	102
53	36 27	42	107	37 09	42	106	37 51	42	105	38 33	41	104	39 14	41	103	39 55	41	102	40 36	40	101
54	35 46	42	106	36 28	42	105	37 10	42	104	37 52	41	103	38 33	41	102	39 14	40	101	39 54	40	100
55	35 05	+42	105	35 47	+42	104	36 29	+41	103	37 10	+41	102	37 51	+41	101	38 32	+40	100	39 12	+40	99
56	34 24	42	104	35 06	42	103	35 48	41	102	36 29	41	101	37 10	40	100	37 50	40	100	38 30	40	99
57	33 43	42	103	34 25	41	102	35 06	41	101	35 47	41	101	36 28	40	100	37 08	40	99	37 48	40	98
58	33 01	42	102	33 43	41	102	34 24	42	101	35 06	40	100	35 46	40	99	36 26	40	98	37 06	39	97
59	32 20	41	102	33 01	42	101	33 43	41	100	34 24	40	99	35 04	40	98	35 44	40	97	36 24	39	96
60	31 38	+42	101	32 20	+41	100	33 01	+41	99	33 42	+40	98	34 22	+40	97	35 02	+40	96	35 42	+39	95
61	30 56	42	100	31 38	41	99	32 19	41	98	33 00	40	97	33 40	40	97	34 20	40	96	35 00	39	95
62	30 15	41	99	30 56	41	98	31 37	41	98	32 18	40	97	32 58	40	96	33 38	39	95	34 17	39	94
63	29 33	41	98	30 14	41	98	30 55	40	97	31 35	41	96	32 16	39	95	32 55	40	94	33 35	39	93
64	28 51	41	98	29 32	41	97	30 13	40	96	30 53	40	95	31 33	40	94	32 13	39	93	32 52	40	93
65	28 09	+41	97	28 50	+40	96	29 30	+41	95	30 11	+40	94	30 51	+40	94	31 31	+39	93	32 10	+39	92
66	27 26	41	96	28 07	41	95	28 48	41	95	29 29	40	94	30 09	39	93	30 48	40	92	31 28	39	91
67	26 44	41	95	27 25	41	95	28 06	40	94	28 46	40	93	29 26	40	92	30 06	39	91	30 45	39	90
68	26 02	41	95	26 43	40	94	27 23	41	93	28 04	40	92	28 44	39	91	29 23	40	91	30 03	39	90
69	25 20	41	94	26 01	40	93	26 41	40	92	27 21	40	92	28 01	40	91	28 41	39	90	29 20	39	89

LHA	22° Hc	22° d	22° Z	23° Hc	23° d	23° Z	24° Hc	24° d	24° Z	25° Hc	25° d	25° Z	26° Hc	26° d	26° Z	27° Hc	27° d	27° Z	28° Hc	28° d	28° Z	29° Hc	29° d	29° Z	LHA
	° ′	′	°	° ′	′	°	° ′	′	°	° ′	′	°	° ′	′	°	° ′	′	°	° ′	′	°	° ′	′	°	
0	67 00	+60	180	68 00	+60	180	69 00	+60	180	70 00	+60	180	71 00	+60	180	72 00	+60	180	73 00	+60	180	74 00	+60	180	360
1	66 59	60	178	67 59	60	178	68 59	60	178	69 59	60	177	70 59	60	177	71 59	60	177	72 59	60	177	73 59	60	177	359
2	66 57	59	175	67 56	60	175	68 56	60	175	69 56	60	175	70 56	60	175	71 56	60	174	72 56	59	174	73 55	60	174	358
3	66 52	60	173	67 52	60	173	68 52	59	172	69 51	60	172	70 51	59	172	71 50	60	171	72 50	60	171	73 50	59	171	357
4	66 46	60	171	67 46	59	170	68 45	59	170	69 44	60	170	70 44	59	169	71 43	59	169	72 42	59	168	73 41	59	168	356
5	66 38	+60	168	67 38	+59	168	68 37	+59	167	69 36	+59	167	70 35	+59	166	71 34	+58	166	72 32	+59	165	73 31	+59	164	355
6	66 29	59	166	67 28	59	166	68 27	58	165	69 25	59	164	70 24	58	164	71 22	59	163	72 21	58	162	73 19	58	161	354
7	66 18	58	164	67 16	59	163	68 15	58	163	69 13	58	162	70 11	58	161	71 09	58	160	72 07	57	160	73 04	57	159	353
8	66 05	58	161	67 03	58	161	68 01	58	160	68 59	57	159	69 56	58	159	70 54	57	158	71 51	57	157	72 48	56	156	352
9	65 51	57	159	66 48	58	159	67 46	57	158	68 43	57	157	69 40	57	156	70 37	56	155	71 33	56	154	72 29	56	153	351
10	65 35	+57	157	66 32	+57	156	67 29	+57	156	68 26	+56	155	69 22	+56	154	70 18	+56	153	71 14	+55	152	72 09	+55	150	350
11	65 18	56	155	66 14	57	154	67 11	56	153	68 07	56	152	69 03	55	151	69 58	55	150	70 53	54	149	71 47	54	148	349
12	64 59	56	153	65 55	56	152	66 51	55	151	67 46	55	150	68 41	55	149	69 36	54	148	70 30	54	147	71 24	53	145	348
13	64 39	56	151	65 35	55	150	66 30	55	149	67 25	54	148	68 19	54	147	69 13	53	146	70 06	53	144	70 59	52	143	347
14	64 18	55	149	65 13	54	148	66 07	54	147	67 01	54	146	67 55	53	145	68 48	53	143	69 41	52	142	70 33	51	141	346
15	63 55	+54	147	64 49	+54	146	65 43	+54	145	66 37	+53	144	67 30	+52	143	68 22	+52	141	69 14	+51	140	70 05	+50	138	345
16	63 31	54	145	64 25	53	144	65 18	53	143	66 11	53	142	67 04	51	141	67 55	51	139	68 46	50	138	69 36	50	136	344
17	63 07	53	143	64 00	52	142	64 52	52	141	65 44	52	140	66 36	51	139	67 27	50	137	68 17	49	136	69 06	49	134	343
18	62 41	52	141	63 33	52	140	64 25	52	139	65 17	50	138	66 07	51	137	66 58	49	135	67 47	48	134	68 35	48	132	342
19	62 14	51	140	63 05	52	139	63 57	51	137	64 48	50	136	65 38	49	135	66 27	49	133	67 16	48	132	68 04	46	130	341
20	61 46	+51	138	62 37	+51	137	63 28	+50	136	64 18	+49	134	65 07	+49	133	65 56	+48	132	66 44	+47	130	67 31	+46	129	340
21	61 17	50	136	62 07	51	135	62 58	49	134	63 47	49	133	64 36	48	131	65 24	47	130	66 11	46	128	66 57	45	127	339
22	60 47	50	135	61 37	50	134	62 27	48	132	63 15	49	131	64 04	47	130	64 51	46	128	65 37	46	127	66 23	44	125	338
23	60 16	50	133	61 06	49	132	61 55	48	131	62 43	48	129	63 31	46	128	64 17	46	127	65 03	45	125	65 48	44	124	337
24	59 45	49	132	60 34	48	130	61 22	48	129	62 10	47	128	62 57	46	127	63 43	45	125	64 28	44	124	65 12	43	122	336
25	59 13	+48	130	60 01	+48	129	60 49	+47	128	61 36	+46	126	62 22	+46	125	63 08	+44	124	63 52	+44	122	64 36	+42	121	335
26	58 40	48	129	59 28	47	127	60 15	47	126	61 02	45	125	61 47	45	124	62 32	44	122	63 16	43	121	63 59	42	119	334
27	58 07	47	127	58 54	47	126	59 41	45	125	60 26	46	124	61 12	44	122	61 56	43	121	62 39	43	119	63 22	41	118	333
28	57 32	47	126	58 19	46	125	59 05	46	123	59 51	44	122	60 35	44	121	61 19	43	119	62 02	42	118	62 44	41	116	332
29	56 58	46	125	57 44	46	123	58 30	45	122	59 15	44	121	59 59	43	119	60 42	42	118	61 24	42	117	62 06	40	115	331
30	56 22	+46	123	57 08	+45	122	57 53	+45	121	58 38	+44	120	59 22	+42	118	60 04	+42	117	60 46	+41	115	61 27	+40	114	330
31	55 47	45	122	56 32	45	121	57 17	44	120	58 01	43	118	58 44	42	117	59 26	42	116	60 08	40	114	60 48	39	113	329
32	55 10	45	121	55 55	45	120	56 40	43	118	57 23	43	117	58 06	42	116	58 48	41	114	59 29	40	113	60 09	39	111	328
33	54 34	44	119	55 18	44	118	56 02	43	117	56 45	42	116	57 27	42	115	58 09	40	113	58 49	40	112	59 29	39	110	327
34	53 57	44	118	54 41	43	117	55 24	43	116	56 07	42	115	56 49	41	113	57 30	40	112	58 10	39	111	58 49	38	109	326
35	53 19	+44	117	54 03	+43	116	54 46	+42	115	55 28	+42	114	56 10	+40	112	56 50	+40	111	57 30	+39	110	58 09	+38	108	325
36	52 41	43	116	53 24	43	115	54 07	42	114	54 49	41	112	55 30	40	111	56 10	40	110	56 50	38	108	57 28	38	107	324
37	52 03	43	115	52 46	42	114	53 28	42	113	54 10	40	111	54 50	40	110	55 30	40	109	56 10	38	107	56 48	37	106	323
38	51 24	43	114	52 07	42	113	52 49	41	112	53 30	40	110	54 10	40	109	54 50	39	108	55 29	38	106	56 07	37	105	322
39	50 45	42	113	51 27	42	112	52 09	41	111	52 50	40	109	53 30	40	108	54 10	38	107	54 48	38	105	55 26	37	104	321
40	50 06	+42	112	50 48	+41	111	51 29	+41	109	52 10	+40	108	52 50	+39	107	53 29	+38	106	54 07	+38	105	54 45	+36	103	320
41	49 26	42	111	50 08	41	110	50 49	40	108	51 29	40	107	52 09	39	106	52 48	38	105	53 26	37	104	54 03	37	102	319
42	48 46	42	110	49 28	41	109	50 09	40	108	50 49	39	106	51 28	39	105	52 07	38	104	52 45	37	103	53 22	36	101	318
43	48 06	42	109	48 48	40	108	49 28	40	107	50 08	39	105	50 47	39	104	51 26	37	103	52 03	37	102	52 40	36	100	317
44	47 26	41	108	48 07	40	107	48 47	40	106	49 27	39	104	50 06	38	103	50 44	38	102	51 22	36	101	51 58	36	100	316
45	46 46	+40	107	47 26	+40	106	48 06	+40	105	48 46	+39	104	49 25	+38	102	50 03	+37	101	50 40	+36	100	51 16	+36	99	315
46	46 05	40	106	46 45	40	105	47 25	40	104	48 05	38	103	48 43	38	102	49 21	37	100	49 58	36	99	50 34	36	98	314
47	45 24	40	105	46 04	40	104	46 44	39	103	47 23	38	102	48 01	38	101	48 39	37	100	49 16	36	98	49 52	36	97	313
48	44 43	40	104	45 23	40	103	46 03	38	102	46 41	39	101	47 20	37	100	47 57	37	99	48 34	36	97	49 10	35	96	312
49	44 02	40	103	44 42	39	102	45 21	39	101	46 00	38	100	46 38	37	99	47 15	37	98	47 52	36	97	48 28	35	95	311
50	43 20	+40	102	44 00	+39	101	44 39	+39	100	45 18	+38	99	45 56	+37	98	46 33	+37	97	47 10	+36	96	47 46	+35	95	310
51	42 39	39	102	43 18	40	101	43 58	38	100	44 36	38	98	45 14	37	97	45 51	37	96	46 28	35	95	47 03	35	94	309
52	41 57	40	101	42 37	39	100	43 16	38	99	43 54	38	98	44 32	37	97	45 09	36	95	45 45	36	94	46 21	35	93	308
53	41 16	39	100	41 55	39	99	42 34	38	98	43 12	38	97	43 50	37	96	44 27	36	95	45 03	36	94	45 39	35	92	307
54	40 34	39	99	41 13	39	98	41 52	38	97	42 30	37	96	43 07	37	95	43 44	37	94	44 21	35	93	44 56	35	92	306
55	39 52	+39	98	40 31	+38	97	41 09	+39	96	41 48	+37	95	42 25	+37	94	43 02	+36	93	43 38	+36	92	44 14	+35	91	305
56	39 10	39	98	39 49	38	97	40 27	38	96	41 05	38	95	41 43	37	94	42 20	36	92	42 56	35	91	43 31	35	90	304
57	38 28	39	97	39 07	38	96	39 45	38	95	40 23	37	94	41 00	37	93	41 37	36	92	42 13	36	91	42 49	35	90	303
58	37 45	39	96	38 24	39	95	39 03	38	94	39 41	37	93	40 18	37	92	40 55	36	91	41 31	36	90	42 07	35	89	302
59	37 03	39	95	37 42	38	94	38 20	38	93	38 58	38	92	39 36	36	91	40 12	37	90	40 49	35	89	41 24	35	88	301
60	36 21	+39	95	37 00	+38	94	37 38	+38	93	38 16	+37	92	38 53	+37	91	39 30	+36	90	40 06	+36	89	40 42	+35	88	300
61	35 39	38	94	36 17	39	93	36 56	37	92	37 33	38	91	38 11	36	90	38 47	37	89	39 24	35	88	39 59	36	87	299
62	34 56	39	93	35 35	38	92	36 13	38	91	36 51	37	90	37 28	37	89	38 05	36	88	38 41	36	87	39 17	35	86	298
63	34 14	39	92	34 53	38	91	35 31	38	90	36 09	37	89	36 46	37	89	37 23	36	88	37 59	36	87	38 35	35	85	297
64	33 32	38	92	34 10	38	91	34 48	38	90	35 26	37	89	36 03	37	88	36 40	37	87	37 17	35	86	37 52	36	85	296
65	32 49	+39	91	33 28	+38	90	34 06	+38	89	34 44	+37	88	35 21	+37	87	35 58	+36	86	36 34	+36	85	37 10	+36	84	295
66	32 07	38	90	32 45	39	89	33 24	37	88	34 01	38	87	34 39	37	86	35 16	36	86	35 52	36	85	36 28	36	84	294
67	31 24	39	89	32 03	38	89	32 41	38	88	33 19	37	87	33 56	37	86	34 33	37	85	35 10	36	84	35 46	36	83	293
68	30 42	38	89	31 20	39	88	31 59	38	87	32 37	37	86	33 14	37	85	33 51	37	84	34 28	36	83	35 04	36	82	292
69	29 59	39	88	30 38	38	87	31 16	38	86	31 54	38	85	32 32	37	84	33 09	37	84	33 46	36	83	34 22	36	82	291

S. Lat. {LHA greater than 180°.......Zn=180−Z; LHA less than 180°..........Zn=180+Z}

DECLINATION (15°-29°) SAME NAME AS LATITUDE

LAT 45°

LAT 45°

DECLINATION (15°-29°) SAME NAME AS LATITUDE

N. Lat. {LHA greater than 180°........ Zn=Z; LHA less than 180°........... Zn=360−Z}

LHA	15° Hc	15° d	15° Z	16° Hc	16° d	16° Z	17° Hc	17° d	17° Z	18° Hc	18° d	18° Z	19° Hc	19° d	19° Z
	° ′	′	°	° ′	′	°	° ′	′	°	° ′	′	°	° ′	′	°
70	24 37	+41	93	25 18	+41	92	25 59	+40	92	26 39	+40	91	27 19	+40	90
71	23 55	41	93	24 36	40	92	25 16	41	91	25 57	40	90	26 37	39	89
72	23 13	40	92	23 53	41	91	24 34	40	90	25 14	40	89	25 54	40	89
73	22 30	41	91	23 11	40	90	23 51	41	89	24 32	40	89	25 12	39	88
74	21 48	40	90	22 28	41	90	23 09	40	89	23 49	40	88	24 29	40	87
75	21 05	+41	90	21 46	+41	89	22 27	+40	88	23 07	+40	87	23 47	+40	86
76	20 23	41	89	21 04	40	88	21 44	41	87	22 25	40	87	23 05	39	86
77	19 40	41	88	20 21	41	87	21 02	40	87	21 42	40	86	22 22	40	85
78	18 58	41	88	19 39	40	87	20 19	41	86	21 00	40	85	21 40	40	84
79	18 16	41	87	18 57	40	86	19 37	41	85	20 18	40	85	20 58	40	84
80	17 33	+41	86	18 14	+41	85	18 55	+40	85	19 35	+41	84	20 16	+40	83
81	16 51	41	85	17 32	41	85	18 13	40	84	18 53	41	83	19 34	40	82
82	16 09	41	85	16 50	41	84	17 31	40	83	18 11	41	82	18 52	40	82
83	15 27	41	84	16 08	40	83	16 48	41	83	17 29	41	82	18 10	40	81
84	14 44	41	83	15 25	41	83	16 06	41	82	16 47	41	81	17 28	40	80
85	14 02	+41	83	14 43	+41	82	15 24	+41	81	16 05	+41	80	16 46	+41	80
86	13 20	41	82	14 01	42	81	14 43	41	81	15 24	40	80	16 04	41	79
87	12 38	42	81	13 20	41	81	14 01	41	80	14 42	41	79	15 23	41	78
88	11 56	42	81	12 38	41	80	13 19	41	79	14 00	41	78	14 41	41	78
89	11 14	42	80	11 56	41	79	12 37	42	79	13 19	41	78	14 00	41	77
90	10 33	+41	79	11 14	+42	79	11 56	+41	78	12 37	+42	77	13 19	+41	76
91	09 51	42	79	10 33	42	78	11 15	41	77	11 56	41	76	12 37	42	76
92	09 10	41	78	09 51	42	77	10 33	42	76	11 15	41	76	11 56	42	75
93	08 28	42	77	09 10	42	77	09 52	42	76	10 34	42	75	11 16	41	74
94	07 47	42	77	08 29	42	76	09 11	42	75	09 53	42	74	10 35	41	74
95	07 06	+42	76	07 48	+42	75	08 30	+42	74	09 12	+42	74	09 54	+42	73
96	06 25	42	75	07 07	42	75	07 49	42	74	08 31	43	73	09 14	42	72
97	05 44	42	75	06 26	43	74	07 09	42	73	07 51	42	72	08 33	42	72
98	05 03	42	74	05 45	43	73	06 28	43	72	07 11	42	72	07 53	42	71
99	04 22	43	73	05 05	43	72	05 48	42	72	06 30	43	71	07 13	43	70
100	03 42	+43	72	04 25	+43	72	05 08	+42	71	05 50	+43	70	06 33	+43	70
101	03 01	43	72	03 44	43	71	04 27	44	70	05 11	43	70	05 54	42	69
102	02 21	43	71	03 04	44	70	03 48	43	70	04 31	43	69	05 14	43	68
103	01 41	43	70	02 24	44	70	03 08	43	69	03 51	44	68	04 35	43	68
104	01 01	44	70	01 45	43	69	02 28	44	68	03 12	44	68	03 56	43	67
105	00 21	+44	69	01 05	+44	68	01 49	+44	68	02 33	+44	67	03 17	+43	66
106	−0 18	44	68	00 26	44	68	01 10	44	67	01 54	44	66	02 38	44	65
107	−0 57	44	68	−0 13	44	67	00 31	44	66	01 15	44	65	01 59	45	65
108	−1 36	44	67	−0 52	44	66	−0 08	45	65	00 37	44	65	01 21	45	64
109	−2 15	44	66	−1 31	45	65	−0 46	45	65	−0 01	44	64	00 43	45	63
110	−2 54	+45	65	−2 09	+45	65	−1 24	+44	64	−0 40	+45	63	00 05	+45	63
111	−3 32	45	65	−2 47	45	64	−2 02	45	63	−1 17	45	63	−0 32	45	62
112	−4 11	46	64	−3 25	45	63	−2 40	45	63	−1 55	45	62	−1 10	46	61
113	−4 49	46	63	−4 03	45	63	−3 18	46	62	−2 32	45	61	−1 47	46	61
114	−5 26	45	62	−4 41	46	62	−3 55	46	61	−3 09	46	60	−2 23	45	60
115	−6 04	+46	62	−5 18	+46	61	−4 32	+46	60	−3 46	+46	60	−3 00	+46	59
116				−5 55	46	60	−5 09	46	60	−4 23	47	59	−3 36	46	58
117							−5 45	46	59	−4 59	47	58	−4 12	46	58
118										−5 35	47	57	−4 48	47	57
119										−6 10	47	57	−5 23	47	56
120													−5 58	+47	55

LHA	20° Hc	20° d	20° Z	21° Hc	21° d	21° Z	22° Hc	22° d	22° Z	23° Hc	23° d	23° Z	24° Hc	24° d	24° Z
	° ′	′	°	° ′	′	°	° ′	′	°	° ′	′	°	° ′	′	°
70	27 59	+39	89	28 38	+39	88	29 17	+39	87	29 56	+38	87	30 34	+38	86
71	27 16	40	88	27 56	39	88	28 35	38	87	29 13	39	86	29 52	38	85
72	26 34	39	88	27 13	39	87	27 52	39	86	28 31	39	85	29 10	38	84
73	25 51	40	87	26 31	39	86	27 10	39	85	27 49	38	84	28 27	39	84
74	25 09	40	86	25 49	39	85	26 28	39	85	27 07	38	84	27 45	38	83
75	24 27	+39	86	25 06	+40	85	25 46	+39	84	26 25	+38	83	27 03	+39	82
76	23 44	40	85	24 24	39	84	25 03	39	83	25 42	39	82	26 21	39	82
77	23 02	40	84	23 42	39	83	24 21	39	83	25 00	39	82	25 39	39	81
78	22 20	40	84	23 00	39	83	23 39	39	82	24 18	39	81	24 57	39	80
79	21 38	40	83	22 18	39	82	22 57	40	81	23 37	39	80	24 16	38	80
80	20 56	+40	82	21 36	+39	81	22 15	+40	81	22 55	+39	80	23 34	+39	79
81	20 14	40	82	20 54	40	81	21 34	39	80	22 13	39	79	22 52	39	78
82	19 32	40	81	20 12	40	80	20 52	39	79	21 31	40	79	22 11	39	78
83	18 50	40	80	19 30	40	79	20 10	40	79	20 50	39	78	21 29	40	77
84	18 08	41	80	18 49	40	79	19 29	39	78	20 08	40	77	20 48	40	76
85	17 27	+40	79	18 07	+40	78	18 47	+40	77	19 27	+40	77	20 07	+40	76
86	16 45	41	78	17 26	40	77	18 06	40	77	18 46	40	76	19 26	40	75
87	16 04	40	78	16 44	41	77	17 25	40	76	18 05	40	75	18 45	40	75
88	15 22	41	77	16 03	41	76	16 44	40	75	17 24	40	75	18 04	40	74
89	14 41	41	76	15 22	41	76	16 03	40	75	16 43	40	74	17 23	41	73
90	14 00	+41	76	14 41	+41	75	15 22	+40	74	16 02	+41	73	16 43	+40	73
91	13 19	41	75	14 00	41	74	14 41	41	73	15 22	41	73	16 03	40	72
92	12 38	41	74	13 19	41	74	14 00	41	73	14 41	41	72	15 22	41	71
93	11 57	42	74	12 39	41	73	13 20	41	72	14 01	41	71	14 42	41	71
94	11 16	42	73	11 58	42	72	12 40	41	71	13 21	41	71	14 02	41	70
95	10 36	+42	72	11 18	+41	72	11 59	+42	71	12 41	+41	70	13 22	+42	69
96	09 56	42	72	10 38	41	71	11 19	42	70	12 01	42	69	12 43	41	69
97	09 15	43	71	09 58	42	70	10 40	42	70	11 22	41	69	12 03	42	68
98	08 35	43	70	09 18	42	70	10 00	42	69	10 42	42	68	11 24	42	67
99	07 56	42	70	08 38	43	69	09 21	42	68	10 03	42	67	10 45	42	67
100	07 16	+43	69	07 59	+42	68	08 41	+43	68	09 24	+42	67	10 06	+43	66
101	06 36	43	68	07 19	43	68	08 02	43	67	08 45	43	66	09 28	42	65
102	05 57	43	68	06 40	43	67	07 23	43	66	08 06	43	65	08 49	43	65
103	05 18	43	67	06 01	44	66	06 45	43	66	07 28	43	65	08 11	43	64
104	04 39	44	66	05 23	43	66	06 06	43	65	06 49	44	64	07 33	43	63
105	04 00	+44	65	04 44	+44	65	05 28	+43	64	06 11	+44	63	06 55	+44	63
106	03 22	44	65	04 06	44	64	04 50	44	63	05 34	43	63	06 17	44	62
107	02 44	44	64	03 28	44	63	04 12	44	63	04 56	44	62	05 40	44	61
108	02 06	44	63	02 50	44	63	03 34	45	62	04 19	44	61	05 03	44	61
109	01 28	44	63	02 12	45	62	02 57	44	61	03 41	45	61	04 26	45	60
110	00 50	+45	62	01 35	+45	61	02 20	+45	61	03 05	+44	60	03 49	+45	59
111	00 13	45	61	00 58	45	61	01 43	45	60	02 28	45	59	03 13	45	59
112	−0 24	45	61	00 21	45	60	01 06	46	59	01 52	45	59	02 37	45	58
113	−1 01	45	60	−0 16	46	59	00 30	46	59	01 16	45	58	02 01	46	57
114	−1 38	46	59	−0 52	46	59	−0 06	46	58	00 40	45	57	01 25	46	57
115	−2 14	+46	58	−1 28	+46	58	−0 42	+46	57	00 04	+46	57	00 50	+46	56
116	−2 50	46	58	−2 04	47	57	−1 17	46	56	−0 31	46	56	00 15	47	55
117	−3 26	47	57	−2 39	46	56	−1 53	47	56	−1 06	47	55	−0 19	46	54
118	−4 01	47	56	−3 14	46	56	−2 28	47	55	−1 41	47	54	−0 54	47	54
119	−4 36	47	56	−3 49	47	55	−3 02	47	54	−2 15	47	54	−1 28	47	53
120	−5 11	+47	55	−4 24	+48	54	−3 36	+47	54	−2 49	+47	53	−2 02	+48	52
121	−5 46	48	54	−4 58	48	53	−4 10	47	53	−3 23	48	52	−2 35	48	52
122				−5 32	48	53	−4 44	48	52	−3 56	48	52	−3 08	48	51
123				−6 06	49	52	−5 17	48	51	−4 29	48	51	−3 41	48	50
124							−5 50	48	51	−5 02	49	50	−4 13	48	49
125										−5 34	+49	49	−4 45	+48	49
126													−5 17	49	48
127													−5 48	49	47

LHA	25° Hc	25° d	25° Z	26° Hc	26° d	26° Z	27° Hc	27° d	27° Z	28° Hc	28° d	28° Z	29° Hc	29° d	29° Z	LHA
	° ′	′	°	° ′	′	°	° ′	′	°	° ′	′	°	° ′	′	°	
70	31 12	+38	85	31 50	+37	84	32 27	+37	83	33 04	+36	82	33 40	+36	81	290
71	30 30	37	84	31 07	38	83	31 45	37	82	32 22	36	81	32 58	36	80	289
72	29 48	37	83	30 25	38	82	31 03	37	82	31 40	36	81	32 16	36	80	288
73	29 06	37	83	29 43	38	82	30 21	37	81	30 58	37	80	31 35	36	79	287
74	28 23	38	82	29 01	38	81	29 39	37	80	30 16	37	79	30 53	36	78	286
75	27 42	+38	81	28 20	+37	81	28 57	+38	80	29 35	+36	79	30 11	+37	78	285
76	27 00	38	81	27 38	38	80	28 16	37	79	28 53	37	78	29 30	37	77	284
77	26 18	38	80	26 56	38	79	27 34	38	78	28 12	37	77	28 49	37	77	283
78	25 36	38	79	26 14	38	79	26 52	38	78	27 30	38	77	28 08	37	76	282
79	24 54	39	79	25 33	38	78	26 11	38	77	26 49	37	76	27 26	38	75	281
80	24 13	+38	78	24 51	+39	77	25 30	+38	76	26 08	+37	76	26 45	+38	75	280
81	23 31	39	78	24 10	39	77	24 49	38	76	25 27	38	75	26 05	37	74	279
82	22 50	39	77	23 29	38	76	24 07	39	75	24 46	38	74	25 24	38	74	278
83	22 09	39	76	22 48	39	75	23 27	38	75	24 05	38	74	24 43	38	73	277
84	21 28	39	76	22 07	39	75	22 46	38	74	23 24	39	73	24 03	38	72	276
85	20 47	+39	75	21 26	+39	74	22 05	+39	73	22 44	+38	73	23 22	+39	72	275
86	20 06	39	74	20 45	39	74	21 24	39	73	22 03	39	72	22 42	39	71	274
87	19 25	40	74	20 05	39	73	20 44	39	72	21 23	39	71	22 02	39	70	273
88	18 44	40	73	19 24	40	72	20 04	39	71	20 43	39	71	21 22	39	70	272
89	18 04	40	72	18 44	40	72	19 24	39	71	20 03	40	70	20 43	39	69	271
90	17 23	+41	72	18 04	+40	71	18 44	+39	70	19 23	+40	69	20 03	+39	69	270
91	16 43	40	71	17 23	41	70	18 04	40	70	18 44	40	69	19 24	39	68	269
92	16 03	41	71	16 44	40	70	17 24	40	69	18 04	40	68	18 44	40	67	268
93	15 23	41	70	16 04	41	69	16 45	40	68	17 25	40	68	18 05	40	67	267
94	14 43	41	69	15 24	41	68	16 05	41	68	16 46	40	67	17 26	41	66	266
95	14 04	+41	69	14 45	+41	68	15 26	+41	67	16 07	+41	66	16 48	+40	66	265
96	13 24	42	68	14 06	41	67	14 47	41	66	15 28	41	66	16 09	41	65	264
97	12 45	42	67	13 27	41	67	14 08	42	66	14 50	41	65	15 31	41	64	263
98	12 06	42	67	12 48	42	66	13 30	41	65	14 11	42	64	14 53	41	64	262
99	11 27	42	66	12 09	42	65	12 51	42	65	13 33	42	64	14 15	41	63	261
100	10 49	+42	65	11 31	+42	65	12 13	+42	64	12 55	+42	63	13 37	+42	62	260
101	10 10	43	65	10 53	42	64	11 35	42	63	12 17	43	63	13 00	42	62	259
102	09 32	43	64	10 15	42	63	10 57	43	63	11 40	42	62	12 22	43	61	258
103	08 54	43	63	09 37	43	63	10 20	43	62	11 03	42	61	11 45	43	61	257
104	08 16	43	63	08 59	43	62	09 42	43	61	10 25	43	61	11 08	43	60	256
105	07 39	+43	62	08 22	+43	61	09 05	+44	61	09 49	+43	60	10 32	+43	59	255
106	07 01	44	61	07 45	43	61	08 28	44	60	09 12	43	59	09 55	44	59	254
107	06 24	44	61	07 08	44	60	07 52	44	59	08 36	43	59	09 19	44	58	253
108	05 47	44	60	06 31	44	59	07 15	45	59	08 00	44	58	08 44	44	57	252
109	05 11	44	59	05 55	44	59	06 39	45	58	07 24	44	57	08 08	44	57	251
110	04 34	+45	59	05 19	+45	58	06 04	+44	57	06 48	+45	57	07 33	+44	56	250
111	03 58	45	58	04 43	45	57	05 28	45	57	06 13	45	56	06 58	44	55	249
112	03 22	45	57	04 07	46	57	04 53	45	56	05 38	45	55	06 23	45	55	248
113	02 47	45	57	03 32	46	56	04 18	45	55	05 03	45	55	05 48	46	54	247
114	02 11	46	56	02 57	46	55	03 43	46	55	04 29	45	54	05 14	46	53	246
115	01 36	+46	55	02 22	+46	55	03 08	+46	54	03 54	+46	53	04 40	+46	53	245
116	01 02	46	55	01 48	46	54	02 34	46	53	03 20	47	53	04 07	46	52	244
117	00 27	47	54	01 14	46	53	02 00	47	53	02 47	46	52	03 33	47	51	243
118	−0 07	47	53	00 40	47	53	01 27	47	52	02 14	46	51	03 00	47	51	242
119	−0 41	47	52	00 06	48	52	00 54	47	51	01 41	47	51	02 28	47	50	241
120	−1 14	+47	52	−0 27	+48	51	00 21	+47	51	01 08	+47	50	01 55	+48	49	240
121	−1 47	47	51	−1 00	48	50	−0 12	48	50	00 36	48	49	01 24	47	49	239
122	−2 20	48	50	−1 32	48	50	−0 44	48	49	00 04	48	48	00 52	48	48	238
123	−2 53	49	50	−2 04	48	49	−1 16	48	48	−0 28	49	48	00 21	48	47	237
124	−3 25	49	49	−2 36	48	48	−1 48	49	48	−0 59	49	47	−0 10	48	46	236
125	−3 57	+49	48	−3 08	+49	47	−2 19	+49	47	−1 30	+49	46	−0 41	+49	46	235
126	−4 28	49	47	−3 39	49	47	−2 50	50	46	−2 00	49	46	−1 11	49	45	234
127	−4 59	50	47	−4 09	49	46	−3 20	49	45	−2 31	50	45	−1 41	49	44	233
128	−5 30	50	46	−4 40	50	45	−3 50	50	45	−3 00	50	44	−2 10	49	44	232
129	−6 00	50	45	−5 10	50	44	−4 20	50	44	−3 30	50	43	−2 40	51	43	231
130				−5 39	+50	44	−4 49	+50	43	−3 59	+51	43	−3 08	+50	42	230
131							−5 18	51	42	−4 27	51	42	−3 36	50	41	229
132							−5 46	51	42	−4 55	51	41	−4 04	51	41	228
133										−5 23	51	40	−4 32	52	40	227
134										−5 50	51	40	−4 59	52	39	226
135													−5 25	+52	38	225
136													−5 52	53	38	224

DECLINATION (15°-29°) CONTRARY NAME TO LATITUDE

S. Lat. {LHA greater than 180°........ Zn=180−Z; LHA less than 180°........... Zn=180+Z}

LHA	15° Hc	15° d	15° Z	16° Hc	16° d	16° Z	17° Hc	17° d	17° Z	18° Hc	18° d	18° Z	19° Hc	19° d	19° Z	20° Hc	20° d	20° Z	21° Hc	21° d	21° Z
83	−5 44	42	105	277																	
82	−5 03	42	106	−5 45	43	107	278														
81	−4 22	43	107	−5 05	43	108	−5 48	42	108	279											
80	−3 42	−43	108	−4 25	−43	108	−5 08	−42	109	−5 50	−43	110	280								
79	−3 01	43	108	−3 44	43	109	−4 27	44	110	−5 11	43	110	−5 54	42	111	281					
78	−2 21	43	109	−3 04	44	110	−3 48	43	110	−4 31	43	111	−5 14	43	112	−5 57	43	112	282		
77	−1 41	43	110	−2 24	44	110	−3 08	43	111	−3 51	44	112	−4 35	43	112	−5 18	43	113	−6 01	44	114
76	−1 01	44	110	−1 45	43	111	−2 28	44	112	−3 12	44	112	−3 56	43	113	−4 39	44	114	−5 23	43	114
75	−0 21	−44	111	−1 05	−44	112	−1 49	−44	112	−2 33	−44	113	−3 17	−43	114	−4 00	−44	115	−4 44	−44	115
74	00 18	44	112	−0 26	44	112	−1 10	44	113	−1 54	44	114	−2 38	44	115	−3 22	44	115	−4 06	44	116
73	00 57	44	112	00 13	44	113	−0 31	44	114	−1 15	44	115	−1 59	45	115	−2 44	44	116	−3 28	44	117
72	01 36	44	113	00 52	44	114	00 08	45	115	−0 37	44	115	−1 21	45	116	−2 06	44	117	−2 50	44	117
71	02 15	44	114	01 31	45	115	00 46	45	115	00 01	44	116	−0 43	45	117	−1 28	44	117	−2 12	45	118
70	02 54	−45	115	02 09	−45	115	01 24	−44	116	00 40	−45	117	−0 05	−45	117	−0 50	−45	118	−1 35	−45	119

LHA	22° Hc	22° d	22° Z	23° Hc	23° d	23° Z	24° Hc	24° d	24° Z	25° Hc	25° d	25° Z	26° Hc	26° d	26° Z	27° Hc	27° d	27° Z	28° Hc	28° d	28° Z
77	283																				
76	−6 06	43	115	284																	
75	−5 28	−43	116	−6 11	−44	117	285														
74	−4 50	44	117	−5 34	43	117	286														
73	−4 12	44	117	−4 56	44	118	−5 40	44	119	287											
72	−3 34	45	118	−4 19	44	119	−5 03	44	119	−5 47	44	120	288								
71	−2 57	44	119	−3 41	45	119	−4 26	45	120	−5 11	44	121	−5 55	44	121	289					
70	−2 20	−45	119	−3 05	−44	120	−3 49	−45	121	−4 34	−45	121	−5 19	−45	122	−6 04	−44	123	290		

LAT 45°

N. Lat. {LHA greater than 180°........ Zn=Z; LHA less than 180°............ Zn=360−Z}

DECLINATION (15°-29°) CONTRARY NAME TO LATITUDE

LHA	15°			16°			17°			18°			19°			20°			21°		
	Hc	d	Z	Hc	d	Z	Hc	d	Z	Hc	d	Z	Hc	d	Z	Hc	d	Z	Hc	d	Z
	° ′	′	°	° ′	′	°	° ′	′	°	° ′	′	°	° ′	′	°	° ′	′	°	° ′	′	°
69	03 32	45	115	02 47	45	116	02 02	45	117	01 17	45	117	00 32	45	118	−0 13	45	119	−0 58	45	119
68	04 11	46	116	03 25	45	117	02 40	45	117	01 55	45	118	01 10	46	119	00 24	45	119	−0 21	45	120
67	04 49	46	117	04 03	45	117	03 18	46	118	02 32	45	119	01 47	46	119	01 01	45	120	00 16	46	121
66	05 26	45	118	04 41	46	118	03 55	46	119	03 09	46	120	02 23	45	120	01 38	46	121	00 52	46	121
65	06 04	−46	118	05 18	−46	119	04 32	−46	120	03 46	−46	120	03 00	−46	121	02 14	−46	122	01 28	−46	122
64	06 41	46	119	05 55	46	120	05 09	46	120	04 23	47	121	03 36	46	122	02 50	46	122	02 04	47	123
63	07 18	46	120	06 32	47	120	05 45	46	121	04 59	47	122	04 12	46	122	03 26	47	123	02 39	46	124
62	07 55	47	121	07 08	47	121	06 21	46	122	05 35	47	123	04 48	47	123	04 01	47	124	03 14	46	124
61	08 31	47	121	07 44	47	122	06 57	47	123	06 10	47	123	05 23	47	124	04 36	47	124	03 49	47	125
60	09 07	−47	122	08 20	−47	123	07 33	−47	123	06 46	−48	124	05 58	−47	125	05 11	−47	125	04 24	−48	126
59	09 43	47	123	08 56	48	124	08 08	47	124	07 21	48	125	06 33	47	125	05 46	48	126	04 58	48	127
58	10 18	47	124	09 31	48	124	08 43	48	125	07 55	47	126	07 08	48	126	06 20	48	127	05 32	48	127
57	10 54	48	124	10 06	48	125	09 18	48	126	08 30	48	126	07 42	48	127	06 54	48	128	06 06	49	128
56	11 28	48	125	10 40	48	126	09 52	48	126	09 04	48	127	08 16	49	128	07 27	48	128	06 39	49	129
55	12 03	−48	126	11 15	−49	127	10 26	−48	127	09 38	−49	128	08 49	−49	128	08 00	−48	129	07 12	−49	130
54	12 37	49	127	11 48	48	127	11 00	49	128	10 11	49	129	09 22	49	129	08 33	49	130	07 44	49	130
53	13 11	49	128	12 22	49	128	11 33	49	129	10 44	49	129	09 55	49	130	09 06	50	131	08 16	49	131
52	13 44	49	128	12 55	49	129	12 06	49	130	11 17	50	130	10 27	49	131	09 38	50	131	08 48	49	132
51	14 17	49	129	13 28	50	130	12 38	49	130	11 49	50	131	10 59	50	132	10 09	49	132	09 20	50	133
50	14 50	−50	130	14 00	−49	131	13 11	−50	131	12 21	−50	132	11 31	−50	132	10 41	−50	133	09 51	−51	134
49	15 22	50	131	14 32	50	132	13 42	50	132	12 52	50	133	12 02	50	133	11 12	51	134	10 21	50	134
48	15 54	50	132	15 04	50	132	14 14	51	133	13 23	50	133	12 33	51	134	11 42	51	135	10 51	50	135
47	16 26	51	133	15 35	51	133	14 44	50	134	13 54	51	134	13 03	51	135	12 12	51	135	11 21	51	136
46	16 57	51	133	16 06	51	134	15 15	51	135	14 24	51	135	13 33	51	136	12 42	52	136	11 50	51	137
45	17 27	−51	134	16 36	−51	135	15 45	−51	135	14 54	−52	136	14 02	−51	136	13 11	−52	137	12 19	−51	138
44	17 57	51	135	17 06	51	136	16 15	52	136	15 23	52	137	14 31	51	137	13 40	52	138	12 48	52	138
43	18 27	52	136	17 35	51	137	16 44	52	137	15 52	52	138	15 00	52	138	14 08	52	139	13 16	52	139
42	18 56	52	137	18 04	52	137	17 12	52	138	16 20	52	139	15 28	52	139	14 36	53	140	13 43	52	140
41	19 25	52	138	18 33	52	138	17 41	53	139	16 48	52	139	15 56	53	140	15 03	53	140	14 10	52	141
40	19 53	−52	139	19 01	−53	139	18 08	−53	140	17 15	−52	140	16 23	−53	141	15 30	−53	141	14 37	−53	142
39	20 21	53	140	19 28	53	140	18 35	53	141	17 42	53	141	16 49	53	142	15 56	53	142	15 03	53	143
38	20 48	53	141	19 55	53	141	19 02	53	142	18 09	54	142	17 15	53	142	16 22	54	143	15 28	53	143
37	21 15	53	141	20 22	54	142	19 28	53	142	18 35	54	143	17 41	54	143	16 47	53	144	15 54	54	144
36	21 41	53	142	20 48	54	143	19 54	54	143	19 00	54	144	18 06	54	144	17 12	54	145	16 18	54	145
35	22 07	−54	143	21 13	−54	144	20 19	−54	144	19 25	−54	145	18 31	−55	145	17 36	−54	146	16 42	−54	146
34	22 32	54	144	21 38	55	145	20 43	54	145	19 49	54	146	18 55	55	146	18 00	55	147	17 05	54	147
33	22 57	55	145	22 02	55	146	21 07	54	146	20 13	55	147	19 18	55	147	18 23	55	147	17 28	55	148
32	23 21	55	146	22 26	55	147	21 31	55	147	20 36	55	147	19 41	55	148	18 46	55	148	17 51	55	149
31	23 44	55	147	22 49	55	148	21 54	56	148	20 58	55	148	20 03	55	149	19 08	56	149	18 12	55	150
30	24 07	−56	148	23 11	−55	149	22 16	−56	149	21 20	−55	149	20 25	−56	150	19 29	−55	150	18 34	−56	151
29	24 29	56	149	23 33	55	149	22 38	56	150	21 42	56	150	20 46	56	151	19 50	56	151	18 54	56	151
28	24 50	56	150	23 54	55	150	22 59	56	151	22 03	57	151	21 06	56	152	20 10	56	152	19 14	56	152
27	25 11	56	151	24 15	56	151	23 19	56	152	22 23	57	152	21 26	56	153	20 30	56	153	19 34	57	153
26	25 31	56	152	24 35	56	152	23 39	57	153	22 42	56	153	21 46	57	154	20 49	57	154	19 52	56	154
25	25 51	−57	153	24 54	−56	153	23 58	−57	154	23 01	−57	154	22 04	−57	155	21 07	−56	155	20 11	−57	155
24	26 10	57	154	25 13	57	154	24 16	57	155	23 19	57	155	22 22	57	155	21 25	57	156	20 28	57	156
23	26 28	57	155	25 31	57	155	24 34	57	156	23 37	57	156	22 40	58	156	21 42	57	157	20 45	57	157
22	26 46	58	156	25 48	57	156	24 51	57	157	23 54	58	157	22 56	57	157	21 59	58	158	21 01	57	158
21	27 03	58	157	26 05	58	157	25 07	57	158	24 10	58	158	23 12	58	158	22 14	57	159	21 17	58	159
20	27 19	−58	158	26 21	−58	159	25 23	−58	159	24 25	−58	159	23 27	−57	159	22 30	−58	160	21 32	−58	160
19	27 34	58	159	26 36	58	160	25 38	58	160	24 40	58	160	23 42	58	160	22 44	58	161	21 46	58	161
18	27 49	58	160	26 51	59	161	25 52	58	161	24 54	58	161	23 56	58	161	22 58	59	162	21 59	58	162
17	28 03	59	161	27 04	58	162	26 06	58	162	25 08	59	162	24 09	58	162	23 11	59	163	22 12	58	163
16	28 16	59	162	27 17	58	163	26 19	59	163	25 20	58	163	24 22	59	163	23 23	59	164	22 24	58	164
15	28 28	−58	164	27 30	−59	164	26 31	−59	164	25 32	−59	164	24 33	−58	164	23 35	−59	165	22 36	−59	165
14	28 40	59	165	27 41	59	165	26 42	59	165	25 43	59	165	24 44	58	165	23 46	59	166	22 47	59	166
13	28 51	59	166	27 52	59	166	26 53	59	166	25 54	59	166	24 55	59	166	23 56	59	167	22 57	59	167
12	29 01	59	167	28 02	59	167	27 03	59	167	26 04	60	167	25 04	59	168	24 05	59	168	23 06	59	168
11	29 10	59	168	28 11	59	168	27 12	59	168	26 13	60	168	25 13	59	169	24 14	59	169	23 15	60	169
10	29 19	−59	169	28 20	−60	169	27 20	−59	169	26 21	−60	169	25 21	−59	170	24 22	−60	170	23 22	−59	170
9	29 27	60	170	28 27	59	170	27 28	60	170	26 28	59	170	25 29	60	171	24 29	59	171	23 30	60	171
8	29 34	60	171	28 34	60	171	27 34	59	171	26 35	60	172	25 35	59	172	24 36	60	172	23 36	60	172
7	29 40	60	172	28 40	60	172	27 40	59	172	26 41	60	173	25 41	60	173	24 41	59	173	23 42	60	173
6	29 45	60	173	28 45	59	173	27 46	60	174	26 46	60	174	25 46	60	174	24 46	60	174	23 46	59	174
5	29 50	−60	174	28 50	−60	175	27 50	−60	175	26 50	−60	175	25 50	−60	175	24 50	−59	175	23 51	−60	175
4	29 53	59	176	28 54	60	176	27 54	60	176	26 54	60	176	25 54	60	176	24 54	60	176	23 54	60	176
3	29 56	60	177	28 56	60	177	27 56	60	177	26 56	59	177	25 57	60	177	24 57	60	177	23 57	60	177
2	29 58	60	178	28 58	60	178	27 58	60	178	26 58	60	178	25 58	59	178	24 59	60	178	23 59	60	178
1	30 00	60	179	29 00	60	179	28 00	60	179	27 00	60	179	26 00	60	179	25 00	60	179	24 00	60	179
0	30 00	−60	180	29 00	−60	180	28 00	−60	180	27 00	−60	180	26 00	−60	180	25 00	−60	180	24 00	−60	180
	15°			16°			17°			18°			19°			20°			21°		

LHA	22°			23°			24°			25°			26°			27°			28°			29°			LHA
	Hc	d	Z	Hc	d	Z	Hc	d	Z	Hc	d	Z	Hc	d	Z	Hc	d	Z	Hc	d	Z	Hc	d	Z	
	° ′	′	°	° ′	′	°	° ′	′	°	° ′	′	°	° ′	′	°	° ′	′	°	° ′	′	°	° ′	′	°	
69	−1 43	45	120	−2 28	45	121	−3 13	45	121	−3 58	45	122	−4 43	45	123	−5 28	45	123	291						
68	−1 06	46	121	−1 52	45	121	−2 37	45	122	−3 22	45	123	−4 07	46	123	−4 53	45	124	−5 38	45	125	292			
67	−0 30	46	121	−1 16	45	122	−2 01	46	123	−2 47	45	123	−3 32	46	124	−4 18	45	125	−5 03	45	125	−5 48	46	126	293
66	00 06	46	122	−0 40	45	123	−1 25	46	123	−2 11	46	124	−2 57	46	125	−3 43	46	125	−4 29	45	126	−5 14	46	127	294
65	00 42	−46	123	−0 04	−46	123	−0 50	−46	124	−1 36	−46	125	−2 22	−46	125	−3 08	−46	126	−3 54	−46	127	−4 40	−46	127	295
64	01 17	46	124	00 31	46	124	−0 15	47	125	−1 02	46	125	−1 48	46	126	−2 34	46	127	−3 20	47	127	−4 07	46	128	296
63	01 53	47	124	01 06	47	125	00 19	46	126	−0 27	47	126	−1 14	46	127	−2 00	47	127	−2 47	46	128	−3 33	47	129	297
62	02 28	47	125	01 41	47	126	00 54	47	126	00 07	47	127	−0 40	47	127	−1 27	47	128	−2 14	46	129	−3 00	47	129	298
61	03 02	47	126	02 15	47	126	01 28	47	127	00 41	47	128	−0 06	48	128	−0 54	47	129	−1 41	47	129	−2 28	47	130	299
60	03 36	−47	126	02 49	−47	127	02 02	−48	128	01 14	−47	128	00 27	−48	129	−0 21	−47	129	−1 08	−47	130	−1 55	−48	131	300
59	04 10	47	127	03 23	48	128	02 35	48	128	01 47	47	129	01 00	48	130	00 12	48	130	−0 36	48	131	−1 24	47	131	301
58	04 44	48	128	03 56	48	128	03 08	48	129	02 20	48	130	01 32	48	130	00 44	48	131	−0 04	48	132	−0 52	48	132	302
57	05 17	48	129	04 29	48	129	03 41	48	130	02 53	49	130	02 04	48	131	01 16	48	132	00 28	49	132	−0 21	48	133	303
56	05 50	48	129	05 02	49	130	04 13	48	131	03 25	49	131	02 36	48	132	01 48	49	132	00 59	49	133	00 10	48	134	304
55	06 23	−49	130	05 34	−49	131	04 45	−48	131	03 57	−49	132	03 08	−49	133	02 19	−49	133	01 30	−49	134	00 41	−49	134	305
54	06 55	49	131	06 06	49	132	05 17	49	132	04 28	49	133	03 39	49	133	02 50	50	134	02 00	49	134	01 11	49	135	306
53	07 27	49	132	06 38	50	132	05 48	49	133	04 59	50	133	04 09	49	134	03 20	49	135	02 31	50	135	01 41	49	136	307
52	07 59	50	133	07 09	50	133	06 19	49	134	05 30	50	134	04 40	50	135	03 50	50	135	03 00	50	136	02 10	49	136	308
51	08 30	50	133	07 40	50	134	06 50	50	134	06 00	50	135	05 10	50	136	04 20	50	136	03 30	50	137	02 40	51	137	309
50	09 00	−50	134	08 10	−50	135	07 20	−50	135	06 30	−51	136	05 39	−50	136	04 49	−50	137	03 59	−51	137	03 08	−50	138	310
49	09 31	51	135	08 40	50	135	07 50	51	136	06 59	50	136	06 09	51	137	05 18	51	138	04 27	51	138	03 36	50	139	311
48	10 01	51	136	09 10	51	136	08 19	51	137	07 28	51	137	06 37	51	138	05 46	51	138	04 55	51	139	04 04	51	139	312
47	10 30	51	136	09 39	51	137	08 48	51	138	07 57	51	138	07 06	52	139	06 14	51	139	05 23	51	140	04 32	52	140	313
46	10 59	51	137	10 08	52	138	09 16	51	138	08 25	52	139	07 33	51	139	06 42	52	140	05 50	51	140	04 59	52	141	314
45	11 28	−52	138	10 36	−52	139	09 44	−51	139	08 53	−52	140	08 01	−52	140	07 09	−52	141	06 17	−52	141	05 25	−52	142	315
44	11 56	52	139	11 04	52	139	10 12	52	140	09 20	52	140	08 28	52	141	07 36	52	141	06 44	52	142	05 52	53	142	316
43	12 24	53	140	11 31	52	140	10 39	52	141	09 47	53	141	08 54	52	142	08 02	52	142	07 10	53	143	06 17	52	143	317
42	12 51	53	141	11 58	52	141	11 06	53	142	10 13	52	142	09 21	53	142	08 28	53	143	07 35	53	143	06 42	52	144	318
41	13 18	53	141	12 25	53	142	11 32	53	142	10 39	53	143	09 46	53	143	08 53	53	144	08 00	53	144	07 07	53	145	319
40	13 44	−53	142	12 51	−53	143	11 58	−53	143	11 05	−54	144	10 11	−53	144	09 18	−53	145	08 25	−53	145	07 32	−54	146	320
39	14 10	54	143	13 16	53	144	12 23	54	144	11 29	53	144	10 36	54	145	09 42	53	145	08 49	54	146	07 55	53	146	321
38	14 35	54	144	13 41	53	144	12 48	54	145	11 54	54	145	11 00	54	146	10 06	53	146	09 13	54	147	08 19	54	147	322
37	15 00	54	145	14 06	54	145	13 12	54	146	12 18	54	146	11 24	54	147	10 30	54	147	09 36	54	147	08 42	55	148	323
36	15 24	54	146	14 30	54	146	13 36	55	147	12 41	54	147	11 47	54	147	10 53	55	148	09 58	54	148	09 04	55	149	324
35	15 48	−55	146	14 53	−54	147	13 59	−55	147	13 04	−54	148	12 10	−55	148	11 15	−55	149	10 20	−54	149	09 26	−55	149	325
34	16 11	55	147	15 16	55	148	14 21	54	148	13 27	55	149	12 32	55	149	11 37	55	149	10 42	55	150	09 47	55	150	326
33	16 33	55	148	15 38	55	149	14 43	55	149	13 48	55	149	12 53	55	150	11 58	55	150	11 03	55	151	10 08	55	151	327
32	16 56	56	149	16 00	55	150	15 05	55	150	14 10	56	150	13 14	55	151	12 19	55	151	11 24	56	152	10 28	55	152	328
31	17 17	55	150	16 22	56	150	15 26	56	151	14 30	55	151	13 35	56	152	12 39	56	152	11 43	55	152	10 48	56	153	329
30	17 38	−56	151	16 42	−56	151	15 46	−55	152	14 51	−56	152	13 55	−56	152	12 59	−56	153	12 03	−56	153	11 07	−56	154	330
29	17 58	56	152	17 02	56	152	16 06	56	153	15 10	56	153	14 14	56	153	13 18	56	154	12 22	56	154	11 26	57	154	331
28	18 18	56	153	17 22	56	153	16 26	57	153	15 29	56	154	14 33	56	154	13 37	57	155	12 40	56	155	11 44	57	155	332
27	18 37	56	154	17 41	57	154	16 44	56	154	15 48	57	155	14 51	57	155	13 54	56	155	12 58	57	156	12 01	57	156	333
26	18 56	57	155	17 59	57	155	17 02	56	155	16 06	57	156	15 09	57	156	14 12	57	156	13 15	57	157	12 18	57	157	334
25	19 14	−57	156	18 17	−57	156	17 20	−57	156	16 23	−57	157	15 26	−57	157	14 29	−57	157	13 32	−58	157	12 34	−57	158	335
24	19 31	57	156	18 34	57	157	17 37	58	157	16 39	57	157	15 42	57	158	14 45	57	158	13 48	58	158	12 50	57	159	336
23	19 48	58	157	18 50	57	158	17 53	58	158	16 55	57	158	15 58	58	159	15 00	57	159	14 03	58	159	13 05	57	160	337
22	20 04	58	158	19 06	58	159	18 08	57	159	17 11	58	159	16 13	58	160	15 15	57	160	14 18	58	160	13 20	58	160	338
21	20 19	58	159	19 21	58	160	18 23	57	160	17 26	58	160	16 28	58	160	15 30	58	161	14 32	58	161	13 34	58	161	339
20	20 34	−58	160	19 36	−58	161	18 38	−58	161	17 40	−58	161	16 42	−58	161	15 44	−59	162	14 45	−58	162	13 47	−58	162	340
19	20 48	58	161	19 50	59	161	18 51	58	162	17 53	58	162	16 55	58	162	15 57	59	162	14 58	58	163	14 00	58	163	341
18	21 01	58	162	20 03	59	162	19 04	58	163	18 06	58	163	17 08	59	163	16 09	58	163	15 11	59	164	14 12	58	164	342
17	21 14	59	163	20 15	58	163	19 17	59	164	18 18	58	164	17 20	59	164	16 21	59	164	15 22	58	165	14 24	59	165	343
16	21 26	59	164	20 27	59	164	19 28	58	165	18 30	59	165	17 31	59	165	16 32	59	165	15 33	58	165	14 35	59	166	344
15	21 37	−59	165	20 38	−59	165	19 39	−59	166	18 40	−58	166	17 42	−59	166	16 43	−59	166	15 44	−59	166	14 45	−59	167	345
14	21 48	59	166	20 49	59	166	19 50	59	166	18 51	59	167	17 52	59	167	16 53	59	167	15 54	59	167	14 55	60	167	346
13	21 58	60	167	20 58	59	167	19 59	59	167	19 00	59	168	18 01	59	168	17 02	59	168	16 03	60	168	15 03	59	168	347
12	22 07	60	168	21 07	59	168	20 08	59	168	19 09	59	169	18 10	60	169	17 10	59	169	16 11	59	169	15 12	59	169	348
11	22 15	59	169	21 16	60	169	20 16	59	169	19 17	59	169	18 18	60	170	17 18	59	170	16 19	60	170	15 19	59	170	349
10	22 23	−60	170	21 23	−59	170	20 24	−60	170	19 24	−59	170	18 25	−59	171	17 26	−60	171	16 26	−60	171	15 26	−59	171	350
9	22 30	60	171	21 30	59	171	20 31	60	171	19 31	59	171	18 32	60	172	17 32	60	172	16 32	59	172	15 33	60	172	351
8	22 36	59	172	21 37	60	172	20 37	60	172	19 37	59	172	18 38	60	172	17 38	60	173	16 38	59	173	15 39	60	173	352
7	22 42	60	173	21 42	60	173	20 42	59	173	19 43	60	173	18 43	60	173	17 43	60	174	16 43	59	174	15 44	60	174	353
6	22 47	60	174	21 47	60	174	20 47	60	174	19 47	60	174	18 47	59	174	17 48	60	174	16 48	60	175	15 48	60	175	354
5	22 51	−60	175	21 51	−60	175	20 51	−60	175	19 51	−60	175	18 51	−60	175	17 51	−59	175	16 52	−60	175	15 52	−60	176	355
4	22 54	60	176	21 54	60	176	20 54	60	176	19 54	60	176	18 54	59	176	17 55	60	176	16 55	60	176	15 55	60	176	356
3	22 57	60	177	21 57	60	177	20 57	60	177	19 57	60	177	18 57	60	177	17 57	60	177	16 57	60	177	15 57	60	177	357
2	22 59	60	178	21 59	60	178	20 59	60	178	19 59	60	178	18 59	60	178	17 59	60	178	16 59	60	178	15 59	60	178	358
1	23 00	60	179	22 00	60	179	21 00	60	179	20 00	60	179	19 00	60	179	18 00	60	179	17 00	60	179	16 00	60	179	359
0	23 00	−60	180	22 00	−60	180	21 00	−60	180	20 00	−60	180	19 00	−60	180	18 00	−60	180	17 00	−60	180	16 00	−60	180	360
	22°			23°			24°			25°			26°			27°			28°			29°			

S. Lat. {LHA greater than 180°........ Zn=180−Z; LHA less than 180°............ Zn=180+Z}

DECLINATION (15°-29°) CONTRARY NAME TO LATITUDE

LAT 45°

TABLE 5.—Correction to Tabulated Altitude for Minutes of Declination

d / ′	1	2	3	4	5	6	7	8	9	10	11	12	13	14	15	16	17	18	19	20	21	22	23	24	25	26	27	28	29	30
0	0	0	0	0	0	0	0	0	0	0	0	0	0	0	0	0	0	0	0	0	0	0	0	0	0	0	0	0	0	0
1	0	0	0	0	0	0	0	0	0	0	0	0	0	0	0	0	0	0	0	0	0	0	0	0	0	0	0	0	0	0
2	0	0	0	0	0	0	0	0	0	0	0	0	0	0	0	1	1	1	1	1	1	1	1	1	1	1	1	1	1	1
3	0	0	0	0	0	0	0	0	0	0	1	1	1	1	1	1	1	1	1	1	1	1	1	1	1	1	1	1	1	2
4	0	0	0	0	0	0	0	1	1	1	1	1	1	1	1	1	1	1	1	1	1	1	2	2	2	2	2	2	2	2
5	0	0	0	0	0	0	1	1	1	1	1	1	1	1	1	1	1	2	2	2	2	2	2	2	2	2	2	2	2	2
6	0	0	0	0	0	1	1	1	1	1	1	1	1	1	2	2	2	2	2	2	2	2	2	2	2	3	3	3	3	3
7	0	0	0	0	1	1	1	1	1	1	1	1	2	2	2	2	2	2	2	2	2	3	3	3	3	3	3	3	3	4
8	0	0	0	1	1	1	1	1	1	1	1	2	2	2	2	2	2	2	3	3	3	3	3	3	3	3	4	4	4	4
9	0	0	0	1	1	1	1	1	1	2	2	2	2	2	2	2	3	3	3	3	3	3	3	4	4	4	4	4	4	4
10	0	0	0	1	1	1	1	1	2	2	2	2	2	2	2	3	3	3	3	3	4	4	4	4	4	4	4	5	5	5
11	0	0	1	1	1	1	1	1	2	2	2	2	2	3	3	3	3	3	3	4	4	4	4	4	5	5	5	5	5	6
12	0	0	1	1	1	1	1	2	2	2	2	2	3	3	3	3	3	4	4	4	4	4	5	5	5	5	5	6	6	6
13	0	0	1	1	1	1	2	2	2	2	2	3	3	3	3	3	4	4	4	4	5	5	5	5	5	6	6	6	6	6
14	0	0	1	1	1	1	2	2	2	2	3	3	3	3	4	4	4	4	4	5	5	5	5	6	6	6	6	7	7	7
15	0	0	1	1	1	2	2	2	2	2	3	3	3	4	4	4	4	4	5	5	5	6	6	6	6	6	7	7	7	8
16	0	1	1	1	1	2	2	2	2	3	3	3	3	4	4	4	5	5	5	5	6	6	6	6	7	7	7	7	8	8
17	0	1	1	1	1	2	2	2	3	3	3	3	4	4	4	5	5	5	5	6	6	6	7	7	7	7	8	8	8	8
18	0	1	1	1	2	2	2	2	3	3	3	4	4	4	4	5	5	5	6	6	6	7	7	7	8	8	8	8	9	9
19	0	1	1	1	2	2	2	3	3	3	3	4	4	4	5	5	5	6	6	6	7	7	7	8	8	8	9	9	9	10
20	0	1	1	1	2	2	2	3	3	3	4	4	4	5	5	5	6	6	6	7	7	7	8	8	8	9	9	9	10	10
21	0	1	1	1	2	2	2	3	3	4	4	4	5	5	5	6	6	6	7	7	7	8	8	8	9	9	9	10	10	10
22	0	1	1	1	2	2	3	3	3	4	4	4	5	5	6	6	6	7	7	7	8	8	8	9	9	10	10	10	11	11
23	0	1	1	2	2	2	3	3	3	4	4	5	5	5	6	6	7	7	7	8	8	8	9	9	10	10	10	11	11	12
24	0	1	1	2	2	2	3	3	4	4	4	5	5	6	6	6	7	7	8	8	8	9	9	10	10	10	11	11	12	12
25	0	1	1	2	2	2	3	3	4	4	5	5	5	6	6	7	7	8	8	8	9	9	10	10	10	11	11	12	12	12
26	0	1	1	2	2	3	3	3	4	4	5	5	6	6	6	7	7	8	8	9	9	10	10	10	11	11	12	12	13	13
27	0	1	1	2	2	3	3	4	4	4	5	5	6	6	7	7	8	8	9	9	9	10	10	11	11	12	12	13	13	14
28	0	1	1	2	2	3	3	4	4	5	5	6	6	7	7	7	8	8	9	9	10	10	11	11	12	12	13	13	14	14
29	0	1	1	2	2	3	3	4	4	5	5	6	6	7	7	8	8	9	9	10	10	11	11	12	12	13	13	14	14	14
30	0	1	2	2	2	3	4	4	4	5	6	6	6	7	8	8	8	9	10	10	10	11	12	12	12	13	14	14	14	15
31	1	1	2	2	3	3	4	4	5	5	6	6	7	7	8	8	9	9	10	10	11	11	12	12	13	13	14	14	15	16
32	1	1	2	2	3	3	4	4	5	5	6	6	7	7	8	9	9	10	10	11	11	12	12	13	13	14	14	15	15	16
33	1	1	2	2	3	3	4	4	5	6	6	7	7	8	8	9	9	10	10	11	12	12	13	13	14	14	15	15	16	16
34	1	1	2	2	3	3	4	5	5	6	6	7	7	8	8	9	10	10	11	11	12	12	13	14	14	15	15	16	16	17
35	1	1	2	2	3	4	4	5	5	6	6	7	8	8	9	9	10	10	11	12	12	13	13	14	15	15	16	16	17	18
36	1	1	2	2	3	4	4	5	5	6	7	7	8	8	9	10	10	11	11	12	13	13	14	14	15	16	16	17	17	18
37	1	1	2	2	3	4	4	5	6	6	7	7	8	9	9	10	10	11	12	12	13	14	14	15	15	16	17	17	18	18
38	1	1	2	3	3	4	4	5	6	6	7	8	8	9	10	10	11	11	12	13	13	14	15	15	16	16	17	18	18	19
39	1	1	2	3	3	4	5	5	6	6	7	8	8	9	10	10	11	12	12	13	14	14	15	16	16	17	18	18	19	20
40	1	1	2	3	3	4	5	5	6	7	7	8	9	9	10	11	11	12	13	13	14	15	15	16	17	17	18	19	19	20
41	1	1	2	3	3	4	5	5	6	7	8	8	9	10	10	11	12	12	13	14	14	15	16	16	17	18	18	19	20	20
42	1	1	2	3	4	4	5	6	6	7	8	8	9	10	10	11	12	13	13	14	15	15	16	17	18	18	19	20	20	21
43	1	1	2	3	4	4	5	6	6	7	8	9	9	10	11	11	12	13	14	14	15	16	16	17	18	19	19	20	21	22
44	1	1	2	3	4	4	5	6	7	7	8	9	10	10	11	12	12	13	14	15	15	16	17	18	18	19	20	21	21	22
45	1	2	2	3	4	4	5	6	7	8	8	9	10	10	11	12	13	14	14	15	16	16	17	18	19	20	20	21	22	22
46	1	2	2	3	4	5	5	6	7	8	8	9	10	11	12	12	13	14	15	15	16	17	18	18	19	20	21	21	22	23
47	1	2	2	3	4	5	5	6	7	8	9	9	10	11	12	13	13	14	15	16	16	17	18	19	20	20	21	22	23	24
48	1	2	2	3	4	5	6	6	7	8	9	10	10	11	12	13	14	14	15	16	17	18	18	19	20	21	22	22	23	24
49	1	2	2	3	4	5	6	7	7	8	9	10	11	11	12	13	14	15	16	16	17	18	19	20	20	21	22	23	24	24
50	1	2	2	3	4	5	6	7	8	8	9	10	11	12	12	13	14	15	16	17	18	18	19	20	21	22	22	23	24	25
51	1	2	3	3	4	5	6	7	8	8	9	10	11	12	13	14	14	15	16	17	18	19	20	20	21	22	23	24	25	26
52	1	2	3	3	4	5	6	7	8	9	10	10	11	12	13	14	15	16	16	17	18	19	20	21	22	23	23	24	25	26
53	1	2	3	4	4	5	6	7	8	9	10	11	11	12	13	14	15	16	17	18	19	19	20	21	22	23	24	25	26	26
54	1	2	3	4	4	5	6	7	8	9	10	11	12	13	14	14	15	16	17	18	19	20	21	22	22	23	24	25	26	27
55	1	2	3	4	5	6	6	7	8	9	10	11	12	13	14	15	16	16	17	18	19	20	21	22	23	24	25	26	27	28
56	1	2	3	4	5	6	7	7	8	9	10	11	12	13	14	15	16	17	18	19	20	21	21	22	23	24	25	26	27	28
57	1	2	3	4	5	6	7	8	9	10	10	11	12	13	14	15	16	17	18	19	20	21	22	23	24	25	26	27	28	28
58	1	2	3	4	5	6	7	8	9	10	11	12	13	14	14	15	16	17	18	19	20	21	22	23	24	25	26	27	28	29
59	1	2	3	4	5	6	7	8	9	10	11	12	13	14	15	16	17	18	19	20	21	22	23	24	25	26	27	28	29	30

d / ′	31	32	33	34	35	36	37	38	39	40	41	42	43	44	45	46	47	48	49	50	51	52	53	54	55	56	57	58	59	60	d / ′
0	0	0	0	0	0	0	0	0	0	0	0	0	0	0	0	0	0	0	0	0	0	0	0	0	0	0	0	0	0	0	0
1	1	1	1	1	1	1	1	1	1	1	1	1	1	1	1	1	1	1	1	1	1	1	1	1	1	1	1	1	1	1	1
2	1	1	1	1	1	1	1	1	1	1	1	1	1	1	2	2	2	2	2	2	2	2	2	2	2	2	2	2	2	2	2
3	2	2	2	2	2	2	2	2	2	2	2	2	2	2	2	2	2	2	2	2	3	3	3	3	3	3	3	3	3	3	3
4	2	2	2	2	2	2	2	3	3	3	3	3	3	3	3	3	3	3	3	3	3	3	4	4	4	4	4	4	4	4	4
5	3	3	3	3	3	3	3	3	3	3	3	4	4	4	4	4	4	4	4	4	4	4	4	4	5	5	5	5	5	5	5
6	3	3	3	3	4	4	4	4	4	4	4	4	4	4	4	5	5	5	5	5	5	5	5	5	6	6	6	6	6	6	6
7	4	4	4	4	4	4	4	4	5	5	5	5	5	5	5	5	5	6	6	6	6	6	6	6	6	7	7	7	7	7	7
8	4	4	4	5	5	5	5	5	5	5	5	6	6	6	6	6	6	6	7	7	7	7	7	7	7	7	8	8	8	8	8
9	5	5	5	5	5	5	6	6	6	6	6	6	6	7	7	7	7	7	7	8	8	8	8	8	8	8	9	9	9	9	9
10	5	5	6	6	6	6	6	6	6	7	7	7	7	7	8	8	8	8	8	8	8	9	9	9	9	9	10	10	10	10	10
11	6	6	6	6	6	7	7	7	7	7	8	8	8	8	8	8	9	9	9	9	9	10	10	10	10	10	10	11	11	11	11
12	6	6	7	7	7	7	7	8	8	8	8	8	9	9	9	9	9	10	10	10	10	10	11	11	11	11	11	12	12	12	12
13	7	7	7	7	8	8	8	8	8	9	9	9	9	10	10	10	10	10	11	11	11	11	11	12	12	12	12	13	13	13	13
14	7	7	8	8	8	8	9	9	9	9	10	10	10	10	10	11	11	11	11	12	12	12	12	13	13	13	13	14	14	14	14
15	8	8	8	8	9	9	9	10	10	10	10	10	11	11	11	12	12	12	12	12	13	13	13	14	14	14	14	14	15	15	15
16	8	9	9	9	9	10	10	10	10	11	11	11	11	12	12	12	13	13	13	13	14	14	14	14	15	15	15	15	16	16	16
17	9	9	9	10	10	10	10	11	11	11	12	12	12	12	13	13	13	14	14	14	14	15	15	15	16	16	16	16	17	17	17
18	9	10	10	10	10	11	11	11	12	12	12	13	13	13	14	14	14	14	15	15	15	16	16	16	16	17	17	17	18	18	18
19	10	10	10	11	11	11	12	12	12	13	13	13	14	14	14	15	15	15	16	16	16	16	17	17	17	18	18	18	19	19	19
20	10	11	11	11	12	12	12	13	13	13	14	14	14	15	15	15	16	16	16	17	17	17	18	18	18	19	19	19	20	20	20
21	11	11	12	12	12	13	13	13	14	14	14	15	15	15	16	16	16	17	17	18	18	18	19	19	19	20	20	20	21	21	21
22	11	12	12	12	13	13	14	14	14	15	15	15	16	16	16	17	17	18	18	18	19	19	19	20	20	21	21	21	22	22	22
23	12	12	13	13	13	14	14	15	15	15	16	16	16	17	17	18	18	18	19	19	20	20	20	21	21	21	22	22	23	23	23
24	12	13	13	14	14	14	15	15	16	16	16	17	17	18	18	18	19	19	20	20	20	21	21	22	22	22	23	23	24	24	24
25	13	13	14	14	15	15	15	16	16	17	17	18	18	18	19	19	20	20	20	21	21	22	22	22	23	23	24	24	25	25	25
26	13	14	14	15	15	16	16	16	17	17	18	18	19	19	20	20	20	21	21	22	22	23	23	23	24	24	25	25	26	26	26
27	14	14	15	15	16	16	17	17	18	18	18	19	19	20	20	21	21	22	22	22	23	23	24	24	25	25	26	26	27	27	27
28	14	15	15	16	16	17	17	18	18	19	19	20	20	21	21	21	22	22	23	23	24	24	25	25	26	26	27	27	28	28	28
29	15	15	16	16	17	17	18	18	19	19	20	20	21	21	22	22	23	23	24	24	25	25	26	26	27	27	28	28	29	29	29
30	16	16	16	17	18	18	18	19	20	20	20	21	22	22	22	23	24	24	24	25	26	26	26	27	28	28	28	29	30	30	30
31	16	17	17	18	18	19	19	20	20	21	21	22	22	23	23	24	24	25	25	26	26	27	27	28	28	29	29	30	30	31	31
32	17	17	18	18	19	19	20	20	21	21	22	22	23	23	24	25	25	26	26	27	27	28	28	29	29	30	30	31	31	32	32
33	17	18	18	19	19	20	20	21	21	22	23	23	24	24	25	25	26	26	27	28	28	29	29	30	30	31	31	32	32	33	33
34	18	18	19	19	20	20	21	22	22	23	23	24	24	25	26	26	27	27	28	28	29	29	30	31	31	32	32	33	33	34	34
35	18	19	19	20	20	21	22	22	23	23	24	24	25	26	26	27	27	28	29	29	30	30	31	32	32	33	33	34	34	35	35
36	19	19	20	20	21	22	22	23	23	24	25	25	26	26	27	28	28	29	29	30	31	31	32	32	33	34	34	35	35	36	36
37	19	20	20	21	22	22	23	23	24	25	25	26	27	27	28	28	29	30	30	31	31	32	33	33	34	35	35	36	36	37	37
38	20	20	21	22	22	23	23	24	25	25	26	27	27	28	28	29	30	30	31	32	32	33	34	34	35	35	36	37	37	38	38
39	20	21	21	22	23	23	24	25	25	26	27	27	28	29	29	30	31	31	32	32	33	34	34	35	36	36	37	38	38	39	39
40	21	21	22	23	23	24	25	25	26	27	27	28	29	29	30	31	31	32	33	33	34	35	35	36	37	37	38	39	39	40	40
41	21	22	23	23	24	25	25	26	27	27	28	29	29	30	31	31	32	33	33	34	35	36	36	37	38	38	39	40	40	41	41
42	22	22	23	24	24	25	26	27	27	28	29	29	30	31	32	32	33	34	34	35	36	36	37	38	38	39	40	41	41	42	42
43	22	23	24	24	25	26	27	27	28	29	29	30	31	32	32	33	34	34	35	36	37	37	38	39	39	40	41	42	42	43	43
44	23	23	24	25	26	26	27	28	29	29	30	31	32	32	33	34	34	35	36	37	37	38	39	40	40	41	42	43	43	44	44
45	23	24	25	26	26	27	28	28	29	30	31	32	32	33	34	34	35	36	37	38	38	39	40	40	41	42	43	44	44	45	45
46	24	25	25	26	27	28	28	29	30	31	31	32	33	34	34	35	36	37	38	38	39	40	41	41	42	43	44	44	45	46	46
47	24	25	26	27	27	28	29	30	31	31	32	33	34	34	35	36	37	38	38	39	40	41	42	42	43	44	45	45	46	47	47
48	25	26	26	27	28	29	30	30	31	32	33	34	34	35	36	37	38	38	39	40	41	42	42	43	44	45	46	46	47	48	48
49	25	26	27	28	29	29	30	31	32	33	33	34	35	36	37	38	38	39	40	41	42	42	43	44	45	46	47	47	48	49	49
50	26	27	28	28	29	30	31	32	32	33	34	35	36	37	38	38	39	40	41	42	42	43	44	45	46	47	48	48	49	50	50
51	26	27	28	29	30	31	31	32	33	34	35	36	37	37	38	39	40	41	42	42	43	44	45	46	47	48	48	49	50	51	51
52	27	28	29	29	30	31	32	33	34	35	36	36	37	38	39	40	41	42	42	43	44	45	46	47	48	49	49	50	51	52	52
53	27	28	29	30	31	32	33	34	34	35	36	37	38	39	40	41	42	42	43	44	45	46	47	48	49	49	50	51	52	53	53
54	28	29	30	31	32	32	33	34	35	36	37	38	39	40	40	41	42	43	44	45	46	47	48	49	50	50	51	52	53	54	54
55	28	29	30	31	32	33	34	35	36	37	38	38	39	40	41	42	43	44	45	46	47	48	49	50	50	51	52	53	54	55	55
56	29	30	31	32	33	34	35	35	36	37	38	39	40	41	42	43	44	45	46	47	48	49	49	50	51	52	53	54	55	56	56
57	29	30	31	32	33	34	35	36	37	38	39	40	41	42	43	44	45	46	47	48	48	49	50	51	52	53	54	55	56	57	57
58	30	31	32	33	34	35	36	37	38	39	40	41	42	43	44	44	45	46	47	48	49	50	51	52	53	54	55	56	57	58	58
59	30	31	32	33	34	35	36	37	38	39	40	41	42	43	44	45	46	47	48	49	50	51	52	53	54	55	56	57	58	59	59

276

POLARIS (POLE STAR) TABLES, 1978

FOR DETERMINING LATITUDE FROM SEXTANT ALTITUDE AND FOR AZIMUTH

L.H.A. ARIES	240°–249°	250°–259°	260°–269°	270°–279°	280°–289°	290°–299°	300°–309°	310°–319°	320°–329°	330°–339°	340°–349°	350°–359°
	a_0	a_0	a_0	a_0	a_0	a_0	a_0	a_0	a_0	a_0	a_0	a_0
°	° ′	° ′	° ′	° ′	° ′	° ′	° ′	° ′	° ′	° ′	° ′	° ′
0	1 43·3	1 38·8	1 33·0	1 26·2	1 18·5	1 10·3	1 01·6	0 52·9	0 44·4	0 36·3	0 28·8	0 22·3
1	42·9	38·2	32·3	25·4	17·7	09·4	1 00·8	52·1	43·5	35·5	28·1	21·7
2	42·5	37·7	31·7	24·7	16·9	08·6	0 59.9	51·2	42·7	34·7	27·4	21·1
3	42·1	37·2	31·0	24·0	16·1	07·7	59·0	50·3	41·9	33·9	26·8	20·5
4	41·7	36·6	30·4	23·2	15·3	06·8	58·2	49·5	41·1	33·2	26·1	20·0
5	1 41·2	1 36·0	1 29·7	1 22·4	1 14·5	1 06·0	0 57·3	0 48·6	0 40·3	0 32·4	0 25·4	0 19·4
6	40·8	35·4	29·0	21·7	13·6	05·1	56·4	47·8	39·4	31·7	24·8	18·9
7	40·3	34·8	28·3	20·9	12·8	04·3	55·5	46·9	38·6	31·0	24·1	18·4
8	39·8	34·2	27·6	20·1	11·9	03·4	54·7	46·1	37·8	30·2	23·5	17·9
9	39·3	33·6	26·9	19·3	11·1	02·5	53·8	45·2	37·0	29·5	22·9	17·4
10	1 38·8	1 33·0	1 26·2	1 18·5	1 10·3	1 01·6	0 52·9	0 44·4	0 36·3	0 28·8	0 22·3	0 16·9
Lat.	a_1	a_1	a_1	a_1	a_1	a_1	a_1	a_1	a_1	a_1	a_1	a_1
°	′	′	′	′	′	′	′	′	′	′	′	′
0	0·5	0·4	0·3	0·3	0·2	0·2	0·2	0·2	0·2	0·3	0·4	0·4
10	·5	·4	·4	·3	·3	·2	·2	·2	·3	·3	·4	·5
20	·5	·5	·4	·4	·3	·3	·3	·3	·3	·4	·4	·5
30	·5	·5	·5	·4	·4	·4	·4	·4	·4	·4	·5	·5
40	0·6	0·5	0·5	0·5	0·5	0·5	0·5	0·5	0·5	0·5	0·5	0·6
45	·6	·6	·6	·5	·5	·5	·5	·5	·5	·6	·6	·6
50	·6	·6	·6	·6	·6	·6	·6	·6	·6	·6	·6	·6
55	·6	·6	·7	·7	·7	·7	·7	·7	·7	·7	·6	·6
60	·7	·7	·7	·8	·8	·8	·8	·8	·8	·7	·7	·7
62	0·7	0·7	0·8	0·8	0·8	0·8	0·9	0·8	0·8	0·8	0·7	0·7
64	·7	·7	·8	·8	·9	0·9	0·9	0·9	·9	·8	·8	·7
66	·7	·8	·8	0·9	0·9	1·0	1·0	1·0	0·9	·9	·8	·7
68	0·7	0·8	0·9	1·0	1·0	1·1	1·1	1·0	1·0	0·9	0·9	0·8
Month	a_2	a_2	a_2	a_2	a_2	a_2	a_2	a_2	a_2	a_2	a_2	a_2
	′	′	′	′	′	′	′	′	′	′	′	′
Jan.	0·5	0·5	0·5	0·5	0·5	0·6	0·6	0·6	0·6	0·6	0·7	0·7
Feb.	·4	·4	·4	·4	·4	·4	·4	·5	·5	·5	·5	·6
Mar.	·4	·4	·4	·3	·3	·3	·3	·3	·3	·4	·4	·4
Apr.	0·5	0·5	0·4	0·3	0·3	0·3	0·2	0·2	0·2	0·2	0·3	0·3
May	·7	·6	·5	·4	·4	·3	·3	·2	·2	·2	·2	·2
June	·8	·7	·7	·6	·5	·4	·4	·3	·3	·2	·2	·2
July	0·9	0·9	0·8	0·7	0·7	0·6	0·5	0·5	0·4	0·3	0·3	0·3
Aug.	1·0	·9	·9	·9	·8	·8	·7	·6	·6	·5	·4	·4
Sept.	0·9	·9	·9	·9	·9	·9	·8	·8	·7	·7	·6	·6
Oct.	0·8	0·9	0·9	0·9	0·9	0·9	0·9	0·9	0·9	0·9	0·8	0·8
Nov.	·7	·8	·8	·9	·9	·9	1·0	1·0	1·0	1·0	0·9	0·9
Dec.	0·5	0·6	0·7	0·7	0·8	0·8	0·9	0·9	1·0	1·0	1·0	1·0
Lat.	AZIMUTH											
°	°	°	°	°	°	°	°	°	°	°	°	°
0	0·4	0·6	0·7	0·7	0·8	0·8	0·8	0·8	0·8	0·7	0·6	0·5
20	0·5	0·6	0·7	0·8	0·8	0·9	0·9	0·9	0·8	0·8	0·7	0·5
40	0·6	0·7	0·9	1·0	1·0	1·1	1·1	1·1	1·0	0·9	0·8	0·7
50	0·7	0·9	1·0	1·1	1·2	1·3	1·3	1·3	1·2	1·1	1·0	0·8
55	0·8	1·0	1·1	1·3	1·4	1·4	1·5	1·4	1·4	1·2	1·1	0·9
60	0·9	1·1	1·3	1·5	1·6	1·6	1·7	1·6	1·6	1·4	1·3	1·0
65	1·0	1·3	1·5	1·7	1·9	1·9	2·0	1·9	1·8	1·7	1·5	1·2

Latitude = Apparent altitude (corrected for refraction) $- 1° + a_0 + a_1 + a_2$

The table is entered with L.H.A. Aries to determine the column to be used; each column refers to a range of 10°. a_0 is taken, with mental interpolation, from the upper table with the units of L.H.A. Aries in degrees as argument; a_1, a_2 are taken, without interpolation, from the second and third tables with arguments latitude and month respectively. a_0, a_1, a_2 are always positive. The final table gives the azimuth of *Polaris*.

N. Lat. {LHA greater than 180°....... Zn=Z; LHA less than 180°............ Zn=360−Z}

DECLINATION (15°-29°) CONTRARY NAME TO LATITUDE — LAT 20°

LHA	15° Hc	d	Z	16° Hc	d	Z	17° Hc	d	Z	18° Hc	d	Z	19° Hc	d	Z	20° Hc	d	Z	21° Hc	d	Z	22° Hc	d	Z
29	44 52	47	139	44 05	46	140	43 19	47	140	42 32	48	141	41 44	47	142	40 57	48	143	40 09	49	144	39 20	48	145
28	45 28	46	140	44 42	48	141	43 54	47	142	43 07	48	142	42 19	49	143	41 30	48	144	40 42	49	145	39 53	49	145
27	46 04	47	141	45 17	48	142	44 29	48	143	43 41	49	143	42 52	49	144	42 03	49	145	41 14	50	146	40 24	50	146
26	46 40	49	142	45 51	48	143	45 03	49	144	44 14	49	144	43 25	50	145	42 35	50	146	41 45	50	147	40 55	50	148
25	47 14	−49	143	46 25	−49	144	45 36	−50	145	44 46	−50	146	43 56	−50	146	43 06	−50	147	42 16	−51	148	41 25	−51	149

23° Hc	d	Z	24° Hc	d	Z	25° Hc	d	Z	26° Hc	d	Z	27° Hc	d	Z	28° Hc	d	Z	29° Hc	d	Z	LHA
38 32	49	145	37 43	49	146	36 54	50	147	36 04	49	147	35 15	50	148	34 25	51	149	33 34	50	149	331
39 04	50	146	38 14	50	147	37 24	50	148	36 34	50	148	35 44	51	149	34 53	50	150	34 03	51	150	332
39 34	50	147	38 44	50	148	37 54	51	149	37 03	50	149	36 13	51	150	35 22	52	151	34 30	51	151	333
40 05	51	148	39 14	51	149	38 23	51	150	37 32	52	150	36 40	51	151	35 49	52	152	34 57	52	152	334
40 34	−51	149	39 43	−52	150	38 51	−52	151	37 59	−51	151	37 08	−53	152	36 15	−52	152	35 23	−52	153	335

N. Lat. {LHA greater than 180°....... Zn=Z; LHA less than 180°............ Zn=360−Z}

DECLINATION (15°-29°) CONTRARY NAME TO LATITUDE — LAT 21°

LHA	15° Hc	d	Z	16° Hc	d	Z	17° Hc	d	Z	18° Hc	d	Z	19° Hc	d	Z	20° Hc	d	Z	21° Hc	d	Z	22° Hc	d	Z
29	44 06	47	139	43 19	47	140	42 32	47	141	41 45	48	142	40 57	48	143	40 09	49	143	39 20	49	144	38 31	49	145
28	44 42	47	140	43 55	48	141	43 07	48	142	42 19	48	143	41 31	49	144	40 42	49	144	39 53	50	145	39 03	49	146
27	45 18	48	141	44 30	49	142	43 41	49	143	42 52	49	144	42 03	49	145	41 14	50	145	40 24	50	146	39 34	50	147
26	45 52	49	143	45 03	49	143	44 14	49	144	43 25	50	145	42 35	50	146	41 45	50	147	40 55	51	147	40 04	50	148
25	46 26	−50	144	45 36	−49	145	44 47	−50	145	43 57	−51	146	43 06	−50	147	42 16	−51	148	41 25	−51	148	40 34	−52	149
14	51 28	56	158	50 32	56	159	49 36	57	159	48 39	56	160	47 43	57	160	46 46	56	161	45 50	57	161	44 53	57	162
13	51 48	56	159	50 52	57	160	49 55	57	161	48 58	57	161	48 01	57	162	47 04	57	162	46 07	57	162	45 10	57	163
12	52 07	57	161	51 10	57	161	50 13	57	162	49 16	57	162	48 19	58	163	47 21	57	163	46 24	58	164	45 26	58	164
11	52 25	57	162	51 28	58	163	50 30	58	163	49 32	57	164	48 35	58	164	47 37	58	165	46 39	58	165	45 41	58	165
10	52 41	−58	164	51 43	−58	164	50 45	−58	165	49 47	−58	165	48 49	−58	166	47 51	−58	166	46 53	−59	166	45 54	−58	167

23° Hc	d	Z	24° Hc	d	Z	25° Hc	d	Z	26° Hc	d	Z	27° Hc	d	Z	28° Hc	d	Z	29° Hc	d	Z	LHA
37 42	49	146	36 53	50	146	36 03	49	147	35 14	50	148	34 24	51	148	33 33	50	149	32 43	51	150	331
38 14	50	147	37 24	51	147	36 33	50	148	35 43	51	149	34 52	50	149	34 02	51	150	33 11	52	151	332
38 44	51	148	37 53	50	148	37 03	51	149	36 12	51	150	35 21	52	150	34 29	51	151	33 38	52	152	333
39 14	52	149	38 22	51	149	37 31	51	150	36 40	52	151	35 48	52	151	34 56	52	152	34 04	52	152	334
39 42	−51	150	38 51	−52	150	37 59	−52	151	37 07	−52	152	36 15	−53	152	35 22	−52	153	34 30	−53	153	335
43 56	57	162	42 59	57	162	42 02	57	163	41 05	58	163	40 07	57	164	39 10	57	164	38 13	58	164	346
44 13	58	163	43 15	57	164	42 18	58	164	41 20	57	164	40 23	58	165	39 25	58	165	38 27	58	165	347
44 28	57	164	43 31	58	165	42 33	58	165	41 35	58	166	40 37	58	166	39 39	58	166	38 41	58	167	348
44 43	58	166	43 45	58	166	42 47	59	166	41 48	58	167	40 50	58	167	39 52	59	167	38 53	58	168	349
44 56	−58	167	43 58	−59	167	42 59	−58	168	42 01	−59	168	41 02	−59	168	40 03	−58	168	39 05	−59	169	350

N. Lat. {LHA greater than 180°....... Zn=Z; LHA less than 180°............ Zn=360−Z}

DECLINATION (0°-14°) SAME NAME AS LATITUDE — LAT 21°

LHA	0° Hc	d	Z	1° Hc	d	Z	2° Hc	d	Z	3° Hc	d	Z	4° Hc	d	Z	5° Hc	d	Z	6° Hc	d	Z	7° Hc	d	Z
30	53 57	+36	122	54 33	+35	121	55 08	+34	119	55 42	+33	118	56 15	+32	116	56 47	+31	115	57 18	+30	113	57 48	+28	111
31	53 09	36	121	53 45	34	120	54 19	34	118	54 53	32	117	55 25	31	115	55 56	30	114	56 26	29	112	56 55	28	111
32	52 21	35	120	52 56	33	119	53 29	33	117	54 02	32	116	54 34	31	114	55 05	29	113	55 34	29	111	56 03	27	110
33	51 32	34	119	52 06	33	118	52 39	33	116	53 12	31	115	53 43	30	113	54 13	29	112	54 42	28	110	55 10	27	109
34	50 43	33	118	51 16	33	117	51 49	32	115	52 21	30	114	52 51	30	113	53 21	28	111	53 49	28	110	54 17	26	108

8° Hc	d	Z	9° Hc	d	Z	10° Hc	d	Z	11° Hc	d	Z	12° Hc	d	Z	13° Hc	d	Z	14° Hc	d	Z	LHA
58 16	+27	110	58 43	+26	108	59 09	+24	106	59 33	+22	105	59 55	+21	103	60 16	+20	101	60 36	+18	99	330
57 23	27	109	57 50	25	107	58 15	23	106	58 38	23	104	59 01	20	102	59 21	19	100	59 40	18	98	329
56 30	26	108	56 56	25	106	57 21	23	105	57 44	22	103	58 06	20	101	58 26	19	100	58 45	17	98	328
55 37	25	107	56 02	24	106	56 26	23	104	56 49	22	102	57 11	20	101	57 31	18	99	57 49	17	97	327
54 43	25	107	55 08	24	105	55 32	22	103	55 54	22	102	56 16	19	100	56 35	19	98	56 54	17	97	326

N. Lat. {LHA greater than 180°....... Zn=Z; LHA less than 180°............ Zn=360−Z}

DECLINATION (0°-14°) SAME NAME AS LATITUDE — LAT 22°

LHA	0° Hc	d	Z	1° Hc	d	Z	2° Hc	d	Z	3° Hc	d	Z	4° Hc	d	Z	5° Hc	d	Z	6° Hc	d	Z	7° Hc	d	Z
5	67 28	+59	167	68 27	+58	166	69 25	+58	166	70 23	+59	165	71 22	+58	164	72 20	+57	163	73 17	+58	163	74 15	+57	161
6	67 14	58	164	68 12	58	164	69 10	58	163	70 08	57	162	71 05	57	161	72 02	57	160	72 59	56	159	73 55	56	158
7	66 58	57	162	67 55	57	161	68 52	57	160	69 49	57	159	70 46	56	158	71 42	56	157	72 38	55	156	73 33	55	155
8	66 40	56	159	67 36	56	159	68 32	56	158	69 28	56	157	70 24	55	156	71 19	55	154	72 14	54	153	73 08	53	152
9	66 19	56	157	67 15	55	156	68 10	55	155	69 05	55	154	70 00	54	153	70 54	53	152	71 47	53	150	72 40	52	149
30	53 25	+37	123	54 02	+37	122	54 39	+35	120	55 14	+34	119	55 48	+34	117	56 22	+32	116	56 54	+31	114	57 25	+30	113
31	52 38	37	122	53 15	35	121	53 50	35	119	54 25	34	118	54 59	33	117	55 32	31	115	56 03	31	114	56 34	29	112
32	51 50	36	121	52 26	36	120	53 02	34	118	53 36	33	117	54 09	32	116	54 41	31	114	55 12	30	113	55 42	29	111
33	51 03	35	120	51 38	34	119	52 12	34	117	52 46	32	116	53 18	32	115	53 50	30	113	54 20	30	112	54 50	28	110
34	50 14	35	119	50 49	34	118	51 23	33	116	51 56	32	115	52 28	31	114	52 59	30	112	53 29	29	111	53 58	27	109

8° Hc	d	Z	9° Hc	d	Z	10° Hc	d	Z	11° Hc	d	Z	12° Hc	d	Z	13° Hc	d	Z	14° Hc	d	Z	LHA
75 12	+56	160	76 08	+57	159	77 05	+55	157	78 00	+55	156	78 55	+54	154	79 49	+53	151	80 42	+51	148	355
74 51	56	157	75 47	55	155	76 42	54	153	77 36	53	152	78 29	51	149	79 20	51	147	80 11	48	144	354
74 28	54	153	75 22	53	152	76 15	52	150	77 07	51	148	77 58	50	145	78 48	48	142	79 36	45	139	353
74 01	53	150	74 54	51	148	75 45	51	146	76 36	49	144	77 25	48	141	78 13	45	138	78 58	43	135	352
73 32	51	147	74 23	50	145	75 13	49	143	76 02	47	141	76 49	45	138	77 34	44	135	78 18	40	132	351
57 55	+29	111	58 24	+27	110	58 51	+26	108	59 17	+24	106	59 41	+23	104	60 04	+22	102	60 26	+19	101	330
57 03	28	110	57 31	27	109	57 58	25	107	58 23	24	105	58 47	23	104	59 10	21	102	59 31	19	100	329
56 11	27	110	56 38	27	108	57 05	25	106	57 30	23	105	57 53	22	103	58 15	21	101	58 36	19	99	328
55 18	27	109	55 45	26	107	56 11	25	106	56 36	23	104	56 59	22	102	57 21	20	100	57 41	19	99	327
54 25	27	108	54 52	25	106	55 17	25	105	55 42	22	103	56 04	22	102	56 26	20	100	56 46	19	98	326

N. Lat. { L.H.A. greater than 180°......Zn=Z; L.H.A. less than 180°............Zn=360°−Z }

S. Lat. { L.H.A. greater than 180°......Zn=180°−Z; L.H.A. less than 180°............Zn=180°+Z }

Selected parts of Pub. 249 Sight Reduction Tables for use with Exercise 6.6.
Use Table 5 (T-21) for d correction to Hc.

N. Lat. {LHA greater than 180°....... Zn=Z; LHA less than 180°............ Zn=360−Z}

DECLINATION (15°-29°) SAME NAME AS LATITUDE — LAT 26°

LHA	15°			16°			17°			18°			19°			20°			21°			22°		
	Hc	d	Z	Hc	d	Z	Hc	d	Z	Hc	d	Z	Hc	d	Z	Hc	d	Z	Hc	d	Z	Hc	d	Z
	° ′	′	°	° ′	′	°	° ′	′	°	° ′	′	°	° ′	′	°	° ′	′	°	° ′	′	°	° ′	′	°
10	75 34	+46	138	76 20	+44	135	77 04	+42	132	77 46	+39	129	78 25	+36	125	79 01	+33	121	79 34	+28	117	80 02	+23	112
11	74 57	44	135	75 41	42	132	76 23	40	129	77 03	37	126	77 40	34	122	78 14	31	118	78 45	26	114	79 11	22	109
12	74 18	42	132	75 00	41	129	75 41	38	127	76 19	35	123	76 54	32	120	77 26	29	116	77 55	25	112	78 20	21	108
13	73 37	41	130	74 18	39	127	74 57	36	124	75 33	34	121	76 07	31	118	76 38	27	114	77 05	24	110	77 29	19	106
14	72 55	39	127	73 34	37	125	74 11	35	122	74 46	33	119	75 19	29	116	75 48	26	112	76 14	23	108	76 37	18	104
40	51 08	+22	98	51 30	+22	97	51 52	+21	95	52 13	+19	94	52 32	+18	92	52 50	+17	91	53 07	+16	89	53 23	+14	88
41	50 14	23	98	50 37	21	96	50 58	21	95	51 19	19	93	51 38	18	92	51 56	17	90	52 13	16	89	52 29	14	87
42	49 21	22	97	49 43	22	96	50 05	20	94	50 25	19	93	50 44	18	91	51 02	17	90	51 19	16	88	51 35	15	87
43	48 27	23	97	48 50	21	95	49 11	20	94	49 31	19	92	49 50	19	91	50 09	16	90	50 25	16	88	50 41	15	86
44	47 34	22	96	47 56	21	95	48 17	20	93	48 37	20	92	48 57	18	91	49 15	17	89	49 32	15	88	49 47	15	86

23°			24°			25°			26°			27°			28°			29°			LHA
Hc	d	Z	Hc	d	Z	Hc	d	Z	Hc	d	Z	Hc	d	Z	Hc	d	Z	Hc	d	Z	
° ′	′	°	° ′	′	°	° ′	′	°	° ′	′	°	° ′	′	°	° ′	′	°	° ′	′	°	
80 25	+18	106	80 43	+12	100	80 55	+6	94	81 01	−1	88	81 00	−8	81	80 52	−14	75	80 38	−19	69	350
79 33	17	104	79 50	12	99	80 02	5	93	80 07	0	88	80 07	7	82	80 00	12	76	79 48	18	70	349
78 41	16	103	78 57	11	98	79 08	5	93	79 13	0	87	79 13	5	82	79 08	11	77	78 57	16	72	348
77 48	15	102	78 03	11	97	78 14	5	92	78 19	+1	87	78 20	5	82	78 15	9	77	78 06	15	73	347
76 55	15	100	77 10	10	96	77 20	5	92	77 25	1	87	77 26	4	82	77 22	8	78	77 14	13	73	346
53 37	+13	86	53 50	+12	84	54 02	+10	83	54 12	+8	81	54 20	+8	79	54 28	+6	78	54 34	+4	76	320
52 43	13	86	52 56	12	84	53 08	10	82	53 18	9	81	53 27	8	79	53 35	6	77	53 41	5	76	319
51 50	13	85	52 03	12	84	52 15	10	82	52 25	10	80	52 35	8	79	52 43	6	77	52 49	5	76	318
50 56	13	85	51 09	12	83	51 21	11	82	51 32	10	80	51 42	8	79	51 50	7	77	51 57	6	75	317
50 02	14	85	50 16	12	83	50 28	11	82	50 39	10	80	50 49	8	78	50 57	8	77	51 05	6	75	316

N. Lat. {LHA greater than 180°....... Zn=Z; LHA less than 180°............ Zn=360−Z}

DECLINATION (0°-14°) CONTRARY NAME TO LATITUDE — LAT 27°

LHA	0°			1°			2°			3°			4°			5°			6°			7°		
	Hc	d	Z	Hc	d	Z	Hc	d	Z	Hc	d	Z	Hc	d	Z	Hc	d	Z	Hc	d	Z	Hc	d	Z
	° ′	′	°	° ′	′	°	° ′	′	°	° ′	′	°	° ′	′	°	° ′	′	°	° ′	′	°	° ′	′	°
69	18 37	29	100	18 08	29	101	17 39	29	102	17 10	30	103	16 40	30	104	16 10	30	105	15 40	30	105	15 10	31	106
68	19 30	29	100	19 01	29	101	18 32	30	102	18 02	30	103	17 32	30	104	17 02	30	105	16 32	31	106	16 01	31	107
67	20 22	29	101	19 53	29	102	19 24	30	103	18 54	30	104	18 24	30	105	17 54	31	106	17 23	31	106	16 52	31	107
66	21 15	29	101	20 46	30	102	20 16	30	103	19 46	30	104	19 16	31	105	18 45	31	106	18 14	31	107	17 43	31	108
65	22 07	−29	102	21 38	−30	103	21 08	−30	104	20 38	−31	105	20 07	−31	106	19 36	−31	107	19 05	−31	108	18 34	−31	108

8°			9°			10°			11°			12°			13°			14°			LHA
Hc	d	Z	Hc	d	Z	Hc	d	Z	Hc	d	Z	Hc	d	Z	Hc	d	Z	Hc	d	Z	
° ′	′	°	° ′	′	°	° ′	′	°	° ′	′	°	° ′	′	°	° ′	′	°	° ′	′	°	
14 39	30	107	14 09	31	108	13 38	31	109	13 07	32	110	12 35	31	111	12 04	32	112	11 32	32	112	291
15 30	31	108	14 59	31	109	14 28	31	109	13 57	32	110	13 25	31	111	12 54	32	112	12 22	33	113	292
16 21	31	108	15 50	31	109	15 19	32	110	14 47	32	111	14 15	32	112	13 43	32	113	13 11	33	114	293
17 12	32	109	16 40	31	110	16 09	32	111	15 37	32	111	15 05	33	112	14 32	32	113	14 00	33	114	294
18 03	−32	109	17 31	−32	110	16 59	−33	111	16 26	−32	112	15 54	−33	113	15 21	−33	114	14 48	−33	115	295

N. Lat. {LHA greater than 180°....... Zn=Z; LHA less than 180°............ Zn=360−Z}

DECLINATION (0°-14°) CONTRARY NAME TO LATITUDE — LAT 28°

LHA	0°			1°			2°			3°			4°			5°			6°			7°		
	Hc	d	Z	Hc	d	Z	Hc	d	Z	Hc	d	Z	Hc	d	Z	Hc	d	Z	Hc	d	Z	Hc	d	Z
26	52 31	46	134	51 45	47	135	50 58	48	136	50 10	48	137	49 22	48	138	48 34	49	139	47 45	49	140	46 56	50	140
25	53 09	−47	135	52 22	−48	136	51 34	−48	137	50 46	−49	138	49 57	−49	139	49 08	−49	140	48 19	−50	141	47 29	−50	142
24	53 46	48	137	52 58	48	138	52 10	49	139	51 21	49	139	50 32	50	140	49 42	50	141	48 52	51	142	48 01	50	143
23	54 22	49	138	53 33	49	139	52 44	49	140	51 55	50	141	51 05	50	142	50 15	51	143	49 24	51	143	48 33	52	144
22	54 57	49	139	54 08	50	140	53 18	50	141	52 28	51	142	51 37	51	143	50 46	51	144	49 55	52	145	49 03	52	145
21	55 31	50	141	54 41	50	142	53 51	51	143	53 00	51	144	52 09	52	144	51 17	52	145	50 25	52	146	49 33	53	147
20	56 04	−51	142	55 13	−51	143	54 22	−51	144	53 31	−52	145	52 39	−52	146	51 47	−53	147	50 54	−53	147	50 01	−53	148
9	60 42	58	161	59 44	57	162	58 47	58	162	57 49	58	163	56 51	58	163	55 53	58	164	54 55	59	164	53 56	58	165
8	60 58	58	163	60 00	58	164	59 02	58	164	58 04	59	165	57 05	58	165	56 07	59	166	55 08	59	166	54 09	58	166
7	61 12	58	165	60 14	59	166	59 15	58	166	58 17	59	167	57 18	59	167	56 19	59	167	55 20	59	168	54 21	59	168
6	61 25	59	167	60 26	59	168	59 27	59	168	58 28	59	169	57 29	59	169	56 30	59	169	55 31	60	169	54 31	59	170
5	61 36	−60	169	60 36	−59	170	59 37	−59	170	58 38	−60	170	57 38	−59	171	56 39	−59	171	55 40	−60	171	54 40	−59	171

8°			9°			10°			11°			12°			13°			14°			LHA
Hc	d	Z	Hc	d	Z	Hc	d	Z	Hc	d	Z	Hc	d	Z	Hc	d	Z	Hc	d	Z	
46 06	50	141	45 16	50	142	44 26	51	143	43 35	51	144	42 44	51	144	41 53	51	145	41 02	52	146	334
46 39	−51	142	45 48	−51	143	44 57	−51	144	44 06	−51	145	43 15	−52	145	42 23	−52	146	41 31	−52	147	335
47 11	52	144	46 19	51	144	45 28	52	145	44 36	52	146	43 44	52	147	42 52	52	147	42 00	53	148	336
47 41	51	145	46 50	52	146	45 58	52	146	45 06	53	147	44 13	53	148	43 20	53	148	42 27	53	149	337
48 11	52	146	47 19	52	147	46 27	53	148	45 34	53	148	44 41	53	149	43 48	54	150	42 54	53	150	338
48 40	52	148	47 48	53	148	46 55	54	149	46 01	53	150	45 08	54	150	44 14	54	151	43 20	54	151	339
49 08	−53	149	48 15	−54	150	47 21	−53	150	46 28	−54	151	45 34	−55	152	44 39	−54	152	43 45	−55	153	340
52 58	59	165	51 59	58	166	51 01	59	166	50 02	58	166	49 04	59	167	48 05	59	167	47 06	58	167	351
53 11	59	167	52 12	59	167	51 13	59	167	50 14	59	168	49 15	59	168	48 16	58	168	47 18	60	169	352
53 22	59	168	52 23	59	169	51 24	59	169	50 25	59	169	49 26	59	169	48 27	60	170	47 27	59	170	353
53 32	59	170	52 33	59	170	51 34	60	171	50 34	59	171	49 35	60	171	48 35	59	171	47 36	59	171	354
53 41	−60	172	52 41	−59	172	51 42	−60	172	50 42	−59	172	49 43	−60	172	48 43	−60	173	47 43	−59	173	355

N. Lat. {LHA greater than 180°....... Zn=Z; LHA less than 180°............ Zn=360−Z}

DECLINATION (15°-29°) SAME NAME AS LATITUDE — LAT 28°

LHA	15°			16°			17°			18°			19°			20°			21°			22°		
	Hc	d	Z	Hc	d	Z	Hc	d	Z	Hc	d	Z	Hc	d	Z	Hc	d	Z	Hc	d	Z	Hc	d	Z
	° ′	′	°	° ′	′	°	° ′	′	°	° ′	′	°	° ′	′	°	° ′	′	°	° ′	′	°	° ′	′	°
25	63 26	+33	114	63 59	+31	112	64 30	+29	110	64 59	+27	108	65 26	+26	106	65 52	+23	104	66 15	+22	102	66 37	+19	99
26	62 38	31	113	63 09	31	111	63 40	28	109	64 08	27	107	64 35	25	105	65 00	23	103	65 23	21	101	65 44	19	99
27	61 49	31	112	62 20	29	110	62 49	28	108	63 17	27	106	63 44	24	104	64 08	23	102	64 31	21	100	64 52	19	98
28	60 59	31	111	61 30	29	109	61 59	27	107	62 26	26	105	62 52	24	103	63 16	23	101	63 39	20	99	63 59	19	97
29	60 10	30	110	60 40	28	108	61 08	27	106	61 35	26	104	62 01	23	102	62 24	22	100	62 46	21	98	63 07	18	96

23°			24°			25°			26°			27°			28°			29°			LHA
Hc	d	Z	Hc	d	Z	Hc	d	Z	Hc	d	Z	Hc	d	Z	Hc	d	Z	Hc	d	Z	
° ′	′	°	° ′	′	°	° ′	′	°	° ′	′	°	° ′	′	°	° ′	′	°	° ′	′	°	
66 56	+17	97	67 13	+15	94	67 28	+12	92	67 40	+10	89	67 50	+8	87	67 58	+5	84	68 03	+2	81	335
66 03	17	96	66 20	15	94	66 35	13	91	66 48	10	89	66 58	7	86	67 05	6	84	67 11	2	81	334
65 11	16	96	65 27	15	93	65 42	13	91	65 55	10	88	66 05	8	86	66 13	5	84	66 18	3	81	333
64 18	17	95	64 35	14	93	64 49	13	90	65 02	10	88	65 12	8	86	65 20	6	83	65 26	3	81	332
63 25	17	94	63 42	14	92	63 56	13	90	64 09	10	88	64 19	8	85	64 27	7	83	64 34	4	81	331

N. Lat. {LHA greater than 180°....... Zn=Z; LHA less than 180°............ Zn=360−Z}

DECLINATION (15°-29°) SAME NAME AS LATITUDE — LAT 27°

LHA	15°			16°			17°			18°			19°			20°			21°			22°		
	Hc	d	Z	Hc	d	Z	Hc	d	Z	Hc	d	Z	Hc	d	Z	Hc	d	Z	Hc	d	Z	Hc	d	Z
	° ′	′	°	° ′	′	°	° ′	′	°	° ′	′	°	° ′	′	°	° ′	′	°	° ′	′	°	° ′	′	°
5	77 08	+56	158	78 04	+55	156	78 59	+54	154	79 53	+53	152	80 46	+52	149	81 38	+50	146	82 28	+47	142	83 15	+42	137
6	76 46	54	154	77 40	54	152	78 34	52	150	79 26	51	147	80 17	49	144	81 06	47	141	81 53	43	136	82 36	39	131
7	76 21	53	150	77 14	51	148	78 05	50	146	78 55	49	143	79 44	46	140	80 30	44	136	81 14	40	132	81 54	36	127
8	75 53	51	147	76 44	50	144	77 34	48	142	78 22	46	139	79 08	44	136	79 52	41	132	80 33	37	128	81 10	33	123
9	75 22	49	143	76 11	48	141	76 59	46	138	77 45	45	135	78 30	41	132	79 11	39	128	79 50	35	124	80 25	30	120
10	74 49	+47	140	75 36	+47	138	76 23	+44	135	77 07	+42	132	77 49	+39	129	78 28	+37	125	79 05	+32	121	79 37	+29	117
11	74 14	46	137	75 00	44	135	75 44	42	132	76 26	40	129	77 06	38	126	77 44	34	123	78 18	31	119	78 49	27	114
12	73 36	45	135	74 21	43	132	75 04	40	130	75 44	39	127	76 23	35	123	76 58	33	120	77 31	29	116	78 00	25	112
13	72 58	42	132	73 40	42	130	74 22	39	127	75 01	36	124	75 37	34	121	76 11	31	118	76 42	28	114	77 10	24	110
14	72 17	42	130	72 59	39	127	73 38	38	125	74 16	35	122	74 51	33	119	75 24	29	116	75 53	27	112	76 20	22	108
40	50 58	+25	100	51 23	+23	98	51 46	+22	97	52 08	+21	95	52 29	+20	94	52 49	+18	92	53 07	+18	91	53 25	+16	89
41	50 05	25	99	50 30	23	98	50 53	22	96	51 15	21	95	51 36	19	93	51 55	19	92	52 14	17	90	52 31	16	89
42	49 13	24	98	49 37	23	97	50 00	21	96	50 21	21	94	50 42	20	93	51 02	18	91	51 20	18	90	51 38	16	88
43	48 20	23	98	48 43	23	96	49 06	22	95	49 28	21	94	49 49	19	92	50 08	19	91	50 27	17	89	50 44	16	88
44	47 27	23	97	47 50	23	96	48 13	22	95	48 35	20	93	48 55	20	92	49 15	19	90	49 34	17	89	49 51	16	87

23°			24°			25°			26°			27°			28°			29°			LHA
Hc	d	Z	Hc	d	Z	Hc	d	Z	Hc	d	Z	Hc	d	Z	Hc	d	Z	Hc	d	Z	
° ′	′	°	° ′	′	°	° ′	′	°	° ′	′	°	° ′	′	°	° ′	′	°	° ′	′	°	
83 57	+38	130	84 35	+30	123	85 05	+20	113	85 25	+8	102	85 33	−6	89	85 27	−18	76	85 09	−28	65	355
83 15	34	125	83 49	26	118	84 15	17	109	84 32	7	99	84 39	4	89	84 35	15	78	84 20	24	68	354
82 30	31	121	83 01	23	114	83 24	15	106	83 39	7	98	83 46	3	88	83 43	13	79	63 30	20	70	353
81 43	28	117	82 11	21	111	82 32	14	104	82 46	6	96	82 52	2	88	82 50	10	80	82 40	18	72	352
80 55	26	114	81 21	19	108	81 40	13	102	81 53	6	95	81 59	2	88	81 57	8	81	81 49	16	74	351
80 06	+24	112	80 30	+18	106	80 48	+12	100	81 00	+6	94	81 06	−1	88	81 05	−8	81	80 57	−14	75	350
79 16	22	110	79 38	17	104	79 55	12	99	80 07	5	93	80 12	0	88	80 12	7	82	80 05	12	76	349
78 25	21	108	78 46	16	103	79 02	11	98	79 13	6	93	79 19	0	87	79 19	6	82	79 13	10	77	348
77 34	20	106	77 54	15	102	78 09	11	97	78 20	5	92	78 25	+1	87	78 26	5	82	78 21	9	77	347
76 42	19	104	77 01	15	100	77 16	10	96	77 26	6	91	77 32	1	87	77 33	4	82	77 29	8	78	346
53 41	+14	87	53 55	+14	86	54 09	+11	84	54 20	+11	82	54 31	+9	81	54 40	+8	79	54 48	+6	77	320
52 47	15	87	53 02	13	85	53 15	12	84	53 27	11	82	53 38	10	80	53 48	7	79	53 55	7	77	319
51 54	15	87	52 09	13	85	52 22	13	83	52 35	11	82	52 46	9	80	52 55	8	79	53 03	7	77	318
51 00	15	86	51 15	14	85	51 29	13	83	51 42	11	81	51 53	10	80	52 03	8	78	52 11	8	77	317
50 07	15	86	50 22	14	84	50 36	13	83	50 49	11	81	51 00	10	80	51 10	9	78	51 19	8	77	316

LAT 28°

DECLINATION (15°-29°) CONTRARY NAME TO LATITUDE

N. Lat. {LHA greater than 180°........ Zn=Z; LHA less than 180°............ Zn=360−Z}

LHA	15°	16°	17°	18°	19°	20°	21°	22°	23°	24°	25°	26°	27°	28°	29°	LHA
	Hc d Z	Hc d Z	Hc d Z	Hc d Z	Hc d Z	Hc d Z	Hc d Z	Hc d Z	Hc d Z	Hc d Z	Hc d Z	Hc d Z	Hc d Z	Hc d Z	Hc d Z	
	° ′ ′ °	° ′ ′ °	° ′ ′ °	° ′ ′ °	° ′ ′ °	° ′ ′ °	° ′ ′ °	° ′ ′ °	° ′ ′ °	° ′ ′ °	° ′ ′ °	° ′ ′ °	° ′ ′ °	° ′ ′ °	° ′ ′ °	
34	35 51 48 138	35 03 48 139	34 15 48 140	33 27 49 140	32 38 49 141	31 49 49 142	31 00 49 143	30 11 49 143	29 22 50 144	28 32 49 144	27 43 50 145	26 53 50 146	26 03 50 146	25 13 51 147	24 22 50 148	326
33	36 26 49 139	35 37 48 140	34 49 49 141	34 00 49 141	33 11 49 142	32 22 50 143	31 32 49 143	30 43 50 144	29 53 50 145	29 03 50 145	28 13 51 146	27 22 50 147	26 32 51 147	25 41 51 148	24 50 51 148	327
32	37 00 49 140	36 11 49 141	35 22 49 142	34 33 50 142	33 43 49 143	32 54 50 144	32 04 50 144	31 14 51 145	30 23 50 146	29 33 51 146	28 42 51 147	27 51 51 147	27 00 51 148	26 09 51 149	25 18 52 149	328
31	37 33 49 141	36 44 49 142	35 55 50 143	35 05 50 143	34 15 50 144	33 25 51 145	32 34 50 145	31 44 51 146	30 53 51 147	30 02 51 147	29 11 52 148	28 19 51 148	27 28 52 149	26 36 51 149	25 45 52 150	329
30	38 06 −49 142	37 17 −51 143	36 26 −50 144	35 36 −50 144	34 46 −51 145	33 55 −51 146	33 04 −51 146	32 13 −51 147	31 22 −52 147	30 30 −51 148	29 39 −52 149	28 47 −52 149	27 55 −52 150	27 03 −52 150	26 11 −53 151	330
9	46 08 59 167	45 09 59 168	44 10 59 168	43 11 59 168	42 12 59 169	41 13 59 169	40 14 59 169	39 15 59 169	38 16 59 169	37 17 59 170	36 18 59 170	35 19 59 170	34 20 60 170	33 20 59 171	32 21 59 171	351
8	46 18 59 169	45 19 59 169	44 20 59 169	43 21 59 170	42 22 59 170	41 23 59 170	40 24 60 170	39 24 59 170	38 25 59 171	37 26 59 171	36 27 60 171	35 27 59 171	34 28 59 171	33 29 60 172	32 29 59 172	352
7	46 28 59 170	45 29 59 170	44 30 60 171	43 30 59 171	42 31 59 171	41 32 60 171	40 32 59 171	39 33 60 172	38 33 59 172	37 34 60 172	36 34 59 172	35 35 59 172	34 36 60 172	33 36 59 173	32 37 60 173	353
6	46 37 60 172	45 37 59 172	44 38 60 172	43 38 59 172	42 39 60 172	41 39 59 172	40 40 60 173	39 40 60 173	38 40 59 173	37 41 60 173	36 41 59 173	35 42 60 173	34 42 60 174	33 42 59 174	32 43 60 174	354
5	46 44 −60 173	45 44 −60 173	44 44 −59 173	43 45 −60 173	42 45 −60 174	41 45 −59 174	40 46 −60 174	39 46 −60 174	38 46 −59 174	37 47 −60 174	36 47 −60 174	35 47 −59 175	34 48 −60 175	33 48 −60 175	32 48 −60 175	355

LAT 29°

DECLINATION (0°-14°) CONTRARY NAME TO LATITUDE

N. Lat. {LHA greater than 180°....... Zn=Z; LHA less than 180°........... Zn=360−Z}

LHA	0°	1°	2°	3°	4°	5°	6°	7°	8°	9°	10°	11°	12°	13°	14°	LHA
	Hc d Z	Hc d Z	Hc d Z	Hc d Z	Hc d Z	Hc d Z	Hc d Z	Hc d Z	Hc d Z	Hc d Z	Hc d Z	Hc d Z	Hc d Z	Hc d Z	Hc d Z	
	° ′ ′ °	° ′ ′ °	° ′ ′ °	° ′ ′ °	° ′ ′ °	° ′ ′ °	° ′ ′ °	° ′ ′ °	° ′ ′ °	° ′ ′ °	° ′ ′ °	° ′ ′ °	° ′ ′ °	° ′ ′ °	° ′ ′ °	
49	35 01 36 113	34 25 36 114	33 49 37 115	33 12 37 116	32 35 37 117	31 58 38 118	31 20 38 119	30 42 39 119	30 03 39 120	29 24 39 121	28 45 40 122	28 05 40 123	27 25 40 124	26 45 41 125	26 04 41 125	311
48	35 49 36 114	35 13 36 115	34 37 38 116	33 59 37 117	33 22 38 117	32 44 38 118	32 06 39 119	31 27 39 120	30 48 39 121	30 09 40 122	29 29 40 123	28 49 40 124	28 09 41 125	27 28 41 125	26 47 41 126	312
47	36 37 36 114	36 01 37 115	35 24 38 116	34 46 38 117	34 08 38 118	33 30 39 119	32 51 39 120	32 12 39 121	31 33 40 122	30 53 40 123	30 13 41 124	29 32 40 124	28 52 42 125	28 10 41 126	27 29 42 127	313
46	37 25 37 115	36 48 37 116	36 11 38 117	35 33 38 118	34 55 39 119	34 16 39 120	33 37 40 121	32 57 40 122	32 17 40 123	31 37 41 124	30 56 40 124	30 16 42 125	29 34 41 126	28 53 42 127	28 11 42 128	314
45	38 12 −37 116	37 35 −38 117	36 57 −38 118	36 19 −39 119	35 40 −39 120	35 01 −39 121	34 22 −40 122	33 42 −41 123	33 01 −40 123	32 21 −41 124	31 40 −42 125	30 58 −42 126	30 16 −42 127	29 34 −42 128	28 52 −42 128	315
14	58 04 55 153	57 09 56 154	56 13 55 154	55 18 56 155	54 22 56 156	53 26 56 156	52 30 57 157	51 33 56 157	50 37 57 158	49 40 56 158	48 44 57 159	47 47 57 159	46 50 57 160	45 53 58 160	44 55 57 161	346
13	58 27 56 155	57 31 55 155	56 36 57 156	55 39 56 157	54 43 56 157	53 47 57 158	52 50 57 158	51 53 57 159	50 56 57 159	49 59 57 160	49 02 57 160	48 05 58 161	47 07 57 161	46 10 58 162	45 12 57 162	347
12	58 49 56 156	57 53 57 157	56 56 56 158	56 00 57 158	55 03 57 159	54 06 57 159	53 09 58 160	52 11 57 160	51 14 57 161	50 17 58 161	49 19 58 162	48 21 57 162	47 24 58 163	46 26 58 163	45 28 58 163	348
11	59 09 57 158	58 12 57 159	57 15 57 159	56 18 57 160	55 21 57 160	54 24 58 161	53 26 58 161	52 28 57 162	51 31 58 162	50 33 58 163	49 35 58 163	48 37 58 164	47 39 58 164	46 41 59 164	45 42 58 165	349
10	59 28 −57 160	58 31 −58 161	57 33 −57 161	56 36 −58 162	55 38 −58 162	54 40 −58 163	53 42 −58 163	52 44 −58 164	51 46 −58 164	50 48 −59 164	49 49 −58 165	48 51 −58 165	47 53 −59 165	46 54 −58 166	45 56 −59 166	350

LAT 30°

DECLINATION (0°-14°) CONTRARY NAME TO LATITUDE

N. Lat. {LHA greater than 180°........ Zn=Z; LHA less than 180°........... Zn=360−Z}

LHA	0°	1°	2°	3°	4°	5°	6°	7°	8°	9°	10°	11°	12°	13°	14°	LHA
	Hc d Z	Hc d Z	Hc d Z	Hc d Z	Hc d Z	Hc d Z	Hc d Z	Hc d Z	Hc d Z	Hc d Z	Hc d Z	Hc d Z	Hc d Z	Hc d Z	Hc d Z	
	° ′ ′ °	° ′ ′ °	° ′ ′ °	° ′ ′ °	° ′ ′ °	° ′ ′ °	° ′ ′ °	° ′ ′ °	° ′ ′ °	° ′ ′ °	° ′ ′ °	° ′ ′ °	° ′ ′ °	° ′ ′ °	° ′ ′ °	
29	49 14 46 132	48 28 46 133	47 42 48 134	46 54 47 135	46 07 48 136	45 19 48 137	44 31 49 138	43 42 49 138	42 53 49 139	42 04 50 140	41 14 50 141	40 24 50 141	39 34 51 142	38 43 50 143	37 53 51 143	331
28	49 53 47 133	49 06 47 134	48 19 48 135	47 31 48 136	46 43 49 137	45 54 49 138	45 05 49 139	44 16 49 139	43 27 50 140	42 37 50 141	41 47 51 142	40 56 51 142	40 05 50 143	39 15 52 144	38 23 51 145	332
27	50 30 47 135	49 43 48 135	48 55 48 136	48 07 49 137	47 18 49 138	46 29 50 139	45 39 49 140	44 50 51 141	43 59 50 141	43 09 51 142	42 18 51 143	41 27 51 144	40 36 51 144	39 45 52 145	38 53 52 146	333
26	51 07 48 136	50 19 49 137	49 30 49 138	48 41 49 139	47 52 50 139	47 02 50 140	46 12 50 141	45 22 50 142	44 32 51 143	43 41 52 143	42 49 51 144	41 58 52 145	41 06 52 145	40 14 52 146	39 22 52 147	334
25	51 43 −49 137	50 54 −49 138	50 05 −50 139	49 15 −49 140	48 26 −51 141	47 35 −50 141	46 45 −51 142	45 54 −51 143	45 03 −52 144	44 11 −51 144	43 20 −52 145	42 28 −53 146	41 35 −52 146	40 43 −53 147	39 50 −53 148	335

N. Lat. { L.H.A. greater than 180° ......Zn=Z
L.H.A. less than 180° ....Zn=360°−Z }

S. Lat. { L.H.A. greater than 180° ......Zn=180°−Z
L.H.A. less than 180° ....Zn=180°+Z }

Selected parts of Pub. 249 Sight Reduction Tables for use with special running fix problems

* * * use Table 5, page 116 for the d-corr to Hc * * *

LAT 10°

DECLINATION (**0° – 14°**) **SAME** NAME AS LATITUDE

LHA	8° Hc	d	Z	9° Hc	d	Z	10° Hc	d	Z	11° Hc	d	Z	12° Hc	d	Z	LHA
	° ′	′	°	° ′	′	°	° ′	′	°	° ′	′	°	° ′	′	°	
0	88 00	60	180	89 00	60	180	90 00	-60	90	89 00	-60	0	88 00	-60	0	360
1	87 46	50	154	88 36	25	135	89 01	-25	90	88 36	-50	44	87 46	-55	26	359
2	87 11	36	135	87 47	15	117	88 02	-14	90	87 48	-36	63	87 12	-47	44	358
3	86 26	27	124	86 53	10	108	87 03	-10	90	86 53	-27	71	86 26	-38	56	357
4	85 34	22	117	85 56	08	104	86 04	-07	90	85 57	-21	75	85 36	-32	63	356

LAT 17°

DECLINATION (**0° – 14°**)
CONTRARY NAME TO LATITUDE

LHA	1° Hc	d	Z	2° Hc	d	Z	3° Hc	d	Z	4° Hc	d	Z	5° Hc	d	Z	LHA
	° ′	′	°	° ′	′	°	° ′	′	°	° ′	′	°	° ′	′	°	
4	71 34	-58	167	70 36	-59	168	69 37	-59	168	68 38	-59	169	67 39	-59	169	356
3	71 46	-60	170	70 46	-59	171	69 47	-59	171	68 48	-60	172	67 48	-59	172	357
2	71 54	-60	174	70 54	-60	174	69 54	-60	174	68 54	-59	174	67 55	-60	175	358
1	71 58	-60	177	70 58	-59	177	69 59	-60	177	68 59	-60	177	67 59	-60	177	359
0	72 00	-60	180	71 00	-60	180	70 00	-60	180	69 00	-60	180	68 00	-60	180	360

LAT 23°

DECLINATION (**0° – 14°**) **SAME** NAME AS LATITUDE

LHA	0° Hc	d	Z	1° Hc	d	Z	2° Hc	d	Z	3° Hc	d	Z	4° Hc	d	Z	LHA
	° ′	′	°	° ′	′	°	° ′	′	°	° ′	′	°	° ′	′	°	
0	67 00	60	180	68 00	60	180	69 00	60	180	70 00	60	180	71 00	60	180	360
1	66 59	60	177	67 59	60	177	68 59	60	177	69 59	60	177	70 59	59	177	359
2	66 55	60	175	67 55	60	175	68 55	59	174	69 54	60	174	70 54	60	174	358
3	66 49	59	172	67 48	60	172	68 48	59	172	69 47	60	171	70 47	59	171	357
4	66 40	60	170	67 40	59	169	68 39	59	169	69 38	59	168	70 37	58	168	356

LAT 27°

DECLINATION (**0° – 14°**) **SAME** NAME AS LATITUDE

LHA	10° Hc	d	Z	11° Hc	d	Z	12° Hc	d	Z	13° Hc	d	Z	14° Hc	d	Z	LHA
	° ′	′	°	° ′	′	°	° ′	′	°	° ′	′	°	° ′	′	°	
0	73 00	60	180	74 00	60	180	75 00	60	180	76 00	60	180	77 00	60	180	360
1	72 58	60	177	73 58	60	176	74 58	60	176	75 58	60	176	76 58	60	176	359
2	72 54	59	173	73 53	60	173	74 53	60	172	75 53	59	172	76 52	59	171	358
3	72 46	59	170	73 45	59	169	74 44	59	169	75 43	59	168	76 42	59	167	357
4	72 35	59	167	73 34	58	166	74 32	58	165	75 30	58	164	76 28	58	163	356

LAT 29°

DECLINATION (**15° – 29°**)
CONTRARY NAME TO LATITUDE

LHA	17° Hc	d	Z	18° Hc	d	Z	19° Hc	d	Z	20° Hc	d	Z	21° Hc	d	Z	LHA
	° ′	′	°	° ′	′	°	° ′	′	°	° ′	′	°	° ′	′	°	
4	43 50	-60	175	42 50	-59	175	41 51	-60	175	40 51	-60	175	39 51	-60	175	356
3	43 55	-60	176	42 55	-60	176	41 55	-60	176	40 55	-60	176	39 55	-60	176	357
2	43 58	-60	177	42 58	-60	177	41 58	-60	178	40 58	-60	177	39 58	-60	178	358
1	43 59	-60	179	42 59	-60	179	41 59	-60	179	40 59	-60	179	39 59	-60	179	359
0	44 00	-60	180	43 00	-60	180	42 00	-60	180	41 00	-60	180	40 00	-60	180	360

LAT 34°

DECLINATION (**0° – 14°**)
CONTRARY NAME TO LATITUDE

LHA	10° Hc	d	Z	11° Hc	d	Z	12° Hc	d	Z	13° Hc	d	Z	14° Hc	d	Z	LHA
	° ′	′	°	° ′	′	°	° ′	′	°	° ′	′	°	° ′	′	°	
4	45 50	-60	174	44 50	-59	174	43 51	-60	175	42 51	-60	175	41 51	-60	175	356
3	45 54	-59	176	44 55	-60	176	43 55	-60	176	42 55	-60	176	41 55	-60	176	357
2	45 58	-60	177	44 58	-60	177	43 58	-60	177	42 58	-60	177	41 58	-60	177	358
1	45 59	-60	179	44 59	-60	179	43 59	-60	179	42 59	-60	179	41 59	-60	179	359
0	46 00	-60	180	45 00	-60	180	44 00	-60	180	43 00	-60	180	42 00	-60	180	360

LAT 36°

DECLINATION (**0° – 14°**)
CONTRARY NAME TO LATITUDE

LHA	9° Hc	d	Z	10° Hc	d	Z	11° Hc	d	Z	12° Hc	d	Z	13° Hc	d	Z	LHA
	° ′	′	°	° ′	′	°	° ′	′	°	° ′	′	°	° ′	′	°	
4	44 51	-60	174	43 51	-60	175	42 51	-60	175	41 51	-60	175	40 51	-60	175	356
3	44 55	-60	176	43 55	-60	176	42 55	-60	176	41 55	-60	176	40 55	-60	176	357
2	44 58	-60	177	43 58	-60	177	42 58	-60	177	41 58	-60	177	40 58	-60	177	358
1	44 59	-60	179	43 59	-60	179	42 59	-60	179	41 59	-60	179	40 59	-60	179	359
0	45 00	-60	180	44 00	-60	180	43 00	-60	180	42 00	-60	180	41 00	-60	180	360

LAT 38°

DECLINATION (**0° – 14°**) **SAME** NAME AS LATITUDE

LHA	0° Hc	d	Z	1° Hc	d	Z	2° Hc	d	Z	3° Hc	d	Z	4° Hc	d	Z	LHA
	° ′	′	°	° ′	′	°	° ′	′	°	° ′	′	°	° ′	′	°	
0	52 00	60	180	53 00	60	180	54 00	60	180	55 00	60	180	56 00	60	180	360
1	51 59	60	178	52 59	60	178	53 59	60	178	54 59	60	178	55 59	60	178	359
2	51 57	60	177	52 57	60	177	53 57	60	177	54 57	60	177	55 57	60	176	358
3	51 54	60	175	52 54	60	175	53 54	60	175	54 54	59	175	55 53	60	175	357
4	51 49	60	174	52 49	60	173	53 49	60	173	54 49	59	173	55 48	60	173	356

LAT 44°

DECLINATION (**15° – 29°**) **SAME** NAME AS LATITUDE

LHA	17° Hc	d	Z	18° Hc	d	Z	19° Hc	d	Z	20° Hc	d	Z	21° Hc	d	Z	LHA
	° ′	′	°	° ′	′	°	° ′	′	°	° ′	′	°	° ′	′	°	
0	63 00	60	180	64 00	60	180	65 00	60	180	66 00	60	180	67 00	60	180	360
1	62 59	60	178	63 59	60	178	64 59	60	178	65 59	60	178	66 59	60	178	359
2	62 57	60	176	63 57	60	176	64 57	60	176	65 57	59	175	66 56	60	175	358
3	62 53	60	174	63 53	59	174	64 52	60	173	65 52	60	173	66 52	60	173	357
4	62 47	60	172	63 47	60	171	64 47	59	171	65 46	60	171	66 46	59	170	356

LAT 56°

DECLINATION (**15° – 29°**) **SAME** NAME AS LATITUDE

LHA	17° Hc	d	Z	18° Hc	d	Z	19° Hc	d	Z	20° Hc	d	Z	21° Hc	d	Z	LHA
	° ′	′	°	° ′	′	°	° ′	′	°	° ′	′	°	° ′	′	°	
0	51 00	60	180	52 00	60	180	53 00	60	180	54 00	60	180	55 00	60	180	360
1	51 00	60	178	52 00	60	178	53 00	60	178	54 00	60	178	55 00	60	178	359
2	50 58	60	177	51 58	60	177	52 58	60	177	53 58	60	177	54 58	60	177	358
3	50 56	60	175	51 56	60	175	52 56	60	175	53 56	60	175	54 56	60	175	357
4	50 53	60	174	51 53	60	174	52 53	60	174	53 53	59	174	54 52	60	174	356

T-27

N(x) Table for Emergency Sight Reduction

This table can be used for several calculations in celestial navigation. Examples are given in Section 11.5 and in the Answers section.

The phrase "C = N(20)" means that C equals the N value that is listed beside x = 20, or C = 1073. The phrase "N(B) =56" means that B equals the x value that is listed beside N = 56, or B = 71 Some applications require interpolation of the table.

This table uses meridian angle instead of local hour angle. Meridian angle (t) is defined as: t west = LHA for LHA < 180 and t east = 360 - LHA for LHA > 180.

x	N(x)	x	N(x)	x	N(x)
1	4048	31	664	61	134
2	3355	32	635	62	124
3	2950	33	608	63	115
4	2663	34	581	64	107
5	2440	35	556	65	98
6	2258	36	531	66	90
7	2105	37	508	67	83
8	1972	38	485	68	76
9	1855	39	463	69	69
10	1751	40	442	70	62
11	1656	41	422	71	56
12	1571	42	402	72	50
13	1492	43	383	73	45
14	1419	44	364	74	40
15	1352	45	347	75	35
16	1289	46	329	76	30
17	1230	47	313	77	26
18	1174	48	297	78	22
19	1122	49	281	79	19
20	1073	50	267	80	15
21	1026	51	252	81	12
22	982	52	238	82	10
23	940	53	225	83	7
24	900	54	212	84	5
25	861	55	199	85	4
26	825	56	187	86	2
27	790	57	176	87	1
28	756	58	165	88	1
29	724	59	154	89	0
30	693	60	144		

SIGHT REDUCTION WITH N(X) TABLE

Find v from:

N(v) = N(90 - dec) + N(t); if t > 90, use t = 180 - t.

Find w from:

N(w) = N(dec) - N(90 - v);

If original t > 90, use w = 180 – w.

Find u from:

u = 90 - w + Lat, for same name.

u = 90 - w - Lat, for contrary name.

If u > 90 (either name), use u = 180 - u.

Find Hc from:

N(Hc) = N(90 - v) + N(u).

Find Z from:

N(Z) = N(v) - N(90 - Hc);

for all Contrary Names or for Same Names with original u > 90, use Z = 180 - Z.

This method of sight reduction lies somewhere between a tool for emergency use and a novelty. We developed it for use with the equally short Emergency Almanac for the Sun. The idea was to have all that is needed for emergency navigation on one small card. We first published this in 1987 and since then (now 2015) we have had exactly zero feedback on its use. That is, we have no idea if anyone has ever used it for anything! It remains, however, the world's shortest sight reduction tables that will indeed give usably accurate results for any sight—which, together with three dollars will get you a cup of coffee in Seattle. It has been discussed in forums by experts in celestial navigation, but always from a formal point of view, i.e., how it works, accuracy, and so on, but not the actual application.

Emergency Almanac for the Sun

GHA (– 175°) and Declination given as degrees-minutes for 0000 UTC.

day	January		February		March	
01	4-11	S 23-01	1-38	S 17-10	1-54	S 07-41
04	3-50	S 22-45	1-33	S 16-18	2-03	S 06-33
07	3-30	S 22-24	1-29	S 15-23	2-13	S 05-23
10	3-11	S 22-00	1-28	S 14-26	2-25	S 04-13
13	2-53	S 21-31	1-28	S 13-27	2-36	S 03-02
16	2-37	S 20-59	1-29	S 12-25	2-49	S 01-51
19	2-22	S 20-23	1-33	S 11-22	3-02	S 00-40
22	2-09	S 19-44	1-37	S 10-18	3-15	N 00-31
25	1-58	S 19-02	1-44	S 09-11	3-29	N 01-42
28	1-48	S 18-16	1-51	S 08-04	3-42	N 02-53

day	April		May		June	
01	4-00	N 04-26	5-43	N 15-00	5-34	N 22-01
04	4-13	N 05-35	5-48	N 15-53	5-27	N 22-24
07	4-26	N 06-44	5-52	N 16-44	5-19	N 22-43
10	4-39	N 07-51	5-54	N 17-33	5-10	N 22-59
13	4-51	N 08-57	5-55	N 18-19	5-01	N 23-12
16	5-02	N 10-02	5-55	N 19-02	4-52	N 23-20
19	5-12	N 11-05	5-54	N 19-42	4-42	N 23-25
22	5-21	N 12-06	5-51	N 20-20	4-32	N 23-26
25	5-30	N 13-06	5-47	N 20-54	4-23	N 23-24
28	5-37	N 14-04	5-42	N 21-25	4-13	N 23-17

day	July		August		September	
01	4-04	N 23-07	3-25	N 18-05	4-58	N 08-23
04	3-56	N 22-54	3-28	N 17-18	5-13	N 07-17
07	3-48	N 22-37	3-33	N 16-30	5-28	N 06-10
10	3-41	N 22-16	3-39	N 15-38	5-43	N 05-02
13	3-35	N 21-52	3-46	N 14-45	5-59	N 03-54
16	3-30	N 21-24	3-55	N 13-49	6-15	N 02-45
19	3-26	N 20-53	4-05	N 12-51	6-31	N 01-35
22	3-24	N 20-19	4-15	N 11-52	6-47	N 00-25
25	3-23	N 19-42	4-27	N 10-51	7-03	S 00-45
28	3-23	N 19-02	4-40	N 09-48	7-18	S 01-55

day	October		November		December	
01	7-33	S 03-05	9-07	S 14-20	7-48	S 21-45
04	7-48	S 04-15	9-07	S 15-17	7-31	S 22-12
07	8-01	S 05-24	9-06	S 16-12	7-12	S 22-34
10	8-14	S 06-32	9-03	S 17-04	6-53	S 22-53
13	8-25	S 07-40	8-58	S 17-53	6-32	S 23-07
16	8-36	S 08-47	8-51	S 18-40	6-10	S 23-18
19	8-45	S 09-53	8-42	S 19-23	5-48	S 23-24
22	8-52	S 10-57	8-31	S 20-04	5-26	S 23-26
25	8-59	S 12-00	8-18	S 20-41	5-04	S 23-24
28	9-03	S 13-01	8-04	S 21-15	4-41	S 23-18

Procedure

For declination, interpolate for hour and day as follows: Find Dec at 1400 (14h 00m) on Nov 6. At 00h on Nov 4 the value is S 15° 17' and on Nov 7 it is S 16° 12', so for 72h the increase was 55'.

The time wanted is 62h past 00h on Nov 4, so the correction is (62/72) x 55' = 47' and the Dec = S 15° 17' + 47' = S 16° 04' at 1400 on Nov 6.

For GHA, interpolate the table for the 00h value on the proper date, add 175°, and then add the UTC converted to angle using standard **Arc to Time Conversion.** If needed, subtract 360°.

Example: Find GHA at 14h 22m 13s on Nov 27. From Nov 25 to 28, the 00h value decreases from 8° 18' to 8° 04', or 4.7' per day, so the 00h value on Nov 27 is 8° 08.6'. To convert UTC to angle, use: 14h = 14h x (15°/1h) = 210°; 22m = 22m x (15'/1 m) = 330' = 5° 30'; and 13s = 13s x (1'/4s) = 3'. So GHA at 14h 22m 13s on Nov 27 = 8° 08.6' + 175° + 210° + 5° 30' + 3' = 398° 41.6' = 38° 41.6'.

The accuracy of the interpolated values for any year should be within 10' in most cases. The error is primarily due to an average over the leap year cycle. For more accurate perpetual data for sun and stars, see the *Long Term Almanac* by Geoffrey Kolbe.

Appendix 4
WORK FORMS

Contents

Overview of Starpath Work Forms

Not all celestial navigators use work forms to help with the paperwork, but I think it fair to say that most do. Or at least most—even very experienced navigators—like to have the forms at hand just in case they are needed. There are a lot of steps in the process, and we may have to do the work when very tired and not feeling well, as the boat rocks around in the seas. Having a guide that takes you step by step, with little thought required, can be a blessing. So even if you do not use them routinely, it is good to add them to your checklist and have at least one of each type tucked away in the almanac. Also, these days we rely mainly on GPS; so we might be rusty when we need to do the sights. For those who want to use them routinely, you can copy the ones in this book, or download from www.starpath.com/celnavbook.

The course presented in this book proceeds by giving annotated step-by-step instructions for filling out the forms. That we might think of as the *first pass* through the materials—the place you learn it and practice it. The detailed form instructions (to follow) is a summary of the process. So these form instructions are a *second pass* through the process.

The *third and final pass* is the set of forms themselves. After you have worked a few examples, you will find that the form itself, without any further instructions, will guide you through the process for each of the celestial bodies.

We have heard back many times from navigators who have been away from the subject for a long time, who told us how easy it was to recall the paperwork with the use of these forms. This was, of course, an intention of the forms, along with the main design criteria that they be such that all sights are done essentially the same way. Another goal was to have a place to write in every step of the process, and to have some reasonable element of smooth flow though the process. Alternative designs that one sees are typically vertical strip forms that usually do not meet any of these criteria.

The Form 106 that we have for the NAO Tables is especially valuable because the original instructions for the process given in the *Nautical Almanac* are difficult to follow. As a result of that problem, these valuable tables have not been used as much as they deserve. Some instructors go so far as to ridicule the NAO Tables for their complexity, driving new users away before they even get to try them. Misguided magazine articles have not helped. Our Form 106 makes the process very simple, and with just a few samples worked, you will be doing them automatically.

We postpone the use of NAO Tables till the end of the course simply because they do introduce a few extra steps at a time you are already learning a lot of new tables. Once you have had the experience of sight reductions with Pub 249, however, it takes just 20 minutes or so to master these new ones. These tables have a great virtue these days when cel nav is often just a back up to GPS. Since there is a full set of the NAO Tables in every *Nautical Almanac*, you just need buy one book to have a complete solution. Pub 249, and especially Pub 229, are large, heavy books when it comes to stowage on a small boat at sea. Also if you choose to do cel nav by computation, then the NAO Tables as part of the Almanac are a natural back up.

NOTE: The dates and latitudes used for the examples in these form instructions are different from those we use in the book for other examples. If you want extra practice confirming these sight reductions you will need to refer to the full sets of Sight Reduction Tables and obtain the almanac data for the times and dates listed. All of this can be downloaded from www.starpath.com/celnavbook.

Sun Sights with Form 104

BOX 1–Sight Data

Record the watch time (WT), watch date, log reading, celestial body, measured index correction, and sextant reading (Hs) for the sight. Find the watch error (WE) and the zone description of the watch (ZD) from WWV radio broadcasts or chronometer logbook, and apply these to WT to get the universal time (UTC) of the sight. Use the extra space provided to adjust time and date if necessary. Choose and record a LOP (line of position) label for the sight. From your DR (dead reckoning) track on a chart or plotting sheet, figure your DR position (DR-Lat and DR-Lon) and log reading at the time of the sight. Record your height of eye (HE) for the sight.

BOX 2–*Nautical Almanac* Daily Pages

From the *Nautical Almanac* daily pages, record the Greenwich hour angle (GHA-hr) and declination (Dec-hr) of the sun at the exact hour of the UTC. Record the declination d-value, and label it "+" if declination is increasing with time, or "-" if decreasing. Cross out the spaces for v-value and UP; they do not apply to the sun.

BOX 3–Increments and Corrections

From the increments and corrections pages of the *Nautical Almanac*, record the sun's increment of GHA (GHA-m,s) for the minutes and seconds part of the UTC. Also record the d-correction to the declination based on the d-value given in Box 2. Cross out the SHA or v-correction space; these do not apply to the sun.

Add GHA-hr to GHA-m,s to find GHA and record it. Apply the d-corr to Dec-hr to find Dec and record it. The sign (±) of d-corr is the same as that of d-value. Use the extra space provided to adjust minutes to less than 60 if necessary. You now have the GHA and Dec that apply for your precise UTC. For later use, record the degrees part of the declination (Dec-deg) in Box 4 with a prominent N or S label, and also record the minutes part (Dec-min) just below Box 5.

Assumed Position and Hour Angle

Figure the assumed longitude (a-Lon) from your DR-Lon and the minutes part of GHA. In western longitudes, it should be the one longitude that lies within 30' of your DR-Lon that has the same minutes as the minutes part of GHA. In eastern longitudes, it should be the one longitude that lies within 30' of your DR-Lon that has minutes equal to 60 minus the minutes part of GHA. Record a-Lon below GHA and also in Box 6. Figure the local hour angle (LHA) from:

LHA = GHA - a-Lon(W)

in western longitudes or

LHA = GHA + a-Lon(E)

in eastern longitudes. With the proper choice of a-Lon, LHA will always be in whole degrees with no minutes left over. Record LHA in Box 4.

Choose the assumed latitude (a-Lat) as your DR-Lat rounded off to the nearest whole degree. Record a-Lat in Box 4 with a prominent N or S label. Also record a-Lat in Box 6.

BOX 4 and BOX 5–Sight Reduction Tables

Box 4 now contains all data needed to enter the Sight Reduction Tables, Pubs. 249 or 229. Same or Contrary Name labels of Dec and a-Lat are clear at a glance.

From the Sight Reduction Tables, record in Box 5 the tabulated value of the calculated altitude (tab He), the d-value with its tabulated sign (±), and the azimuth angle (Z).

Convert the azimuth angle (Z) to the azimuth (Zn) using the rules on the work form (also given on each page of the Sight Reduction Tables) and record it in Box 6. CAUTION: For "high-altitude" sights, meaning Hc above 70° or so, you should interpolate for Z to account for the minutes part of Dec. Use:

Z = Z(Dec-deg) + dZ,

where

dZ = [Z(Dec-deg + 1°) - Z(Dec-deg)] x (Dec-min)/60.

Hs to Ho

The upper right side of the work form is used for converting the sextant altitude (Hs) to the observed altitude (Ho). Altitude corrections are inside the covers of the *Nautical Almanac*. Record the dip correction and apply dip and index corr to Hs to get the apparent altitude (Ha).

Cross out the additional altitude corr space and the upper limb moon space; these do not apply to the sun.

Record the altitude correction for the sun and apply it to Ha to get Ho. Compare Hc and Ho in the space provided above Box 6. Subtract the smaller from the larger to get the altitude intercept (a). Extra space is provided to rewrite Ho or Hc if necessary for this subtraction. Choose the label, A for Away or T for Toward, which is beside the larger of Hc or Ho, and record the a-value and mark its label in Box 6.

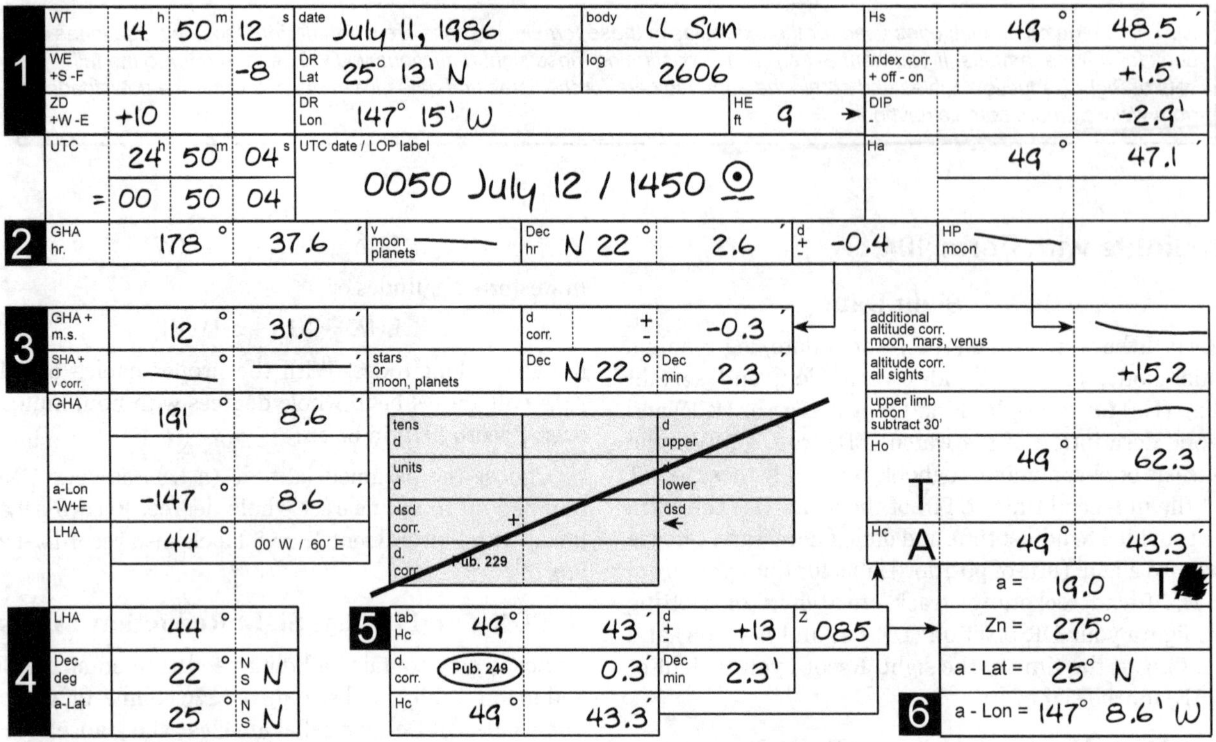

WT 14h 50m 12s
date July 11, 1986
body LL Sun
Hs 49° 48.5'
WE +S -F -8
DR Lat 25° 13' N
log 2606
index corr. + off - on +1.5'
ZD +W -E +10
DR Lon 147° 15' W
HE ft 9
DIP -2.9'
UTC 24h 50m 04s = 00 50 04
UTC date / LOP label
0050 July 12 / 1450 ☉
Ha 49° 47.1'
GHA hr. 178° 37.6'
v moon planets
Dec hr N 22° 2.6'
d + - -0.4
HP moon
GHA + m.s. 12° 31.0'
d corr. + - -0.3'
additional altitude corr. moon, mars, venus
SHA + or v corr.
stars or moon, planets
Dec N 22°
Dec min 2.3
altitude corr. all sights +15.2
GHA 191° 8.6'
tens d
units d
dsd corr.
d. corr.
Pub. 229
d upper
lower
dsd
upper limb moon subtract 30'
Ho 49° 62.3'
a-Lon -W+E -147° 8.6'
LHA 44°
00' W / 60' E
T
Hc A 49° 43.3'
a = 19.0 T
LHA 44°
tab Hc 49° 43'
d + - +13
Z 085
Zn = 275°
Dec deg 22° N S N
d. corr. Pub. 249 0.3'
Dec min 2.3'
a - Lat = 25° N
a-Lat 25° N S N
Hc 49° 43.3'
a - Lon = 147° 8.6' W
1
2
3
4
5
6

Figure WF-1 Sun #9. *Sight reduction of the sun using Form 104 and Pub 249. The crossed out box is for Pub 229 only.*

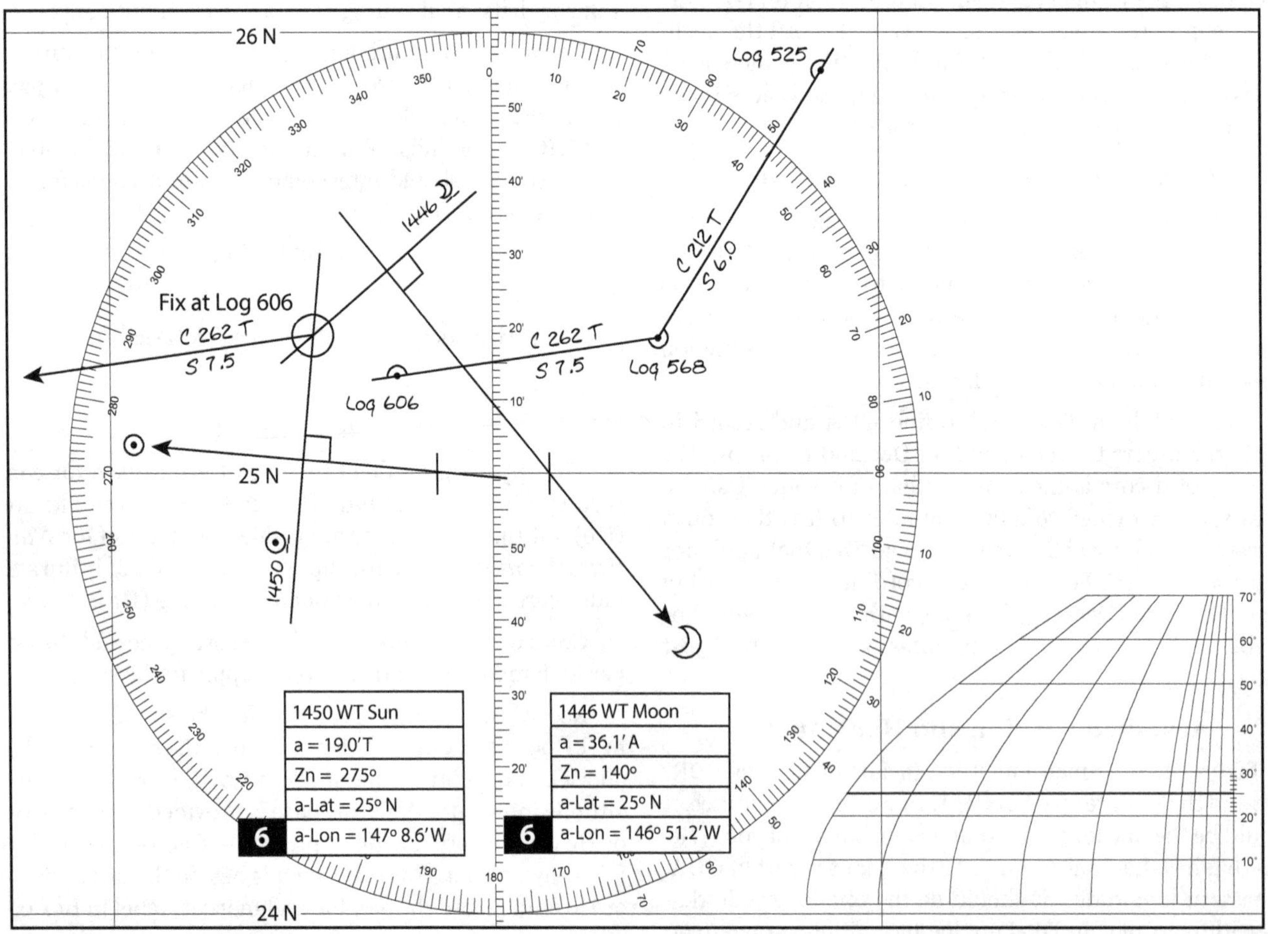

Figure WF-2 *Plot of a celestial fix from a sun and moon sight. The work form for the sun is shown in Figure WF-1. The moon sight is shown worked out on the next page in Figure WF-3.*

Pub. 249 Versus Pub. 229

Although the tables are arranged differently and the values in Pub. 229 are given to a higher precision, the practical use of Pubs. 249 and 229 differs only in the determination of the d-correction to tab Hc. In Pub. 249 this is done in one step, whereas in Pub. 229 this must be done in several steps. The extra steps are required for the extra precision.

d-Corr from Pub. 249

From Table 5 of Pub. 249, record the d-correction. It depends on the d-value and Dec-min (recorded together in Box 5 for convenience). Apply this d-corr to tab Hc to find Hc and record it. The sign (±) of d-corr is the same as the sign of the d-value given in the Sight Reduction Tables. Also record Hc above Box 6. You can interpolate the d-correction to Hc for the minutes of the declination to potentially gain a tenth or two in precision. (Use of Pub 229 is given in the star and planet examples.)

BOX 6–Plotting the Line of Position

Box 6 now contains all data needed to plot the LOP on a plotting sheet. Plotting procedure:

(1) Set up a plotting sheet with mid-latitude equal to a-Lat and mid-longitude equal to a-Lon rounded off to the nearest whole degree. Plot a point at the assumed position (a-Lat, a-Lon).

(2) Draw a line through this point in the direction of Zn (this is the true bearing of the object at the sight time). We call this line the "azimuth line."

(3) Put a mark on the azimuth line at a distance of "a" nautical miles from the assumed position, where "a" is the a-value in Box 6 expressed in minutes of arc (get this distance from the latitude scale on the plotting sheet). Mark the point on the azimuth line in the direction toward Zn, when "a" is labeled T; go the opposite direction along the azimuth line (away from Zn) when "a" is labeled A.

(4) Finally, draw a line perpendicular to the azimuth line passing through the point just marked. This perpendicular line is your LOP. This sight and sight reduction have told you that you are located somewhere on this line. Label the LOP with the name of the celestial body, the log reading, and the UTC.

Moon Sights with Form 104

BOX 2–*Nautical Almanac* Daily Pages

From the *Nautical Almanac* daily pages, record the Greenwich Hour Angle (GHA-hr), v-value, declination (Dec-hr), d-value, and horizontal parallax (UP) for the moon at the exact hour of the UTC. These values are simply transferred to the work form in the exact order they are listed in the *Nautical Almanac*. Figure and record the label of the d-value: label it "+" if declination is increasing with time, or "-" if it is decreasing. CAUTION: The d-value label is found from the trend in *declination* not from the trend in the d-value itself.

BOX 3–Increments and Corrections

From the increments and corrections pages of the *Nautical Almanac*, record the moon's increment of GHA (GHA-m,s) for the minutes and seconds part of the UTC. Also record the d-correction to the declination (based on the d-value given in Box 2) and the v-correction (based on the v-value of Box 2). Cross out the space label "SHA+"; for the moon this space contains v-corr.

Add GHA-hr, GHA-m,s, and v-corr to find GHA and record it. Add the d-corr to Dec-hr to find Dec and record it. For the moon v-corr is always positive; d-corr has the same sign as d-value.

ALL THE REST IS THE SAME AS FOR SUN LINES except that the altitude corrections for the moon are taken from the special moon tables on the back cover of the *Nautical Almanac*. Because of the way the tables are organized, the moon's additional altitude correction (needed for all moon sights) must be found after finding the altitude correction. For upper limb noon sights (and only for these) subtract 30' from the altitude corrections using the labeled space provided.

Star Sights with Form 104

BOX 2–*Nautical Almanac* Daily Pages

From the *Nautical Almanac* daily pages, record in Box 2 the Greenwich Hour Angle (GHA-hr) of Aries at the exact hour of the UTC. Record the declination (Dec) and sidereal hour angle (SHA) of the star in Box 3. Cross out the spaces for v-value, Dec-hr, d-value, and HP; they do not apply to stars.

BOX 3–Increments and Corrections

From the increments and corrections pages of the *Nautical Almanac*, record the Aries increment of GHA (GHA-m,s) for the minutes and seconds part of the UTC. Cross out the d-corr space; stars have no d-corr. And cross out the space label "v-corr"; for stars this space contains SHA.

Add GHA-hr, GHA-m,s, and SHA to find the GHA of the star and record it. Use the extra space provided to adjust minutes to less than 60 and degrees to less than 360, if necessary.

ALL THE REST IS THE SAME AS FOR SUN LINES except that the altitude correction for stars is taken from the stars and planets table instead of the sun table.

d-Corr from Pub. 229

Pub 229 can be used to reduce any sight (Pub 249 is only for declinations less than 29°). It provides a higher precision (0.1' on Hc) compared to Pub 249 (1'), but it takes a few extra steps to obtain this. In Form 104, we use the middle box for these extra steps to finding the d-correction

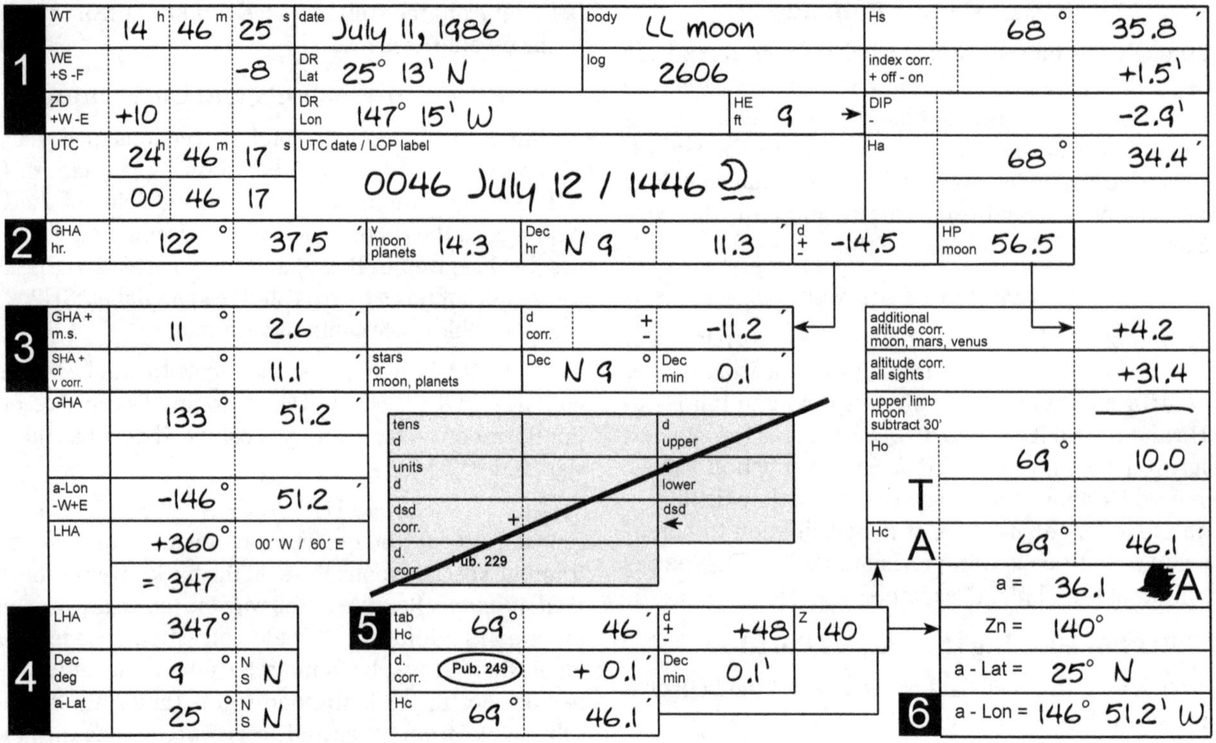

Figure WF-3 Moon #5. *Sight reduction of the moon using Form 104 and Pub 249. The center box crossed out is only for use with Pub 229.*

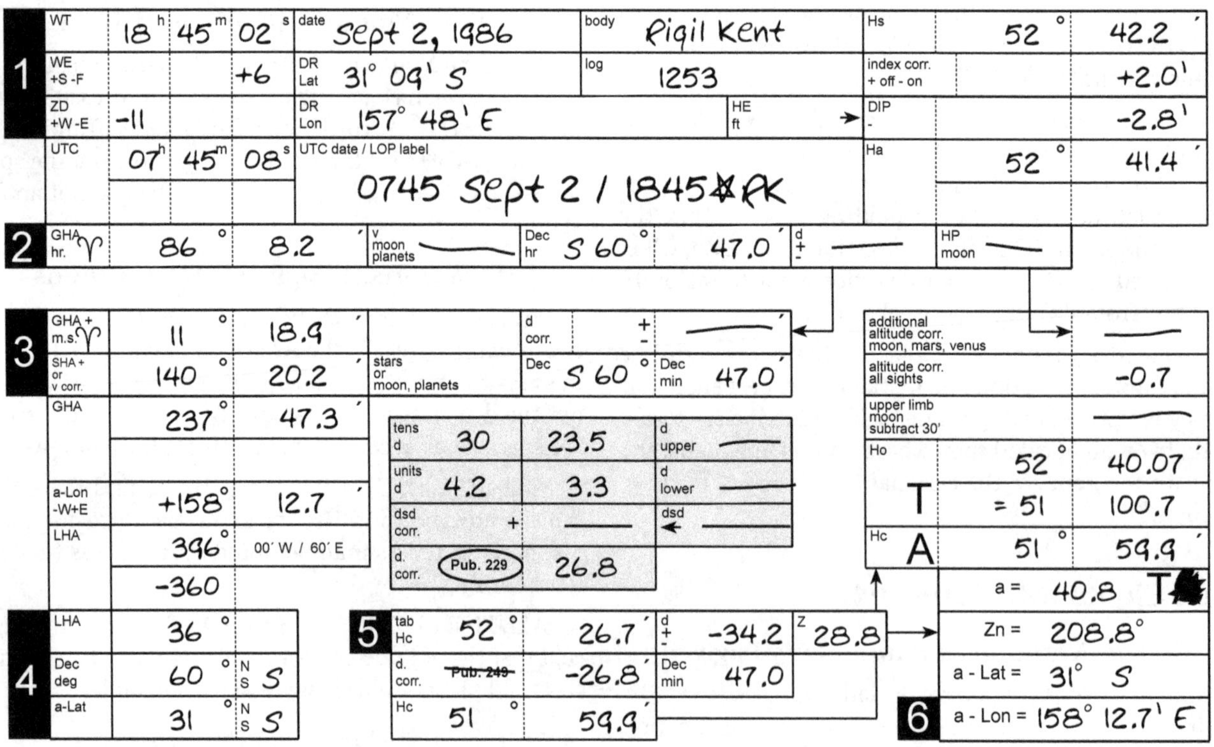

Figure WF-4 Star #10. *Sight reduction of a star (Rigil Kentarus) using Form 104 and Pub 229. The only difference between Pub 229 and Pub 249 for this form is the box in the middle of the form used to figure the d correction to Hc*

to Hc. The star and planet sights shown in Figures 5 and 6 use this method.

First, record the tens and units parts of the d-value in the spaces above Box 5. From the Interpolation Table on the inside covers of Pub. 229, record the tens and units corrections with their tabulated signs (±) in the spaces next to the d-value parts. These corrections depend on the d-value parts and on Dec-min, which is called the *declination increment* in Pub. 229. Add the tens and units corrections to get the d-corr and then apply this correction to tab Hc to get the final Hc. Also record Hc in the space above Box 6.

If (when first recording tab Hc, d, and Z) the d-value is listed with an asterisk (*), a further correction is needed for maximum precision. Proceed as above, but also record the d-values just above and just below (d-upper and d-lower) the tabulated d-value. These are the d-values that correspond to Dec values 1° above and below the Dec-deg recorded in Box 4. Next figure the *double second difference* (dsd), which equals the difference between d-upper and d-lower, and record it. Find the dsd-correction in the small table, inset next to the tens and units corrections table. Record this small dsd correction and add it to the tens and units correction to find the final d-corr. The dsd-corr is always positive, regardless of the sign of the tens and units corrections.

NOTE: dsd corrections are only needed for high-altitude sights, and for these you must interpolate for the azimuth angle Z as explained in the earlier caution note. Hence an asterisk signaling a dsd correction is also your signal to interpolate for Z. Pub. 249 does not have this built-in warning.

Planet Sights with Form 104

BOX 2–*Nautical Almanac* Daily Pages

From the *Nautical Almanac* daily pages, record the Greenwich Hour Angle (GHA-hr) and declination (Dec-hr) of the planet at the exact hour of the UTC. Record the declination d-value, and label it "+" if declination is increasing with time, or "-" if decreasing. Record the v-value, it is positive for all planets except Venus, which can sometimes be negative. If it is negative, it is listed as such, and the v-corr found from it should be subtracted. Cross out the space for HP; it does not apply to planets.

BOX 3–Increments and Corrections

From the increments and corrections pages of the *Nautical Almanac*, record the planet's increment of GHA (GHA-m,s) for the minutes and seconds part of the UTC. Also, record the d-correction to the declination (based on the d-value of Box 2) and the v-correction to the GHA (based on the v-value in Box 2). Cross out the space label "SHA"; for planets this space contains v-corr. Add GHA-hr, GHA-m,s, and v-corr to find GHA and record it.

If v-value is negative for Venus, the v-corr is negative. Apply d-corr to Dec-hr to find Dec and record it. The sign of d-corr is the same as that of d-value.

ALL THE REST IS THE SAME AS FOR SUN LINES except that the altitude correction for planets is taken from the stars and planets table instead of the sun table. Also there is a small additional altitude correction in the *Nautical Almanac* for the planets Mars and Venus. A labeled space is provided for this additional correction.

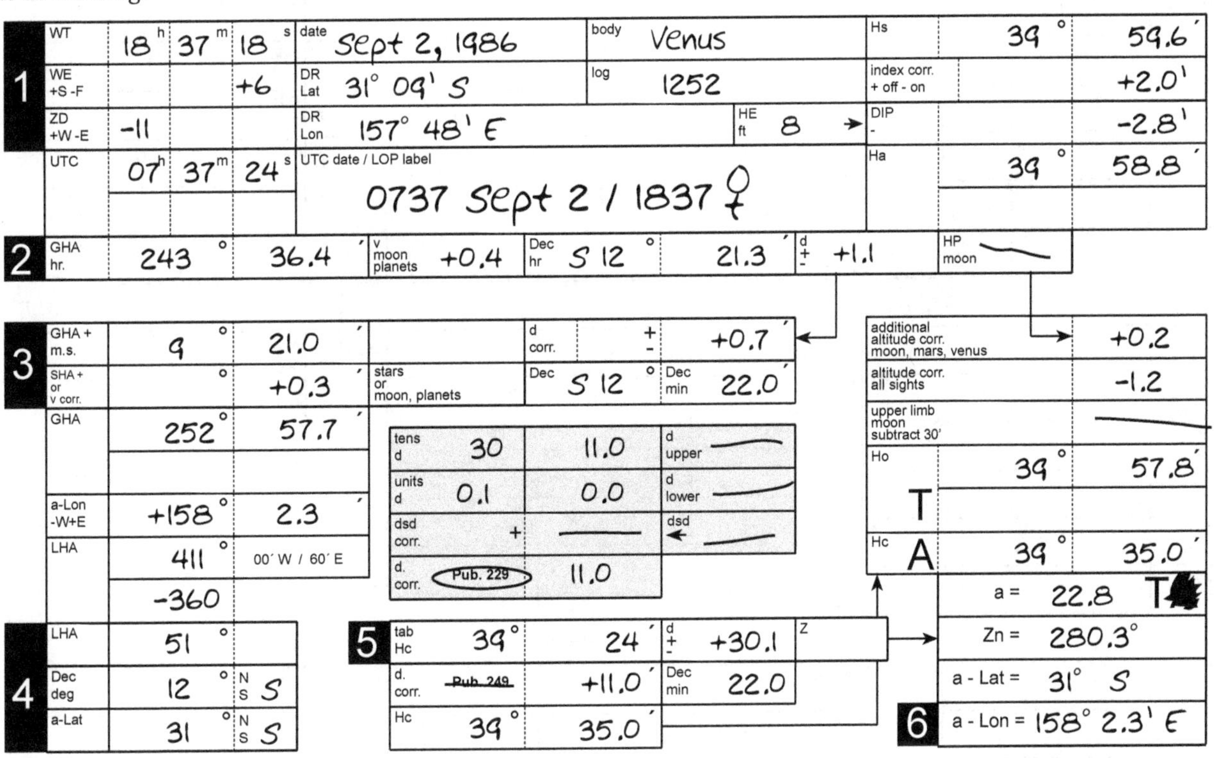

Figure WF-5 Planet #4. *Sight reduction of the Venus using Form 104 and Pub 229. The only difference between Pub 229 and Pub 249 for this form is the box in the middle of the form used to figure the d correction to Hc*

1
WT h m s | date | body | Hs ° ′
WE +S -F | DR Lat | log | index corr. + off - on
ZD +W -E | DR Lon | HE ft → | DIP -
UTC h m s | UTC date / LOP label | Ha ° ′

2
GHA hr. ° ′ | v moon planets | Dec hr ° ′ | d + - | HP moon

3
GHA + m.s. ° ′ | d corr. + - ′ | additional altitude corr. moon, mars, venus
SHA + or v corr. ° ′ | stars or moon, planets | Dec ° Dec min ′ | altitude corr. all sights
GHA ° ′ | upper limb moon subtract 30′
a-Lon -W+E ° ′ | Ho ° ′
LHA ° 00′ W / 60′ E | Hc ° ′

Pub. 229: tens d | d upper
units d | d lower
dsd corr. + | dsd ←
d. corr.

T A

4
LHA °
Dec deg ° N S
a-Lat ° N S

5
tab Hc ° ′ | d + - | Z
d. corr. Pub. 249 ′ | Dec min
Hc ° ′

6
a = TA
Zn =
a - Lat =
a - Lon =

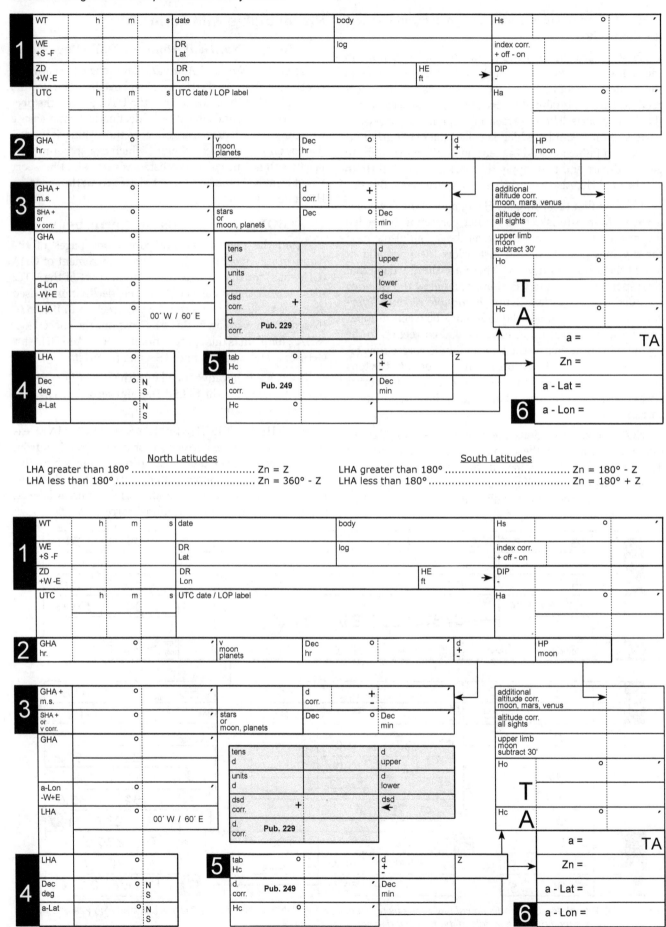

<u>North Latitudes</u>		<u>South Latitudes</u>	
LHA greater than 180°	Zn = Z	LHA greater than 180°	Zn = 180° - Z
LHA less than 180°	Zn = 360° - Z	LHA less than 180°	Zn = 180° + Z

1
WT h m s | date | body | Hs ° ′
WE +S -F | DR Lat | log | index corr. + off - on
ZD +W -E | DR Lon | HE ft → | DIP -
UTC h m s | UTC date / LOP label | Ha ° ′

2
GHA hr. ° ′ | v moon planets | Dec hr ° ′ | d + - | HP moon

3
GHA + m.s. ° ′ | d corr. + - ′ | additional altitude corr. moon, mars, venus
SHA + or v corr. ° ′ | stars or moon, planets | Dec ° Dec min ′ | altitude corr. all sights
GHA ° ′ | upper limb moon subtract 30′
a-Lon -W+E ° ′ | Ho ° ′
LHA ° 00′ W / 60′ E | Hc ° ′

Pub. 229: tens d | d upper
units d | d lower
dsd corr. + | dsd ←
d. corr.

T A

4
LHA °
Dec deg ° N S
a-Lat ° N S

5
tab Hc ° ′ | d + - | Z
d. corr. Pub. 249 ′ | Dec min
Hc ° ′

6
a = TA
Zn =
a - Lat =
a - Lon =

← Form 104 — for Sight Reduction using Pub 249 or Pub 229

Form 106 — Sight Reduction using the NAO Tables

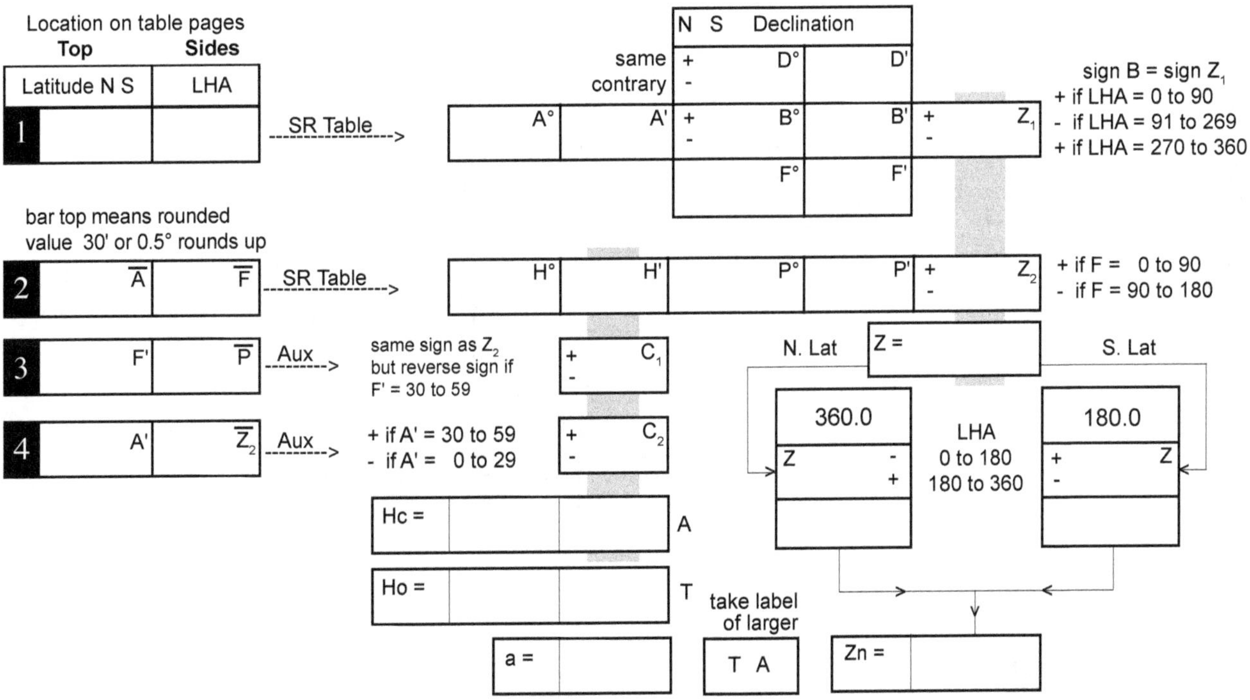

Short Instructions

1 In row 1, record assumed Lat, LHA, and Dec (D). Mark the signs of D, B, and Z1.

2 In row 1, with Lat and LHA, enter Sight Reduction (SR) Table and record A, B, and Z1.

3 Add D and B to get F, and record it in row 1.

4 Copy A' to row 4 and mark the sign of C2.

5 Round off A to nearest whole degree and record it as A-bar in row 2.

6 Mark the signs of Z2 and C1 in rows 2 and 3.

7 Round off F to nearest whole degree and record it as F-bar in row 2.

8 With A-bar and F-bar, enter SR table and record H, P, and Z2 in row 2.

9 Round off P and Z2 to nearest whole degrees and record them as as P-bar and Z2-bar in rows 3 and 4.

10 With F' and P-bar, enter Auxiliary Table (Aux) and record C1 in row 3.

11 With A' and Z2-bar, enter Aux table and record C2 in row 4.

12 Add C1 and C2 to H to get Hc.

13 Add Z1 and Z2 to get Z. Copy Z to space below it, rounding to nearest degree. Drop minus sign if present.

14 Convert Z to Zn by choosing appropriate Z sign next to LHA.

15 Record Ho below Hc; take their difference and record it as "a" with the proper label.

Detailed instructions on the use of these forms, with several examples, are given in Section 11.29.

Form 106 — Sight Reduction using the NAO Tables

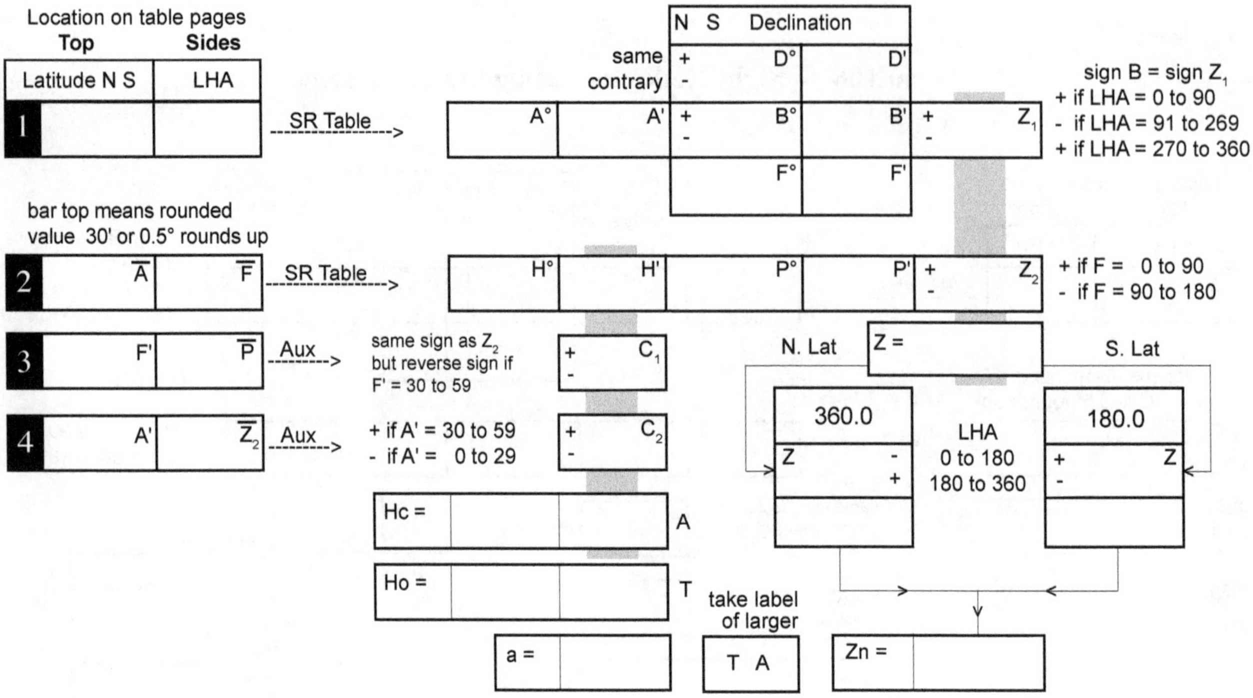

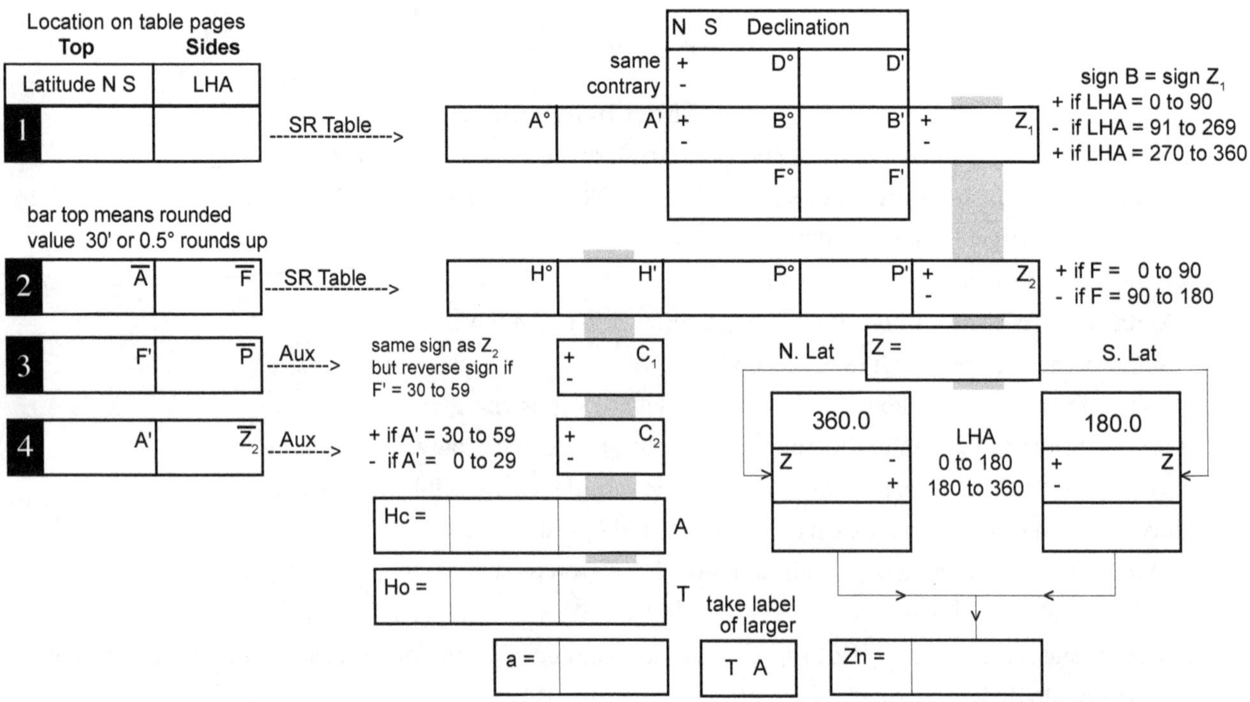

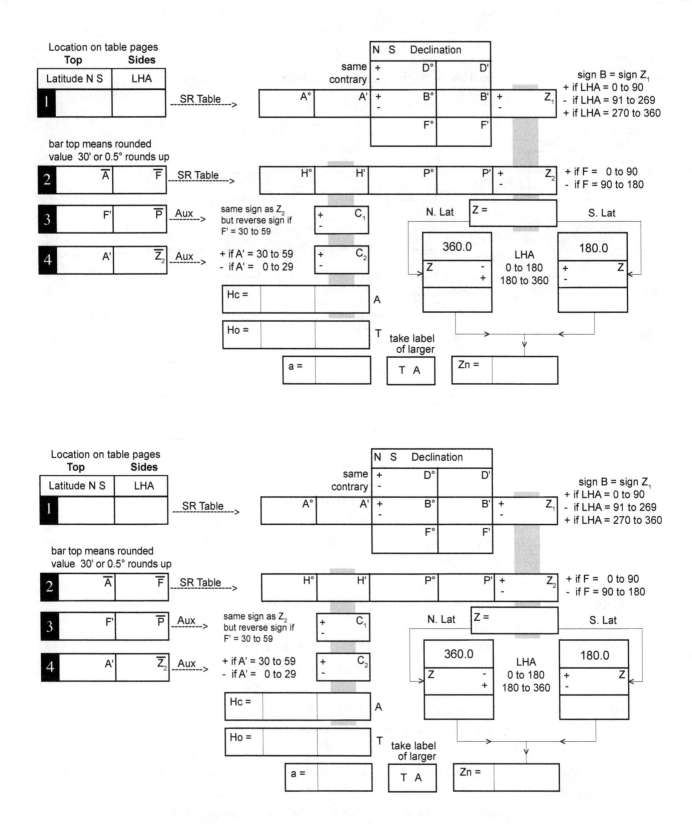

Detailed instructions on the use of these forms, with several examples, are given in Section 11.29.

Form 104 and Form 106 — Almanac Daily Pages plus NAO Tables

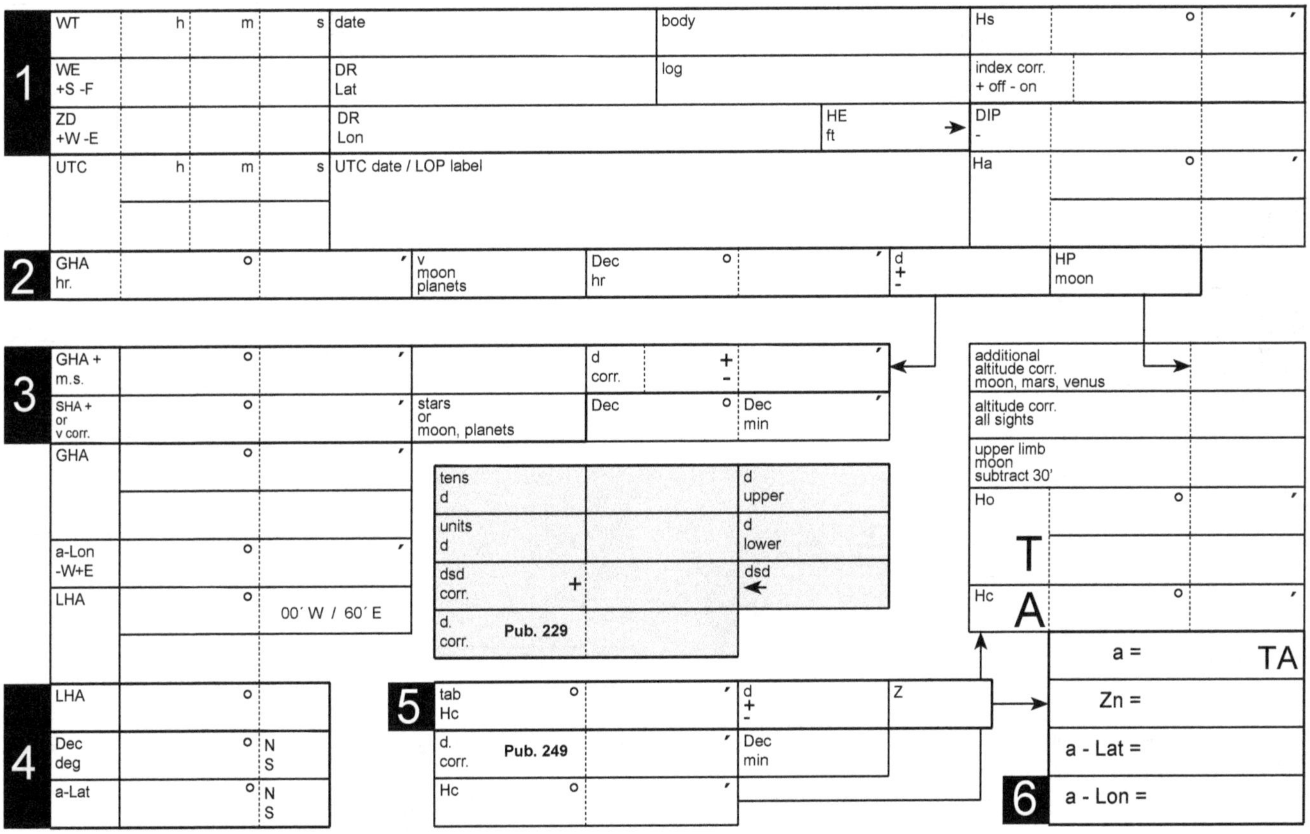

North Latitudes	
LHA greater than 180°	Zn = Z
LHA less than 180°	Zn = 360° - Z

South Latitudes	
LHA greater than 180°	Zn = 180° - Z
LHA less than 180°	Zn = 180° + Z

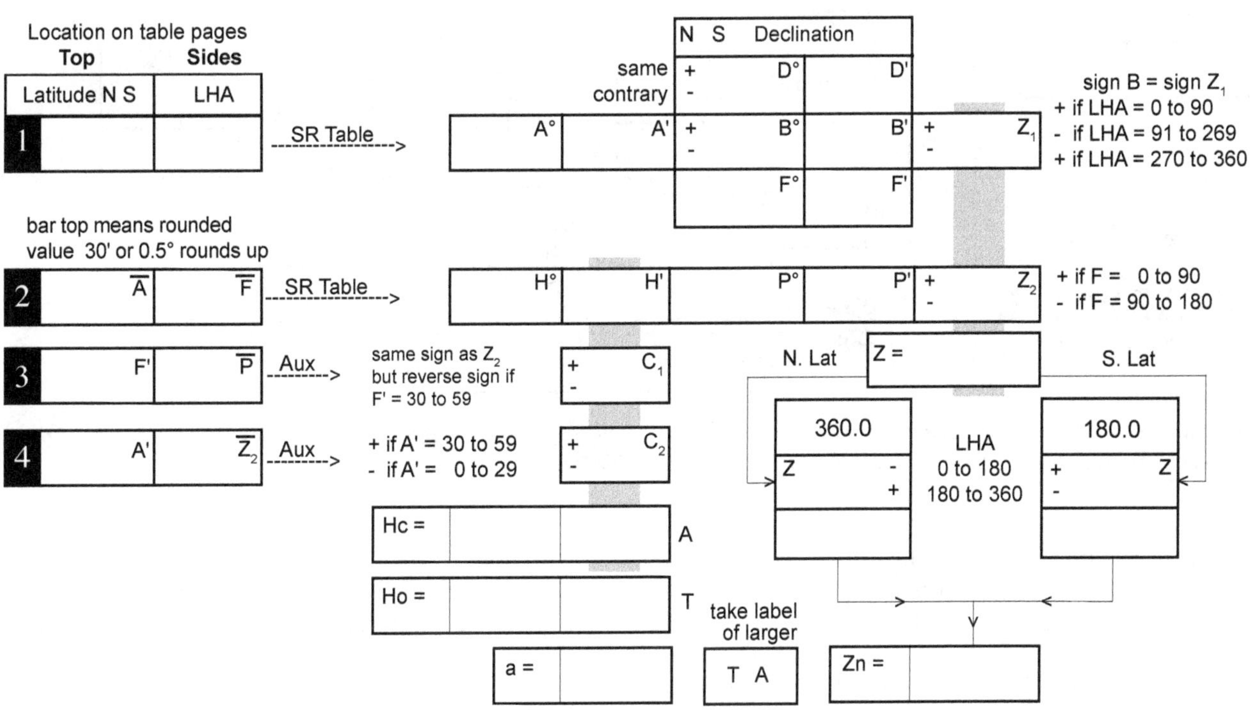

Form 108 — Combined form for Almanac Daily Pages plus NAO Tables

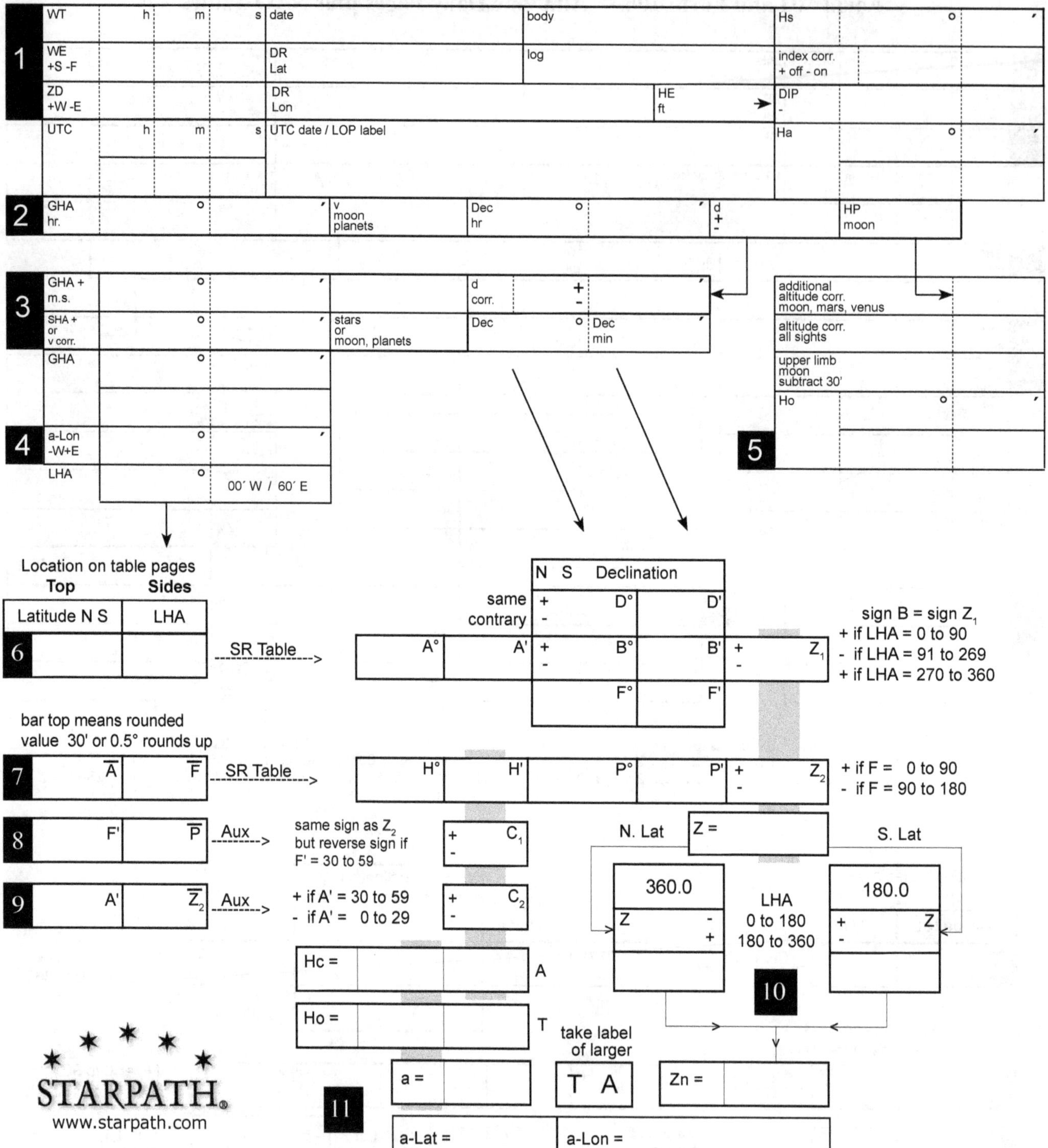

This is a combined form for those using NAO tables. The instructions for the top part are essentially the same as for Form 104. Instructions for the bottom part are the same as for the NAO tables.

[1] Fill in sight data.
[2] Get GP data from daily pages for whole hour.
[3] Get minutes and seconds corrections. Sum for GHA, Sum for Dec. Copy Dec to line in 6. Mark N or S.
[4] Choose a-Lon and find LHA. Copy to line [6]. Choose a-Lat, record in line [5]. Record a-Lat and a-Lon in line [11].
[5] Apply altitude corrections to get Ho. Copy Ho to space above [11].
[6] to [10] Follow standard NAO Form 106 instructions.
[11] Find a-value as difference between Hc and Ho, and choose its label. Now all data needed to plot the LOP is at hand.

Form 107 — for Finding Latitude from Local Apparent Noon

	Step 1 Correct Hs to get Ho			
1-1	Record Maximum Sextant Height (Hs = peak height of the sun at noon), and mark limb	Lower / Upper Hs	°	'
1-2	Record Index Correction (mark sign + if off, - if on)	IC	Off + / On -	'
1-3	Record eye height (HE) and Look up Dip Correction on the right-hand side of Table A2, front of the Almanac (T-8 in notes)	Dip / HE (ft)	-	'
1-4	Sum the above three numbers to get Apparent Height	Ha	°	'
1-5	Look up altitude correction on lefthand side of Table A2, front of the Almanac (T-8 in notes) (correction depends on Ha, Limb, and month) (mark sign + for lower limb, - for upper limb)	Alt corr.	+ / -	'
1-6	Sum the above two numbers to get Observed Height	Ho	°	'

	Step 2 Determine the Zenith Distance		89°	60.0'
2-1	Record Ho from Step 1, above, and then subtract it from 90° to get the zenith distance.	Ho	- °	'
2-2	Zenith distance	z	°	'

	Step 3 Use the Almanac to Find Sun's Declination	UTC date =		
3-1	Record the date and UTC of the sight (the time the sun reached its peak height)	UTC (hr) =	UTC(min) =	
3-2	Turn to the daily page of the Almanac for the date of the sight, and find the sun's declination (dec) for the hour of the sight (line 3-1) and record it here.	Dec (hr)	N / S °	'
3-3	Record the d-value from the bottom of the dec column in the Almanac. Mark the signs of the d-value and d-corr + if the dec for the next hour is larger, or - if it is smaller.	d-value = + / -	d-corr = + / -	'
3-4	Turn to the Increments and Corrections pages at the back of the Almanac (T-9 to 12, in the notes) and find the minutes table for the UTC minutes (line 3-1). On the right-hand side of the double line in the table, find the d-corr corresponding to the d-value of line 3-3	Declination =	N / S °	'
		3-5 Apply the d-corr to the dec(hr) and record it above.		

Step 4 Find Latitude from Zenith Distance and Declination

Record DR Latitude to use as a guide, and then take the sum or difference of zenith distance and declination to find your true Latitute at LAN.

Declination or Zenith distance	°	'
Zenith distance or Declination	°	'
Latitude =	°	'

Form 109 — Finding Index Correction from the Sun by the Solar Method

Toward or Away		Date	
On	Off	Diff	Check SD
sight #	-	-	+
	=	= ÷2	= ÷4
SD=		=	=

Toward or Away		Date	
On	Off	Diff	Check SD
sight #	-	-	+
	=	= ÷2	= ÷4
SD=		=	=

Toward or Away		Date	
On	Off	Diff	Check SD
sight #	-	-	+
	=	= ÷2	= ÷4
SD=		=	=

Toward or Away		Date	
On	Off	Diff	Check SD
sight #	-	-	+
	=	= ÷2	= ÷4
SD=		=	=

Toward or Away		Date	
On	Off	Diff	Check SD
sight #	-	-	+
	=	= ÷2	= ÷4
SD=		=	=

Toward or Away		Date	
On	Off	Diff	Check SD
sight #	-	-	+
	=	= ÷2	= ÷4
SD=		=	=

Toward or Away		Date	
On	Off	Diff	Check SD
sight #	-	-	+
	=	= ÷2	= ÷4
SD=		=	=

Toward or Away		Date	
On	Off	Diff	Check SD
sight #	-	-	+
	=	= ÷2	= ÷4
SD=		=	=

Toward or Away		Date	
On	Off	Diff	Check SD
sight #	-	-	+
	=	= ÷2	= ÷4
SD=		=	=

Toward or Away		Date	
On	Off	Diff	Check SD
sight #	-	-	+
	=	= ÷2	= ÷4
SD=		=	=

Toward or Away		Date	
On	Off	Diff	Check SD
sight #	-	-	+
	=	= ÷2	= ÷4
SD=		=	=

Toward or Away		Date	
On	Off	Diff	Check SD
sight #	-	-	+
	=	= ÷2	= ÷4
SD=		=	=

Detailed instructions for the use of this form are in Section 11.7. This form covers 12 sights.

Index

T

U

V

W

Z

About the Author

David Burch is a Fellow of the Royal Institute of Navigation in London and a Fellow of the Institute of Navigation, Washington, DC, from whom he received the Superior Achievement Award for outstanding performance as a practicing navigator. He has logged more than 70,000 miles at sea including twelve transoceanic yacht races, with several first place victories and a passage record for boats under 36 feet that lasted 16 years. He also navigated the only American entry in the storm-ridden 1993 Sydney to Hobart Race.

On the academic side, he is a past Fulbright Scholar with a PhD in Physics. As Founding Director of Starpath School of Navigation in Seattle he has designed courses and taken part in the teaching of marine weather and navigation for more than 30 years. He continues to work on the development of online training materials, which are presented at www.starpath.com. Articles on special topics in navigation and weather appear at davidburchnavigation.blogspot.com

Other books related to celestial navigation

Emergency Navigation
The Star Finder Book
Hawaii By Sextant
How to Use Plastic Sextants
GPS Backup with a Mark 3 Sextant
Starpath Celestial Navigation Work Forms

Other books on navigation and weather

Modern Marine Weather
Introduction to Electronic Chart Navigation
Inland and Coastal Navigation
The Barometer Handbook
Radar for Mariners
Fundamentals of Kayak Navigation
Sailor's Logbook

CPSIA information can be obtained
at www.ICGtesting.com
Printed in the USA
BVHW050205291220
596565BV00008B/51

9 780914 025467